GOOD NEWS
NEW TESTAMENT

Today's English Version

CANADIAN BIBLE SOCIETY

10 Carnforth Road
Toronto, Ontario   M4A 2S4

British usage edition
Text, illustrations and all helps for the reader
© American Bible Society
New York 1966, 1971 and 4th edition 1976
ISBN 0-88834-606-9 (paperback)

Permission to reproduce any part of the British edition
should be requested from:
Bible Society (Publishing)
Stonehill Green, Westlea Down
Swindon SN5 7DG
United Kingdom

Text set by computer by
C. R. Barber and Partners, Wrotham, Kent, U.K.

Printed in Canada by
Gagné Printing, Louiseville, Québec

Authorized by the
Canadian Conference
of Catholic Bishops
May 1986

The *United Bible Societies* is a worldwide fellowship of
National Bible Societies working in more than 180 countries.
Their aim is to reach every person with the Bible or some part
of it in a language he or she can understand and at an affordable
price. Between them the Bible Societies distribute many millions
of copies of the Holy Scriptures every year. You are invited to
share this work by your prayers and gifts.

The Canadian Bible Society will be very happy to provide
details of its activity.

TEV260PN 21104   CBS-1987-75M

Preface

THE NEW TESTAMENT is the book about Jesus Christ. Its name means that it is the record of God's new covenant with his people. This covenant, or agreement, is the good news of God's promise to save those who believe in Jesus Christ as Lord and Saviour.

The twenty-seven books which make up the New Testament were written by perhaps as many as twelve different authors over a period of some fifty years.

The four Gospels tell the story of the life, teaching, deeds, death, and resurrection of Jesus. They are followed by the Acts of the Apostles, which traces the spread of the gospel for some thirty years from Jerusalem to Rome, the capital of the Empire. The letters of Paul were all written to meet specific needs faced by early Christians. The eight books that follow, known as the General Letters, are varied: some of them are addressed to believers everywhere, while others are written to individual churches or persons.

The last book in the New Testament is different from all the others. Its teaching concerning the victory of the Kingdom of God and the lordship of Christ is conveyed by means of visions, images, and symbols, many of which are very difficult for the modern reader to understand. But its central message, which may also be taken as the theme of the whole New Testament, is clearly proclaimed: "The power to rule over the world belongs now to our Lord and his Messiah, and he will rule for ever and ever!" (Revelation 11.15).

This translation of the New Testament has been prepared by the United Bible Societies for people who speak English either as their mother tongue or as an acquired language. As a distinctively new translation, it does not conform to traditional vocabulary or style, but seeks to express the meaning of the Greek text in words and forms accepted as standard by people everywhere who employ English as a means of communication.

The translator, Dr Robert G. Bratcher, was assisted in his task by a panel of specialists, and the translation

PREFACE

was reviewed and approved by the Translations Committee and the Board of the American Bible Society.

In view of the differences in vocabulary and form which exist between the American and the British use of the English language, this British edition has been published, incorporating such changes as are in keeping with British usage. Final approval of this text was given by the General Committee of the British and Foreign Bible Society.

A *Word List* at the end of the volume explains technical terms and rarely used words, and identifies a number of places and persons in the New Testament, in order to enable the reader to understand the text better in its historical setting. An *Index* is provided which locates some of the more important subjects, persons, places, and events. Finally, there are a few line *Maps* designed to help the reader visualize the geographical setting of the countries and places mentioned. The line drawings were specially prepared by Miss Annie Vallotton to accompany the text.

The text from which this translation was made is the Third Edition (1975) of the Greek New Testament prepared by an international committee of New Testament scholars, sponsored by the United Bible Societies. There are many places in the New Testament where the various Greek manuscripts and ancient versions have different texts; some of the more important of these *variant readings* appear in the footnotes. In many places the Greek text may be understood and translated in two or more different ways; and some of these *alternative renderings* are also given in footnotes.

Contents

List of Maps

(To help the reader these maps can also be found
at the end of the book on pages 690-695)

JERUSALEM IN
NEW TESTAMENT TIMES

To Caesarea

Present City Wall

To Jericho

Damascus Gate

Pool of
Bethzatha

PRAETORIUM

Ancient
City Wall

FORT

Gate

TEMPLE

To Bethany

Golgotha

Gethsemane

Gate

Beautiful
Gate

Gate

Court of
Gentiles

Solomon's
Porch

Gennath
Gate

Bridge

Gates

HEROD'S
PALACE

Present City Wall

Pool

K I D R O N   V A L L E Y

Pool of
Siloam

To Joppa

To Bethlehem

Gate

To Dead Sea

V A L L E Y   O F   H I N N O M

0   250   500 Metres

Roads

THE GOSPEL ACCORDING TO
MATTHEW

INTRODUCTION

The Gospel according to Matthew tells the good news that Jesus is the promised Saviour, the one through whom God fulfilled the promises he made to his people in the Old Testament. This good news is not only for the Jewish people, among whom Jesus was born and lived, but for the whole world.

Matthew is carefully arranged. It begins with the birth of Jesus, describes his baptism and temptation, and then takes up his ministry of preaching, teaching, and healing in Galilee. After this the Gospel records Jesus' journey from Galilee to Jerusalem and the events of Jesus' last week, culminating in his crucifixion and resurrection.

This Gospel presents Jesus as the great Teacher, who has the authority to interpret the Law of God, and who teaches about God's kingdom. Much of his teaching is gathered by subject matter into five collections: (1) the Sermon on the Mount, which concerns the character, duties, privileges, and destiny of the citizens of the Kingdom of heaven (chapters 5–7); (2) instructions to the twelve disciples for their mission (chapter 10); (3) parables about the Kingdom of heaven (chapter 13); (4) teaching on the meaning of discipleship (chapter 18); and (5) teaching about the end of the present age and the coming of the Kingdom of heaven (chapters 24–25).

Outline of Contents

The last week in and near Jerusalem   21.1—27.66
The resurrection and appearances of the
**   Lord   28.1-20**

The Ancestors of Jesus Christ
(Luke 3.23-38)

1 This is the list of the ancestors of Jesus Christ, a descendant of David, who was a descendant of Abraham.

2-6a From Abraham to King David, the following ancestors are listed: Abraham, Isaac, Jacob, Judah and his brothers; then Perez and Zerah (their mother was Tamar), Hezron, Ram, Amminadab, Nahshon, Salmon, Boaz (his mother was Rahab), Obed (his mother was Ruth), Jesse, and King David.

6b-11 From David to the time when the people of Israel were taken into exile in Babylon, the following ancestors are listed: David, Solomon (his mother was the woman who had been Uriah's wife), Rehoboam, Abijah, Asa, Jehoshaphat, Jehoram, Uzziah, Jotham, Ahaz, Hezekiah, Manasseh, Amon, Josiah, and Jehoiachin and his brothers.

12-16 From the time after the exile in Babylon to the birth of Jesus, the following ancestors are listed: Jehoiachin, Shealtiel, Zerubbabel, Abiud, Eliakim, Azor, Zadok, Achim, Eliud, Eleazar, Matthan, Jacob, and Joseph, who married Mary, the mother of Jesus, who was called the Messiah.

17 So then, there were fourteen generations from Abraham to David, and fourteen from David to the exile in Babylon, and fourteen from then to the birth of the Messiah.

The Birth of Jesus Christ
(Luke 2.1-7)

18 This was how the birth of Jesus Christ took place. His mother Mary was engaged to Joseph, but before they were married, she found out that she was going to have a baby by the Holy Spirit. 19 Joseph

was a man who always did what was right, but he did not want to disgrace Mary publicly; so he made plans to break the engagement privately. 20 While he was thinking about this, an angel of the Lord appeared to him in a dream and said, "Joseph, descendant of David, do not be afraid to take Mary to be your wife. For it is by the Holy Spirit that she has conceived. 21 She will have a son, and you will name him Jesus—because he will save his people from their sins."

22 Now all this happened in order to make what the Lord had said through the prophet come true, 23 "A virgin will become pregnant and have a son, and he will be called Immanuel" (which means, "God is with us").

24 So when Joseph woke up, he married Mary, as the angel of the Lord had told him to do. 25 But he had no sexual relations with her before she gave birth to her son. And Joseph named him Jesus.

Visitors from the East

2 Jesus was born in the town of Bethlehem in Judaea, during the time when Herod was king. Soon afterwards, some men who studied the stars came from the east to Jerusalem 2 and asked, "Where is the baby born to be the king of the Jews? We saw his star when it came up in the east, and we have come to worship him."

3 When King Herod heard about this, he was very upset, and so was everyone else in Jerusalem. 4 He called together all the chief priests and the teachers of the Law and asked them, "Where will the Messiah be born?"

5 "In the town of Bethlehem in Judaea," they answered. "For this is what the prophet wrote:
6 'Bethlehem in the land of Judah,
   you are by no means the least of the leading
      cities of Judah;
for from you will come a leader
   who will guide my people Israel.' "

7 So Herod called the visitors from the east to a secret meeting and found out from them the exact time the star had appeared. 8 Then he sent them to Bethlehem with these instructions: "Go and make a

careful search for the child, and when you find him, let me know, so that I too may go and worship him."

The same star...went ahead of them (2.9-10)

9-10 And so they left, and on their way they saw the same star they had seen in the east. When they saw it, how happy they were, what joy was theirs! It went ahead of them until it stopped over the place where the child was. ¹¹They went into the house, and when they saw the child with his mother Mary, they knelt down and worshipped him. They brought out their gifts of gold, frankincense, and myrrh, and presented them to him.

12 Then they returned to their country by another road, since God had warned them in a dream not to go back to Herod.

The Escape to Egypt

13 After they had left, an angel of the Lord appeared in a dream to Joseph and said, "Herod will be looking for the child in order to kill him. So get up, take the child and his mother and escape to Egypt, and stay there until I tell you to leave."

14 Joseph got up, took the child and his mother,

and left during the night for Egypt, ¹⁵where he stayed until Herod died. This was done to make what the Lord had said through the prophet come true, "I called my Son out of Egypt."

The Killing of the Children

16 When Herod realized that the visitors from the east had tricked him, he was furious. He gave orders to kill all the boys in Bethlehem and its neighbourhood who were two years old and younger—this was done in accordance with what he had learned from the visitors about the time when the star had appeared.

17 In this way what the prophet Jeremiah had said came true:

¹⁸ "A sound is heard in Ramah,
the sound of bitter weeping.
Rachel is crying for her children;
she refuses to be comforted,
for they are dead."

The Return from Egypt

19 After Herod died, an angel of the Lord appeared in a dream to Joseph in Egypt ²⁰and said, "Get up, take the child and his mother, and go back to the land of Israel, because those who tried to kill the child are dead." ²¹So Joseph got up, took the child and his mother, and went back to Israel.

22 But when Joseph heard that Archelaus had succeeded his father Herod as king of Judaea, he was afraid to go there. He was given more instructions in a dream, so he went to the province of Galilee ²³and made his home in a town named Nazareth. And so what the prophets had said came true: "He will be called a Nazarene."

The Preaching of John the Baptist
(Mark 1.1–8; Luke 3.1–18; John 1.19–28)

3 At that time John the Baptist came to the desert of Judaea and started preaching. ²"Turn away from your sins," he said, "because the Kingdom of heaven is near!" ³John was the man the prophet Isaiah was talking about when he said,

"Someone is shouting in the desert,

'Prepare a road for the Lord;
make a straight path for him to travel!' "

4 John's clothes were made of camel's hair; he wore a leather belt round his waist, and his food was locusts and wild honey. 5 People came to him from Jerusalem, from the whole province of Judaea, and from all the country near the River Jordan. 6 They confessed their sins, and he baptized them in the Jordan.

7 When John saw many Pharisees and Sadducees coming to him to be baptized, he said to them, "You snakes—who told you that you could escape from the punishment God is about to send? 8 Do those things that will show that you have turned from your sins. 9 And don't think you can escape punishment by saying that Abraham is your ancestor. I tell you that God can take these stones and make descendants for Abraham! 10 The axe is ready to cut down the trees at the roots; every tree that does not bear good fruit will be cut down and thrown in the fire. 11 I baptize you with water to show that you have repented, but the one who will come after me will baptize you with the Holy Spirit and fire. He is much greater than I am; and I am not good enough even to carry his sandals. 12 He has his winnowing shovel with him to thresh out all the grain. He will gather his wheat into his barn, but he will burn the chaff in a fire that never goes out."

The Baptism of Jesus
(Mark 1.9-11; Luke 3.21-22)

13 At that time Jesus arrived from Galilee and came to John at the Jordan to be baptized by him. 14 But John tried to make him change his mind. "I ought to be baptized by you," John said, "and yet you have come to me!"

15 But Jesus answered him, "Let it be so for now. For in this way we shall do all that God requires." So John agreed.

16 As soon as Jesus was baptized, he came up out of the water. Then heaven was opened to him, and he saw the Spirit of God coming down like a dove and alighting on him. 17 Then a voice said from

heaven, "This is my own dear Son, with whom I am pleased."

The Temptation of Jesus
(Mark 1.12–13; Luke 4.1–13)

4 Then the Spirit led Jesus into the desert to be tempted by the Devil. ²After spending forty days and nights without food, Jesus was hungry. ³Then

Order these stones to turn into bread (4.3)

the Devil came to him and said, "If you are God's Son, order these stones to turn into bread."

4 But Jesus answered, "The scripture says, 'Man cannot live on bread alone, but needs every word that God speaks.' "

5 Then the Devil took Jesus to Jerusalem, the Holy City, set him on the highest point of the Temple, ⁶and said to him, "If you are God's Son, throw yourself down, for the scripture says,

'God will give orders to his angels about you;
   they will hold you up with their hands,

so that not even your feet will be hurt on the
    stones.' "

7 Jesus answered, "But the scripture also says, 'Do
not put the Lord your God to the test.' "

8 Then the Devil took Jesus to a very high mountain
and showed him all the kingdoms of the world in
all their greatness. 9 "All this I will give you," the
Devil said, "if you kneel down and worship me."

10 Then Jesus answered, "Go away, Satan! The scripture says, 'Worship the Lord your God and serve
only him!' "

11 Then the Devil left Jesus; and angels came and
helped him.

Jesus Begins His Work in Galilee
(Mark 1.14–15; Luke 4.14–15)

12 When Jesus heard that John had been put in
prison, he went away to Galilee. 13 He did not stay
in Nazareth, but went to live in Capernaum, a town
by Lake Galilee, in the territory of Zebulun and
Naphtali. 14 This was done to make what the prophet
Isaiah had said come true,

15 "Land of Zebulun and land of Naphtali,
    on the road to the sea, on the other side of
      the Jordan,
    Galilee, land of the Gentiles!
16 The people who live in darkness
    will see a great light.
  On those who live in the dark land of death
    the light will shine."

17 From that time Jesus began to preach his message: "Turn away from your sins, because the Kingdom
of heaven is near!"

Jesus Calls Four Fishermen
(Mark 1.16–20; Luke 5.1–11)

18 As Jesus walked along the shore of Lake Galilee,
he saw two brothers who were fishermen, Simon
(called Peter) and his brother Andrew, catching fish
in the lake with a net. 19 Jesus said to them, "Come
with me, and I will teach you to catch men." 20 At
once they left their nets and went with him.

21 He went on and saw two other brothers, James

Teaching about Anger

21 "You have heard that people were told in the past, 'Do not commit murder; anyone who does will be brought to trial.' 22 But now I tell you: whoever is angry[b] with his brother will be brought to trial, whoever calls his brother 'You good-for-nothing!' will be brought before the Council, and whoever calls his brother a worthless fool will be in danger of going to the fire of hell. 23 So if you are about to offer your gift to God at the altar and there you remember that your brother has something against you, 24 leave your gift there in front of the altar, go at once and make peace with your brother, and then come back and offer your gift to God.

25 "If someone brings a lawsuit against you and takes you to court, settle the dispute with him while there is time, before you get to court. Once you are there, he will hand you over to the judge, who will hand you over to the police, and you will be put in jail. 26 There you will stay, I tell you, until you pay the last penny of your fine.

Teaching about Adultery

27 "You have heard that it was said, 'Do not commit adultery.' 28 But now I tell you: anyone who looks at a woman and wants to possess her is guilty of committing adultery with her in his heart. 29 So if your right eye causes you to sin, take it out and throw it away! It is much better for you to lose a part of your body than to have your whole body thrown into hell. 30 If your right hand causes you to sin, cut it off and throw it away! It is much better for you to lose one of your limbs than for your whole body to go to hell.

Teaching about Divorce
(Matt. 19.9; Mark 10.11-12; Luke 16.18)

31 "It was also said, 'Anyone who divorces his wife must give her a written notice of divorce.' 32 But now

---

[b]whoever is angry; *some manuscripts have* whoever without cause is angry.

I tell you: if a man divorces his wife for any cause other than her unfaithfulness, then he is guilty of making her commit adultery if she marries again; and the man who marries her commits adultery also.

Teaching about Vows

33 "You have also heard that people were told in the past, 'Do not break your promise, but do what you have vowed to the Lord to do.' 34 But now I tell you: do not use any vow when you make a promise. Do not swear by heaven, for it is God's throne; 35 nor by earth, for it is the resting place for his feet; nor by Jerusalem, for it is the city of the great King. 36 Do not even swear by your head, because you cannot make a single hair white or black. 37 Just say 'Yes' or 'No'—anything else you say comes from the Evil One.

Teaching about Revenge
(Luke 6.29-30)

38 "You have heard that it was said, 'An eye for an eye, and a tooth for a tooth.' 39 But now I tell you: do not take revenge on someone who wrongs you. If anyone slaps you on the right cheek, let him slap your left cheek too. 40 And if someone takes you to court to sue you for your shirt, let him have your coat as well. 41 And if one of the occupation troops forces you to carry his pack one kilometre, carry it two kilometres. 42 When someone asks you for something, give it to him; when someone wants to borrow something, lend it to him.

Love for Enemies
(Luke 6.27-28, 32-36)

43 "You have heard that it was said, 'Love your friends, hate your enemies.' 44 But now I tell you: love your enemies and pray for those who persecute you, 45 so that you may become the sons of your Father in heaven. For he makes his sun to shine on bad and good people alike, and gives rain to those who do good and to those who do evil. 46 Why should God reward you if you love only the people who love you? Even the tax collectors do that! 47 And

if you speak only to your friends, have you done anything out of the ordinary? Even the pagans do that! 48You must be perfect—just as your Father in heaven is perfect!

Teaching about Charity

6 "Make certain you do not perform your religious duties in public so that people will see what you do. If you do these things publicly, you will not have any reward from your Father in heaven.

2 "So when you give something to a needy person,

Do not make a big show of it (6.2)

do not make a big show of it, as the hypocrites do in the houses of worship and on the streets. They do it so that people will praise them. I assure you, they have already been paid in full. 3But when you help a needy person, do it in such a way that even your closest friend will not know about it. 4Then it will be a private matter. And your Father, who sees what you do in private, will reward you.

Teaching about Prayer
(Luke 11.2–4)

5 "When you pray, do not be like the hypocrites! They love to stand up and pray in the houses of worship and on the street corners, so that everyone will see them. I assure you, they have already been paid in full. 6 But when you pray, go to your room, close the door, and pray to your Father, who is unseen. And your Father, who sees what you do in private, will reward you.

7 "When you pray, do not use a lot of meaningless words, as the pagans do, who think that their gods will hear them because their prayers are long. 8 Do not be like them. Your Father already knows what you need before you ask him. 9 This, then, is how you should pray:

'Our Father in heaven:
　　May your holy name be honoured;
10　　may your Kingdom come;
　　may your will be done on earth as it is in heaven.
11　　Give us today the food we need. c
12　　Forgive us the wrongs we have done,
　　　as we forgive the wrongs that others have done to us.
13　　Do not bring us to hard testing,
　　but keep us safe from the Evil One.' x

14 "If you forgive others the wrongs they have done to you, your Father in heaven will also forgive you. 15 But if you do not forgive others, then your Father will not forgive the wrongs you have done.

Teaching about Fasting

16 "And when you fast, do not put on a sad face as the hypocrites do. They neglect their appearance so that everyone will see that they are fasting. I assure you, they have already been paid in full. 17 When you go without food, wash your face and comb your hair, 18 so that others cannot know that you are fasting—only your Father, who is unseen, will know. And

c we need; or for today; or for tomorrow.
x Some manuscripts add For yours is the kingdom, and the power, and the glory for ever. Amen.

your Father, who sees what you do in private, will reward you.

Riches in Heaven
(Luke 12.33–34)

19 "Do not store up riches for yourselves here on earth, where moths and rust destroy, and robbers break in and steal. 20 Instead, store up riches for yourselves in heaven, where moths and rust cannot destroy, and robbers cannot break in and steal. 21 For your heart will always be where your riches are.

The Light of the Body
(Luke 11.34–36)

22 "The eyes are like a lamp for the body. If your eyes are sound, your whole body will be full of light; 23 but if your eyes are no good, your body will be in darkness. So if the light in you is darkness, how terribly dark it will be!

God and Possessions
(Luke 16.13; 12.22–31)

24 "No one can be a slave of two masters; he will hate one and love the other; he will be loyal to one and despise the other. You cannot serve both God and money.

25 "This is why I tell you not to be worried about the food and drink you need in order to stay alive, or about clothes for your body. After all, isn't life worth more than food? And isn't the body worth more than clothes? 26 Look at the birds: they do not sow seeds, gather a harvest and put it in barns; yet your Father in heaven takes care of them! Aren't you worth much more than birds? 27 Can any of you live a bit longer *d* by worrying about it?

28 "And why worry about clothes? Look how the wild flowers grow: they do not work or make clothes for themselves. 29 But I tell you that not even King Solomon with all his wealth had clothes as beautiful as one of these flowers. 30 It is God who clothes the

---

d live a bit longer; *or* grow a bit taller.

Aren't you worth much more than birds? (6.26)

wild grass—grass that is here today and gone
tomorrow, burnt up in the oven. Won't he be all
the more sure to clothe you? How little faith you
have!

31 "So do not start worrying: 'Where will my food
come from? or my drink? or my clothes?' ³²(These
are the things the pagans are always concerned about.)
Your Father in heaven knows that you need all these
things. ³³Instead, be concerned above everything else
with the Kingdom of God and with what he requires
of you, and he will provide you with all these other
things. ³⁴So do not worry about tomorrow; it will have
enough worries of its own. There is no need to add
to the troubles each day brings.

Judging Others
(Luke 6.37-38, 41-42)

7 "Do not judge others, so that God will not judge
you, ²for God will judge you in the same way
as you judge others, and he will apply to you the
same rules you apply to others. ³Why, then, do you
look at the speck in your brother's eye, and pay
no attention to the log in your own eye? ⁴How dare
you say to your brother, 'Please, let me take that

speck out of your eye,' when you have a log in your own eye? 5 You hypocrite! First take the log out of your own eye, and then you will be able to see clearly to take the speck out of your brother's eye.

6 "Do not give what is holy to dogs—they will only turn and attack you. Do not throw your pearls in front of pigs—they will only trample them underfoot.

Ask, Seek, Knock
(Luke 11.9-13)

7 "Ask, and you will receive; seek, and you will find; knock, and the door will be opened to you. 8 For everyone who asks will receive, and anyone who seeks will find, and the door will be opened to him who knocks. 9 Would any of you who are fathers give your son a stone when he asks for bread? 10 Or would you give him a snake when he asks for a fish? 11 Bad as you are, you know how to give good things to your children. How much more, then, will your Father in heaven give good things to those who ask him!

12 "Do for others what you want them to do for you: this is the meaning of the Law of Moses and of the teachings of the prophets.

The Narrow Gate
(Luke 13.24)

13 "Go in through the narrow gate, because the gate to hell is wide and the road that leads to it is easy, and there are many who travel it. 14 But the gate to life is narrow and the way that leads to it is hard, and there are few people who find it.

A Tree and Its Fruit
(Luke 6.43-44)

15 "Be on your guard against false prophets; they come to you looking like sheep on the outside, but on the inside they are really like wild wolves. 16 You will know them by what they do. Thorn bushes do not bear grapes, and briars do not bear figs. 17 A healthy tree bears good fruit, but a poor tree bears

bad fruit. ¹⁸A healthy tree cannot bear bad fruit, and a poor tree cannot bear good fruit. ¹⁹And any tree that does not bear good fruit is cut down and thrown in the fire. ²⁰So then, you will know the false prophets by what they do.

I Never Knew You
(Luke 13.25–27)

21 "Not everyone who calls me 'Lord, Lord' will enter the Kingdom of heaven, but only those who do what my Father in heaven wants them to do. ²²When Judgement Day comes, many will say to me, 'Lord, Lord! In your name we spoke God's message, by your name we drove out many demons and performed many miracles!' ²³Then I will say to them, 'I never knew you. Get away from me, you wicked people!'

The Two House Builders
(Luke 6.47–49)

24 "So then, anyone who hears these words of mine and obeys them is like a wise man who built his house on rock. ²⁵The rain poured down, the rivers overflowed, and the wind blew hard against that house. But it did not fall, because it was built on rock.

26 "But anyone who hears these words of mine and does not obey them is like a foolish man who built his house on sand. ²⁷The rain poured down, the rivers overflowed, the wind blew hard against that house, and it fell. And what a terrible fall that was!"

The Authority of Jesus

28 When Jesus finished saying these things, the crowd was amazed at the way he taught. ²⁹He wasn't like the teachers of the Law; instead, he taught with authority.

Jesus Heals a Man
(Mark 1.40–45; Luke 5.12–16)

8 When Jesus came down from the hill, large crowds followed him. ²Then a man suffering from a dreaded skin-disease came to him, knelt down before him, and said, "Sir, if you want to, you can make me clean." *e*

3 Jesus stretched out his hand and touched him. "I do want to," he answered. "Be clean!" At once the man was healed of his disease. 4 Then Jesus said to him, "Listen! Don't tell anyone, but go straight to the priest and let him examine you; then in order to prove to everyone that you are cured, offer the sacrifice that Moses ordered."

Jesus Heals a Roman Officer's Servant
(Luke 7.1–10)

5 When Jesus entered Capernaum, a Roman officer met him and begged for help: 6 "Sir, my servant is sick in bed at home, unable to move and suffering terribly."

7 "I will go and make him well," Jesus said.

8 "Oh no, sir," answered the officer. "I do not deserve to have you come into my house. Just give the order, and my servant will get well. 9 I, too, am a man under the authority of superior officers, and I have soldiers under me. I order this one, 'Go!' and he goes; and I order that one, 'Come!' and he comes; and I order my slave, 'Do this!' and he does it."

10 When Jesus heard this, he was surprised and said to the people following him, "I tell you, I have never found anyone in Israel with faith like this. 11 I assure you that many will come from the east and the west and sit down with Abraham, Isaac, and Jacob at the feast in the Kingdom of heaven. 12 But those who should be in the Kingdom will be thrown out into the darkness, where they will cry and grind their teeth." 13 Then Jesus said to the officer, "Go home, and what you believe will be done for you."

And the officer's servant was healed that very moment.

Jesus Heals Many People
(Mark 1.29–34; Luke 4.38–41)

14 Jesus went to Peter's home, and there he saw

---

*e*MAKE ME CLEAN: *This disease was considered to make a person ritually unclean.*

Peter's mother-in-law sick in bed with a fever. [15] He touched her hand; the fever left her, and she got up and began to wait on him.

16 When evening came, people brought to Jesus many who had demons in them. Jesus drove out the evil spirits with a word and healed all who were sick. [17] He did this to make what the prophet Isaiah had said come true, "He himself took our sickness and carried away our diseases."

The Would-be Followers of Jesus
(Luke 9.57–62)

18 When Jesus noticed the crowd round him, he ordered his disciples to go to the other side of the lake. [19] A teacher of the Law came to him. "Teacher," he said, "I am ready to go with you wherever you go."

20 Jesus answered him, "Foxes have holes, and birds have nests, but the Son of Man has nowhere to lie down and rest."

21 Another man, who was a disciple, said, "Sir, first let me go back and bury my father."

22 "Follow me," Jesus answered, "and let the dead bury their own dead."

Jesus Calms a Storm
(Mark 4.35–41; Luke 8.22–25)

23 Jesus got into a boat, and his disciples went with him. [24] Suddenly a fierce storm hit the lake, and the boat was in danger of sinking. But Jesus was asleep. [25] The disciples went to him and woke him up. "Save us, Lord!" they said. "We are about to die!"

26 "Why are you so frightened?" Jesus answered. "How little faith you have!" Then he got up and ordered the winds and the waves to stop, and there was a great calm.

27 Everyone was amazed. "What kind of man is this?" they said. "Even the winds and the waves obey him!"

Jesus Heals Two Men with Demons
(Mark 5.1–20; Luke 8.26–39)

28 When Jesus came to the territory of Gadara on the other side of the lake, he was met by two men who came out of the burial caves there. These men had demons in them and were so fierce that no one dared travel on that road. 29 At once they screamed, "What do you want with us, you Son of God? Have you come to punish us before the right time?"

30 Not far away there was a large herd of pigs feeding. 31 So the demons begged Jesus, "If you are going to drive us out, send us into that herd of pigs."

32 "Go," Jesus told them; so they left and went off into the pigs. The whole herd rushed down the side of the cliff into the lake and was drowned.

33 The men who had been taking care of the pigs ran away and went into the town, where they told the whole story and what had happened to the men with the demons. 34 So everyone from the town went out to meet Jesus; and when they saw him, they begged him to leave their territory.

Jesus Heals a Paralysed Man
(Mark 2.1–12; Luke 5.17–26)

9 Jesus got into the boat and went back across the lake to his own town,*f* 2 where some people brought to him a paralysed man, lying on a bed. When Jesus saw how much faith they had, he said to the paralysed man, "Courage, my son! Your sins are forgiven."

3 Then some teachers of the Law said to themselves, "This man is speaking blasphemy!"

4 Jesus perceived what they were thinking, so he said, "Why are you thinking such evil things? 5 Is it easier to say, 'Your sins are forgiven,' or to say, 'Get up and walk'? 6 I will prove to you, then, that the Son of Man has authority on earth to forgive sins." So he said to the paralysed man, "Get up, pick up your bed, and go home!"

7 The man got up and went home. 8 When the people

---

f HIS OWN TOWN: *Capernaum (see 4.13).*

saw it, they were afraid, and praised God for giving such authority to men.

Jesus Calls Matthew
(Mark 2.13–17; Luke 5.27–32)

9 Jesus left that place, and as he walked along, he saw a tax collector, named Matthew, sitting in his office. He said to him, "Follow me."

Matthew got up and followed him.

10 While Jesus was having a meal in Matthew's house,g many tax collectors and other outcasts came and joined Jesus and his disciples at the table. 11 Some Pharisees saw this and asked his disciples, "Why does your teacher eat with such people?"

12 Jesus heard them and answered, "People who are well do not need a doctor, but only those who are sick. 13 Go and find out what is meant by the scripture that says: 'It is kindness that I want, not animal sacrifices.' I have not come to call respectable people, but outcasts."

The Question about Fasting
(Mark 2.18–22; Luke 5.33–39)

14 Then the followers of John the Baptist came to Jesus, asking, "Why is it that we and the Pharisees fast often, but your disciples don't fast at all?"

15 Jesus answered, "Do you expect the guests at a wedding party to be sad as long as the bridegroom is with them? Of course not! But the day will come when the bridegroom will be taken away from them, and then they will fast.

16 "No one patches up an old coat with a piece of new cloth, for the new patch will shrink and make an even bigger hole in the coat. 17 Nor does anyone pour new wine into used wineskins, for the skins will burst, the wine will pour out, and the skins will be ruined. Instead, new wine is poured into fresh wineskins, and both will keep in good condition."

gin Matthew's house; or in his (that is, Jesus') house.

**The Official's Daughter and the Woman
Who Touched Jesus' Cloak**
(Mark 5.21–43; Luke 8.40–56)

18 While Jesus was saying this, a Jewish official came to him, knelt down before him, and said, "My daughter has just died; but come and place your hands on her, and she will live."

19 So Jesus got up and followed him, and his disciples went along with him.

20 A woman who had suffered from severe bleeding for twelve years came up behind Jesus and touched the edge of his cloak. 21 She said to herself, "If I

If I only touch his cloak (9.21)

only touch his cloak, I will get well."

22 Jesus turned round and saw her, and said, "Courage, my daughter! Your faith has made you well." At that very moment the woman became well.

23 Then Jesus went into the official's house. When he saw the musicians for the funeral and the people all stirred up, 24 he said, "Get out, everybody! The little girl is not dead—she is only sleeping!" Then they all laughed at him. 25 But as soon as the people had been put out, Jesus went into the girl's room and took hold of her hand, and she got up. 26 The news about this spread all over that part of the country.

Jesus Heals Two Blind Men

27 Jesus left that place, and as he walked along, two blind men started following him. "Take pity on us, Son of David!" they shouted.

28 When Jesus had gone indoors, the two blind men came to him, and he asked them, "Do you believe that I can heal you?"

"Yes, sir!" they answered.

29 Then Jesus touched their eyes and said, "Let it happen, then, just as you believe!"—30 and their sight was restored. Jesus spoke sternly to them, "Don't tell this to anyone!"

31 But they left and spread the news about Jesus all over that part of the country.

Jesus Heals a Dumb Man

32 As the men were leaving, some people brought to Jesus a man who could not talk because he had a demon. 33 But as soon as the demon was driven out, the man started talking, and everyone was amazed. "We have never seen anything like this in Israel!" they exclaimed.

34 But the Pharisees said, "It is the chief of the demons who gives him the power to drive out demons."

Jesus Has Pity for the People

35 Jesus went round visiting all the towns and villages. He taught in the synagogues, preached the Good News about the Kingdom, and healed people with every kind of disease and sickness. 36 As he saw the crowds, his heart was filled with pity for them, because they were worried and helpless, like sheep without a shepherd. 37 So he said to his disciples, "The harvest is large, but there are few workers to gather it in. 38 Pray to the owner of the harvest that he will send out workers to gather in his harvest."

The Twelve Apostles
(Mark 3.13–19; Luke 6.12–16)

10 Jesus called his twelve disciples together and gave them authority to drive out evil spirits and to heal every disease and every sickness. 2 These are the names of the twelve apostles: first, Simon (called Peter) and his brother Andrew; James and his brother John, the sons of Zebedee; 3 Philip and Bartholomew; Thomas and Matthew, the tax collector; James son of Alphaeus, and Thaddaeus; 4 Simon the Patriot, and Judas Iscariot, who betrayed Jesus.

The Mission of the Twelve
(Mark 6.7-13; Luke 9.1-6)

5 These twelve men were sent out by Jesus with the following instructions: "Do not go to any Gentile territory or any Samaritan towns. 6 Instead, you are to go to the lost sheep of the people of Israel. 7 Go and preach, 'The Kingdom of heaven is near!' 8 Heal the sick, bring the dead back to life, heal those who suffer from dreaded skin-diseases, and drive out demons. You have received without paying, so give without being paid. 9 Do not carry any gold, silver, or copper money in your pockets; 10 do not carry a beggar's bag for the journey or an extra shirt or shoes or a stick. A worker should be given what he needs.

11 "When you come to a town or village, go in and look for someone who is willing to welcome you, and stay with him until you leave that place. 12 When you go into a house, say, 'Peace be with you.' 13 If the people in that house welcome you, let your greeting of peace remain; but if they do not welcome you, then take back your greeting. 14 And if some home or town will not welcome you or listen to you, then leave that place and shake the dust off your feet. 15 I assure you that on the Judgement Day God will show more mercy to the people of Sodom and Gomorrah than to the people of that town!

Coming Persecutions
(Mark 13.9-13; Luke 21.12-17)

16 "Listen! I am sending you out just like sheep to a pack of wolves. You must be as cautious as snakes and as gentle as doves. 17 Watch out, for there will be men who will arrest you and take you to court, and they will whip you in the synagogues. 18 For my sake you will be brought to trial before rulers and kings, to tell the Good News to them

and to the Gentiles. [19]When they bring you to trial, do not worry about what you are going to say or how you will say it; when the time comes, you will be given what you will say. [20]For the words you will speak will not be yours; they will come from the Spirit of your Father speaking through you.

21 "Men will hand over their own brothers to be put to death, and fathers will do the same to their children; children will turn against their parents and have them put to death. [22]Everyone will hate you because of me. But whoever holds out to the end will be saved. [23]When they persecute you in one town, run away to another one. I assure you that you will not finish your work in all the towns of Israel before the Son of Man comes.

24 "No pupil is greater than his teacher; no slave is greater than his master. [25]So a pupil should be satisfied to become like his teacher, and a slave like his master. If the head of the family is called Beelzebul, the members of the family will be called even worse names!

Whom to Fear
(Luke 12.2-7)

26 "So do not be afraid of people. Whatever is now covered up will be uncovered, and every secret will be made known. [27]What I am telling you in the dark you must repeat in broad daylight, and what you have heard in private you must announce from the housetops. [28]Do not be afraid of those who kill the body but cannot kill the soul; rather be afraid of God, who can destroy both body and soul in hell. [29]For only a penny you can buy two sparrows, yet not one sparrow falls to the ground without your Father's consent. [30]As for you, even the hairs of your head have all been counted. [31]So do not be afraid; you are worth much more than many sparrows!

Confessing and Rejecting Christ
(Luke 12.8-9)

32 "If anyone declares publicly that he belongs to me, I will do the same for him before my Father

in heaven. 33 But if anyone rejects me publicly, I wi.. reject him before my Father in heaven.

Not Peace, but a Sword
(Luke 12.51–53; 14.26–27)

34 "Do not think that I have come to bring peace to the world. No, I did not come to bring peace, but a sword. 35 I came to set sons against their fathers, daughters against their mothers, daughters-in-law against their mothers-in-law; 36 a man's worst enemies will be the members of his own family.

37 "Whoever loves his father or mother more than me is not fit to be my disciple; whoever loves his son or daughter more than me is not fit to be my disciple. 38 Whoever does not take up his cross and follow in my steps is not fit to be my disciple. 39 Whoever tries to gain his own life will lose it; but whoever loses his life for my sake will gain it.

Rewards
(Mark 9.41)

40 "Whoever welcomes you welcomes me; and whoever welcomes me welcomes the one who sent me. 41 Whoever welcomes God's messenger because he is God's messenger, will share in his reward. And whoever welcomes a good man because he is good, will share in his reward. 42 You can be sure that whoever gives even a drink of cold water to one of the least of these my followers because he is my follower, will certainly receive a reward."

The Messengers from John the Baptist
(Luke 7.18–35)

11 When Jesus finished giving these instructions to his twelve disciples, he left that place and went off to teach and preach in the towns near there.

2 When John the Baptist heard in prison about the things that Christ was doing, he sent some of his disciples to him. 3 "Tell us," they asked Jesus, "are you the one John said was going to come, or should we expect someone else?"

4 Jesus answered, "Go back and tell John what you are hearing and seeing: 5 the blind can see, the

lame can walk, those who suffer from dreaded skin-
diseases are made clean,[h] the deaf hear, the dead
are brought back to life, and the Good News is
preached to the poor. [6]How happy are those who
have no doubts about me!"

7 While John's disciples were leaving, Jesus spoke
about him to the crowds: "When you went out to
John in the desert, what did you expect to see? A
blade of grass bending in the wind? [8]What did you
go out to see? A man dressed up in fancy clothes?
People who dress like that live in palaces! [9]Tell me,
what did you go out to see? A prophet? Yes indeed,
but you saw much more than a prophet. [10]For John
is the one of whom the scripture says: 'God said,
I will send my messenger ahead of you to open the
way for you.' [11]I assure you that John the Baptist is
greater than any man who has ever lived. But he
who is least in the Kingdom of heaven is greater
than John. [12]From the time John preached his message
until this very day the Kingdom of heaven has suffered
violent attacks,[i] and violent men try to seize it. [13]Until
the time of John all the prophets and the Law of
Moses spoke about the Kingdom; [14]and if you are
willing to believe their message, John is Elijah, whose
coming was predicted. [15]Listen, then, if you have ears!

16 "Now, to what can I compare the people of
this day? They are like children sitting in the market-
place. One group shouts to the other, [17]'We played
wedding music for you, but you wouldn't dance! We
sang funeral songs, but you wouldn't cry!' [18]When
John came, he fasted and drank no wine, and everyone
said, 'He has a demon in him!' [19]When the Son of
Man came, he ate and drank, and everyone said, 'Look
at this man! He is a glutton and a drinker, a friend
of tax collectors and other outcasts!' God's wisdom,
however, is shown to be true by its results."

The Unbelieving Towns
(Luke 10.13–15)

20 The people in the towns where Jesus had per-

[h]MADE CLEAN: See 8.2.
[i]has suffered violent attacks; or has been coming violently.

Come to me, all of you who are tired (11.28)

formed most of his miracles did not turn from their sins, so he reproached those towns. 21"How terrible it will be for you, Chorazin! How terrible for you too, Bethsaida! If the miracles which were performed in you had been performed in Tyre and Sidon, the people there would long ago have put on sackcloth and sprinkled ashes on themselves, to show that they had turned from their sins! 22I assure you that on the Judgement Day God will show more mercy to the people of Tyre and Sidon than to you! 23And as for you, Capernaum! Did you want to lift yourself up to heaven? You will be thrown down to hell! If the miracles which were performed in you had been performed in Sodom, it would still be in existence today! 24You can be sure that on the Judgement Day God will show more mercy to Sodom than to you!"

Come to Me and Rest
(Luke 10.21-22)

25 At that time Jesus said, "Father, Lord of heaven and earth! I thank you because you have shown to the unlearned what you have hidden from the wise and learned. 26Yes, Father, this was how you wanted it to happen.

27 "My Father has given me all things. No one knows the Son except the Father, and no one knows the Father except the Son and those to whom the Son chooses to reveal him.

28 "Come to me, all of you who are tired from

carrying heavy loads, and I will give you rest. 29 Take my yoke and put it on you, and learn from me, because I am gentle and humble in spirit; and you will find rest. 30 For the yoke I will give you is easy, and the load I will put on you is light."

The Question about the Sabbath
(Mark 2.23–28; Luke 6.1–5)

12 Not long afterwards Jesus was walking through some cornfields on the Sabbath. His disciples were hungry, so they began to pick ears of corn and eat the grain. 2 When the Pharisees saw this, they said to Jesus, "Look, it is against our Law for your disciples to do this on the Sabbath!"

3 Jesus answered, "Have you never read what David did that time when he and his men were hungry? 4 He went into the house of God, and he and his men ate the bread offered to God, even though it was against the Law for them to eat it—only the priests were allowed to eat that bread. 5 Or have you not read in the Law of Moses that every Sabbath the priests in the Temple actually break the Sabbath law, yet they are not guilty? 6 I tell you that there is something here greater than the Temple. 7 The scripture says, 'It is kindness that I want, not animal sacrifices.' If you really knew what this means, you would not condemn people who are not guilty; 8 for the Son of Man is Lord of the Sabbath."

The Man with a Paralysed Hand
(Mark 3.1–6; Luke 6.6–11)

9 Jesus left that place and went to a synagogue, 10 where there was a man who had a paralysed hand. Some people were there who wanted to accuse Jesus of doing wrong, so they asked him, "Is it against our Law to heal on the Sabbath?"

11 Jesus answered, "What if one of you has a sheep and it falls into a deep hole on the Sabbath? Will he not take hold of it and lift it out? 12 And a man is worth much more than a sheep! So then, our Law does allow us to help someone on the Sabbath." 13 Then he said to the man with the paralysed hand, "Stretch out your hand."

He stretched it out, and it became well again, just like the other one. [14] Then the Pharisees left and made plans to kill Jesus.

God's Chosen Servant

15 When Jesus heard about the plot against him, he went away from that place; and large crowds followed him. He healed all those who were ill [16] and gave them orders not to tell others about him. [17] He did this so as to make what God had said through the prophet Isaiah come true:

[18] "Here is my servant, whom I have chosen,
    the one I love, and with whom I am pleased.
I will send my Spirit upon him,
    and he will announce my judgement to the nations.
[19] He will not argue or shout,
    or make loud speeches in the streets.
[20] He will not break off a bent reed,
    or put out a flickering lamp.
He will persist until he causes justice to triumph,
[21] and in him all peoples will put their hope."

Jesus and Beelzebul
(Mark 3.20-30; Luke 11.14-23)

22 Then some people brought to Jesus a man who was blind and could not talk because he had a demon. Jesus healed the man, so that he was able to talk and see. [23] The crowds were all amazed at what Jesus had done. "Could he be the Son of David?" they asked.

24 When the Pharisees heard this, they replied, "He drives out demons only because their ruler Beelzebul gives him power to do so."

25 Jesus knew what they were thinking, so he said to them, "Any country that divides itself into groups which fight each other will not last very long. And any town or family that divides itself into groups which fight each other will fall apart. [26] So if one group is fighting another in Satan's kingdom, this means that it is already divided into groups and will soon fall apart! [27] You say that I drive out demons because Beelzebul gives me the power to do so. Well, then, who gives your followers the power to drive

them out? What your own followers do proves that you are wrong! 28No, it is not Beelzebul, but God's Spirit, who gives me the power to drive out demons, which proves that the Kingdom of God has already come upon you.

29 "No one can break into a strong man's house and take away his belongings unless he first ties up the strong man; then he can plunder his house.

30 "Anyone who is not for me is really against me; anyone who does not help me gather is really scattering. 31And so I tell you that people can be forgiven any sin and any evil thing they say;*j* but whoever says evil things against the Holy Spirit will not be forgiven. 32Anyone who says something against the Son of Man can be forgiven; but whoever says something against the Holy Spirit will not be forgiven—now or ever.

A Tree and Its Fruit
(Luke 6.43–45)

33 "To have good fruit you must have a healthy tree; if you have a poor tree, you will have bad fruit. A tree is known by the kind of fruit it bears. 34You snakes—how can you say good things when you are evil? For the mouth speaks what the heart is full of. 35A good person brings good things out of his treasure of good things; a bad person brings bad things out of his treasure of bad things.

36 "You can be sure that on Judgement Day everyone will have to give account of every useless word he has ever spoken. 37Your words will be used to judge you—to declare you either innocent or guilty."

The Demand for a Miracle
(Mark 8.11–12; Luke 11.29–32)

38 Then some teachers of the Law and some Pharisees spoke up. "Teacher," they said, "we want to see you perform a miracle."

39 "How evil and godless are the people of this day!" Jesus exclaimed. "You ask me for a miracle? No! The only miracle you will be given is the miracle

*j*evil thing they say; or evil thing they say against God.

of the prophet Jonah. 40 In the same way that Jonah spent three days and nights in the big fish, so will the Son of Man spend three days and nights in the depths of the earth. 41 On Judgement Day the people of Nineveh will stand up and accuse you, because they turned from their sins when they heard Jonah preach; and I tell you that there is something here greater than Jonah! 42 On Judgement Day the Queen of Sheba will stand up and accuse you, because she travelled all the way from her country to listen to King Solomon's wise teaching; and I assure you that there is something here greater than Solomon!

The Return of the Evil Spirit
(Luke 11.24–26)

43 "When an evil spirit goes out of a person, it travels over dry country looking for a place to rest. If it can't find one, 44 it says to itself, 'I will go back to my house.' So it goes back and finds the house empty, clean, and all tidy. 45 Then it goes out and brings along seven other spirits even worse than itself, and they come and live there. So when it is all over, that person is in a worse state than he was at the beginning. This is what will happen to the evil people of this day."

Jesus' Mother and Brothers
(Mark 3.31–35; Luke 8.19–21)

46 Jesus was still talking to the people when his mother and brothers arrived. They stood outside, asking to speak with him. 47 So one of the people there said to him, "Look, your mother and brothers are standing outside, and they want to speak with you." k

48 Jesus answered, "Who is my mother? Who are my brothers?" 49 Then he pointed to his disciples and said, "Look! Here are my mother and my brothers! 50 Whoever does what my Father in heaven wants him to do is my brother, my sister, and my mother."

k Some manuscripts do not have verse 47.

The Parable of the Sower
(Mark 4.1–9; Luke 8.4–8)

13 That same day Jesus left the house and went to the 1ake-side, where he sat down to teach. ²The crowd that gathered round him was so large that he got into a boat and sat in it, while the crowd stood on the shore. ³He used parables to tell them many things.

"Once there was a man who went out to sow corn. ⁴As he scattered the seed in the field, some of it fell along the path, and the birds came and ate it up. ⁵Some of it fell on rocky ground, where there was little soil. The seeds soon sprouted, because the soil wasn't deep. ⁶But when the sun came up, it burnt the young plants; and because the roots had not grown deep enough, the plants soon dried up. ⁷Some of the seed fell among thorn bushes, which grew up and choked the plants. ⁸But some seeds fell in good soil, and the plants produced corn; some produced a hundred grains, others sixty, and others thirty."

9 And Jesus concluded, "Listen, then, if you have ears!"

The Purpose of the Parables
(Mark 4.10–12; Luke 8.9–10)

10 Then the disciples came to Jesus and asked him, "Why do you use parables when you talk to the people?"

11 Jesus answered, "The knowledge about the secrets of the Kingdom of heaven has been given to you, but not to them. ¹²For the person who has something will be given more, so that he will have more than enough; but the person who has nothing will have taken away from him even the little he has. ¹³The reason I use parables in talking to them is that they look, but do not see, and they listen, but do not hear or understand. ¹⁴So the prophecy of Isaiah applies to them:

'This people will listen and listen, but not understand;
    they will look and look, but not see,
¹⁵ because their minds are dull,

and they have stopped up their ears
and have closed their eyes.
Otherwise, their eyes would see,
their ears would hear,
their minds would understand,
and they would turn to me, says God,
and I would heal them.'

16 "As for you, how fortunate you are! Your eyes see and your ears hear. 17 I assure you that many prophets and many of God's people wanted very much to see what you see, but they could not, and to hear what you hear, but they did not.

Jesus Explains the Parable of the Sower
(Mark 4.13–20; Luke 8.11–15)

18 "Listen, then, and learn what the parable of the sower means. 19 Those who hear the message about the Kingdom but do not understand it are like the seeds that fell along the path. The Evil One comes and snatches away what was sown in them. 20 The seeds that fell on rocky ground stand for those who receive the message gladly as soon as they hear it. 21 But it does not sink deep into them, and they don't last long. So when trouble or persecution comes because of the message, they give up at once. 22 The seeds that fell among thorn bushes stand for those who hear the message; but the worries about this life and the love for riches choke the message, and they don't bear fruit. 23 And the seeds sown in the good soil stand for those who hear the message and understand it: they bear fruit, some as much as a hundred, others sixty, and others thirty."

The Parable of the Weeds

24 Jesus told them another parable: "The Kingdom of heaven is like this. A man sowed good seed in his field. 25 One night, when everyone was asleep, an enemy came and sowed weeds among the wheat and went away. 26 When the plants grew and the ears of corn began to form, then the weeds showed up. 27 The man's servants came to him and said, 'Sir, it was good seed you sowed in your field; where did the weeds come from?' 28 'It was some enemy who

did this,' he answered. 'Do you want us to go and pull up the weeds?' they asked him. 29 'No,' he answered, 'because as you gather the weeds you might pull up some of the wheat along with them. 30 Let the wheat and the weeds both grow together until harvest. Then I will tell the harvest workers to pull up the weeds first, tie them in bundles and burn them, and then to gather in the wheat and put it in my barn.' "

The Parable of the Mustard Seed
(Mark 4.30–32; Luke 13.18–19)

31 Jesus told them another parable: "The Kingdom of heaven is like this. A man takes a mustard seed and sows it in his field. 32 It is the smallest of all seeds, but when it grows up, it is the biggest of all plants. It becomes a tree, so that birds come and make their nests in its branches."

The Parable of the Yeast
(Luke 13.20–21)

33 Jesus told them still another parable: "The Kingdom of heaven is like this. A woman takes some yeast and mixes it with forty litres of flour until the whole batch of dough rises."

Jesus' Use of Parables
(Mark 4.33–34)

34 Jesus used parables to tell all these things to the crowds; he would not say a thing to them without using a parable. 35 He did this to make what the prophet had said come true,

"I will use parables when I speak to them;
　I will tell them things unknown since the creation
　　of the world."

Jesus Explains the Parable of the Weeds

36 When Jesus had left the crowd and gone indoors, his disciples came to him and said, "Tell us what the parable about the weeds in the field means."

37 Jesus answered, "The man who sowed the good seed is the Son of Man; 38 the field is the world; the good seed is the people who belong to the King-

dom; the weeds are the people who belong to the Evil One; [39] and the enemy who sowed the weeds is the Devil. The harvest is the end of the age, and the harvest workers are angels. [40] Just as the weeds are gathered up and burnt in the fire, so the same thing will happen at the end of the age: [41] the Son of Man will send out his angels to gather up out of his Kingdom all those who cause people to sin and all others who do evil things, [42] and they will throw them into the fiery furnace, where they will cry and grind their teeth. [43] Then God's people will shine like the sun in their Father's Kingdom. Listen, then, if you have ears!

The Parable of the Hidden Treasure

[44] "The Kingdom of heaven is like this. A man happens to find a treasure hidden in a field. He covers it up again, and is so happy that he goes and sells everything he has, and then goes back and buys that field.

The Parable of the Pearl

[45] "Also, the Kingdom of heaven is like this. A man is looking for fine pearls, [46] and when he finds one that is unusually fine, he goes and sells everything he has, and buys that pearl.

The Parable of the Net

[47] "Also, the Kingdom of heaven is like this. Some fishermen throw their net out in the lake and catch all kinds of fish. [48] When the net is full, they pull it to shore and sit down to divide the fish: the good ones go into their buckets, the worthless ones are thrown away. [49] It will be like this at the end of the age: the angels will go out and gather up the evil people from among the good [50] and will throw them into the fiery furnace, where they will cry and grind their teeth.

New Truths and Old

[51] "Do you understand these things?" Jesus asked them.

"Yes," they answered.

52 So he replied, "This means, then, that every teacher of the Law who becomes a disciple in the Kingdom of heaven is like the owner of a house who takes new and old things out of his storeroom."

Jesus is Rejected at Nazareth
(Mark 6.1–6; Luke 4.16–30)

53 When Jesus finished telling these parables, he left that place 54 and went back to his home town. He taught in the synagogue, and those who heard him were amazed. "Where did he get such wisdom?" they asked. "And what about his miracles? 55 Isn't he the carpenter's son? Isn't Mary his mother, and aren't James, Joseph, Simon, and Judas his brothers? 56 Aren't all his sisters living here? Where did he get all this?" 57 And so they rejected him.

Jesus said to them, "A prophet is respected everywhere except in his home town and by his own family." 58 Because they did not have faith, he did not perform many miracles there.

The Death of John the Baptist
(Mark 6.14–29; Luke 9.7–9)

14 At that time Herod, the ruler of Galilee, heard about Jesus. 2 "He is really John the Baptist, who has come back to life," he told his officials. "That is why he has this power to perform miracles."

3 For Herod had earlier ordered John's arrest, and he had him chained and put in prison. He had done this because of Herodias, his brother Philip's wife. 4 For some time John the Baptist had told Herod, "It isn't right for you to be married to Herodias!" 5 Herod wanted to kill him, but he was afraid of the Jewish people, because they considered John to be a prophet.

6 On Herod's birthday the daughter of Herodias danced in front of the whole group. Herod was so pleased 7 that he promised her, "I swear that I will give you anything you ask for!"

8 At her mother's suggestion she asked him, "Give me here and now the head of John the Baptist on a dish!"

9 The king was sad, but because of the promise

he had made in front of all his guests he gave orders that her wish be granted. ¹⁰ So he had John beheaded in prison. ¹¹ The head was brought in on a dish and given to the girl, who took it to her mother. ¹² John's disciples came, carried away his body, and buried it; then they went and told Jesus.

Jesus Feeds Five Thousand Men
(Mark 6.30–44; Luke 9.10–17; John 6.1–14)

13 When Jesus heard the news about John, he left there in a boat and went to a lonely place by himself. The people heard about it, so they left their towns and followed him by land. ¹⁴ Jesus got out of the boat, and when he saw the large crowd, his heart was filled with pity for them, and he healed those who were ill.

15 That evening his disciples came to him and said, "It is already very late, and this is a lonely place. Send the people away and let them go to the villages to buy food for themselves."

16 "They don't have to leave," answered Jesus. "You yourselves give them something to eat!"

17 "All we have here are five loaves and two fish," they replied.

18 "Then bring them here to me," Jesus said. ¹⁹ He ordered the people to sit down on the grass; then he took the five loaves and the two fish, looked up to heaven, and gave thanks to God. He broke the loaves and gave them to the disciples, and the disciples gave them to the people. ²⁰ Everyone ate and had enough. Then the disciples took up twelve baskets full of what was left over. ²¹ The number of men who ate was about five thousand, not counting the women and children.

Jesus Walks on the Water
(Mark 6.45–52; John 6.15–21)

22 Then Jesus made the disciples get into the boat and go on ahead to the other side of the lake, while he sent the people away. ²³ After sending the people away, he went up a hill by himself to pray. When evening came, Jesus was there alone; ²⁴ and by this time the boat was far out in the lake, tossed about by

the waves, because the wind was blowing against it.

25 Between three and six o'clock in the morning Jesus came to the disciples, walking on the water. 26 When they saw him walking on the water, they were terrified. "It's a ghost!" they said, and screamed with fear.

27 Jesus spoke to them at once. "Courage!" he said. "It is I. Don't be afraid!"

28 Then Peter spoke up. "Lord, if it is really you, order me to come out on the water to you."

29 "Come!" answered Jesus. So Peter got out of the boat and started walking on the water to Jesus. 30 But when he noticed the strong wind, he was afraid and started to sink down in the water. "Save me, Lord!" he cried.

31 At once Jesus reached out and grabbed hold of him and said, "How little faith you have! Why did you doubt?"

32 They both got into the boat, and the wind died down. 33 Then the disciples in the boat worshipped Jesus. "Truly you are the Son of God!" they exclaimed.

Jesus Heals the Sick in Gennesaret
(Mark 6.53–56)

34 They crossed the lake and came to land at Gennesaret, 35 where the people recognized Jesus. So they sent for the sick people in all the surrounding country and brought them to Jesus. 36 They begged him to let those who were ill at least touch the edge of his cloak; and all who touched it were made well.

The Teaching of the Ancestors
(Mark 7.1–13)

15 Then some Pharisees and teachers of the Law came from Jerusalem to Jesus and asked him, 2 "Why is it that your disciples disobey the teaching handed down by our ancestors? They don't wash their hands in the proper way before they eat!"

3 Jesus answered, "And why do you disobey God's command and follow your own teaching? 4 For God said, 'Respect your father and your mother,' and 'Whoever curses his father or his mother is to be put

to death.' [5] But you teach that if a person has something he could use to help his father or mother, but says, 'This belongs to God,' [6] he does not need to honour his father.[1] In this way you disregard God's command, in order to follow your own teaching. [7] You hypocrites! How right Isaiah was when he prophesied about you!

[8] 'These people, says God, honour me with their words,
    but their heart is really far away from me.
[9] It is no use for them to worship me,
    because they teach man-made rules as though they
      were my laws!' "

The Things That Make a Person Unclean
(Mark 7.14–23)

10 Then Jesus called the crowd to him and said to them, "Listen and understand! [11] It is not what goes into a person's mouth that makes him ritually unclean; rather, what comes out of it makes him unclean."

12 Then the disciples came to him and said, "Do you know that the Pharisees had their feelings hurt by what you said?"

13 "Every plant which my Father in heaven did not plant will be pulled up," answered Jesus. [14] "Don't worry about them! They are blind leaders of the blind; and when one blind man leads another, both fall into a ditch."

15 Peter spoke up, "Explain this saying to us."

16 Jesus said to them, "You are still no more intelligent than the others. [17] Don't you understand? Anything that goes into a person's mouth goes into his stomach and then on out of his body. [18] But the things that come out of the mouth come from the heart, and these are the things that make a person ritually unclean. [19] For from his heart come the evil ideas which lead him to kill, commit adultery, and do other immoral things; to rob, lie, and slander others. [20] These are the things that make a person unclean. But to eat without washing your hands as they say you should—this doesn't make a person unclean."

[1] his father; *some manuscripts have* his father or mother.

They are blind leaders of the blind (15.14)

A Woman's Faith
(Mark 7.24-30)

21 Jesus left that place and went off to the territory near the cities of Tyre and Sidon. 22 A Canaanite woman who lived in that region came to him. "Son of David!" she cried out. "Have mercy on me, sir! My daughter has a demon and is in a terrible condition."

23 But Jesus did not say a word to her. His disciples came to him and begged him, "Send her away! She is following us and making all this noise!"

24 Then Jesus replied, "I have been sent only to the lost sheep of the people of Israel."

25 At this the woman came and fell at his feet. "Help me, sir!" she said.

26 Jesus answered, "It isn't right to take the children's food and throw it to the dogs."

27 "That's true, sir," she answered; "but even the dogs eat the leftovers that fall from their masters' table."

28 So Jesus answered her, "You are a woman of

great faith! What you want will be done for you."
And at that very moment her daughter was healed.

Jesus Heals Many People

29 Jesus left there and went along by Lake Galilee.
He climbed a hill and sat down. ³⁰Large crowds came
to him, bringing with them the lame, the blind, the
crippled, the dumb, and many other sick people, whom
they placed at Jesus' feet; and he healed them. ³¹The
people were amazed as they saw the dumb speaking,
the crippled made whole, the lame walking, and the
blind seeing; and they praised the God of Israel.

Jesus Feeds Four Thousand Men
(Mark 8.1-10)

32 Jesus called his disciples to him and said, "I
feel sorry for these people, because they have been
with me for three days and now have nothing to
eat. I don't want to send them away without feeding
them, for they might faint on their way home."

33 The disciples asked him, "Where will we find
enough food in this desert to feed this crowd?"

34 "How much bread have you?" Jesus asked.

"Seven loaves," they answered, "and a few small
fish."

35 So Jesus ordered the crowd to sit down on the
ground. ³⁶Then he took the seven loaves and the fish,
gave thanks to God, broke them, and gave them to
the disciples; and the disciples gave them to the people.
³⁷They all ate and had enough. Then the disciples
took up seven baskets full of pieces left over. ³⁸The
number of men who ate was four thousand, not counting the women and children.

39 Then Jesus sent the people away, got into a
boat, and went to the territory of Magadan.

The Demand for a Miracle
(Mark 8.11-13; Luke 12.54-56)

16 Some Pharisees and Sadducees who came to
Jesus wanted to trap him, so they asked him
to perform a miracle for them, to show that God
approved of him. ²But Jesus answered, "When the
sun is setting, you say, 'We are going to have fine

weather, because the sky is red.' ³And early in the morning you say, 'It is going to rain, because the sky is red and dark.' You can predict the weather by looking at the sky, but you cannot interpret the signs concerning these times!ᵐ ⁴How evil and godless are the people of this day! You ask me for a miracle? No! The only miracle you will be given is the miracle of Jonah."

So he left them and went away.

The Yeast of the Pharisees and Sadducees
(Mark 8.14–21)

5 When the disciples crossed over to the other side of the lake, they forgot to take any bread. ⁶Jesus said to them, "Take care; be on your guard against the yeast of the Pharisees and Sadducees."

7 They started discussing among themselves, "He says this because we didn't bring any bread."

8 Jesus knew what they were saying, so he asked them, "Why are you discussing among yourselves about not having any bread? How little faith you have! ⁹Don't you understand yet? Don't you remember when I broke the five loaves for the five thousand men? How many baskets did you fill? ¹⁰And what about the seven loaves for the four thousand men? How many baskets did you fill? ¹¹How is it that you don't understand that I was not talking to you about bread? Guard yourselves from the yeast of the Pharisees and Sadducees!"

12 Then the disciples understood that he was not warning them to guard themselves from the yeast used in bread but from the teaching of the Pharisees and Sadducees.

Peter's Declaration about Jesus
(Mark 8.27–30; Luke 9.18–21)

13 Jesus went to the territory near the town of Caesarea Philippi, where he asked his disciples, "Who do people say the Son of Man is?"

14 "Some say John the Baptist," they answered.

ᵐ Some manuscripts do not have the words of Jesus in verses 2 and 3.

"Others say Elijah, while others say Jeremiah or some other prophet."

15 "What about you?" he asked them. "Who do you say I am?"

16 Simon Peter answered, "You are the Messiah, the Son of the living God."

17 "Good for you, Simon son of John!" answered Jesus. "For this truth did not come to you from any human being, but it was given to you directly by my Father in heaven. 18 And so I tell you, Peter: you are a rock, and on this rock foundation I will build my church, and not even death will ever be able to overcome it. 19 I will give you the keys of the Kingdom of heaven; what you prohibit on earth will be prohibited in heaven, and what you permit on earth will be permitted in heaven."

20 Then Jesus ordered his disciples not to tell anyone that he was the Messiah.

Jesus Speaks about His Suffering and Death
(Mark 8.31—9.1; Luke 9.22-27)

21 From that time on Jesus began to say plainly to his disciples, "I must go to Jerusalem and suffer much from the elders, the chief priests, and the teachers of the Law. I will be put to death, but three days later I will be raised to life."

22 Peter took him aside and began to rebuke him. "God forbid it, Lord!" he said. "That must never happen to you!"

23 Jesus turned around and said to Peter, "Get away from me, Satan! You are an obstacle in my way, because these thoughts of yours don't come from God, but from man."

24 Then Jesus said to his disciples, "If anyone wants to come with me, he must forget self, carry his cross, and follow me. 25 For whoever wants to save his own life will lose it; but whoever loses his life for my sake will find it. 26 Will a person gain anything if he wins the whole world but loses his life? Of course not! There is nothing he can give to regain his life. 27 For the Son of Man is about to come in the glory of his Father with his angels, and then he will reward each one according to his deeds. 28 I assure you that

there are some here who will not die until they have seen the Son of Man come as King."

The Transfiguration
(Mark 9.2–13; Luke 9.28–36)

17 Six days later Jesus took with him Peter and the brothers James and John and led them up a high mountain where they were alone. ²As they looked on, a change came over Jesus: his face was shining like the sun, and his clothes were dazzling white. ³Then the three disciples saw Moses and Elijah talking with Jesus. ⁴So Peter spoke up and said to Jesus, "Lord, how good it is that we are here! If you wish, I will make three tents here, one for you, one for Moses, and one for Elijah."

5 While he was talking, a shining cloud came over them, and a voice from the cloud said, "This is my own dear Son, with whom I am pleased—listen to him!"

6 When the disciples heard the voice, they were so terrified that they threw themselves face downwards on the ground. ⁷Jesus came to them and touched them. "Get up," he said. "Don't be afraid!" ⁸So they looked up and saw no one there but Jesus.

9 As they came down the mountain, Jesus ordered them, "Don't tell anyone about this vision you have seen until the Son of Man has been raised from death."

10 Then the disciples asked Jesus, "Why do the teachers of the Law say that Elijah has to come first?"

11 "Elijah is indeed coming first," answered Jesus, "and he will get everything ready. ¹²But I tell you that Elijah has already come and people did not recognize him, but treated him just as they pleased. In the same way they will also ill-treat the Son of Man."

13 Then the disciples understood that he was talking to them about John the Baptist.

Jesus Heals a Boy with a Demon
(Mark 9.14–29; Luke 9.37–43a)

14 When they returned to the crowd, a man came to Jesus, knelt before him, ¹⁵and said, "Sir, have mercy on my son! He is an epileptic and has such terrible

fits that he often falls in the fire or into water. [16]I brought him to your disciples, but they could not heal him."

17 Jesus answered, "How unbelieving and wrong you people are! How long must I stay with you? How long do I have to put up with you? Bring the boy here to me!" [18]Jesus gave a command to the demon, and it went out of the boy, and at that very moment he was healed.

19 Then the disciples came to Jesus in private and asked him, "Why couldn't we drive the demon out?"

20 "It was because you haven't enough faith," answered Jesus. "I assure you that if you have faith as big. as a mustard seed, you can say to this hill, 'Go from here to there!' and it will go. You could do anything!"[n]

Jesus Speaks Again about His Death
(Mark 9.30–32; Luke 9.43b–45)

22 When the disciples all came together in Galilee, Jesus said to them, "The Son of Man is about to be handed over to men [23]who will kill him; but three days later he will be raised to life."

The disciples became very sad.

Payment of the Temple-Tax

24 When Jesus and his disciples came to Capernaum, the collectors of the temple-tax came to Peter and asked, "Does your teacher pay the temple-tax?"

25 "Of course," Peter answered.

When Peter went into the house, Jesus spoke up first, "Simon, what is your opinion? Who pays duties or taxes to the kings of this world? The citizens of the country or the foreigners?"

26 "The foreigners," answered Peter.

"Well, then," replied Jesus, "that means that the citizens don't have to pay. [27]But we don't want to offend these people. So go to the lake and drop in a line. Pull up the first fish you hook, and in its mouth

[n] *Some manuscripts add verse 21:* But only prayer and fasting can drive this kind out; nothing else can *(see Mk 9.29).*

you will find a coin worth enough for my temple-tax and yours. Take it and pay them our taxes."

Who Is the Greatest?
(Mark 9.33–37; Luke 9.46–48)

18 At that time the disciples came to Jesus, asking, "Who is the greatest in the Kingdom of heaven?"

2 So Jesus called a child, made him stand in front of them, ³and said, "I assure you that unless you

Unless you change and become like children (18.3)

change and become like children, you will never enter the Kingdom of heaven. ⁴The greatest in the Kingdom of heaven is the one who humbles himself and becomes like this child. ⁵And whoever welcomes in my name one such child as this, welcomes me.

Temptations to Sin
(Mark 9.42–48; Luke 17.1–2)

6 "If anyone should cause one of these little ones to lose his faith in me, it would be better for that person to have a large millstone tied round his neck and be drowned in the deep sea. ⁷How terrible for the world that there are things that make people lose their faith! Such things will always happen—but how terrible for the one who causes them!

8 "If your hand or your foot makes you lose your

faith, cut it off and throw it away! It is better for
you to enter life without a hand or a foot than to
keep both hands and both feet and be thrown into
the eternal fire. 9 And if your eye makes you lose
your faith, take it out and throw it away! It is better
for you to enter life with only one eye than to keep
both eyes and be thrown into the fire of hell.

The Parable of the Lost Sheep
(Luke 15.3–7)

10 "See that you don't despise any of these little
ones. Their angels in heaven, I tell you, are always
in the presence of my Father in heaven. *o*

12 "What do you think a man does who has a

*o Some manuscripts add verse 11: For the Son of Man came to
save the lost (see Lk 19.10).*

He will...go and look for the lost sheep (18.12)

hundred sheep and one of them gets lost? He will leave the other ninety-nine grazing on the hillside and go and look for the lost sheep. [13]When he finds it, I tell you, he feels far happier over this one sheep than over the ninety-nine that did not get lost. [14]In just the same way your[p] Father in heaven does not want any of these little ones to be lost.

A Brother Who Sins

[15] "If your brother sins against you,[q] go to him and show him his fault. But do it privately, just between yourselves. If he listens to you, you have won your brother back. [16]But if he will not listen to you, take one or two other persons with you, so that every accusation may be upheld by the testimony of two or more witnesses,' as the scripture says. [17]And if he will not listen to them, then tell the whole thing to the church. Finally, if he will not listen to the church, treat him as though he were a pagan or a tax collector.

Prohibiting and Permitting

[18] "And so I tell all of you: what you prohibit on earth will be prohibited in heaven, and what you permit on earth will be permitted in heaven.

[19] "And I tell you more: whenever two of you on earth agree about anything you pray for, it will be done for you by my Father in heaven. [20]For where two or three come together in my name, I am there with them."

The Parable of the Unforgiving Servant

[21] Then Peter came to Jesus and asked, "Lord, if my brother keeps on sinning against me, how many times do I have to forgive him? Seven times?"

[22] "No, not seven times," answered Jesus, "but seventy times seven,[r] [23]because the Kingdom of heaven is like this. Once there was a king who decided to check on his servants' accounts. [24]He had just begun to

[p]your; *some manuscripts have* my.
[q]*Some manuscripts do not have* against you.
[r]seventy times seven; *or* seventy-seven times.

do so when one of them was brought in who owed him millions of pounds. 25 The servant did not have enough to pay his debt, so the king ordered him to be sold as a slave, with his wife and his children and all that he had, in order to pay the debt. 26 The servant fell on his knees before the king. 'Be patient with me,' he begged, 'and I will pay you everything!' 27 The king felt sorry for him, so he forgave him the debt and let him go.

28 "Then the man went out and met one of his fellow-servants who owed him a few pounds. He grabbed him and started choking him. 'Pay back what you owe me!' he said. 29 His fellow-servant fell down and begged him, 'Be patient with me, and I will pay you back!' 30 But he refused; instead, he had him thrown into jail until he should pay the debt. 31 When the other servants saw what had happened, they were very upset and went to the king and told him everything. 32 So he called the servant in. 'You worthless slave!' he said. 'I forgave you the whole amount you owed me, just because you asked me to. 33 You should have had mercy on your fellow-servant, just as I had mercy on you.' 34 The king was very angry, and he sent the servant to jail to be punished until he should pay back the whole amount."

35 And Jesus concluded, "That is how my Father in heaven will treat every one of you unless you forgive your brother from your heart."

Jesus Teaches About Divorce
(Mark 10.1–12)

19 When Jesus finished saying these things, he left Galilee and went to the territory of Judaea on the other side of the River Jordan. 2 Large crowds followed him, and he healed them there.

3 Some Pharisees came to him and tried to trap him by asking, "Does our Law allow a man to divorce his wife for whatever reason he wishes?"

4 Jesus answered, "Haven't you read the scripture that says that in the beginning the Creator made people male and female? 5 And God said, 'For this reason a man will leave his father and mother and unite with his wife, and the two will become one.'

6 So they are no longer two, but one. Man must not separate, then, what God has joined together."

7 The Pharisees asked him, "Why, then, did Moses give the law for a man to hand his wife a divorce notice and send her away?"

8 Jesus answered, "Moses gave you permission to divorce your wives because you are so hard to teach. But it was not like that at the time of creation. 9 I tell you, then, that any man who divorces his wife for any cause other than her unfaithfulness, commits adultery if he marries some other woman."

10 His disciples said to him, "If this is how it is between a man and his wife, it is better not to marry."

11 Jesus answered, "This teaching does not apply to everyone, but only to those to whom God has given it. 12 For there are different reasons why men cannot marry: some, because they were born that way; others, because men made them that way; and others do not marry for the sake of the Kingdom of heaven. Let him who can accept this teaching do so."

Jesus Blesses Little Children
(Mark 10.13-16; Luke 18.15-17)

13 Some people brought children to Jesus for him to place his hands on them and to pray for them, but the disciples scolded the people. 14 Jesus said, "Let the children come to me and do not stop them, because the Kingdom of heaven belongs to such as these."

15 He placed his hands on them and then went away.

The Rich Young Man
(Mark 10.17-31; Luke 18.18-30)

16 Once a man came to Jesus. "Teacher," he asked, "what good thing must I do to receive eternal life?"

17 "Why do you ask me concerning what is good?" answered Jesus. "There is only One who is good. Keep the commandments if you want to enter life."

18 "What commandments?" he asked.

Jesus answered, "Do not commit murder; do not commit adultery; do not steal; do not accuse anyone falsely; [19] respect your father and your mother; and love your neighbour as you love yourself."

20 "I have obeyed all these commandments," the young man replied. "What else do I need to do?"

21 Jesus said to him, "If you want to be perfect, go and sell all you have and give the money to the poor, and you will have riches in heaven; then come and follow me."

22 When the young man heard this, he went away sad, because he was very rich.

23 Jesus then said to his disciples, "I assure you: it will be very hard for rich people to enter the Kingdom of heaven. [24] I repeat: it is much harder for a rich person to enter the Kingdom of God than for a camel to go through the eye of a needle."

25 When the disciples heard this, they were completely amazed. "Who, then, can be saved?" they asked.

26 Jesus looked straight at them and answered, "This is impossible for man, but for God everything is possible."

27 Then Peter spoke up. "Look," he said, "we have left everything and followed you. What will we have?"

28 Jesus said to them, "You can be sure that when the Son of Man sits on his glorious throne in the New Age, then you twelve followers of mine will also sit on thrones, to rule the twelve tribes of Israel. [29] And everyone who has left houses or brothers or sisters or father or mother or children or fields for my sake, will receive a hundred times more and will be given eternal life. [30] But many who now are first will be last, and many who now are last will be first.

The Workers in the Vineyard

20 "The Kingdom of heaven is like this. Once there was a man who went out early in the morning to hire some men to work in his vineyard. [2] He agreed to pay them the regular wage, a silver coin a day, and sent them to work in his vineyard. [3] He went out again to the market place at nine o'clock and saw some men standing there doing nothing, [4] so he told them, 'You also go and work in the vineyard, and I will pay you a fair wage.' [5] So they went. Then at twelve o'clock and again at three o'clock he did the same thing. 6 It was nearly five o'clock when he went to the market place and saw some other men still standing there. 'Why are you wasting the whole day here doing nothing?' he asked them. 7 'No one hired us,' they answered. 'Well, then, you also go and work in the vineyard,' he told them.

8 "When evening came, the owner told his foreman, 'Call the workers and pay them their wages, starting with those who were hired last and ending with those who were hired first.' 9 The men who had begun to work at five o'clock were paid a silver coin each. 10 So when the men who were the first to be hired came to be paid, they thought they would get more; but they too were given a silver coin each. 11 They took their money and started grumbling against the employer. 12 'These men who were hired last worked only one hour,' they said, 'while we put up with a whole day's work in the hot sun—yet you paid them the same as you paid us!'

13 " 'Listen, friend,' the owner answered one of them, 'I have not cheated you. After all, you agreed to do a day's work for one silver coin. 14 Now take your pay and go home. I want to give this man who was hired last as much as I have given you. 15 Don't I have the right to do as I wish with my own money? Or are you jealous because I am generous?' "

16 And Jesus concluded, "So those who are last will be first, and those who are first will be last."

Jesus Speaks a Third Time about His Death
(Mark 10.32-34; Luke 18.31-34)

17 As Jesus was going up to Jerusalem, he took the twelve disciples aside and spoke to them privately, as they walked along. 18 "Listen," he told them, "we are going up to Jerusalem, where the Son of Man will be handed over to the chief priests and the teachers of the Law. They will condemn him to death 19 and then hand him over to the Gentiles, who will mock him, whip him, and crucify him; but three days later he will be raised to life."

A Mother's Request
(Mark 10.35–45)

20 Then the wife of Zebedee came to Jesus with her two sons, bowed before him, and asked him a favour.

21 "What do you want?" Jesus asked her.

She answered, "Promise me that these two sons of mine will sit at your right and your left when you are King."

22 "You don't know what you are asking for," Jesus answered the sons. "Can you drink the cup of suffering that I am about to drink?"

"We can," they answered.

23 "You will indeed drink from my cup," Jesus told them, "but I do not have the right to choose who will sit at my right and my left. These places belong to those for whom my Father has prepared them."

24 When the other ten disciples heard about this, they became angry with the two brothers. 25 So Jesus called them all together and said, "You know that the rulers of the heathen have power over them, and the leaders have complete authority. 26 This, however, is not the way it shall be among you. If one of you wants to be great, he must be the servant of the rest; 27 and if one of you wants to be first, he must be your slave—28 like the Son of Man, who did not come to be served, but to serve and to give his life to redeem many people."

Jesus Heals Two Blind Men
(Mark 10.46–52; Luke 18.35–43)

29 As Jesus and his disciples were leaving Jericho, a large crowd was following. 30 Two blind men who were sitting by the road heard that Jesus was passing by, so they began to shout, "Son of David! Take pity on us, sir!"

31 The crowd scolded them and told them to be quiet. But they shouted even more loudly, "Son of David! Take pity on us, sir!"

32 Jesus stopped and called them. "What do you want me to do for you?" he asked them.

God bless him who comes in the name of the Lord! (21.9)

33 "Sir," they answered, "we want you to give us our sight!"

34 Jesus had pity on them and touched their eyes; at once they were able to see, and they followed him.

The Triumphant Entry into Jerusalem
(Mark 11.1–11; Luke 19.28–40; John 12.12–19)

21 As Jesus and his disciples approached Jerusalem, they came to Bethphage at the Mount of Olives. There Jesus sent two of the disciples on ahead ²with these instructions: "Go to the village there ahead of you, and at once you will find a donkey tied up with her colt beside her. Untie them and bring them to me. ³And if anyone says anything, tell him, 'The Master⁵ needs them'; and then he will let them go at once."

4 This happened in order to make what the prophet had said come true:

⁵ "Tell the city of Zion,
   Look, your king is coming to you!
He is humble and rides on a donkey
   and on a colt, the foal of a donkey."

6 So the disciples went and did what Jesus had told them to do: ⁷they brought the donkey and the colt, threw their cloaks over them, and Jesus got on. ⁸A large crowd of people spread their cloaks on the road while others cut branches from the trees and spread them on the road. ⁹The crowds walking in front of Jesus and those walking behind began to shout, "Praise to David's Son! God bless him who comes in the name of the Lord! Praise God!"

10 When Jesus entered Jerusalem, the whole city was thrown into an uproar. "Who is he?" the people asked.

11 "This is the prophet Jesus, from Nazareth in Galilee," the crowds answered.

Jesus Goes to the Temple
(Mark 11.15–19; Luke 19.45–48; John 2.13–22)

12 Jesus went into the Temple and drove out all

⁵The Master; or Their owner.

those who were buying and selling there. He overturned the tables of the money-changers and the stools of those who sold pigeons, 13 and said to them, "It is written in the Scriptures that God said, 'My Temple will be called a house of prayer.' But you are making it a hideout for thieves!"

14 The blind and the crippled came to him in the Temple, and he healed them. 15 The chief priests and the teachers of the Law became angry when they saw the wonderful things he was doing and the children shouting in the Temple, "Praise to David's Son!" 16 So they asked Jesus, "Do you hear what they are saying?"

"Indeed I do," answered Jesus. "Haven't you ever read this scripture? 'You have trained children and babies to offer perfect praise.' "

17 Jesus left them and went out of the city to Bethany, where he spent the night.

Jesus Curses the Fig-Tree
(Mark 11.12–14, 20–24)

18 On his way back to the city early next morning, Jesus was hungry. 19 He saw a fig-tree by the side of the road and went to it, but found nothing on it except leaves. So he said to the tree, "You will never again bear fruit!" At once the fig-tree dried up.

20 The disciples saw this and were astounded. "How did the fig-tree dry up so quickly?" they asked.

21 Jesus answered, "I assure you that if you believe and do not doubt, you will be able to do what I have done to this fig-tree. And not only this, but you will even be able to say to this hill, 'Get up and throw yourself in the sea,' and it will. 22 If you believe, you will receive whatever you ask for in prayer."

The Question about Jesus' Authority
(Mark 11.27–33; Luke 20.1–8)

23 Jesus came back to the Temple; and as he taught, the chief priests and the elders came to him and asked, "What right have you to do these things? Who gave you this right?"

24 Jesus answered them, "I will ask you just one question, and if you give me an answer, I will tell

you what right I have to do these things. 25 Where did John's right to baptize come from: was it from God or from man?"

They started to argue among themselves, "What shall we say? If we answer, 'From God,' he will say to us, 'Why, then, did you not believe John?' 26 But if we say, 'From man,' we are afraid of what the people might do, because they are all convinced that John was a prophet." 27 So they answered Jesus, "We don't know."

And he said to them, "Neither will I tell you, then, by what right I do these things.

The Parable of the Two Sons

28 "Now, what do you think? There was once a man who had two sons. He went to the elder one and said, 'Son, go and work in the vineyard today.' 29 'I don't want to,' he answered, but later he changed his mind and went. 30 Then the father went to the other son and said the same thing. 'Yes, sir,' he answered, but he did not go. 31 Which one of the two did what his father wanted?"

"The elder one," they answered.

So Jesus said to them, "I tell you: the tax collectors and the prostitutes are going into the Kingdom of God ahead of you. 32 For John the Baptist came to you showing you the right path to take, and you would not believe him; but the tax collectors and the prostitutes believed him. Even when you saw this, you did not later change your minds and believe him.

The Parable of the Tenants in the Vineyard
(Mark 12.1–12; Luke 20.9–19)

33 "Listen to another parable," Jesus said. "There was once a landowner who planted a vineyard, put a fence around it, dug a hole for the winepress, and built a watch-tower. Then he let out the vineyard to tenants and went on a journey. 34 When the time came to gather the grapes, he sent his slaves to the tenants to receive his share of the harvest. 35 The tenants seized his slaves, beat one, killed another, and stoned another. 36 Again the man sent other slaves, more than the first time, and the tenants treated them

the same way. 36 Last of all he sent his son to them. 'Surely they will respect my son,' he said. 38 But when the tenants saw the son, they said to themselves, 'This is the owner's son. Come on, let's kill him, and we will get his property!' 39 So they seized him, threw him out of the vineyard, and killed him.

40 "Now, when the owner of the vineyard comes, what will he do to those tenants?" Jesus asked.

41 "He will certainly kill those evil men," they answered, "and let the vineyard out to other tenants, who will give him his share of the harvest at the right time."

42 Jesus said to them, "Haven't you ever read what the Scriptures say?

'The stone which the builders rejected as worthless
    turned out to be the most important of all.
This was done by the Lord;
    what a wonderful sight it is!'

43 "And so I tell you," added Jesus, "the Kingdom of God will be taken away from you and given to a people who will produce the proper fruits." *t*

45 The chief priests and the Pharisees heard Jesus' parables and knew that he was talking about them, 46 so they tried to arrest him. But they were afraid of the crowds, who considered Jesus to be a prophet.

The Parable of the Wedding Feast
(Luke 14.15-24)

22 Jesus again used parables in talking to the people. 2 "The Kingdom of heaven is like this. Once there was a king who prepared a wedding feast for his son. 3 He sent his servants to tell the invited guests to come to the feast, but they did not want to come. 4 So he sent other servants with this message for the guests: 'My feast is ready now; my bullocks and prize calves have been butchered, and everything is ready. Come to the wedding feast!' 5 But the invited guests paid no attention and went about their business: one went to his farm, another to his shop, 6 while

t Some manuscripts add verse 44: Whoever falls on this stone will be cut to pieces; and if the stone falls on someone, it will crush him to dust *(see Lk 20.18).*

others grabbed the servants, beat them, and killed them. 7 The king was very angry; so he sent his soldiers, who killed those murderers and burnt down their city. 8 Then he called his servants and said to them, 'My wedding feast is ready, but the people I invited did not deserve it. 9 Now go to the main streets and invite to the feast as many people as you find.' 10 So the servants went out into the streets and gathered all the people they could find, good and bad alike; and the wedding hall was filled with people.

11 "The king went in to look at the guests and saw a man who was not wearing wedding clothes. 12 'Friend, how did you get in here without wedding clothes?' the king asked him. But the man said nothing. 13 Then the king told the servants, 'Tie him up hand and foot, and throw him outside in the dark. There he will cry and grind his teeth.' "

14 And Jesus concluded, "Many are invited, but few are chosen."

The Question about Paying Taxes
(Mark 12.13–17; Luke 20.20–26)

15 The Pharisees went off and made a plan to trap Jesus with questions. 16 Then they sent to him some of their disciples and some members of Herod's party. "Teacher," they said, "we know that you tell the truth. You teach the truth about God's will for man, without worrying about what people think, because you pay no attention to a man's status. 17 Tell us, then, what do you think? Is it against our Law to pay taxes to the Roman Emperor, or not?"

18 Jesus, however, was aware of their evil plan, and so he said, "You hypocrites! Why are you trying to trap me? 19 Show me the coin for paying the tax!"

They brought him the coin, 20 and he asked them, "Whose face and name are these?"

21 "The Emperor's," they answered.

So Jesus said to them, "Well, then, pay the Emperor what belongs to the Emperor, and pay God what belongs to God."

22 When they heard this, they were amazed; and they left him and went away.

The Question about Rising from Death
(Mark 12.18–27; Luke 20.27–40)

23 That same day some Sadducees came to Jesus and claimed that people will not rise from death. 24 "Teacher," they said, "Moses said that if a man who has no children dies, his brother must marry the widow so that they can have children who will be considered the dead man's children. 25 Now, there were seven brothers who used to live here. The eldest got married and died without having children, so he left his widow to his brother. 26 The same thing happened to the second brother, to the third, and finally to all seven. 27 Last of all, the woman died. 28 Now, on the day when the dead rise to life, whose wife will she be? All of them had married her."

29 Jesus answered them, "How wrong you are! It is because you don't know the Scriptures or God's power. 30 For when the dead rise to life, they will be like the angels in heaven and will not marry. 31 Now, as for the dead rising to life: haven't you ever read what God has told you? He said, 32 'I am the God of Abraham, the God of Isaac, and the God of Jacob.' He is the God of the living, not of the dead."

33 When the crowds heard this, they were amazed at his teaching.

The Great Commandment
(Mark 12.28–34; Luke 10.25–28)

34 When the Pharisees heard that Jesus had silenced the Sadducees, they came together, 35 and one of them, a teacher of the Law, tried to trap him with a question. 36 "Teacher," he asked, "which is the greatest commandment in the Law?"

37 Jesus answered, " 'Love the Lord your God with all your heart, with all your soul, and with all your mind.' 38 This is the greatest and the most important commandment. 39 The second most important commandment is like it: 'Love your neighbour as you love yourself.' 40 The whole Law of Moses and the teachings of the prophets depend on these two commandments."

The Question about the Messiah
(Mark 12.35–37; Luke 20.41–44)

41 When some Pharisees gathered together, Jesus asked them, 42 "What do you think about the Messiah? Whose descendant is he?"

"He is David's descendant," they answered.

43 "Why, then," Jesus asked, "did the Spirit inspire David to call him 'Lord'? David said,

44 'The Lord said to my Lord:

   Sit here on my right

   until I put your enemies under your feet.'

45 If, then, David called him 'Lord,' how can the Messiah be David's descendant?"

46 No one was able to give Jesus any answer, and from that day on no one dared to ask him any more questions.

Jesus Warns against the Teachers of the Law and the Pharisees
(Mark 12.38–39; Luke 11.43, 46; 20.45–46)

23 Then Jesus spoke to the crowds and to his disciples. 2 "The teachers of the Law and the Pharisees are the authorized interpreters of Moses' Law. 3 So you must obey and follow everything they tell you to do; do not, however, imitate their actions, because they don't practise what they preach. 4 They tie on to people's backs loads that are heavy and hard to carry, yet they aren't willing even to lift a finger to help them carry those loads. 5 They do everything so that people will see them. Look at the straps with scripture verses on them which they wear on their foreheads and arms, and notice how large they are! Notice also how long are the tassels on their cloaks!ᵘ 6 They love the best places at feasts and the reserved seats in the synagogues; 7 they love to be greeted with respect in the market-places and to be called 'Teacher.' You must not be called 'Teacher', because you are all brothers of one another and have only one Teacher. 9 And you must not call anyone here on

ᵘTASSELS ON THEIR CLOAKS: *These tassels were worn as a sign of devotion to God (see Num 15.37-41).*

They aren't willing...to help them (23.4)

earth 'Father', because you have only the one Father in heaven. ¹⁰Nor should you be called 'Leader', because your one and only leader is the Messiah. ¹¹The greatest one among you must be your servant. ¹²Whoever makes himself great will be humbled, and whoever humbles himself will be made great.

Jesus Condemns Their Hypocrisy
(Mark 12.40; Luke 11.39–42, 44, 52; 20.47)

13 "How terrible for you, teachers of the Law and Pharisees! You hypocrites! You lock the door to the Kingdom of heaven in people's faces, and you yourselves don't go in, nor do you allow in those who are trying to enter!ᵛ

15 "How terrible for you, teachers of the Law and Pharisees! You hypocrites! You sail the seas and cross whole countries to win one convert; and when you

ᵛ*Some manuscripts add verse 14:* How terrible for you, teachers of the Law and Pharisees! You hypocrites! You take advantage of widows and rob them of their homes, and then make a show of saying long prayers! Because of this your punishment will be all the worse! *(see Mk 12.40).*

succeed, you make him twice as deserving of going to hell as you yourselves are!

16 "How terrible for you, blind guides! You teach,

How terrible for you, blind guides! (23.16)

'If someone swears by the Temple, he isn't bound by his vow; but if he swears by the gold in the Temple, he is bound.' 17Blind fools! Which is more important, the gold or the Temple which makes the gold holy? 18You also teach, 'If someone swears by the altar, he isn't bound by his vow; but if he swears by the gift on the altar, he is bound.' 19How blind you are! Which is the more important, the gift or the altar which makes the gift holy? 20So then, when a person swears by the altar, he is swearing by it and by all the gifts on it; 21and when he swears by the Temple, he is swearing by it and by God, who lives there; 22and when someone swears by heaven, he is swearing by God's throne and by him who sits on it.

23 "How terrible for you, teachers of the Law and Pharisees! You hypocrites! You give to God a tenth even of the seasoning herbs, such as mint, dill, and cumin, but you neglect to obey the really important teachings of the Law, such as justice and mercy and honesty. These you should practise, without neglecting

the others. 24 Blind guides! You strain a fly out of your drink, but swallow a camel!

25 "How terrible for you, teachers of the Law and Pharisees! You hypocrites! You clean the outside of your cup and plate, while the inside is full of what you have obtained by violence and selfishness. 26 Blind Pharisee! Clean what is inside the cup first, and then the outside will be clean too!

27 "How terrible for you, teachers of the Law and Pharisees! You hypocrites! You are like whitewashed tombs, which look fine on the outside but are full of bones and decaying corpses on the inside. 28 In the same way, on the outside you appear good to everybody, but inside you are full of hypocrisy and sins.

Jesus Predicts Their Punishment
(Luke 11.47-51)

29 "How terrible for you, teachers of the Law and Pharisees! You hypocrites! You make fine tombs for the prophets and decorate the monuments of those who lived good lives; 30 and you claim that if you had lived during the time of your ancestors, you would not have done what they did and killed the prophets. 31 So you actually admit that you are the descendants of those who murdered the prophets! 32 Go on, then, and finish what your ancestors started! 33 You snakes and sons of snakes! How do you expect to escape from being condemned to hell? 34 And so I tell you that I will send you prophets and wise men and teachers; you will kill some of them, crucify others, and whip others in the synagogues and chase them from town to town. 35 As a result, the punishment for the murder of all innocent men will fall on you, from the murder of innocent Abel to the murder of Zachariah son of Berachiah, whom you murdered between the Temple and the altar. 36 I tell you indeed: the punishment for all these murders will fall on the people of this day!

Jesus' Love for Jerusalem
(Luke 13.34-35)

37 "Jerusalem, Jerusalem! You kill the prophets and

stone the messengers God has sent you! How many times have I wanted to put my arms round all your people, just as a hen gathers her chicks under her wings, but you would not let me! ³⁸And so your Temple will be abandoned and empty. ³⁹From now on, I tell you, you will never see me again until you say, 'God bless him who comes in the name of the Lord.' "

Jesus Speaks of the Destruction of the Temple
(Mark 13.1-2; Luke 21.5-6)

24 Jesus left and was going away from the Temple when his disciples came to him to call his attention to its buildings. ²"Yes," he said, "you may well look at all these. I tell you this: not a single stone here will be left in its place; every one of them will be thrown down."

Troubles and Persecutions
(Mark 13.3-13; Luke 21.7-19)

3 As Jesus sat on the Mount of Olives, the disciples came to him in private. "Tell us when all this will be," they asked, "and what will happen to show that it is the time for your coming and the end of the age."

4 Jesus answered, "Be on your guard, and do not let anyone deceive you. ⁵Many men, claiming to speak for me, will come and say, 'I am the Messiah!' and they will deceive many people. ⁶You are going to hear the noise of battles close by and the news of battles far away; but do not be troubled. Such things must happen, but they do not mean that the end has come. ⁷Countries will fight each other, kingdoms will attack one another. There will be famines and earthquakes everywhere. ⁸All these things are like the first pains of childbirth.

9 "Then you will be arrested and handed over to be punished and be put to death. All mankind will hate you because of me. ¹⁰Many will give up their faith at that time, they will betray one another and hate one another. ¹¹Then many false prophets will appear and deceive many people. ¹²Such will be the spread of evil that many people's love will grow cold. ¹³But whoever holds out to the end will be saved.

14 And this Good News about the Kingdom will be
preached through all the world for a witness to all
mankind; and then the end will come.

The Awful Horror
(Mark 13.14–23; Luke 21.20–24)

15 "You will see 'The Awful Horror' of which the
prophet Daniel spoke. It will be standing in the holy
place." (Note to the reader: be sure to understand
what this means!) 16 "Then those who are in Judaea
must run away to the hills. 17 A man who is on the
roof of his house must not take the time to go down
and get his belongings from the house. 18 A man who
is in the field must not go back to get his cloak.
19 How terrible it will be in those days for women
who are pregnant and for mothers with little babies!
20 Pray to God that you will not have to run away
during the winter or on a Sabbath! 21 For the trouble at
that time will be far more terrible than any there
has ever been, from the beginning of the world to
this very day. Nor will there ever be anything like
it again. 22 But God has already reduced the number of
days; had he not done so, nobody would survive.
For the sake of his chosen people, however, God
will reduce the days.

23 "Then, if anyone says to you, 'Look, here is
the Messiah!' or 'There he is!'—do not believe him.
24 For false Messiahs and false prophets will appear;
they will perform great miracles and wonders in order
to deceive even God's chosen people, if possible.
25 Listen! I have told you this before the time comes.

26 "Or, if people should tell you, 'Look, he is out
in the desert!'—don't go there; or if they say, 'Look,
he is hiding here!'—don't believe it. 27 For the Son
of Man will come like the lightning which flashes
across the whole sky from the east to the west.

28 "Wherever there is a dead body, the vultures
will gather.

The Coming of the Son of Man
(Mark 13.24–27; Luke 21.25–28)

29 "Soon after the trouble of those days, the sun
will grow dark, the moon will no longer shine, the

stars will fall from heaven, and the powers in space will be driven from their courses. [30]Then the sign of the Son of Man will appear in the sky; and all the peoples of earth will weep as they see the Son of Man coming on the clouds of heaven with power and great glory. [31]The great trumpet will sound, and he will send out his angels to the four corners of the earth, and they will gather his chosen people from one end of the world to the other.

The Lesson of the Fig-Tree
(Mark 13.28–31; Luke 21.29–33)

[32]"Let the fig-tree teach you a lesson. When its branches become green and tender and it starts putting out leaves, you know that summer is near. [33]In the same way, when you see all these things, you will know that the time is near, ready to begin. [w] [34]Remember that all these things will happen before the people now living have all died. [35]Heaven and earth will pass away, but my words will never pass away.

No One Knows the Day and Hour
(Mark 13.32–37; Luke 17.26–30, 34–36)

[36]"No one knows, however, when that day and hour will come—neither the angels in heaven nor the Son; [x] the Father alone knows. [37]The coming of the Son of Man will be like what happened in the time of Noah. [38]In the days before the flood people ate and drank, men and women married, up to the very day Noah went into the boat; [39]yet they did not realize what was happening until the flood came and swept them all away. That is how it will be when the Son of Man comes. [40]At that time two men will be working in a field: one will be taken away, the other will be left behind. [41]Two women will be at a mill grinding meal: one will be taken away, the other will be left behind.

[42]"Be on your guard, then, because you do not know what day your Lord will come. [43]If the owner of a house knew the time when the thief would come,

---

[w]the time is near, ready to begin; *or* he is near, ready to come.
[x]*Some manuscripts do not have* nor the Son.

you can be sure that he would stay awake and not let the thief break into his house. 44 So then, you also must always be ready, because the Son of Man will come at an hour when you are not expecting him.

The Faithful or the Unfaithful Servant
(Luke 12.41–48)

45 "Who, then, is a faithful and wise servant? He is the one that his master has placed in charge of the other servants to give them their food at the proper time. 46 How happy that servant is if his master finds him doing this when he comes home! 47 Indeed, I tell you, the master will put that servant in charge of all his property. 48 But if he is a bad servant, he will tell himself that his master will not come back for a long time, 49 and he will begin to beat his fellow-servants and to eat and drink with drunkards. 50 Then that servant's master will come back one day when the servant does not expect him and at a time he does not know. 51 The master will cut him in pieces^y and make him share the fate of the hypocrites. There he will cry and grind his teeth.

The Parable of the Ten Girls

25 "At that time the Kingdom of heaven will be like this. Once there were ten girls who took their oil lamps and went out to meet the bridegroom. 2 Five of them were foolish, and the other five were wise. 3 The foolish ones took their lamps but did not take any extra oil with them, 4 while the wise ones took containers full of oil for their lamps. 5 The bridegroom was late in coming, so the girls began to nod and fall asleep.

6 "It was already midnight when the cry rang out, 'Here is the bridegroom! Come and meet him!' 7 The ten girls woke up and trimmed their lamps. 8 Then the foolish ones said to the wise ones, 'Let us have some of your oil, because our lamps are going out.' 9 'No, indeed,' the wise ones answered, 'there is not enough for you and for us. Go to the shop and buy some for yourselves.' 10 So the foolish girls went off

^y cut him in pieces; or throw him out.

to buy some oil; and while they were gone, the bridegroom arrived. The five girls who were ready went in with him to the wedding feast, and the door was closed.

11 "Later the other girls arrived. 'Sir, sir! Let us in!' they cried out. 12 'Certainly not! I don't know you,' the bridegroom answered."

13 And Jesus concluded, "Be on your guard, then, because you do not know the day or the hour.

The Parable of the Three Servants
(Luke 19.11–27)

14 "At that time the Kingdom of heaven will be like this. Once there was a man who was about to go on a journey; he called his servants and put them in charge of his property. 15 He gave to each one according to his ability: to one he gave five thousand gold coins, to another he gave two thousand, and to another he gave one thousand. Then he left on his journey. 16 The servant who had received five thousand coins went at once and invested his money and earned another five thousand. 17 In the same way the servant who had received two thousand coins earned another two thousand. 18 But the servant who had received one thousand coins went off, dug a hole in the ground, and hid his master's money.

19 "After a long time the master of those servants came back and settled accounts with them. 20 The servant who had received five thousand coins came in and handed over the other five thousand. 'You gave me five thousand coins, sir,' he said. 'Look! Here are another five thousand that I have earned.' 21 'Well done, you good and faithful servant!' said his master. 'You have been faithful in managing small amounts, so I will put you in charge of large amounts. Come on in and share my happiness!'

22 "Then the servant who had been given two thousand coins came in and said, 'You gave me two thousand coins, sir. Look! Here are another two thousand that I have earned.' 23 'Well done, you good and faithful servant!' said his master. 'You have been faithful in managing small amounts, so I will put

you in charge of large amounts. Come on in and share my happiness!'

24 "Then the servant who had received one thousand coins came in and said, 'Sir, I know you are a hard man; you reap harvests where you did not sow, and you gather crops where you did not scatter seed. 25 I was afraid, so I went off and hid your money in the ground. Look! Here is what belongs to you.'

26 " 'You bad and lazy servant!' his master said. 'You knew, did you, that I reap harvests where I did not sow, and gather crops where I did not scatter seed? 27 Well, then, you should have deposited my money in the bank, and I would have received it all back with interest when I returned. 28 Now, take the money away from him and give it to the one who has ten thousand coins. 29 For to every person who has something, even more will be given, and he will have more than enough; but the person who has nothing, even the little that he has will be taken away from him. 30 As for this useless servant—throw him outside in the darkness; there he will cry and grind his teeth.'

The Final Judgement

31 "When the Son of Man comes as King and all the angels with him, he will sit on his royal throne, 32 and the people of all the nations will be gathered before him. Then he will divide them into two groups, just as a shepherd separates the sheep from the goats. 33 He will put the righteous people on his right and the others on his left. 34 Then the King will say to the people on his right, 'Come, you that are blessed by my Father! Come and possess the kingdom which has been prepared for you ever since the creation of the world. 35 I was hungry and you fed me, thirsty and you gave me a drink; I was a stranger and you received me in your homes, 36 naked and you clothed me; I was sick and you took care of me, in prison and you visited me.'

37 "The righteous will then answer him, 'When, Lord, did we ever see you hungry and feed you, or thirsty and give you a drink? 38 When did we ever see you a stranger and welcome you in our

homes, or naked and clothe you? ³⁹When did we ever see you sick or in prison, and visit you?' ⁴⁰The King will reply, 'I tell you, whenever you did this for one of the least important of these brothers of mine, you did it for me!'

41 "Then he will say to those on his left, 'Away from me, you that are under God's curse! Away to the eternal fire which has been prepared for the Devil and his angels! ⁴²I was hungry but you would not feed me, thirsty but you would not give me a drink; ⁴³I was a stranger but you would not welcome me in your homes, naked but you would not clothe me; I was sick and in prison but you would not take care of me.'

44 "Then they will answer him, 'When, Lord, did we ever see you hungry or thirsty or a stranger or naked or sick or in prison, and would not help you?' ⁴⁵The King will reply, 'I tell you, whenever you refused to help one of these least important ones, you refused to help me.' ⁴⁶These, then, will be sent off to eternal punishment, but the righteous will go to eternal life."

The Plot against Jesus
(Mark 14.1-2; Luke 22.1-2; John 11.45-53)

26 When Jesus had finished teaching all these things, he said to his disciples, ²"In two days, as you know, it will be the Passover Festival, and the Son of Man will be handed over to be crucified."

3 Then the chief priests and the elders met together in the palace of Caiaphas, the High Priest, ⁴and made plans to arrest Jesus secretly and put him to death. ⁵"We must not do it during the festival," they said, "or the people will riot."

Jesus Is Anointed at Bethany
(Mark 14.3-9; John 12.1-8)

6 Jesus was in Bethany at the house of Simon, a man who had suffered from a dreaded skin-disease. ⁷While Jesus was eating, a woman came to him with an alabaster jar filled with an expensive perfume, which she poured on his head. ⁸The disciples saw this and became angry. "Why all this waste?" they

asked. ⁹"This perfume could have been sold for a large amount and the money given to the poor!"

10 Jesus knew what they were saying, so he said to them, "Why are you bothering this woman? It is a fine and beautiful thing that she has done for me. ¹¹You will always have poor people with you, but you will not always have me. ¹²What she did was to pour this perfume on my body to get me ready for burial. ¹³Now, I assure you that wherever this gospel is preached all over the world, what she has done will be told in memory of her."

Judas Agrees to Betray Jesus
(Mark 14.10–11; Luke 22.3–6)

14 Then one of the twelve disciples—the one named Judas Iscariot—went to the chief priests ¹⁵and asked,

Thirty silver coins (26.15)

"What will you give me if I betray Jesus to you?" They counted out thirty silver coins and gave them to him. ¹⁶From then on Judas was looking for a good chance to hand Jesus over to them.

Jesus Eats the Passover Meal with His Disciples
(Mark 14.12–21; Luke 22.7–13, 21–23; John 13.21–30)

17 On the first day of the Festival of Unleavened Bread the disciples came to Jesus and asked him, "Where do you want us to get the Passover meal ready for you?"

18 "Go to a certain man in the city," he said to them, "and tell him: 'The Teacher says, My hour has come; my disciples and I will celebrate the Passover at your house.' "

19 The disciples did as Jesus had told them and prepared the Passover meal.

20 When it was evening, Jesus and the twelve disciples sat down to eat. 21 During the meal Jesus said, "I tell you, one of you will betray me."

22 The disciples were very upset and began to ask him, one after the other, "Surely, Lord, you don't mean me?"

23 Jesus answered, "One who dips his bread in the dish with me will betray me. 24 The Son of Man will die as the Scriptures say he will, but how terrible for that man who betrays the Son of Man! It would have been better for that man if he had never been born!"

25 Judas, the traitor, spoke up. "Surely, Teacher, you don't mean me?" he asked.

Jesus answered, "So you say."

The Lord's Supper
(Mark 14.22–26; Luke 22.14–20; 1 Cor. 11.23–25)

26 While they were eating, Jesus took a piece of bread, gave a prayer of thanks, broke it, and gave it to his disciples. "Take and eat it," he said; "this is my body."

27 Then he took a cup, gave thanks to God, and gave it to them. "Drink it, all of you," he said; 28 "this is my blood, which seals God's covenant, my blood poured out for many for the forgiveness of sins. 29 I tell you, I will never again drink this wine until the day I drink the new wine with you in my Father's Kingdom."

30 Then they sang a hymn and went out to the Mount of Olives.

Jesus Predicts Peter's Denial
(Mark 14.27–31; Luke 22.31–34; John 13.36–38)

31 Then Jesus said to them, "This very night all of you will run away and leave me, for the scripture says, 'God will kill the shepherd, and the sheep of

the flock will be scattered.' ³²But after I am raised to life, I will go to Galilee ahead of you."

33 Peter spoke up and said to Jesus, "I will never leave you, even though all the rest do!"

34 Jesus said to Peter, "I tell you that before the cock crows tonight, you will say three times that you do not know me."

35 Peter answered, "I will never say that, even if I have to die with you!"

And all the other disciples said the same thing.

Jesus Prays in Gethsemane
(Mark 14.32-42; Luke 22.39-46)

36 Then Jesus went with his disciples to a place called Gethsemane, and he said to them, "Sit here while I go over there and pray." ³⁷He took with him Peter and the two sons of Zebedee. Grief and anguish came over him, ³⁸and he said to them, "The sorrow in my heart is so great that it almost crushes me. Stay here and keep watch with me."

39 He went a little farther on, threw himself face

Take this cup of suffering from me! (26.39)

downwards on the ground, and prayed, "My Father, if it is possible, take this cup of suffering from me! Yet not what I want, but what you want."

40 Then he returned to the three disciples and found them asleep; and he said to Peter, "How is it that you three were not able to keep watch with me even for one hour? ⁴¹Keep watch and pray that you will not fall into temptation. The spirit is willing, but the flesh is weak."

42 Once more Jesus went away and prayed, "My Father, if this cup of suffering cannot be taken away unless I drink it, your will be done." 43He returned once more and found the disciples asleep; they could not keep their eyes open.

44 Again Jesus left them, went away, and prayed the third time, saying the same words. 45Then he returned to the disciples and said, "Are you still sleeping and resting? Look! The hour has come for the Son of Man to be handed over to the power of sinful men. 46Get up, let us go. Look, here is the man who is betraying me!"

The Arrest of Jesus
(Mark 14.43–50; Luke 22.47–53; John 18.3–12)

47 Jesus was still speaking when Judas, one of the twelve disciples, arrived. With him was a large crowd armed with swords and clubs and sent by the chief priests and the elders. 48The traitor had given the crowd a signal: "The man I kiss is the one you want. Arrest him!"

49 Judas went straight to Jesus and said, "Peace be with you, Teacher," and kissed him.

50 Jesus answered, "Be quick about it, friend!" z

Then they came up, arrested Jesus, and held him tight. 51One of those who were with Jesus drew his sword and struck at the High Priest's slave, cutting off his ear. 52"Put your sword back in its place," Jesus said to him. "All who take the sword will die by the sword. 53Don't you know that I could call on my Father for help, and at once he would send me more than twelve armies of angels? 54But in that case, how could the Scriptures come true which say that this is what must happen?"

55 Then Jesus spoke to the crowd, "Did you have to come with swords and clubs to capture me, as though I were an outlaw? Every day I sat down and taught in the Temple, and you did not arrest me. 56But all this has happened in order to make what the prophets wrote in the Scriptures come true."

Then all the disciples left him and ran away.

z Be quick about it, friend! or Why are you here, friend?

Jesus Before the Council
(Mark 14.53–65; Luke 22.54–55, 63–71; John 18.13–14, 19–24)

57 Those who had arrested Jesus took him to the house of Caiaphas, the High Priest, where the teachers of the Law and the elders had gathered together. 58 Peter followed from a distance, as far as the courtyard of the High Priest's house. He went into the courtyard and sat down with the guards to see how it would all come out. 59 The chief priests and the whole Council tried to find some false evidence against Jesus to put him to death; 60 but they could not find any, even though many people came forward and told lies about him. Finally two men stepped up 61 and said, "This man said, 'I am able to tear down God's Temple and three days later build it up again.'"

62 The High Priest stood up and said to Jesus, "Have you no answer to give to this accusation against you?" 63 But Jesus kept quiet. Again the High Priest spoke to him, "In the name of the living God I now put you on oath: tell us if you are the Messiah, the Son of God."

64 Jesus answered him, "So you say. But I tell all of you: from this time on you will see the Son of Man sitting on the right of the Almighty and coming on the clouds of heaven!"

65 At this the High Priest tore his clothes and said, "Blasphemy! We don't need any more witnesses! You have just heard his blasphemy! 66 What do you think?"

They answered, "He is guilty and must die."

67 Then they spat in his face and beat him; and those who slapped him 68 said, "Prophesy for us, Messiah! Guess who hit you!"

Peter Denies Jesus
(Mark 14.66–72; Luke 22.56–62; John 18.15–18, 25–27)

69 Peter was sitting outside in the courtyard when one of the High Priest's servant-girls came to him and said, "You, too, were with Jesus of Galilee."

70 But he denied it in front of them all. "I don't know what you are talking about," he answered, 71 and went on out to the entrance of the courtyard. Another

servant-girl saw him and said to the men there, "He was with Jesus of Nazareth."

72 Again Peter denied it and answered, "I swear that I don't know that man!"

73 After a little while the men standing there came to Peter. "Of course you are one of them," they said. "After all, the way you speak gives you away!"

74 Then Peter said, "I swear that I am telling the truth! May God punish me if I am not! I do not know that man!"

Just then a cock crowed, 75 and Peter remembered what Jesus had told him: "Before the cock crows, you will say three times that you do not know me." He went out and wept bitterly.

Jesus Is Taken to Pilate
(Mark 15.1; Luke 23.1-2; John 18.28-32)

27 Early in the morning all the chief priests and the elders made their plans against Jesus to put him to death. 2 They put him in chains, led him off, and handed him over to Pilate, the Roman governor.

The Death of Judas
(Acts 1.18-19)

3 When Judas, the traitor, learnt that Jesus had been condemned, he repented and took back the thirty silver coins to the chief priests and the elders. 4 "I have sinned by betraying an innocent man to death!" he said.

"What do we care about that?" they answered. "That is your business!"

5 Judas threw the coins down in the Temple and left; then he went off and hanged himself.

6 The chief priests picked up the coins and said, "This is blood money, and it is against our Law to put it in the temple treasury." 7 After reaching an agreement about it, they used the money to buy Potter's Field, as a cemetery for foreigners. 8 That is why that field is called "Field of Blood" to this very day.

9 Then what the prophet Jeremiah had said came true: "They took the thirty silver coins, the amount the people of Israel had agreed to pay for him, 10 and

used the money to buy the potter's field, as the Lord
had commanded me."

Pilate Questions Jesus
(Mark 15.2–5; Luke 23.3–5; John 18.33–38)

11 Jesus stood before the Roman governor, who questioned him. "Are you the king of the Jews?" he asked.

"So you say," answered Jesus. 12 But he said nothing
in response to the accusations of the chief priests
and elders.

13 So Pilate said to him, "Don't you hear all these
things they accuse you of?"

14 But Jesus refused to answer a single word, with
the result that the Governor was greatly surprised.

Jesus Is Sentenced to Death
(Mark 15.6–15; Luke 23.13–25; John 18.39—19.16)

15 At every Passover Festival the Roman governor
was in the habit of setting free any one prisoner
the crowd asked for. 16 At that time there was a well-
known prisoner named Jesus Barabbas. 17 So when
the crowd gathered, Pilate asked them, "Which one
do you want me to set free for you? Jesus Barabbas
or Jesus called the Messiah?" 18 He knew very well
that the Jewish authorities had handed Jesus over
to him because they were jealous.

19 While Pilate was sitting in the judgement hall,
his wife sent him a message: "Have nothing to do
with that innocent man, because in a dream last night
I suffered much on account of him."

20 The chief priests and the elders persuaded the
crowd to ask Pilate to set Barabbas free and have
Jesus put to death. 21 But Pilate asked the crowd,
"Which one of these two do you want me to set
free for you?"

"Barabbas!" they answered.

22 "What, then, shall I do with Jesus called the
Messiah?" Pilate asked them.

"Crucify him!" they all answered.

23 But Pilate asked, "What crime has he committed?"

Then they started shouting at the top of their voices:
"Crucify him!"

24 When Pilate saw that it was no use to go on,

but that a riot might break out, he took some water, washed his hands in front of the crowd, and said, "I am not responsible for the death of this man! This is your doing!"

25 The whole crowd answered, "Let the responsibility for his death fall on us and our children!"

26 Then Pilate set Barabbas free for them; and after he had Jesus whipped, he handed him over to be crucified.

The Soldiers Mock Jesus
(Mark 15.16-20; John 19.2-3)

27 Then Pilate's soldiers took Jesus into the governor's palace, and the whole company gathered round him. 28 They stripped off his clothes and put a scarlet robe on him. 29 Then they made a crown out of thorny branches and placed it on his head, and put a stick in his right hand; then they knelt before him and mocked him. "Long live the King of the Jews!" they said. 30 They spat on him, and took the stick and hit him over the head. 31 When they had finished mocking him, they took the robe off and put his own clothes back on him. Then they led him out to crucify him.

Jesus Is Crucified
(Mark 15.21-32; Luke 23.26-43; John 19.17-27)

32 As they were going out, they met a man from Cyrene named Simon, and the soldiers forced him to carry Jesus' cross. 33 They came to a place called Golgotha, which means, "The Place of the Skull." 34 There they offered Jesus wine mixed with a bitter substance; but after tasting it, he would not drink it.

35 They crucified him and then divided his clothes among them by throwing dice. 36 After that they sat there and watched him. 37 Above his head they put the written notice of the accusation against him: "This is Jesus, the King of the Jews." 38 Then they crucified two bandits with Jesus, one on his right and the other on his left.

39 People passing by shook their heads and hurled insults at Jesus: 40 "You were going to tear down

the Temple and build it up again in three days! Save
yourself if you are God's Son! Come on down from
the cross!"

41 In the same way the chief priests and the teachers
of the Law and the elders jeered at him: 42"He saved
others, but he cannot save himself! Isn't he the king
of Israel? If he comes down off the cross now, we
will believe in him! 43He trusts in God and claims
to be God's Son. Well, then, let us see if God wants
to save him now!"

44 Even the bandits who had been crucified with
him insulted him in the same way.

The Death of Jesus
(Mark 15.33–41; Luke 23.44–49; John 19.28–30)

45 At noon the whole country was covered with
darkness, which lasted for three hours. 46At about
three o'clock Jesus cried out with a loud shout, *"Eli,
Eli, lema sabachthani?"* which means, "My God, my
God, why did you abandon me?"

47 Some of the people standing there heard him
and said, "He is calling for Elijah!" 48One of them
ran up at once, took a sponge, soaked it in cheap
wine, put it on the end of a stick, and tried to make
him drink it.

49 But the others said, "Wait, let us see if Elijah
is coming to save him!"

50 Jesus again gave a loud cry and breathed his
last.

51 Then the curtain hanging in the Temple was torn
in two from top to bottom. The earth shook, the
rocks split apart, 52the graves broke open, and many
of God's people who had died were raised to life.
53They left the graves, and after Jesus rose from death,
they went into the Holy City, where many people
saw them.

54 When the army officer and the soldiers with
him who were watching Jesus saw the earthquake
and everything else that happened, they were terrified
and said, "He really was the Son of God!"

55 There were many women there, looking on from
a distance, who had followed Jesus from Galilee and
helped him. 56Among them were Mary Magdalene,

Mary the mother of James and Joseph, and the wife of Zebedee.

The Burial of Jesus
(Mark 15.42–47; Luke 23.50–56; John 19.38–42)

57 When it was evening, a rich man from Arimathea arrived; his name was Joseph, and he also was a disciple of Jesus. 58 He went into the presence of Pilate and asked for the body of Jesus. Pilate gave orders for the body to be given to Joseph. 59 So Joseph took it, wrapped it in a new linen sheet, 60 and placed it in his own tomb, which he had just recently dug out of solid rock. Then he rolled a large stone across the entrance to the tomb and went away. 61 Mary Magdalene and the other Mary were sitting there, facing the tomb.

The Guard at the Tomb

62 The next day, which was a Sabbath, the chief priests and the Pharisees met with Pilate 63 and said, "Sir, we remember that while that liar was still alive he said, 'I will be raised to life three days later.' 64 Give orders, then, for his tomb to be carefully guarded until the third day, so that his disciples will not be able to go and steal the body, and then tell the people that he was raised from death. This last lie would be even worse than the first one."

65 "Take a guard," Pilate told them; "go and make the tomb as secure as you can."

66 So they left and made the tomb secure by putting a seal on the stone and leaving the guard on watch.

The Resurrection
(Mark 16.1–10; Luke 24.1–12; John 20.1–10)

28 After the Sabbath, as Sunday morning was dawning, Mary Magdalene and the other Mary went to look at the tomb. 2 Suddenly there was a violent earthquake; an angel of the Lord came down from heaven, rolled the stone away, and sat on it. 3 His appearance was like lightning, and his clothes were white as snow. 4 The guards were so afraid that they trembled and became like dead men.

5 The angel spoke to the women. "You must not

be afraid," he said. "I know you are looking for Jesus, who was crucified. [6]He is not here; he has been raised, just as he said. Come here and see the place where he was lying. [7]Go quickly now, and tell his disciples, 'He has been raised from death, and now he is going to Galilee ahead of you; there you will see him!' Remember what I have told you."

8 So they left the tomb in a hurry, afraid and yet filled with joy, and ran to tell his disciples.

9 Suddenly Jesus met them and said, "Peace be with you." They came up to him, took hold of his feet, and worshipped him. [10]"Do not be afraid," Jesus said to them. "Go and tell my brothers to go to Galilee, and there they will see me."

The Report of the Guard

11 While the women went on their way, some of the soldiers guarding the tomb went back to the city and told the chief priests everything that had happened. [12]The chief priests met with the elders and made their plan; they gave a large sum of money to the soldiers [13]and said, "You are to say that his disciples came during the night and stole his body while you were asleep. [14]And if the Governor should hear of this, we will convince him that you are innocent, and that you will have nothing to worry about."

15 The guards took the money and did what they were told to do. And so that is the report spread round by the Jews to this very day.

Jesus Appears to His Disciples
(Mark 16.14–18; Luke 24.36–49; John 20.19–23; Acts 1.6–8)

16 The eleven disciples went to the hill in Galilee where Jesus had told them to go. [17]When they saw him, they worshipped him, even though some of them doubted. [18]Jesus drew near and said to them, "I have been given all authority in heaven and on earth. [19]Go, then, to all peoples everywhere and make them my disciples: baptize them in the name of the Father, the Son, and the Holy Spirit, [20]and teach them to obey everything I have commanded you. And I will be with you always, to the end of the age."

THE GOSPEL ACCORDING TO

MARK

INTRODUCTION

The Gospel according to Mark begins with the statement that it is "the Good News about Jesus Christ,
the Son of God." Jesus is pictured as a man of action
and authority. His authority is seen in his teaching,
in his power over demons, and in forgiving people's
sins. Jesus speaks of himself as the Son of Man,
who came to give his life to set people free from
sin.

Mark presents the story of Jesus in a straightforward,
vigorous way, with emphasis on what Jesus did, rather
than on his words and teachings. After a brief prologue
about John the Baptist and the baptism and temptation
of Jesus, the writer immediately takes up Jesus' ministry of healing and teaching. As time goes on, the
followers of Jesus come to understand him better,
but Jesus' opponents become more hostile. The closing
chapters report the events of Jesus' last week of earthly
life, especially his crucifixion and resurrection.

The two endings to the Gospel, which are enclosed
in brackets, are generally regarded as written by someone other than the author of *Mark*.

Outline of Contents

The Preaching of John the Baptist
(Matt. 3.1-12; Luke 3.1-18; John 1.19-28)

1 This is the Good News about Jesus Christ, the Son of God.[a] [2] It began as the prophet Isaiah had written:

"God said, 'I will send my messenger ahead of you
   to clear the way for you.'

[3] Someone is shouting in the desert,
   'Get the road ready for the Lord;
   make a straight path for him to travel!' "

[4] So John appeared in the desert, baptizing and preaching.[b] "Turn away from your sins and be baptized," he told the people, "and God will forgive your sins." [5] Many people from the province of Judaea and the city of Jerusalem went out to hear John. They confessed their sins, and he baptized them in the River Jordan.

[6] John wore clothes made of camel's hair, with a leather belt round his waist, and his food was locusts and wild honey. [7] He announced to the people, "The man who will come after me is much greater than I am. I am not good enough even to bend down and untie his sandals. [8] I baptize you with water, but he will baptize you with the Holy Spirit."

The Baptism and Temptation of Jesus
(Matt. 3.13—4.11; Luke 3.21-22; 4.1-13)

[9] Not long afterwards Jesus came from Nazareth in the province of Galilee, and was baptized by John in the Jordan. [10] As soon as Jesus came up out of the water, he saw heaven opening and the Spirit coming down on him like a dove. [11] And a voice came from heaven, "You are my own dear Son. I am pleased with you."

[12] At once the Spirit made him go into the desert, [13] where he stayed forty days, being tempted by Satan.

---

[a] Some manuscripts do not have the Son of God.
[b] John appeared in the desert, baptizing and preaching; some manuscripts have John the Baptist appeared in the desert, preaching.

Wild animals were there also, but angels came and helped him.

Jesus Calls Four Fishermen
(Matt. 4.12–22; Luke 4.14–15; 5.1–11)

14 After John had been put in prison, Jesus went to Galilee and preached the Good News from God. 15"The right time has come," he said, "and the Kingdom of God is near! Turn away from your sins and believe the Good News!"

16 As Jesus walked along the shore of Lake Galilee, he saw two fishermen, Simon and his brother Andrew, catching fish with a net. 17 Jesus said to them, "Come with me, and I will teach you to catch men." 18 At once

At once they left their nets (1.18)

they left their nets and went with him.

19 He went a little farther on and saw two other brothers, James and John, the sons of Zebedee. They were in their boat getting their nets ready. 20 As soon as Jesus saw them, he called them; they left their father Zebedee in the boat with the hired men and went with Jesus.

A Man with an Evil Spirit
(Luke 4.31–37)

21 Jesus and his disciples came to the town of Capernaum, and on the next Sabbath Jesus went to the synagogue and began to teach. 22 The people who heard him were amazed at the way he taught, for

he wasn't like the teachers of the Law; instead, he taught with authority.

23 Just then a man with an evil spirit in him came into the synagogue and screamed, 24"What do you want with us, Jesus of Nazareth? Are you here to destroy us? I know who you are—you are God's holy messenger!"

25 Jesus ordered the spirit, "Be quiet, and come out of the man!"

26 The evil spirit shook the man hard, gave a loud scream, and came out of him. 27The people were all so amazed that they started saying to one another, "What is this? Is it some kind of new teaching? This man has authority to give orders to the evil spirits, and they obey him!"

28 And so the news about Jesus spread quickly everywhere in the province of Galilee.

Jesus Heals Many People
(Matt. 8.14–17; Luke 4.38–41)

29 Jesus and his disciples, including James and John, left the synagogue and went straight to the home of Simon and Andrew. 30Simon's mother-in-law was sick in bed with a fever, and as soon as Jesus arrived, he was told about her. 31He went to her, took her by the hand, and helped her up. The fever left her, and she began to wait on them.

32 After the sun had set and evening had come, people brought to Jesus all the sick and those who had demons. 33All the people of the town gathered in front of the house. 34Jesus healed many who were sick with all kinds of diseases and drove out many demons. He would not let the demons say anything, because they knew who he was.

Jesus Preaches in Galilee
(Luke 4.42–44)

35 Very early the next morning, long before daylight, Jesus got up and left the house. He went out of the town to a lonely place, where he prayed. 36But Simon and his companions went out searching for him, 37and when they found him, they said, "Everyone is looking for you."

Took her by the hand, and...the fever left her (1.31)

38 But Jesus answered, "We must go on to the other villages round here. I have to preach in them also, because that is why I came."

39 So he travelled all over Galilee, preaching in the synagogues and driving out demons.

Jesus Heals a Man
(Matt. 8.1–4; Luke 5.12–16)

40 A man suffering from a dreaded skin-disease came to Jesus, knelt down, and begged him for help. "If you want to," he said, "you can make me clean."*c*

41 Jesus was filled with pity,*d* and stretched out his hand and touched him. "I do want to," he answered. "Be clean!" 42 At once the disease left the man, and he was clean. 43 Then Jesus spoke sternly to him and sent him away at once, 44 after saying to him, "Listen, don't tell anyone about this. But go straight to the priest and let him examine you; then in order to prove to everyone that you are cured, offer the sacrifice that Moses ordered."

45 But the man went away and began to spread

*c*MAKE ME CLEAN: *This disease was considered to make a person ritually unclean.*   *d*pity; *some manuscripts have* anger.

the news everywhere. Indeed, he talked so much that Jesus could not go into a town publicly. Instead, he stayed out in lonely places, and people came to him from everywhere.

Jesus Heals a Paralysed Man
(Matt. 9.1–8; Luke 5.17–26)

2 A few days later Jesus went back to Capernaum, and the news spread that he was at home. ²So many people came together that there was no room left, not even out in front of the door. Jesus was preaching the message to them ³when four men arrived, carrying a paralysed man to Jesus. ⁴Because of the crowd, however, they could not get the man to him. So they made a hole in the roof right above the place where Jesus was. When they had made an opening, they let the man down, lying on his mat. ⁵Seeing how much faith they had, Jesus said to the paralysed man, "My son, your sins are forgiven."

6 Some teachers of the Law who were sitting there thought to themselves, ⁷"How does he dare· to talk like this? This is blasphemy! God is the only one who can forgive sins!"

8 At once Jesus knew what they were thinking, so he said to them, "Why do you think such things? ⁹Is it easier to say to this paralysed man, 'Your sins are forgiven', or to say, 'Get up, pick up your mat, and walk'? ¹⁰I will prove to you, then, that the Son of Man has authority on earth to forgive sins." So he said to the paralysed man, ¹¹"I tell you, get up, pick up your mat, and go home!"

12 While they all watched, the man got up, picked up his mat, and hurried away. They were all completely amazed and praised God, saying, "We have never seen anything like this!"

Jesus Calls Levi
(Matt. 9.9–13; Luke 5.27–32)

13 Jesus went back again to the shore of Lake Galilee. A crowd came to him, and he started teaching them. ¹⁴As he walked along, he saw a tax collector, Levi son of Alphaeus, sitting in his office. Jesus said to him, "Follow me." Levi got up and followed him.

15 Later on Jesus was having a meal in Levi's house.[e] A large number of tax collectors and other outcasts were following Jesus, and many of them joined him and his disciples at the table. 16 Some teachers of the Law, who were Pharisees, saw that Jesus was eating with these outcasts and tax collectors, so they asked his disciples, "Why does he eat with such people?"

17 Jesus heard them and answered, "People who are well do not need a doctor, but only those who are sick. I have not come to call respectable people, but outcasts."

The Question about Fasting
(Matt. 9.14–17; Luke 5.33–39)

18 On one occasion the followers of John the Baptist and the Pharisees were fasting. Some people came to Jesus and asked him, "Why is it that the disciples of John the Baptist and the disciples of the Pharisees fast, but yours do not?"

19 Jesus answered, "Do you expect the guests at a wedding party to go without food? Of course not! As long as the bridegroom is with them, they will not do that. 20 But the day will come when the bridegroom will be taken away from them, and then they will fast.

21 "No one uses a piece of new cloth to patch up an old coat, because the new patch will shrink and tear off some of the old cloth, making an even bigger hole. 22 Nor does anyone pour new wine into used wineskins, because the wine will burst the skins, and both the wine and the skins will be ruined. Instead, new wine must be poured into fresh wineskins."

The Question about the Sabbath
(Matt. 12.1–8; Luke 6.1–5)

23 Jesus was walking through some cornfields on the Sabbath. As his disciples walked along with him, they began to pick the ears of corn. 24 So the Pharisees said to Jesus, "Look, it is against our Law for your disciples to do that on the Sabbath!"

[e] in Levi's house; or in his (*that is,* Jesus') house.

25 Jesus answered, "Have you never read what David did that time when he needed something to eat? He and his men were hungry, 26 so he went into the house of God and ate the bread offered to God. This happened when Abiathar was the High Priest. According to our Law only the priests may eat this bread—but David ate it and even gave it to his men."

27 And Jesus concluded, "The Sabbath was made for the good of man; man was not made for the Sabbath. 28 So the Son of Man is Lord even of the Sabbath."

The Man with a Paralysed Hand
(Matt. 12.9-14; Luke 6.6-11)

3 Then Jesus went back to the synagogue, where there was a man who had a paralysed hand. 2 Some people were there who wanted to accuse Jesus of doing wrong; so they watched him closely to see whether he would heal the man on the Sabbath. 3 Jesus said to the man, "Come up here to the front." 4 Then he asked the people, "What does our Law allow us to do on the Sabbath? To help or to harm? To save a man's life or to destroy it?"

But they did not say a thing. 5 Jesus was angry as he looked round at them, but at the same time he felt sorry for them, because they were so stubborn and wrong. Then he said to the man, "Stretch out your hand." He stretched it out, and it became well again. 6 So the Pharisees left the synagogue and met at once with some members of Herod's party, and they made plans to kill Jesus.

A Crowd by the Lake

7 Jesus and his disciples went away to Lake Galilee, and a large crowd followed him. They had come from Galilee, from Judaea, 8 from Jerusalem, from the territory of Idumea, from the territory on the east side of the Jordan, and from the region round the cities of Tyre and Sidon. All these people came to Jesus because they had heard of the things he was doing. 9 The crowd was so large that Jesus told his disciples to get a boat ready for him, so that the people would not crush him. 10 He had healed many people, and

The crowd was so large (3.9)

all those who were ill kept pushing their way to him in order to touch him. 11 And whenever the people who had evil spirits in them saw him, they would fall down before him and scream, "You are the Son of God!"

12 Jesus sternly ordered the evil spirits not to tell anyone who he was.

Jesus Chooses the Twelve Apostles
(Matt. 10.1–4; Luke 6.12–16)

13 Then Jesus went up a hill and called to himself the men he wanted. They came to him, 14 and he chose twelve, whom he named apostles. "I have chosen you to be with me," he told them. "I will also send you out to preach, 15 and you will have authority to drive out demons."

16 These are the twelve he chose: Simon (Jesus gave him the name Peter); 17 James and his brother John, the sons of Zebedee (Jesus gave them the name Boanerges, which means "Men of Thunder"); 18 Andrew, Philip, Bartholomew, Matthew, Thomas,

James son of Alphaeus, Thaddaeus, Simon the Patriot, [19] and Judas Iscariot, who betrayed Jesus.

Jesus and Beelzebul
(Matt. 12.22–32; Luke 11.14–23; 12.10)

20 Then Jesus went home. Again such a large crowd gathered that Jesus and his disciples had no time to eat. [21] When his family heard about it, they set out to take charge of him, because people were saying, "He's gone mad!"

22 Some teachers of the Law who had come from Jerusalem were saying, "He has Beelzebul in him! It is the chief of the demons who gives him the power to drive them out."

23 So Jesus called them to him and spoke to them in parables: "How can Satan drive out Satan? [24] If a country divides itself into groups which fight each other, that country will fall apart. [25] If a family divides itself into groups which fight each other, that family will fall apart. [26] So if Satan's kingdom divides into groups, it cannot last, but will fall apart and come to an end.

27 "No one can break into a strong man's house and take away his belongings unless he first ties up the strong man; then he can plunder his house

28 "I assure you that people can be forgiven all their sins and all the evil things they may say. [f] [29] But whoever says evil things against the Holy Spirit will never be forgiven, because he has committed an eternal sin." [30] (Jesus said this because some people were saying, "He has an evil spirit in him.")

Jesus' Mother and Brothers
(Matt. 12.46–50; Luke 8.19–21)

31 Then Jesus' mother and brothers arrived. They stood outside the house and sent in a message, asking for him. [32] A crowd was sitting round Jesus, and they said to him, "Look, your mother and your brothers and sisters are outside, and they want you."

33 Jesus answered, "Who is my mother? Who are

[f] evil things they may say; or evil things they may say against God.

my brothers?" [34] He looked at the people sitting round him and said, "Look! Here are my mother and my brothers! [35] Whoever does what God wants him to do is my brother, my sister, my mother."

The Parable of the Sower
(Matt. 13.1–9; Luke 8.4–8)

4 Again Jesus began to teach beside Lake Galilee. The crowd that gathered round him was so large that he got into a boat and sat in it. The boat was out in the water, and the crowd stood on the shore at the water's edge. [2] He used parables to teach them many things, saying to them:

3 "Listen! Once there was a man who went out to sow corn. [4] As he scattered the seed in the field, some of it fell along the path, and the birds came and ate it up. [5] Some of it fell on rocky ground, where there was little soil. The seeds soon sprouted, because the soil wasn't deep. [6] Then, when the sun came up, it burnt the young plants; and because the roots had not grown deep enough, the plants soon dried up. [7] Some of the seed fell among thorn bushes, which grew up and choked the plants, and they didn't produce any corn. [8] But some seeds fell in good soil, and the plants sprouted, grew, and produced corn: some had thirty grains, others sixty, and others a hundred."

9 And Jesus concluded, "Listen, then, if you have ears!"

The Purpose of the Parables
(Matt. 13.10–17; Luke 8.9–10)

10 When Jesus was alone, some of those who had heard him came to him with the twelve disciples and asked him to explain the parables. [11] "You have been given the secret of the Kingdom of God," Jesus answered. "But the others, who are on the outside, hear all things by means of parables, [12] so that,

'They may look and look,
    yet not see;
they may listen and listen,
    yet not understand.
For if they did, they would turn to God,
    and he would forgive them.' "

Jesus Explains the Parable of the Sower
(Matt. 13.18-23; Luke 8.11-15)

13 Then Jesus asked them, "Don't you understand this parable? How, then, will you ever understand any parable? ¹⁴The sower sows God's message. ¹⁵Some people are like the seeds that fall along the path; as soon as they hear the message, Satan comes and takes it away. ¹⁶Other people are like the seeds that fall on rocky ground. As soon as they hear the message, they receive it gladly. ¹⁷But it does not sink deep into them, and they don't last long. So when trouble or persecution comes because of the message, they give up at once. ¹⁸Other people are like the seeds sown among the thorn bushes. These are the ones who hear the message, ¹⁹but the worries about this life, the love for riches, and all other kinds of desires crowd in and choke the message, and they don't bear fruit. ²⁰But other people are like the seeds sown in good soil. They hear the message, accept it, and bear fruit: some thirty, some sixty, and some a hundred."

A Lamp under a Bowl
(Luke 8.16-18)

21 Jesus continued, "Does anyone ever bring in a lamp and put it under a bowl or under the bed? Doesn't he put it on the lampstand? ²²Whatever is hidden away will be brought out into the open, and whatever is covered up will be uncovered. ²³Listen, then, if you have ears!"

24 He also said to them, "Pay attention to what you hear! The same rules you use to judge others will be used by God to judge you—but with even greater severity. ²⁵The person who has something will be given more, and the person who has nothing will have taken away from him even the little he has."

The Parable of the Growing Seed

26 Jesus went on to say, "The Kingdom of God is like this. A man scatters seed in his field. ²⁷He sleeps at night, is up and about during the day, and all the while the seeds are sprouting and growing. Yet he does not know how it happens. ²⁸The soil itself

makes the plants grow and bear fruit; first the tender stalk appears, then the ear, and finally the ear full of corn. 29 When ⸓the corn is ripe, the man starts cutting it with his sickle, because harvest time has come.

The Parable of the Mustard Seed
(Matt. 13.31-32, 34; Luke 13.18-19)

30 "What shall we say the Kingdom of God is like?" asked Jesus. "What parable shall we use to explain it? 31 It is like this. A man takes a mustard seed, the smallest seed in the world, and plants it in the ground. 32 After a while it grows up and becomes the biggest of all plants. It puts out such large branches that the birds come and make their nests in its shade."

33 Jesus preached his message to the people, using many other parables like these; he told them as much as they could understand. 34 He would not speak to them without using parables, but when he was alone with his disciples, he would explain everything to them.

Jesus Calms a Storm
(Matt. 8.23-27; Luke 8.22-25)

35 On the evening of that same day Jesus said to his disciples, "Let us go across to the other side of the lake." 36 So they left the crowd; the disciples got into the boat in which Jesus was already sitting, and they took him with them. Other boats were there too. 37 Suddenly a strong wind blew up, and the waves began to spill over into the boat, so that it was about to fill with water. 38 Jesus was in the back of the boat, sleeping with his head on a pillow. The disciples woke him up and said, "Teacher, don't you care that we are about to die?"

39 Jesus stood up and commanded the wind, "Be quiet!" and he said to the waves, "Be still!" The wind died down, and there was a great calm. 40 Then Jesus said to his disciples, "Why are you frightened? Have you still no faith?"

41 But they were terribly afraid and said to one another, "Who is this man? Even the wind and the waves obey him!"

Waves began to spill over into the boat (4.37)

Jesus Heals a Man with Evil Spirits
(Matt. 8.28–34; Luke 8.26–39)

5 Jesus and his disciples arrived on the other side of Lake Galilee, in the territory of Gerasa. ²As soon as Jesus got out of the boat, he was met by a man who came out of the burial caves there. This man had an evil spirit in him ³and lived among the

And there was a great calm (4.39)

tombs. Nobody could keep him chained up any more; [4] many times his feet and hands had been chained, but every time he broke the chains and smashed the irons on his feet. He was too strong for anyone to control him. [5] Day and night he wandered among the tombs and through the hills, screaming and cutting himself with stones.

6 He was some distance away when he saw Jesus; so he ran, fell on his knees before him, [7] and screamed in a loud voice, "Jesus, Son of the Most High God! What do you want with me? For God's sake, I beg you, don't punish me!" [8] (He said this because Jesus was saying, "Evil spirit, come out of this man!")

9 So Jesus asked him, "What is your name?"

The man answered, "My name is 'Mob'—there are so many of us!" [10] And he kept begging Jesus not to send the evil spirits out of that region.

11 There was a large herd of pigs near by, feeding on a hillside. [12] So the spirits begged Jesus, "Send us to the pigs, and let us go into them." [13] He let them go, and the evil spirits went out of the man and entered the pigs. The whole herd—about two thousand pigs in all—rushed down the side of the cliff into the lake and was drowned.

14 The men who had been taking care of the pigs ran away and spread the news in the town and among the farms. People went out to see what had happened, [15] and when they came to Jesus, they saw the man who used to have the mob of demons in him. He was sitting there, clothed and in his right mind; and they were all afraid. [16] Those who had seen it told the people what had happened to the man with the demons, and about the pigs.

17 So they asked Jesus to leave their territory.

18 As Jesus was getting into the boat, the man who had had the demons begged him, "Let me go with you!"

19 But Jesus would not let him. Instead, he told him, "Go back home to your family and tell them how much the Lord has done for you and how kind he has been to you."

20 So the man left and went all through the Ten

Towns, telling what Jesus had done for him. And
all who heard it were amazed.

Jairus' Daughter and the Woman
Who Touched Jesus' Cloak
(Matt. 9.18–26; Luke 8.40–56)

21 Jesus went back across to the other side of the
lake. There at the lakeside a large crowd gathered
round him. ²² Jairus, an official of the local synagogue,
arrived, and when he saw Jesus, he threw himself down
at his feet ²³ and begged him earnestly, "My little
daughter is very ill. Please come and place your hands
on her, so that she will get well and live!"

24 Then Jesus started off with him. So many people
were going along with Jesus that they were crowding
him from every side.

25 There was a woman who had suffered terribly
from severe bleeding for twelve years, ²⁶ even though
she had been treated by many doctors. She had spent
all her money, but instead of getting better she got
worse all the time. ²⁷ She had heard about Jesus, so
she came in the crowd behind him, ²⁸ saying to herself,
"If I just touch his clothes, I will get well."

29 She touched his cloak, and her bleeding stopped
at once; and she had the feeling inside herself that
she was healed of her trouble. ³⁰ At once Jesus knew
that power had gone out of him, so he turned round in
the crowd and asked, "Who touched my clothes?"

31 His disciples answered, "You see how the people
are crowding you; why do you ask who touched you?"

32 But Jesus kept looking round to see who had
done it. ³³ The woman realized what had happened
to her, so she came, trembling with fear, knelt at
his feet, and told him the whole truth. ³⁴ Jesus said
to her, "My daughter, your faith has made you well.
Go in peace, and be healed of your trouble."

35 While Jesus was saying this, some messengers
came from Jairus' house and told him, "Your daughter
has died. Why bother the Teacher any longer?"

36 Jesus paid no attention to^g what they said, but
told him, "Don't be afraid, only believe." ³⁷ Then he

^gpaid no attention to; or overheard.

did not let anyone else go on with him except Peter and James and his brother John. [38]They arrived at Jairus' house, where Jesus saw the confusion and heard all the loud crying and wailing. [39]He went in and said to them, "Why all this confusion? Why are you crying? The child is not dead—she is only sleeping!"

40 They laughed at him, so he put them all out, took the child's father and mother and his three disciples, and went into the room where the child was lying. [41]He took her by the hand and said to her, "*Talitha, koum,*" which means, "Little girl, I tell you to get up!"

42 She got up at once and started walking around. (She was twelve years old.) When this happened, they were completely amazed. [43]But Jesus gave them strict orders not to tell anyone, and he said, "Give her something to eat."

Jesus Is Rejected at Nazareth
(Matt. 13.53-58; Luke 4.16-30)

6 Jesus left that place and went back to his home town, followed by his disciples. [2]On the Sabbath he began to teach in the synagogue. Many people were there; and when they heard him, they were all amazed. "Where did he get all this?" they asked. "What wisdom is this that has been given him? How does he perform miracles? [3]Isn't he the carpenter, the son of Mary, and the brother of James, Joseph, Judas, and Simon? Aren't his sisters living here?" And so they rejected him.

4 Jesus said to them, "A prophet is respected everywhere except in his own home town and by his relatives and his family."

5 He was not able to perform any miracles there, except that he placed his hands on a few sick people and healed them. [6]He was greatly surprised, because the people did not have faith.

Jesus Sends out the Twelve Disciples
(Matt. 10.5-15; Luke 9.1-6)

Then Jesus went to the villages round there, teaching the people. [7]He called the twelve disciples together and sent them out two by two. He gave them authority over the evil spirits [8]and ordered them, "Don't take anything with you on your journey except a stick—no bread, no beggar's bag, no money in your pockets. [9]Wear sandals, but don't carry an extra shirt." [10]He also said, "Wherever you are welcomed, stay in the same house until you leave that place. [11]If you come to a town where people do not welcome you or will not listen to you, leave it and shake the dust off your feet. That will be a warning to them!"

12 So they went out and preached that people should turn away from their sins. [13]They drove out many demons, and rubbed olive-oil on many sick people and healed them.

The Death of John the Baptist
(Matt. 14.1–12; Luke 9.7–9)

14 Now King Herod[h] heard about all this, because Jesus' reputation had spread everywhere. Some people were saying, "John the Baptist has come back to life! That is why he has this power to perform miracles."

15 Others, however, said, "He is Elijah."

Others said, "He is a prophet, like one of the prophets of long ago."

16 When Herod heard it, he said, "He is John the Baptist! I had his head cut off, but he has come back to life!" [17]Herod himself had ordered John's arrest, and he had him chained and put in prison. Herod did this because of Herodias, whom he had married, even though she was the wife of his brother Philip. [18]John the Baptist kept telling Herod, "It isn't right for you to be married to your brother's wife!"

19 So Herodias held a grudge against John and wanted to kill him, but she could not because of Herod. [20]Herod was afraid of John because he knew that John was a good and holy man, and so he kept him safe. He liked to listen to him, even though he became greatly disturbed every time he heard him.

21 Finally Herodias got her chance. It was on Herod's birthday, when he gave a feast for all the chief govern-

[h]KING HEROD: *Herod Antipas, ruler of Galilee.*

ment officials, the military commanders, and the leading citizens of Galilee. [22] The daughter of Herodias[i] came in and danced, and pleased Herod and his guests. So the king said to the girl, "What would you like to have? I will give you anything you want." [23] With many vows he said to her, "I swear that I will give you anything you ask for, even as much as half my kingdom!"

24 So the girl went out and asked her mother, "What shall I ask for?"

"The head of John the Baptist," she answered.

25 The girl hurried back at once to the king and demanded, "I want you to give me here and now the head of John the Baptist on a dish!"

26 This made the king very sad, but he could not refuse her because of the vows he had made in front of all his guests. [27] So he sent off a guard at once with orders to bring John's head. The guard left, went to the prison, and cut John's head off; [28] then he brought it on a dish and gave it to the girl, who gave it to her mother. [29] When John's disciples heard about this, they came and took away his body, and buried it.

Jesus Feeds Five Thousand Men
(Matt. 14.13-21; Luke 9.10-17; John 6.1-14)

30 The apostles returned and met with Jesus, and told him all they had done and taught. [31] There were so many people coming and going that Jesus and his disciples didn't even have time to eat. So he said to them, "Let us go off by ourselves to some place where we will be alone and you can rest for a while." [32] So they started out in a boat by themselves for a lonely place.

33 Many people, however, saw them leave and knew at once who they were; so they went from all the towns and ran ahead by land and arrived at the place ahead of Jesus and his disciples. [34] When Jesus got out of the boat, he saw this large crowd, and his heart was filled with pity for them, because they

[i]The daughter of Herodias; *some manuscripts have* His daughter Herodias.

were like sheep without a shepherd. So he began to teach them many things. [35]When it was getting late, his disciples came to him and said, "It is already very late, and this is a lonely place. [36]Send the people away, and let them go to the nearby farms and villages in order to buy themselves something to eat."

37 "You yourselves give them something to eat," Jesus answered.

They asked, "Do you want us to go and spend two hundred silver coins[j] on bread in order to feed them?"

38 So Jesus asked them, "How much bread have you got? Go and see."

When they found out, they told him, "Five loaves and also two fish."

39 Jesus then told his disciples to make all the people divide into groups and sit down on the green grass. [40]So the people sat down in rows, in groups of a hundred and groups of fifty. [41]Then Jesus took the five loaves and the two fish, looked up to heaven, and gave thanks to God. He broke the loaves and gave them to his disciples to distribute to the people. He also divided the two fish among them all. [42]Everyone ate and had enough. [43]Then the disciples took up twelve baskets full of what was left of the bread and the fish. [44]The number of men who were fed was five thousand.

Jesus Walks on the Water
(Matt. 14.22–33; John 6.15–21)

45 At once Jesus made his disciples get into the boat and go ahead of him to Bethsaida, on the other side of the lake, while he sent the crowd away. [46]After saying good-bye to the people he went away to a hill to pray. [47]When evening came, the boat was in the middle of the lake, while Jesus was alone on land. [48]He saw that his disciples were straining at the oars, because they were rowing against the wind; so some time between three and six o'clock in the morning he came to them, walking on the water.

[j]SILVER COINS: *A silver coin was the daily wage of a rural worker (see Mt 20.2).*

It's a ghost! (6.49)

He was going to pass them by,[k] [49]but they saw him walking on the water. "It's a ghost!" they thought, and screamed. [50]They were all terrified when they saw him.

Jesus spoke to them at once, "Courage!" he said. "It is I. Don't be afraid!" [51]Then he got into the boat with them, and the wind died down. The disciples were completely amazed, [52]because they had not understood the real meaning of the feeding of the five thousand; their minds could not grasp it.

Jesus Heals the Sick in Gennesaret
(Matt. 14.34-36)

[53] They crossed the lake and came to land at Gennesaret, where they tied up the boat. [54]As they left the boat, people recognized Jesus at once. [55]So they ran throughout the whole region; and wherever they heard he was, they brought to him sick people lying on their mats. [56]And everywhere Jesus went, to villages, towns, or farms, people would take those who were ill to the market places and beg him to

[k]pass them by; *or* join them.

let them at least touch the edge of his cloak; and all who touched it were made well.

The Teaching of the Ancestors
(Matt. 15.1-9)

7 Some Pharisees and teachers of the Law who had come from Jerusalem gathered round Jesus. ²They noticed that some of his disciples were eating their food with hands that were ritually unclean—that is, they had not washed them in the way the Pharisees said people should.

3 (For the Pharisees, as well as the rest of the Jews, follow the teaching they received from their ancestors: they do not eat unless they wash their hands in the proper way; ⁴nor do they eat anything that comes from the market unless they wash it first.[l] And they follow many other rules which they have received, such as the proper way to wash cups, pots, copper bowls, and beds.[m])

5 So the Pharisees and the teachers of the Law asked Jesus, "Why is it that your disciples do not follow the teaching handed down by our ancestors, but instead eat with ritually unclean hands?"

6 Jesus answered them, "How right Isaiah was when he prophesied about you! You are hypocrites, just as he wrote:

'These people, says God, honour me with their words,
    but their heart is really far away from me.
⁷ It is no use for them to worship me,
    because they teach man-made rules
    as though they were God's laws!'

8 "You put aside God's command and obey the teachings of men."

9 And Jesus continued, "You have a clever way of rejecting God's law in order to uphold your own teaching. ¹⁰For Moses commanded, 'Respect your father and your mother,' and, 'Whoever curses his father or his mother is to be put to death.' ¹¹But

---

[l] anything that comes from the market unless they wash it first; *or* anything after they come from the market unless they wash themselves first.
[m] *Some manuscripts do not have* and beds.

you teach that if a person has something he could use to help his father or mother, but says, 'This is Corban' (which means, it belongs to God), [12]he is excused from helping his father or mother. [13]In this way the teaching you pass on to others cancels out the word of God. And there are many other things like this that you do."

The Things that Make a Person Unclean
(Matt. 15.10-20)

14 Then Jesus called the crowd to him once more and said to them, "Listen to me, all of you, and understand. [15]There is nothing that goes into a person from the outside which can make him ritually unclean. Rather, it is what comes out of a person that makes him unclean."[n]

17 When he left the crowd and went into the house, his disciples asked him to explain this saying. [18]"You are no more intelligent than the others," Jesus said to them. "Don't you understand? Nothing that goes into a person from the outside can really make him unclean, [19]because it does not go into his heart but into his stomach and then goes on out of the body." (In saying this, Jesus declared that all foods are fit to be eaten.)

20 And he went on to say, "It is what comes out of a person that makes him unclean. [21]For from the inside, from a person's heart, come the evil ideas which lead him to do immoral things, to rob, kill, [22]commit adultery, be greedy, and do all sorts of evil things; deceit, indecency, jealousy, slander, pride, and folly— [23]all these evil things come from inside a person and make him unclean."

A Woman's Faith
(Matt. 15.21-28)

24 Then Jesus left and went away to the territory near the city of Tyre. He went into a house and did not want anyone to know he was there, but he could not stay hidden. [25]A woman, whose daughter

[n] Some manuscripts add verse 16: Listen, then, if you have ears! (see 4.23).

had an evil spirit in her, heard about Jesus and came to him at once and fell at his feet. ²⁶The woman was a Gentile, born in the region of Phoenicia in Syria. She begged Jesus to drive the demon out of her daughter. ²⁷But Jesus answered, "Let us first feed the children. It isn't right to take the children's food and throw it to the dogs."

28 "Sir," she answered, "even the dogs under the table eat the children's leftovers!"

29 So Jesus said to her, "Because of that answer, go back home, where you will find that the demon has gone out of your daughter!"

30 She went home and found her child lying on the bed; the demon had indeed gone out of her.

Jesus Heals a Deaf-Mute

31 Jesus then left the neighbourhood of Tyre and went on through Sidon to Lake Galilee, going by way of the territory of the Ten Towns. ³²Some people brought him a man who was deaf and could hardly speak, and they begged Jesus to place his hands on him. ³³So Jesus took him off alone, away from the crowd, put his fingers in the man's ears, spat, and touched the man's tongue. ³⁴Then Jesus looked up to heaven, gave a deep groan, and said to the man, "*Ephphatha*," which means, "Open up!"

35 At once the man was able to hear, his speech impediment was removed, and he began to talk without any trouble. ³⁶Then Jesus ordered the people not to speak of it to anyone; but the more he ordered them not to, the more they spoke. ³⁷And all who heard were completely amazed. "How well he does everything!" they exclaimed. "He even causes the deaf to hear and the dumb to speak!"

Jesus Feeds Four Thousand People
(Matt. 15.32–39)

8 Not long afterwards another large crowd came together. When the people had nothing left to eat, Jesus called the disciples to him and said, ²"I feel sorry for these people, because they have been with me for three days and now have nothing to eat. ³If I send them home without feeding them, they

will faint as they go, because some of them have
come a long way."

4 His disciples asked him, "Where in this desert
can anyone find enough food to feed all these people?"

5 "How much bread have you got?" Jesus asked.

"Seven loaves," they answered.

6 He ordered the crowd to sit down on the ground.
Then he took the seven loaves, gave thanks to God,
broke them, and gave them to his disciples to distribute
to the crowd; and the disciples did so. 7 They also had
a few small fish. Jesus gave thanks for these and
told the disciples to distribute them too. 8-9 Everybody
ate and had enough—there were about four thousand
people. Then the disciples took up seven baskets full
of pieces left over. Jesus sent the people away 10 and
at once got into a boat with his disciples and went
to the district of Dalmanutha.

The Pharisees Ask for a Miracle
(Matt. 16.1-4)

11 Some Pharisees came to Jesus and started to
argue with him. They wanted to trap him, so they
asked him to perform a miracle to show that God
approved of him. 12 But Jesus gave a deep groan and
said, "Why do the people of this day ask for a miracle?
No, I tell you! No such proof will be given to these
people!"

13 He left them, got back into the boat, and started
across to the other side of the lake.

The Yeast of the Pharisees and of Herod
(Matt. 16.5-12)

14 The disciples had forgotten to bring enough bread
and had only one loaf with them in the boat. 15 "Take
care," Jesus warned them, "and be on your guard
against the yeast of the Pharisees and the yeast of
Herod."

16 They started discussing among themselves: "He
says this because we haven't any bread."

17 Jesus knew what they were saying, so he asked
them, "Why are you discussing about not having any
bread? Don't you know or understand yet? Are your
minds so dull? 18 You have eyes—can't you see? You

have ears—can't you hear? Don't you remember
¹⁹ when I broke the five loaves for the five thousand
people? How many baskets full of leftover pieces did
you take up?"

"Twelve," they answered.

20 "And when I broke the seven loaves for the
four thousand people," asked Jesus, "how many baskets full of leftover pieces did you take up?"

"Seven," they answered.

21 "And you still don't understand?" he asked them.

Jesus Heals a Blind Man at Bethsaida

22 They came to Bethsaida, where some people
brought a blind man to Jesus and begged him to
touch him. ²³ Jesus took the blind man by the hand
and led him out of the village. After spitting on the
man's eyes, Jesus placed his hands on him and asked
him, "Can you see anything?"

24 The man looked up and said, "Yes, I can see
people, but they look like trees walking about."

25 Jesus again placed his hands on the man's eyes.
This time the man looked intently, his eyesight
returned, and he saw everything clearly. ²⁶ Jesus then
sent him home with the order, "Don't go back into
the village."

Peter's Declaration about Jesus
(Matt. 16.13–20; Luke 9.18–21)

27 Then Jesus and his disciples went away to the
villages near Caesarea Philippi. On the way he asked

He must forget self, carry his cross, and follow me (8.34)

them, "Tell me, who do people say I am?"

28 "Some say that you are John the Baptist," they answered; "others say that you are Elijah, while others say that you are one of the prophets."

29 "What about you?" he asked them. "Who do you say I am?"

Peter answered, "You are the Messiah."

30 Then Jesus ordered them, "Do not tell anyone about me."

Jesus Speaks about His Suffering and Death
(Matt. 16.21-28; Luke 9.22-27)

31 Then Jesus began to teach his disciples: "The Son of Man must suffer much and be rejected by the elders, the chief priests, and the teachers of the Law. He will be put to death, but three days later he will rise to life." 32 He made this very clear to them. So Peter took him aside and began to rebuke him. 33 But Jesus turned round, looked at his disciples, and rebuked Peter. "Get away from me, Satan," he said. "Your thoughts don't come from God but from man!"

34 Then Jesus called the crowd and his disciples to him. "If anyone wants to come with me," he told them, "he must forget self, carry his cross, and follow me. 35 For whoever wants to save his own life will lose it; but whoever loses his life for me and for the gospel will save it. 36 Does a person gain anything if he wins the whole world but loses his life? Of course not! 37 There is nothing he can give to regain

his life. [38]If a person is ashamed of me and of my teaching in this godless and wicked day, then the Son of Man will be ashamed of him when he comes in the glory of his Father with the holy angels."

9 And he went on to say, "I tell you, there are some here who will not die until they have seen the Kingdom of God come with power."

The Transfiguration
(Matt. 17.1–13; Luke 9.28–36)

2 Six days later Jesus took with him Peter, James, and John, and led them up a high mountain, where they were alone. As they looked on, a change came over Jesus, [3]and his clothes became shining white— whiter than anyone in the world could wash them. [4]Then the three disciples saw Elijah and Moses talking with Jesus. [5]Peter spoke up and said to Jesus, "Teacher, how good it is that we are here! We will make three tents, one for you, one for Moses, and one for Elijah." [6]He and the others were so frightened that he did not know what to say.

7 Then a cloud appeared and covered them with its shadow, and a voice came from the cloud, "This is my own dear Son—listen to him!" [8]They took a quick look round but did not see anyone else; only Jesus was with them.

9 As they came down the mountain, Jesus ordered them, "Don't tell anyone what you have seen, until the Son of Man has risen from death."

10 They obeyed his order, but among themselves they started discussing the matter, "What does this 'rising from death' mean?" [11]And they asked Jesus, "Why do the teachers of the Law say that Elijah has to come first?"

12 His answer was, "Elijah is indeed coming first in order to get everything ready. Yet why do the Scriptures say that the Son of Man will suffer much and be rejected? [13]I tell you, however, that Elijah has already come and that people treated him just as they pleased, as the Scriptures say about him."

Jesus Heals a Boy with an Evil Spirit
(Matt. 17.14–21; Luke 9.37–43a)

14 When they joined the rest of the disciples, they saw a large crowd round them and some teachers of the Law arguing with them. 15 When the people saw Jesus, they were greatly surprised, and ran to him and greeted him. 16 Jesus asked his disciples, "What are you arguing with them about?"

17 A man in the crowd answered, "Teacher, I brought my son to you, because he has an evil spirit in him and cannot talk. 18 Whenever the spirit attacks him, it throws him to the ground, and he foams at the mouth, grits his teeth, and becomes stiff all over. I asked your disciples to drive the spirit out, but they could not."

19 Jesus said to them, "How unbelieving you people are! How long must I stay with you? How long do I have to put up with you? Bring the boy to me!" 20 They brought him to Jesus.

As soon as the spirit saw Jesus, it threw the boy into a fit, so that he fell on the ground and rolled round, foaming at the mouth. 21 "How long has he been like this?" Jesus asked the father.

"Ever since he was a child," he replied. 22 "Many times the evil spirit has tried to kill him by throwing him in the fire and into water. Have pity on us and help us, if you possibly can!"

23 "Yes," said Jesus, "if you yourself can! Everything is possible for the person who has faith."

24 The father at once cried out, "I do have faith, but not enough. Help me to have more!"

25 Jesus noticed that the crowd was closing in on them, so he gave a command to the evil spirit. "Deaf and dumb spirit," he said, "I order you to come out of the boy and never go into him again!"

26 The spirit screamed, threw the boy into a bad fit, and came out. The boy looked like a corpse, and everyone said, "He is dead!" 27 But Jesus took the boy by the hand and helped him to rise, and he stood up.

28 After Jesus had gone indoors, his disciples asked him privately, "Why couldn't we drive the spirit out?"

29 "Only prayer can drive this kind out," answered Jesus; "nothing else can."

Jesus Speaks Again about His Death
(Matt. 17.22–23; Luke 9.43b–45)

30 Jesus and his disciples left that place and went on through Galilee. Jesus did not want anyone to know where he was, 31because he was teaching his disciples: "The Son of Man will be handed over to men who will kill him. Three days later, however, he will rise to life."

32 But they did not understand what this teaching meant, and they were afraid to ask him.

Who Is the Greatest?
(Matt. 18.1–5; Luke 9.46–48)

33 They came to Capernaum, and after going indoors Jesus asked his disciples, "What were you arguing about on the road?"

34 But they would not answer him, because on the road they had been arguing among themselves about who was the greatest. 35Jesus sat down, called the twelve disciples, and said to them, "Whoever wants to be first must place himself last of all and be the servant of all." 36Then he took a child and made him stand in front of them. He put his arms round him and said to them, 37"Whoever welcomes in my name one of these children, welcomes me; and whoever welcomes me, welcomes not only me but also the one who sent me."

Whoever Is Not against Us Is for Us
(Luke 9.49–50)

38 John said to him, "Teacher, we saw a man who was driving out demons in your name, and we told him to stop, because he doesn't belong to our group."

39 "Do not try to stop him," Jesus told them, "because no one who performs a miracle in my name will be able soon afterwards to say evil things about me. 40For whoever is not against us is for us. 41I assure you that anyone who gives you a drink of water because you belong to me will certainly receive his reward.

Temptations to Sin
(Matt. 18.6–9; Luke 17.1–2)

42 "If anyone should cause one of these little ones to lose his faith in me, it would be better for that person to have a large millstone tied round his neck and be thrown into the sea. 43 So if your hand makes you lose your faith, cut it off! It is better for you to enter life without a hand than to keep both hands and go off to hell, to the fire that never goes out. *o* 45 And if your foot makes you lose your faith, cut it off! It is better for you to enter life without a foot than to keep both feet and be thrown into hell. *p* 47 And if your eye makes you lose your faith, take it out! It is better for you to enter the Kingdom of God with only one eye than to keep both eyes and be thrown into hell. 48 There 'the worms that eat them never die, and the fire that burns them is never put out.'

49 "Everyone will be purified by fire as a sacrifice is purified by salt.

50 "Salt is good; but if it loses its saltiness, how can you make it salty again?

"Have the salt of friendship among yourselves, and live in peace with one another."

Jesus Teaches about Divorce
(Matt. 19.1–12; Luke 16.18)

10 Then Jesus left that place, went to the province of Judaea, and crossed the River Jordan. Crowds came flocking to him again, and he taught them, as he always did.

2 Some Pharisees came to him and tried to trap him. "Tell us," they asked, "does our Law allow a man to divorce his wife?"

o Some manuscripts add verse 44: There 'the worms that eat them never die, and the fire that burns them is never put out' (see verse 48).
p Some manuscripts add verse 46: There 'the worms that eat them never die, and the fire that burns them is never put out' (see verse 48).

3 Jesus answered with a question, "What law did Moses give you?"

4 Their answer was, "Moses gave permission for a man to write a divorce notice and send his wife away."

5 Jesus said to them, "Moses wrote this law for you because you are so hard to teach. 6 But in the beginning, at the time of creation, 'God made them male and female,' as the scripture says. 7 'And for this reason a man will leave his father and mother and unite with his wife,*q* 8 and the two will become one.' So they are no longer two, but one. 9 Man must not separate, then, what God has joined together."

10 When they went back into the house, the disciples asked Jesus about this matter. 11 He said to them, "A man who divorces his wife and marries another woman commits adultery against his wife. 12 In the same way, a woman who divorces her husband and marries another man commits adultery."

Jesus Blesses Little Children
(Matt. 19.13–15; Luke 18.15–17)

13 Some people brought children to Jesus for him to place his hands on them, but the disciples scolded the people. 14 When Jesus noticed this, he was angry and said to his disciples, "Let the children come to me, and do not stop them, because the Kingdom of God belongs to such as these. 15 I assure you that whoever does not receive the Kingdom of God like a child will never enter it." 16 Then he took the children in his arms, placed his hands on each of them, and blessed them.

The Rich Man
(Matt. 19.16–30; Luke 18.18–30)

17 As Jesus was starting on his way again, a man ran up, knelt before him, and asked him, "Good Teacher, what must I do to receive eternal life?"

18 "Why do you call me good?" Jesus asked him. "No one is good except God alone. 19 You know the commandments: 'Do not commit murder; do not com-

---

*q*Some manuscripts do not have and unite with his wife.

mit adultery; do not steal; do not accuse anyone falsely; do not cheat; respect your father and your mother.' "

20 "Teacher," the man said, "ever since I was young, I have obeyed all these commandments."

21 Jesus looked straight at him with love and said, "You need only one thing. Go and sell all you have and give the money to the poor, and you will have riches in heaven; then come and follow me." 22 When the man heard this, gloom spread over his face, and he went away sad, because he was very rich.

23 Jesus looked round at his disciples and said to them, "How hard it will be for rich people to enter the Kingdom of God!"

24 The disciples were shocked at these words, but Jesus went on to say, "My children, how hard it is to enter the Kingdom of God! 25 It is much harder for a rich person to enter the Kingdom of God than for a camel to go through the eye of a needle."

26 At this the disciples were completely amazed and asked one another, "Who, then, can be saved?"

27 Jesus looked straight at them and answered, "This is impossible for man, but not for God; everything is possible for God."

28 Then Peter spoke up, "Look, we have left everything and followed you."

29 "Yes," Jesus said to them, "and I tell you that anyone who leaves home or brothers or sisters or mother or father or children or fields for me and for the gospel, 30 will receive much more in this present age. He will receive a hundred times more houses, brothers, sisters, mothers, children and fields—and persecutions as well; and in the age to come he will receive eternal life. 31 But many who now are first will be last, and many who now are last will be first."

Jesus Speaks a Third Time about His Death
(Matt. 20.17-19; Luke 18.31-34)

32 Jesus and his disciples were now on the road going up to Jerusalem. Jesus was going ahead of the disciples, who were filled with alarm; the people who followed behind were afraid. Once again Jesus

took the twelve disciples aside and spoke of the things that were going to happen to him. ³³"Listen," he told them, "we are going up to Jerusalem where the Son of Man will be handed over to the chief priests and the teachers of the Law. They will condemn him to death and then hand him over to the Gentiles, ³⁴who will mock him, spit on him, whip him, and kill him; but three days later he will rise to life."

The Request of James and John
(Matt. 20.20–28)

35 Then James and John, the sons of Zebedee, came to Jesus. "Teacher," they said, "there is something we want you to do for us."

36 "What is it?" Jesus asked them.

37 They answered, "When you sit on your throne in your glorious Kingdom, we want you to let us sit with you, one at your right and one at your left."

38 Jesus said to them, "You don't know what you are asking for. Can you drink the cup of suffering that I must drink? Can you be baptized in the way I must be baptized?"

39 "We can," they answered.

Jesus said to them, "You will indeed drink the cup I must drink and be baptized in the way I must be baptized. ⁴⁰But I do not have the right to choose who will sit at my right and my left. It is God who will give these places to those for whom he has prepared them."

41 When the other ten disciples heard about it, they became angry with James and John. ⁴²So Jesus called them all together to him and said, "You know that the men who are considered rulers of the heathen have power over them, and the leaders have complete authority. ⁴³This, however, is not the way it is among you. If one of you wants to be great, he must be the servant of the rest; ⁴⁴and if one of you wants to be first, he must be the slave of all. ⁴⁵For even the Son of Man did not come to be served; he came to serve and to give his life to redeem many people."

Jesus Heals Blind Bartimaeus
(Matt. 20.29-34; Luke 18.35-43)

46 They came to Jericho, and as Jesus was leaving with his disciples and a large crowd, a blind beggar named Bartimaeus son of Timaeus was sitting by the road. 47When he heard that it was Jesus of Nazareth, he began to shout, "Jesus! Son of David! Take pity on me!"

48 Many of the people scolded him and told him to be quiet. But he shouted even more loudly, "Son of David, take pity on me!"

49 Jesus stopped and said, "Call him."

So they called the blind man. "Cheer up!" they said. "Get up, he is calling you."

50 He threw off his cloak, jumped up, and came to Jesus.

51 "What do you want me to do for you?" Jesus asked him.

"Teacher," the blind man answered, "I want to see again."

52 "Go," Jesus told him, "your faith has made you well."

At once he was able to see and followed Jesus on the road.

The Triumphant Entry into Jerusalem
(Matt. 21.1-11; Luke 19.28-40; John 12.12-19)

11 As they approached Jerusalem, near the towns of Bethphage and Bethany, they came to the Mount of Olives. Jesus sent two of his disciples on ahead 2with these instructions: "Go to the village there ahead of you. As soon as you get there, you will find a colt tied up that has never been ridden. Untie it and bring it here. 3And if someone asks you why you are doing that, tell him that the Master*r* needs it and will send it back at once."

4 So they went and found a colt out in the street, tied to the door of a house. As they were untying it, 5some of the bystanders asked them, "What are you doing, untying that colt?"

*r*the Master; *or* its owner.

6 They answered just as Jesus had told them, and the men let them go. 7They brought the colt to Jesus, threw their cloaks over the animal, and Jesus got on. 8Many people spread their cloaks on the road, while others cut branches in the fields and spread them on the road. 9The people who were in front and those who followed behind began to shout, "Praise God! God bless him who comes in the name of the Lord! 10God bless the coming kingdom of King David, our father! Praise God!"

11 Jesus entered Jerusalem, went into the Temple, and looked round at everything. But since it was already late in the day, he went out to Bethany with the twelve disciples.

Jesus Curses the Fig-Tree
(Matt. 21.18–19)

12 The next day, as they were coming back from Bethany, Jesus was hungry. 13He saw in the distance a fig-tree covered with leaves, so he went to see if he could find any figs on it. But when he came to it, he found only leaves, because it was not the right time for figs. 14Jesus said to the fig-tree, "No one shall ever eat figs from you again!"

And his disciples heard him.

Jesus Goes to the Temple
(Matt. 21.12–17; Luke 19.45–48; John 2.13–22)

15 When they arrived in Jerusalem, Jesus went to the Temple and began to drive out all those who were buying and selling. He overturned the tables of the money-changers and the stools of those who sold pigeons, 16and he would not let anyone carry anything through the temple courtyards. 17He then taught the people: "It is written in the Scriptures that God said, 'My Temple will be called a house of prayer for the people of all nations.' But you have turned it into a hideout for thieves!"

18 The chief priests and the teachers of the Law heard of this, so they began looking for some way to kill Jesus. They were afraid of him, because the whole crowd was amazed at his teaching.

19 When evening came, Jesus and his disciples left the city.

The Lesson from the Fig-Tree
(Matt. 21.20–22)

20 Early next morning, as they walked along the road, they saw the fig-tree. It was dead all the way down to its roots. 21 Peter remembered what had happened and said to Jesus, "Look, Teacher, the fig-tree you cursed has died!"

22 Jesus answered them, "Have faith in God. 23 I assure you that whoever tells this hill to get up and throw itself in the sea and does not doubt in his heart, but believes that what he says will happen, it will be done for him. 24 For this reason I tell you: When you pray and ask for something, believe that you have received it, and you will be given whatever you ask for. 25 And when you stand and pray, forgive anything you may have against anyone, so that your Father in heaven will forgive the wrongs you have done." s

The Question about Jesus' Authority
(Matt. 21.23–27; Luke 20.1–8)

27 They arrived once again in Jerusalem. As Jesus was walking in the Temple, the chief priests, the teachers of the Law, and the elders came to him 28 and asked him, "What right have you to do these things? Who gave you this right?"

29 Jesus answered them, "I will ask you just one question, and if you give me an answer, I will tell you what right I have to do these things. 30 Tell me, where did John's right to baptize come from: was it from God or from man?"

31 They started to argue among themselves: "What shall we say? If we answer, 'From God,' he will say, 'Why, then, did you not believe John?' 32 But if we say, 'From man . . .'" (They were afraid of the people, because everyone was convinced that John

---

s Some manuscripts add verse 26: If you do not forgive others, your Father in heaven will not forgive the wrongs you have done (see Mt 6.15).

had been a prophet.) 33 So their answer to Jesus was, "We don't know."

Jesus said to them, "Neither will I tell you, then, by what right I do these things."

The Parable of the Tenants in the Vineyard
(Matt. 21.33–46; Luke 20.9–19)

12 Then Jesus spoke to them in parables: "Once there was a man who planted a vineyard, put a fence round it, dug a hole for the winepress, and built a watch-tower. Then he let out the vineyard to tenants and left home on a journey. 2 When the time came to gather the grapes, he sent a slave to the tenants to receive from them his share of the harvest. 3 The tenants seized the slave, beat him, and sent him back without a thing. 4 Then the owner sent another slave; the tenants beat him over the head and treated him shamefully. 5 The owner sent another slave, and they killed him; and they treated many others the same way, beating some and killing others. 6 The only one left to send was the man's own dear son. Last of all, then, he sent his son to the tenants. 'I am sure they will respect my son,' he said. 7 But those tenants said to one another, 'This is the owner's son. Come on, let's kill him, and his property will be ours!' 8 So they seized the son and killed him and threw his body out of the vineyard.

9 "What, then, will the owner of the vineyard do?" asked Jesus. "He will come and kill those men and hand the vineyard over to other tenants. 10 Surely you have read this scripture?

'The stone which the builders rejected as worthless
    turned out to be the most important of all.
11 This was done by the Lord;
    what a wonderful sight it is!' "

12 The Jewish leaders tried to arrest Jesus, because they knew that he had told this parable against them. But they were afraid of the crowd, so they left him and went away.

The Question about Paying Taxes
(Matt. 22.15–22; Luke 20.20–26)

13 Some Pharisees and some members of Herod's

party were sent to Jesus to trap him with questions.
14 They came to him and said, "Teacher, we know
that you tell the truth, without worrying about what
people think. You pay no attention to a man's status,
but teach the truth about God's will for man. Tell
us, is it against our Law to pay taxes to the Roman
Emperor? Should we pay them or not?"

15 But Jesus saw through their trick and answered,
"Why are you trying to trap me? Bring a silver coin,
and let me see it."

16 They brought him one, and he asked, "Whose
face and name are these?"

"The Emperor's," they answered.

17 So Jesus said, "Well, then, pay the Emperor what
belongs to the Emperor, and pay God what belongs
to God."

And they were amazed at Jesus.

The Question about Rising from Death
(Matt. 22.23–33; Luke 20.27–40)

18 Then some Sadducees, who say that people will
not rise from death, came to Jesus and said,
19 "Teacher, Moses wrote this law for us: 'If a man
dies and leaves a wife but no children, that man's
brother must marry the widow so that they can have
children who will be considered the dead man's children.' 20 Once there were seven brothers; the eldest got
married and died without having children. 21 Then the
second one married the woman, and he also died
without having children. The same thing happened
to the third brother, 22 and then to the rest: all seven
brothers married the woman and died without having
children. Last of all, the woman died. 23 Now, when
all the dead rise to life on the day of resurrection,
whose wife will she be? All seven of them had married
her."

24 Jesus answered them, "How wrong you are! And
do you know why? It is because you don't know
the Scriptures or God's power. 25 For when the dead
rise to life, they will be like the angels in heaven
and will not marry. 26 Now, as for the dead being
raised: haven't you ever read in the Book of Moses
the passage about the burning bush? There it is written

that God said to Moses, 'I am the God of Abraham, the God of Isaac, and the God of Jacob.' 27 He is the God of the living, not of the dead. You are completely wrong!'"

The Great Commandment
(Matt. 22.34–40; Luke 10.25–28)

28 A teacher of the Law was there who heard the discussion. He saw that Jesus had given the Sadducees a good answer, so he came to him with a question: "Which commandment is the most important of all?"

29 Jesus replied, "The most important one is this: 'Listen, Israel! The Lord our God is the only Lord.[t] 30 Love the Lord your God with all your heart, with all your soul, with all your mind, and with all your strength.' 31 The second most important commandment is this: 'Love your neighbour as you love yourself.' There is no other commandment more important than these two."

32 The teacher of the Law said to Jesus, "Well done, Teacher! It is true, as you say, that only the Lord is God and that there is no other god but he. 33 And man must love God with all his heart and with all his mind and with all his strength; and he must love his neighbour as he loves himself. It is more important to obey these two commandments than to offer animals and other sacrifices to God."

34 Jesus noticed how wise his answer was, and so he told him, "You are not far from the Kingdom of God."

After this nobody dared to ask Jesus any more questions.

The Question about the Messiah
(Matt. 22.41–46; Luke 20.41–44)

35 As Jesus was teaching in the Temple, he asked the question, "How can the teachers of the Law say that the Messiah will be the descendant of David? 36 The Holy Spirit inspired David to say:

'The Lord said to my Lord:

[t] The Lord our God is the only Lord; *or* The Lord is our God, the Lord alone.

Sit here on my right
until I put your enemies under your feet.'
37 David himself called him 'Lord'; so how can the
Messiah be David's descendant?"

Jesus Warns against the Teachers of the Law
(Matt. 23.1–36; Luke 20.45–47)

A large crowd was listening to Jesus gladly. 38 As
he taught them, he said, "Watch out for the teachers
of the Law, who like to walk around in their long
robes and be greeted with respect in the market-place,
39 who choose the reserved seats in the synagogues
and the best places at feasts. 40 They take advantage
of widows and rob them of their homes, and then
make a show of saying long prayers. Their punishment
will be all the worse!"

The Widow's Offering
(Luke 21.1–4)

41 As Jesus sat near the temple treasury, he watched
the people as they dropped in their money. Many
rich men dropped in a lot of money; 42 then a poor
widow came along and dropped in two little copper

A poor widow came along (12.42)

coins, worth about a penny. 43 He called his disciples together and said to them, "I tell you that this poor widow put more in the offering box than all the others. 44 For the others put in what they had to spare of their riches; but she, poor as she is, put in all she had—she gave all she had to live on."

Jesus Speaks of the Destruction of the Temple
(Matt. 24.1-2; Luke 21.5-6)

13 As Jesus was leaving the Temple, one of his disciples said, "Look, Teacher! What wonderful stones and buildings!"

2 Jesus answered, "You see these great buildings? Not a single stone here will be left in its place; every one of them will be thrown down."

Troubles and Persecutions
(Matt. 24.3-14; Luke 21.7-19)

3 Jesus was sitting on the Mount of Olives, across from the Temple, when Peter, James, John, and Andrew came to him in private. 4 "Tell us when this will be," they said, "and tell us what will happen to show that the time has come for all these things to take place."

5 Jesus said to them, "Be on guard, and don't let anyone deceive you. 6 Many men, claiming to speak for me, will come and say, 'I am he!' and they will deceive many people. 7 And don't be troubled when you hear the noise of battles close by and news of battles far away. Such things must happen, but they do not mean that the end has come. 8 Countries will fight each other; kingdoms will attack one another. There will be earthquakes everywhere, and there will be famines. These things are like the first pains of childbirth.

9 "You yourselves must be on guard. You will be arrested and taken to court. You will be beaten in the synagogues; you will stand before rulers and kings for my sake to tell them the Good News. 10 But before the end comes, the gospel must be preached to all peoples. 11 And when you are arrested and taken to court, do not worry beforehand about what you are going to say; when the time comes, say whatever

is then given to you. For the words you speak will not be yours; they will come from the Holy Spirit. [12] Men will hand over their own brothers to be put to death, and fathers will do the same to their children. Children will turn against their parents and have them put to death. [13] Everyone will hate you because of me. But whoever holds out to the end will be saved.

The Awful Horror
(Matt. 24.15–28; Luke 21.20–24)

14 "You will see 'The Awful Horror' standing in the place where he should not be." (Note to the reader: be sure to understand what this means!) "Then those who are in Judaea must run away to the hills. [15] A man who is on the roof of his house must not lose time by going down into the house to get anything to take with him. [16] A man who is in the field must not go back to the house for his cloak. [17] How terrible it will be in those days for women who are pregnant and for mothers with little babies! [18] Pray to God that these things will not happen in the winter! [19] For the trouble of those days will be far worse than any the world has ever known from the very beginning when God created the world until the present time. Nor will there ever be anything like it again. [20] But the Lord has reduced the number of those days; if he had not, nobody would survive. For the sake of his chosen people, however, he has reduced those days.

21 "Then, if anyone says to you, 'Look, here is the Messiah!' or, 'Look, there he is!'—do not believe him. [22] For false Messiahs and false prophets will appear. They will perform miracles and wonders in order to deceive even God's chosen people, if possible. [23] Be on your guard! I have told you everything before the time comes.

The Coming of the Son of Man
(Matt. 24.29–31; Luke 21.25–28)

24 "In the days after that time of trouble the sun will grow dark, the moon will no longer shine, [25] the stars will fall from heaven, and the powers in space will be driven from their courses. [26] Then the Son of

Man will appear, coming in the clouds with great power and glory. ²⁷He will send the angels out to the four corners of the earth to gather God's chosen people from one end of the world to the other.

The Lesson of the Fig-Tree
(Matt. 24.32–35; Luke 21.29–33)

28 "Let the fig-tree teach you a lesson. When its branches become green and tender and it starts putting out leaves, you know that summer is near. ²⁹In the same way, when you see these things happening, you will know that the time is near, ready to begin.ᵘ ³⁰Remember that all these things will happen before the people now living have all died. ³¹Heaven and earth will pass away, but my words will never pass away.

No One Knows the Day or Hour
(Matt. 24.36–44)

32 "No one knows, however, when that day or hour will come—neither the angels in heaven, nor the Son; only the Father knows. ³³Be on watch, be alert, for you do not know when the time will come. ³⁴It will be like a man who goes away from home on a journey and leaves his servants in charge, after giving to each one his own work to do and after telling the doorkeeper to keep watch. ³⁵Be on guard, then, because you do not know when the master of the house is coming—it might be in the evening or at midnight or before dawn or at sunrise. ³⁶If he comes suddenly, he must not find you asleep. ³⁷What I say to you, then, I say to all: Watch!"

The Plot against Jesus
(Matt. 26.1–5; Luke 22.1–2; John 11.45–53)

14 It was now two days before the Festival of Passover and Unleavened Bread. The chief priests and the teachers of the Law were looking for a way to arrest Jesus secretly and put him to death. ²"We must not do it during the festival," they said, "or the people might riot."

ᵘthe time is near, ready to begin; or he is near, ready to come.

Jesus Is Anointed at Bethany
(Matt. 26.6-13; John 12.1-8)

3 Jesus was in Bethany at the house of Simon, a man who had suffered from a dreaded skin-disease. While Jesus was eating, a woman came in with an alabaster jar full of a very expensive perfume made of pure nard. She broke the jar and poured the perfume on Jesus' head. 4 Some of the people there became angry and said to one another, "What was the use of wasting the perfume? 5 It could have been sold for more than three hundred silver coins[v] and the money given to the poor!" And they criticized her harshly.

6 But Jesus said, "Leave her alone! Why are you bothering her? She has done a fine and beautiful thing for me. 7 You will always have poor people with you, and any time you want to, you can help them. But you will not always have me. 8 She did what she could; she poured perfume on my body to prepare it ahead of time for burial. 9 Now, I assure you that wherever the gospel is preached all over the world, what she has done will be told in memory of her."

Judas Agrees to Betray Jesus
(Matt. 26.14-16; Luke 22.3-6)

10 Then Judas Iscariot, one of the twelve disciples, went off to the chief priests in order to betray Jesus to them. 11 They were pleased to hear what he had to say, and promised to give him money. So Judas started looking for a good chance to hand Jesus over to them.

Jesus Eats the Passover Meal with His Disciples
(Matt. 26.17-25; Luke 22.7-14, 21-23; John 13.21-30)

12 On the first day of the Festival of Unleavened Bread, the day the lambs for the Passover meal were killed, Jesus' disciples asked him, "Where do you want us to go and get the Passover meal ready for you?"

13 Then Jesus sent two of them with these instructions: "Go into the city, and a man carrying a jar

[v] SILVER COINS: See 6.37.

of water will meet you. Follow him ¹⁴to the house
he enters, and say to the owner of the house: 'The
Teacher says, Where is the room where my disciples
and I will eat the Passover meal?' ¹⁵Then he will
show you a large upstairs room, prepared and furnished, where you will get everything ready for us."

16 The disciples left, went to the city, and found
everything just as Jesus had told them; and they
prepared the Passover meal.

17 When it was evening, Jesus came with the twelve
disciples. ¹⁸While they were at the table eating, Jesus
said, "I tell you that one of you will betray me—one
who is eating with me."

19 The disciples were upset and began to ask him,
one after the other, "Surely you don't mean me, do
you?"

20 Jesus answered, "It will be one of you twelve,
one who dips his bread in the dish with me. ²¹The
Son of Man will die as the Scriptures say he will;
but how terrible for that man who betrays the Son
of Man! It would have been better for that man
if he had never been born!"

The Lord's Supper
(Matt. 26.26–30; Luke 22.14–20; I Cor. 11.23–25)

22 While they were eating, Jesus took a piece of
bread, gave a prayer of thanks, broke it, and gave

This is my body (14.22)

it to his disciples. "Take it," he said, "this is my body."

23 Then he took a cup, gave thanks to God, and handed it to them; and they all drank from it. ²⁴Jesus said, "This is my blood which is poured out for many, my blood which seals God's covenant. ²⁵I tell you, I will never again drink this wine until the day I drink the new wine in the Kingdom of God."

26 Then they sang a hymn and went out to the Mount of Olives.

Jesus Predicts Peter's Denial
(Matt. 26.31–35; Luke 22.31–34; John 13.36–38)

27 Jesus said to them, "All of you will run away and leave me, for the scripture says, 'God will kill the shepherd, and the sheep will all be scattered.' ²⁸But after I am raised to life, I will go to Galilee ahead of you."

29 Peter answered, "I will never leave you, even though all the rest do!"

30 Jesus said to Peter, "I tell you that before the cock crows twice tonight, you will say three times that you do not know me."

31 Peter answered even more strongly, "I will never say that, even if I have to die with you!"

And all the other disciples said the same thing.

Jesus Prays in Gethsemane
(Matt. 26.36–46; Luke 22.39–46)

32 They came to a place called Gethsemane, and Jesus said to his disciples, "Sit here while I pray." ³³He took Peter, James, and John with him. Distress and anguish came over him, ³⁴and he said to them, "The sorrow in my heart is so great that it almost crushes me. Stay here and keep watch."

35 He went a little farther on, threw himself on the ground, and prayed that, if possible, he might not have to go through that time of suffering. ³⁶"Father," he prayed, "my Father! All things are possible for you. Take this cup of suffering away from me. Yet not what I want, but what you want."

37 Then he returned and found the three disciples asleep. He said to Peter, "Simon, are you asleep?

Weren't you able to stay awake even for one hour?" 38 And he said to them, "Keep watch, and pray that you will not fall into temptation. The spirit is willing, but the flesh is weak."

39 He went away once more and prayed, saying the same words. 40 Then he came back to the disciples and found them asleep; they could not keep their eyes open. And they did not know what to say to him.

41 When he came back the third time, he said to them, "Are you still sleeping and resting? Enough! The hour has come! Look, the Son of Man is now being handed over to the power of sinful men. 42 Get up, let us go. Look, here is the man who is betraying me!"

The Arrest of Jesus
(Matt. 26.47-56; Luke 22.47-53; John 18.3-12)

43 Jesus was still speaking when Judas, one of the twelve disciples, arrived. With him was a crowd armed with swords and clubs, and sent by the chief priests, the teachers of the Law, and the elders. 44 The traitor had given the crowd a signal: "The man I kiss is the one you want. Arrest him and take him away under guard."

45 As soon as Judas arrived, he went up to Jesus and said, "Teacher!" and kissed him. 46 So they arrested Jesus and held him tight. 47 But one of those standing there drew his sword and struck at the High Priest's slave, cutting off his ear. 48 Then Jesus spoke up and said to them, "Did you have to come with swords and clubs to capture me, as though I were an outlaw? 49 Day after day I was with you teaching in the Temple, and you did not arrest me. But the Scriptures must come true."

50 Then all the disciples left him and ran away.

51 A certain young man, dressed only in a linen cloth, was following Jesus. They tried to arrest him, 52 but he ran away naked, leaving the cloth behind.

Jesus before the Council
(Matt. 26.57-68; Luke 22.54-55, 63-71; John 18.13-14, 19-24)

53 Then Jesus was taken to the High Priest's house,

So they arrested Jesus and held him tight (14.46)

where all the chief priests, the elders, and the teachers of the Law were gathering. 54 Peter followed from a distance and went into the courtyard of the High Priest's house. There he sat down with the guards, keeping himself warm by the fire. 55 The chief priests and the whole Council tried to find some evidence against Jesus in order to put him to death, but they could not find any. 56 Many witnesses told lies against Jesus, but their stories did not agree.

57 Then some men stood up and told this lie against Jesus: 58 "We heard him say, 'I will tear down this Temple which men have made, and after three days I will build one that is not made by men.' " 59 Not even they, however, could make their stories agree.

60 The High Priest stood up in front of them all and questioned Jesus, "Have you no answer to the accusation they bring against you?"

61 But Jesus kept quiet and would not say a word. Again the High Priest questioned him, "Are you the Messiah, the Son of the Blessed God?"

62 "I am," answered Jesus, "and you will all see

the Son of Man seated on the right of the Almighty and coming with the clouds of heaven!"

63 The High Priest tore his robes and said, "We don't need any more witnesses! 64 You heard his blasphemy. What is your decision?"

They all voted against him: he was guilty and should be put to death.

65 Some of them began to spit on Jesus, and they blindfolded him and hit him. "Guess who hit you!" they said. And the guards took him and slapped him.

Peter Denies Jesus
(Matt. 26.69–75; Luke 22.56–62; John 18.15–18, 25–27)

66 Peter was still down in the courtyard when one of the High Priest's servant-girls came by. 67 When she saw Peter warming himself, she looked straight at him and said, "You, too, were with Jesus of Nazareth."

68 But he denied it. "I don't know... I don't understand what you are talking about," he answered, and went out into the passage. Just then a cock crowed. w

69 The servant-girl saw him there and began to repeat to the bystanders, "He is one of them!" 70 But Peter denied it again.

A little while later the bystanders accused Peter again, "You can't deny that you are one of them, because you, too, are from Galilee."

71 Then Peter said, "I swear that I am telling the truth! May God punish me if I am not! I do not know the man you are talking about!"

72 Just then a cock crowed a second time, and Peter remembered how Jesus had said to him, "Before the cock crows twice, you will say three times that you do not know me." And he broke down and cried.

Jesus Is Brought before Pilate
(Matt. 27.1–2, 11–14; Luke 23.1–5; John 18.28–38)

15 Early in the morning the chief priests met hurriedly with the elders, the teachers of the Law, and the whole Council, and made their plans. They put Jesus in chains, led him away, and handed him

w *Some manuscripts do not have* Just then a cock crowed.

A cock crowed...and Peter remembered (14.72)

over to Pilate. ²Pilate questioned him, "Are you the king of the Jews?"

Jesus answered, "So you say."

3 The chief priests were accusing Jesus of many things, ⁴so Pilate questioned him again, "Aren't you going to answer? Listen to all their accusations!"

5 Again Jesus refused to say a word, and Pilate was amazed.

Jesus Is Sentenced to Death
(Matt. 27.15-26; Luke 23.13-25; John 18.39—19.16)

6 At every Passover Festival Pilate was in the habit of setting free any one prisoner the people asked for. ⁷At that time a man named Barabbas was in prison with the rebels who had committed murder in the riot. ⁸When the crowd gathered and began to ask Pilate for the usual favour, ⁹he asked them, "Do you want me to set free for you the king of the Jews?" ¹⁰He knew very well that the chief priests had handed Jesus over to him because they were jealous.

11 But the chief priests stirred up the crowd to ask, instead, for Pilate to set Barabbas free for them.

12 Pilate spoke again to the crowd, "What, then, do you want me to do with the one you call the king of the Jews?"

13 They shouted back, "Crucify him!"

14 "But what crime has he committed?" Pilate asked. They shouted all the louder, "Crucify him!"

15 Pilate wanted to please the crowd, so he set Barabbas free for them. Then he had Jesus whipped and handed him over to be crucified.

The Soldiers Mock Jesus
(Matt. 27.27-31; John 19.2-3)

16 The soldiers took Jesus inside to the courtyard of the governor's palace and called together the rest of the company. 17 They put a purple robe on Jesus, made a crown out of thorny branches, and put it on his head. 18 Then they began to salute him: "Long live the King of the Jews!" 19 They beat him over the head with a stick, spat on him, fell on their knees, and bowed down to him. 20 When they had finished mocking him, they took off the purple robe and put his own clothes back on him. Then they led him out to crucify him.

Jesus Is Crucified
(Matt. 27.32-44; Luke 23.26-43; John 19.17-27)

21 On the way they met a man named Simon, who was coming into the city from the country, and the soldiers forced him to carry Jesus' cross. (Simon was from Cyrene and was the father of Alexander and Rufus.) 22 They took Jesus to a place called Golgotha, which means "The Place of the Skull." 23 There they tried to give him wine mixed with a drug called myrrh, but Jesus would not drink it. 24 Then they crucified him and divided his clothes among themselves, throwing dice to see who would get which piece of clothing. 25 It was nine o'clock in the morning when they crucified him. 26 The notice of the accusation against him said: "The King of the Jews." 27 They also crucified

two bandits with Jesus, one on his right and the other on his left.^x

29 People passing by shook their heads and hurled insults at Jesus: "Aha! You were going to tear down the Temple and build it up again in three days! ³⁰Now come down from the cross and save yourself!"

Throwing dice (15.24)

31 In the same way the chief priests and the teachers of the Law jeered at Jesus, saying to each other, "He saved others, but he cannot save himself! ³²Let us see the Messiah, the king of Israel, come down from the cross now, and we will believe in him!"

And the two who were crucified with Jesus insulted him also.

The Death of Jesus
(Matt. 27.45–56; Luke 23.44–49; John 19.28–30)

33 At noon the whole country was covered with darkness, which lasted for three hours. ³⁴At three o'clock Jesus cried out with a loud shout, *"Eloi, Eloi,*

---

^x*Some manuscripts add verse 28:* In this way the scripture came true which says, "He shared the fate of criminals" *(see Lk 22.37).*

Aha! ...come down from the cross (15.29,30)

lema sabachthani?" which means, "My God, my God, why did you abandon me?"

35 Some of the people there heard him and said, "Listen, he is calling for Elijah!" 36 One of them ran up with a sponge, soaked it in cheap wine, and put it on the end of a stick. Then he held it up to Jesus' lips and said, "Wait! Let us see if Elijah is coming to bring him down from the cross!"

37 With a loud cry Jesus died.

38 The curtain hanging in the Temple was torn in two, from top to bottom. 39 The army officer who was standing there in front of the cross saw how Jesus had died.[y] "This man was really the Son of God!" he said.

40 Some women were there, looking on from a distance. Among them were Mary Magdalene, Mary the

[y] had died; *some manuscripts have* had cried out and died.

mother of the younger James and of Joseph, and
Salome. [41] They had followed Jesus while he was in
Galilee and had helped him. Many other women who
had come to Jerusalem with him were there also.

The Burial of Jesus
(Matt. 27.57-61; Luke 23.50-56; John 19.38-42)

[42-43] It was towards evening when Joseph of
Arimathea arrived. He was a respected member of
the Council, who was waiting for the coming of the
Kingdom of God. It was Preparation day (that is,
the day before the Sabbath), so Joseph went boldly
into the presence of Pilate and asked him for the
body of Jesus. [44] Pilate was surprised to hear that
Jesus was already dead. He called the army officer
and asked him if Jesus had been dead a long time.
[45] After hearing the officer's report, Pilate told Joseph
he could have the body. [46] Joseph bought a linen sheet,
took the body down, wrapped it in the sheet, and
placed it in a tomb which had been dug out of solid
rock. Then he rolled a large stone across the entrance
to the tomb. [47] Mary Magdalene and Mary the mother
of Joseph were watching and saw where the body
of Jesus was placed.

The Resurrection
(Matt. 28.1-8; Luke 24.1-12; John 20.1-10)

16 After the Sabbath was over, Mary Magdalene,
Mary the mother of James, and Salome bought
spices to go and anoint the body of Jesus. [2] Very
early on Sunday morning, at sunrise, they went to
the tomb. [3-4] On the way they said to one another,
"Who will roll away the stone for us from the entrance
to the tomb?" (It was a very large stone.) Then they
looked up and saw that the stone had already been
rolled back. [5] So they entered the tomb, where they
saw a young man sitting on the right, wearing a
white robe—and they were alarmed.

[6] "Don't be alarmed," he said. "I know you are
looking for Jesus of Nazareth, who was crucified.
He is not here—he has been raised! Look, here is
the place where they put him. [7] Now go and give
this message to his disciples, including Peter: 'He is

going to Galilee ahead of you; there you will see him, just as he told you.' "

8 So they went out and ran from the tomb, distressed

So they went out and ran (16.8)

and terrified. They said nothing to anyone, because they were afraid.

AN OLD ENDING TO THE GOSPEL[z]
Jesus Appears to Mary Magdalene
(Matt. 28.9–10; John 20.11–18)

[[9] After Jesus rose from death early on Sunday, he appeared first to Mary Magdalene, from whom he had driven out seven demons. [10] She went and told his companions. They were mourning and crying; [11] and when they heard her say that Jesus was alive and that she had seen him, they did not believe her.

Jesus Appears to Two Disciples
(Luke 24.13–35)

12 After this, Jesus appeared in a different manner to two of them while they were on their way to the country. [13] They returned and told the others, but they would not believe it.

[z] *Some manuscripts and ancient translations do not have this ending to the Gospel (verses 9–20).*

Jesus Appears to the Eleven
(Matt. 28.16–20; Luke 24.36–49; John 20.19–23; Acts 1.6–8)

14 Last of all, Jesus appeared to the eleven disciples as they were eating. He scolded them, because they did not have faith and because they were too stubborn to believe those who had seen him alive. 15 He said to them, "Go throughout the whole world and preach the gospel to all mankind. 16 Whoever believes and is baptized will be saved; whoever does not believe will be condemned. 17 Believers will be given the power to perform miracles: they will drive out demons in my name; they will speak in strange tongues; 18 if they pick up snakes or drink any poison, they will not be harmed; they will place their hands on sick people, who will get well."

Jesus Is Taken up to Heaven
(Luke 24.50–53; Acts 1.9–11)

19 After the Lord Jesus had talked with them, he was taken up to heaven and sat at the right side of God. 20 The disciples went and preached everywhere, and the Lord worked with them and proved that their preaching was true by the miracles that were performed.]

ANOTHER OLD ENDING[a]

[9 The women went to Peter and his friends and gave them a brief account of all they had been told. 10 After this, Jesus himself sent out through his disciples from the east to the west the sacred and ever-living message of eternal salvation.]

[a] Some manuscripts and ancient translations have this shorter ending to the Gospel in addition to the longer ending (verses 9–20).

THE GOSPEL ACCORDING TO

LUKE

INTRODUCTION

The Gospel according to Luke presents Jesus as both the promised Saviour of Israel and as the Saviour of all mankind. *Luke* records that Jesus was called by the Spirit of the Lord to "preach the Good News to the poor," and this Gospel is filled with a concern for people with all kinds of need. The note of joy is also prominent in *Luke,* especially in the opening chapters that announce the coming of Jesus, and again at the conclusion, when Jesus ascends to heaven. The story of the growth and spread of the Christian faith after the ascension of Jesus is told by the same writer in the book of *Acts.*

Parts 2 and 6 (see the outline below) contain much material that is found only in this Gospel, such as the stories about the song of the angels and the shepherds' visit at the birth of Jesus, Jesus in the Temple as a boy, and the parables of the Good Samaritan and the Lost Son. Throughout the Gospel great emphasis is placed on prayer, the Holy Spirit, the role of women in the ministry of Jesus, and God's forgiveness of sins.

1 Dear Theophilus:
Many people have done their best to write a report
of the things that have taken place among us. [2]They
wrote what we have been told by those who saw
these things from the beginning and who proclaimed
the message. [3]And so, your Excellency, because I have
carefully studied all these matters from their beginning,
I thought it would be good to write an orderly account
for you. [4]I do this so that you will know the full truth
about everything which you have been taught.

The Birth of John the Baptist Is Announced

5 During the time when Herod was king of Judaea,[a]
there was a priest named Zechariah, who belonged
to the priestly order of Abijah. His wife's name was
Elizabeth; she also belonged to a priestly family. [6]They
both lived good lives in God's sight and obeyed fully
all the Lord's laws and commands. [7]They had no
children because Elizabeth could not have any, and
she and Zechariah were both very old.

8 One day Zechariah was doing his work as a priest
in the Temple, taking his turn in the daily service.
[9]According to the custom followed by the priests,
he was chosen by lot to burn incense on the altar.
So he went into the Temple of the Lord, [10]while
the crowd of people outside prayed during the hour
when the incense was burnt.

11 An angel of the Lord appeared to him, standing
on the right of the altar where the incense was burnt.
[12]When Zechariah saw him, he was alarmed and felt
afraid. [13]But the angel said to him, "Don't be afraid,
Zechariah! God has heard your prayer, and your wife
Elizabeth will bear you a son. You are to name him
John. [14]How glad and happy you will be, and how
happy many others will be when he is born! [15]He will
be a great man in the Lord's sight. He must not
drink any wine or strong drink. From his very birth

---

[a]JUDAEA: *The term here refers to the whole land of Palestine.*

he will be filled with the Holy Spirit, [16]and he will bring back many of the people of Israel to the Lord their God. [17]He will go ahead of the Lord, strong and mighty like the prophet Elijah. He will bring fathers and children together again; he will turn disobedient people back to the way of thinking of the righteous; he will get the Lord's people ready for him."

18 Zechariah said to the angel, "How shall I know if this is so? I am an old man, and my wife is old also."

19 "I am Gabriel," the angel answered. "I stand in the presence of God, who sent me to speak to you and tell you this good news. [20]But you have not believed my message, which will come true at the right time. Because you have not believed, you will be unable to speak; you will remain silent until the day my promise to you comes true."

21 In the meantime the people were waiting for Zechariah and wondering why he was spending such a long time in the Temple. [22]When he came out, he could not speak to them, and so they knew that he had seen a vision in the Temple. Unable to say a word, he made signs to them with his hands.

23 When his period of service in the Temple was over, Zechariah went back home. [24]Some time later his wife Elizabeth became pregnant and did not leave the house for five months. [25]"Now at last the Lord has helped me," she said. "He has taken away my public disgrace!"

The Birth of Jesus Is Announced

26 In the sixth month of Elizabeth's pregnancy God sent the angel Gabriel to a town in Galilee named Nazareth. [27]He had a message for a girl promised in marriage to a man named Joseph, who was a descendant of King David. The girl's name was Mary. [28]The angel came to her and said, "Peace be with you! The Lord is with you and has greatly blessed you!"

29 Mary was deeply troubled by the angel's message, and she wondered what his words meant. [30]The angel said to her, "Don't be afraid, Mary; God has been gracious to you. [31]You will become pregnant and give

birth to a son, and you will name him Jesus. [32] He will be great and will be called the Son of the Most High God. The Lord God will make him a king, as his ancestor David was, [33] and he will be the king of the descendants of Jacob for ever; his kingdom will never end!"

34 Mary said to the angel, "I am a virgin. How, then, can this be?"

35 The angel answered, "The Holy Spirit will come on you, and God's power will rest upon you. For this reason the holy child will be called the Son of God. [36] Remember your relative Elizabeth. It is said that she cannot have children, but she herself is now six months pregnant, even though she is very old. [37] For there is nothing that God cannot do."

38 "I am the Lord's servant," said Mary; "may it happen to me as you have said." And the angel left her.

Mary Visits Elizabeth

39 Soon afterwards Mary got ready and hurried off to a town in the hill-country of Judaea. [40] She went into Zechariah's house and greeted Elizabeth. [41] When Elizabeth heard Mary's greeting, the baby moved within her. Elizabeth was filled with the Holy Spirit [42] and said in a loud voice, "You are the most blessed of all women, and blessed is the child you will bear! [43] Why should this great thing happen to me, that my Lord's mother comes to visit me? [44] For as soon as I heard your greeting, the baby within me jumped with gladness. [45] How happy you are to believe that the Lord's message to you will come true!"

Mary's Song of Praise

46 Mary said,
"My heart praises the Lord;
[47]   my soul is glad because of God my Saviour,
[48]   for he has remembered me, his lowly servant!
From now on all people will call me happy,
[49]   because of the great things the Mighty God has
      done for me.
His name is holy;
[50]   from one generation to another

he shows mercy to those who honour him.
51 He has stretched out his mighty arm
     and scattered the proud with all their plans.
52 He has brought down mighty kings from their
         thrones,
     and lifted up the lowly.
53 He has filled the hungry with good things,
     and sent the rich away with empty hands.
54 He has kept the promise he made to our ancestors,
     and has come to the help of his servant Israel.
55 He has remembered to show mercy to Abraham
     and to all his descendants for ever!''

56 Mary stayed about three months with Elizabeth
and then went back home.

The Birth of John the Baptist

57 The time came for Elizabeth to have her baby,
and she gave birth to a son. 58 Her neighbours and
relatives heard how wonderfully good the Lord had
been to her, and they all rejoiced with her.

59 When the baby was a week old, they came to
circumcise him, and they were going to name him
Zechariah, after his father. 60 But his mother said, "No!
His name is to be John."

61 They said to her, "But you have no relatives
with that name!" 62 Then they made signs to his father,
asking him what name he would like the boy to
have.

63 Zechariah asked for a writing tablet and wrote,
"His name is John." How surprised they all were!
64 At that moment Zechariah was able to speak again,
and he started praising God. 65 The neighbours were all
filled with fear, and the news about these things spread
through all the hill-country of Judaea. 66 Everyone who
heard of it thought about it and asked, "What is
this child going to be?" For it was plain that the
Lord's power was upon him.

Zechariah's Prophecy

67 John's father Zechariah was filled with the Holy
Spirit, and he spoke God's message:
68 "Let us praise the Lord, the God of Israel!

He has come to the help of his people and has
   set them free.
69 He has provided for us a mighty Saviour,
   a descendant of his servant David.
70 He promised through his holy prophets long ago
71   that he would save us from our enemies,
   from the power of all those who hate us.
72 He said he would show mercy to our ancestors
   and remember his sacred covenant.
73-74 With a solemn oath to our ancestor Abraham
   he promised to rescue us from our enemies
   and allow us to serve him without fear,
75 so that we might be holy and righteous before
      him
   all the days of our life.

76 "You, my child, will be called a prophet of the
      Most High God.
   You will go ahead of the Lord
   to prepare his road for him,
77 to tell his people that they will be saved
   by having their sins forgiven.
78 Our God is merciful and tender.
   He will cause the bright dawn of salvation to rise
      on us
79   and to shine from heaven on all those who live
   in the dark shadow of death,
   to guide our steps into the path of peace."

80 The child grew and developed in body and spirit.
He lived in the desert until the day when he appeared
publicly to the people of Israel.

The Birth of Jesus
(Matt. 1.18-25)

2 At that time the Emperor Augustus ordered a
   census to be taken throughout the Roman Empire.
2 When this first census took place, Quirinius was the
governor of Syria. 3 Everyone, then, went to register
himself, each to his own town.

4 Joseph went from the town of Nazareth in Galilee
to the town of Bethlehem in Judaea, the birthplace
of King David. Joseph went there because he was
a descendant of David. 5 He went to register with

Mary, who was promised in marriage to him. She was pregnant, 6 and while they were in Bethlehem, the time came for her to have her baby. 7 She gave birth to her first son, wrapped him in strips of cloth and laid him in a manger—there was no room for them to stay in the inn.

The Shepherds and the Angels

8 There were some shepherds in that part of the country who were spending the night in the fields, taking care of their flocks. 9 An angel of the Lord appeared to them, and the glory of the Lord shone over them. They were terribly afraid, 10 but the angel said to them, "Don't be afraid! I am here with good news for you, which will bring great joy to all the people. 11 This very day in David's town your Saviour was born—Christ the Lord! 12 And this is what will prove it to you: you will find a baby wrapped in strips of cloth and lying in a manger."

13 Suddenly a great army of heaven's angels appeared with the angel, singing praises to God:
14 "Glory to God in the highest heaven,
　　and peace on earth to those with whom he is
　　　　pleased!"

15 When the angels went away from them back into heaven, the shepherds said to one another, "Let's go to Bethlehem and see this thing that has happened, which the Lord has told us."

16 So they hurried off and found Mary and Joseph and saw the baby lying in the manger. 17 When the shepherds saw him, they told them what the angel had said about the child. 18 All who heard it were amazed at what the shepherds said. 19 Mary remembered all these things and thought deeply about them. 20 The shepherds went back, singing praises to God for all they had heard and seen; it had been just as the angel had told them.

Jesus Is Named

21 A week later, when the time came for the baby to be circumcised, he was named Jesus, the name which the angel had given him before he had been conceived.

Mary remembered all these things (2.19)

Jesus Is Presented in the Temple

22 The time came for Joseph and Mary to perform the ceremony of purification, as the Law of Moses commanded. So they took the child to Jerusalem to present him to the Lord, 23 as it is written in the law of the Lord: "Every first-born male is to be dedicated to the Lord." 24 They also went to offer a sacrifice of a pair of doves or two young pigeons, as required by the law of the Lord.

25 At that time there was a man named Simeon living in Jerusalem. He was a good, God-fearing man and was waiting for Israel to be saved. The Holy Spirit was with him 26 and had assured him that he would not die before he had seen the Lord's promised Messiah. 27 Led by the Spirit, Simeon went into the Temple. When the parents brought the child Jesus into the Temple to do for him what the Law required, 28 Simeon took the child in his arms and gave thanks to God:

29 "Now, Lord, you have kept your promise,
    and you may let your servant go in peace.
30 With my own eyes I have seen your salvation,
31   which you have prepared in the presence of all
        peoples:

³² A light to reveal your will to the Gentiles
and bring glory to your people Israel."

33 The child's father and mother were amazed at the things Simeon said about him. ³⁴ Simeon blessed them and said to Mary, his mother, "This child is chosen by God for the destruction and the salvation of many in Israel. He will be a sign from God which many people will speak against ³⁵ and so reveal their secret thoughts. And sorrow, like a sharp sword, will break your own heart."

36–37 There was a very old prophetess, a widow named Anna, daughter of Phanuel of the tribe of Asher. She had been married for only seven years and was now eighty-four years old.*b* She never left the Temple; day and night she worshipped God, fasting and praying. ³⁸ That very same hour she arrived and gave thanks to God and spoke about the child to all who were waiting for God to set Jerusalem free.

The Return to Nazareth

39 When Joseph and Mary had finished doing all that was required by the law of the Lord, they returned to their home town of Nazareth in Galilee. ⁴⁰ The child grew and became strong; he was full of wisdom, and God's blessings were upon him.

The Boy Jesus in the Temple

41 Every year the parents of Jesus went to Jerusalem for the Passover Festival. ⁴² When Jesus was twelve years old, they went to the festival as usual. ⁴³ When the festival was over, they started back home, but the boy Jesus stayed in Jerusalem. His parents did not know this; ⁴⁴ they thought that he was with the group, so they travelled a whole day and then started looking for him among their relatives and friends. ⁴⁵ They did not find him, so they went back to Jerusalem looking for him. ⁴⁶ On the third day they found him in the Temple, sitting with the Jewish teachers, listening to them and asking questions. ⁴⁷ All who heard him were amazed at his intelligent answers. ⁴⁸ His parents were

*b*was now eighty-four years old; *or* had been a widow eighty-four years.

Sitting with the Jewish teachers (2.46)

astonished when they saw him, and his mother said to him, "My son, why have you done this to us? Your father and I have been terribly worried trying to find you."

49 He answered them, "Why did you have to look for me? Didn't you know that I had to be in my Father's house?" 50 But they did not understand his answer.

51 So Jesus went back with them to Nazareth, where he was obedient to them. His mother treasured all these things in her heart. 52 Jesus grew both in body and in wisdom, gaining favour with God and men.

The Preaching of John the Baptist
(Matt. 3.1-12; Mark 1.1-8; John 1.19-28)

3 It was the fifteenth year of the rule of the Emperor Tiberius; Pontius Pilate was governor of Judaea, Herod was ruler of Galilee, and his brother Philip was ruler of the territory of Iturea and Trachonitis; Lysanias was ruler of Abilene, 2 and Annas and Caiaphas were high priests. At that time the word of God came to John son of Zechariah in the desert. 3 So John went throughout the whole territory of the River Jordan, preaching, "Turn away from your sins and

be baptized, and God will forgive your sins." ⁴As
it is written in the book of the prophet Isaiah:

"Someone is shouting in the desert:
  'Get the road ready for the Lord;
  make a straight path for him to travel!
⁵ Every valley must be filled up,
  every hill and mountain levelled off.
The winding roads must be made straight,
  and the rough paths made smooth.
⁶ All mankind will see God's salvation!' "

7 Crowds of people came out to John to be baptized
by him. "You snakes!" he said to them. "Who told
you that you could escape from the punishment God
is about to send? ⁸Do those things that will show
that you have turned from your sins. And don't start
saying among yourselves that Abraham is your
ancestor. I tell you that God can take these stones and
make descendants for Abraham! ⁹The axe is ready
to cut down the trees at the roots; every tree that
does not bear good fruit will be cut down and thrown
in the fire."

10 The people asked him, "What are we to do,
then?"

11 He answered, "Whoever has two shirts must give
one to the man who has none, and whoever has
food must share it."

12 Some tax collectors came to be baptized, and
they asked him, "Teacher, what are we to do?"

13 "Don't collect more than is legal," he told them.

14 Some soldiers also asked him, "What about us?
What are we to do?"

He said to them, "Don't take money from anyone
by force or accuse anyone falsely. Be content with
your pay."

15 People's hopes began to rise, and they began
to wonder whether John perhaps might be the Messiah.
¹⁶So John said to all of them, "I baptize you with
water, but someone is coming who is much greater
than I am. I am not good enough even to untie his
sandals. He will baptize you with the Holy Spirit
and fire. ¹⁷He has his winnowing shovel with him,
to thresh out all the grain and gather the wheat

into his barn; but he will burn the chaff in a fire that never goes out."

18 In many different ways John preached the Good News to the people and urged them to change their ways. 19 But John reprimanded Herod, the governor, because he had married Herodias, his brother's wife, and had done many other evil things. 20 Then Herod did an even worse thing by putting John in prison.

The Baptism of Jesus
(Matt. 3.13-17; Mark 1.9-11)

21 After all the people had been baptized, Jesus also was baptized. While he was praying, heaven was opened, 22 and the Holy Spirit came down upon him in bodily form like a dove. And a voice came from heaven, "You are my own dear Son. I am pleased with you."

The Ancestors of Jesus
(Matt. 1.1-17)

23 When Jesus began his work, he was about thirty years old. He was the son, so people thought, of Joseph, who was the son of Heli, 24 the son of Matthat, the son of Levi, the son of Melchi, the son of Jannai, the son of Joseph, 25 the son of Mattathias, the son of Amos, the son of Nahum, the son of Esli, the son of Naggai, 26 the son of Maath, the son of Mattathias, the son of Semein, the son of Josech, the son of Joda, 27 the son of Joanan, the son of Rhesa, the son of Zerubbabel, the son of Shealtiel, the son of Neri, 28 the son of Melchi, the son of Addi, the son of Cosam, the son of Elmadam, the son of Er, 29 the son of Joshua, the son of Eliezer, the son of Jorim, the son of Matthat, the son of Levi, 30 the son of Simeon, the son of Judah, the son of Joseph, the son of Jonam, the son of Eliakim, 31 the son of Melea, the son of Menna, the son of Mattatha, the son of Nathan, the son of David, 32 the son of Jesse, the son of Obed, the son of Boaz, the son of Salmon, the son of Nahshon, 33 the son of Amminadab, the son of Admin, the son of Arni, the son of Hezron, the son of Perez, the son of Judah, 34 the son of Jacob, the son of Isaac, the son of Abraham, the

PALESTINE IN THE TIME OF JESUS

Sidon

Zarephath

ITUREA

ABILENE

Tyre

PHOENICIA

Caesarea Philippi

GALILEE

TRACHONITIS

Chorazin

Capernaum

Bethsaida

LAKE GALILEE

Cana

Tiberias

Mount Carmel △

Nazareth

Nain

Gadara

MEDITERRANEAN SEA

Caesarea

D E C A P O L I S (The Ten Towns)

Salim

Aenon

Samaria

Mount Gerizim △

Sychar

Gerasa

SAMARIA

River Jordan

Arimathea

Ephraim

PEREA

Emmaus

Jericho

Bethphage

Jerusalem

Bethany

JUDAEA

Qumran

Bethlehem

DEAD SEA

IDUMEA

0 10 20 30 40

Kilometres

son of Terah, the son of Nahor, 35the son of Serug, the son of Reu, the son of Peleg, the son of Eber, the son of Shelah, 36the son of Cainan, the son of Arphaxad, the son of Shem, the son of Noah, the son of Lamech, 37the son of Methuselah, the son of Enoch, the son of Jared, the son of Mahalaleel, the son of Kenan, 38the son of Enosh, the son of Seth, the son of Adam, the son of God.

The Temptation of Jesus
(Matt. 4.1–11; Mark 1.12–13)

4 Jesus returned from the Jordan full of the Holy Spirit and was led by the Spirit into the desert, 2where he was tempted by the Devil for forty days. In all that time he ate nothing, so that he was hungry when it was over.

3 The Devil said to him, "If you are God's Son, order this stone to turn into bread."

4 But Jesus answered, "The scripture says, 'Man cannot live on bread alone.' "

5 Then the Devil took him up and showed him in a second all the kingdoms of the world. 6"I will give you all this power and all this wealth," the Devil told him. "It has all been handed over to me, and I can give it to anyone I choose. 7All this will be yours, then, if you worship me."

8 Jesus answered, "The scripture says, 'Worship the Lord your God and serve only him!' "

9 Then the Devil took him to Jerusalem and set him on the highest point of the Temple, and said to him, "If you are God's Son, throw yourself down from here. 10For the scripture says, 'God will order his angels to take good care of you.' 11It also says, 'They will hold you up with their hands so that not even your feet will be hurt on the stones.' "

12 But Jesus answered, "The scripture says, 'Do not put the Lord your God to the test.' "

13 When the Devil finished tempting Jesus in every way, he left him for a while.

Jesus Begins His Work in Galilee
(Matt. 4.12–17; Mark 1.14–15)

14 Then Jesus returned to Galilee, and the power

of the Holy Spirit was with him. The news about him spread throughout all that territory. ¹⁵He taught in the synagogues and was praised by everyone.

Jesus Is Rejected at Nazareth
(Matt. 13.53–58; Mark 6.1–6)

16 Then Jesus went to Nazareth, where he had been brought up, and on the Sabbath he went as usual to the synagogue. He stood up to read the Scriptures ¹⁷and was handed the book of the prophet Isaiah. He unrolled the scroll and found the place where it is written,

¹⁸ "The Spirit of the Lord is upon me,
    because he has chosen me to bring good news
      to the poor.
He has sent me to proclaim liberty to the captives
    and recovery of sight to the blind;
to set free the oppressed
¹⁹   and announce that the time has come
    when the Lord will save his people."

20 Jesus rolled up the scroll, gave it back to the attendant, and sat down. All the people in the synagogue had their eyes fixed on him, ²¹as he said to them, "This passage of scripture has come true today, as you heard it being read."

22 They were all well impressed with him and marvelled at the eloquent words that he spoke. They said, "Isn't he the son of Joseph?"

23 He said to them, "I am sure that you will quote this proverb to me, 'Doctor, heal yourself.' You will also tell me to do here in my home town the same things you heard were done in Capernaum. ²⁴I tell you this," Jesus added, "a prophet is never welcomed in his home town.

25 "Listen to me: it is true that there were many widows in Israel during the time of Elijah, when there was no rain for three and a half years and a severe famine spread throughout the whole land. ²⁶Yet Elijah was not sent to anyone in Israel, but only to a widow living in Zarephath in the territory of Sidon. ²⁷And there were many people suffering from a dreaded skin-disease who lived in Israel during the time of the

prophet Elisha; yet not one of them was healed, but only Naaman the Syrian."

28 When the people in the synagogue heard this, they were filled with anger. 29 They rose up, dragged Jesus out of the town, and took him to the top of the hill on which their town was built. They meant to throw him over the cliff, 30 but he walked through the middle of the crowd and went his way.

A Man with an Evil Spirit
(Mark 1.21-28)

31 Then Jesus went to Capernaum, a town in Galilee, where he taught the people on the Sabbath. 32 They were all amazed at the way he taught, because he spoke with authority. 33 In the synagogue was a man who had the spirit of an evil demon in him; he screamed out in a loud voice, 34 "Ah! What do you want with us, Jesus of Nazareth? Are you here to destroy us? I know who you are: you are God's holy messenger!"

35 Jesus ordered the spirit, "Be quiet and come out of the man!" The demon threw the man down in front of them and went out of him without doing him any harm.

36 The people were all amazed and said to one another, "What kind of words are these? With authority and power this man gives orders to the evil spirits, and they come out!" 37 And the report about Jesus spread everywhere in that region.

Jesus Heals Many People
(Matt. 8.14-17; Mark 1.29-34)

38 Jesus left the synagogue and went to Simon's house. Simon's mother-in-law was sick with a high fever, and they spoke to Jesus about her. 39 He went and stood at her bedside and ordered the fever to leave her. The fever left her, and she got up at once and began to wait on them.

40 After sunset all who had friends who were sick with various diseases brought them to Jesus; he placed his hands on every one of them and healed them all. 41 Demons also went out from many people, screaming, "You are the Son of God!"

Jesus gave the demons an order and would not let them speak, because they knew that he was the Messiah.

Jesus Preaches in the Synagogues
(Mark 1.35-39)

42 At daybreak Jesus left the town and went off to a lonely place. The people started looking for him, and when they found him, they tried to keep him from leaving. 43 But he said to them, "I must preach the Good News about the Kingdom of God in other towns also, because that is what God sent me to do."

44 So he preached in the synagogues throughout the country.

Jesus Calls the First Disciples
(Matt. 4.18-22; Mark 1.16-20)

5 One day Jesus was standing on the shore of Lake Gennesaret while the people pushed their way up to him to listen to the word of God. 2 He saw two boats pulled up on the beach; the fishermen had left them and were washing the nets. 3 Jesus got into one of the boats—it belonged to Simon—and asked him to push off a little from the shore. Jesus sat in the boat and taught the crowd.

4 When he finished speaking, he said to Simon, "Push the boat out further to the deep water, and you and your partners let down your nets for a catch."

5 "Master," Simon answered, "we worked hard all night long and caught nothing. But if you say so, I will let down the nets." 6 They let them down and caught such a large number of fish that the nets were about to break. 7 So they motioned to their partners in the other boat to come and help them. They came and filled both boats so full of fish that the boats were about to sink. 8 When Simon Peter saw what had happened, he fell on his knees before Jesus and said, "Go away from me, Lord! I am a sinful man!"

9 He and the others with him were all amazed at the large number of fish they had caught. 10 The same was true of Simon's partners, James and John, the

The nets were about to break (5.6)

sons of Zebedee. Jesus said to Simon, "Don't be afraid; from now on you will be catching men."

11 They pulled the boats up on the beach, left everything, and followed Jesus.

Jesus Heals a Man
(Matt. 8.1–4; Mark 1.40–45)

12 Once Jesus was in a town where there was a man who was suffering from a dreaded skin-disease. When he saw Jesus, he threw himself down and begged him, "Sir, if you want to, you can make me clean!" *c*

13 Jesus stretched out his hand and touched him. "I do want to," he answered. "Be clean!" At once the disease left the man. 14 Jesus ordered him, "Don't tell anyone, but go straight to the priest and let him examine you; then to prove to everyone that you are cured, offer the sacrifice as Moses ordered."

15 But the news about Jesus spread all the more widely, and crowds of people came to hear him and be healed from their diseases. 16 But he would go away to lonely places, where he prayed.

c MAKE ME CLEAN: *This disease was considered to make a person ritually unclean.*

Jesus Heals a Paralysed Man
(Matt. 9.1–8; Mark 2.1–12)

17 One day when Jesus was teaching, some Pharisees and teachers of the Law were sitting there who had come from every town in Galilee and Judaea and from Jerusalem. The power of the Lord was present for Jesus to heal the sick. 18 Some men came carrying a paralysed man on a bed, and they tried to take him into the house and put him in front of Jesus. 19 Because of the crowd, however, they could find no

Let him down on his bed into the middle of the group (5.19)

way to take him in. So they carried him up on the roof, made an opening in the tiles, and let him down on his bed into the middle of the group in front of Jesus. 20 When Jesus saw how much faith they had, he said to the man, "Your sins are forgiven, my friend."

21 The teachers of the Law and the Pharisees began

to say to themselves, "Who is this man who speaks such blasphemy! God is the only one who can forgive sins!"

22 Jesus knew their thoughts and said to them, "Why do you think such things? 23 Is it easier to say, 'Your sins are forgiven you,' or to say, 'Get up and walk'? 24 I will prove to you, then, that the Son of Man has authority on earth to forgive sins." So he said to the paralysed man, "I tell you, get up, pick up your bed, and go home!"

25 At once the man got up in front of them all, took the bed he had been lying on, and went home, praising God. 26 They were all completely amazed! Full of fear, they praised God, saying, "What marvellous things we have seen today!"

Jesus Calls Levi
(Matt. 9.9–13; Mark 2.13–17)

27 After this, Jesus went out and saw a tax collector named Levi, sitting in his office. Jesus said to him, "Follow me." 28 Levi got up, left everything, and followed him.

29 Then Levi had a big feast in his house for Jesus, and among the guests was a large number of tax collectors and other people. 30 Some Pharisees and some teachers of the Law who belonged to their group complained to Jesus' disciples. "Why do you eat and drink with tax collectors and other outcasts?" they asked.

31 Jesus answered them, "People who are well do not need a doctor, but only those who are sick. 32 I have not come to call respectable people to repent, but outcasts."

The Question about Fasting
(Matt. 9.14–17; Mark 2.18–22)

33 Some people said to Jesus, "The disciples of John fast frequently and offer prayers, and the disciples of the Pharisees do the same; but your disciples eat and drink."

34 Jesus answered, "Do you think you can make the guests at a wedding party go without food as long as the bridegroom is with them? Of course not!

35 But the day will come when the bridegroom will be taken away from them, and then they will fast."

36 Jesus also told them this parable: "No one tears a piece off a new coat to patch up an old coat. If he does, he will have torn the new coat, and the piece of new cloth will not match the old. 37 Nor does anyone pour new wine into used wineskins, because the new wine will burst the skins, the wine will pour out, and the skins will be ruined. 38 Instead, new wine must be poured into fresh wineskins! 39 And no one wants new wine after drinking old wine. 'The old is better,' he says."

The Question about the Sabbath
(Matt. 12.1-8; Mark 2.23-28)

6 Jesus was walking through some cornfields on the Sabbath. His disciples began to pick the ears of corn, rub them in their hands, and eat the grain. 2 Some Pharisees asked, "Why are you doing what our Law says you cannot do on the Sabbath?"

3 Jesus answered them, "Haven't you read what David did when he and his men were hungry? 4 He went into the house of God, took the bread offered to God, ate it, and gave it also to his men. Yet it is against our Law for anyone except the priests to eat that bread."

5 And Jesus concluded, "The Son of Man is Lord of the Sabbath."

The Man with a Paralysed Hand
(Matt. 12.9-14; Mark 3.1-6)

6 On another Sabbath Jesus went into a synagogue and taught. A man was there whose right hand was paralysed. 7 Some teachers of the Law and some Pharisees wanted a reason to accuse Jesus of doing wrong, so they watched him closely to see if he would heal on the Sabbath. 8 But Jesus knew their thoughts and said to the man, "Stand up and come here to the front." The man got up and stood there. 9 Then Jesus said to them, "I ask you: What does our Law allow us to do on the Sabbath? To help or to harm? To save a man's life or destroy it?" 10 He looked around

at them all; then he said[d] to the man, "Stretch out your hand." He did so, and his hand became well again.

11 They were filled with rage and began to discuss among themselves what they could do to Jesus.

Jesus Chooses the Twelve Apostles
(Matt. 10.1-4; Mark 3.13-19)

12 At that time Jesus went up a hill to pray and spent the whole night there praying to God. 13 When day came, he called his disciples to him and chose twelve of them, whom he named apostles: 14 Simon (whom he named Peter) and his brother Andrew; James and John, Philip and Bartholomew, 15 Matthew and Thomas, James son of Alphaeus, and Simon (who was called the Patriot), 16 Judas son of James, and Judas Iscariot, who became the traitor.

Jesus Teaches and Heals
(Matt. 4.23-25)

17 When Jesus had come down from the hill with the apostles, he stood on a level place with a large number of his disciples. A large crowd of people was there from all over Judaea and from Jerusalem and from the coastal cities of Tyre and Sidon; 18 they had come to hear him and to be healed of their diseases. Those who were troubled by evil spirits also came and were healed. 19 All the people tried to touch him, for power was going out from him and healing them all.

Happiness and Sorrow
(Matt. 5.1-12)

20 Jesus looked at his disciples and said,
"Happy are you poor;
  the Kingdom of God is yours! .
21 "Happy are you who are hungry now;
  you will be filled!
"Happy are you who weep now;
  you will laugh!
22 "Happy are you when people hate you, reject .

---

[d]said; *some manuscripts have* said angrily.

you, insult you, and say that you are evil, all because of the Son of Man! 23 Be glad when that happens, and dance for joy, because a great reward is kept for you in heaven. For their ancestors did the very same things to the prophets.

24 "But how terrible for you who are rich now;
   you have had your easy life!

25 "How terrible for you who are full now;
   you will go hungry!

"How terrible for you who laugh now;
   you will mourn and weep!

26 "How terrible when all people speak well of you; their ancestors said the very same things about the false prophets.

Love for Enemies
(Matt. 5.38–48; 7.12a)

27 "But I tell you who hear me: Love your enemies, do good to those who hate you, 28 bless those who curse you, and pray for those who ill-treat you. 29 If anyone hits you on one cheek, let him hit the other one too; if someone takes your coat, let him have your shirt as well. 30 Give to everyone who asks you for something, and when someone takes what is yours, do not ask for it back. 31 Do for others just what you want them to do for you.

32 "If you love only the people who love you, why should you receive a blessing? Even sinners love those who love them! 33 And if you do good only to those who do good to you, why should you receive a blessing? Even sinners do that! 34 And if you lend only to those from whom you hope to get it back, why should you receive a blessing? Even sinners lend to sinners, to get back the same amount! 35 No! Love your enemies and do good to them; lend and expect nothing back. You will then have a great reward, and you will be sons of the Most High God. For he is good to the ungrateful and the wicked. 36 Be merciful just as your Father is merciful.

Judging Others
(Matt. 7.1–5)

37 "Do not judge others, and God will not judge

you; do not condemn others, and God will not condemn you; forgive others, and God will forgive you. [38]Give to others, and God will give to you. Indeed, you will receive a full measure, a generous helping, poured into your hands—all that you can hold. The measure you use for others is the one that God will use for you."

39 And Jesus told them this parable: "One blind man cannot lead another one; if he does, both will fall into a ditch. [40]No pupil is greater than his teacher; but every pupil, when he has completed his training, will be like his teacher.

41 "Why do you look at the speck in your brother's eye, but pay no attention to the log in your own eye? [42]How can you say to your brother, 'Please, brother, let me take that speck out of your eye,' yet cannot even see the log in your own eye? You hypocrite! First take the log out of your own eye, and then you will be able to see clearly to take the speck out of your brother's eye.

A Tree and Its Fruit
(Matt. 7.16–20; 12.33–35)

43 "A healthy tree does not bear bad fruit, nor does a poor tree bear good fruit. [44]Every tree is known by the fruit it bears; you do not pick figs from thorn bushes or gather grapes from bramble bushes. [45]A good person brings good out of the treasure of good things in his heart; a bad person brings bad out of his treasure of bad things. For the mouth speaks what the heart is full of.

The Two House Builders
(Matt. 7.24–27)

46 "Why do you call me, 'Lord, Lord,' and yet don't do what I tell you? [47]Anyone who comes to me and listens to my words and obeys them—I will show you what he is like. [48]He is like a man who, in building his house, dug deep and laid the foundation on rock. The river overflowed and hit that house but could not shake it, because it was well built. [49]But anyone who hears my words and does not obey them is like a man who built his house without laying

a foundation; when the flood hit that house it fell at once—and what a terrible crash that was!"

Jesus Heals a Roman Officer's Servant
(Matt. 8.5–13)

7 When Jesus had finished saying all these things to the people, he went to Capernaum. ²A Roman officer there had a servant who was very dear to him; the man was sick and about to die. ³When the officer heard about Jesus, he sent some Jewish elders to ask him to come and heal his servant. ⁴They came to Jesus and begged him earnestly, "This man really deserves your help. ⁵He loves our people and he himself built a synagogue for us."

6 So Jesus went with them. He was not far from the house when the officer sent friends to tell him, "Sir, don't trouble yourself. I do not deserve to have you come into my house, ⁷neither do I consider myself worthy to come to you in person. Just give the order, and my servant will get well. ⁸I, too, am a man placed under the authority of superior officers, and I have soldiers under me. I order this one, 'Go!' and he goes; I order that one, 'Come!' and he comes; and I order my slave, 'Do this!' and he does it."

9 Jesus was surprised when he heard this; he turned round and said to the crowd following him, "I tell you, I have never found faith like this, not even in Israel!"

10 The messengers went back to the officer's house and found his servant well.

Jesus Raises a Widow's Son

11 Soon afterwards[e] Jesus went to a town called Nain, accompanied by his disciples and a large crowd. ¹²Just as he arrived at the gate of the town, a funeral procession was coming out. The dead man was the only son of a woman who was a widow, and a large crowd from the town was with her. ¹³When the Lord saw her, his heart was filled with pity for her, and he said to her, "Don't cry." ¹⁴Then he walked over and touched the coffin, and the men carrying it

[e]Soon afterwards; *some manuscripts have* The next day.

stopped. Jesus said, "Young man! Get up, I tell you!" 15 The dead man sat up and began to talk, and Jesus gave him back to his mother.

16 They all were filled with fear and praised God. "A great prophet has appeared among us!" they said; "God has come to save his people!"

17 This news about Jesus went out through all the country and the surrounding territory.

The Messengers from John the Baptist
(Matt. 11.2–19)

18 When John's disciples told him about all these things, he called two of them 19 and sent them to the Lord to ask him, "Are you the one John said was going to come, or should we expect someone else?"

20 When they came to Jesus, they said, "John the Baptist sent us to ask if you are the one he said was going to come, or if we should expect someone else."

21 At that very time Jesus cured many people of their sicknesses, diseases, and evil spirits, and gave sight to many blind people. 22 He answered John's messengers, "Go back and tell John what you have seen and heard: the blind can see, the lame can walk, those who suffer from dreaded skin-diseases are made clean,f the deaf can hear, the dead are raised to life, and the Good News is preached to the poor. 23 How happy are those who have no doubts about me!"

24 After John's messengers had left, Jesus began to speak about him to the crowds: "When you went out to John in the desert, what did you expect to see? A blade of grass bending in the wind? 25 What did you go out to see? A man dressed up in fancy clothes? People who dress like that and live in luxury are found in palaces! 26 Tell me, what did you go out to see? A prophet? Yes indeed, but you saw much more than a prophet. 27 For John is the one of whom the scripture says: 'God said, I will send my messenger ahead of you to open the way for

---

f MADE CLEAN: *See 5.12.*

you.' ²⁸I tell you," Jesus added, "John is greater than any man who has ever lived. But he who is least in the Kingdom of God is greater than John."

29 All the people heard him; they and especially the tax collectors were the ones who had obeyed God's righteous demands and had been baptized by John. ³⁰But the Pharisees and the teachers of the Law rejected God's purpose for themselves and refused to be baptized by John.

31 Jesus continued, "Now to what can I compare the people of this day? What are they like? ³²They are like children sitting in the market-place. One group shouts to the other, 'We played wedding music for you, but you wouldn't dance! We sang funeral songs, but you wouldn't cry!' ³³John the Baptist came, and he fasted and drank no wine, and you said, 'He has a demon in him!' ³⁴The Son of Man came, and he ate and drank, and you said, 'Look at this man! He is a glutton and a drinker, a friend of tax collectors and other outcasts!' ³⁵God's wisdom, however, is shown to be true by all who accept it."

Jesus at the Home of Simon the Pharisee

36 A Pharisee invited Jesus to have dinner with him, and Jesus went to his house and sat down to eat. ³⁷In that town was a woman who lived a sinful life. She heard that Jesus was eating in the Pharisee's house, so she brought an alabaster jar full of perfume ³⁸and stood behind Jesus, by his feet, crying and wetting his feet with her tears. Then she dried his feet with her hair, kissed them, and poured the perfume on them. ³⁹When the Pharisee saw this, he said to himself, "If this man really were a prophet, he would know who this woman is who is touching him; he would know what kind of sinful life she lives!"

40 Jesus spoke up and said to him, "Simon, I have something to tell you."

"Yes, Teacher," he said, "tell me."

41 "There were two men who owed money to a money-lender," Jesus began. "One owed him five hundred silver coins, and the other owed him fifty. ⁴²Neither of them could pay him back, so he cancelled the debts of both. Which one, then, will love him more?"

43 "I suppose," answered Simon, "that it would be the one who was forgiven more."

"You are right," said Jesus. 44 Then he turned to the woman and said to Simon, "Do you see this woman? I came into your home, and you gave me no water for my feet, but she has washed my feet with her tears and dried them with her hair. 45 You did not welcome me with a kiss, but she has not stopped kissing my feet since I came. 46 You provided no olive-oil for my head, but she has covered my feet with perfume. 47 I tell you, then, the great love she has shown proves that her many sins have been forgiven. But whoever has been forgiven little shows only a little love."

48 Then Jesus said to the woman, "Your sins are forgiven."

49 The others sitting at the table began to say to themselves, "Who is this, who even forgives sins?"

50 But Jesus said to the woman, "Your faith has saved you; go in peace."

Women Who Accompanied Jesus

8 Some time later Jesus travelled through towns and villages, preaching the Good News about the Kingdom of God. The twelve disciples went with him, 2 and so did some women who had been healed of evil spirits and diseases: Mary (who was called Magdalene), from whom seven demons had been driven out; 3 Joanna, whose husband Chuza was an officer in Herod's court; and Susanna, and many other women who used their own resources to help Jesus and his disciples.

The Parable of the Sower
(Matt. 13.1-9; Mark 4.1-9)

4 People kept coming to Jesus from one town after another; and when a great crowd gathered, Jesus told this parable:

5 "Once there was a man who went out to sow corn. As he scattered the seed in the field, some of it fell along the path, where it was stepped on, and the birds ate it up. 6 Some of it fell on rocky ground, and when the plants sprouted, they dried up

because the soil had no moisture. ⁷Some of the seed fell among thorn bushes, which grew up with the plants and choked them. ⁸And some seeds fell in good soil; the plants grew and produced corn, a hundred grains each."

And Jesus concluded, "Listen, then, if you have ears!"

The Purpose of the Parables
(Matt. 13.10-17; Mark 4.10-12)

9 His disciples asked Jesus what this parable meant, ¹⁰and he answered, "The knowledge of the secrets of the Kingdom of God has been given to you, but to the rest it comes by means of parables, so that they may look but not see, and listen but not understand.

Jesus Explains the Parable of the Sower
(Matt. 13.18-23; Mark 4.13-20)

11 "This is what the parable means: the seed is the word of God. ¹²The seeds that fell along the path stand for those who hear; but the Devil comes and takes the message away from their hearts in order to keep them from believing and being saved. ¹³The seeds that fell on rocky ground stand for those who hear the message and receive it gladly. But it does not sink deep into them; they believe only for a while but when the time of testing comes, they fall away. ¹⁴The seeds that fell among thorn bushes stand for those who hear; but the worries and riches and pleasures of this life crowd in and choke them, and their fruit never ripens. ¹⁵The seeds that fell in good soil stand for those who hear the message and retain it in a good and obedient heart, and they persist until they bear fruit.

A Lamp under a Bowl
(Mark 4.21-25)

16 "No one lights a lamp and covers it with a bowl or puts it under a bed. Instead, he puts it on the lampstand, so that people will see the light as they come in.

17 "Whatever is hidden away will be brought out

into the open, and whatever is covered up will be found and brought to light.

18 "Be careful, then, how you listen; because whoever has something will be given more, but whoever has nothing will have taken away from him even the little he thinks he has."

Jesus' Mother and Brothers
(Matt. 12.46–50; Mark 3.31–35)

19 Jesus' mother and brothers came to him, but were unable to join him because of the crowd. 20 Someone said to Jesus, "Your mother and brothers are standing outside and want to see you."

21 Jesus said to them all, "My mother and brothers are those who hear the word of God and obey it."

Jesus Calms a Storm
(Matt. 8.23–27; Mark 4.35–41)

22 One day Jesus got into a boat with his disciples and said to them, "Let us go across to the other side of the lake." So they started out. 23 As they were sailing, Jesus fell asleep. Suddenly a strong wind blew down on the lake, and the boat began to fill with water, so that they were all in great danger. 24 The disciples went to Jesus and woke him up, saying, "Master, Master! We are about to die!"

Jesus got up and gave an order to the wind and the stormy water; they died down, and there was a great calm. 25 Then he said to the disciples, "Where is your faith?"

But they were amazed and afraid, and said to one another, "Who is this man? He gives orders to the winds and waves, and they obey him!"

Jesus Heals a Man with Demons
(Matt. 8.28–34; Mark 5.1–20)

26 Jesus and his disciples sailed on over to the territory of Gerasa,ᵍ which is across the lake from Galilee. 27 As Jesus stepped ashore, he was met by a man from the town who had demons in him. For

ᵍGerasa; *some manuscripts have* Gadara (*see Mt 8.28*); *others have* Gergesa.

a long time this man had gone without clothes and would not stay at home, but spent his time in the burial caves. [28] When he saw Jesus, he gave a loud cry, threw himself down at his feet, and shouted, "Jesus, Son of the Most High God! What do you want with me? I beg you, don't punish me!" [29] He said this because Jesus had ordered the evil spirit to go out of him. Many times it had seized him, and even though he was kept a prisoner, his hands and feet fastened with chains, he would break the chains and be driven by the demon out into the desert.

30 Jesus asked him, "What is your name?"

"My name is 'Mob,' " he answered—because many demons had gone into him. [31] The demons begged Jesus not to send them into the abyss. [h]

32 There was a large herd of pigs near by, feeding on a hillside. So the demons begged Jesus to let them go into the pigs, and he let them. [33] They went out of the man and into the pigs. The whole herd rushed down the side of the cliff into the lake and was drowned.

34 The men who had been taking care of the pigs saw what happened, so they ran off and spread the news in the town and among the farms. [35] People went out to see what had happened, and when they came to Jesus, they found the man from whom the demons had gone out sitting at the feet of Jesus, clothed and in his right mind; and they were all afraid. [36] Those who had seen it told the people how the man had been cured. [37] Then all the people from that territory asked Jesus to go away, because they were terribly afraid. So Jesus got into the boat and left. [38] The man from whom the demons had gone out begged Jesus, "Let me go with you."

But Jesus sent him away, saying, [39] "Go back home and tell what God has done for you."

The man went through the town, telling what Jesus had done for him.

[h]ABYSS: *It was thought that the demons were to be imprisoned in the depths of the earth until their final punishment.*

Jairus' Daughter and the Woman
Who Touched Jesus' Cloak
(Matt. 9.18–26; Mark 5.21–43)

40 When Jesus returned to the other side of the lake, the people welcomed him, because they had all been waiting for him. 41 Then a man named Jairus arrived; he was an official in the local synagogue. He threw himself down at Jesus' feet and begged him to go to his home, 42 because his only daughter, who was twelve years old, was dying.

As Jesus went along, the people were crowding him from every side. 43 Among them was a woman who had suffered from severe bleeding for twelve years; she had spent all she had on doctors,*i* but no one had been able to cure her. 44 She came up in the crowd behind Jesus and touched the edge of his cloak, and her bleeding stopped at once. 45 Jesus asked, "Who touched me?"

Everyone denied it, and Peter said, "Master, the people are all round you and crowding in on you."

46 But Jesus said, "Someone touched me, for I knew it when power went out of me." 47 The woman saw that she had been found out, so she came trembling and threw herself at Jesus' feet. There in front of everybody, she told him why she had touched him and how she had been healed at once. 48 Jesus said to her, "My daughter, your faith has made you well. Go in peace."

49 While Jesus was saying this, a messenger came from the official's house. "Your daughter has died," he told Jairus; "don't bother the Teacher any longer."

50 But Jesus heard it and said to Jairus, "Don't be afraid; only believe, and she will be well."

51 When he arrived at the house, he would not let anyone go in with him except Peter, John, and James, and the child's father and mother. 52 Everyone there was crying and mourning for the child. Jesus said, "Don't cry; the child is not dead—she is only sleeping!"

---

i Some manuscripts do not have she had spent all she had on doctors.

53 They all laughed at him, because they knew that she was dead. [54] But Jesus took her by the hand and called out, "Get up, my child!" [55] Her life returned, and she got up at once, and Jesus ordered them to give her something to eat. [56] Her parents were astounded, but Jesus commanded them not to tell anyone what had happened.

Jesus Sends Out the Twelve Disciples
(Matt. 10.5–15; Mark 6.7–13)

9 Jesus called the twelve disciples together and gave them power and authority to drive out all demons and to cure diseases. [2] Then he sent them out to preach the Kingdom of God and to heal the sick, [3] after saying to them, "Take nothing with you for the journey: no stick, no beggar's bag, no food, no money, not even an extra shirt. [4] Wherever you are welcomed, stay in the same house until you leave that town; [5] wherever people don't welcome you, leave that town and shake the dust off your feet as a warning to them."

6 The disciples left and travelled through all the villages, preaching the Good News and healing people everywhere.

Herod's Confusion
(Matt. 14.1–12; Mark 6.14–29)

7 When Herod, the ruler of Galilee, heard about all the things that were happening, he was very confused, because some people were saying that John the Baptist had come back to life. [8] Others were saying that Elijah had appeared, and still others that one of the prophets of long ago had come back to life. [9] Herod said, "I had John's head cut off; but who is this man I hear these things about?" And he kept trying to see Jesus.

Jesus Feeds Five Thousand Men
(Matt. 14.13–21; Mark 6.30–44; John 6.1–14)

10 The apostles came back and told Jesus everything they had done. He took them with him, and they went off by themselves to a town called Bethsaida. [11] When the crowds heard about it, they followed him.

He welcomed them, spoke to them about the Kingdom of God, and healed those who needed it.

12 When the sun was beginning to set, the twelve disciples came to him and said, "Send the people away so that they can go to the villages and farms round here and find food and lodging, because this is a lonely place."

13 But Jesus said to them, "You yourselves give them something to eat."

They answered, "All we have are five loaves and two fish. Do you want us to go and buy food for this whole crowd?" 14 (There were about five thousand men there.)

Jesus said to his disciples, "Make the people sit down in groups of about fifty each."

15 After the disciples had done so, 16 Jesus took the five loaves and two fish, looked up to heaven, thanked God for them, broke them, and gave them to the disciples to distribute to the people. 17 They all

They all ate and had enough (9.17)

ate and had enough, and the disciples took up twelve baskets of what was left over.

Peter's Declaration about Jesus
(Matt. 16.13–19; Mark 8.27–29)

18 One day when Jesus was praying alone, the disciples came to him. "Who do the crowds say I am?" he asked them.

19 "Some say that you are John the Baptist," they answered. "Others say that you are Elijah, while others say that one of the prophets of long ago has come back to life."

20 "What about you?" he asked them. "Who do you say I am?"

Peter answered, "You are God's Messiah."

Jesus Speaks about His Suffering and Death
(Matt. 16.20–28; Mark 8.30—9.1)

21 Then Jesus gave them strict orders not to tell this to anyone. 22 He also said to them, "The Son of Man must suffer much and be rejected by the elders, the chief priests, and the teachers of the Law. He will be put to death, but three days later he will be raised to life."

23 And he said to them all, "If anyone wants to come with me, he must forget self, take up his cross every day, and follow me. 24 For whoever wants to save his own life will lose it, but whoever loses his life for my sake will save it. 25 Will a person gain anything if he wins the whole world but is himself lost or defeated? Of course not! 26 If a person is ashamed of me and of my teaching, then the Son of Man will be ashamed of him when he comes in his glory and in the glory of the Father and of the holy angels. 27 I assure you that there are some here who will not die until they have seen the Kingdom of God."

The Transfiguration
(Matt. 17.1–8; Mark 9.2–8)

28 About a week after he had said these things, Jesus took Peter, John, and James with him and went up a hill to pray. 29 While he was praying, his face

changed its appearance, and his clothes became dazzling white. [30] Suddenly two men were there talking with him. They were Moses and Elijah, [31] who appeared in heavenly glory and talked with Jesus about the way in which he would soon fulfil God's purpose by dying in Jerusalem. [32] Peter and his companions were sound asleep, but they woke up and saw Jesus' glory and the two men who were standing with him. [33] As the men were leaving Jesus, Peter said to him, "Master, how good it is that we are here! We will make three tents, one for you, one for Moses, and one for Elijah." (He did not really know what he was saying.)

34 While he was still speaking, a cloud appeared and covered them with its shadow; and the disciples were afraid as the cloud came over them. [35] A voice said from the cloud, "This is my Son, whom I have chosen—listen to him!"

36 When the voice stopped, there was Jesus all alone. The disciples kept quiet about all this, and told no one at that time anything they had seen.

Jesus Heals a Boy with an Evil Spirit
(Matt. 17.14–18; Mark 9.14–27)

37 The next day Jesus and the three disciples went down from the hill, and a large crowd met Jesus. [38] A man shouted from the crowd, "Teacher! I beg you, look at my son—my only son! [39] A spirit attacks him with a sudden shout and throws him into a fit, so that he foams at the mouth; it keeps on hurting him and will hardly let him go! [40] I begged your disciples to drive it out, but they couldn't."

41 Jesus answered, "How unbelieving and wrong you people are! How long must I stay with you? How long do I have to put up with you?" Then he said to the man, "Bring your son here."

42 As the boy was coming, the demon knocked him to the ground and threw him into a fit. Jesus gave a command to the evil spirit, healed the boy, and gave him back to his father. [43] All the people were amazed at the mighty power of God.

Jesus Speaks Again about His Death
(Matt. 17.22–23; Mark 9.30–32)

The people were still marvelling at everything Jesus was doing, when he said to his disciples, 44 "Don't forget what I am about to tell you! The Son of Man is going to be handed over to the power of men." 45 But the disciples did not know what this meant. It had been hidden from them so that they could not understand it, and they were afraid to ask him about the matter.

Who Is the Greatest?
(Matt. 18.1–5; Mark 9.33–37)

46 An argument broke out among the disciples as to which one of them was the greatest. 47 Jesus knew what they were thinking, so he took a child, stood him by his side, 48 and said to them, "Whoever welcomes this child in my name, welcomes me; and whoever welcomes me, also welcomes the one who sent me. For he who is least among you all is the greatest."

Whoever Is Not against You Is for You
(Mark 9.38–40)

49 John spoke up, "Master, we saw a man driving out demons in your name, and we told him to stop, because he doesn't belong to our group."

50 "Do not try to stop him," Jesus said to him and to the other disciples, "because whoever is not against you is for you."

A Samaritan Village Refuses to Receive Jesus

51 As the time drew near when Jesus would be taken up to heaven, he made up his mind and set out on his way to Jerusalem. 52 He sent messengers ahead of him, who went into a village in Samaria to get everything ready for him. 53 But the people there would not receive him, because it was clear that he was on his way to Jerusalem. 54 When the disciples James and John saw this, they said, "Lord,

do you want us to call fire down from heaven to destroy them?"[j]

55 Jesus turned and rebuked them.[k] 56 Then Jesus and his disciples went on to another village.

The Would-be Followers of Jesus
(Matt. 8.19–22)

57 As they went on their way, a man said to Jesus, "I will follow you wherever you go."

58 Jesus said to him, "Foxes have holes, and birds have nests, but the Son of Man has nowhere to lie down and rest."

59 He said to another man, "Follow me."

But that man said, "Sir, first let me go back and bury my father."

60 Jesus answered, "Let the dead bury their own dead. You go and proclaim the Kingdom of God."

61 Another man said, "I will follow you, sir; but first let me go and say good-bye to my family."

62 Jesus said to him, "Anyone who starts to plough and then keeps looking back is of no use to the Kingdom of God."

Jesus Sends Out the Seventy-two

10 After this the Lord chose another seventy-two[l] men and sent them out two by two, to go ahead of him to every town and place where he himself was about to go. 2 He said to them, "There is a large harvest, but few workers to gather it in. Pray to the owner of the harvest that he will send out workers to gather in his harvest. 3 Go! I am sending you like lambs among wolves. 4 Don't take a purse or a beggar's bag or shoes; don't stop to greet anyone on the road. 5 Whenever you go into a house, first say, 'Peace be with this house.' 6 If a peace-loving man lives there, let your greeting of peace remain on him; if not, take back your greeting of peace. 7 Stay in that same house, eating and drinking whatever

[j] Some manuscripts add as Elijah did.
[k] Some manuscripts add and said, "You don't know what kind of a Spirit you belong to; for the Son of Man did not come to destroy men's lives, but to save them."
[l] seventy-two; some manuscripts have seventy.

they offer you, for a worker should be given his pay. Don't move round from one house to another. ⁸Whenever you go into a town and are made welcome, eat what is set before you, ⁹heal the sick in that town, and say to the people there, 'The Kingdom of God has come near you.' ¹⁰But whenever you go into a town and are not welcomed, go out in the streets and say, ¹¹'Even the dust from your town that sticks to our feet we wipe off against you. But remember that the Kingdom of God has come near you!' ¹²I assure you that on Judgement Day God will show more mercy to Sodom than to that town!

The Unbelieving Towns
(Matt. 11.20–24)

13 "How terrible it will be for you, Chorazin! How terrible for you too, Bethsaida! If the miracles which were performed in you had been performed in Tyre and Sidon, the people there would long ago have sat down, put on sackcloth, and sprinkled ashes on themselves, to show that they had turned from their sins! ¹⁴God will show more mercy on Judgement Day to Tyre and Sidon than to you. ¹⁵And as for you, Capernaum! Did you want to lift yourself up to heaven? You will be thrown down to hell!"

16 Jesus said to his disciples, "Whoever listens to you listens to me; whoever rejects you rejects me; and whoever rejects me rejects the one who sent me."

The Return of the Seventy-two

17 The seventy-two*ᵐ* men came back in great joy. "Lord," they said, "even the demons obeyed us when we gave them a command in your name!"

18 Jesus answered them, "I saw Satan fall like lightning from heaven. ¹⁹Listen! I have given you authority, so that you can walk on snakes and scorpions and overcome all the power of the Enemy, and nothing will hurt you. ²⁰But don't be glad because the evil spirits obey you; rather be glad because your names are written in heaven."

ᵐseventy-two; *some manuscripts have* seventy *(see verse 1)*.

Jesus Rejoices
(Matt. 11.25–27; 13.16–17)

21 At that time Jesus was filled with joy by the Holy Spirit[n] and said, "Father, Lord of heaven and earth! I thank you because you have shown to the unlearned what you have hidden from the wise and learned. Yes, Father, this was how you wanted it to happen.

22 "My Father has given me all things. No one knows who the Son is except the Father, and no one knows who the Father is except the Son and those to whom the Son chooses to reveal him."

23 Then Jesus turned to the disciples and said to them privately, "How fortunate you are to see the things you see! 24 I tell you that many prophets and kings wanted to see what you see, but they could not, and to hear what you hear, but they did not."

The Parable of the Good Samaritan

25 A teacher of the Law came up and tried to trap Jesus. "Teacher," he asked, "what must I do to receive eternal life?"

26 Jesus answered him, "What do the Scriptures say? How do you interpret them?"

27 The man answered, " 'Love the Lord your God with all your heart, with all your soul, with all your strength, and with all your mind'; and 'Love your neighbour as you love yourself.' "

28 "You are right," Jesus replied; "do this and you will live."

29 But the teacher of the Law wanted to justify himself, so he asked Jesus, "Who is my neighbour?"

30 Jesus answered, "There was once a man who was going down from Jerusalem to Jericho when robbers attacked him, stripped him, and beat him up, leaving him half dead. 31 It so happened that a priest was going down that road; but when he saw the man, he walked on by, on the other side. 32 In the same way a Levite also came along, went over and

[n] by the Holy Spirit; *some manuscripts have* by the Spirit; *others have* in his spirit.

looked at the man, and then walked on by, on the other side. ³³But a Samaritan who was travelling that

His heart was filled with pity (10.33)

way came upon the man, and when he saw him, his heart was filled with pity. ³⁴He went over to him, poured oil and wine on his wounds and bandaged them; then he put the man on his own animal and took him to an inn, where he took care of him. ³⁵The next day he took out two silver coins and gave them to the innkeeper. 'Take care of him,' he told the innkeeper, 'and when I come back this way, I will pay you whatever else you spend on him.' "

36 And Jesus concluded, "In your opinion, which one of these three acted like a neighbour towards the man attacked by the robbers?"

37 The teacher of the Law answered, "The one who was kind to him."

Jesus replied, "You go, then, and do the same."

Jesus Visits Martha and Mary

38 As Jesus and his disciples went on their way, he came to a village where a woman named Martha welcomed him in her home. ³⁹She had a sister named

Mary, who sat down at the feet of the Lord and listened to his teaching. 40 Martha was upset over all the work she had to do, so she came and said, "Lord, don't you care that my sister has left me to do all the work by myself? Tell her to come and help me!"

41 The Lord answered her, "Martha, Martha! You are worried and troubled over so many things, 42 but just one is needed. Mary has chosen the right thing, and it will not be taken away from her."

Jesus' Teaching on Prayer
(Matt. 6.9-13; 7.7-11)

11 One day Jesus was praying in a certain place. When he had finished, one of his disciples said to him, "Lord, teach us to pray, just as John taught his disciples."

2 Jesus said to them, "When you pray, say this:
'Father:
  May your holy name be honoured;
  may your Kingdom come.
3   Give us day by day the food we need. *o*
4   Forgive us our sins,
    for we forgive everyone who does us wrong.
  And do not bring us to hard testing.' "

5 And Jesus said to his disciples, "Suppose one of you should go to a friend's house at midnight and say to him, 'Friend, let me borrow three loaves of bread. 6 A friend of mine who is on a journey has just come to my house, and I haven't got any food for him!' 7 And suppose your friend should answer from inside, 'Don't bother me! The door is already locked, and my children and I are in bed. I can't get up and give you anything.' 8 Well, what then? I tell you that even if he will not get up and give you the bread because you are his friend, yet he will get up and give you everything you need because you are not ashamed to keep on asking.

9 "And so I say to you: Ask, and you will receive; seek, and you will find; knock, and the door will be opened to you. 10 For everyone who asks will receive, and he who seeks will find, and the door will be opened

*o*the food we need; *or* food for the next day.

to anyone who knocks. ¹¹Would any of you who are fathers give your son a snake when he asks for fish? ¹²Or would you give him a scorpion when he asks for an egg? ¹³Bad as you are, you know how to give good things to your children. How much more, then, will the Father in heaven give the Holy Spirit to those who ask him!"

Jesus and Beelzebul
(Matt. 12.22–30; Mark 3.20–27)

14 Jesus was driving out a demon that could not talk; and when the demon went out, the man began to talk. The crowds were amazed, ¹⁵but some of the people said, "It is Beelzebul, the chief of the demons, who gives him the power to drive them out."

16 Others wanted to trap Jesus, so they asked him to perform a miracle to show that God approved of him. ¹⁷But Jesus knew what they were thinking, so he said to them, "Any country that divides itself into groups which fight each other will not last very long; a family divided against itself falls apart. ¹⁸So if Satan's kingdom has groups fighting each other, how can it last? You say that I drive out demons because Beelzebul gives me the power to do so. ¹⁹If this is how I drive them out, how do your followers drive them out? Your own followers prove that you are wrong! ²⁰No, it is rather by means of God's power that I drive out demons, and this proves that the Kingdom of God has already come to you.

21 "When a strong man, with all his weapons ready, guards his own house, all his belongings are safe. ²²But when a stronger man attacks him and defeats him, he carries away all the weapons the owner was depending on and divides up what he stole.

23 "Anyone who is not for me is really against me; anyone who does not help me gather is really scattering.

The Return of the Evil Spirit
(Matt. 12.43–45)

24 "When an evil spirit goes out of a person, it travels over dry country looking for a place to rest. If it can't find one, it says to itself, 'I will go back

to my house.' 25 So it goes back and finds the house clean and tidy. 26 Then it goes out and brings seven other spirits even worse than itself, and they come and live there. So when it is all over, that person is in a worse state than he was at the beginning."

True Happiness

27 When Jesus had said this, a woman spoke up from the crowd and said to him, "How happy is the woman who bore you and nursed you!"

28 But Jesus answered, "Rather, how happy are those who hear the word of God and obey it!"

The Demand for a Miracle
(Matt. 12.38–42)

29 As the people crowded round Jesus, he went on to say, "How evil are the people of this day! They ask for a miracle, but none will be given them except the miracle of Jonah. 30 In the same way that the prophet Jonah was a sign for the people of Nineveh, so the Son of Man will be a sign for the people of this day. 31 On Judgement Day the Queen of Sheba will stand up and accuse the people of today, because she travelled all the way from her country to listen to King Solomon's wise teaching; and I tell you there is something here greater than Solomon. 32 On Judgement Day the people of Nineveh will stand up and accuse you, because they turned from their sins when they heard Jonah preach; and I assure you that there is something here greater than Jonah!

The Light of the Body
(Matt. 5.15; 6.22–23)

33 "No one lights a lamp and then hides it or puts it under a bowl; p instead, he puts it on the lampstand, so that people may see the light as they come in. 34 Your eyes are like a lamp for the body. When your eyes are sound, your whole body is full of light; but when your eyes are no good, your whole body will be in darkness. 35 Make certain, then, that the light in you is not darkness. 36 If your whole body is

p Some manuscripts do not have or puts it under a bowl.

full of light, with no part of it in darkness, it will be bright all over, as when a lamp shines on you with its brightness."

Jesus Accuses the Pharisees and the Teachers of the Law
(Matt. 23.1–36; Mark 12.38–40)

37 When Jesus finished speaking, a Pharisee invited him to eat with him; so he went in and sat down to eat. 38 The Pharisee was surprised when he noticed that Jesus had not washed before eating. 39 So the Lord said to him, "Now then, you Pharisees clean the outside of your cup and plate, but inside you are full of violence and evil. 40 Fools! Did not God, who made the outside, also make the inside? 41 But give what is in your cups and plates to the poor, and everything will be ritually clean for you.

42 "How terrible for you Pharisees! You give God a tenth of the seasoning herbs, such as mint and rue and all the other herbs, but you neglect justice and love for God. These you should practise, without neglecting the others.

43 "How terrible for you Pharisees! You love the reserved seats in the synagogues and to be greeted with respect in the market-places. 44 How terrible for you! You are like unmarked graves which people walk on without knowing it."

45 One of the teachers of the Law said to him, "Teacher, when you say this, you insult us too!"

46 Jesus answered, "How terrible also for you teachers of the Law! You put loads on people's backs which are hard to carry, but you yourselves will not stretch out a finger to help them carry those loads. 47 How terrible for you! You make fine tombs for the prophets—the very prophets your ancestors murdered. 48 You yourselves admit, then, that you approve of what your ancestors did; they murdered the prophets, and you build their tombs. 49 For this reason the Wisdom of God said, 'I will send them prophets and messengers; they will kill some of them and persecute others.' 50 So the people of this time will be punished for the murder of all the prophets killed since the creation of the world, 51 from the murder

of Abel to the murder of Zechariah, who was killed
between the altar and the Holy Place. Yes, I tell
you, the people of this time will be punished for
them all!

52 "How terrible for you teachers of the Law! You
have kept the key that opens the door to the house
of knowledge; you yourselves will not go in, and
you stop those who are trying to go in!"

53 When Jesus left that place, the teachers of the
Law and the Pharisees began to criticize him bitterly
and ask him questions about many things, 54trying
to lay traps for him and catch him saying something
wrong.

A Warning against Hypocrisy
(Matt. 10.26-27)

12 As thousands of people crowded together, so
that they were stepping on each other, Jesus
said first to his disciples, "Be on guard against the
yeast of the Pharisees—I mean their hypocrisy. 2Whatever is covered up will be uncovered, and every secret
will be made known. 3So then, whatever you have
said in the dark will be heard in broad daylight, and
whatever you have whispered in private in a closed
room will be shouted from the housetops.

Whom to Fear
(Matt. 10.28-31)

4 "I tell you, my friends, do not be afraid of those
who kill the body but cannot afterwards do anything
worse. 5I will show you whom to fear: fear God,
who, after killing, has the authority to throw into hell.
Believe me, he is the one you must fear!

6 "Aren't five sparrows sold for two pennies? Yet
not one sparrow is forgotten by God. 7Even the hairs
of your head have all been counted. So do not be
afraid; you are worth much more than many sparrows!

Confessing and Rejecting Christ
(Matt. 10.32-33; 12.32; 10.19-20)

8 "I assure you that whoever declares publicly that
he belongs to me, the Son of Man will do the same
for him before the angels of God. 9But whoever rejects

me publicly, the Son of Man will also reject him before the angels of God.

10 "Anyone who says a word against the Son of Man can be forgiven; but whoever says evil things against the Holy Spirit will not be forgiven.

11 "When they bring you to be tried in the synagogues or before governors or rulers, do not be worried about how you will defend yourself or what you will say. 12 For the Holy Spirit will teach you at that time what you should say."

The Parable of the Rich Fool

13 A man in the crowd said to Jesus, "Teacher, tell my brother to divide with me the property our father left us."

14 Jesus answered him, "My friend, who gave me the right to judge or to divide the property between you two?" 15 And he went on to say to them all, "Watch out and guard yourselves from every kind of greed; because a person's true life is not made up of the things he owns, no matter how rich he may be."

16 Then Jesus told them this parable: "There was once a rich man who had land which bore good crops. 17 He began to think to himself, 'I haven't anywhere to keep all my crops. What can I do? 18 This is what I will do,' he told himself; 'I will tear down my barns and build bigger ones, where I will store my corn and all my other goods. 19 Then I will say to myself, Lucky man! You have all the good things you need for many years. Take life easy, eat, drink, and enjoy yourself!' 20 But God said to him, 'You fool! This very night you will have to give up your life; then who will get all these things you have kept for yourself?' "

21 And Jesus concluded, "This is how it is with those who pile up riches for themselves but are not rich in God's sight."

Trust in God
(Matt. 6.25-34)

22 Then Jesus said to the disciples, "And so I tell you not to worry about the food you need to stay

And so I tell you not to worry (12.22)

alive or about the clothes you need for your body. 23 Life is much more important than food, and the body much more important than clothes. 24 Look at the crows: they don't sow seeds or gather a harvest; they don't have store-rooms or barns; God feeds them! You are worth so much more than birds! 25 Can any of you live a bit longerq by worrying about it? 26 If you can't manage even such a small thing, why worry about the other things? 27 Look how the wild flowers grow: they don't work or make clothes for themselves. But I tell you that not even King Solomon with all his wealth had clothes as beautiful as one of these flowers. 28 It is God who clothes the wild grass—grass that is here today and gone tomorrow, burnt up in the oven. Won't he be all the more sure to clothe you? How little faith you have!

29 "So don't be all upset, always concerned about what you will eat and drink. 30 (For the pagans of this world are always concerned about all these things.) Your Father knows that you need these things. 31 Instead, be concerned with his Kingdom, and he will provide you with these things.

Riches in Heaven
(Matt. 6.19–21)

32 "Do not be afraid, little flock, for your Father is pleased to give you the Kingdom. 33 Sell all your belongings and give the money to the poor. Provide for yourselves purses that don't wear out, and save

qlive a bit longer; *or* grow a bit taller.

your riches in heaven, where they will never decrease, because no thief can get to them, and no moth can destroy them. ³⁴ For your heart will always be where your riches are.

Watchful Servants

35 "Be ready for whatever comes, dressed for action and with your lamps lit, ³⁶ like servants who are waiting for their master to come back from a wedding feast. When he comes and knocks, they will open the door for him at once. ³⁷ How happy are those servants whose master finds them awake and ready when he returns! I tell you, he will take off his coat, ask them to sit down, and will wait on them. ³⁸ How happy they are if he finds them ready, even if he should come at midnight or even later! ³⁹ And you can be sure that if the owner of a house knew the time when the thief would come, he would not let the thief break into his house. ⁴⁰ And you, too, must be ready, because the Son of Man will come at an hour when you are not expecting him."

The Faithful or the Unfaithful Servant
(Matt. 24.45-51)

41 Peter said, "Lord does this parable apply to us, or do you mean it for everyone?"

42 The Lord answered, "Who, then, is the faithful and wise servant? He is the one that his master will put in charge, to run the household and give the other servants their share of the food at the proper time. ⁴³ How happy that servant is if his master finds him doing this when he comes home! ⁴⁴ Indeed, I tell you, the master will put that servant in charge of all his property. ⁴⁵ But if that servant says to himself that his master is taking a long time to come back and if he begins to beat the other servants, both the men and the women, and eats and drinks and gets drunk, ⁴⁶ then the master will come back one day when the servant does not expect him and at a time he does not know. The master will cut him

in pieces^r and make him share the fate of the disobedient.

47 "The servant who knows what his master wants him to do, but does not get himself ready and do it, will be punished with a heavy whipping. 48 But the servant who does not know what his master wants, and yet does something for which he deserves a whipping, will be punished with a light whipping. Much is required from the person to whom much is given; much more is required from the person to whom much more is given.

Jesus the Cause of Division
(Matt. 10.34–36)

49 "I came to set the earth on fire, and how I wish it were already kindled! 50 I have a baptism to receive, and how distressed I am until it is over! 51 Do you suppose that I came to bring peace to the world? No, not peace, but division. 52 From now on a family of five will be divided, three against two and two against three. 53 Fathers will be against their sons, and sons against their fathers; mothers will be against their daughters, and daughters against their mothers; mothers-in-law will be against their daughters-in-law, and daughters-in-law against their mothers-in-law."

Understanding the Time
(Matt. 16.2–3)

54 Jesus said also to the people, "When you see a cloud coming up in the west, at once you say that it is going to rain—and it does. 55 And when you feel the south wind blowing, you say that it is going to get hot—and it does. 56 Hypocrites! You can look at the earth and the sky and predict the weather; why, then, don't you know the meaning of this present time?

Settle with Your Opponent
(Matt. 5.25–26)

57 "Why do you not judge for yourselves the right thing to do? 58 If someone brings a lawsuit against you and takes you to court, do your best to settle

^{r}cut him in pieces; *or* throw him out.

the dispute with him before you get to court. If you don't, he will drag you before the judge, who will hand you over to the police, and you will be put in jail. ⁵⁹There you will stay, I tell you, until you pay the last penny of your fine."

Turn from Your Sins or Die

13 At that time some people were there who told Jesus about the Galileans whom Pilate had killed while they were offering sacrifices to God. ²Jesus answered them, "Because those Galileans were killed in that way, do you think it proves that they were worse sinners than all the other Galileans? ³No indeed! And I tell you that if you do not turn from your sins, you will all die as they did. ⁴What about those eighteen people in Siloam who were killed when the tower fell on them? Do you suppose this proves that they were worse than all the other people living in Jerusalem? ⁵No indeed! And I tell you that if you do not turn from your sins, you will all die as they did."

The Parable of the Unfruitful Fig-Tree

6 Then Jesus told them this parable: "There was once a man who had a fig-tree growing in his vineyard. He went looking for figs on it but found none. ⁷So he said to his gardener, 'Look, for three years I have been coming here looking for figs on this fig-tree, and I haven't found any. Cut it down! Why should it go on using up the soil?' ⁸But the gardener answered, 'Leave it alone, sir, just one more year; I will dig round it and put in some manure. ⁹Then if the tree bears figs next year, so much the better; if not, then you can have it cut down.' "

Jesus Heals a Crippled Woman on the Sabbath

10 One Sabbath Jesus was teaching in a synagogue. ¹¹A woman there had an evil spirit that had made her ill for eighteen years; she was bent over and could not straighten up at all. ¹²When Jesus saw her, he called out to her, "Woman, you are free from your illness!" ¹³He placed his hands on her, and at once she straightened herself up and praised God.

14 The official of the synagogue was angry that Jesus had healed on the Sabbath, so he spoke up and said to the people, "There are six days in which we should work; so come during those days and be healed, but not on the Sabbath!"

15 The Lord answered him, "You hypocrites! Any one of you would untie his ox or his donkey from the stall and take it out to give it water on the Sabbath. 16 Now here is this descendant of Abraham whom Satan has kept bound up for eighteen years; should she not be released on the Sabbath?" 17 His answer made his enemies ashamed of themselves, while the people rejoiced over all the wonderful things that he did.

The Parable of the Mustard Seed
(Matt. 13.31–32; Mark 4.30–32)

18 Jesus asked, "What is the Kingdom of God like? What shall I compare it with? 19 It is like this. A man takes a mustard seed and sows it in his field. The plant grows and becomes a tree, and the birds make their nests in its branches."

The Parable of the Yeast
(Matt. 13.33)

20 Again Jesus asked, "What shall I compare the Kingdom of God with? 21 It is like this. A woman takes some yeast and mixes it with forty litres of flour until the whole batch of dough rises."

The Narrow Door
(Matt. 7.13–14, 21–23)

22 Jesus went through towns and villages, teaching the people and making his way towards Jerusalem. 23 Someone asked him, "Sir, will just a few people be saved?"

Jesus answered them, 24 "Do your best to go in through the narrow door; because many people will surely try to go in but will not be able. 25 The master of the house will get up and close the door; then when you stand outside and begin to knock on the door and say, 'Open the door for us, sir!' he will answer you, 'I don't know where you come from!'

26 Then you will answer, 'We ate and drank with you; you taught in our town!' 27 But he will say again, 'I don't know where you come from. Get away from me, all you wicked people!' 28 How you will cry and grind your teeth when you see Abraham, Isaac, and Jacob, and all the prophets in the Kingdom of God, while you are thrown out! 29 People will come from the east and the west, from the north and the south, and sit down at the feast in the Kingdom of God. 30 Then those who are now last will be first, and those who are now first will be last."

Jesus' Love for Jerusalem
(Matt. 23.37–39)

31 At that same time some Pharisees came to Jesus and said to him, "You must get out of here and go somewhere else, because Herod wants to kill you."

32 Jesus answered them, "Go and tell that fox: 'I am driving out demons and performing cures today and tomorrow, and on the third day I shall finish my work.' 33 Yet I must be on my way today, tomorrow, and the next day; it is not right for a prophet to be killed anywhere except in Jerusalem.

34 "Jerusalem, Jerusalem! You kill the prophets, you stone the messengers God has sent you! How many times have I wanted to put my arms round all your people, just as a hen gathers her chicks under her wings, but you would not let me! 35 And so your Temple will be abandoned. I assure you that you will not see me until the time comes when you say, 'God bless him who comes in the name of the Lord.' "

Jesus Heals a Sick Man

14 One Sabbath Jesus went to eat a meal at the home of one of the leading Pharisees; and people were watching Jesus closely. 2 A man whose legs and arms were swollen came to Jesus, 3 and Jesus asked the teachers of the Law and the Pharisees, "Does our Law allow healing on the Sabbath or not?"

4 But they would not say anything. Jesus took the man, healed him, and sent him away. 5 Then he said to them, "If any one of you had a son or an ox

that happened to fall in a well on a Sabbath, would you not pull him out at once on the Sabbath itself?"

6 But they were not able to answer him about this.

Humility and Hospitality

7 Jesus noticed how some of the guests were choosing the best places, so he told this parable to all of them: 8"When someone invites you to a wedding feast, do not sit down in the best place. It could happen that someone more important than you has been invited, 9 and your host, who invited both of you, would have to come and say to you, 'Let him have this place.' Then you would be embarrassed and have to sit in the lowest place. 10 Instead, when you are invited, go and sit in the lowest place, so that your host will come to you and say, 'Come on up, my friend, to a better place.' This will bring you honour in the presence of all the other guests. 11 For everyone who makes himself great will be humbled, and everyone who humbles himself will be made great."

12 Then Jesus said to his host, "When you give a lunch or a dinner, do not invite your friends or your brothers or your relatives or your rich neighbours—for they will invite you back, and in this way you will be paid for what you did. 13 When you give a feast, invite the poor, the crippled, the lame, and the blind; 14 and you will be blessed, because they are not able to pay you back. God will repay you on the day the good people rise from death."

The Parable of the Great Feast
(Matt. 22.1-10)

15 When one of the men sitting at table heard this, he said to Jesus, "How happy are those who will sit down at the feast in the Kingdom of God!"

16 Jesus said to him, "There was once a man who was giving a great feast to which he invited many people. 17 When it was time for the feast, he sent his servant to tell his guests, 'Come, everything is ready!' 18 But they all began, one after another, to make excuses. The first one told the servant, 'I have bought a field and must go and look at it; please accept my apologies.' 19 Another one said, 'I have

bought five pairs of oxen and am on my way to try them out; please accept my apologies.' 20 Another one said, 'I have just got married, and for that reason I cannot come.'

21 "The servant went back and told all this to his master. The master was furious and said to his servant, 'Hurry out to the streets and alleys of the town, and bring back the poor, the crippled, the blind, and the lame.' 22 Soon the servant said, 'Your order has been carried out, sir, but there is room for more.' 23 So the master said to the servant, 'Go out to the country roads and lanes and make people come in, so that my house will be full. 24 I tell you all that none of those men who were invited will taste my dinner!' "

The Cost of Being a Disciple
(Matt. 10.37–38)

25 Once when large crowds of people were going along with Jesus, he turned and said to them, 26 "Whoever comes to me cannot be my disciple unless he loves me more than he loves his father and his mother, his wife and his children, his brothers and his sisters, and himself as well. 27 Whoever does not carry his own cross and come after me cannot be my disciple.

28 "If one of you is planning to build a tower, he sits down first and works out what it will cost, to see if he has enough money to finish the job. 29 If he doesn't, he will not be able to finish the tower after laying the foundation; and all who see what happened will laugh at him. 30 'This man began to build but can't finish the job!' they will say.

31 "If a king goes out with ten thousand men to fight another king who comes against him with twenty thousand men, he will sit down first and decide if he is strong enough to face that other king. 32 If he isn't, he will send messengers to meet the other king, to ask for terms of peace while he is still a long way off. 33 In the same way," concluded Jesus, "none of you can be my disciple unless he gives up everything he has.

Worthless Salt
(Matt. 5.13; Mark 9.50)

34 "Salt is good, but if it loses its saltiness, there is no way to make it salty again. 35 It is no good for the soil or for the manure heap; it is thrown away. Listen, then, if you have ears!"

The Lost Sheep
(Matt. 18.12–14)

15 One day when many tax collectors and other outcasts came to listen to Jesus, 2 the Pharisees and the teachers of the Law started grumbling, "This man welcomes outcasts and even eats with them!" 3 So Jesus told them this parable:

4 "Suppose one of you has a hundred sheep and loses one of them—what does he do? He leaves the other ninety-nine sheep in the pasture and goes looking for the one that got lost until he finds it. 5 When he finds it, he is so happy that he puts it on his shoulders 6 and carries it back home. Then he calls his friends and neighbours together and says to them, 'I am so happy I found my lost sheep. Let us celebrate!' 7 In the same way, I tell you, there will be more joy in heaven over one sinner who repents than over ninety-nine respectable people who do not need to repent.

The Lost Coin

8 "Or suppose a woman who has ten silver coins loses one of them—what does she do? She lights a lamp, sweeps her house, and looks carefully everywhere until she finds it. 9 When she finds it, she calls her friends and neighbours together, and says to them, 'I am so happy I found the coin I lost. Let us celebrate!' 10 In the same way, I tell you, the angels of God rejoice over one sinner who repents."

The Lost Son

11 Jesus went on to say, "There was once a man who had two sons. 12 The younger one said to him, 'Father, give me my share of the property now.' So the man divided his property between his two sons.

¹³After a few days the younger son sold his part of the property and left home with the money. He went to a country far away, where he wasted his money in reckless living. ¹⁴He spent everything he had. Then a severe famine spread over that country, and he was left without a thing. ¹⁵So he went to work for one of the citizens of that country, who sent him out to his farm to take care of the pigs. ¹⁶He wished he could fill himself with the bean pods the pigs ate, but no one gave him anything to eat. ¹⁷At

Here I am about to starve! (15.17)

last he came to his senses and said, 'All my father's hired workers have more than they can eat, and here I am about to starve! ¹⁸I will get up and go to my father and say, Father, I have sinned against God and against you. ¹⁹I am no longer fit to be called your son; treat me as one of your hired workers.' ²⁰So he got up and started back to his father.

"He was still a long way from home when his father saw him; his heart was filled with pity, and he ran, threw his arms round his son, and kissed him. ²¹'Father,' the son said, 'I have sinned against God and against you. I am no longer fit to be called your son.' ²²But the father called his servants. 'Hurry!' he said. 'Bring the best robe and put it on him. Put a ring on his finger and shoes on his feet. ²³Then go and get the prize calf and kill it, and let us celebrate with a feast! ²⁴For this son of mine was dead, but now he is alive; he was lost, but now he has been found.' And so the feasting began.

25 "In the meantime the elder son was out in the

field. On his way back, when he came close to the house, he heard the music and dancing. ²⁶So he called one of the servants and asked him, 'What's going on?' ²⁷'Your brother has come back home,' the servant answered, 'and your father has killed the prize calf, because he got him back safe and sound.'

28 "The elder brother was so angry that he would not go into the house; so his father came out and begged him to come in. ²⁹But he answered his father, 'Look, all these years I have worked for you like a slave, and I have never disobeyed your orders. What have you given me? Not even a goat for me to have a feast with my friends! ³⁰But this son of yours wasted all your property on prostitutes, and when he comes back home, you kill the prize calf for him!' ³¹'My son,' the father answered, 'you are always here with me, and everything I have is yours. ³²But we had to cele-

But now he is alive (15.32)

brate and be happy, because your brother was dead, but now he is alive; he was lost, but now he has been found.' "

The Shrewd Manager

16 Jesus said to his disciples, "There was once a rich man who had a servant who managed his property. The rich man was told that the manager was wasting his master's money, ²so he called him in and said, 'What is this I hear about you? Hand in a complete account of your handling of my property, because you cannot be my manager any longer.' ³The servant said to himself, 'My master is going to dismiss me from my job. What shall I do? I am not strong enough to dig ditches, and I am ashamed to beg. ⁴Now I know what I will do! Then when my job is gone, I shall have friends who will welcome me in their homes.'

5 "So he called in all the people who were in debt to his master. He asked the first one, 'How much do you owe my master?' ⁶'One hundred barrels of olive-oil,' he answered. 'Here is your account,' the manager told him; 'sit down and write fifty.' ⁷Then he asked another one, 'And you—how much do you owe?' 'A thousand sacks of wheat,' he answered. 'Here is your account,' the manager told him; 'write eight hundred.'

8 "As a result the master of this dishonest manager praised him for doing such a shrewd thing; because the people of this world are much more shrewd in handling their affairs than the people who belong to the light."

9 And Jesus went on to say, "And so I tell you: make friends for yourselves with worldly wealth, so that when it gives out, you will be welcomed in the eternal home. ¹⁰Whoever is faithful in small matters will be faithful in large ones; whoever is dishonest in small matters will be dishonest in large ones. ¹¹If, then, you have not been faithful in handling worldly wealth, how can you be trusted with true wealth? ¹²And if you have not been faithful with what belongs to someone else, who will give you what belongs to you?

13 "No servant can be the slave of two masters; he will hate one and love the other; he will be loyal to one and despise the other. You cannot serve both God and money."

Some Sayings of Jesus —
(Matt. 11.12–13; 5.31–32; Mark 10.11–12)

14 When the Pharisees heard all this, they sneered at Jesus, because they loved money. 15 Jesus said to them, "You are the ones who make yourselves look right in other people's sight, but God knows your hearts. For the things that are considered of great value by man are worth nothing in God's sight.

16 "The Law of Moses and the writings of the prophets were in effect up to the time of John the Baptist; since then the Good News about the Kingdom of God is being told, and everyone forces his way in. 17 But it is easier for heaven and earth to disappear than for the smallest detail of the Law to be done away with.

18 "Any man who divorces his wife and marries another woman commits adultery; and the man who marries a divorced woman commits adultery.

The Rich Man and Lazarus

19 "There was once a rich man who dressed in the most expensive clothes and lived in great luxury every day. 20 There was also a poor man named Lazarus, covered with sores, who used to be brought to the rich man's door, 21 hoping to eat the bits of food that fell from the rich man's table. Even the dogs would come and lick his sores.

22 "The poor man died and was carried by the angels to sit beside Abraham at the feast in heaven. The rich man died and was buried, 23 and in Hades,^{s} where he was in great pain, he looked up and saw Abraham, far away, with Lazarus at his side. 24 So he called out, 'Father Abraham! Take pity on me, and send Lazarus to dip his finger in some water and cool my tongue, because I am in great pain in this fire!'

25 "But Abraham said, 'Remember, my son, that in your lifetime you were given all the good things, while Lazarus got all the bad things. But now he is enjoying himself here, while you are in pain. 26 Be-

---

^{s}HADES: *The world of the dead.*

sides all that, there is a deep pit lying between us, so that those who want to cross over from here to you cannot do so, nor can anyone cross over to us from where you are.' ²⁷The rich man said, 'Then I beg you, father Abraham, send Lazarus to my father's house, ²⁸where I have five brothers. Let him go and warn them so that they, at least, will not come to this place of pain.'

29 "Abraham said, 'Your brothers have Moses and the prophets to warn them; your brothers should listen to what they say.' ³⁰The rich man answered, 'That is not enough, father Abraham! But if someone were to rise from death and go to them, then they would turn from their sins.' ³¹But Abraham said, 'If they will not listen to Moses and the prophets, they will not be convinced even if someone were to rise from death.' "

Sin
(Matt. 18.6-7, 21-22; Mark 9.42)

17 Jesus said to his disciples, "Things that make people fall into sin are bound to happen, but how terrible for the one who makes them happen! ²It would be better for him if a large millstone were tied round his neck and he were thrown into the sea than for him to cause one of these little ones to sin. ³So watch what you do!

"If your brother sins, rebuke him, and if he repents, forgive him. ⁴If he sins against you seven times in one day, and each time he comes to you saying, 'I repent,' you must forgive him."

Faith

5 The apostles said to the Lord, "Make our faith greater."

6 The Lord answered, "If you had faith as big as a mustard seed, you could say to this mulberry tree, 'Pull yourself up by the roots and plant yourself in the sea!' and it would obey you.

A Servant's Duty

7 "Suppose one of you has a servant who is plough-ing or looking after the sheep. When he comes in

from the field, do you tell him to hurry and eat his meal? 8 Of course not! Instead, you say to him, 'Get my supper ready, then put on your apron and wait on me while I eat and drink; after that you may have your meal.' 9 The servant does not deserve thanks for obeying orders, does he? 10 It is the same with you; when you have done all you have been told to do, say, 'We are ordinary servants; we have only done our duty.' "

Jesus Heals Ten Men

11 As Jesus made his way to Jerusalem, he went along the border between Samaria and Galilee. 12 He was going into a village when he was met by ten men suffering from a dreaded skin-disease. They stood at a distance 13 and shouted, "Jesus! Master! Take pity on us!"

14 Jesus saw them and said to them, "Go and let the priests examine you."

On the way they were made clean.*t* 15 When one of them saw that he was healed, he came back, praising God in a loud voice. 16 He threw himself to the ground at Jesus' feet and thanked him. The man was a Samaritan. 17 Jesus said, "There were ten men who were healed; where are the other nine? 18 Why is this foreigner the only one who came back to give thanks to God?" 19 And Jesus said to him, "Get up and go; your faith has made you well."

The Coming of the Kingdom
(Matt. 24.23–28, 37–41)

20 Some Pharisees asked Jesus when the Kingdom of God would come. His answer was, "The Kingdom of God does not come in such a way as to be seen. 21 No one will say, 'Look, here it is!' or, 'There it is!'; because the Kingdom of God is within you."*u*

22 Then he said to the disciples, "The time will come when you will wish you could see one of the days of the Son of Man, but you will not see it. 23 There will be those who will say to you, 'Look,

---

t MADE CLEAN: *See 5.12.*
u is within you; *or* is among you, *or* will suddenly appear among you.

Where are the other nine? (17.17)

over there!' or, 'Look, over here!' But don't go out looking for it. ²⁴As the lightning flashes across the sky and lights it up from one side to the other, so will the Son of Man be in his day. ²⁵But first he must suffer much and be rejected by the people of this day. ²⁶As it was in the time of Noah so shall it be in the days of the Son of Man. ²⁷Everybody kept on eating and drinking, and men and women married, up to the very day Noah went into the boat and the flood came and killed them all. ²⁸It will be as it was in the time of Lot. Everybody kept on eating and drinking, buying and selling, planting and building. ²⁹On the day Lot left Sodom, fire and sulphur rained down from heaven and killed them all. ³⁰That is how it will be on the day the Son of Man is revealed.

31 "On that day the man who is on the roof of his house must not go down into the house to get his belongings; in the same way the man who is out in the field must not go back to the house. ³²Remember Lot's wife! ³³Whoever tries to save his own life will lose it; whoever loses his life will save it. ³⁴On that night, I tell you, there will be two people sleeping in the same bed: one will be taken away, the other will be left behind. ³⁵Two women will be grinding corn together: one will be taken away, the other will be left behind." ᵛ

37 The disciples asked him, "Where, Lord?"

Jesus answered, "Wherever there is a dead body, the vultures will gather."

The Parable of the Widow and the Judge

18 Then Jesus told his disciples a parable to teach them that they should always pray and never become discouraged. ²"In a certain town there was a judge who neither feared God nor respected man. ³And there was a widow in that same town who kept coming to him and pleading for her rights, saying, 'Help me against my opponent!' ⁴For a long time the judge refused to act, but at last he said to himself, 'Even though I don't fear God or respect man, ⁵yet because of all the trouble this widow is giving me, I will see to it that she gets her rights. If I don't, she will keep on coming and finally wear me out!' "

6 And the Lord continued, "Listen to what that corrupt judge said. ⁷Now, will God not judge in favour of his own people who cry to him day and night for help? Will he be slow to help them? ⁸I tell you, he will judge in their favour and do it quickly. But will the Son of Man find faith on earth when he comes?"

The Parable of the Pharisee and the Tax Collector

9 Jesus also told this parable to people who were sure of their own goodness and despised everybody

ᵛ *Some manuscripts add verse 36:* Two men will be working in a field: one will be taken away, the other will be left behind *(see Mt 24.40).*

else. [10] "Once there were two men who went up to the Temple to pray: one was a Pharisee, the other a tax collector.

11 "The Pharisee stood apart by himself and prayed,[w] 'I thank you, God, that I am not greedy, dishonest, or an adulterer, like everybody else. I thank you that I am not like that tax collector over there. [12] I fast two days a week, and I give you a tenth of all my income.'

13 "But the tax collector stood at a distance and would not even raise his face to heaven, but beat on his breast and said, 'God, have pity on me, a sinner!' [14] I tell you," said Jesus, "the tax collector, and not the Pharisee, was in the right with God when he went home. For everyone who makes himself great will be humbled, and everyone who humbles himself will be made great."

Jesus Blesses Little Children
(Matt. 19.13–15; Mark 10.13–16)

15 Some people brought their babies to Jesus for him to place his hands on them. The disciples saw them and scolded them for doing so, [16] but Jesus called the children to him and said, "Let the children come to me and do not stop them, because the Kingdom of God belongs to such as these. [17] Remember this! Whoever does not receive the Kingdom of God like a child will never enter it."

The Rich Man
(Matt. 19.16–30; Mark 10.17–31)

18 A Jewish leader asked Jesus, "Good Teacher, what must I do to receive eternal life?"

19 "Why do you call me good?" Jesus asked him. "No one is good except God alone. [20] You know the commandments: 'Do not commit adultery; do not commit murder; do not steal; do not accuse anyone falsely; respect your father and your mother.' "

21 The man replied, "Ever since I was young, I have obeyed all these commandments."

---

[w] stood apart by himself and prayed; *some manuscripts have* stood up and prayed to himself.

22 When Jesus heard this, he said to him, "There is still one more thing you need to do. Sell all you have and give the money to the poor, and you will have riches in heaven; then come and follow me." 23 But when the man heard this, he became very sad, because he was very rich.

24 Jesus saw that he was sad and said, "How hard it is for rich people to enter the Kingdom of God! 25 It is much harder for a rich person to enter the Kingdom of God than for a camel to go through the eye of a needle."

26 The people who heard him asked, "Who, then, can be saved?"

27 Jesus answered, "What is impossible for man is possible for God."

28 Then Peter said, "Look! We have left our homes to follow you."

29 "Yes," Jesus said to them, "and I assure you that anyone who leaves home or wife or brothers or parents or children for the sake of the Kingdom of God 30 will receive much more in this present age and eternal life in the age to come."

Jesus Speaks a Third Time about His Death
(Matt. 20.17–19; Mark 10.32–34)

31 Jesus took the twelve disciples aside and said to them, "Listen! We are going to Jerusalem where everything the prophets wrote about the Son of Man will come true. 32 He will be handed over to the Gentiles, who will mock him, insult him, and spit on him. 33 They will whip him and kill him, but three days later he will rise to life."

34 But the disciples did not understand any of these things; the meaning of the words was hidden from them, and they did not know what Jesus was talking about.

Jesus Heals a Blind Beggar
(Matt. 20.29–34; Mark 10.46–52)

35 As Jesus was coming near Jericho, there was a blind man sitting by the road, begging. 36 When he heard the crowd passing by, he asked, "What is this?"

37 "Jesus of Nazareth is passing by," they told him.

38 He cried out, "Jesus! Son of David! Take pity on me!"

39 The people in front scolded him and told him to be quiet. But he shouted even more loudly, "Son of David! Take pity on me!"

40 So Jesus stopped and ordered the blind man to be brought to him. When he came near, Jesus asked him, 41 "What do you want me to do for you?"

"Sir," he answered, "I want to see again."

42 Jesus said to him, "Then see! Your faith has made you well."

43 At once he was able to see, and he followed Jesus, giving thanks to God. When the crowd saw it, they all praised God.

Jesus and Zacchaeus

19 Jesus went on into Jericho and was passing through. 2 There was a chief tax collector there named Zacchaeus, who was rich. 3 He was trying to see who Jesus was, but he was a little man and could not see Jesus because of the crowd. 4 So he ran ahead of the crowd and climbed a sycomore tree to see Jesus, who was going to pass that way. 5 When Jesus came to that place, he looked up and said to Zacchaeus, "Hurry down, Zacchaeus, because I must stay in your house today."

6 Zacchaeus hurried down and welcomed him with great joy. 7 All the people who saw it started grumbling, "This man has gone as a guest to the home of a sinner!"

8 Zacchaeus stood up and said to the Lord, "Listen, sir! I will give half my belongings to the poor, and if I have cheated anyone, I will pay him back four times as much."

9 Jesus said to him, "Salvation has come to this house today, for this man, also, is a descendant of Abraham. 10 The Son of Man came to seek and to save the lost."

The Parable of the Gold Coins
(Matt. 25.14-30)

11 While the people were listening to this, Jesus

He...could not see Jesus because of the crowd (19.3)

continued and told them a parable. He was now almost at Jerusalem, and they supposed that the Kingdom of God was just about to appear. [12] So he said, "There was once a man of high rank who was going to a country far away to be made king, after which he planned to come back home. [13] Before he left, he called his ten servants and gave them each a gold coin and told them, 'See what you can earn with this while I am gone.' [14] Now, his countrymen hated him, and so they sent messengers after him to say, 'We don't want this man to be our king.'

15 "The man was made king and came back. At

once he ordered his servants to appear before him, in order to find out how much they had earned. 16 The first one came and said, 'Sir, I have earned ten gold coins with the one you gave me.' 17 'Well done,' he said; 'you are a good servant! Since you were faithful in small matters, I will put you in charge of ten cities.' 18 The second servant came and said, 'Sir, I have earned five gold coins with the one you gave me.' 19 To this one he said, 'You will be in charge of five cities.'

20 "Another servant came and said, 'Sir, here is your gold coin; I kept it hidden in a handkerchief. 21 I was afraid of you, because you are a hard man. You take what is not yours and reap what you did not sow.' 22 He said to him, 'You bad servant! I will use your own words to condemn you! You know that I am a hard man, taking what is not mine and reaping what I have not sown. 23 Well, then, why didn't you put my money in the bank? Then I would have received it back with interest when I returned.'

24 "Then he said to those who were standing there, 'Take the gold coin away from him and give it to the servant who has ten coins.' 25 But they said to him, 'Sir, he already has ten coins!' 26 'I tell you,' he replied, 'that to every person who has something, even more will be given; but the person who has nothing, even the little that he has will be taken away from him. 27 Now, as for those enemies of mine who did not want me to be their king, bring them here and kill them in my presence!' "

The Triumphant Approach to Jerusalem
(Matt. 21.1–11; Mark 11.1–11; John 12.12–19)

28 Jesus said this and then went on to Jerusalem ahead of them. 29 As he came near Bethphage and Bethany at the Mount of Olives, he sent two disciples ahead 30 with these instructions: "Go to the village there ahead of you; as you go in, you will find a colt tied up that has never been ridden. Untie it and bring it here. 31 If someone asks you why you are untying it, tell him that the Master x needs it."

x the Master; *or* its owner.

32 They went on their way and found everything just as Jesus had told them. 33 As they were untying the colt, its owners said to them, "Why are you untying it?"

34 "The Master*x* needs it," they answered, 35 and they took the colt to Jesus. Then they threw their cloaks over the animal and helped Jesus get on. 36 As he rode on, people spread their cloaks on the road.

37 When he came near Jerusalem, at the place where the road went down the Mount of Olives, the large crowd of his disciples began to thank God and praise him in loud voices for all the great things that they had seen: 38 "God bless the king who comes in the name of the Lord! Peace in heaven and glory to God!"

39 Then some of the Pharisees in the crowd spoke to Jesus. "Teacher," they said, "command your disciples to be quiet!"

40 Jesus answered, "I tell you that if they keep quiet, the stones themselves will start shouting."

Jesus Weeps over Jerusalem

41 He came closer to the city, and when he saw it, he wept over it, 42 saying, "If you only knew today what is needed for peace! But now you cannot see it! 43 The time will come when your enemies will surround you with barricades, blockade you, and close in on you from every side. 44 They will completely destroy you and the people within your walls; not a single stone will they leave in its place, because you did not recognize the time when God came to save you!"

Jesus Goes to the Temple
(Matt. 21.12–17; Mark 11.15–19; John 2.13–22)

45 Then Jesus went into the Temple and began to drive out the merchants, 46 saying to them, "It is written in the Scriptures that God said, 'My Temple will be called a house of prayer.' But you have turned it into a hideout for thieves!"

47 Every day Jesus taught in the Temple. The chief priests, the teachers of the Law, and the leaders of the people wanted to kill him, 48 but they could not

find a way to do it, because all the people kept listening to him, not wanting to miss a single word.

The Question about Jesus' Authority
(Matt. 21.23–27; Mark 11.27–33)

20 One day when Jesus was in the Temple teaching the people and preaching the Good News, the chief priests and the teachers of the Law, together with the elders, came ²and said to him, "Tell us, what right have you to do these things? Who gave you this right?"

3 Jesus answered them, "Now let me ask you a question. Tell me, ⁴did John's right to baptize come from God or from man?"

5 They started to argue among themselves, "What shall we say? If we say, 'From God,' he will say, 'Why, then, did you not believe John?' ⁶But if we say 'From man,' this whole crowd here will stone us, because they are convinced that John was a prophet." ⁷So they answered, "We don't know where it came from."

8 And Jesus said to them, "Neither will I tell you, then, by what right I do these things."

The Parable of the Tenants in the Vineyard
(Matt. 21.33–46; Mark 12.1–12)

9 Then Jesus told the people this parable: "There was once a man who planted a vineyard, let it out to tenants, and then left home for a long time. ¹⁰When the time came to gather the grapes, he sent a slave to the tenants to receive from them his share of the harvest. But the tenants beat the slave and sent him back without a thing. ¹¹So he sent another slave; but the tenants beat him also, treated him shamefully, and sent him back without a thing. ¹²Then he sent a third slave; the tenants wounded him, too, and threw him out. ¹³Then the owner of the vineyard said, 'What shall I do? I will send my own dear son; surely they will respect him!' ¹⁴But when the tenants saw him, they said to one another, 'This is the owner's son. Let's kill him, and his property will be ours!' ¹⁵So they threw him out of the vineyard and killed him.

"What, then, will the owner of the vineyard do to the tenants?" Jesus asked. 16 "He will come and kill those men, and hand the vineyard over to other tenants."

When the people heard this, they said, "Surely not!"

17 Jesus looked at them and asked, "What, then, does this scripture mean?

'The stone which the builders rejected as worthless
    turned out to be the most important of all.'

18 Everyone who falls on that stone will be cut to pieces; and if that stone falls on someone, it will crush him to dust."

The Question about Paying Taxes
(Matt. 22.15-22; Mark 12.13-17)

19 The teachers of the Law and the chief priests tried to arrest Jesus on the spot, because they knew that he had told this parable against them; but they were afraid of the people. 20 So they looked for an opportunity. They bribed some men to pretend they were sincere, and they sent them to trap Jesus with questions, so that they could hand him over to the authority and power of the Roman Governor. 21 These spies said to Jesus, "Teacher, we know that what you say and teach is right. We know that you pay no attention to a man's status, but teach the truth about God's will for man. 22 Tell us, is it against our Law for us to pay taxes to the Roman Emperor, or not?"

23 But Jesus saw through their trick and said to them, 24 "Show me a silver coin. Whose face and name are these on it?"

"The Emperor's," they answered.

25 So Jesus said, "Well, then, pay the Emperor what belongs to the Emperor, and pay God what belongs to God."

26 There before the people they could not catch him out in anything, so they kept quiet, amazed at his answer.

The Question about Rising from Death
(Matt. 22.23-33; Mark 12.18-27)

27 Then some Sadducees, who say that people will

not rise from death, came to Jesus and said,
28 "Teacher, Moses wrote this law for us: 'If a man
dies and leaves a wife but no children, that man's
brother must marry the widow so that they can have
children who will be considered the dead man's children.' 29 Once there were seven brothers; the eldest got
married and died without having children. 30 Then the
second one married the woman, 31 and then the third.
The same thing happened to all seven—they died without having children. 32 Last of all, the woman died.
33 Now, on the day when the dead rise to life, whose
wife will she be? All seven of them had married
her."

34 Jesus answered them, "The men and women of
this age marry, 35 but the men and women who are
worthy to rise from death and live in the age to
come will not then marry. 36 They will be like angels
and cannot die. They are the sons of God, because
they have risen from death. 37 And Moses clearly proves
that the dead are raised to life. In the passage about
the burning bush he speaks of the Lord as 'the God
of Abraham, the God of Isaac, and the God of Jacob.'
38 He is the God of the living, not of the dead, for
to him all are alive."

39 Some of the teachers of the Law spoke up, "A
good answer, Teacher!" 40 For they did not dare ask
him any more questions.

The Question about the Messiah
(Matt. 22.41-46; Mark 12.35-37)

41 Jesus asked them, "How can it be said that the
Messiah will be the descendant of David? 42 For David
himself says in the book of Psalms,

    'The Lord said to my Lord:
      Sit here on my right
43   until I put your enemies as a footstool under your
      feet.'

44 David called him 'Lord'; how, then, can the Messiah
be David's descendant?"

Jesus Warns against the Teachers of the Law
(Matt. 23.1-36; Mark 12.38-40)

45 As all the people listened to him, Jesus said

to his disciples, 46"Be on your guard against the teachers of the Law, who like to walk about in their long robes and love to be greeted with respect in the market-place; who choose the reserved seats in the synagogues and the best places at feasts; 47who take advantage of widows and rob them of their homes, and then make a show of saying long prayers! Their punishment will be all the worse!"

The Widow's Offering
(Mark 12.41–44)

21 Jesus looked round and saw rich men dropping their gifts in the temple treasury, 2and he also saw a very poor widow dropping in two little copper coins. 3He said, "I tell you that this poor widow put in more than all the others. 4For the others offered their gifts from what they had to spare of their riches; but she, poor as she is, gave all she had to live on."

Jesus Speaks of the Destruction of the Temple
(Matt. 24.1–2; Mark 13.1–2)

5 Some of the disciples were talking about the Temple, how beautiful it looked with its fine stones and the gifts offered to God. Jesus said, 6"All this you see—the time will come when not a single stone here will be left in its place; every one will be thrown down."

Troubles and Persecutions
(Matt. 24.3–14; Mark 13.3–13)

7 "Teacher," they asked, "when will this be? And what will happen in order to show that the time has come for it to take place?"

8 Jesus said, "Be on guard; don't be deceived. Many men, claiming to speak for me, will come and say, 'I am he!' and, 'The time has come!' But don't follow them. 9Don't be afraid when you hear of wars and revolutions; such things must happen first, but they do not mean that the end is near."

10 He went on to say, "Countries will fight each other; kingdoms will attack one another. 11There will be terrible earthquakes, famines, and plagues every-

where; there will be strange and terrifying things coming from the sky. 12 Before all these things take place, however, you will be arrested and persecuted; you will be handed over to be tried in synagogues and be put in prison; you will be brought before kings and rulers for my sake. 13 This will be your chance to tell the Good News. 14 Make up your minds beforehand not to worry about how you will defend yourselves, 15 because I will give you such words and wisdom that none of your enemies will be able to refute or contradict what you say. 16 You will be handed over by your parents, your brothers, your relatives, and your friends; and some of you will be put to death. 17 Everyone will hate you because of me. 18 But not a single hair from your heads will be lost. 19 Stand firm, and you will save yourselves.

Jesus Speaks of the Destruction of Jerusalem
(Matt. 24.15-21; Mark 13.14-19)

20 "When you see Jerusalem surrounded by armies, then you will know that she will soon be destroyed. 21 Then those who are in Judaea must run away to the hills; those who are in the city must leave, and those who are out in the country must not go into the city. 22 For those will be 'The Days of Punishment,' to make all that the Scriptures say come true. 23 How terrible it will be in those days for women who are pregnant and for mothers with little babies! Terrible distress will come upon this land, and God's punishment will fall on this people. 24 Some will be killed by the sword, and others will be taken as prisoners to all countries; and the heathen will trample over Jerusalem until their time is up.

The Coming of the Son of Man
(Matt. 24.29-31; Mark 13.24-27)

25 "There will be strange things happening to the sun, the moon, and the stars. On earth whole countries will be in despair, afraid of the roar of the sea and the raging tides. 26 People will faint from fear as they wait for what is coming over the whole earth, for the powers in space will be driven from their courses. 27 Then the Son of Man will appear, coming in a

cloud with great power and glory. 28 When these things begin to happen, stand up and raise your heads, because your salvation is near."

The Lesson of the Fig-Tree
(Matt. 24.32–35; Mark 13.28–31)

29 Then Jesus told them this parable: "Think of the fig-tree and all the other trees. 30 When you see their leaves beginning to appear, you know that summer is near. 31 In the same way, when you see these things happening, you will know that the Kingdom of God is about to come.

32 "Remember that all these things will take place before the people now living have all died. 33 Heaven and earth will pass away, but my words will never pass away.

The Need to Watch

34 "Be on your guard! Don't let yourselves become occupied with too much feasting and drinking and with the worries of this life, or that Day may suddenly catch you 35 like a trap. For it will come upon all people everywhere on earth. 36 Be on the alert and pray always that you will have the strength to go safely through all those things that will happen and to stand before the Son of Man."

37 Jesus spent those days teaching in the Temple, and when evening came, he would go out and spend the night on the Mount of Olives. 38 Early each morning all the people went to the Temple to listen to him.

The Plot against Jesus
(Matt. 26.1–5; Mark 14.1–2; John 11.45–53)

22 The time was near for the Festival of Unleavened Bread, which is called the Passover. 2 The chief priests and the teachers of the Law were afraid of the people, and so they were trying to find a way of putting Jesus to death secretly.

Judas Agrees to Betray Jesus
(Matt. 26.14–16; Mark 14.10–11)

3 Then Satan entered Judas, called Iscariot, who was one of the twelve disciples. 4 So Judas went off

and spoke with the chief priests and the officers of
the temple guard about how he could betray Jesus
to them. ⁵They were pleased and offered to pay him
money. ⁶Judas agreed to it and started looking for
a good chance to hand Jesus over to them without
the people knowing about it.

Jesus Prepares to Eat the Passover Meal
(Matt. 26.17–25; Mark 14.12–21; John 13.21–30)

7 The day came during the Festival of Unleavened
Bread when the lambs for the Passover meal were
to be killed. ⁸Jesus sent off Peter and John with
these instructions: "Go and get the Passover meal
ready for us to eat."

9 "Where do you want us to get it ready?" they
asked him.

10 He answered, "As you go into the city, a man
carrying a jar of water will meet you. Follow him
into the house that he enters, ¹¹and say to the owner
of the house: 'The Teacher says to you, Where is
the room where my disciples and I will eat the Passover
meal?' ¹²He will show you a large furnished room
upstairs, where you will get everything ready."

13 They went off and found everything just as Jesus
had told them, and they prepared the Passover meal.

The Lord's Supper
(Matt. 26.26–30; Mark 14.22–26; 1 Cor. 11.23–25)

14 When the hour came, Jesus took his place at
the table with the apostles. ¹⁵He said to them, "I
have wanted so much to eat this Passover meal with
you before I suffer! ¹⁶For I tell you, I will never
eat it until it is given its full meaning in the Kingdom
of God."

17 Then Jesus took a cup, gave thanks to God,
and said, "Take this and share it among yourselves.
¹⁸I tell you that from now on I will not drink this
wine until the Kingdom of God comes."

19 Then he took a piece of bread, gave thanks to
God, broke it, and gave it to them, saying, "This
is my body, which is given for you. Do this in memory
of me." ²⁰In the same way, he gave them the cup after

the supper, saying, "This cup is God's new covenant sealed with my blood, which is poured out for you. *y*

21 "But, look! The one who betrays me is here at the table with me! 22 The Son of Man will die as God has decided, but how terrible for that man who betrays him!"

23 Then they began to ask among themselves which one of them it could be who was going to do this.

The Argument about Greatness

24 An argument broke out among the disciples as to which one of them should be thought of as the greatest. 25 Jesus said to them, "The kings of the pagans have power over their people, and the rulers claim the title 'Friends of the People.' 26 But this is not the way it is with you; rather, the greatest one among you must be like the youngest, and the leader must be like the servant. 27 Who is greater, the one who sits down to eat or the one who serves him? The one who sits down, of course. But I am among you as one who serves.

28 "You have stayed with me all through my trials; 29 and just as my Father has given me the right to rule, so I will give you the same right. 30 You will eat and drink at my table in my Kingdom, and you will sit on thrones to rule over the twelve tribes of Israel.

Jesus Predicts Peter's Denial
(Matt. 26.31–35; Mark 14.27–31; John 13.36–38)

31 "Simon, Simon! Listen! Satan has received permission to test all of you, to separate the good from the bad, as a farmer separates the wheat from the chaff. 32 But I have prayed for you, Simon, that your faith will not fail. And when you turn back to me, you must strengthen your brothers."

33 Peter answered, "Lord, I am ready to go to prison with you and to die with you!"

34 "I tell you, Peter," Jesus said, "the cock will not crow tonight until you have said three times that you do not know me."

y Some manuscripts do not have the words of Jesus after *This is my body* in verse 19, and all of verse 20.

Purse, Bag, and Sword

35 Then Jesus asked his disciples, "When I sent you out that time without purse, bag, or shoes, did you lack anything?"

"Not a thing," they answered.

36 "But now," Jesus said, "whoever has a purse or a bag must take it; and whoever has no sword must sell his coat and buy one. 37 For I tell you that the scripture which says, 'He shared the fate of criminals,' must come true about me, because what was written about me is coming true."

38 The disciples said, "Look! Here are two swords, Lord!"

"That is enough!" [z] he replied.

Jesus Prays on the Mount of Olives
(Matt. 26.36–46; Mark 14.32–42)

39 Jesus left the city and went, as he usually did, to the Mount of Olives; and the disciples went with him. 40 When he arrived at the place, he said to them, "Pray that you will not fall into temptation."

41 Then he went off from them about the distance of a stone's throw and knelt down and prayed. 42 "Father," he said, "if you will, take this cup of suffering away from me. Not my will, however, but your will be done." 43 An angel from heaven appeared to him and strengthened him. 44 In great anguish he prayed even more fervently; his sweat was like drops of blood falling to the ground. [a]

45 Rising from his prayer, he went back to the disciples and found them asleep, worn out by their grief. 46 He said to them, "Why are you sleeping? Get up and pray that you will not fall into temptation."

The Arrest of Jesus
(Matt. 26.47–56; Mark 14.43–50; John 18.3–11)

47 Jesus was still speaking when a crowd arrived, led by Judas, one of the twelve disciples. He came

[z] That is enough; or Enough of this.
[a] Some manuscripts do not have verses 43–44.

up to Jesus to kiss him. ⁴⁸But Jesus said, "Judas, is it with a kiss that you betray the Son of Man?"

49 When the disciples who were with Jesus saw what was going to happen, they asked, "Shall we use our swords, Lord?" ⁵⁰And one of them struck the High Priest's slave and cut off his right ear.

51 But Jesus said, "Enough of this!" He touched the man's ear and healed him.

52 Then Jesus said to the chief priests and the officers of the temple guard and the elders who had come there to get him, "Did you have to come with swords and clubs, as though I were an outlaw? ⁵³I was with you in the Temple every day, and you did not try to arrest me. But this is your hour to act, when the power of darkness rules."

Peter Denies Jesus
(Matt. 26.57–58, 69–75; Mark 14.53–54, 66–72;
John 18.12–18, 25–27)

54 They arrested Jesus and took him away into the house of the High Priest; and Peter followed at a distance. ⁵⁵A fire had been lit in the centre of the courtyard, and Peter joined those who were sitting round it. ⁵⁶When one of the servant-girls saw him

This man too was with Jesus! (22.56)

sitting there at the fire, she looked straight at him and said, "This man too was with Jesus!"

57 But Peter denied it, "Woman, I don't even know him!"

58 After a little while a man noticed Peter and said, "You are one of them, too!"

But Peter answered, "Man, I am not!"

59 And about an hour later another man insisted strongly, "There isn't any doubt that this man was with Jesus, because he also is a Galilean!"

60 But Peter answered, "Man, I don't know what you are talking about!"

At once, while he was still speaking, a cock crowed. 61 The Lord turned round and looked straight at Peter, and Peter remembered that the Lord had said to him, "Before the cock crows tonight, you will say three times that you do not know me." 62 Peter went out and wept bitterly.

Jesus Is Mocked and Beaten
(Matt. 26.67-68; Mark 14.65)

63 The men who were guarding Jesus mocked him and beat him. 64 They blindfolded him and asked him, "Who hit you? Guess!" 65 And they said many other insulting things to him.

Jesus Is Brought Before the Council
(Matt. 26.59-66; Mark 14.55-64; John 18.19-24)

66 When day came, the elders, the chief priests, and the teachers of the Law met together, and Jesus was brought before the Council. 67 "Tell us," they said, "are you the Messiah?"

He answered, "If I tell you, you will not believe me; 68 and if I ask you a question, you will not answer. 69 But from now on the Son of Man will be seated on the right of Almighty God."

70 They all said, "Are you, then, the Son of God?"

He answered them, "You say that I am."

71 And they said, "We don't need any witnesses! We ourselves have heard what he said!"

Jesus Is Brought Before Pilate
(Matt. 27.1-2, 11-14; Mark 15.1-5; John 18.28-38)

23 The whole group rose up and took Jesus before Pilate, 2 where they began to accuse him: "We caught this man misleading our people, telling them not to pay taxes to the Emperor and claiming that he himself is the Messiah, a king."

3 Pilate asked him, "Are you the king of the Jews?"

"So you say," answered Jesus.

4 Then Pilate said to the chief priests and the crowds, "I find no reason to condemn this man."

5 But they insisted even more strongly, "With his teaching he is starting a riot among the people all through Judaea. He began in Galilee and now has come here."

Jesus Is Sent to Herod

6 When Pilate heard this, he asked, "Is this man a Galilean?" 7 When he learnt that Jesus was from the region ruled by Herod, he sent him to Herod, who was also in Jerusalem at that time. 8 Herod was very pleased when he saw Jesus, because he had heard about him and had been wanting to see him for a long time. He was hoping to see Jesus perform some miracle. 9 So Herod asked Jesus many questions, but Jesus made no answer. 10 The chief priests and the teachers of the Law stepped forward and made strong accusations against Jesus. 11 Herod and his soldiers mocked Jesus and treated him with contempt; then they put a fine robe on him and sent him back to Pilate. 12 On that very day Herod and Pilate became friends; before this they had been enemies.

Jesus Is Sentenced to Death
(Matt. 27.15-26; Mark 15.6-15; John 18.39-19.16)

13 Pilate called together the chief priests, the leaders, and the people, 14 and said to them, "You brought this man to me and said that he was misleading the people. Now, I have examined him here in your presence, and I have not found him guilty of any of the crimes you accuse him of. 15 Nor did Herod find him guilty, for he sent him back to us. There is

nothing this man has done to deserve death. [16]So I will have him whipped and let him go."[b]

18 The whole crowd cried out, "Kill him! Set Barabbas free for us!" [19](Barabbas had been put in prison for a riot that had taken place in the city, and for murder.)

20 Pilate wanted to set Jesus free, so he appealed to the crowd again. [21]But they shouted back, "Crucify him! Crucify him!"

22 Pilate said to them the third time, "But what crime has he committed? I cannot find anything he has done to deserve death! I will have him whipped and set him free."

23 But they kept on shouting at the top of their voices that Jesus should be crucified, and finally their shouting succeeded. [24]So Pilate passed the sentence on Jesus that they were asking for. [25]He set free the man they wanted, the one who had been put in prison for riot and murder, and he handed Jesus over for them to do as they wished.

Jesus Is Crucified
(Matt. 27.32–44; Mark 15.21–32; John 19.17–27)

26 The soldiers led Jesus away, and as they were going, they met a man from Cyrene named Simon who was coming into the city from the country. They seized him, put the cross on him, and made him carry it behind Jesus.

27 A large crowd of people followed him; among them were some women who were weeping and wailing for him. [28]Jesus turned to them and said, "Women of Jerusalem! Don't cry for me, but for yourselves and your children. [29]For the days are coming when people will say, 'How lucky are the women who never had children, who never bore babies, who never nursed them!' [30]That will be the time when people will say to the mountains, 'Fall on us!' and to the hills, 'Hide us!' [31]For if such things as these are done when the wood is green, what will happen when it is dry?"

32 Two other men, both of them criminals, were

[b] Some manuscripts add verse 17: At every Passover Festival Pilate had to set free one prisoner for them (see Mk 15.6).

They...put the cross on him, and made him carry it (23.26)

also led out to be put to death with Jesus. [33]When they came to the place called "The Skull," they crucified Jesus there, and the two criminals, one on his right and the other on his left. [34]Jesus said, "Forgive them, Father! They don't know what they are doing."[c]

They divided his clothes among themselves by throwing dice. [35]The people stood there watching while the Jewish leaders jeered at him: "He saved others; let him save himself if he is the Messiah whom God has chosen!"

[36]The soldiers also mocked him: they came up to him and offered him cheap wine, [37]and said, "Save yourself if you are the king of the Jews!"

[38]Above him were written these words: "This is the King of the Jews."

[39]One of the criminals hanging there hurled insults at him: "Aren't you the Messiah? Save yourself and us!"

[40]The other one, however, rebuked him, saying "Don't you fear God? You received the same sentence he did. [41]Ours, however, is only right, because we are getting what we deserve for what we did; but

[c]*Some manuscripts do not have* Jesus said, "Forgive them, Father! They don't know what they are doing."

he has done no wrong." 42 And he said to Jesus, "Remember me, Jesus, when you come as King!"

43 Jesus said to him, "I promise you that today you will be in Paradise with me."

The Death of Jesus
(Matt. 27.45–56; Mark 15.33–41; John 19.28–30)

44 It was about twelve o'clock when the sun stopped shining and darkness covered the whole country until three o'clock; 45 and the curtain hanging in the Temple was torn in two. 46 Jesus cried out in a loud voice,

Father! In your hands I place my spirit! (23.46)

"Father! In your hands I place my spirit!" He said this and died.

47 The army officer saw what had happened, and he praised God, saying, "Certainly he was a good man!"

48 When the people who had gathered there to watch the spectacle saw what happened, they all went back home, beating their breasts in sorrow. 49 All those who knew Jesus personally, including the women who had followed him from Galilee, stood at a distance to watch.

The Burial of Jesus
(Matt. 27.57–61; Mark 15.42–47; John 19.38–42)

50–51 There was a man named Joseph from Arimathea, a town in Judaea. He was a good and honourable man, who was waiting for the coming of the Kingdom of God. Although he was a member of the Council, he had not agreed with their decision and action. ⁵²He went into the presence of Pilate and asked for the body of Jesus. ⁵³Then he took the body down, wrapped it in a linen sheet, and placed it in a tomb which had been dug out of solid rock and which had never been used. ⁵⁴It was Friday, and the Sabbath was about to begin.

55 The women who had followed Jesus from Galilee went with Joseph and saw the tomb and how Jesus' body was placed in it. ⁵⁶Then they went back home and prepared the spices and perfumes for the body.

On the Sabbath they rested, as the Law commanded.

The Resurrection
(Matt. 28.1–10; Mark 16.1–8; John 20.1–10)

24 Very early on Sunday morning the women went to the tomb, carrying the spices they had prepared. ²They found the stone rolled away from the entrance to the tomb, ³so they went in; but they did not find the body of the Lord Jesus. ⁴They stood there puzzled about this, when suddenly two men in bright shining clothes stood by them. ⁵Full of fear, the women bowed down to the ground, as the men said to them, "Why are you looking among the dead for one who is alive? ⁶He is not here; he has been raised. Remember what he said to you while he was in Galilee: ⁷'The Son of Man must be handed over to sinful men, be crucified, and three days later rise to life.' "

8 Then the women remembered his words, ⁹returned from the tomb, and told all these things to the eleven disciples and all the rest. ¹⁰The women were Mary Magdalene, Joanna, and Mary the mother of James; they and the other women with them told these things to the apostles. ¹¹But the apostles thought that what the women said was nonsense, and they did not believe them. ¹²But Peter got up and ran to the tomb; he bent down and saw the linen wrappings but nothing else. Then he went back home amazed at what had happened. *d*

d Some manuscripts do not have verse 12.

He is not here; he has been raised (24.6)

The Walk to Emmaus
(Mark 16.12–13)

13 On that same day two of Jesus' followers were going to a village named Emmaus, about eleven kilometres from Jerusalem, ¹⁴and they were talking to each other about all the things that had happened. ¹⁵As they talked and discussed, Jesus himself drew near and walked along with them; ¹⁶they saw him, but somehow did not recognize him. ¹⁷Jesus said to them, "What are you talking about to each other, as you walk along?"

They stood still, with sad faces. ¹⁸One of them, named Cleopas, asked him, "Are you the only visitor in Jerusalem who doesn't know the things that have been happening there these last few days?"

19 "What things?" he asked.

"The things that happened to Jesus of Nazareth," they answered. "This man was a prophet and was considered by God and by all the people to be powerful in everything he said and did. ²⁰Our chief priests and rulers handed him over to be sentenced to death, and he was crucified. ²¹And we had hoped that he would be the one who was going to set Israel free! Besides all that, this is now the third day since it happened. [22] Some of the women of our group surprised us; they went at dawn to the tomb, [23] but could not find his body. They came back saying they had seen a vision of angels who told them that he is alive. [24] Some of our group went to the tomb and found it exactly as the women had said, but they did not see him."

25 Then Jesus said to them, "How foolish you are, how slow you are to believe everything the prophets said! [26] Was it not necessary for the Messiah to suffer these things and then to enter his glory?" [27] And Jesus explained to them what was said about himself in all the Scriptures, beginning with the books of Moses and the writings of all the prophets.

28 As they came near the village to which they were going, Jesus acted as if he were going farther; [29] but they held him back, saying, "Stay with us; the day is almost over and it is getting dark." So he went in to stay with them. [30] He sat down to eat with them, took the bread, and said the blessing; then he broke the bread and gave it to them. [31] Then their eyes were opened and they recognized him, but he disappeared from their sight. [32] They said to each other, "Wasn't it like a fire burning in us when he talked to us on the road and explained the Scriptures to us?"

33 They got up at once and went back to Jerusalem, where they found the eleven disciples gathered together with the others [34] and saying, "The Lord is risen indeed! He has appeared to Simon!"

35 The two then explained to them what had happened on the road, and how they had recognized the Lord when he broke the bread.

Jesus Appears to His Disciples
(Matt. 28.16–20; Mark 16.14–18; John 20.19–23; Acts 1.6–8)

36 While the two were telling them this, suddenly the Lord himself stood among them and said to them, "Peace be with you." [e]

37 They were terrified, thinking that they were seeing

[e] Some manuscripts do not have and said to them, "Peace be with you."

a ghost. 38 But he said to them, "Why are you alarmed? Why are these doubts coming up in your minds? 39 Look at my hands and my feet, and see that it is I myself. Feel me, and you will know, for a ghost doesn't have flesh and bones, as you can see I have."

40 He said this and showed them his hands and his feet.f 41 They still could not believe, they were so full of joy and wonder; so he asked them, "Have you anything here to eat?" 42 They gave him a piece of cooked fish, 43 which he took and ate in their presence.

44 Then he said to them, "These are the very things I told you about while I was still with you: everything written about me in the Law of Moses, the writings of the prophets, and the Psalms had to come true."

45 Then he opened their minds to understand the Scriptures, 46 and said to them, "This is what is written: the Messiah must suffer and must rise from death three days later, 47 and in his name the message about repentance and the forgiveness of sins must be preached to all nations, beginning in Jerusalem. 48 You are witnesses of these things. 49 And I myself will send upon you what my Father has promised. But you must wait in the city until the power from above comes down upon you."

Jesus Is Taken up to Heaven
(Mark 16.19-20; Acts 1.9-11)

50 Then he led them out of the city as far as Bethany, where he raised his hands and blessed them. 51 As he was blessing them, he departed from them and was taken up into heaven.g 52 They worshipped him and went back into Jerusalem, filled with great joy, 53 and spent all their time in the Temple giving thanks to God.

---

f Some manuscripts do not have verse 40.

g Some manuscripts do not have and was taken up into heaven.

THE GOSPEL ACCORDING TO

JOHN

INTRODUCTION

The Gospel according to John presents Jesus as the eternal Word of God, who "became a human being and lived among us." As the book itself says, this Gospel was written so that its readers might believe that Jesus is the promised Saviour, the Son of God, and that through their faith in him they might have life (20.31).

After an introduction that identifies the eternal Word of God with Jesus, the first part of the Gospel presents various miracles which show that Jesus is the promised Saviour, the Son of God. These are followed by discourses that explain what is revealed by the miracles. This part of the book tells how some people believed in Jesus and became his followers, while others opposed him and refused to believe. Chapters 13–17 record at length the close fellowship of Jesus with his disciples on the night of his arrest, and his words of preparation and encouragement to them on the eve of his crucifixion. The closing chapters tell of Jesus' arrest and trial, his crucifixion and resurrection, and his appearances to his disciples after the resurrection.

The story of the woman caught in adultery (8.1–11) is placed in brackets because many manuscripts and early translations omit it, while others include it in other places.

John emphasizes the gift of eternal life through Christ, a gift which begins now and which comes to those who respond to Jesus as the way, the truth, and the life. A striking feature of *John* is the symbolic use of common things from everyday life to point to spiritual realities, such as water, bread, light, the shepherd and his sheep, and the grapevine and its fruit.

Outline of Contents

The Word of Life

1 Before the world was created, the Word already existed; he was with God, and he was the same as God. ²From the very beginning the Word was with God. ³Through him God made all things; not one thing in all creation was made without him. ⁴The Word was the source of life,ᵃ and this life brought light to mankind. ⁵The light shines in the darkness, and the darkness has never put it out.

6 God sent his messenger, a man named John, ⁷who came to tell people about the light, so that all should hear the message and believe. ⁸He himself was not the light; he came to tell about the light. ⁹This was the real light—the light that comes into the world and shines on all mankind.

10 The Word was in the world, and though God made the world through him, yet the world did not recognize him. ¹¹He came to his own country, but his own people did not receive him. ¹²Some, however, did receive him and believed in him; so he gave them the right to become God's children. ¹³They did not become God's children by natural means, that is, by being born as the children of a human father; God himself was their Father.

14 The Word became a human being and, full of

ᵃThe Word was the source of life; *or* What was made had life in union with the Word.

grace and truth, lived among us. We saw his glory,
the glory which he received as the Father's only Son.

15 John spoke about him. He cried out, "This is
the one I was talking about when I said, 'He comes
after me, but he is greater than I am, because he
existed before I was born.'"

16 Out of the fullness of his grace he has blessed
us all, giving us one blessing after another. [17] God
gave the Law through Moses, but grace and truth
came through Jesus Christ. [18] No one has ever seen
God. The only Son, who is the same as God and
is at the Father's side, he has made him known.

John the Baptist's Message
(Matt. 3.1-12; Mark 1.1-8; Luke 3.1-18)

19 The Jewish authorities in Jerusalem sent some
priests and Levites to John, to ask him, "Who are
you?"

20 John did not refuse to answer, but spoke out
openly and clearly, saying: "I am not the Messiah."

21 "Who are you, then?" they asked. "Are you
Elijah?"

"No, I am not," John answered.

"Are you the Prophet?" [b] they asked.

"No," he replied.

22 "Then tell us who you are," they said. "We have
to take an answer back to those who sent us. What
do you say about yourself?"

23 John answered by quoting the prophet Isaiah:
" I am 'the voice of someone shouting in the desert:
Make a straight path for the Lord to travel!'"

24 The messengers, who had been sent by the Pharisees, [25] then [c] asked John, "If you are not the Messiah
nor Elijah nor the Prophet, why do you baptize?"

26 John answered, "I baptize with water, but among
you stands the one you do not know. [27] He is coming
after me, but I am not good enough even to untie
his sandals."

---

[b] THE PROPHET: *The one who was expected to appear and
announce the coming of the Messiah.*
[c] The messengers, who had been sent by the Pharisees, then; *or*
Those who had been sent were Pharisees; they.

28 All this happened in Bethany on the east side of the River Jordan, where John was baptizing.

The Lamb of God

29 The next day John saw Jesus coming to him, and said, "There is the Lamb of God, who takes away the sin of the world! 30 This is the one I was talking about when I said, 'A man is coming after me, but he is greater than I am, because he existed before I was born.' 31 I did not know who he would be, but I came baptizing with water in order to make him known to the people of Israel."

32 And John gave this testimony: "I saw the Spirit come down like a dove from heaven and stay on him. 33 I still did not know that he was the one, but God, who sent me to baptize with water, had said to me, 'You will see the Spirit come down and stay on a man; he is the one who baptizes with the Holy Spirit.' 34 I have seen it," said John, "and I tell you that he is the Son of God."

The First Disciples of Jesus

35 The next day John was standing there again with two of his disciples, 36 when he saw Jesus walking by. "There is the Lamb of God!" he said.

37 The two disciples heard him say this and went with Jesus. 38 Jesus turned, saw them following him, and asked, "What are you looking for?"

They answered, "Where do you live, Rabbi?" (This word means "Teacher.")

39 "Come and see," he answered. (It was then about four o'clock in the afternoon.) So they went with him and saw where he lived, and spent the rest of that day with him.

40 One of them was Andrew, Simon Peter's brother. 41 At once he found his brother Simon and told him, "We have found the Messiah." (This word means "Christ.") 42 Then he took Simon to Jesus.

Jesus looked at him and said, "Your name is Simon son of John, but you will be called Cephas." (This is the same as Peter and means "a rock.")

I saw the Spirit come down like a dove (1.32)

Jesus Calls Philip and Nathanael

43 The next day Jesus decided to go to Galilee. He found Philip and said to him, "Come with me!" 44 (Philip was from Bethsaida, the town where Andrew and Peter lived.) 45 Philip found Nathanael and told him, "We have found the one whom Moses wrote

about in the book of the Law and whom the prophets also wrote about. He is Jesus son of Joseph, from Nazareth."

46 "Can anything good come from Nazareth?" Nathanael asked.

"Come and see," answered Philip.

47 When Jesus saw Nathanael coming to him, he said about him, "Here is a real Israelite; there is nothing false in him!"

48 Nathanael asked him, "How do you know me?"

Jesus answered, "I saw you when you were under the fig-tree before Philip called you."

49 "Teacher," answered Nathanael, "you are the Son of God! You are the King of Israel!"

50 Jesus said, "Do you believe just because I told you I saw you when you were under the fig-tree? You will see much greater things than this!" 51 And he said to them, "I am telling you the truth: you will see heaven open and God's angels going up and coming down on the Son of Man."

The Wedding in Cana

2 Two days later there was a wedding in the town of Cana in Galilee. Jesus' mother was there, 2 and Jesus and his disciples had also been invited to the wedding. 3 When the wine had given out, Jesus' mother said to him, "They have no wine left."

4 "You must not tell me what to do," Jesus replied. "My time has not yet come."

5 Jesus' mother then told the servants, "Do whatever he tells you."

6 The Jews have rules about ritual washing, and for this purpose six stone water jars were there, each one large enough to hold about a hundred litres. 7 Jesus said to the servants, "Fill these jars with water." They filled them to the brim, 8 and then he told them, "Now draw some water out and take it to the man in charge of the feast." They took him the water, 9 which now had turned into wine, and he tasted it. He did not know where this wine had come from (but, of course, the servants who had drawn out the water knew); so he called the bridegroom 10 and said to him, "Everyone else serves the best wine first, and

Fill these jars with water (2.7)

after the guests have had plenty to drink, he serves the ordinary wine. But you have kept the best wine until now!"

11 Jesus performed this first miracle in Cana in Galilee; there he revealed his glory, and his disciples believed in him.

12 After this, Jesus and his mother, brothers, and disciples went to Capernaum and stayed there a few days.

Jesus Goes to the Temple
(Matt. 21.12-13; Mark 11.15-17; Luke 19.45-46)

13 It was almost time for the Passover Festival, so Jesus went to Jerusalem. 14 There in the Temple he found men selling cattle, sheep, and pigeons, and also the money-changers sitting at their tables. 15 So he made a whip from cords and drove all the animals out of the Temple, both the sheep and the cattle;

he overturned the tables of the money-changers and scattered their coins; 16 and he ordered the men who sold the pigeons, "Take them out of here! Stop making my Father's house a market-place!" 17 His disciples remembered that the scripture says, "My devotion to your house, O God, burns in me like a fire."

18 The Jewish authorities replied with a question, "What miracle can you perform to show us that you have the right to do this?"

19 Jesus answered, "Tear down this Temple, and in three days I will build it again."

20 "Are you going to build it again in three days?" they asked him. "It has taken forty-six years to build this Temple!"

21 But the temple Jesus was speaking about was his body. 22 So when he was raised from death, his disciples remembered that he had said this, and they believed the scripture and what Jesus had said.

Jesus' Knowledge of Human Nature

23 While Jesus was in Jerusalem during the Passover Festival, many believed in him as they saw the miracles he performed. 24 But Jesus did not trust himself to them, because he knew them all. 25 There was no need for anyone to tell him about them, because he himself knew what was in their hearts.

Jesus and Nicodemus

3 There was a Jewish leader named Nicodemus, who belonged to the party of the Pharisees. 2 One night he went to Jesus and said to him, "Rabbi, we know that you are a teacher sent by God. No one could perform the miracles you are doing unless God were with him."

3 Jesus answered, "I am telling you the truth: no one can see the Kingdom of God unless he is born again."*d*

4 "How can a grown man be born again?" Nicodemus asked. "He certainly cannot enter his mother's womb and be born a second time!"

5 "I am telling you the truth," replied Jesus. "No

*d*again; *or* from above.

one can enter the Kingdom of God unless he is born of water and the Spirit. 6 A person is born physically of human parents, but he is born spiritually of the Spirit. 7 Do not be surprised because I tell you that you must all be born again.[e] 8 The wind blows wherever it wishes; you hear the sound it makes, but you do not know where it comes from or where it is going. It is like that with everyone who is born of the Spirit."

9 "How can this be?" asked Nicodemus.

10 Jesus answered, "You are a great teacher in Israel, and you don't know this? 11 I am telling you the truth: we speak of what we know and report what we have seen, yet none of you is willing to accept our message. 12 You do not believe me when I tell you about the things of this world; how will you ever believe me, then, when I tell you about the things of heaven? 13 And no one has ever gone up to heaven except the Son of Man, who came down from heaven."[x]

14 As Moses lifted up the bronze snake on a pole in the desert, in the same way the Son of Man must be lifted up, 15 so that everyone who believes in him may have eternal life. 16 For God loved the world so much that he gave his only Son, so that everyone who believes in him may not die but have eternal life. 17 For God did not send his Son into the world to be its judge, but to be its saviour.

18 Whoever believes in the Son is not judged; but whoever does not believe has already been judged, because he has not believed in God's only Son. 19 This is how the judgement works: the light has come into the world, but people love the darkness rather than the light, because their deeds are evil. 20 Anyone who does evil things hates the light and will not come to the light, because he does not want his evil deeds to be shown up. 21 But whoever does what is true comes to the light in order that the light may show that what he did was in obedience to God.

[e] again; or from above.
[x] The quotation may continue through verse 21.

Jesus and John

22 After this, Jesus and his disciples went to the
province of Judaea, where he spent some time with
them and baptized. 23 John also was baptizing in Aenon,
not far from Salim, because there was plenty of water
in that place. People were going to him, and he was
baptizing them. 24 (This was before John had been
put in prison.)

25 Some of John's disciples began arguing with a
Jew[f] about the matter of ritual washing. 26 So they
went to John and said, "Teacher, you remember the
man who was with you on the east side of the Jordan,
the one you spoke about? Well, he is baptizing now,
and everyone is going to him!"

27 John answered, "No one can have anything unless
God gives it to him. 28 You yourselves are my witnesses
that I said, 'I am not the Messiah, but I have been
sent ahead of him.' 29 The bridegroom is the one to
whom the bride belongs; but the bridegroom's friend,
who stands by and listens, is glad when he hears
the bridegroom's voice. This is how my own happiness
is made complete. 30 He must become more important
while I become less important."

He Who Comes from Heaven

31 He who comes from above is greater than all.
He who is from the earth belongs to the earth and
speaks about earthly matters, but he who comes from
heaven is above all. 32 He tells what he has seen
and heard, yet no one accepts his message. 33 But
whoever accepts his message confirms by this that
God is truthful. 34 The one whom God has sent speaks
God's words, because God gives him the fullness of his
Spirit. 35 The Father loves his Son and has put everything in his power. 36 Whoever believes in the Son
has eternal life; whoever disobeys the Son will not
have life, but will remain under God's punishment.

[f] a Jew; *some manuscripts have* some Jews.

Jesus and the Samaritan Woman

4 The Pharisees heard that Jesus was winning and baptizing more disciples than John. [2](Actually, Jesus himself did not baptize anyone; only his disciples did.) [3]So when Jesus heard what was being said, he left Judaea and went back to Galilee; [4]on his way there he had to go through Samaria.

5 In Samaria he came to a town named Sychar, which was not far from the field that Jacob had given to his son Joseph. [6]Jacob's well was there, and Jesus, tired out by the journey, sat down by the well. It was about noon.

7 A Samaritan woman came to draw some water,

Give me a drink of water (4.7)

and Jesus said to her, "Give me a drink of water." [8](His disciples had gone into town to buy food.)

9 The woman answered, "You are a Jew, and I am a Samaritan—so how can you ask me for a drink?" (Jews will not use the same cups and bowls that Samaritans use.)[g]

10 Jesus answered, "If only you knew what God

[g]Jews will not use the same cups and bowls that Samaritans use; *or* Jews will have nothing to do with Samaritans.

gives and who it is that is asking you for a drink, you would ask him, and he would give you life-giving water."

11 "Sir," the woman said, "you haven't got a bucket, and the well is deep. Where would you get that life-giving water? 12 It was our ancestor Jacob who gave us this well; he and his sons and his flocks all drank from it. You don't claim to be greater than Jacob, do you?"

13 Jesus answered, "Whoever drinks this water will be thirsty again, 14 but whoever drinks the water that I will give him will never be thirsty again. The water that I will give him will become in him a spring which will provide him with life-giving water and give him eternal life."

15 "Sir," the woman said, "give me that water! Then I will never be thirsty again, nor will I have to come here to draw water."

16 "Go and call your husband," Jesus told her, "and come back."

17 "I haven't got a husband," she answered.

Jesus replied, "You are right when you say you haven't got a husband. 18 You have been married to five men, and the man you live with now is not really your husband. You have told me the truth."

19 "I see you are a prophet, sir," the woman said. 20 "My Samaritan ancestors worshipped God on this mountain, but you Jews say that Jerusalem is the place where we should worship God."

21 Jesus said to her, "Believe me, woman, the time will come when people will not worship the Father either on this mountain or in Jerusalem. 22 You Samaritans do not really know whom you worship; but we Jews know whom we worship, because it is from the Jews that salvation comes. 23 But the time is coming and is already here, when by the power of God's Spirit people will worship the Father as he really is, offering him the true worship that he wants. 24 God is Spirit, and only by the power of his Spirit can people worship him as he really is."

25 The woman said to him, "I know that the Messiah will come, and when he comes, he will tell us everything."

26 Jesus answered, "I am he, I who am talking with you."

27 At that moment Jesus' disciples returned, and they were greatly surprised to find him talking with a woman. But none of them said to her, "What do you want?" or asked him, "Why are you talking with her?"

28 Then the woman left her water jar, went back to the town, and said to the people there, 29 "Come and see the man who told me everything I have ever done. Could he be the Messiah?" 30 So they left the town and went to Jesus.

31 In the meantime the disciples were begging Jesus, "Teacher, have something to eat!"

32 But he answered, "I have food to eat that you know nothing about."

33 So the disciples started asking among themselves, "Could somebody have brought him food?"

34 "My food," Jesus said to them, "is to obey the will of the one who sent me and to finish the work he gave me to do. 35 You have a saying, 'Four more months and then the harvest.' But I tell you, take a good look at the fields; the crops are now ripe and ready to be harvested! 36 The man who reaps the harvest is being paid and gathers the crops for eternal life; so the man who sows and the man who reaps will be glad together. 37 The saying is true, 'One man sows, another man reaps.' 38 I have sent you to reap a harvest in a field where you did not work; others worked there, and you profit from their work."

39 Many of the Samaritans in that town believed in Jesus because the woman had said, "He told me everything I have ever done." 40 So when the Samaritans came to him, they begged him to stay with them, and Jesus stayed there two days.

41 Many more believed because of his message, 42 and they said to the woman, "We believe now, not because of what you said, but because we ourselves have heard him, and we know that he really is the Saviour of the world."

Jesus Heals an Official's Son

43 After spending two days there, Jesus left and

went to Galilee. [44] For he himself had said, "A prophet
is not respected in his own country." [45] When he arrived
in Galilee, the people there welcomed him, because
they had gone to the Passover Festival in Jerusalem
and had seen everything that he had done during
the festival.

46 Then Jesus went back to Cana in Galilee, where
he had turned the water into wine. A government
official was there whose son was ill in Capernaum.
[47] When he heard that Jesus had come from Judaea
to Galilee, he went to him and asked him to go
to Capernaum and heal his son, who was about to
die. [48] Jesus said to him, "None of you will ever believe
unless you see miracles and wonders."

49 "Sir," replied the official, "come with me before
my child dies."

50 Jesus said to him, "Go, your son will live!"

The man believed Jesus' words and went. [51] On his
way home his servants met him with the news, "Your
boy is going to live!"

52 He asked them what time it was when his son
got better, and they answered, "It was one o'clock
yesterday afternoon when the fever left him." [53] Then
the father remembered that it was at that very hour
when Jesus had told him, "Your son will live." So
he and all his family believed.

54 This was the second miracle that Jesus performed
after coming from Judaea to Galilee.

The Healing at the Pool

5 After this, Jesus went to Jerusalem for a religious
festival. [2] Near the Sheep Gate in Jerusalem there
is a pool [h] with five porches; in Hebrew it is called
Bethzatha. [i] [3] A large crowd of sick people were lying
in the porches—the blind, the lame, and the paralysed. [j]

---

[h] Near the Sheep Gate...a pool; or Near the Sheep Pool...a place.
[i] Bethzatha; some manuscripts have Bethesda.
[j] Some manuscripts add verses 3b–4: They were waiting for the
water to move, [4] because every now and then an angel of the
Lord went down into the pool and stirred up the water. The first
sick person to go into the pool after the water was stirred up
was healed from whatever disease he had.

5 A man was there who had been ill for thirty-eight years. 6 Jesus saw him lying there, and he knew that the man had been ill for such a long time; so he asked him, "Do you want to get well?"

7 The sick man answered, "Sir, I have no one here to put me in the pool when the water is stirred up; while I am trying to get in, somebody else gets there first."

8 Jesus said to him, "Get up, pick up your mat, and walk." 9 Immediately the man got well; he picked up his mat and started walking.

The day this happened was a Sabbath, 10 so the Jewish authorities told the man who had been healed, "This is a Sabbath, and it is against our Law for you to carry your mat."

11 He answered, "The man who made me well told me to pick up my mat and walk."

12 They asked him, "Who is the man who told you to do this?"

13 But the man who had been healed did not know who Jesus was, for there was a crowd in that place, and Jesus had slipped away.

14 Afterwards, Jesus found him in the Temple and said, "Listen, you are well now; so stop sinning or something worse may happen to you."

15 Then the man left and told the Jewish authorities that it was Jesus who had healed him. 16 So they began to persecute Jesus, because he had done this healing on a Sabbath. 17 Jesus answered them, "My Father is always working, and I too must work."

18 This saying made the Jewish authorities all the more determined to kill him; not only had he broken the Sabbath law, but he had said that God was his own Father and in this way had made himself equal with God.

The Authority of the Son

19 So Jesus answered them, "I am telling you the truth: the Son can do nothing on his own; he does only what he sees his Father doing. What the Father does, the Son also does. 20 For the Father loves the Son and shows him all that he himself is doing. He will show him even greater things to do than this, and

you will all be amazed. 21 Just as the Father raises the dead and gives them life, in the same way the Son gives life to those he wants to. 22 Nor does the Father himself judge anyone. He has given his Son the full right to judge, 23 so that all will honour the Son in the same way as they honour the Father. Whoever does not honour the Son does not honour the Father who sent him.

24 "I am telling you the truth: whoever hears my words and believes in him who sent me has eternal life. He will not be judged, but has already passed from death to life. 25 I am telling you the truth: the time is coming—the time has already come—when the dead will hear the voice of the Son of God, and those who hear it will come to life. 26 Just as the Father is himself the source of life, in the same way he has made his Son to be the source of life. 27 And he has given the Son the right to judge, because he is the Son of Man. 28 Do not be surprised at this; the time is coming when all the dead will hear his voice 29 and come out of their graves: those who have done good will rise and live, and those who have done evil will rise and be condemned.

Witnesses to Jesus

30 "I can do nothing on my own authority; I judge only as God tells me, so my judgement is right, because I am not trying to do what I want, but only what he who sent me wants.

31 "If I testify on my own behalf, what I say is not to be accepted as real proof. 32 But there is someone else who testifies on my behalf, and I know that what he says about me is true. 33 John is the one to whom you sent your messengers, and he spoke on behalf of the truth. 34 It is not that I must have a man's witness; I say this only in order that you may be saved. 35 John was like a lamp, burning and shining, and you were willing for a while to enjoy his light. 36 But I have a witness on my behalf which is even greater than the witness that John gave: what I do, that is, the deeds my Father gave me to do, these speak on my behalf and show that the Father has sent me. 37 And the Father, who sent me, also

testifies on my behalf. You have never heard his voice or seen his face, ³⁸ and you do not keep his message in your hearts, for you do not believe in the one whom he sent. ³⁹ You study the Scriptures, because you think that in them you will find eternal life. And these very Scriptures speak about me! ⁴⁰ Yet you are not willing to come to me in order to have life.

41 "I am not looking for human praise. ⁴² But I know what kind of people you are, and I know that you have no love for God in your hearts. ⁴³ I have come with my Father's authority, but you have not received me; when, however, someone comes with his own authority, you will receive him. ⁴⁴ You like to receive praise from one another, but you do not try to win praise from the one who alone is God; how, then, can you believe me? ⁴⁵ Do not think, however, that I am the one who will accuse you to my Father. Moses, in whom you have put your hope, is the very one who will accuse you. ⁴⁶ If you had really believed Moses, you would have believed me, because he wrote about me. ⁴⁷ But since you do not believe what he wrote, how can you believe what I say?"

Jesus Feeds Five Thousand Men
(Matt. 14.13–21; Mark 6.30–44; Luke 9.10–17)

6 After this, Jesus went across Lake Galilee (or, Lake Tiberias, as it is also called). ² A large crowd followed him, because they had seen his miracles of healing those who were ill. ³ Jesus went up a hill and sat down with his disciples. ⁴ The time for the Passover Festival was near. ⁵ Jesus looked round and saw that a large crowd was coming to him, so he asked Philip, "Where can we buy enough food to feed all these people?" ⁶ (He said this to test Philip; actually he already knew what he would do.)

7 Philip answered, "For everyone to have even a little, it would take more than two hundred silver coins^k to buy enough bread."

---

^k SILVER COINS: *A silver coin was the daily wage of a rural worker (see Mt 20.2).*

8 Another of his disciples, Andrew, who was Simon Peter's brother, said, 9"There is a boy here who has five loaves of barley bread and two fish. But they will certainly not be enough for all these people."

10 "Make the people sit down," Jesus told them. (There was a lot of grass there.) So all the people sat down; there were about five thousand men. 11 Jesus took the bread, gave thanks to God, and distributed it to the people who were sitting there. He did the same with the fish, and they all had as much as they wanted. 12 When they were all full, he said to his disciples, "Gather the pieces left over; let us not waste any." 13 So they gathered them all up and filled twelve baskets with the pieces left over from the five barley loaves which the people had eaten.

14 Seeing this miracle that Jesus had performed, the people there said, "Surely this is the Prophet*l* who was to come into the world!" 15 Jesus knew that they were about to come and seize him in order to make him king by force; so he went off again to the hills by himself.

Jesus Walks on the Water
(Matt. 14.22–33; Mark 6.45–52)

16 When evening came, Jesus' disciples went down to the lake, 17 got into a boat, and went back across the lake towards Capernaum. Night came on, and Jesus still had not come to them. 18 By then a strong wind was blowing and stirring up the water. 19 The disciples had rowed about five or six kilometres when they saw Jesus walking on the water, coming near the boat, and they were terrified. 20"Don't be afraid," Jesus told them, "it is I!" 21 Then they willingly took him into the boat, and immediately the boat reached land at the place they were heading for.

The People Seek Jesus

22 Next day the crowd which had stayed on the other side of the lake realized that there had been only one boat there. They knew that Jesus had not gone in it with his disciples, but that they had left

*l*THE PROPHET: *See 1.21.*

without him. [23] Other boats, which were from Tiberias, came to shore near the place where the crowd had eaten the bread after the Lord had given thanks. [24] When the crowd saw that Jesus was not there, nor his disciples, they got into those boats and went to Capernaum, looking for him.

Jesus the Bread of Life

25 When the people found Jesus on the other side of the lake, they said to him, "Teacher, when did you get here?"

26 Jesus answered, "I am telling you the truth: you are looking for me because you ate the bread and had all you wanted, not because you understood my miracles. [27] Do not work for food that goes bad; instead, work for the food that lasts for eternal life. This is the food which the Son of Man will give you, because God, the Father, has put his mark of approval on him."

28 So they asked him, "What can we do in order to do what God wants us to do?"

29 Jesus answered, "What God wants you to do is to believe in the one he sent."

30 They replied, "What miracle will you perform so that we may see it and believe you? What will you do? [31] Our ancestors ate manna in the desert, just as the scripture says, 'He gave them bread from heaven to eat.'"

32 "I am telling you the truth," Jesus said. "What Moses gave you was not[m] the bread from heaven; it is my Father who gives you the real bread from heaven. [33] For the bread that God gives is he who comes down from heaven and gives life to the world."

34 "Sir," they asked him, "give us this bread always."

35 "I am the bread of life," Jesus told them. "He who comes to me will never be hungry; he who believes in me will never be thirsty. [36] Now, I told you that you have seen me but will not believe. [37] Everyone whom my Father gives me will come to me. I will never turn away anyone who comes to me,

---

[m] What Moses gave you was not; or It was not Moses who gave you.

38because I have come down from heaven to do not my own will but the will of him who sent me. 39And it is the will of him who sent me that I should not lose any of all those he has given me, but that I should raise them all to life on the last day. 40For what my Father wants is that all who see the Son and believe in him should have eternal life. And I will raise them to life on the last day."

41 The people started grumbling about him, because he said, "I am the bread that came down from heaven." 42So they said, "This man is Jesus son of Joseph, isn't he? We know his father and mother. How, then, does he now say he came down from heaven?"

43 Jesus answered, "Stop grumbling among yourselves. 44No one can come to me unless the Father who sent me draws him to me; and I will raise him to life on the last day. 45The prophets wrote, 'Everyone will be taught by God.' Anyone who hears the Father and learns from him comes to me. 46This does not mean that anyone has seen the Father; he who is from God is the only one who has seen the Father. 47I am telling you the truth: he who believes has eternal life. 48I am the bread of life. 49Your ancestors ate manna in the desert, but they died. 50But the bread that comes down from heaven is of such a kind that whoever eats it will not die. 51I am the living bread that came down from heaven. If anyone eats this bread, he will live for ever. The bread that I will give him is my flesh, which I give so that the world may live."

52 This started an angry argument among them. "How can this man give us his flesh to eat?" they asked.

53 Jesus said to them, "I am telling you the truth: if you do not eat the flesh of the Son of Man and drink his blood, you will not have life in yourselves. 54Whoever eats my flesh and drinks my blood has eternal life, and I will raise him to life on the last day. 55For my flesh is the real food; my blood is the real drink. 56Whoever eats my flesh and drinks my blood lives in me, and I live in him. 57The living Father sent me, and because of him I live also. In the same way whoever eats me will live because of

me. ⁵⁸This, then, is the bread that came down from heaven; it is not like the bread that your ancestors ate, but then later died. The one who eats this bread will live for ever."

59 Jesus said this as he taught in the synagogue in Capernaum.

The Words of Eternal Life

60 Many of his followers heard this and said, "This teaching is too hard. Who can listen to it?"

61 Without being told, Jesus knew that they were grumbling about this, so he said to them, "Does this make you want to give up? ⁶²Suppose, then, that you should see the Son of Man go back up to the place where he was before? ⁶³What gives life is God's Spirit; man's power is of no use at all. The words I have spoken to you bring God's life-giving Spirit. ⁶⁴Yet some of you do not believe." (Jesus knew from the very beginning who were the ones that would not believe and which one would betray him.) ⁶⁵And he added, "This is the very reason I told you that no one can come to me unless the Father makes it possible for him to do so."

66 Because of this, many of Jesus' followers turned back and would not go with him any more. ⁶⁷So he asked the twelve disciples, "And you—would you also like to leave?"

68 Simon Peter answered him, "Lord, to whom would we go? You have the words that give eternal life. ⁶⁹And now we believe and know that you are the Holy One who has come from God."

70 Jesus replied, "I chose the twelve of you, didn't I? Yet one of you is a devil!" ⁷¹He was talking about Judas, the son of Simon Iscariot. For Judas, even though he was one of the twelve disciples, was going to betray him.

Jesus and His Brothers

7 After this, Jesus travelled in Galilee; he did not want to travel in Judaea, because the Jewish authorities there were wanting to kill him. ²The time for the Festival of Shelters was near, ³so Jesus' brothers said to him, "Leave this place and go to Judaea,

so that your followers will see the things that you are doing. [4]No one hides what he is doing if he wants to be well known. Since you are doing these things, let the whole world know about you!" [5](Not even his brothers believed in him.)

6 Jesus said to them, "The right time for me has not yet come. Any time is right for you. [7]The world cannot hate you, but it hates me, because I keep telling it that its ways are bad. [8]You go on to the festival. I am not going[n] to this festival, because the right time has not come for me." [9]He said this, and then stayed on in Galilee.

Jesus at the Festival of Shelters

10 After his brothers had gone to the festival, Jesus also went; however, he did not go openly, but secretly. [11]The Jewish authorities were looking for him at the festival. "Where is he?" they asked.

12 There was much whispering about him in the crowd. "He is a good man," some people said. "No," others said, "he is misleading the people." [13]But no one talked about him openly, because they were afraid of the Jewish authorities.

14 The festival was nearly half over when Jesus went to the Temple and began teaching. [15]The Jewish authorities were greatly surprised and said, "How does this man know so much when he has never had any training?"

16 Jesus answered, "What I teach is not my own teaching, but it comes from God, who sent me. [17]Whoever is willing to do what God wants will know whether what I teach comes from God or whether I speak on my own authority. [18]A person who speaks on his own authority is trying to gain glory for himself. But he who wants glory for the one who sent him is honest, and there is nothing false in him. [19]Moses gave you the Law, didn't he? But not one of you obeys the Law. Why are you trying to kill me?"

20 "You have a demon in you!" the crowd answered. "Who is trying to kill you?"

21 Jesus answered, "I performed one miracle, and

[n]I am not going; *some manuscripts have* I am not yet going.

you were all surprised. 22 Moses ordered you to circumcise your sons (although it was not Moses but your ancestors who started it), and so you circumcise a boy on the Sabbath. 23 If a boy is circumcised on the Sabbath so that Moses' Law is not broken, why are you angry with me because I made a man completely well on the Sabbath? 24 Stop judging by external standards, and judge by true standards."

Is He the Messiah?

25 Some of the people of Jerusalem said, "Isn't this the man the authorities are trying to kill? 26 Look! He is talking in public, and they say nothing against him! Can it be that they really know that he is the Messiah? 27 But when the Messiah comes, no one will know where he is from. And we all know where this man comes from."

28 As Jesus taught in the Temple, he said in a loud voice, "Do you really know me and know where I am from? I have not come on my own authority. He who sent me, however, is truthful. You do not know him, 29 but I know him, because I come from him and he sent me."

30 Then they tried to seize him, but no one laid a hand on him, because his hour had not yet come. 31 But many in the crowd believed in him and said, "When the Messiah comes, will he perform more miracles than this man has?"

Guards Are Sent to Arrest Jesus

32 The Pharisees heard the crowd whispering these things about Jesus, so they and the chief priests sent some guards to arrest him. 33 Jesus said, "I shall be with you a little while longer, and then I shall go away to him who sent me. 34 You will look for me, but you will not find me, because you cannot go where I will be."

35 The Jewish authorities said among themselves, "Where is he about to go so that we shall not find him? Will he go to the Greek cities where our people live, and teach the Greeks? 36 He says that we will look for him but will not find him, and that we cannot go where he will be. What does he mean?"

Streams of Life-Giving Water

37 On the last and most important day of the festival Jesus stood up and said in a loud voice, "Whoever is thirsty should come to me and drink. 38 As the scripture says, 'Whoever believes in me, streams of life-giving water will pour out from his heart.' "o 39 Jesus said this about the Spirit, which those who believed in him were going to receive. At that time the Spirit had not yet been given, because Jesus had not been raised to glory.

Division among the People

40 Some of the people in the crowd heard him say this and said, "This man is really the Prophet!"p
41 Others said, "He is the Messiah!"
But others said, "The Messiah will not come from Galilee! 42 The scripture says that the Messiah will be a descendant of King David and will be born in Bethlehem, the town where David lived." 43 So there was a division in the crowd because of Jesus. 44 Some wanted to seize him, but no one laid a hand on him.

The Unbelief of the Jewish Authorities

45 When the guards went back, the chief priests and Pharisees asked them, "Why did you not bring him?"
46 The guards answered, "Nobody has ever talked like this man!"
47 "Did he fool you, too?" the Pharisees asked them. 48 "Have you ever known one of the authorities or one Pharisee to believe in him? 49 This crowd does not know the Law of Moses, so they are under God's curse!"
50 One of the Pharisees there was Nicodemus, the man who had gone to see Jesus before. He said to

o Jesus' words in verses 37–38 may be translated: "Whoever is thirsty should come to me, and whoever believes in me should drink. 38 As the scripture says, 'Streams of life-giving water will pour out from his heart.' "
p THE PROPHET: See 1.21.

the others, ⁵¹"According to our Law we cannot condemn a man before hearing him and finding out what he has done."

52 "Well," they answered, "are you also from Galilee? Study the Scriptures and you will learn that no prophet ever comes *q* from Galilee."

The Woman Caught in Adultery

8 [Then everyone went home, but Jesus went to the Mount of Olives. ²Early the next morning he went back to the Temple. All the people gathered round him, and he sat down and began to teach them. ³The teachers of the Law and the Pharisees brought in a woman who had been caught committing adultery, and they made her stand before them all. ⁴"Teacher," they said to Jesus, "this woman was caught in the very act of committing adultery. ⁵In our Law Moses commanded that such a woman must be stoned to death. Now, what do you say?" ⁶They said this to trap Jesus, so that they could accuse him. But he bent over and wrote on the ground with his finger.

7 As they stood there asking him questions, he straightened himself up and said to them, "Whichever one of you has committed no sin may throw the first stone at her." ⁸Then he bent over again and wrote on the ground. ⁹When they heard this, they all left, one by one, the older ones first. Jesus was left alone, with the woman still standing there. ¹⁰He straightened himself up and said to her, "Where are they? Is there no one left to condemn you?"

11 "No one, sir," she answered.

"Well, then," Jesus said, "I do not condemn you either. Go, but do not sin again."]*r*

Jesus the Light of the World

12 Jesus spoke to the Pharisees again. "I am the

---

q no prophet ever comes; *one manuscript has* the Prophet will not come.

r *Many manuscripts and early translations do not have this passage (8.1–11); others have it after Jn 21.24; others have it after Lk 21.38; one manuscript has it after Jn 7.36.*

light of the world," he said. "Whoever follows me will have the light of life and will never walk in darkness."

13 The Pharisees said to him, "Now you are testifying on your own behalf; what you say proves nothing."

14 "No," Jesus answered, "even though I do testify on my own behalf, what I say is true, because I know where I came from and where I am going. You do not know where I came from or where I am going. 15 You make judgements in a purely human way; I pass judgement on no one. 16 But if I were to do so, my judgement would be true, because I am not alone in this; the Father who sent me is with me. 17 It is written in your Law that when two witnesses agree, what they say is true. 18 I testify on my own behalf, and the Father who sent me also testifies on my behalf."

19 "Where is your father?" they asked him.

"You know neither me nor my Father," Jesus answered. "If you knew me, you would know my Father also."

20 Jesus said all this as he taught in the Temple, in the room where the offering boxes were placed. And no one arrested him, because his hour had not come.

You Cannot Go Where I Am Going

21 Again Jesus said to them, "I will go away; you will look for me, but you will die in your sins. You cannot go where I am going."

22 So the Jewish authorities said, "He says that we cannot go where he is going. Does this mean that he will kill himself?"

23 Jesus answered, "You belong to this world here below, but I come from above. You are from this world, but I am not from this world. 24 That is why I told you that you will die in your sins. And you will die in your sins if you do not believe that 'I Am Who I Am'."

25 "Who are you?" they asked him.

Jesus answered, "What I have told you from the

very beginning.*s* 26 I have much to say about you,
much to condemn you for. The one who sent me,
however, is truthful, and I tell the world only what
I have heard from him."

27 They did not understand that Jesus was talking
to them about the Father. 28 So he said to them, "When
you lift up the Son of Man, you will know that 'I
Am Who I Am'; then you will know that I do nothing
on my own authority, but I say only what the Father
has instructed me to say. 29 And he who sent me
is with me; he has not left me alone, because I
always do what pleases him."

30 Many who heard Jesus say these things believed
in him.

Free Men and Slaves

31 So Jesus said to those who believed in him,
"If you obey my teaching, you are really my disciples;
32 you will know the truth, and the truth will set
you free."

33 "We are the descendants of Abraham," they
answered, "and we have never been anybody's slaves.
What do you mean, then, by saying, 'You will be
free'?"

34 Jesus said to them, "I am telling you the truth:
everyone who sins is a slave of sin. 35 A slave does
not belong to a family permanently, but a son belongs
there for ever. 36 If the Son sets you free, then you
will be really free. 37 I know you are Abraham's descendants. Yet you are trying to kill me, because you
will not accept my teaching. 38 I talk about what my
Father has shown me, but you do what your father has
told you."

39 They answered him, "Our father is Abraham."

"If you really were Abraham's children," Jesus replied, "you would do*t* the same things that he did.
40 All I have ever done is to tell you the truth I
heard from God, yet you are trying to kill me. Abraham

---

s What I have told you from the very beginning; *or* Why should
I speak to you at all?
t If you really were...you would do; *some manuscripts have* If
you are...do.

did nothing like this! [41] You are doing what your father did."

"God himself is the only Father we have," they answered, "and we are his true sons."

42 Jesus said to them, "If God really were your Father, you would love me, because I came from God and now I am here. I did not come on my own authority, but he sent me. [43] Why do you not understand what I say? It is because you cannot bear to listen to my message. [44] You are the children of your father, the Devil, and you want to follow your father's desires. From the very beginning he was a murderer and has never been on the side of truth, because there is no truth in him. When he tells a lie, he is only doing what is natural to him, because he is a liar and the father of all lies. [45] But I tell the truth, and that is why you do not believe me. [46] Which one of you can prove that I am guilty of sin? If I tell the truth, then why do you not believe me? [47] He who comes from God listens to God's words. You, however, are not from God, and that is why you will not listen."

Jesus and Abraham

48 They asked Jesus, "Were we not right in saying that you are a Samaritan and have a demon in you?"

49 "I have no demon," Jesus answered. "I honour my Father, but you dishonour me. [50] I am not seeking honour for myself. But there is one who is seeking it and who judges in my favour. [51] I am telling you the truth: whoever obeys my teaching will never die."

52 They said to him, "Now we are certain that you have a demon! Abraham died, and the prophets died, yet you say that whoever obeys your teaching will never die. [53] Our father Abraham died; you do not claim to be greater than Abraham, do you? And the prophets also died. Who do you think you are?"

54 Jesus answered, "If I were to honour myself, that honour would be worth nothing. The one who honours me is my Father—the very one you say is your God. [55] You have never known him, but I know him. If I were to say that I do not know him, I would be a liar like you. But I do know him, and

I obey his word. [56] Your father Abraham rejoiced that he was to see the time of my coming; he saw it and was glad."

57 They said to him, "You are not even fifty years old—and you have seen Abraham?" [u]

58 "I am telling you the truth," Jesus replied. "Before Abraham was born, 'I Am'."

59 Then they picked up stones to throw at him, but Jesus hid himself and left the Temple.

Jesus Heals a Man Born Blind

9 As Jesus was walking along, he saw a man who had been born blind. [2] His disciples asked him, "Teacher, whose sin caused him to be born blind? Was it his own or his parents' sin?"

3 Jesus answered, "His blindness has nothing to do with his sins or his parents' sins. He is blind so that God's power might be seen at work in him. [4] As long as it is day, we must keep on doing the work of him who sent me; night is coming when no one can work. [5] While I am in the world, I am the light for the world."

6 After he said this, Jesus spat on the ground and made some mud with the spittle; he rubbed the mud on the man's eyes [7] and said, "Go and wash your face in the Pool of Siloam." (This name means "Sent.") So the man went, washed his face, and came back seeing.

8 His neighbours, then, and the people who had seen him begging before this, asked, "Isn't this the man who used to sit and beg?"

9 Some said, "He is the one," but others said, "No he isn't; he just looks like him."

So the man himself said, "I am the man."

10 "How is it that you can now see?" they asked him.

11 He answered, "The man called Jesus made some mud, rubbed it on my eyes, and told me to go to Siloam and wash my face. So I went, and as soon as I washed, I could see."

[u]you have seen Abraham?; *some manuscripts have* has Abraham seen you?

12 "Where is he?" they asked.
"I don't know," he answered.

The Pharisees Investigate the Healing

13 Then they took to the Pharisees the man who
had been blind. 14 The day that Jesus made the mud
and cured him of his blindness was a Sabbath. 15 The
Pharisees, then, asked the man again how he had
received his sight. He told them, "He put some mud
on my eyes; I washed my face, and now I can see."

16 Some of the Pharisees said, "The man who did
this cannot be from God, for he does not obey the
Sabbath law."

Others, however, said, "How could a man who is
a sinner perform such miracles as these?" And there
was a division among them.

17 So the Pharisees asked the man once more, "You
say he cured you of your blindness—well, what do
you say about him?"

"He is a prophet," the man answered.

18 The Jewish authorities, however, were not willing
to believe that he had been blind and could now
see, until they called his parents 19 and asked them,
"Is this your son? You say that he was born blind;
how is it, then, that he can now see?"

20 His parents answered, "We know that he is our
son, and we know that he was born blind. 21 But
we do not know how it is that he is now able to
see, nor do we know who cured him of his blindness.
Ask him; he is old enough, and he can answer for
himself!" 22 His parents said this because they were
afraid of the Jewish authorities, who had already
agreed that anyone who said he believed that Jesus
was the Messiah would be expelled from the synagogue. 23 That is why his parents said, "He is old
enough; ask him!"

24 A second time they called back the man who
had been born blind, and said to him, "Promise before
God that you will tell the truth! We know that this
man who cured you is a sinner."

25 "I do not know if he is a sinner or not," the
man replied. "One thing I do know: I was blind,
and now I see."

26 "What did he do to you?" they asked. "How did he cure you of your blindness?"

27 "I have already told you," he answered, "and you would not listen. Why do you want to hear it again? Maybe you, too, would like to be his disciples?"

28 They cursed him and said, "You are that fellow's disciple; but we are Moses' disciples. 29 We know that God spoke to Moses; as for that fellow, however, we do not even know where he comes from!"

30 The man answered, "What a strange thing that is! You do not know where he comes from, but he cured me of my blindness! 31 We know that God does not listen to sinners; he does listen to people who respect him and do what he wants them to do. 32 Since the beginning of the world nobody has ever heard of anyone giving sight to a person born blind. 33 Unless this man came from God, he would not be able to do a thing."

34 They answered, "You were born and brought up in sin—and you are trying to teach us?" And they expelled him from the synagogue.

Spiritual Blindness

35 When Jesus heard what had happened, he found the man and asked him, "Do you believe in the Son of Man?"

36 The man answered, "Tell me who he is, sir, so that I can believe in him!"

37 Jesus said to him, "You have already seen him, and he is the one who is talking with you now."

38 "I believe, Lord!" the man said, and knelt down before Jesus.

39 Jesus said, "I came to this world to judge, so that the blind should see and those who see should become blind."

40 Some Pharisees who were there with him heard him say this and asked him, "Surely you don't mean that we are blind, too?"

41 Jesus answered, "If you were blind, then you would not be guilty; but since you claim that you can see, this means that you are still guilty."

The Parable of the Shepherd

10 Jesus said, "I am telling you the truth: the man who does not enter the sheepfold by the gate, but climbs in some other way, is a thief and a robber. ²The man who goes in through the gate is the shepherd of the sheep. ³The gatekeeper opens the gate for him; the sheep hear his voice as he calls his own sheep by name, and he leads them out. ⁴When he has brought them out, he goes ahead of them, and the sheep follow him, because they know his voice. ⁵They will not follow someone else; instead, they will run away from such a person, because they do not know his voice."

6 Jesus told them this parable, but they did not understand what he meant.

Jesus the Good Shepherd

7 So Jesus said again, "I am telling you the truth: I am the gate for the sheep. ⁸All others who came before me are thieves and robbers, but the sheep did not listen to them. ⁹I am the gate. Whoever comes in by me will be saved; he will come in and go out and find pasture. ¹⁰The thief comes only in order to steal, kill, and destroy. I have come in order that you might have life—life in all its fullness.

11 "I am the good shepherd, who is willing to die for the sheep. ¹²When the hired man, who is not a shepherd and does not own the sheep, sees a wolf coming, he leaves the sheep and runs away; so the wolf snatches the sheep and scatters them. ¹³The hired man runs away because he is only a hired man and does not care about the sheep. ¹⁴⁻¹⁵I am the good shepherd. As the Father knows me and I know the Father, in the same way I know my sheep and they know me. And I am willing to die for them. ¹⁶There are other sheep which belong to me that are not in this sheepfold. I must bring them, too; they will listen to my voice, and they will become ᵛ one flock with one shepherd.

17 "The Father loves me because I am willing to

ᵛthey will become; *some manuscripts have* there will be.

give up my life, in order that I may receive it back again. 18No one takes my life away from me. I give it up of my own free will. I have the right to give it up, and I have the right to take it back. This is what my Father has commanded me to do."

19 Again there was a division among the people because of these words. 20Many of them were saying, "He has a demon! He is mad! Why do you listen to him?"

21 But others were saying, "A man with a demon could not talk like this! How could a demon give sight to blind people?"

Jesus Is Rejected

22 It was winter, and the Festival of the Dedication of the Temple was being celebrated in Jerusalem. 23Jesus was walking in Solomon's Porch in the Temple, 24when the people gathered round him and asked, "How long are you going to keep us in suspense? Tell us the plain truth: are you the Messiah?"

25 Jesus answered, "I have already told you, but you would not believe me. The things I do by my Father's authority speak on my behalf; 26but you will not believe, for you are not my sheep. 27My sheep listen to my voice; I know them, and they follow me. 28I give them eternal life, and they shall never die. No one can snatch them away from me. 29What my Father has given me is greater w than everything, and no one can snatch them away from the Father's care. 30The Father and I are one."

31 Then the people again picked up stones to throw at him. 32Jesus said to them, "I have done many good deeds in your presence which the Father gave me to do; for which one of these do you want to stone me?"

33 They replied, "We do not want to stone you because of any good deeds, but because of your blasphemy! You are only a man, but you are trying to make yourself God!"

34 Jesus answered, "It is written in your own Law

wWhat my Father has given me is greater; *some manuscripts have* My Father, who gave them to me, is greater.

that God said, 'You are gods.' 35 We know that what the scripture says is true for ever; and God called those people gods, the people to whom his message was given. 36 As for me, the Father chose me and sent me into the world. How, then, can you say that I blaspheme because I said that I am the Son of God? 37 Do not believe me, then, if I am not doing the things my Father wants me to do. 38 But if I do them, even though you do not believe me, you should at least believe my deeds, in order that you may know once and for all that the Father is in me and that I am in the Father."

39 Once more they tried to seize Jesus, but he slipped out of their hands.

40 Jesus then went back again across the River Jordan to the place where John had been baptizing, and he stayed there. 41 Many people came to him. "John performed no miracles," they said, "but everything he said about this man was true." 42 And many people there believed in him.

The Death of Lazarus

11 A man named Lazarus, who lived in Bethany, was ill. Bethany was the town where Mary and her sister Martha lived. 2 (This Mary was the one who poured the perfume on the Lord's feet and wiped them with her hair; it was her brother Lazarus who was ill.) 3 The sisters sent Jesus a message: "Lord, your dear friend is ill."

4 When Jesus heard it, he said, "The final result of this illness will not be the death of Lazarus; this has happened in order to bring glory to God, and it will be the means by which the Son of God will receive glory."

5 Jesus loved Martha and her sister and Lazarus. 6 Yet when he received the news that Lazarus was ill, he stayed where he was for two more days. 7 Then he said to the disciples, "Let us go back to Judaea."

8 "Teacher," the disciples answered, "just a short time ago the people there wanted to stone you; and are you planning to go back?"

9 Jesus said, "A day has twelve hours, hasn't it? So whoever walks in broad daylight does not stumble,

for he sees the light of this world. [10] But if he walks during the night he stumbles, because he has no light." [11] Jesus said this and then added, "Our friend Lazarus has fallen asleep, but I will go and wake him up."

12 The disciples answered, "If he is asleep, Lord, he will get well."

13 Jesus meant that Lazarus had died, but they thought he meant natural sleep. [14] So Jesus told them plainly, "Lazarus is dead, [15] but for your sake I am glad that I was not with him, so that you will believe. Let us go to him."

16 Thomas (called the Twin) said to his fellow-disciples, "Let us all go with the Teacher, so that we may die with him!"

Jesus the Resurrection and the Life

17 When Jesus arrived, he found that Lazarus had been buried four days before. [18] Bethany was less than three kilometres from Jerusalem, [19] and many Judaeans had come to see Martha and Mary to comfort them over their brother's death.

20 When Martha heard that Jesus was coming, she went out to meet him, but Mary stayed in the house. [21] Martha said to Jesus, "If you had been here, Lord, my brother would not have died! [22] But I know that even now God will give you whatever you ask him for."

23 "Your brother will rise to life," Jesus told her.

24 "I know," she replied, "that he will rise to life on the last day."

25 Jesus said to her, "I am the resurrection and the life. Whoever believes in me will live, even though he dies; [26] and whoever lives and believes in me will never die. Do you believe this?"

27 "Yes, Lord!" she answered. "I do believe that you are the Messiah, the Son of God, who was to come into the world."

Jesus Weeps

28 After Martha said this, she went back and called her sister Mary privately. "The Teacher is here," she told her, "and is asking for you." [29] When Mary heard this, she got up and hurried out to meet him. [30] (Jesus

had not yet arrived in the village, but was still in the place where Martha had met him.) 31 The people who were in the house with Mary, comforting her, followed her when they saw her get up and hurry out. They thought that she was going to the grave to weep there.

32 Mary arrived where Jesus was, and as soon as she saw him, she fell at his feet. "Lord," she said, "if you had been here, my brother would not have died!"

33 Jesus saw her weeping, and he saw how the people who were with her were weeping also; his heart was touched, and he was deeply moved. 34 "Where have you buried him?" he asked them.

"Come and see, Lord," they answered.

35 Jesus wept. 36 "See how much he loved him!" the people said.

37 But some of them said, "He gave sight to the blind man, didn't he? Could he not have kept Lazarus from dying?"

Lazarus Is Brought to Life

38 Deeply moved once more, Jesus went to the tomb, which was a cave with a stone placed at the entrance. 39 "Take the stone away!" Jesus ordered.

Martha, the dead man's sister, answered, "There will be a bad smell, Lord. He has been buried four days!"

40 Jesus said to her, "Didn't I tell you that you would see God's glory if you believed?" 41 They took the stone away. Jesus looked up and said, "I thank you, Father, that you listen to me. 42 I know that you always listen to me, but I say this for the sake of the people here, so that they will believe that you sent me." 43 After he had said this, he called out in a loud voice, "Lazarus, come out!" 44 He came out, his hands and feet wrapped in grave clothes, and with a cloth round his face. "Untie him," Jesus told them, "and let him go."

The Plot against Jesus
(Matt. 26.1-5; Mark 14.1-2; Luke 22.1-2)

45 Many of the people who had come to visit Mary

Lazarus, come out! (11.43)

saw what Jesus did, and they believed in him. 46 But
some of them returned to the Pharisees and told them
what Jesus had done. 47 So the Pharisees and the
chief priests met with the Council and said, "What
shall we do? Look at all the miracles this man is
performing! 48 If we let him go on in this way, everyone
will believe in him, and the Roman authorities will take
action and destroy our Temple and our nation!"

49 One of them, named Caiaphas, who was High
Priest that year, said, "What fools you are! 50 Don't
you realize that it is better for you to let one man
die for the people, instead of having the whole nation
destroyed?" 51 Actually, he did not say this of his
own accord; rather, as he was High Priest that year,
he was prophesying that Jesus was going to die for
the Jewish people, 52 and not only for them, but also to
bring together into one body all the scattered people
of God.

53 From that day on the Jewish authorities made
plans to kill Jesus. 54 So Jesus did not travel openly
in Judaea, but left and went to a place near the
desert, to a town named Ephraim, where he stayed
with the disciples.

55 The time for the Passover Festival was near,
and many people went up from the country to Jerusalem to perform the ritual of purification before the
festival. 56 They were looking for Jesus, and as they

gathered in the Temple, they asked one another, "What do you think? Surely he will not come to the festival, will he?" [57] The chief priests and the Pharisees had given orders that if anyone knew where Jesus was, he must report it, so that they could arrest him.

Jesus Is Anointed at Bethany
(Matt. 26.6–13; Mark 14.3–9)

12 Six days before the Passover, Jesus went to Bethany, the home of Lazarus, the man he had raised from death. [2] They prepared a dinner for him there, which Martha helped to serve; Lazarus was one of those who were sitting at the table with Jesus. [3] Then Mary took half a litre of a very expensive perfume made of pure nard, poured it on Jesus' feet, and wiped them with her hair. The sweet smell of the perfume filled the whole house. [4] One of Jesus' disciples, Judas Iscariot—the one who was going to betray him—said, [5] "Why wasn't this perfume sold for three hundred silver coins[x] and the money given to the poor?" [6] He said this, not because he cared about the poor, but because he was a thief. He carried the money bag and would help himself from it.

7 But Jesus said, "Leave her alone! Let her keep what she has for the day of my burial. [8] You will always have poor people with you, but you will not always have me."

The Plot against Lazarus

9 A large number of people heard that Jesus was in Bethany, so they went there, not only because of Jesus but also to see Lazarus, whom Jesus had raised from death. [10] So the chief priests made plans to kill Lazarus too, [11] because on his account many Jews were rejecting them and believing in Jesus.

The Triumphant Entry into Jerusalem
(Matt. 21.1–11; Mark 11.1–11; Luke 19.28–40)

12 The next day the large crowd that had come to the Passover Festival heard that Jesus was coming to Jerusalem. [13] So they took branches of palm-trees

[x] SILVER COINS: *See 6.7.*

and went out to meet him, shouting, "Praise God!
God bless him who comes in the name of the Lord!
God bless the King of Israel!"

14 Jesus found a donkey and rode on it, just as
the scripture says,

15 "Do not be afraid, city of Zion!
Here comes your king,
    riding on a young donkey."

16 His disciples did not understand this at the time;
but when Jesus had been raised to glory, they remembered that the scripture said this about him and that
they had done this for him.

17 The people who had been with Jesus when he
called Lazarus out of the grave and raised him from
death had reported what had happened. 18 That was
why the crowd met him—because they heard that
he had performed this miracle. 19 The Pharisees then
said to one another, "You see, we are not succeeding
at all! Look, the whole world is following him!"

Some Greeks Seek Jesus

20 Some Greeks were among those who had gone
to Jerusalem to worship during the festival. 21 They
went to Philip (he was from Bethsaida in Galilee)
and said, "Sir, we want to see Jesus."

22 Philip went and told Andrew, and the two of
them went and told Jesus. 23 Jesus answered them,
"The hour has now come for the Son of Man to
receive great glory. 24 I am telling you the truth: a
grain of wheat remains no more than a single grain
unless it is dropped into the ground and dies. If it
does die, then it produces many grains. 25 Whoever
loves his own life will lose it; whoever hates his
own life in this world will keep it for life eternal.
26 Whoever wants to serve me must follow me, so
that my servant will be with me where I am. And my
Father will honour anyone who serves me.

Jesus Speaks about His Death

27 "Now my heart is troubled—and what shall I
say? Shall I say, 'Father, do not let this hour come
upon me'? But that is why I came—so that I might

go through this hour of suffering. [28] Father, bring glory to your name!"

Then a voice spoke from heaven, "I have brought glory to it, and I will do so again."

29 The crowd standing there heard the voice, and some of them said it was thunder, while others said, "An angel spoke to him!"

30 But Jesus said to them, "It was not for my sake that this voice spoke, but for yours. [31] Now is the time for this world to be judged; now the ruler of this world will be overthrown. [32] When I am lifted up from the earth, I will draw everyone to me." [33] (In saying this he indicated the kind of death he was going to suffer.)

34 The crowd answered, "Our Law tells us that the Messiah will live for ever. How, then, can you say that the Son of Man must be lifted up? Who is this Son of Man?"

35 Jesus answered, "The light will be among you a little longer. Continue on your way while you have the light, so that the darkness will not come upon you; for the one who walks in the dark does not know where he is going. [36] Believe in the light, then, while you have it, so that you will be the people of the light."

The Unbelief of the People

After Jesus said this, he went off and hid himself from them. [37] Even though he had performed all these miracles in their presence, they did not believe in him, [38] so that what the prophet Isaiah had said might come true:

"Lord, who believed the message we told?
    To whom did the Lord reveal his power?"

39 And so they were not able to believe, because Isaiah also said,

[40] "God has blinded their eyes
    and closed their minds,
so that their eyes would not see,
    and their minds would not understand,
    and they would not turn to me, says God,
    for me to heal them."

41 Isaiah said this because he saw Jesus' glory and spoke about him.

42 Even then, many of the Jewish authorities believed in Jesus; but because of the Pharisees they did not talk about it openly, so as not to be expelled from the synagogue. 43 They loved the approval of men rather than the approval of God.

Judgement by Jesus' Words

44 Jesus said in a loud voice, "Whoever believes in me believes not only in me but also in him who sent me. 45 Whoever sees me sees also him who sent me. 46 I have come into the world as light, so that everyone who believes in me should not remain in the darkness. 47 If anyone hears my message and does not obey it, I will not judge him. I came, not to judge the world, but to save it. 48 Whoever rejects me and does not accept my message has one who will judge him. The words I have spoken will be his judge on the last day! 49 This is true, because I have not spoken on my own authority, but the Father who sent me has commanded me what I must say and speak. 50 And I know that his command brings eternal life. What I say, then, is what the Father has told me to say."

Jesus Washes His Disciples' Feet

13 It was now the day before the Passover Festival. Jesus knew that the hour had come for him to leave this world and go to the Father. He had always loved those in the world who were his own, and he loved them to the very end.

2 Jesus and his disciples were at supper. The Devil had already put into the heart of Judas, the son of Simon Iscariot, the thought of betraying Jesus.y 3 Jesus knew that the Father had given him complete power; he knew that he had come from God and was going to God. 4 So he rose from the table, took off his outer garment, and tied a towel round his waist. 5 Then he poured some water into a basin and began to

yThe Devil...betraying Jesus; *or* The Devil had already decided that Judas, the son of Simon Iscariot, would betray Jesus.

wash the disciples' feet and dry them with the towel round his waist. ⁶He came to Simon Peter, who said to him, "Are you going to wash my feet, Lord?"

7 Jesus answered him, "You do not understand now what I am doing, but you will understand later."

8 Peter declared, "Never at any time will you wash my feet!"

"If I do not wash your feet," Jesus answered, "you will no longer be my disciple."

9 Simon Peter answered, "Lord, do not wash only my feet, then! Wash my hands and head, too!"

10 Jesus said, "Anyone who has had a bath is completely clean and does not have to wash himself, except for his feet.ᶻ All of you are clean—all except one."
¹¹(Jesus already knew who was going to betray him; that is why he said, "All of you, except one, are clean.")

12 After Jesus had washed their feet, he put his outer garment back on and returned to his place at the table. "Do you understand what I have just done to you?" he asked. ¹³"You call me Teacher and Lord, and it is right that you do so, because that is what I am. ¹⁴I, your Lord and Teacher, have just washed your feet. You, then, should wash one another's feet. ¹⁵I have set an example for you, so that you will do just what I have done for you. ¹⁶I am telling you the truth: no slave is greater than his master, and no messenger is greater than the one who sent him. ¹⁷Now that you know this truth, how happy you will be if you put it into practice!

18 "I am not talking about all of you; I know those I have chosen. But the scripture must come true that says, 'The man who shared my food turned against me.' ¹⁹I tell you this now before it happens, so that when it does happen, you will believe that 'I Am Who I Am.' ²⁰I am telling you the truth: whoever receives anyone I send receives me also; and whoever receives me receives him who sent me."

ᶻ Some manuscripts do not have except for his feet.

Jesus Predicts His Betrayal
(Matt. 26.20–25; Mark 14.17–21; Luke 22.21–23)

21 After Jesus had said this, he was deeply troubled and declared openly, "I am telling you the truth: one of you is going to betray me."

22 The disciples looked at one another, completely

The disciples looked at one another (13.22)

puzzled about whom he meant. 23 One of the disciples, the one whom Jesus loved, was sitting next to Jesus. 24 Simon Peter motioned to him and said, "Ask him whom he is talking about."

25 So that disciple moved closer to Jesus' side and asked, "Who is it, Lord?"

26 Jesus answered, "I will dip some bread in the sauce and give it to him; he is the man." So he took a piece of bread, dipped it, and gave it to Judas, the son of Simon Iscariot. 27 As soon as Judas took the bread, Satan entered him. Jesus said to him, "Be quick about what you are doing!" 28 None of the others at the table understood why Jesus said this to him. 29 Since Judas was in charge of the money bag, some of the disciples thought that Jesus had told him to go and buy what they needed for the festival, or to give something to the poor.

The New Commandment

30 Judas accepted the bread and went out at once. It was night.

31 After Judas had left, Jesus said, "Now the Son of Man's glory is revealed; now God's glory is revealed through him. 32 And if God's glory is revealed through him, then God will reveal the glory of the Son of Man in himself, and he will do so at once. 33 My children, I shall not be with you very much longer. You will look for me; but I tell you now what I

told the Jewish authorities, 'You cannot go where I am going.' [34] And now I give you a new commandment: love one another. As I have loved you, so you must love one another. [35] If you have love for one another, then everyone will know that you are my disciples."

Jesus Predicts Peter's Denial
(Matt. 26.31–35; Mark 14.27–31; Luke 22.31–34)

36 "Where are you going, Lord?" Simon Peter asked him.

"You cannot follow me now where I am going," answered Jesus; "but later you will follow me."

37 "Lord, why can't I follow you now?" asked Peter. "I am ready to die for you!"

38 Jesus answered, "Are you really ready to die for me? I am telling you the truth: before the cock crows you will say three times that you do not know me.

Jesus the Way to the Father

14 "Do not be worried and upset," Jesus told them. "Believe[a] in God and believe also in me. [2] There are many rooms in my Father's house, and I am going to prepare a place for you. I would not tell you this if it were not so.[b] [3] And after I go and prepare a place for you, I will come back and take you to myself, so that you will be where I am. [4] You know the way that leads to the place where I am going."

5 Thomas said to him, "Lord, we do not know where you are going; so how can we know the way to get there?"

6 Jesus answered him, "I am the way, the truth, and the life; no one goes to the Father except by me. [7] Now that you have known me," he said to them, "you will know[c] my Father also, and from

[a] Believe; *or* You believe.
[b] There are...were not so; *or* There are many rooms in my Father's house; if it were not so, would I tell you that I am going to prepare a place for you?
[c] Now that you have known me...you will know; *some manuscripts have* If you had known me...you would know.

now on you do know him and you have seen him."

8 Philip said to him, "Lord, show us the Father; that is all we need."

9 Jesus answered, "For a long time I have been with you all; yet you do not know me, Philip? Whoever has seen me has seen the Father. Why, then, do you say, 'Show us the Father'? 10 Do you not believe, Philip, that I am in the Father and the Father is in me? The words that I have spoken to you," Jesus said to his disciples, "do not come from me. The Father, who remains in me, does his own work. 11 Believe me when I say that I am in the Father and the Father is in me. If not, believe because of the things I do. 12 I am telling you the truth: whoever believes in me will do what I do—yes, he will do even greater things, because I am going to the Father. 13 And I will do whatever you ask for in my name, so that the Father's glory will be shown through the Son. 14 If you ask me*d* for anything in my name, I will do it.

The Promise of the Holy Spirit

15 "If you love me, you will obey my commandments. 16 I will ask the Father, and he will give you another Helper, who will stay with you for ever. 17 He is the Spirit who reveals the truth about God. The world cannot receive him, because it cannot see him or know him. But you know him, because he remains with you and is*e* in you.

18 "When I go, you will not be left all alone; I will come back to you. 19 In a little while the world will see me no more, but you will see me; and because I live, you also will live. 20 When that day comes, you will know that I am in my Father and that you are in me, just as I am in you.

21 "Whoever accepts my commandments and obeys them is the one who loves me. My Father will love whoever loves me; I too will love him and reveal myself to him."

d Some manuscripts do not have me.
e is; some manuscripts have will be.

22 Judas (not Judas Iscariot) said, "Lord, how can it be that you will reveal yourself to us and not to the world?"

23 Jesus answered him, "Whoever loves me will obey my teaching. My Father will love him, and my Father and I will come to him and live with him. 24 Whoever does not love me does not obey my teaching. And the teaching you have heard is not mine, but comes from the Father, who sent me.

25 "I have told you this while I am still with you. 26 The Helper, the Holy Spirit, whom the Father will send in my name, will teach you everything and make you remember all that I have told you.

27 "Peace is what I leave with you; it is my own peace that I give you. I do not give it as the world does. Do not be worried and upset; do not be afraid. 28 You heard me say to you, 'I am leaving, but I will come back to you.' If you loved me, you would be glad that I am going to the Father; for he is greater than I. 29 I have told you this now before it all happens, so that when it does happen, you will believe. 30 I cannot talk with you much longer, because the ruler of this world is coming. He has no power over me, 31 but the world must know that I love the Father; that is why I do everything as he commands me.

"Come, let us go from this place.

Jesus the Real Vine

15 "I am the real vine, and my Father is the gardener. 2 He breaks off every branch in me that does not bear fruit, and he prunes every branch that does bear fruit, so that it will be clean and bear more fruit. 3 You have been made clean already by the teaching I have given you. 4 Remain united to me, and I will remain united to you. A branch cannot bear fruit by itself; it can do so only if it remains in the vine. In the same way you cannot bear fruit unless you remain in me.

5 "I am the vine, and you are the branches. Whoever remains in me, and I in him, will bear much fruit; for you can do nothing without me. 6 Whoever does not remain in me is thrown out like a branch and

dries up; such branches are gathered up and thrown into the fire, where they are burnt. [7] If you remain in me and my words remain in you, then you will ask for anything you wish, and you shall have it. [8] My Father's glory is shown by your bearing much fruit; and in this way you become my disciples. [9] I love you just as the Father loves me; remain in my love. [10] If you obey my commands, you will remain in my love, just as I have obeyed my Father's commands and remain in his love.

11 "I have told you this so that my joy may be in you and that your joy may be complete. [12] My commandment is this: love one another, just as I love you. [13] The greatest love a person can have for his friends is to give his life for them. [14] And you are my friends if you do what I command you. [15] I do not call you servants any longer, because a servant does not know what his master is doing. Instead, I call you friends, because I have told you everything I have heard from my Father. [16] You did not choose me; I chose you and appointed you to go and bear much fruit, the kind of fruit that endures. And so the Father will give you whatever you ask of him in my name. [17] This, then, is what I command you: love one another.

The World's Hatred

18 "If the world hates you, just remember that it has hated me first. [19] If you belonged to the world, then the world would love you as its own. But I chose you from this world, and you do not belong to it; that is why the world hates you. [20] Remember what I told you: 'No slave is greater than his master.' If they persecuted me, they will persecute you too; if they obeyed my teaching, they will obey yours too. [21] But they will do all this to you because you are mine; for they do not know the one who sent me. [22] They would not have been guilty of sin if I had not come and spoken to them; as it is, they no longer have any excuse for their sin. [23] Whoever hates me hates my Father also. [24] They would not have been guilty of sin if I had not done among them the things that no one else ever did; as it is, they have seen

what I did, and they hate both me and my Father. [25] This, however, was bound to happen so that what is written in their Law may come true: 'They hated me for no reason at all.'

26 "The Helper will come—the Spirit, who reveals the truth about God and who comes from the Father. I will send him to you from the Father, and he will speak about me. [27] And you, too, will speak about me, because you have been with me from the very beginning.

16 "I have told you this, so that you will not give up your faith. [2] You will be expelled from the synagogues, and the time will come when anyone who kills you will think that by doing this he is serving God. [3] People will do these things to you because they have not known either the Father or me. [4] But I have told you this, so that when the time comes for them to do these things, you will remember that I told you.

The Work of the Holy Spirit

"I did not tell you these things at the beginning, for I was with you. [5] But now I am going to him who sent me, yet none of you asks me where I am going. [6] And now that I have told you, your hearts are full of sadness. [7] But I am telling you the truth: it is better for you that I go away, because if I do not go, the Helper will not come to you. But if I do go away, then I will send him to you. [8] And when he comes, he will prove to the people of the world that they are wrong about sin and about what is right and about God's judgement. [9] They are wrong about sin, because they do not believe in me; [10] they are wrong about what is right, because I am going to the Father and you will not see me any more; [11] and they are wrong about judgement, because the ruler of this world has already been judged.

12 "I have much more to tell you, but now it would be too much for you to bear. [13] When, however, the Spirit comes, who reveals the truth about God, he will lead you into all the truth. He will not speak on his own authority, but he will speak of what he hears, and will tell you of things to come. [14] He will

give me glory, because he will take what I say and tell it to you. ¹⁵All that my Father has is mine; that is why I said that the Spirit will take what I give him and tell it to you.

Sadness and Gladness

16 "In a little while you will not see me any more, and then a little while later you will see me."

17 Some of his disciples asked among themselves, "What does this mean? He tells us that in a little while we will not see him, and then a little while later we will see him; and he also says, 'It is because I am going to the Father.' ¹⁸What does this 'a little while' mean? We don't know what he is talking about!"

19 Jesus knew that they wanted to question him, so he said to them, "I said, 'In a little while you will not see me, and then a little while later you will see me.' Is this what you are asking about among yourselves? ²⁰I am telling you the truth: you will cry and weep, but the world will be glad; you will be sad, but your sadness will turn into gladness. ²¹When a woman is about to give birth, she is sad because her hour of suffering has come; but when the baby is born, she forgets her suffering, because she is happy that a baby has been born into the world. ²²That is how it is with you: now you are sad, but I will see you again, and your hearts will be filled with gladness, the kind of gladness that no one can take away from you.

23 "When that day comes, you will not ask me for anything. I am telling you the truth: the Father will give you whatever you ask him for in my name.ᶠ ²⁴Until now you have not asked for anything in my name; ask and you will receive, so that your happiness may be complete.

Victory over the World

25 "I have used figures of speech to tell you these things. But the time will come when I will not use

---

ᶠthe Father will give you whatever you ask him for in my name; *some manuscripts have* if you ask the Father for anything, he will give it to you in my name.

figures of speech, but will speak to you plainly about the Father. 26When that day comes, you will ask him in my name; and I do not say that I will ask him on your behalf, 27for the Father himself loves you. He loves you because you love me and have believed that I came from God. 28I did come from the Father, and I came into the world; and now I am leaving the world and going to the Father."

29 Then his disciples said to him, "Now you are speaking plainly, without using figures of speech. 30We know now that you know everything; you do not need someone to ask you questions. This makes us believe that you came from God."

31 Jesus answered them, "Do you believe now? 32The time is coming, and is already here, when all of you will be scattered, each one to his own home, and I will be left all alone. But I am not really alone, because the Father is with me. 33I have told you this so that you will have peace by being united to me. The world will make you suffer. But be brave! I have defeated the world!"

Jesus Prays for His Disciples

17 After Jesus finished saying this, he looked up to heaven and said, "Father, the hour has come. Give glory to your Son, so that the Son may give glory to you. 2For you gave him authority over all mankind, so that he might give eternal life to all those you gave him. 3And eternal life means knowing you, the only true God, and knowing Jesus Christ, whom you sent. 4I have shown your glory on earth; I have finished the work you gave me to do. 5Father! Give me glory in your presence now, the same glory I had with you before the world was made.

6 "I have made you known to those you gave me out of the world. They belonged to you, and you gave them to me. They have obeyed your word, 7and now they know that everything you gave me comes from you. 8I gave them the message that you gave me, and they received it; they know that it is true that I came from you, and they believe that you sent me.

9 "I pray for them. I do not pray for the world

Father, the hour has come (17.1)

but for those you gave me, for they belong to you. ¹⁰All I have is yours, and all you have is mine; and my glory is shown through them. ¹¹And now I am coming to you; I am no longer in the world, but they are in the world. Holy Father! Keep them safe by the power of your name, the name you gave me,ᵍ so that they may be one just as you and I are one. ¹²While I was with them, I kept them safe by the power of your name, the name you gave me.ʰ I protected them, and not one of them was lost, except the man who was bound to be lost—so that the scripture might come true. ¹³And now I am coming to you, and I say these things in the world so that they might have my joy in their hearts in all its fullness. ¹⁴I gave them your message, and the world hated them, because they do not belong to the world, just as I do not belong to the world. ¹⁵I do not ask you

ᵍKeep them safe by the power of your name, the name you gave me; *some manuscripts have* By the power of your name keep safe those you have given me.
ʰI kept them safe by the power of your name, the name you gave me; *some manuscripts have* By the power of your name I kept safe those you have given me.

to take them out of the world, but I do ask you to keep them safe from the Evil One. [16] Just as I do not belong to the world, they do not belong to the world. [17] Dedicate them to yourself by means of the truth; your word is truth. [18] I sent them into the world, just as you sent me into the world. [19] And for their sake I dedicate myself to you, in order that they, too, may be truly dedicated to you.

20 "I pray not only for them, but also for those who believe in me because of their message. [21] I pray that they may all be one. Father! May they be in us, just as you are in me and I am in you. May they be one, so that the world will believe that you sent me. [22] I gave them the same glory you gave me, so that they may be one, just as you and I are one: [23] I in them and you in me, so that they may be completely one, in order that the world may know that you sent me and that you love them as you love me.

24 "Father! You have given them to me, and I want them to be with me where I am, so that they may see my glory, the glory you gave me; for you loved me before the world was made. [25] Righteous Father! The world does not know you, but I know you, and these know that you sent me. [26] I made you known to them, and I will continue to do so, in order that the love you have for me may be in them, and so that I also may be in them."

The Arrest of Jesus
(Matt. 26.47-56; Mark 14.43-50; Luke 22.47-53)

18 After Jesus had said this prayer, he left with his disciples and went across the brook called Kidron. There was a garden in that place, and Jesus and his disciples went in. [2] Judas, the traitor, knew where it was, because many times Jesus had met there with his disciples. [3] So Judas went to the garden, taking with him a group of Roman soldiers, and some temple guards sent by the chief priests and the Pharisees; they were armed and carried lanterns and torches. [4] Jesus knew everything that was going to happen to him, so he stepped forward and asked them, "Who is it you are looking for?"

5 "Jesus of Nazareth," they answered.

"I am he," he said.

Judas, the traitor, was standing there with them.
6 When Jesus said to them, "I am he," they moved
back and fell to the ground. 7 Again Jesus asked them,
"Who is it you are looking for?"

"Jesus of Nazareth," they said.

8 "I have already told you that I am he," Jesus
said. "If, then, you are looking for me, let these others
go." 9 (He said this so that what he had said might
come true: "Father, I have not lost even one of those
you gave me.")

10 Simon Peter, who had a sword, drew it and
struck the High Priest's slave, cutting off his right
ear. The name of the slave was Malchus. 11 Jesus
said to Peter, "Put your sword back in its place!
Do you think that I will not drink the cup of suffering
which my Father has given me?"

Jesus before Annas

12 Then the Roman soldiers with their commanding
officer and the Jewish guards arrested Jesus, bound
him, 13 and took him first to Annas. He was the father-
in-law of Caiaphas, who was High Priest that year. 14 It
was Caiaphas who had advised the Jewish authorities
that it was better that one man should die for all
the people.

Peter Denies Jesus
(Matt. 26.69-70; Mark 14.66-68; Luke 22.55-57)

15 Simon Peter and another disciple followed Jesus.
That other disciple was well known to the High Priest,
so he went with Jesus into the courtyard of the High
Priest's house, 16 while Peter stayed outside by the
gate. Then the other disciple went back out, spoke
to the girl at the gate, and brought Peter inside.
17 The girl at the gate said to Peter, "Aren't you also
one of the disciples of that man?"

"No, I am not," answered Peter.

18 It was cold, so the servants and guards had
built a charcoal fire and were standing round it, warming themselves. So Peter went over and stood with
them, warming himself.

The High Priest Questions Jesus
(Matt. 26.59-66; Mark 14.55-64; Luke 22.66-71)

19 The High Priest questioned Jesus about his disciples and about his teaching. 20 Jesus answered, "I have always spoken publicly to everyone; all my teaching was done in the synagogues and in the Temple, where all the people come together. I have never said anything in secret. 21 Why, then, do you question me? Question the people who heard me. Ask them what I told them—they know what I said."

22 When Jesus said this, one of the guards there slapped him and said, "How dare you talk like that to the High Priest!"

23 Jesus answered him, "If I have said anything wrong, tell everyone here what it was. But if I am right in what I have said, why do you hit me?"

24 Then Annas sent him, still bound, to Caiaphas the High Priest.

Peter Denies Jesus Again
(Matt. 26.71-75; Mark 14.69-72; Luke 22.58-62)

25 Peter was still standing there keeping himself warm. So the others said to him, "Aren't you also one of the disciples of that man?"

But Peter denied it. "No, I am not," he said.

26 One of the High Priest's slaves, a relative of the man whose ear Peter had cut off, spoke up. "Didn't I see you with him in the garden?" he asked.

27 Again Peter said "No"—and at once a cock crowed.

Jesus is Brought Before Pilate
(Matt. 27.1-2, 11-14; Mark 15.1-5; Luke 23.1-5)

28 Early in the morning Jesus was taken from Caiaphas' house to the governor's palace. The Jewish authorities did not go inside the palace, for they wanted to keep themselves ritually clean, in order to be able to eat the Passover meal. 29 So Pilate went outside to them and asked, "What do you accuse this man of?"

30 Their answer was, "We would not have brought him to you if he had not committed a crime."

31 Pilate said to them, "Then you yourselves take him and try him according to your own law."

They replied, "We are not allowed to put anyone to death." ³²(This happened in order to make the words of Jesus come true, the words he used when he indicated the kind of death he would die.)

33 Pilate went back into the palace and called Jesus. "Are you the King of the Jews?" he asked him.

34 Jesus answered, "Does this question come from you or have others told you about me?"

35 Pilate replied, "Do you think I am a Jew? It was your own people and the chief priests who handed you over to me. What have you done?"

36 Jesus said, "My kingdom does not belong to this world; if my kingdom belonged to this world, my followers would fight to keep me from being handed over to the Jewish authorities. No, my kingdom does not belong here!"

37 So Pilate asked him, "Are you a king, then?"

Jesus answered, "You say that I am a king. I was born and came into the world for this one purpose, to speak about the truth. Whoever belongs to the truth listens to me."

38 "And what is truth?" Pilate asked.

And what is truth? (18.38)

Jesus Is Sentenced to Death
(Matt. 27.15–31; Mark 15.6–20; Luke 23.13–25)

Then Pilate went back outside to the people and said to them, "I cannot find any reason to condemn him. 39 But according to the custom you have, I always set free a prisoner for you during the Passover. Do you want me to set free for you the King of the Jews?"

40 They answered him with a shout, "No, not him! We want Barabbas!" (Barabbas was a bandit.)

19 Then Pilate took Jesus and had him whipped. 2 The soldiers made a crown out of thorny branches and put it on his head; then they put a purple robe on him 3 and came to him and said, "Long live the King of the Jews!" And they went up and slapped him.

4 Pilate went out once more and said to the crowd, "Look, I will bring him out here to you to let you see that I cannot find any reason to condemn him." 5 So Jesus came out, wearing the crown of thorns and the purple robe. Pilate said to them, "Look! Here is the man!"

6 When the chief priests and the temple guards saw him, they shouted, "Crucify him! Crucify him!"

Pilate said to them, "You take him, then, and crucify him. I find no reason to condemn him."

7 The crowd answered back, "We have a law that says he ought to die, because he claimed to be the Son of God."

8 When Pilate heard this, he was even more afraid. 9 He went back into the palace and asked Jesus, "Where do you come from?"

But Jesus did not answer. 10 Pilate said to him, "You will not speak to me? Remember, I have the authority to set you free and also to have you crucified."

11 Jesus answered, "You have authority over me only because it was given to you by God. So the man who handed me over to you is guilty of a worse sin."

12 When Pilate heard this, he tried to find a way to set Jesus free. But the crowd shouted back, "If you set him free, that means that you are not the

No, not him! We want Barabbas! (18.40)

Emperor's friend! Anyone who claims to be a king is a rebel against the Emperor!''

13 When Pilate heard these words, he took Jesus outside and sat down on the judge's seat in the place called "The Stone Pavement." (In Hebrew the name is "Gabbatha.") 14 It was then almost noon of the day before the Passover. Pilate said to the people, "Here is your king!"

15 They shouted back, "Kill him! Kill him! Crucify him!"

Pilate asked them, "Do you want me to crucify your king?"

The chief priests answered, "The only king we have is the Emperor!"

16 Then Pilate handed Jesus over to them to be crucified.

Jesus Is Crucified
(Matt. 27.32–44; Mark 15.21–32; Luke 23.26–43)

So they took charge of Jesus. 17 He went out, carrying his cross, and came to "The Place of the Skull," as it is called. (In Hebrew it is called "Golgotha.") 18 There they crucified him; and they also crucified two other men, one on each side, with Jesus between them. ¹⁹Pilate wrote a notice and had it put on the cross. "Jesus of Nazareth, the King of the Jews," is what he wrote. ²⁰Many people read it, because the place where Jesus was crucified was not far from the city. The notice was written in Hebrew, Latin, and Greek. ²¹The chief priests said to Pilate, "Do not write 'The King of the Jews,' but rather, 'This man said, I am the King of the Jews.' "

22 Pilate answered, "What I have written stays written."

23 After the soldiers had crucified Jesus, they took his clothes and divided them into four parts, one part for each soldier. They also took the robe, which was made of one piece of woven cloth without any seams in it. ²⁴The soldiers said to one another, "Let's not tear it; let's throw dice to see who will get it." This happened in order to make the scripture come true:

"They divided my clothes among themselves
    and gambled for my robe."

And this is what the soldiers did.

25 Standing close to Jesus' cross were his mother, his mother's sister, Mary the wife of Clopas, and Mary Magdalene. ²⁶Jesus saw his mother and the disciple he loved standing there; so he said to his mother, "He is your son."

27 Then he said to the disciple, "She is your mother." From that time the disciple took her to live in his home.

The Death of Jesus
(Matt. 27.45–56; Mark 15.33–41; Luke 23.44–49)

28 Jesus knew that by now everything had been completed; and in order to make the scripture come true, he said, "I am thirsty."

29 A bowl was there, full of cheap wine; so a sponge was soaked in the wine, put on a stalk of hyssop, and lifted up to his lips. ³⁰Jesus drank the wine and said, "It is finished!"

Then he bowed his head and died.

Jesus' Side Is Pierced

31 Then the Jewish authorities asked Pilate to allow them to break the legs of the men who had been

crucified, and to take the bodies down from the crosses. They requested this because it was Friday, and they did not want the bodies to stay on the crosses on the Sabbath, since the coming Sabbath was especially holy. ³²So the soldiers went and broke the legs of the first man and then of the other man who had been crucified with Jesus. ³³But when they came to Jesus, they saw that he was already dead, so they did not break his legs. ³⁴One of the soldiers, however, plunged his spear into Jesus' side, and at once blood and water poured out. ³⁵(The one who saw this happen has spoken of it, so that you also may believe.*i* What he said is true, and he knows that he speaks the truth.) ³⁶This was done to make the scripture come true: "Not one of his bones will be broken." ³⁷And there is another scripture that says, "People will look at him whom they pierced."

The Burial of Jesus
(Matt. 27.57-61; Mark 15.42-47; Luke 23.50-56)

38 After this, Joseph, who was from the town of Arimathea, asked Pilate if he could take Jesus' body. (Joseph was a follower of Jesus, but in secret, because he was afraid of the Jewish authorities.) Pilate told him he could have the body, so Joseph went and took it away. ³⁹Nicodemus, who at first had gone to see Jesus at night, went with Joseph, taking with him about thirty kilogrammes of spices, a mixture of myrrh and aloes. ⁴⁰The two men took Jesus' body and wrapped it in linen with the spices according to the Jewish custom of preparing a body for burial. ⁴¹There was · a garden in the place where Jesus had been put to death, and in it there was a new tomb where no one had ever been buried. ⁴²Since it was the day before the Sabbath and because the tomb was close by, they placed Jesus' body there.

The Empty Tomb
(Matt. 28.1-8; Mark 16.1-8; Luke 24.1-12)

20 Early on Sunday morning, while it was still dark, Mary Magdalene went to the tomb and

believe; *some manuscripts have* continue to believe.

The two men took Jesus' body (19.40)

saw that the stone had been taken away from the
entrance. ²She went running to Simon Peter and the
other disciple, whom Jesus loved, and told them, "They
have taken the Lord from the tomb, and we don't
know where they have put him!"

3 Then Peter and the other disciple went to the
tomb. ⁴The two of them were running, but the other
disciple ran faster than Peter and reached the tomb
first. ⁵He bent over and saw the linen wrappings, but
he did not go in. ⁶Behind him came Simon Peter,
and he went straight into the tomb. He saw the linen
wrappings lying there ⁷and the cloth which had been
round Jesus' head. It was not lying with the linen
wrappings but was rolled up by itself. ⁸Then the other
disciple, who had reached the tomb first, also went
in; he saw and believed. ⁹(They still did not understand
the scripture which said that he must rise from death.)
¹⁰Then the disciples went back home.

Jesus Appears to Mary Magdalene
(Matt. 28.9–10; Mark 16.9–11)

11 Mary stood crying outside the tomb. While she

was still crying, she bent over and looked in the tomb 12 and saw two angels there dressed in white, sitting where the body of Jesus had been, one at the head and the other at the feet. 13 "Woman, why are you crying?" they asked her.

She answered, "They have taken my Lord away, and I do not know where they have put him!"

14 Then she turned round and saw Jesus standing there; but she did not know that it was Jesus. 15 "Woman, why are you crying?" Jesus asked her. "Who is it that you are looking for?"

She thought he was the gardener, so she said to him, "If you took him away, sir, tell me where you have put him, and I will go and get him."

16 Jesus said to her, "Mary!"

She turned towards him and said in Hebrew, "Rabboni!" (This means "Teacher.")

17 "Do not hold on to me," Jesus told her, "because I have not yet gone back up to the Father. But go to my brothers and tell them that I am returning to him who is my Father and their Father, my God and their God."

18 So Mary Magdalene went and told the disciples that she had seen the Lord and related to them what he had told her.

Jesus Appears to His Disciples
(Matt. 28.16-20; Mark 16.14-18; Luke 24.36-49)

19 It was late that Sunday evening, and the disciples were gathered together behind locked doors, because they were afraid of the Jewish authorities. Then Jesus came and stood among them. "Peace be with you," he said. 20 After saying this, he showed them his hands and his side. The disciples were filled with joy at seeing the Lord. 21 Jesus said to them again, "Peace be with you. As the Father sent me, so I send you." 22 Then he breathed on them and said, "Receive the Holy Spirit. 23 If you forgive people's sins, they are forgiven; if you do not forgive them, they are not forgiven."

Jesus and Thomas

24 One of the twelve disciples, Thomas (called the

Jesus came and stood among them (20.19)

Twin), was not with them when Jesus came. ²⁵ So
the other disciples told him, "We have seen the Lord!"

Thomas said to them, "Unless I see the scars of
the nails in his hands and put my finger on those
scars and my hand in his side, I will not believe."

26 A week later the disciples were together again
indoors, and Thomas was with them. The doors were
locked, but Jesus came and stood among them and
said, "Peace be with you." ²⁷ Then he said to Thomas,
"Put your finger here, and look at my hands; then
stretch out your hand and put it in my side. Stop
your doubting, and believe!"

28 Thomas answered him, "My Lord and my God!"

29 Jesus said to him, "Do you believe because you
see me? How happy are those who believe without
seeing me!"

The Purpose of This Book

30 In his disciples' presence Jesus performed many
other miracles which are not written down in this
book. ³¹ But these have been written in order that
you may believeʲ that Jesus is the Messiah, the Son of

ʲbelieve; *some manuscripts have* continue to believe.

God, and that through your faith in him you may
have life.

Jesus Appears to Seven Disciples

21 After this, Jesus appeared once more to his
disciples at Lake Tiberias. This is how it
happened. ²Simon Peter, Thomas (called the Twin),
Nathanael (the one from Cana in Galilee), the sons
of Zebedee, and two other disciples of Jesus were
all together. ³Simon Peter said to the others, "I am
going fishing."

"We will come with you," they told him. So they
went out in a boat, but all that night they did not
catch a thing. ⁴As the sun was rising, Jesus stood
at the water's edge, but the disciples did not know
that it was Jesus. ⁵Then he asked them, "Young men,
haven't you caught anything?"

"Not a thing," they answered.

6 He said to them, "Throw your net out on the
right side of the boat, and you will catch some."
So they threw the net out and could not pull it back
in, because they had caught so many fish.

7 The disciple whom Jesus loved said to Peter, "It
is the Lord!" When Peter heard that it was the Lord,
he wrapped his outer garment round him (for he
had taken his clothes off) and jumped into the water.
⁸The other disciples came to shore in the boat, pulling
the net full of fish. They were not very far from
land, about a hundred metres away. ⁹When they
stepped ashore, they saw a charcoal fire there with
fish on it and some bread. ¹⁰Then Jesus said to them,
"Bring some of the fish you have just caught."

11 Simon Peter went aboard and dragged the net
ashore full of big fish, a hundred and fifty-three in
all; even though there were so many, still the net
did not tear. ¹²Jesus said to them, "Come and eat."
None of the disciples dared ask him, "Who are you?"
because they knew it was the Lord. ¹³So Jesus went
over, took the bread, and gave it to them; he did
the same with the fish.

14 This, then, was the third time Jesus appeared
to the disciples after he was raised from death.

Simon Peter...dragged the net ashore (21.11)

Jesus and Peter

15 After they had eaten, Jesus said to Simon Peter, "Simon son of John, do you love me more than these others do?"

"Yes, Lord," he answered, "you know that I love you."

Jesus said to him, "Take care of my lambs." 16A second time Jesus said to him, "Simon son of John, do you love me?"

"Yes, Lord," he answered, "you know that I love you."

Jesus said to him, "Take care of my sheep." 17A third time Jesus said, "Simon son of John, do you love me?"

Peter was sad because Jesus asked him the third time, "Do you love me?" so he said to him, "Lord, you know everything; you know that I love you!"

Jesus said to him, "Take care of my sheep. [18] I am telling you the truth: when you were young, you used to get ready and go anywhere you wanted to; but when you are old, you will stretch out your hands and someone else will bind you and take you where you don't want to go." [19] (In saying this, Jesus was indicating the way in which Peter would die and bring glory to God.) Then Jesus said to him, "Follow me!"

Jesus and the Other Disciple

20 Peter turned round and saw behind him that other disciple, whom Jesus loved—the one who had leaned close to Jesus at the meal and had asked, "Lord, who is going to betray you?" [21] When Peter saw him, he asked Jesus, "Lord, what about this man?"

22 Jesus answered him, "If I want him to live until I come, what is that to you? Follow me!"

23 So a report spread among the followers of Jesus that this disciple would not die. But Jesus did not say that he would not die; he said, "If I want him to live until I come, what is that to you?"

24 He is the disciple who spoke of these things, the one who also wrote them down; and we know that what he said is true.

Conclusion

25 Now, there are many other things that Jesus did. If they were all written down one by one, I suppose that the whole world could not hold the books that would be written.

THE ACTS

OF THE APOSTLES

INTRODUCTION

The Acts of the Apostles is a continuation of *The Gospel according to Luke*. Its chief purpose is to tell how Jesus' early followers, led by the Holy Spirit, spread the Good News about him "in Jerusalem, in all Judaea and Samaria, and to the ends of the earth" (1.8). It is the story of the Christian movement as it began among the Jewish people and went on to become a faith for the whole world. The writer was also concerned to reassure his readers that the Christians were not a subversive political threat to the Roman Empire, and that the Christian faith was the fulfilment of the Jewish religion.

Acts may be divided into three principal parts, reflecting the ever widening area in which the Good News about Jesus was proclaimed and the church established: (1) the beginning of the Christian movement in Jerusalem following the ascension of Jesus; (2) expansion into other parts of Palestine; and (3) further expansion, into the Mediterranean world as far as Rome.

An important feature of *Acts* is the activity of the Holy Spirit, who comes with power upon the believers in Jerusalem on the day of Pentecost and continues to guide and strengthen the church and its leaders throughout the events reported in the book. The early Christian message is summarized in a number of sermons, and the events recorded in *Acts* show the power of this message in the lives of the believers and in the fellowship of the church.

Outline of Contents

---

1 Dear Theophilus:
In my first book I wrote about all the things that Jesus did and taught from the time he began his work ²until the day he was taken up to heaven. Before he was taken up, he gave instructions by the power of the Holy Spirit to the men he had chosen as his apostles. ³For forty days after his death he appeared to them many times in ways that proved beyond doubt that he was alive. They saw him, and he talked with them about the Kingdom of God. ⁴And when they came together,*ᵃ* he gave them this order: "Do not leave Jerusalem, but wait for the gift I told you about, the gift my Father promised. ⁵John baptized with water, but in a few days you will be baptized with the Holy Spirit."

Jesus Is Taken up to Heaven

6 When the apostles met together with Jesus, they asked him, "Lord, will you at this time give the Kingdom back to Israel?"

7 Jesus said to them, "The times and occasions are set by my Father's own authority, and it is not for you to know when they will be. ⁸But when the Holy Spirit comes upon you, you will be filled with power, and you will be witnesses for me in Jerusalem, in all Judaea and Samaria, and to the ends of the earth." ⁹After saying this, he was taken up to heaven as

ᵃwhen they came together; *or* while he was staying with them; *or* while he was eating with them.

they watched him, and a cloud hid him from their sight.

10 They still had their eyes fixed on the sky as he went away, when two men dressed in white suddenly stood beside them [11] and said, "Galileans, why are you standing there looking up at the sky? This Jesus, who was taken from you into heaven, will come back in the same way that you saw him go to heaven."

Judas' Successor

12 Then the apostles went back to Jerusalem from the Mount of Olives, which is about a kilometre away from the city. [13] They entered the city and went up to the room where they were staying: Peter, John, James and Andrew, Philip and Thomas, Bartholomew and Matthew, James son of Alphaeus, Simon the Patriot, and Judas son of James. [14] They gathered frequently to pray as a group, together with the women and with Mary the mother of Jesus and with his brothers.

15 A few days later there was a meeting of the believers, about a hundred and twenty in all, and Peter stood up to speak. [16] "My brothers," he said, "the scripture had to come true in which the Holy Spirit, speaking through David, made a prediction about Judas, who was the guide for those who arrested Jesus. [17] Judas was a member of our group, for he had been chosen to have a part in our work."

18 (With the money that Judas got for his evil act he bought a field, where he fell to his death; he burst open and all his bowels spilt out. [19] All the people living in Jerusalem heard about it, and so in their own language they call that field Akeldama, which means "Field of Blood.")

20 "For it is written in the book of Psalms,

'May his house become empty;
    may no one live in it.'

It is also written,

'May someone else take his place of service.'

21-22 "So then, someone must join us as a witness to the resurrection of the Lord Jesus. He must be one of the men who were in our group during the whole time that the Lord Jesus travelled about with us, beginning from the time John preached his message of baptism[b] until the day Jesus was taken up from us to heaven."

23 So they proposed two men: Joseph, who was called Barsabbas (also known as Justus), and Matthias. 24 Then they prayed, "Lord, you know the thoughts of everyone, so show us which of these two you have chosen 25 to serve as an apostle in the place of Judas, who left to go to the place where he belongs." 26 Then they drew lots to choose between the two men, and the one chosen was Matthias, who was added to the group of eleven apostles.

The Coming of the Holy Spirit

2 When the day of Pentecost came, all the believers were gathered together in one place. 2 Suddenly there was a noise from the sky which sounded like a strong wind blowing, and it filled the whole house where they were sitting. 3 Then they saw what looked like tongues of fire which spread out and touched each person there. 4 They were all filled with the Holy Spirit and began to talk in other languages, as the Spirit enabled them to speak.

5 There were Jews living in Jerusalem, religious men who had come from every country in the world. 6 When they heard this noise, a large crowd gathered. They were all excited, because each one of them heard the believers speaking in his own language. 7 In amazement and wonder they exclaimed, "These people who are talking like this are Galileans! 8 How is it, then, that all of us hear them speaking in our own native languages? 9 We are from Parthia, Media, and Elam; from Mesopotamia, Judaea, and Cappadocia; from Pontus and Asia, 10 from Phrygia and Pamphylia, from Egypt and the regions of Libya near Cyrene. Some of us are from Rome, 11 both Jews and Gentiles converted to Judaism, and some of us are from Crete and Arabia—yet all of us hear them speaking in our own languages about the great things that God has

_b_ John preached his message of baptism; _or_ John baptized him.

CILICIA

● Tarsus

Antioch
● Seleucia

SYRIA

Salamis ●

CYPRUS

● Paphos

PHOENICIA

PALESTINE AND SYRIA
IN ACTS

● Damascus

MEDITERRANEAN
SEA

Caesarea ●

Samaria ●

River Jordan

● Joppa
● Lydda

Jerusalem

DEAD
SEA

● Gaza
JUDAEA

0   50   100

Kilometres

done!" ¹² Amazed and confused, they kept asking each other, "What does this mean?"

13 But others made fun of the believers, saying, "These people are drunk!"

Peter's Message

14 Then Peter stood up with the other eleven apostles

Fellow-Jews...listen to me! (2.14)

and in a loud voice began to speak to the crowd: "Fellow-Jews and all of you who live in Jerusalem, listen to me and let me tell you what this means. ¹⁵ These people are not drunk, as you suppose; it is only nine o'clock in the morning. ¹⁶ Instead, this is what the prophet Joel spoke about:

¹⁷ 'This is what I will do in the last days, God says:
I will pour out my Spirit on everyone.
Your sons and daughters will proclaim my message;
your young men will see visions,
and your old men will have dreams.
¹⁸ Yes, even on my servants, both men and women,
I will pour out my Spirit in those days,
and they will proclaim my message.

19 I will perform miracles in the sky above
   and wonders on the earth below.
There will be blood, fire, and thick smoke;
20   the sun will be darkened,
   and the moon will turn red as blood,
   before the great and glorious Day of the Lord
      comes.
21 And then, whoever calls out to the Lord for help
   will be saved.'

22 "Listen to these words, fellow-Israelites!. Jesus of Nazareth was a man whose divine authority was clearly proven to you by all the miracles and wonders which God performed through him. You yourselves know this, for it happened here among you. 23 In accordance with his own plan God had already decided that Jesus would be handed over to you; and you killed him by letting sinful men crucify him. 24 But God raised him from death, setting him free from its power, because it was impossible that death should hold him prisoner. 25 For David said about him,

'I saw the Lord before me at all times;
   he is near me, and I will not be troubled.
26 And so I am filled with gladness,
   and my words are full of joy.
And I, mortal though I am,
   will rest assured in hope,
27 because you will not abandon me in the world
      of the dead;
   you will not allow your faithful servant to rot
      in the grave.
28 You have shown me the paths that lead to life,
   and your presence will fill me with joy.'

29 "My brothers, I must speak to you plainly about our famous ancestor King David. He died and was buried, and his grave is here with us to this very day. 30 He was a prophet, and he knew what God had promised him: God had made a vow that he would make one of David's descendants a king, just as David was. 31 David saw what God was going to do in the future, and so he spoke about the resurrection of the Messiah when he said,

'He was not abandoned in the world of the dead;
 his body did not rot in the grave.'
32 God has raised this very Jesus from death, and
we are all witnesses to this fact. 33 He has been raised
to the right-hand side of God, his Father, and has
received from him the Holy Spirit, as he had promised.
What you now see and hear is his gift that he has
poured out on us. 34 For it was not David who went
up into heaven; rather he said,
'The Lord said to my Lord:
 Sit here at my right
35 until I put your enemies as a footstool under your
 feet.'
36 "All the people of Israel, then, are to know for
sure that this Jesus, whom you crucified, is the one
that God has made Lord and Messiah!"

37 When the people heard this, they were deeply
troubled and said to Peter and the other apostles,
"What shall we do, brothers?"

38 Peter said to them, "Each one of you must turn
away from his sins and be baptized in the name
of Jesus Christ, so that your sins will be forgiven;
and you will receive God's gift, the Holy Spirit. 39 For
God's promise was made to you and your children,
and to all who are far away—all whom the Lord
our God calls to himself."

40 Peter made his appeal to them and with many
other words he urged them, saying, "Save yourselves
from the punishment coming on this wicked people!"
41 Many of them believed his message and were baptized, and about three thousand people were added
to the group that day. 42 They spent their time in
learning from the apostles, taking part in the fellowship, and sharing in the fellowship meals and the
prayers.

Life among the Believers

43 Many miracles and wonders were being done
through the apostles, and everyone was filled with
awe. 44 All the believers continued together in close
fellowship and shared their belongings with one

another. ⁴⁵They would sell their property and posses-
sions, and distribute the money among all, according
to what each one needed. ⁴⁶Day after day they met
as a group in the Temple, and they had their meals
together in their homes, eating with glad and humble
hearts, ⁴⁷praising God, and enjoying the good will
of all the people. And every day the Lord added
to their group those who were being saved.

A Lame Man Is Healed

3 One day Peter and John went to the Temple at
three o'clock in the afternoon, the hour for prayer.
²There at the Beautiful Gate, as it was called, was
a man who had been lame all his life. Every day
he was carried to the gate to beg for money from
the people who were going into the Temple. ³When
he saw Peter and John going in, he begged them to
give him something. ⁴They looked straight at him,
and Peter said, "Look at us!" ⁵So he looked at them,
expecting to get something from them. ⁶But Peter

I give you what I have (3.6)

said to him, "I have no money at all, but I give you
what I have: in the name of Jesus Christ of Nazareth
I order you to get up and walk!" ⁷Then he took
him by his right hand and helped him up. At once

the man's feet and ankles became strong; 8he jumped up, stood on his feet, and started walking around. Then he went into the Temple with them, walking and jumping and praising God. 9The people there saw him walking and praising God, 10and when they recognized him as the beggar who had sat at the Beautiful Gate, they were all surprised and amazed at what had happened to him.

Peter's Message in the Temple

11 As the man held on to Peter and John in Solomon's Porch, as it was called, the people were amazed and ran to them. 12When Peter saw the people, he said to them, "Fellow-Israelites, why are you surprised at this, and why do you stare at us? Do you think that it was by means of our own power or godliness that we made this man walk? 13The God of Abraham, Isaac, and Jacob, the God of our ancestors, has given divine glory to his Servant Jesus. But you handed him over to the authorities, and you rejected him in Pilate's presence, even after Pilate had decided to set him free. 14He was holy and good, but you rejected him, and instead you asked Pilate to do you the favour of turning loose a murderer. 15You killed the one who leads to life, but God raised him from death—and we are witnesses to this. 16It was the power of his name that gave strength to this lame man. What you see and know was done by faith in his name; it was faith in Jesus that has made him well, as you can all see.

17 "And now, my brothers, I know that what you and your leaders did to Jesus was due to your ignorance. 18God announced long ago through all the prophets that his Messiah had to suffer; and he made it come true in this way. 19Repent, then, and turn to God, so that he will forgive your sins. If you do, 20times of spiritual strength will come from the Lord, and he will send Jesus, who is the Messiah he has already chosen for you. 21He must remain in heaven until the time comes for all things to be made new, as God announced through his holy prophets who lived long ago. 22For Moses said, 'The

Lord your God will send you a prophet, just as he sent me, *d* and he will be one of your own people. You are to obey everything that he tells you to do. 23 Anyone who does not obey that prophet shall be separated from God's people and destroyed.' 24 And all the prophets who had a message, including Samuel and those who came after him, also announced what has been happening these days. 25 The promises of God through his prophets are for you, and you share in the covenant which God made with your ancestors. As he said to Abraham, 'Through your descendants I will bless all the people on earth.' 26 And so God chose his Servant and sent him first to you, to bless you by making every one of you turn away from his wicked ways."

Peter and John before the Council

4 Peter and John were still speaking to the people when some priests, *e* the officer in charge of the temple guards, and some Sadducees arrived. 2 They were annoyed because the two apostles were teaching the people that Jesus had risen from death, which proved that the dead will rise to life. 3 So they arrested them and put them in jail until the next day, since it was already late. 4 But many who heard the message believed; and the number of men grew to about five thousand.

5 The next day the Jewish leaders, the elders, and the teachers of the Law gathered in Jerusalem. 6 They met with the High Priest Annas and with Caiaphas, John, Alexander, and the others who belonged to the High Priest's family. 7 They made the apostles stand before them and asked them, "How did you do this? What power have you got or whose name did you use?"

8 Peter, full of the Holy Spirit, answered them, "Leaders of the people and elders: 9 if we are being questioned today about the good deed done to the lame man and how he was healed, 10 then you should all know, and all the people of Israel should know,

---

*d*just as he sent me; *or* like me.
*e*priests; *some manuscripts have* chief priests.

that this man stands here before you completely well through the power of the name of Jesus Christ of Nazareth—whom you crucified and whom God raised from death. 11 Jesus is the one of whom the scripture says,

'The stone that you the builders despised
turned out to be the most important of all.'

12 Salvation is to be found through him alone; in all the world there is no one else whom God has given who can save us."

13 The members of the Council were amazed to see how bold Peter and John were and to learn that they were ordinary men of no education. They realized then that they had been companions of Jesus. 14 But there was nothing that they could say, because they saw the man who had been healed standing there with Peter and John. 15 So they told them to leave the Council room, and then they started discussing among themselves. 16 "What shall we do with these men?" they asked. "Everyone in Jerusalem knows that this extraordinary miracle has been performed by them, and we cannot deny it. 17 But to keep this matter from spreading any further among the people, let us warn these men never again to speak to anyone in the name of Jesus."

18 So they called them back in and told them that on no condition were they to speak or to teach in the name of Jesus. 19 But Peter and John answered them, "You yourselves judge which is right in God's sight—to obey you or to obey God. 20 For we cannot stop speaking of what we ourselves have seen and heard." 21 So the Council warned them even more strongly and then set them free. They saw that it was impossible to punish them, because the people were all praising God for what had happened. 22 The man on whom this miracle of healing had been performed was over forty years old.

The Believers Pray for Boldness

23 As soon as Peter and John were set free, they returned to their group and told them what the chief priests and the elders had said. 24 When the believers heard it, they all joined together in prayer to God:

"Master and Creator of heaven, earth, and sea, and all that is in them! 25 By means of the Holy Spirit you spoke through our ancestor David, your servant, when he said,

'Why were the Gentiles furious;
    why did people make their useless plots?
26 The kings of the earth prepared themselves,
    and the rulers met together
    against the Lord and his Messiah.'

27 For indeed Herod and Pontius Pilate met together in this city with the Gentiles and the people of Israel against Jesus, your holy Servant, whom you made Messiah. 28 They gathered to do everything that you by your power and will had already decided would happen. 29 And now, Lord, take notice of the threats they have made, and allow us, your servants, to speak your message with all boldness. 30 Stretch out your hand to heal, and grant that wonders and miracles may be performed through the name of your holy Servant Jesus."

31 When they finished praying, the place where they were meeting was shaken. They were all filled with the Holy Spirit and began to proclaim God's message with boldness.

The Believers Share Their Possessions

32 The group of believers was one in mind and heart. No one said that any of his belongings was his own, but they all shared with one another everything they had. 33 With great power the apostles gave witness to the resurrection of the Lord Jesus, and God poured rich blessings on them all. 34 There was no one in the group who was in need. Those who owned fields or houses would sell them, bring the money received from the sale, 35 and hand it over to the apostles; and the money was distributed to each one according to his need.

36 And so it was that Joseph, a Levite born in Cyprus, whom the apostles called Barnabas (which means "One who Encourages"), 37 sold a field he owned, brought the money, and handed it over to the apostles.

Ananias and Sapphira

5 But there was a man named Ananias, who with his wife Sapphira sold some property that belonged to them. ²But with his wife's agreement he kept part of the money for himself and handed the rest over to the apostles. ³Peter said to him, "Ananias, why did you let Satan take control of you and make you lie to the Holy Spirit by keeping part of the money you received for the property? ⁴Before you sold the property, it belonged to you; and after you sold it, the money was yours. Why, then, did you decide to do such a thing? You have not lied to men—you have lied to God!" ⁵As soon as Ananias heard this, he fell down dead; and all who heard about it were terrified. ⁶The young men came in, wrapped up his body, carried him out, and buried him.

7 About three hours later his wife, not knowing what had happened, came in. ⁸Peter asked her, "Tell me, was this the full amount you and your husband received for your property?"

"Yes," she answered, "the full amount."

9 So Peter said to her, "Why did you and your husband decide to put the Lord's Spirit to the test? The men who buried your husband are now at the door, and they will carry you out too!" ¹⁰At once she fell down at his feet and died. The young men came in and saw that she was dead, so they carried her out and buried her beside her husband. ¹¹The whole church and all the others who heard of this were terrified.

Miracles and Wonders

12 Many miracles and wonders were being performed among the people by the apostles. All the believers met together in Solomon's Porch. ¹³Nobody outside the group dared to join them, even though the people spoke highly of them. ¹⁴But more and more people were added to the group—a crowd of men and women who believed in the Lord. ¹⁵As a result of what the apostles were doing, sick people were carried out into the streets and placed on beds and mats so that at least Peter's shadow might fall on some of them

So that at least Peter's shadow might fall on some of them (5.15)

as he passed by. ¹⁶And crowds of people came in from the towns around Jerusalem, bringing those who were ill or who had evil spirits in them; and they were all healed.

The Apostles Are Persecuted

17 Then the High Priest and all his companions, members of the local party of the Sadducees, became extremely jealous of the apostles; so they decided to take action. ¹⁸They arrested the apostles and put them in the public jail. ¹⁹But that night an angel of the Lord opened the prison gates, led the apostles out, and said to them, ²⁰"Go and stand in the Temple, and tell the people all about this new life." ²¹The

apostles obeyed, and at dawn they entered the Temple and started teaching.

The High Priest and his companions called together all the Jewish elders for a full meeting of the Council; then they sent orders to the prison to have the apostles brought before them. 22 But when the officials arrived, they did not find the apostles in prison, so they returned to the Council and reported. 23 "When we arrived at the jail, we found it locked up tight and all the guards on watch at the gates; but when we opened the gates, we found no one inside!" 24 When the chief priests and the officer in charge of the temple guards heard this, they wondered what had happened to the apostles. 25 Then a man came in and said to them, "Listen! The men you put in prison are in the Temple teaching the people!" 26 So the officer went off with his men and brought the apostles back. They did not use force, however, because they were afraid that the people might stone them.

27 They brought the apostles in, made them stand before the Council, and the High Priest questioned them. 28 "We gave you strict orders not to teach in the name of this man," he said; "but see what you have done! You have spread your teaching all over Jerusalem, and you want to make us responsible for his death!"

29 Peter and the other apostles replied, "We must obey God, not men. 30 The God of our ancestors raised Jesus from death, after you had killed him by nailing him to a cross. 31 God raised him to his right-hand side as Leader and Saviour, to give the people of Israel the opportunity to repent and have their sins forgiven. 32 We are witnesses to these things—we and the Holy Spirit, who is God's gift to those who obey him."

33 When the members of the Council heard this, they were so furious that they wanted to have the apostles put to death. 34 But one of them, a Pharisee named Gamaliel, who was a teacher of the Law and was highly respected by all the people, stood up in the Council. He ordered the apostles to be taken out for a while, 35 and then he said to the Council, "Fellow-Israelites, be careful what you do to these men. 36 You remember that Theudas appeared some time ago, claim-

ing to be somebody great, and about four hundred men joined him. But he was killed, all his followers were scattered, and his movement died out. [37]After that, Judas the Galilean appeared during the time of the census; he drew a crowd after him, but he also was killed, and all his followers were scattered. [38]And so in this case, I tell you, do not take any action against these men. Leave them alone! If what they have planned and done is of human origin, it will disappear, [39]but if it comes from God, you cannot possibly defeat them. You could find yourselves fighting against God!"

The Council followed Gamaliel's advice. [40]They called the apostles in, had them whipped, and ordered them never again to speak in the name of Jesus; and then they set them free. [41]As the apostles left the Council, they were happy, because God had considered them worthy to suffer disgrace for the sake of Jesus. [42]And every day in the Temple and in people's homes they continued to teach and preach the Good News about Jesus the Messiah.

The Seven Helpers

6 Some time later, as the number of disciples kept growing, there was a quarrel between the Greek-speaking Jews and the native Jews. The Greek-speaking Jews claimed that their widows were being neglected in the daily distribution of funds. [2]So the twelve apostles called the whole group of believers together and said, "It is not right for us to neglect the preaching of God's word in order to handle finances. [3]So then, brothers, choose seven men among you who are known to be full of the Holy Spirit and wisdom, and we will put them in charge of this matter. [4]We ourselves, then, will give our full time to prayer and the work of preaching."

[5]The whole group was pleased with the apostles' proposal, so they chose Stephen, a man full of faith and the Holy Spirit, and Philip, Prochorus, Nicanor, Timon, Parmenas, and Nicolaus, a Gentile from Antioch who had earlier been converted to Judaism. [6]The group presented them to the apostles, who prayed and placed their hands on them.

[7]And so the word of God continued to spread.

The number of disciples in Jerusalem grew larger and larger, and a great number of priests accepted the faith.

The Arrest of Stephen

8 Stephen, a man richly blessed by God and full of power, performed great miracles and wonders among the people. 9But he was opposed by some men who were members of the synagogue of the Freedmen *f* (as it was called), which included Jews from Cyrene and Alexandria. They and other Jews from the provinces of Cilicia and Asia started arguing with Stephen. 10But the Spirit gave Stephen such wisdom that when he spoke, they could not refute him. 11So they bribed some men to say, "We heard him speaking against Moses and against God!" 12In this way they stirred up the people, the elders, and the teachers of the Law. They seized Stephen and took him before the Council. 13Then they brought in some men to tell lies about him. "This man," they said, "is always talking against our sacred Temple and the Law of Moses. 14We heard him say that this Jesus of Nazareth will tear down the Temple and change all the customs which have come down to us from Moses!" 15All those sitting in the Council fixed their eyes on Stephen and saw that his face looked like the face of an angel.

Stephen's Speech

7 The High Priest asked Stephen, "Is this true?"
2 Stephen answered, "Brothers and fathers, listen to me! Before our ancestor Abraham had gone to live in Haran, the God of glory appeared to him in Mesopotamia 3and said to him, 'Leave your family and country and go to the land that I will show you.' 4And so he left his country and went to live in Haran. After Abraham's father died, God made him move to this land where you now live. 5God did not then give Abraham any part of it as his own, not even a square metre of ground, but God pro-

---

*f*FREEDMEN: *These were Jews who had been slaves, but had bought or been given their freedom.*

mised to give it to him, and that it would belong
to him and to his descendants. At the time God made
this promise, Abraham had no children. 6 This is what
God said to him: 'Your descendants will live in a
foreign country, where they will be slaves and will
be badly treated for four hundred years. 7 But I will
pass judgement on the people that they will serve,
and afterwards they will come out of that country
and will worship me in this place.' 8 Then God gave
Abraham the ceremony of circumcision as a sign of
the covenant. So Abraham circumcised Isaac a week
after he was born; Isaac circumcised his son, Jacob,
and Jacob circumcised his twelve sons, the famous
ancestors of our race.

9 "Jacob's sons became jealous of their brother
Joseph and sold him to be a slave in Egypt. But
God was with him 10 and brought him safely through
all his troubles. When Joseph appeared before the
king of Egypt, God gave him a pleasing manner and
wisdom, and the king made Joseph governor over
the country and the royal household. 11 Then there
was a famine all over Egypt and Canaan, which caused
much suffering. Our ancestors could not find any food,
12 and when Jacob heard that there was corn in Egypt,
he sent his sons, our ancestors, on their first visit there.
13 On the second visit Joseph made himself known
to his brothers, and the king of Egypt came to know
about Joseph's family. 14 So Joseph sent a message
to his father Jacob, telling him and the whole family,
seventy-five people in all, to come to Egypt. 15 Then
Jacob went to Egypt, where he and his sons died.
16 Their bodies were taken to Shechem, where they
were buried in the grave which Abraham had bought
from the clan of Hamor for a sum of money.

17 "When the time drew near for God to keep the
promise he had made to Abraham, the number of
our people in Egypt had grown much larger. 18 At
last a king who did not know about Joseph began
to rule in Egypt. 19 He tricked our ancestors and was
cruel to them, forcing them to put their babies out
of their homes, so that they would die. 20 It was at
this time that Moses was born, a very beautiful child.
He was cared for at home for three months, 21 and

when he was put out of his home, the king's daughter adopted him and brought him up as her own son. 22 He was taught all the wisdom of the Egyptians and became a great man in words and deeds.

23 "When Moses was forty years old, he decided to find out how his fellow-Israelites were being treated. 24 He saw one of them being ill-treated by an Egyptian, so he went to his help and took revenge on the Egyptian by killing him. 25 (He thought that his own people would understand that God was going to use him to set them free, but they did not understand.) 26 The next day he saw two Israelites fighting, and he tried to make peace between them. 'Listen, men,' he said, 'you are fellow-Israelites; why are you fighting like this?' 27 But the one who was ill-treating the other pushed Moses aside. 'Who made you ruler and judge over us?' he asked. 28 'Do you want to kill me, just as you killed that Egyptian yesterday?' 29 When Moses heard this, he fled from Egypt and went to live in the land of Midian. There he had two sons.

30 "After forty years had passed, an angel appeared to Moses in the flames of a burning bush in the desert near Mount Sinai. 31 Moses was amazed by what he saw, and went near the bush to get a better look. But he heard the Lord's voice: 32 'I am the God of your ancestors, the God of Abraham, Isaac, and Jacob.' Moses trembled with fear and dared not look. 33 The Lord said to him, 'Take your sandals off, for the place where you are standing is holy ground. 34 I have seen the cruel suffering of my people in Egypt. I have heard their groans, and I have come down to set them free. Come now; I will send you to Egypt.'

35 "Moses is the one who was rejected by the people of Israel. 'Who made you ruler and judge over us?' they asked. He is the one whom God sent to rule the people and set them free with the help of the angel who appeared to him in the burning bush. 36 He led the people out of Egypt, performing miracles and wonders in Egypt and at the Red Sea and for forty years in the desert. 37 Moses is the one who said to the people of Israel, 'God will send you a prophet,

just as he sent me,^{g} and he will be one of your own people.' ^{38}He is the one who was with the people of Israel assembled in the desert; he was there with our ancestors and with the angel who spoke to him on Mount Sinai, and he received God's living messages to pass on to us.

39 "But our ancestors refused to obey him; they pushed him aside and wished that they could go back to Egypt. ^{40}So they said to Aaron, 'Make us some gods who will lead us. We do not know what has happened to that man Moses, who brought us out of Egypt.' ^{41}It was then that they made an idol in the shape of a bull, offered sacrifice to it, and had a feast in honour of what they themselves had made. ^{42}So God turned away from them and gave them over to worship the stars of heaven, as it is written in the book of the prophets:

'People of Israel! It was not to me
    that you slaughtered and sacrificed animals
    for forty years in the desert.
^{43}It was the tent of the god Molech that you carried,
    and the image of Rephan, your star god;
    they were idols that you had made to worship.
And so I will send you into exile beyond Babylon.'

44 "Our ancestors had the Tent of God's presence with them in the desert. It had been made as God had told Moses to make it, according to the pattern that Moses had been shown. ^{45}Later on, our ancestors who received the tent from their fathers carried it with them when they went with Joshua and took over the land from the nations that God drove out as they advanced. And it stayed there until the time of David. ^{46}He won God's favour and asked God to allow him to provide a dwelling place for the God of Jacob.^{h} ^{47}But it was Solomon who built him a house.

48 "But the Most High God does not live in houses built by men; as the prophet says,
^{49}'Heaven is my throne, says the Lord,
    and the earth is my footstool.
What kind of house would you build for me?

---

^{g}just as he sent me; or like me.
^{h}the God of Jacob; some manuscripts have the people of Israel.

Where is the place for me to live in?
50 Did not I myself make all these things?'

51 "How stubborn you are!" Stephen went on to say. "How heathen your hearts, how deaf you are to God's message! You are just like your ancestors: you too have always resisted the Holy Spirit! 52 Was there any prophet that your ancestors did not persecute? They killed God's messengers, who long ago announced the coming of his righteous Servant. And now you have betrayed and murdered him. 53 You are the ones who received God's law, that was handed down by angels—yet you have not obeyed it!"

The Stoning of Stephen

54 As the members of the Council listened to Stephen, they became furious and ground their teeth at him in anger. 55 But Stephen, full of the Holy Spirit, looked up to heaven and saw God's glory and Jesus standing at the right-hand side of God. 56 "Look!" he said. "I see heaven opened and the Son of Man standing at the right-hand side of God!"

57 With a loud cry the members of the Council covered their ears with their hands. Then they all rushed at him at once, 58 threw him out of the city, and stoned him. The witnesses left their cloaks in the care of a young man named Saul. 59 They kept on stoning Stephen as he called out to the Lord, "Lord Jesus, receive my spirit!" 60 He knelt down and cried out in a loud voice, "Lord! Do not remember this sin against them!" He said this and died.

8 And Saul approved of his murder.

Saul Persecutes the Church

That very day the church in Jerusalem began to suffer cruel persecution. All the believers, except the apostles, were scattered throughout the provinces of Judaea and Samaria. 2 Some devout men buried Stephen, mourning for him with loud cries.

3 But Saul tried to destroy the church; going from house to house, he dragged out the believers, both men and women, and threw them into jail.

And Saul approved of his murder (8.1)

The Gospel Is Preached in Samaria

4 The believers who were scattered went everywhere, preaching the message. 5 Philip went to the principal city[i] in Samaria and preached the Messiah to the people there. 6 The crowds paid close attention to what Philip said, as they listened to him and saw the miracles that he performed. 7 Evil spirits came out from many people with a loud cry, and many paralysed and lame people were healed. 8 So there was great joy in that city.

9 A man named Simon lived there, who for some time had astounded the Samaritans with his magic. He claimed that he was someone great, 10 and everyone in the city, from all classes of society, paid close attention to him. "He is that power of God known as 'The Great Power', " they said. 11 They paid this attention to him because for such a long time he had astonished them with his magic. 12 But when they believed Philip's message about the good news of the Kingdom of God and about Jesus Christ, they were baptized, both men and women. 13 Simon himself also

[i] the principal city; *some manuscripts have* a city.

believed; and after being baptized, he stayed close to Philip and was astounded when he saw the great wonders and miracles that were being performed.

14 The apostles in Jerusalem heard that the people of Samaria had received the word of God, so they sent Peter and John to them. [15]When they arrived, they prayed for the believers that they might receive the Holy Spirit. [16]For the Holy Spirit had not yet come down on any of them; they had only been baptized in the name of the Lord Jesus. [17]Then Peter and John placed their hands on them, and they received the Holy Spirit.

18 Simon saw that the Spirit had been given to the believers when the apostles placed their hands on them. So he offered money to Peter and John, [19]and said, "Give this power to me too, so that anyone I place my hands on will receive the Holy Spirit."

20 But Peter answered him, "May you and your money go to hell, for thinking that you can buy God's gift with money! [21]You have no part or share in our work, because your heart is not right in God's sight. [22]Repent, then, of this evil plan of yours, and pray to the Lord that he will forgive you for thinking such a thing as this. [23]For I see that you are full of bitter envy and are a prisoner of sin."

24 Simon said to Peter and John, "Please pray to the Lord for me, so that none of these things you spoke of will happen to me."

25 After they had given their testimony and proclaimed the Lord's message, Peter and John went back to Jerusalem. On their way they preached the Good News in many villages of Samaria.

Philip and the Ethiopian Official

26 An angel of the Lord said to Philip, "Get ready and go south[j] to the road that goes from Jerusalem to Gaza." (This road is not used nowadays.)[k] [27-28]So Philip got ready and went. Now an Ethiopian eunuch, who was an important official in charge of the treasury of the queen of Ethiopia, was on his way home. He

---

[j] south; or at midday.
[k] This road is not used nowadays; or This is the desert road.

had been to Jerusalem to worship God and was going back home in his carriage. As he rode along, he was reading from the book of the prophet Isaiah. [29] The Holy Spirit said to Philip, "Go over to that carriage and stay close to it." [30] Philip ran over and heard him reading from the book of the prophet Isaiah. He asked him, "Do you understand what you are reading?"

31 The official replied, "How can I understand unless someone explains it to me?" And he invited Philip to climb up and sit in the carriage with him. [32] The passage of scripture which he was reading was this:

"Like a sheep that is taken to be slaughtered,
   like a lamb that makes no sound when its wool
      is cut off,
   he did not say a word.
[33] He was humiliated, and justice was denied him.
   No one will be able to tell about his descendants,
   because his life on earth has come to an end."

34 The official asked Philip, "Tell me, of whom is the prophet saying this? Of himself or of someone else?" [35] Then Philip began to speak; starting from this passage of scripture, he told him the Good News about Jesus. [36] As they travelled down the road, they came to a place where there was some water, and the official said, "Here is some water. What is to keep me from being baptized?"[1]

38 The official ordered the carriage to stop, and both Philip and the official went down into the water, and Philip baptized him. [39] When they came up out of the water, the Spirit of the Lord took Philip away. The official did not see him again, but continued on his way, full of joy. [40] Philip found himself in Azotus; he went on to Caesarea, and on the way he preached the Good News in every town.

The Conversion of Saul
(Acts 22.6–16; 26.12–18)

9 In the meantime Saul kept up his violent threats of murder against the followers of the Lord. He

[1] *Some manuscripts add verse 37:* Philip said to him, "You may be baptized if you believe with all your heart." "I do," he answered; "I believe that Jesus Christ is the Son of God."

went to the High Priest ²and asked for letters of introduction to the synagogues in Damascus, so that if he should find there any followers of the Way of the Lord, he would be able to arrest them, both men and women, and bring them back to Jerusalem.

3 As Saul was coming near the city of Damascus, suddenly a light from the sky flashed round him. ⁴He fell to the ground and heard a voice saying to him, "Saul, Saul! Why do you persecute me?"

5 "Who are you, Lord?" he asked.

Who are you, Lord? (9.5)

"I am Jesus, whom you persecute," the voice said. ⁶"But get up and go into the city, where you will be told what you must do."

7 The men who were travelling with Saul had stopped, not saying a word; they heard the voice but could not see anyone. ⁸Saul got up from the ground and opened his eyes, but could not see a thing. So they took him by the hand and led him into Damascus. ⁹For three days he was not able to

see, and during that time he did not eat or drink anything.

10 There was a Christian in Damascus named Ananias. He had a vision, in which the Lord said to him, "Ananias!"

"Here I am, Lord," he answered.

11 The Lord said to him, "Get ready and go to Straight Street, and at the house of Judas ask for a man from Tarsus named Saul. He is praying, 12 and in a vision he has seen a man named Ananias come in and place his hands on him so that he might see again."

13 Ananias answered, "Lord, many people have told me about this man and about all the terrible things he has done to your people in Jerusalem. 14 And he has come to Damascus with authority from the chief priests to arrest all who worship you."

15 The Lord said to him, "Go, because I have chosen him to serve me, to make my name known to Gentiles and kings and to the people of Israel. 16 And I myself will show him all that he must suffer for my sake."

17 So Ananias went, entered the house where Saul was, and placed his hands on him. "Brother Saul," he said, "the Lord has sent me—Jesus himself, who appeared to you on the road as you were coming here. He sent me so that you might see again and be filled with the Holy Spirit." 18 At once something like fish scales fell from Saul's eyes, and he was able to see again. He stood up and was baptized; 19 and after he had eaten, his strength came back.

Saul Preaches in Damascus

Saul stayed for a few days with the believers in Damascus. 20 He went straight to the synagogues and began to preach that Jesus was the Son of God.

21 All who heard him were amazed and asked, "Isn't he the one who in Jerusalem was killing those who worship that man Jesus? And didn't he come here for the very purpose of arresting those people and taking them back to the chief priests?"

22 But Saul's preaching became even more powerful, and his proofs that Jesus was the Messiah were so

convincing that the Jews who lived in Damascus could not answer him.

23 After many days had gone by, the Jews met together and made plans to kill Saul, 24 but he was told of their plan. Day and night they watched the city gates in order to kill him. 25 But one night Saul's followers took him and let him down through an opening in the wall, lowering him in a basket.

Saul in Jerusalem

26 Saul went to Jerusalem and tried to join the disciples. But they would not believe that he was a disciple, and they were all afraid of him. 27 Then Barnabas came to his help and took him to the apostles. He explained to them how Saul had seen the Lord on the road and that the Lord had spoken to him. He also told them how boldly Saul had preached in the name of Jesus in Damascus. 28 And so Saul stayed with them and went all over Jerusalem, preaching boldly in the name of the Lord. 29 He also talked and disputed with the Greek-speaking Jews, but they tried to kill him. 30 When the believers found out about this, they took Saul to Caesarea and sent him away to Tarsus.

31 And so it was that the church throughout Judaea, Galilee, and Samaria had a time of peace. Through the help of the Holy Spirit it was strengthened and grew in numbers, as it lived in reverence for the Lord.

Peter in Lydda and Joppa

32 Peter travelled everywhere, and on one occasion he went to visit God's people who lived in Lydda. 33 There he met a man named Aeneas, who was paralysed and had not been able to get out of bed for eight years. 34 "Aeneas," Peter said to him, "Jesus Christ makes you well. Get up and make your bed." At once Aeneas got up. 35 All the people living in Lydda and Sharon saw him, and they turned to the Lord.

36 In Joppa there was a woman named Tabitha, who was a believer. (Her name in Greek is Dorcas, meaning "a deer.") She spent all her time doing good

and helping the poor. 37At that time she became ill
and died. Her body was washed and laid in a room
upstairs. 38Joppa was not very far from Lydda, and
when the believers in Joppa heard that Peter was
in Lydda, they sent two men to him with the message,
"Please hurry and come to us." 39So Peter got ready
and went with them. When he arrived, he was taken
to the room upstairs, where all the widows crowded
round him, crying and showing him all the shirts
and coats that Dorcas had made while she was alive.
40Peter put them all out of the room, and knelt down
and prayed; then he turned to the body and said,
"Tabitha, get up!" She opened her eyes, and when
she saw Peter, she sat up. 41Peter reached over and
helped her get up. Then he called all the believers,
including the widows, and presented her alive to them.
42The news about this spread all over Joppa, and
many people believed in the Lord. 43Peter stayed on
in Joppa for many days with a tanner of leather
named Simon.

Peter and Cornelius

10 There was a man in Caesarea named Cornelius,
who was a captain in the Roman regiment called
"The Italian Regiment." 2He was a religious man;
he and his whole family worshipped God. He also
did much to help the Jewish poor people and was
constantly praying to God. 3It was about three o'clock
one afternoon when he had a vision, in which he clearly
saw an angel of God come in and say to him,
"Cornelius!"

4 He stared at the angel in fear and said, "What
is it, sir?"

The angel answered, "God is pleased with your
prayers and works of charity, and is ready to answer
you. 5And now send some men to Joppa for a certain
man whose full name is Simon Peter. 6He is a guest
in the home of a tanner of leather named Simon,
who lives by the sea." 7Then the angel went away,
and Cornelius called two of his house servants and
a soldier, a religious man who was one of his personal
attendants. 8He told them what had happened and
sent them off to Joppa.

9 The next day, as they were on their way and coming near Joppa, Peter went up on the roof of the house about noon in order to pray. ¹⁰He became hungry and wanted something to eat; while the food was being prepared, he had a vision. ¹¹He saw heaven opened and something coming down that looked like a large sheet being lowered by its four corners to the earth. ¹²In it were all kinds of animals, reptiles, and wild birds. ¹³A voice said to him, "Get up, Peter; kill and eat!"

14 But Peter said, "Certainly not, Lord! I have never eaten anything ritually unclean or defiled."

15 The voice spoke to him again, "Do not consider anything unclean that God has declared clean." ¹⁶This happened three times, and then the thing was taken back up into heaven.

17 While Peter was wondering about the meaning of this vision, the men sent by Cornelius had learnt where Simon's house was, and they were now standing in front of the gate. ¹⁸They called out and asked, "Is there a guest here by the name of Simon Peter?"

19 Peter was still trying to understand what the vision meant, when the Spirit said, "Listen! Three*m* men are here looking for you. ²⁰So get ready and go down, and do not hesitate to go with them, for I have sent them." ²¹So Peter went down and said to the men, "I am the man you are looking for. Why have you come?"

22 "Captain Cornelius sent us," they answered. "He is a good man who worships God and is highly respected by all the Jewish people. An angel of God told him to invite you to his house, so that he could hear what you have to say." ²³Peter invited the men in and persuaded them to spend the night there.

The next day he got ready and went with them; and some of the believers from Joppa went along with him. ²⁴The following day he arrived in Caesarea, where Cornelius was waiting for him, together with relatives and close friends that he had invited. ²⁵As Peter was about to go in, Cornelius met him, fell

*m*Three; *some manuscripts have* Some; *one manuscript has* Two.

at his feet, and bowed down before him. [26] But Peter made him rise. "Stand up," he said; "I myself am only a man." [27] Peter kept on talking to Cornelius as he went into the house, where he found many people gathered. [28] He said to them, "You yourselves know very well that a Jew is not allowed by his religion to visit or associate with Gentiles. But God has shown me that I must not consider any person ritually unclean or defiled. [29] And so when you sent for me, I came without any objection. I ask you, then, why did you send for me?"

30 Cornelius said, "It was about this time three days ago that I was praying[n] in my house at three o'clock in the afternoon. Suddenly a man dressed in shining clothes stood in front of me [31] and said: 'Cornelius! God has heard your prayer and has taken notice of your works of charity. [32] Send someone to Joppa for a man whose full name is Simon Peter. He is a guest in the home of Simon the tanner of leather, who lives by the sea.' [33] And so I sent for you at once, and you have been good enough to come. Now we are all here in the presence of God, waiting to hear anything that the Lord has instructed you to say."

Peter's Speech

34 Peter began to speak: "I now realize that it is true that God treats everyone on the same basis. [35] Whoever worships him and does what is right is acceptable to him, no matter what race he belongs to. [36] You know the message he sent to the people of Israel, proclaiming the Good News of peace through Jesus Christ, who is Lord of all. [37] You know of the great event that took place throughout the land of Israel, beginning in Galilee after John preached his message of baptism. [38] You know about Jesus of Nazareth and how God poured out on him the Holy Spirit and power. He went everywhere, doing good and healing all who were under the power of the Devil, for God was with him. [39] We are witnesses of everything that he did in the land of Israel and in

[n]praying; *some manuscripts have* praying and fasting.

Jerusalem. Then they put him to death by nailing him to a cross. 40But God raised him from death three days later and caused him to appear, 41not to everyone, but only to the witnesses that God had already chosen, that is, to us who ate and drank with him after he rose from death. 42And he commanded us to preach the gospel to the people and to testify that he is the one whom God has appointed judge of the living and the dead. 43All the prophets spoke about him, saying that everyone who believes in him will have his sins forgiven through the power of his name."

The Gentiles Receive the Holy Spirit

44 While Peter was still speaking, the Holy Spirit came down on all those who were listening to his message. 45The Jewish believers who had come from Joppa with Peter were amazed that God had poured out his gift of the Holy Spirit on the Gentiles also. 46For they heard them speaking in strange tongues and praising God's greatness. Peter spoke up: 47"These people have received the Holy Spirit, just as we also did. Can anyone, then, stop them from being baptized with water?" 48So he ordered them to be baptized in the name of Jesus Christ. Then they asked him to stay with them for a few days.

Peter's Report to the Church at Jerusalem

11 The apostles and the other believers throughout Judaea heard that the Gentiles also had received the word of God. 2When Peter went to Jerusalem, those who were in favour of circumcising Gentiles criticized him, saying, 3"You were a guest in the home of uncircumcised Gentiles, and you even ate with them!" 4So Peter gave them a complete account of what had happened from the very beginning:

5 "While I was praying in the city of Joppa, I had a vision. I saw something coming down that looked like a large sheet being lowered by its four corners from heaven, and it stopped next to me. 6I looked closely inside and saw domesticated and wild animals, reptiles, and wild birds. 7Then I heard a voice saying to me, 'Get up, Peter; kill and eat!' 8But I said,

'Certainly not, Lord! No ritually unclean or defiled food has ever entered my mouth.' ⁹The voice spoke again from heaven, 'Do not consider anything unclean that God has declared clean.' ¹⁰This happened three times, and finally the whole thing was drawn back up into heaven. ¹¹At that very moment three men who had been sent to me from Caesarea arrived at the house where I was⁰ staying. ¹²The Spirit told me to go with them without hesitation. These six fellow-believers from Joppa accompanied me to Caesarea, and we all went into the house of Cornelius. ¹³He told us how he had seen an angel standing in his house, who said to him, 'Send someone to Joppa for a man whose full name is Simon Peter. ¹⁴He will speak words to you by which you and all your family will be saved.' ¹⁵And when I began to speak, the Holy Spirit came down on them just as on us at the beginning. ¹⁶Then I remembered what the Lord had said: 'John baptized with water, but you will be baptized with the Holy Spirit.' ¹⁷It is clear that God gave those Gentiles the same gift that he gave us when we believed in the Lord Jesus Christ; who was I, then, to try to stop God!''

18 When they heard this, they stopped their criticism and praised God, saying, "Then God has given to the Gentiles also the opportunity to repent and live!"

The Church at Antioch

19 Some of the believers who were scattered by the persecution which took place when Stephen was killed went as far as Phoenicia, Cyprus, and Antioch, telling the message to Jews only. ²⁰But other believers, men from Cyprus and Cyrene, went to Antioch and proclaimed the message to Gentilesᵖ also, telling them the Good News about the Lord Jesus. ²¹The Lord's power was with them, and a great number of people believed and turned to the Lord.

22 The news about this reached the church in Jerusalem, so they sent Barnabas to Antioch. ²³When

⁰I was; *some manuscripts have* we were.
ᵖGentiles; *some manuscripts have* Greek-speaking Jews *or* Greek-speaking people.

he arrived and saw how God had blessed the people, he was glad and urged them all to be faithful and true to the Lord with all their hearts. [24]Barnabas was a good man, full of the Holy Spirit and faith, and many people were brought to the Lord.

25 Then Barnabas went to Tarsus to look for Saul. [26]When he found him, he took him to Antioch, and for a whole year the two met with the people of the church and taught a large group. It was at Antioch that the believers were first called Christians.

27 About that time some prophets went from Jerusalem to Antioch. [28]One of them, named Agabus, stood up and by the power of the Spirit predicted that a severe famine was about to come over all the earth. (It came when Claudius was emperor.) [29]The disciples decided that each of them would send as much as he could to help their fellow-believers who lived in Judaea. [30]They did this, then, and sent the money to the church elders by Barnabas and Saul.

More Persecution

12 About this time King Herod[q] began to persecute some members of the church. [2]He had James, the brother of John, put to death by the sword. [3]When he saw that this pleased the Jews, he went on to arrest Peter. (This happened during the time of the Festival of Unleavened Bread.) [4]After his arrest Peter was put in jail, where he was handed over to be guarded by four groups of four soldiers each. Herod planned to put him on trial in public after Passover. [5]So Peter was kept in jail, but the people of the church were praying earnestly to God for him.

Peter Is Set Free from Prison

6 The night before Herod was going to bring him out to the people, Peter was sleeping between two guards. He was tied with two chains, and there were guards on duty at the prison gate. [7]Suddenly an angel of the Lord stood there, and a light shone in the cell. The angel shook Peter by the shoulder, woke him up, and said, "Hurry! Get up!" At once the

[q]KING HEROD: *Herod Agrippa I, ruler of all Palestine.*

chains fell off Peter's hands. [8]Then the angel said, "Fasten your belt and put on your sandals." Peter did so, and the angel said, "Put your cloak round you and come with me." [9]Peter followed him out of the prison, not knowing, however, if what the angel was doing was real; he thought he was seeing a vision. [10]They passed by the first guard post and then the second, and came at last to the iron gate leading into the city. The gate opened for them by itself, and they went out. They walked down a street, and suddenly the angel left Peter.

11 Then Peter realized what had happened to him, and said, "Now I know that it is really true! The Lord sent his angel to rescue me from Herod's power and from everything the Jewish people expected to happen."

12 Aware of his situation, he went to the home of Mary, the mother of John Mark, where many people had gathered and were praying. [13]Peter knocked at the outside door, and a servant-girl named Rhoda came to answer it. [14]She recognized Peter's voice and was so happy that she ran back in without opening the door, and announced that Peter was standing outside. [15]"You are mad!" they told her. But she insisted that it was true. So they answered, "It is his angel."

16 Meanwhile Peter kept on knocking. At last they opened the door, and when they saw him, they were amazed. [17]He motioned with his hand for them to be quiet, and he explained to them how the Lord had brought him out of prison. "Tell this to James and the rest of the believers," he said; then he left and went somewhere else.

18 When morning came, there was a tremendous confusion among the guards—what had happened to Peter? [19]Herod gave orders to search for him, but they could not find him. So he had the guards questioned and ordered them to be put to death.

After this, Herod left Judaea and spent some time in Caesarea.

The Death of Herod

20 Herod was very angry with the people of Tyre and Sidon, so they went in a group to see him. First

they convinced Blastus, the man in charge of the palace, that he should help them. Then they went to Herod and asked him for peace, because their country got its food supplies from the king's country.

21 On a chosen day Herod put on his royal robes, sat on his throne, and made a speech to the people. 22 "It isn't a man speaking, but a god!" they shouted. 23 At once the angel of the Lord struck Herod down, because he did not give honour to God. He was eaten by worms and died.

24 Meanwhile the word of God continued to spread and grow.

25 Barnabas and Saul finished their mission and returned from[r] Jerusalem, taking John Mark with them.

Barnabas and Saul Are Chosen and Sent

13 In the church at Antioch there were some prophets and teachers: Barnabas, Simeon (called the Black), Lucius (from Cyrene), Manaen (who had been brought up with Herod[s] the governor), and Saul. 2 While they were serving the Lord and fasting, the Holy Spirit said to them, "Set apart for me Barnabas and Saul, to do the work to which I have called them."

3 They fasted and prayed, placed their hands on them, and sent them off.

In Cyprus

4 Having been sent by the Holy Spirit, Barnabas and Saul went to Seleucia and sailed from there to the island of Cyprus. 5 When they arrived at Salamis, they preached the word of God in the synagogues. They had John Mark with them to help in the work.

6 They went all the way across the island to Paphos, where they met a certain magician named Bar-Jesus, a Jew who claimed to be a prophet. 7 He was a friend of the governor of the island, Sergius Paulus, who was an intelligent man. The governor called Barnabas and Saul before him because he wanted to hear the word of God. 8 But they were opposed by the magician Elymas (that is his name in Greek), who tried to

[r]from; *some manuscripts have* to.
[s]HEROD: *Herod Antipas, ruler of Galilee (see Lk 3.1).*

PAUL'S FIRST MISSIONARY JOURNEY

turn the governor away from the faith. 9 Then Saul—
also known as Paul—was filled with the Holy Spirit;
he looked straight at the magician 10 and said, "You
son of the Devil! You are the enemy of everything
that is good. You are full of all kinds of evil tricks,
and you always keep trying to turn the Lord's truths
into lies! 11 The Lord's hand will come down on you
now; you will be blind and will not see the light
of day for a time."

At once Elymas felt a dark mist cover his eyes,
and he walked about trying to find someone to lead
him by the hand. 12 When the governor saw what
had happened, he believed; for he was greatly amazed
at the teaching about the Lord.

In Antioch in Pisidia

13 Paul and his companions sailed from Paphos and
came to Perga, a city in Pamphylia, where John Mark

left them and went back to Jerusalem. [14]They went on from Perga and arrived in Antioch in Pisidia, and on the Sabbath they went into the synagogue and sat down. [15]After the reading from the Law of Moses and from the writings of the prophets, the officials of the synagogue sent them a message: "Brothers, we want you to speak to the people if you have a message of encouragement for them." [16]Paul stood up, motioned with his hand, and began to speak:

"Fellow-Israelites and all Gentiles here who worship God: hear me! [17]The God of the people of Israel chose our ancestors and made the people a great nation during the time they lived as foreigners in Egypt. God brought them out of Egypt by his great power, [18]and for forty years he endured[t] them in the desert. [19]He destroyed seven nations in the land of Canaan and made his people the owners of the land. [20]All this took about four hundred and fifty years.

"After this[u] he gave them judges until the time of the prophet Samuel. [21]And when they asked for a king, God gave them Saul son of Kish from the tribe of Benjamin, to be their king for forty years. [22]After removing him, God made David their king. This is what God said about him: 'I have found that David son of Jesse is the kind of man I like, a man who will do all I want him to do.' [23]It was Jesus, a descendant of David, whom God made the Saviour of the people of Israel, as he had promised. [24]Before Jesus began his work, John preached to all the people of Israel that they should turn from their sins and be baptized. [25]And as John was about to finish his mission, he said to the people, 'Who do you think I am? I am not the one you are waiting for. But listen! He is coming after me, and I am not good enough to take his sandals off his feet.'

26 "My fellow-Israelites, descendants of Abraham, and all Gentiles here who worship God: it is to us that this message of salvation has been sent! [27]For

---

[t]he endured; *some manuscripts have* he took care of.
[u]All this took about four hundred and fifty years. After this; *or* Some four hundred and fifty years later.

the people who live in Jerusalem and their leaders did not know that he is the Saviour, nor did they understand the words of the prophets that are read every Sabbath. Yet they made the prophets' words come true by condemning Jesus. 28 And even though they could find no reason to pass the death sentence on him, they asked Pilate to have him put to death. 29 And after they had done everything that the Scriptures say about him, they took him down from the cross and placed him in a tomb. 30 But God raised him from death, 31 and for many days he appeared to those who had travelled with him from Galilee to Jerusalem. They are now witnesses for him to the people of Israel. 32-33 And we are here to bring the Good News to you: what God promised our ancestors he would do, he has now done for us, who are their descendants, by raising Jesus to life. As it is written in the second Psalm,

'You are my Son;
    today I have become your Father.'

34 And this is what God said about raising him from death, never to rot away in the grave:

'I will give you the sacred and sure blessings
    that I promised to David.'

35 As indeed he says in another passage,

'You will not allow your devoted servant to rot
    in the grave.'

36 For David served God's purposes in his own time, and then he died, was buried with his ancestors, and his body rotted in the grave. 37 But this did not happen to the one whom God raised from death. 38-39 We want you to know, my fellow-Israelites, that it is through Jesus that the message about forgiveness of sins is preached to you; and that everyone who believes in him is set free from all the sins from which the Law of Moses could not set you free. 40 Take care, then, so that what the prophets said may not happen to you: v

41 'Look, you scoffers! Be astonished and die!
    For what I am doing today
        is something that you will not believe,

---

v Some manuscripts do not have to you.

even when someone explains it to you!' "

42 As Paul and Barnabas were leaving the synagogue, the people invited them to come back the next Sabbath and tell them more about these things. 43 After the people had left the meeting, Paul and Barnabas were followed by many Jews and by many Gentiles who had been converted to Judaism. The apostles spoke to them and encouraged them to keep on living in the grace of God.

44 The next Sabbath nearly everyone in the town came to hear the word of the Lord. 45 When the Jews saw the crowds, they were filled with jealousy; they disputed what Paul was saying and insulted him. 46 But Paul and Barnabas spoke out even more boldly: "It was necessary that the word of God should be spoken first to you. But since you reject it and do not consider yourselves worthy of eternal life, we will leave you and go to the Gentiles. 47 For this is the commandment that the Lord has given us:

'I have made you a light for the Gentiles,
    so that all the world may be saved.' "

48 When the Gentiles heard this, they were glad and praised the Lord's message; and those who had been chosen for eternal life became believers.

49 The word of the Lord spread everywhere in that region. 50 But the Jews stirred up the leading men of the city and the Gentile women of high social standing who worshipped God. They started a persecution against Paul and Barnabas and threw them out of their region. 51 The apostles shook the dust off their feet in protest against them and went on to Iconium. 52 The believers in Antioch were full of joy and the Holy Spirit.

In Iconium

14 The same thing happened in Iconium: Paul and Barnabas went to the synagogue and spoke in such a way that a great number of Jews and Gentiles became believers. 2 But the Jews who would not believe stirred up the Gentiles and turned them against the believers. 3 The apostles stayed there for a long time, speaking boldly about the Lord, who proved that their message about his grace was true by giving them the power to perform miracles and wonders. 4 The people of the city were divided: some were for the Jews, others for the apostles.

5 Then some Gentiles and Jews, together with their leaders, decided to ill-treat the apostles and stone them. 6 When the apostles learnt about it, they fled to the cities of Lystra and Derbe in Lycaonia and to the surrounding territory. 7 There they preached the Good News.

In Lystra and Derbe

8 In Lystra there was a man who had been lame from birth and had never been able to walk. 9 He sat there and listened to Paul's words. Paul saw that he believed and could be healed, so he looked straight at him 10 and said in a loud voice, "Stand up straight on your feet!" The man jumped up and started walking around. 11 When the crowds saw what Paul had done, they started shouting in their own Lycaonian language, "The gods have become like men and have come down to us!" 12 They gave Barnabas the name Zeus, and Paul the name Hermes, because he was the chief speaker. 13 The priest of the god Zeus, whose temple stood just outside the town, brought bulls and flowers to the gate, for he and the crowds wanted to offer sacrifice to the apostles.

14 When Barnabas and Paul heard what they were about to do, they tore their clothes and ran into the middle of the crowd, shouting, 15 "Why are you doing this? We ourselves are only human beings like you! We are here to announce the Good News, to turn you away from these worthless things to the living God, who made heaven, earth, sea, and all that is in them. 16 In the past he allowed all people to go their own way. 17 But he has always given evidence of his existence by the good things he does: he gives you rain from heaven and crops at the right times; he gives you food and fills your hearts with happiness." 18 Even with these words the apostles could hardly keep the crowd from offering a sacrifice to them.

19 Some Jews came from Antioch in Pisidia and from Iconium; they won the crowd over to their side, stoned Paul and dragged him out of the town, thinking

that he was dead. [20] But when the believers gathered round him, he got up and went back into the town. The next day he and Barnabas went to Derbe.

The Return to Antioch in Syria

21 Paul and Barnabas preached the Good News in Derbe and won many disciples. Then they went back to Lystra, to Iconium, and on to Antioch in Pisidia. [22] They strengthened the believers and encouraged them to remain true to the faith. "We must pass through many troubles to enter the Kingdom of God," they taught. [23] In each church they appointed elders, and with prayers and fasting they commended them to the Lord, in whom they had put their trust.

24 After going through the territory of Pisidia, they came to Pamphylia. [25] There they preached the message in Perga and then went to Attalia, [26] and from there they sailed back to Antioch, the place where they had been commended to the care of God's grace for the work they had now completed.

27 When they arrived in Antioch, they gathered the people of the church together and told them about all that God had done with them and how he had opened the way for the Gentiles to believe. [28] And they stayed a long time there with the believers.

The Meeting at Jerusalem

15 Some men came from Judaea to Antioch and started teaching the believers, "You cannot be saved unless you are circumcised as the Law of Moses requires." [2] Paul and Barnabas got into a fierce argument with them about this, so it was decided that Paul and Barnabas and some of the others in Antioch should go to Jerusalem and see the apostles and elders about this matter.

3 They were sent on their way by the church; and as they went through Phoenicia and Samaria, they reported how the Gentiles had turned to God; this news brought great joy to all the believers. [4] When they arrived in Jerusalem, they were welcomed by the church, the apostles, and the elders, to whom they told all that God had done through them. [5] But some of the believers who belonged to the party of

the Pharisees stood up and said, "The Gentiles must be circumcised and told to obey the Law of Moses."

6 The apostles and the elders met together to consider this question. 7 After a long debate Peter stood up and said, "My brothers, you know that a long time ago God chose me from among you to preach the Good News to the Gentiles, so that they could hear and believe. 8 And God, who knows the thoughts of everyone, showed his approval of the Gentiles by giving the Holy Spirit to them, just as he had to us. 9 He made no difference between us and them; he forgave their sins because they believed. 10 So then, why do you now want to put God to the test by laying a load on the backs of the believers which neither our ancestors nor we ourselves were able to carry? 11 No! We believe and are saved by the grace of the Lord Jesus, just as they are."

12 The whole group was silent as they heard Barnabas and Paul report all the miracles and wonders that God had performed through them among the Gentiles. 13 When they had finished speaking, James spoke up: "Listen to me, my brothers! 14 Simon has just explained how God first showed his care for the Gentiles by taking from among them a people to belong to him. 15 The words of the prophets agree completely with this. As the scripture says,

16 'After this I will return, says the Lord,
    and restore the kingdom of David.
  I will rebuild its ruins
    and make it strong again.
17 And so all the rest of mankind will come to me,
    all the Gentiles whom I have called to be my
      own.
18 So says the Lord, who made this known long
      ago.'

19 "It is my opinion," James went on, "that we should not trouble the Gentiles who are turning to God. 20 Instead, we should write a letter telling them not to eat any food that is ritually unclean because it has been offered to idols; to keep themselves from sexual immorality; and not to eat any animal that has been strangled, or any blood. 21 For the Law of Moses has been read for a very long time in the

synagogues every Sabbath, and his words are preached in every town."

The Letter to the Gentile Believers

22 Then the apostles and the elders, together with the whole church, decided to choose some men from the group and send them to Antioch with Paul and Barnabas. They chose two men who were highly respected by the believers, Judas, called Barsabbas, and Silas, 23 and they sent the following letter by them:

"We, the apostles and the elders, your brothers, send greetings to all our brothers of Gentile birth who live in Antioch, Syria, and Cilicia. 24 We have heard that some men who went from our group have troubled and upset you by what they said; they had not, however, received any instruction from us. 25 And so we have met together and have all agreed to choose some messengers and send them to you. They will go with our dear friends Barnabas and Paul, 26 who have risked their lives in the service of our Lord Jesus Christ. 27 We send you, then, Judas and Silas, who will tell you in person the same things we are writing. 28 The Holy Spirit and we have agreed not to put any other burden on you besides these necessary rules: 29 eat no food that has been offered to idols; eat no blood; eat no animal that has been strangled; and keep yourselves from sexual immorality. You will do well if you take care not to do these things. With our best wishes."

30 The messengers were sent off and went to Antioch, where they gathered the whole group of believers and gave them the letter. 31 When the people read it, they were filled with joy by the message of encouragement. 32 Judas and Silas, who were themselves prophets, spoke a long time with them, giving them courage and strength. 33 After spending some time there, they were sent off in peace by the believers and went back to those who had sent them. *w*

35 Paul and Barnabas spent some time in Antioch,

---

w Some manuscripts add verse 34: But Silas decided to stay there.

PAUL'S
SECOND AND THIRD
JOURNEYS

Paul's Second Journey
Paul's Third Journey

0   100   200   300 Kilometres

and together with many others they taught and preached the word of the Lord.

Paul and Barnabas Separate

36 Some time later Paul said to Barnabas, "Let us go back and visit our brothers in every town where we preached the word of the Lord, and let us find out how they are getting on." ³⁷Barnabas wanted to take John Mark with them, ³⁸but Paul did not think it was right to take him, because he had not stayed with them to the end of their mission, but had turned back and left them in Pamphylia. ³⁹There was a sharp argument, and they separated: Barnabas took Mark and sailed off for Cyprus, ⁴⁰while Paul chose Silas and left, commended by the believers to the care of the Lord's grace. ⁴¹He went through Syria and Cilicia, strengthening the churches.

Timothy Goes with Paul and Silas

16 Paul travelled on to Derbe and Lystra, where a Christian named Timothy lived. His mother, who was also a Christian, was Jewish, but his father was a Greek. ²All the believers in Lystra and Iconium spoke well of Timothy. ³Paul wanted to take Timothy along with him, so he circumcised him. He did so because all the Jews who lived in those places knew that Timothy's father was Greek. ⁴As they went through the towns, they delivered to the believers the rules decided upon by the apostles and elders in Jerusalem, and told them to obey those rules. ⁵So the churches were made stronger in the faith and grew in numbers every day.

In Troas: Paul's Vision

6 They travelled through the region of Phrygia and Galatia because the Holy Spirit did not let them preach the message in the province of Asia. ⁷When they reached the border of Mysia, they tried to go into the province of Bithynia, but the Spirit of Jesus did not allow them. ⁸So they travelled right on through˟ Mysia and went to Troas. ⁹That night Paul had a vision

˟travelled right on through; or passed by.

in which he saw a Macedonian standing and begging
him, "Come over to Macedonia and help us!" [10] As
soon as Paul had this vision, we got ready to leave
for Macedonia, because we decided that God had called
us to preach the Good News to the people there.

In Philippi: the Conversion of Lydia

11 We left by ship from Troas and sailed straight
across to Samothrace, and the next day to Neapolis.
[12] From there we went inland to Philippi, a city of
the first district of Macedonia;[y] it is also a Roman
colony. We spent several days there. [13] On the Sabbath
we went out of the city to the river-side, where we
thought there would be a place where Jews gathered
for prayer. We sat down and talked to the women
who gathered there. [14] One of those who heard us
was Lydia from Thyatira, who was a dealer in purple
cloth. She was a woman who worshipped God, and
the Lord opened her mind to pay attention to what
Paul was saying. [15] After she and the people of her
house had been baptized, she invited us, "Come and
stay in my house if you have decided that I am
a true believer in the Lord." And she persuaded us
to go.

In Prison at Philippi

16 One day as we were going to the place of prayer,
we were met by a slave-girl who had an evil spirit
that enabled her to predict the future. She earned
a lot of money for her owners by telling fortunes. [17] She
followed Paul and us, shouting, "These men are servants of the Most High God! They announce to you
how you can be saved!" [18] She did this for many
days, until Paul became so upset that he turned round
and said to the spirit, "In the name of Jesus Christ
I order you to come out of her!" The spirit went
out of her that very moment.

19 When her owners realized that their chance of
making money was gone, they seized Paul and Silas

[y] a city of the first district of Macedonia; *some manuscripts
have* a leading city of the district of Macedonia; *or* a leading
city of that district in Macedonia.

and dragged them to the authorities in the public square. 20 They brought them before the Roman officials and said, "These men are Jews, and they are causing trouble in our city. 21 They are teaching customs that are against our law; we are Roman citizens, and we cannot accept these customs or practise them." 22 And the crowd joined in the attack against Paul and Silas.

Then the officials tore the clothes off Paul and Silas and ordered them to be whipped. 23 After a severe beating, they were thrown into jail, and the jailer was ordered to lock them up tight. 24 Upon receiving this order, the jailer threw them into the inner cell and fastened their feet between heavy blocks of wood.

25 About midnight Paul and Silas were praying and singing hymns to God, and the other prisoners were listening to them. 26 Suddenly there was a violent earthquake, which shook the prison to its foundations. At once all the doors opened, and the chains fell off all the prisoners. 27 The jailer woke up, and when he saw the prison doors open, he thought that the prisoners had escaped; so he pulled out his sword and was about to kill himself. 28 But Paul shouted at the top of his voice, "Don't harm yourself! We are all here!"

29 The jailer called for a light, rushed in, and fell trembling at the feet of Paul and Silas. 30 Then he led them out and asked, "Sirs, what must I do to be saved?"

31 They answered, "Believe in the Lord Jesus, and you will be saved—you and your family." 32 Then they preached the word of the Lord to him and to all the others in his house. 33 At that very hour of the night the jailer took them and washed their wounds; and he and all his family were baptized at once. 34 Then he took Paul and Silas up into his house and gave them some food to eat. He and his family were filled with joy, because they now believed in God.

35 The next morning the Roman authorities sent police officers with the order, "Let those men go."

36 So the jailer told Paul, "The officials have sent an order for you and Silas to be released. You may leave, then, and go in peace."

Sirs, what must I do to be saved? (16.30)

37 But Paul said to the police officers, "We were not found guilty of any crime, yet they whipped us in public—and we are Roman citizens! Then they threw us in prison. And now they want to send us away secretly. Not likely! The Roman officials themselves must come here and let us out."

38 The police officers reported these words to the Roman officials; and when they heard that Paul and Silas were Roman citizens, they were afraid. 39 So they went and apologized to them; then they led them out of the prison and asked them to leave the city. 40 Paul and Silas left the prison and went to Lydia's house. There they met the believers, spoke words of encouragement to them, and left.

In Thessalonica

17 Paul and Silas travelled on through Amphipolis and Apollonia and came to Thessalonica, where

there was a synagogue. [2] According to his usual habit Paul went to the synagogue. There during three Sabbaths he held discussions with the people, quoting [3] and explaining the Scriptures and proving from them that the Messiah had to suffer and rise from death. "This Jesus whom I announce to you," Paul said, "is the Messiah." [4] Some of them were convinced and joined Paul and Silas; so did many of the leading women and a large group of Greeks who worshipped God.

5 But the Jews were jealous and gathered some of the worthless loafers from the streets and formed a mob. They set the whole city in an uproar and attacked the home of a man called Jason, in an attempt to find Paul and Silas and bring them out to the people. [6] But when they did not find them, they dragged Jason and some other believers before the city authorities and shouted, "These men have caused trouble everywhere! Now they have come to our city, [7] and Jason has kept them in his house. They are all breaking the laws of the Emperor, saying that there is another king, whose name is Jesus." [8] With these words they threw the crowd and the city authorities into an uproar. [9] The authorities made Jason and the others pay the required amount of money to be released, and then let them go.

In Berea

10 As soon as night came, the believers sent Paul and Silas to Berea. When they arrived, they went to the synagogue. [11] The people there were more open-minded than the people in Thessalonica. They listened to the message with great eagerness, and every day they studied the Scriptures to see if what Paul said was really true. [12] Many of them believed; and many Greek women of high social standing and many Greek men also believed. [13] But when the Jews in Thessalonica heard that Paul had preached the word of God in Berea also, they came there and started exciting and stirring up the mob. [14] At once the believers sent Paul away to the coast; but both Silas and Timothy stayed in Berea. [15] The men who were taking Paul went with him as far as Athens and then returned to Berea

with instructions from Paul that Silas and Timothy should join him as soon as possible.

In Athens

16 While Paul was waiting in Athens for Silas and Timothy, he was greatly upset when he noticed how full of idols the city was. 17 So he held discussions in the synagogue with the Jews and with the Gentiles who worshipped God, and also in the public square every day with the people who happened to pass by. 18 Certain Epicurean and Stoic teachers also debated with him. Some of them asked, "What is this ignorant show-off trying to say?"

Others answered, "He seems to be talking about foreign gods." They said this because Paul was preaching about Jesus and the resurrection. z 19 So they took Paul, brought him before the city council, the Areopagus, and said, "We would like to know what this new teaching is that you are talking about. 20 Some of the things we hear you say sound strange to us, and we would like to know what they mean." 21 (For all the citizens of Athens and the foreigners who lived there liked to spend all their time telling and hearing the latest new thing.)

22 Paul stood up in front of the city council and said, "I see that in every way you Athenians are very religious. 23 For as I walked through your city and looked at the places where you worship, I found an altar on which is written, 'To an Unknown God'. That which you worship, then, even though you do not know it, is what I now proclaim to you. 24 God, who made the world and everything in it, is Lord of heaven and earth and does not live in man-made temples. 25 Nor does he need anything that we can supply by working for him, since it is he himself who gives life and breath and everything else to everyone. 26 From one man he created all races of mankind and made them live throughout the whole earth. He himself fixed beforehand the exact times and the limits of the places where they would live. 27 He did this so

---

z JESUS AND THE RESURRECTION: *In Greek, the feminine noun "resurrection" could be understood to be the name of a goddess.*

that they would look for him, and perhaps find him as they felt about for him. Yet God is actually not far from any one of us; 28 as someone has said,

'In him we live and move and exist.'

It is as some of your poets have said,

'We too are his children.'

29 Since we are God's children, we should not suppose that his nature is anything like an image of gold or silver or stone, shaped by the art and skill of man. 30 God has overlooked the times when people did not know him, but now he commands all of them everywhere to turn away from their evil ways. 31 For he has fixed a day in which he will judge the whole world with justice by means of a man he has chosen. He has given proof of this to everyone by raising that man from death!"

32 When they heard Paul speak about a raising from death, some of them made fun of him, but others said, "We want to hear you speak about this again." 33 And so Paul left the meeting. 34 Some men joined him and believed, among whom was Dionysius, a member of the council; there was also a woman named Damaris, and some other people.

In Corinth

18 After this, Paul left Athens and went on to Corinth. 2 There he met a Jew named Aquila, born in Pontus, who had recently come from Italy with his wife Priscilla, for the Emperor Claudius had ordered all the Jews to leave Rome. Paul went to see them, 3 and stayed and worked with them, because he earned his living by making tents, just as they did. 4 He held discussions in the synagogue every Sabbath, trying to convince both Jews and Greeks.

5 When Silas and Timothy arrived from Macedonia, Paul gave his whole time to preaching the message, testifying to the Jews that Jesus is the Messiah. 6 When they opposed him and said evil things about him, he protested by shaking the dust from his clothes and saying to them, "If you are lost, you yourselves must take the blame for it! I am not responsible. From now on I will go to the Gentiles." 7 So he left them and went to live in the house of a Gentile named

Titius Justus, who worshipped God; his house was next to the synagogue. [8]Crispus, who was the leader of the synagogue, believed in the Lord, together with all his family; and many other people in Corinth heard the message, believed, and were baptized.

9 One night Paul had a vision in which the Lord said to him, "Do not be afraid, but keep on speaking and do not give up, [10]for I am with you. No one will be able to harm you, for many in this city are my people." [11]So Paul stayed there for a year and a half, teaching the people the word of God.

12 When Gallio was made the Roman governor of Achaia, the Jews got together, seized Paul, and took him into court. [13]"This man," they said, "is trying to persuade people to worship God in a way that is against the law!"

14 Paul was about to speak when Gallio said to the Jews, "If this were a matter of some evil crime or wrong that has been committed, it would be reasonable for me to be patient with you Jews. [15]But since it is an argument about words and names and your own law, you yourselves must settle it. I will not be the judge of such things!" [16]And he drove them out of the court. [17]They all seized Sosthenes, the leader of the synagogue, and beat him in front of the court. But that did not bother Gallio a bit.

The Return to Antioch

18 Paul stayed on with the believers in Corinth for many days, then left them and sailed off with Priscilla and Aquila for Syria. Before sailing from Cenchreae he had his head shaved because of a vow he had taken.[a] [19]They arrived in Ephesus, where Paul left Priscilla and Aquila. He went into the synagogue and held discussions with the Jews. [20]The people asked him to stay longer, but he would not consent. [21]Instead, he told them as he left, "If it is the will of God, I will come back to you." And so he sailed from Ephesus.

22 When he arrived at Caesarea, he went to

---

[a]A VOW HE HAD TAKEN: *This refers to the Jewish custom of shaving the head as a sign that a vow has been kept.*

Jerusalem and greeted the church, and then went to Antioch. 23 After spending some time there, he left and went through the region of Galatia and Phrygia, strengthening all the believers.

Apollos in Ephesus and Corinth

24 At that time a Jew named Apollos, who had been born in Alexandria, came to Ephesus. He was an eloquent speaker and had a thorough knowledge of the Scriptures. 25 He had been instructed in the Way of the Lord, and with great enthusiasm he proclaimed and taught correctly the facts about Jesus. However, he knew only the baptism of John. 26 He began to speak boldly in the synagogue. When Priscilla and Aquila heard him, they took him home with them and explained to him more correctly the Way of God. 27 Apollos then decided to go to Achaia, so the believers in Ephesus helped him by writing to the believers in Achaia, urging them to welcome him. When he arrived, he was a great help to those who through God's grace had become believers. 28 For with his strong arguments he defeated the Jews in public debates by proving from the Scriptures that Jesus is the Messiah.

Paul in Ephesus

19 While Apollos was in Corinth, Paul travelled through the interior of the province and arrived in Ephesus. There he found some disciples 2 and asked them, "Did you receive the Holy Spirit when you became believers?"

"We have not even heard that there is a Holy Spirit," they answered.

3 "Well, then, what kind of baptism did you receive?" Paul asked.

"The baptism of John," they answered.

4 Paul said, "The baptism of John was for those who turned from their sins; and he told the people of Israel to believe in the one who was coming after him—that is, in Jesus."

5 When they heard this, they were baptized in the name of the Lord Jesus. 6 Paul placed his hands on them, and the Holy Spirit came upon them; they

spoke in strange tongues and also proclaimed God's message. [7] They were about twelve men in all.

8 Paul went into the synagogue and during three months spoke boldly with the people, holding discussions with them and trying to convince them about the Kingdom of God. [9] But some of them were stubborn and would not believe, and before the whole group they said evil things about the Way of the Lord. So Paul left them and took the believers with him, and every day[b] he held discussions in the lecture hall of Tyrannus. [10] This went on for two years, so that all the people who lived in the province of Asia, both Jews and Gentiles, heard the word of the Lord.

The Sons of Sceva

11 God was performing unusual miracles through Paul. [12] Even handkerchiefs and aprons he had used were taken to those who were ill, and their diseases were driven away, and the evil spirits would go out of them. [13] Some Jews who travelled round and drove out evil spirits also tried to use the name of the Lord Jesus to do this. They said to the evil spirits, "I command you in the name of Jesus, whom Paul preaches." [14] Seven brothers, who were the sons of a Jewish High Priest named Sceva, were doing this.

15 But the evil spirit said to them, "I know Jesus, and I know about Paul; but you—who are you?"

16 The man who had the evil spirit in him attacked them with such violence that he overpowered them all. They ran away from his house, wounded and with their clothes torn off. [17] All the Jews and Gentiles who lived in Ephesus heard about this; they were all filled with fear, and the name of the Lord Jesus was given greater honour. [18] Many of the believers came, publicly admitting and revealing what they had done. [19] Many of those who had practised magic brought their books together and burnt them in public. They added up the price of the books, and the total came to fifty thousand silver coins.[c] [20] In this powerful

[b] Some manuscripts add from 11a.m. until 4p.m.
[c] SILVER COINS: A silver coin was the daily wage of a rural worker (see Mt 20.2).

way the word of the Lord[d] kept spreading and growing stronger.

The Riot in Ephesus

21 After these things had happened, Paul made up his mind[e] to travel through Macedonia and Achaia and go on to Jerusalem. "After I go there," he said, "I must also see Rome." 22 So he sent Timothy and Erastus, two of his helpers, to Macedonia, while he spent more time in the province of Asia.

23 It was at this time that there was serious trouble in Ephesus because of the Way of the Lord. 24 A certain silversmith named Demetrius made silver models of the temple of the goddess Artemis, and his business brought a great deal of profit to the workers. 25 So he called them all together with others whose work was like theirs and said to them, "Men, you know that our prosperity comes from this work. 26 Now, you can see and hear for yourselves what this fellow Paul is doing. He says that man-made gods are not gods at all, and he has succeeded in convincing many people, both here in Ephesus and in nearly the whole province of Asia. 27 There is the danger, then, that this business of ours will get a bad name. Not only that, but there is also the danger that the temple of the great goddess Artemis will come to mean nothing and that her greatness will be destroyed—the goddess worshipped by everyone in Asia and in all the world!"

28 As the crowd heard these words, they became furious and started shouting, "Great is Artemis of Ephesus!" 29 The uproar spread throughout the whole city. The mob seized Gaius and Aristarchus, two Macedonians who were travelling with Paul, and rushed with them to the theatre. 30 Paul himself wanted to go before the crowd, but the believers would not let him. 31 Some of the provincial authorities, who were his friends, also sent him a message begging

[d] In this...Lord; or And so, by the power of the Lord, the message.
[e] Paul made up his mind; or Paul, led by the Spirit, decided.

him not to show himself in the theatre. ³²Meanwhile the whole meeting was in an uproar: some people were shouting one thing, others were shouting something else, because most of them did not even know why they had come together. ³³Some of the people concluded that Alexander was responsible, since the Jews made him go up to the front. Then Alexander motioned with his hand for the people to be silent, and he tried to make a speech of defence. ³⁴But when they recognized that he was a Jew, they all shouted together the same thing for two hours: "Great is Artemis of Ephesus!"

35 At last the town clerk was able to calm the crowd. "Fellow-Ephesians!" he said. "Everyone knows that the city of Ephesus is the keeper of the temple of the great Artemis and of the sacred stone that fell down from heaven. ³⁶Nobody can deny these things. So then, you must calm down and not do anything reckless. ³⁷You have brought these men here even though they have not robbed temples or said evil things about our goddess. ³⁸If Demetrius and his workers have an accusation against anyone, we have the authorities and the regular days for court; charges can be made there. ³⁹But if there is something more that you want, it will have to be settled in a legal meeting of citizens. ⁴⁰For after what has happened today, there is the danger that we will be accused of a riot. There is no excuse for all this uproar, and we would not be able to give a good reason for it." ⁴¹After saying this, he dismissed the meeting.

To Macedonia and Achaia

20 After the uproar died down, Paul called together the believers and with words of encouragement said goodbye to them. Then he left and went on to Macedonia. ²He went through those regions and encouraged the people with many messages. Then he came to Achaia, ³where he stayed three months. He was getting ready to go to Syria when he discovered that the Jews were plotting against him; so he decided to go back through Macedonia. ⁴Sopater son of Pyrrhus, from Berea, went with him; so did Aristarchus and Secundus, from Thessalonica; Gaius, from Derbe;

Tychicus and Trophimus, from the province of Asia;
and Timothy. ⁵They went ahead and waited for us
in Troas. ⁶We sailed from Philippi after the Festival of
Unleavened Bread, and five days later we joined them
in Troas, where we spent a week.

Paul's Last Visit to Troas

7 On Saturday*f* evening we gathered together for
the fellowship meal. Paul spoke to the people and
kept on speaking until midnight, since he was going
to leave the next day. ⁸Many lamps were burning in
the upstairs room where we were meeting. ⁹A young
man named Eutychus was sitting in the window, and
as Paul kept on talking, Eutychus got sleepier and
sleepier, until he finally went sound asleep and fell
from the third storey to the ground. When they picked
him up, he was dead. ¹⁰But Paul went down and
threw himself on him and hugged him. "Don't worry,"
he said, "he is still alive!" ¹¹Then he went back
upstairs, broke bread, and ate. After talking with them
for a long time, even until sunrise, Paul left. ¹²They
took the young man home alive and were greatly
comforted.

From Troas to Miletus

13 We went on ahead to the ship and sailed off
to Assos, where we were going to take Paul aboard.
He had told us to do this, because he was going
there by land. ¹⁴When he met us in Assos, we took
him aboard and went on to Mitylene. ¹⁵We sailed
from there and arrived off Chios the next day. A
day later we came to Samos, and the following day
we reached Miletus. ¹⁶Paul had decided to sail on
past Ephesus, so as not to lose any time in the province
of Asia. He was in a hurry to arrive in Jerusalem
by the day of Pentecost, if at all possible.

Paul's Farewell Speech to the Elders of Ephesus

17 From Miletus Paul sent a message to Ephesus,
asking the elders of the church to meet him. ¹⁸When
they arrived, he said to them, "You know how I

*f*Saturday; *or* Sunday.

spent the whole time I was with you, from the first day I arrived in the province of Asia. [19] With all humility and many tears I did my work as the Lord's servant during the hard times that came to me because of the plots of the Jews. [20] You know that I did not hold back anything that would be of help to you as I preached and taught in public and in your homes. [21] To Jews and Gentiles alike I gave solemn warning that they should turn from their sins to God and believe in our Lord Jesus. [22] And now, in obedience to the Holy Spirit I am going to Jerusalem, not knowing what will happen to me there. [23] I only know that in every city the Holy Spirit has warned me that prison and troubles wait for me. [24] But I reckon my own life to be worth nothing to me; I only want to complete my mission and finish the work that the Lord Jesus gave me to do, which is to declare the Good News about the grace of God.

25 "I have gone about among all of you, preaching the Kingdom of God. And now I know that none of you will ever see me again. [26] So I solemnly declare to you this very day: if any of you should be lost, I am not responsible. [27] For I have not held back from announcing to you the whole purpose of God. [28] So keep watch over yourselves and over all the flock which the Holy Spirit has placed in your care. Be shepherds of the church of God,[g] which he made his own through the sacrificial death of his Son.[h] [29] I know that after I leave, fierce wolves will come among you, and they will not spare the flock. [30] The time will come when some men from your own group will tell lies to lead the believers away after them. [31] Watch, then, and remember that with many tears, day and night, I taught every one of you for three years.

32 "And now I commend you to the care of God and to the message of his grace, which is able to build you up and give you the blessings God has for all his people. [33] I have not wanted anyone's silver or gold or clothing. [34] You yourselves know that I have worked with these hands of mine to provide

[g] God; *some manuscripts have* the Lord.
[h] the sacrificial death of his Son; *or* his own death.

everything that my companions and I have needed.
³⁵I have shown you in all things that by working
hard in this way we must help the weak, remembering
the words that the Lord Jesus himself said, 'There
is more happiness in giving than in receiving.' "

36 When Paul finished, he knelt down with them
and prayed. ³⁷They were all crying as they hugged
him and kissed him good-bye. ³⁸They were especially
sad because he had said that they would never see
him again. And so they went with him to the ship.

Paul Goes to Jerusalem

21 We said good-bye to them and left. After sailing
straight across, we came to Cos; the next day
we reached Rhodes, and from there we went on to
Patara. ²There we found a ship that was going to
Phoenicia, so we went aboard and sailed away. ³We
came to where we could see Cyprus, and then sailed
south of it on to Syria. We went ashore at Tyre,
where the ship was going to unload its cargo. ⁴There
we found some believers and stayed with them a
week. By the power of the Spirit they told Paul not
to go to Jerusalem. ⁵But when our time with them
was over, we left and went on our way. All of them,
together with their wives and children, went with us
out of the city to the beach, where we all knelt
and prayed. ⁶Then we said good-bye to one another,
and we went on board the ship while they went
back home.

7 We continued our voyage, sailing from Tyre to
Ptolemais, where we greeted the believers and stayed
with them for a day. ⁸On the following day we left
and arrived in Caesarea. There we stayed at the house
of Philip the evangelist, one of the seven men who
had been chosen as helpers in Jerusalem. ⁹He had
four unmarried daughters who proclaimed God's message. ¹⁰We had been there for several days when a
prophet named Agabus arrived from Judaea. ¹¹He came
to us, took Paul's belt, tied up his own feet and
hands with it, and said, "This is what the Holy Spirit
says: The owner of this belt will be tied up in this
way by the Jews in Jerusalem, and they will hand
him over to the Gentiles."

12 When we heard this, we and the others there begged Paul not to go to Jerusalem. 13 But he answered, "What are you doing, crying like this and breaking my heart? I am ready not only to be tied up in Jerusalem but even to die there for the sake of the Lord Jesus."

14 We could not convince him, so we gave up and said, "May the Lord's will be done."

15 After spending some time there, we got our things ready and left for Jerusalem. 16 Some of the disciples from Caesarea also went with us and took us to the house of the man we were going to stay with[i] — Mnason, from Cyprus, who had been a believer since the early days.

Paul Visits James

17 When we arrived in Jerusalem, the believers welcomed us warmly. 18 The next day Paul went with us to see James; and all the church elders were present. 19 Paul greeted them and gave a complete report of everything that God had done among the Gentiles through his work. 20 After hearing him, they all praised God. Then they said, "Brother Paul, you can see how many thousands of Jews have become believers, and how devoted they all are to the Law. 21 They have been told that you have been teaching all the Jews who live in Gentile countries to abandon the Law of Moses, telling them not to circumcise their children or follow the Jewish customs. 22 They are sure to hear that you have arrived. What should be done, then? 23 This is what we want you to do. There are four men here who have taken a vow. 24 Go along with them and join them in the ceremony of purification and pay their expenses; then they will be able to shave their heads.[j] In this way everyone will know that there is no truth in any of the things that they have been told about you, but that you yourself live in accordance with the Law of Moses. 25 But as for

[i] and took us to the house of the man we were going to stay with; or bringing with them the man at whose house we were going to stay.
[j] SHAVE THEIR HEADS: See 18.18.

the Gentiles who have become believers, we have
sent them a letter telling them we decided that they
must not eat any food that has been offered to idols,
or any blood, or any animal that has been strangled,
and that they must keep themselves from sexual
immorality."

26 So Paul took the men and the next day performed
the ceremony of purification with them. Then he went
into the Temple and gave notice of how many days
it would be until the end of the period of purification,
when a sacrifice would be offered for each one of
them.

Paul Is Arrested in the Temple

27 But just when the seven days were about to
come to an end, some Jews from the province of
Asia saw Paul in the Temple. They stirred up the
whole crowd and seized Paul. 28 "Men of Israel!" they
shouted. "Help! This is the man who goes everywhere
teaching everyone against the people of Israel, the
Law of Moses, and this Temple. And now he has even
brought some Gentiles into the Temple and defiled
this holy place!" 29 (They said this because they had
seen Trophimus from Ephesus with Paul in the city,
and they thought that Paul had taken him into the
Temple.)

30 Confusion spread through the whole city, and
the people all ran together, seized Paul, and dragged
him out of the Temple. At once the Temple doors
were closed. 31 The mob was trying to kill Paul, when a
report was sent up to the commander of the Roman
troops that all Jerusalem was rioting. 32 At once the
commander took some officers and soldiers and rushed
down to the crowd. When the people saw him with the
soldiers, they stopped beating Paul. 33 The commander
went over to Paul, arrested him, and ordered him
to be bound with two chains. Then he asked, "Who
is this man, and what has he done?" 34 Some in the
crowd shouted one thing, others something else. There
was such confusion that the commander could not
find out exactly what had happened, so he ordered
his men to take Paul up into the fort. 35 They got
as far as the steps with him, and then the soldiers

had to carry him because the mob was so wild. [36]They were all coming after him and screaming, "Kill him!"

Paul Defends Himself

37 As the soldiers were about to take Paul into the fort, he spoke to the commander: "May I say something to you?"

"You speak Greek, do you?" the commander asked. [38]"Then you are not that Egyptian fellow who some time ago started a revolution and led four thousand armed terrorists out into the desert?"

39 Paul answered, "I am a Jew, born in Tarsus in Cilicia, a citizen of an important city. Please let me speak to the people."

40 The commander gave him permission, so Paul stood on the steps and motioned with his hand for the people to be silent. When they were quiet, Paul spoke to them in Hebrew:

22 "My fellow-Israelites, listen to me as I make my defence before you!" [2]When they heard him speaking to them in Hebrew, they became even quieter; and Paul went on:

3 "I am a Jew, born in Tarsus in Cilicia, but brought up here in Jerusalem as a student of Gamaliel. I received strict instruction in the Law of our ancestors and was just as dedicated to God as are all of you who are here today. [4]I persecuted to the death the people who followed this Way. I arrested men and women and threw them into prison. [5]The High Priest and the whole Council can prove that I am telling the truth. I received from them letters written to fellow-Jews in Damascus, so I went there to arrest these people and bring them back in chains to Jerusalem to be punished.

Paul Tells of His Conversion
(Acts 9.1-19; 26.12-18)

6 "As I was travelling and coming near Damascus, about midday a bright light from the sky flashed suddenly round me. [7]I fell to the ground and heard a voice saying to me, 'Saul, Saul! Why do you persecute me?' [8]'Who are you, Lord?' I asked. 'I am Jesus of Nazareth, whom you persecute,' he said to

me. ⁹The men with me saw the light, but did not hear the voice of the one who was speaking to me. ¹⁰I asked, 'What shall I do, Lord?' and the Lord said to me, 'Get up and go into Damascus, and there you will be told everything that God has determined for you to do.' ¹¹I was blind because of the bright light, and so my companions took me by the hand and led me into Damascus.

12 "In that city was a man named Ananias, a religious man who obeyed our Law and was highly respected by all the Jews living there. ¹³He came to me, stood by me, and said, 'Brother Saul, see again!' At that very moment I saw again and looked at him. ¹⁴He said, 'The God of our ancestors has chosen you to know his will, to see his righteous Servant, and to hear him speaking with his own voice. ¹⁵For you will be a witness for him to tell everyone what you have seen and heard. ¹⁶And now, why wait any longer? Get up and be baptized and have your sins washed away by praying to him.'

Paul's Call to Preach to the Gentiles

17 "I went back to Jerusalem, and while I was praying in the Temple, I had a vision, ¹⁸in which I saw the Lord, as he said to me, 'Hurry and leave Jerusalem quickly, because the people here will not accept your witness about me.' ¹⁹'Lord,' I answered, 'they know very well that I went to the synagogues and arrested and beat those who believe in you. ²⁰And when your witness Stephen was put to death, I myself was there, approving of his murder and taking care of the cloaks of his murderers.' ²¹'Go,' the Lord said to me, 'for I will send you far away to the Gentiles.' "

22 The people listened to Paul until he said this; but then they started shouting at the top of their voices, "Away with him! Kill him! He's not fit to live!" ²³They were screaming, waving their clothes, and throwing dust up in the air. ²⁴The Roman commander ordered his men to take Paul into the fort, and he told them to whip him in order to find out why the Jews were screaming like this against him. ²⁵But when they had tied him up to be whipped, Paul said to the officer standing there, "Is it lawful

for you to whip a Roman citizen who hasn't even been tried for any crime?"

26 When the officer heard this, he went to the commander and asked him, "What are you doing? That man is a Roman citizen!"

27 So the commander went to Paul and asked him, "Tell me, are you a Roman citizen?"

"Yes," answered Paul.

28 The commander said, "I became one by paying a large amount of money."

"But I am one by birth," Paul answered.

29 At once the men who were going to question Paul drew back from him; and the commander was frightened when he realized that Paul was a Roman citizen and that he had put him in chains.

Paul before the Council

30 The commander wanted to find out for certain what the Jews were accusing Paul of; so the next day he had Paul's chains taken off and ordered the chief priests and the whole Council to meet. Then he took Paul and made him stand before them.

23 Paul looked straight at the Council and said, "My fellow-Israelites! My conscience is perfectly clear about the way in which I have lived before God to this very day." 2 The High Priest Ananias ordered those who were standing close to Paul to strike him on the mouth. 3 Paul said to him, "God will certainly strike you—you whitewashed wall! You sit there to judge me according to the Law, yet you break the Law by ordering them to strike me!"

4 The men close to Paul said to him, "You are insulting God's High Priest!"

5 Paul answered, "My fellow-Israelites, I did not know that he was the High Priest. The scripture says, 'You must not speak evil of the ruler of your people.'"

6 When Paul saw that some of the group were Sadducees and the others were Pharisees, he called out in the Council, "Fellow-Israelites! I am a Pharisee, the son of Pharisees. I am on trial here because of the hope I have that the dead will rise to life!"

7 As soon as he said this, the Pharisees and Sadducees started to quarrel, and the group was divided.

8 (For the Sadducees say that people will not rise from death and that there are no angels or spirits; but the Pharisees believe in all three.) 9 The shouting became louder, and some of the teachers of the Law who belonged to the party of the Pharisees stood up and protested strongly: "We cannot find anything wrong with this man! Perhaps a spirit or an angel really did speak to him!"

10 The argument became so violent that the commander was afraid that Paul would be torn to pieces. So he ordered his soldiers to go down into the group, get Paul away from them, and take him into the fort.

11 That night the Lord stood by Paul and said, "Don't be afraid! You have given your witness for me here in Jerusalem, and you must also do the same in Rome."

The Plot against Paul's Life

12 The next morning some Jews met together and made a plan. They took a vow that they would not eat or drink anything until they had killed Paul. 13 There were more than forty who planned this together. 14 Then they went to the chief priests and elders and said, "We have taken a solemn vow not to eat a thing until we have killed Paul. 15 Now then, you and the Council send word to the Roman commander to bring Paul down to you, pretending that you want to get more accurate information about him. But we will be ready to kill him before he ever gets here."

16 But the son of Paul's sister heard about the plot; so he went to the fort and told Paul. 17 Then Paul called one of the officers and said to him, "Take this young man to the commander; he has something to tell him." 18 The officer took him, led him to the commander, and said, "The prisoner Paul called me and asked me to bring this young man to you, because he has something to say to you."

19 The commander took him by the hand, led him off by himself, and asked him, "What have you got to tell me?"

20 He said, "The Jewish authorities have agreed to

ask you tomorrow to take Paul down to the Council, pretending that the Council wants to get more accurate information about him. 21 But don't listen to them, because there are more than forty men who will be hiding and waiting for him. They have taken a vow not to eat or drink until they have killed him. They are now ready to do it and are waiting for your decision."

22 The commander said, "Don't tell anyone that you have reported this to me." And he sent the young man away.

Paul Is Sent to Governor Felix

23 Then the commander called two of his officers and said, "Get two hundred soldiers ready to go to Caesarea, together with seventy horsemen and two hundred spearmen, and be ready to leave by nine o'clock tonight. 24 Provide some horses for Paul to ride and get him safely through to the governor Felix." 25 Then the commander wrote a letter that went like this:

26 "Claudius Lysias to His Excellency, the governor Felix: Greetings. 27 The Jews seized this man and were about to kill him. I learnt that he was a Roman citizen, so I went with my soldiers and rescued him. 28 I wanted to know what they were accusing him of, so I took him down to their Council. 29 I found out that he had not done anything for which he deserved to die or be put in prison; the accusation against him had to do with questions about their own law. 30 And when I was informed that there was a plot against him, at once I decided to send him to you. I have told his accusers to make their charges against him before you."

31 The soldiers carried out their orders. They got Paul and took him that night as far as Antipatris. 32 The next day the foot-soldiers returned to the fort and left the horsemen to go on with him. 33 They took him to Caesarea, delivered the letter to the governor, and handed Paul over to him. 34 The governor read the letter and asked Paul what province he was from. When he found out that he was from Cilicia,

35 he said, "I will hear you when your accusers arrive."
Then he gave orders for Paul to be kept under guard
in the governor's headquarters.

Paul Is Accused by the Jews

24 Five days later the High Priest Ananias went
to Caesarea with some elders and a lawyer
named Tertullus. They appeared before Felix and made
their charges against Paul. 2 Then Paul was called in,
and Tertullus began to make his accusation, as follows:

"Your Excellency! Your wise leadership has brought
us a long period of peace, and many necessary reforms
are being made for the good of our country. 3 We
welcome this everywhere and at all times, and we are
deeply grateful to you. 4 I do not want to take up
too much of your time, however, so I beg you to
be kind and listen to our brief account. 5 We found
this man to be a dangerous nuisance; he starts riots
among the Jews all over the world and is a leader
of the party of the Nazarenes. 6 He also tried to defile
the Temple, and we arrested him. *k* 8 If you question
this man, you yourself will be able to learn from
him all the things that we are accusing him of."
9 The Jews joined in the accusation and said that all
this was true.

Paul's Defence before Felix

10 The governor then motioned to Paul to speak,
and Paul said,

"I know that you have been a judge over this nation
for many years, and so I am happy to defend myself
before you. 11 As you can find out for yourself, it
was no more than twelve days ago that I went to
Jerusalem to worship. 12 The Jews did not find me
arguing with anyone in the Temple, nor did they find
me stirring up the people, either in the synagogues
or anywhere else in the city. 13 Nor can they give you
proof of the accusations they now bring against me.

---

k Some manuscripts add verses 6b–8a: We planned to judge him
according to our own law, 7 but Lysias the commander came,
and with great violence took him from us. 8 Then Lysias gave
orders that his accusers should come before you.

¹⁴I do admit this to you: I worship the God of our ancestors by following that Way which they say is false. But I also believe in everything written in the Law of Moses and the books of the prophets. ¹⁵I have the same hope in God that these themselves have, namely, that all people, both the good and the bad, will rise from death. ¹⁶And so I do my best always to have a clear conscience before God and man.

17 "After being away from Jerusalem for several years, I went there to take some money to my own people and to offer sacrifices. ¹⁸It was while I was doing this that they found me in the Temple after I had completed the ceremony of purification. There was no crowd with me and no disorder. ¹⁹But some Jews from the province of Asia were there; they themselves ought to come before you and make their accusations if they have anything against me. ²⁰Or let these men here tell what crime they found me guilty of when I stood before the Council—²¹except for the one thing I called out when I stood before them: 'I am being tried by you today for believing that the dead will rise to life.' "

22 Then Felix, who was well informed about the Way, brought the hearing to a close. "When Lysias the commander arrives," he told them, "I will decide your case." ²³He ordered the officer in charge of Paul to keep him under guard, but to give him some freedom and allow his friends to provide for his needs.

Paul before Felix and Drusilla

24 After some days Felix came with his wife Drusilla, who was Jewish. He sent for Paul and listened to him as he talked about faith in Christ Jesus. ²⁵But as Paul went on discussing about goodness, self-control, and the coming Day of Judgement, Felix was afraid and said, "You may leave now. I will call you again when I get the chance." ²⁶At the same time he was hoping that Paul would give him some money; and for this reason he would often send for him and talk with him.

27 After two years had passed, Porcius Festus suc-

ceeded Felix as governor. Felix wanted to gain favour with the Jews so he left Paul in prison.

Paul Appeals to the Emperor

25 Three days after Festus arrived in the province, he went from Caesarea to Jerusalem, ²where the chief priests and the Jewish leaders brought their charges against Paul. They begged Festus ³to do them the favour of bringing Paul to Jerusalem, for they had made a plot to kill him on the way. ⁴Festus answered, "Paul is being kept a prisoner in Caesarea, and I myself will be going back there soon. ⁵Let your leaders go to Caesarea with me and accuse the man if he has done anything wrong."

6 Festus spent another eight or ten days with them and then went to Caesarea. On the next day he sat down in the court of judgement and ordered Paul to be brought in. ⁷When Paul arrived, the Jews who had come from Jerusalem stood round him and started making many serious charges against him, which they were not able to prove. ⁸But Paul defended himself: "I have done nothing wrong against the Law of the Jews or against the Temple or against the Roman Emperor."

9 But Festus wanted to gain favour with the Jews, so he asked Paul, "Would you be willing to go to Jerusalem and be tried on these charges before me there?"

10 Paul said, "I am standing before the Emperor's own court of judgement, where I should be tried. I have done no wrong to the Jews, as you yourself well know. ¹¹If I have broken the law and done something for which I deserve the death penalty, I do not ask to escape it. But if there is no truth in the charges they bring against me, no one can hand me over to them. I appeal to the Emperor."

12 Then Festus, after conferring with his advisers, answered, "You have appealed to the Emperor, so to the Emperor you will go."

Paul before Agrippa and Bernice

13 Some time later King Agrippa and Bernice came to Caesarea to pay a visit of welcome to Festus.

¹⁴ After they had been there several days, Festus
explained Paul's situation to the king: "There is a
man here who was left a prisoner by Felix; ¹⁵ and
when I went to Jerusalem, the Jewish chief priests
and elders brought charges against him and asked me
to condemn him. ¹⁶ But I told them that we Romans
are not in the habit of handing over any man accused
of a crime before he has met his accusers face to
face and has had the chance of defending himself
against the accusation. ¹⁷ When they came here, then,
I lost no time, but on the very next day I sat in
the court and ordered the man to be brought in.
¹⁸ His opponents stood up, but they did not accuse
him of any of the evil crimes that I thought they
would. ¹⁹ All they had were some arguments with him
about their own religion and about a man named
Jesus, who has died; but Paul claims that he is alive.
²⁰ I was undecided about how I could get information
on these matters, so I asked Paul if he would be
willing to go to Jerusalem and be tried there on these
charges. ²¹ But Paul appealed; he asked to be kept
under guard and to let the Emperor decide his case.
So I gave orders for him to be kept under guard
until I could send him to the Emperor."

22 Agrippa said to Festus, "I would like to hear
this man myself."

"You will hear him tomorrow," Festus answered.

23 The next day Agrippa and Bernice came with
great pomp and ceremony and entered the audience
hall with the military chiefs and the leading men of
the city. Festus gave the order, and Paul was brought
in. ²⁴ Festus said, "King Agrippa and all who are here
with us: You see this man against whom all the
Jewish people, both here and in Jerusalem, have
brought complaints to me. They scream that he should
not live any longer. ²⁵ But I could not find that he
had done anything for which he deserved the death
sentence. And since he himself made an appeal to
the Emperor, I have decided to send him. ²⁶ But I
have nothing definite about him to write to the
Emperor. So I have brought him here before you—and
especially before you, King Agrippa!—so that, after
investigating his case, I may have something to write.

27 For it seems unreasonable to me to send a prisoner without clearly indicating the charges against him."

Paul Defends Himself before Agrippa

26 Agrippa said to Paul, "You have permission to speak on your own behalf." Paul stretched out his hand and defended himself as follows:

2 "King Agrippa! I consider myself fortunate that today I am to defend myself before you from all the things the Jews accuse me of, 3 particularly since you know so well all the Jewish customs and disputes. I ask you, then, to listen to me with patience.

4 "All the Jews know how I have lived ever since I was young. They know how I have spent my whole life, at first in my own country and then in Jerusalem. 5 They have always known, if they are willing to testify, that from the very first I have lived as a member of the strictest party of our religion, the Pharisees. 6 And now I stand here to be tried because of the hope I have in the promise that God made to our ancestors— 7 the very thing that the twelve tribes of our people hope to receive, as they worship God day and night. And it is because of this hope, Your Majesty, that I am being accused by the Jews! 8 Why do you who are here find it impossible to believe that God raises the dead?

9 "I myself thought that I should do everything I could against the cause of Jesus of Nazareth. 10 That is what I did in Jerusalem. I received authority from the chief priests and put many of God's people in prison; and when they were sentenced to death, I also voted against them. 11 Many times I had them punished in the synagogues and tried to make them deny their faith. I was so furious with them that I even went to foreign cities to persecute them.

Paul Tells of His Conversion
(Acts 9.1–19; 22.6–16)

12 "It was for this purpose that I went to Damascus with authority and orders from the chief priests. 13 It was on the road at midday, Your Majesty, that I saw a light much brighter than the sun, coming from the sky and shining round me and the men travelling

with me. ¹⁴All of us fell to the ground, and I heard a voice say to me in Hebrew, 'Saul, Saul! Why are you persecuting me? You are hurting yourself by hitting back, like an ox kicking against its owner's stick.' ¹⁵'Who are you, Lord?' I asked. And the Lord answered, 'I am Jesus, whom you persecute. ¹⁶But get up and stand on your feet. I have appeared to you to appoint you as my servant. You are to tell others what you have seen of me[1] today and what I will show you in the future. ¹⁷I will rescue you from the people of Israel and from the Gentiles to whom I will send you. ¹⁸You are to open their eyes and turn them from the darkness to the light and from the power of Satan to God, so that through their faith in me they will have their sins forgiven and receive their place among God's chosen people.'

Paul Tells of His Work

19 "And so, King Agrippa, I did not disobey the vision I had from heaven. ²⁰First in Damascus and in Jerusalem and then in all Judaea and among the Gentiles, I preached that they must repent of their sins and turn to God and do the things that would show they had repented. ²¹It was for this reason that the Jews seized me while I was in the Temple, and they tried to kill me. ²²But to this very day I have been helped by God, and so I stand here giving my witness to all, to small and great alike. What I say is the very same thing which the prophets and Moses said was going to happen: ²³that the Messiah must suffer and be the first one to rise from death, to announce the light of salvation to the Jews and to the Gentiles."

24 As Paul defended himself in this way, Festus shouted at him, "You are mad, Paul! Your great learning is driving you mad!"

25 Paul answered, "I am not mad, Your Excellency! I am speaking the sober truth. ²⁶King Agrippa! I can speak to you with all boldness, because you know about these things. I am sure that you have taken notice of every one of them, for this thing has not

---

[1] Some manuscripts do not have of me.

happened hidden away in a corner. [27]King Agrippa, do you believe the prophets? I know that you do!"

28 Agrippa said to Paul, "In this short time do you think you will make me a Christian?"

29 "Whether a short time or a long time," Paul answered, "my prayer to God is that you and all the rest of you who are listening to me today might become what I am—except, of course, for these chains!"

30 Then the king, the governor, Bernice, and all the others got up, [31]and after leaving they said to each other, "This man has not done anything for which he should die or be put in prison." [32]And Agrippa said to Festus, "This man could have been released if he had not appealed to the Emperor."

Paul Sails for Rome

27 When it was decided that we should sail to Italy, they handed Paul and some other prisoners over to Julius, an officer in the Roman regiment called "The Emperor's Regiment." [2]We went aboard a ship from Adramyttium, which was ready to leave for the seaports of the province of Asia, and we sailed away. Aristarchus, a Macedonian from Thessalonica, was with us. [3]The next day we arrived at Sidon. Julius was kind to Paul and allowed him to go and see his friends, to be given what he needed. [4]We went on from there, and because the winds were blowing against us, we sailed on the sheltered side of the island of Cyprus. [5]We crossed over the sea off Cilicia and Pamphylia and came to Myra in Lycia. [6]There the officer found a ship from Alexandria that was going to sail for Italy, so he put us aboard.

7 We sailed slowly for several days and with great difficulty finally arrived off the town of Cnidus. The wind would not let us go any further in that direction, so we sailed down the sheltered side of the island of Crete, passing by Cape Salmone. [8]We kept close to the coast and with great difficulty came to a place called Safe Harbours, not far from the town of Lasea.

9 We spent a long time there, until it became

PAUL'S JOURNEY
TO ROME

dangerous to continue the voyage, for by now the Day of Atonement*m* was already past. So Paul gave them this advice: 10 "Men, I see that our voyage from here on will be dangerous; there will be great damage to the cargo and to the ship, and loss of life as well." 11 But the army officer was convinced by what the captain and the owner of the ship said, and not by what Paul said. 12 The harbour was not a good one to spend the winter in; so most of the men were in favour of putting out to sea and trying to reach Phoenix, if possible, in order to spend the winter there. Phoenix is a harbour in Crete that faces south-west and north-west.*n*

The Storm at Sea

13 A soft wind from the south began to blow, and the men thought that they could carry out their plan, so they pulled up the anchor and sailed as close as possible along the coast of Crete. 14 But soon a very strong wind—the one called "North-easter"—blew down from the island. 15 It hit the ship, and since it was impossible to keep the ship headed into the wind, we gave up trying and let it be carried along by the wind. 16 We got some shelter when we passed to the south of the little island of Cauda. There, with some difficulty, we managed to make the ship's boat secure. 17 They pulled it aboard and then fastened some ropes tight round the ship. They were afraid that they might run into the sandbanks off the coast of Libya, so they lowered the sail and let the ship be carried by the wind. 18 The violent storm continued, so on the next day they began to throw some of the ship's cargo overboard, 19 and on the following day they threw part of the ship's equipment overboard. 20 For many days we could not see the sun or the stars, and the wind kept on blowing very hard. We finally gave up all hope of being saved.

21 After the men had gone a long time without

m DAY OF ATONEMENT: *This was celebrated towards the end of September or beginning of October, at which time bad weather made sailing dangerous.*
n south-west and north-west; *or* north-east and south-east.

food, Paul stood before them and said, "Men, you should have listened to me and not have sailed from Crete; then we would have avoided all this damage and loss. 22But now I beg you, take heart! Not one of you will lose his life; only the ship will be lost. 23For last night an angel of the God to whom I belong and whom I worship came to me 24and said, 'Don't be afraid, Paul! You must stand before the Emperor. And God in his goodness to you has spared the lives of all those who are sailing with you.' 25So take heart, men! For I trust in God that it will be just as I was told. 26But we will be driven ashore on some island."

27 It was the fourteenth night, and we were being driven about in the Mediterranean by the storm. About midnight the sailors suspected that we were getting close to land. 28So they dropped a line with a weight tied to it and found that the water was forty metres deep; a little later they did the same and found that it was thirty metres deep. 29They were afraid that the ship would go on the rocks, so they lowered four anchors from the back of the ship and prayed for daylight. 30Then the sailors tried to escape from the ship; they lowered the boat into the water and pretended that they were going to put out some anchors from the front of the ship. 31But Paul said to the army officer and soldiers, "If the sailors don't stay on board, you have no hope of being saved." 32So the soldiers cut the ropes that held the boat and let it go.

33 Just before dawn, Paul begged them all to eat some food: "You have been waiting for fourteen days now, and all this time you have not eaten anything. 34I beg you, then, eat some food; you need it in order to survive. Not even a hair of your heads will be lost." 35After saying this, Paul took some bread, gave thanks to God before them all, broke it, and began to eat. 36They took heart, and every one of them also ate some food. 37There was a total of 276p of us on board. 38After everyone had eaten enough,

p276; *some manuscripts have* 275; *others have* about 76.

they lightened the ship by throwing all the wheat into the sea.

The Shipwreck

39 When day came, the sailors did not recognize the coast, but they noticed a bay with a beach and decided that, if possible, they would run the ship aground there. 40 So they cut off the anchors and let them sink in the sea, and at the same time they untied the ropes that held the steering oars. Then they raised the sail at the front of the ship so that the wind would blow the ship forward, and we headed for shore. 41 But the ship hit a sandbank and went

But the ship hit a sandbank (27.41)

aground; the front part of the ship got stuck and could not move, while the back part was being broken to pieces by the violence of the waves.

42 The soldiers made a plan to kill all the prisoners, in order to keep them from swimming ashore and escaping. 43 But the army officer wanted to save Paul, so he stopped them from doing this. Instead, he ordered all the men who could swim to jump overboard first and swim ashore; 44 the rest were to follow, holding on to the planks or to some broken pieces of the ship. And this was how we all got safely ashore.

In Malta

28 When we were safely ashore, we learnt that the island was called Malta. ²The natives there were very friendly to us. It had started to rain and was cold, so they lit a fire and made us all welcome. ³Paul gathered up a bundle of sticks and was putting them on the fire when a snake came out on account of the heat and fastened itself to his hand. ⁴The natives saw the snake hanging on Paul's hand and said to one another, "This man must be a murderer, but Fate will not let him live, even though he escaped from the sea." ⁵But Paul shook the snake off into the fire without being harmed at all. ⁶They were waiting for him to swell up or suddenly fall down dead. But after waiting for a long time and not seeing anything unusual happening to him, they changed their minds and said, "He is a god!"

7 Not far from that place were some fields that belonged to Publius, the chief official of the island. He welcomed us kindly and for three days we were his guests. ⁸Publius' father was in bed, sick with fever and dysentery. Paul went into his room, prayed, placed his hands on him, and healed him. ⁹When this happened, all the other sick people on the island came and were healed. ¹⁰They gave us many gifts, and when we sailed, they put on board what we needed for the voyage.

From Malta to Rome .

11 After three months we sailed away on a ship from Alexandria, called "The Twin Gods," which had spent the winter in the island. ¹²We arrived in the city of Syracuse and stayed there for three days. ¹³From there we sailed on and arrived in the city of Rhegium. The next day a wind began to blow from the south, and in two days we came to the town of Puteoli. ¹⁴We found some believers there who asked us to stay with them a week. And so we came to Rome. ¹⁵The believers in Rome heard about us and came as far as the towns of Market of Appius and Three Inns to meet us. When Paul saw them, he thanked God and was greatly encouraged.

In Rome

16 When we arrived in Rome, Paul was allowed to live by himself with a soldier guarding him.

17 After three days Paul called the local Jewish leaders to a meeting. When they had gathered, he said to them, "My fellow-Israelites, even though I did nothing against our people or the customs that we received from our ancestors, I was made a prisoner in Jerusalem and handed over to the Romans. 18 After questioning me, the Romans wanted to release me, because they found that I had done nothing for which I deserved to die. 19 But when the Jews opposed this, I was forced to appeal to the Emperor, even though I had no accusation to make against my own people. 20 That is why I asked to see you and talk with you. As a matter of fact, I am bound in chains like this for the sake of him for whom the people of Israel hope."

21 They said to him, "We have not received any letters from Judaea about you, nor have any of our people come from there with any news or anything bad to say about you. 22 But we would like to hear your ideas, because we know that everywhere people speak against this party to which you belong."

23 So they fixed a date with Paul, and a large number of them came that day to the place where Paul was staying. From morning till night he explained to them his message about the Kingdom of God, and he tried to convince them about Jesus by quoting from the Law of Moses and the writings of the prophets. 24 Some of them were convinced by his words, but others would not believe. 25 So they left, disagreeing among themselves, after Paul had said this one thing: "How well the Holy Spirit spoke through the prophet Isaiah to your ancestors! 26 For he said,

'Go and say to this people:
You will listen and listen, but not understand;
    you will look and look, but not see,
27 because this people's minds are dull,
    and they have stopped up their ears
    and closed their eyes.
Otherwise, their eyes would see,

their ears would hear,
their minds would understand,
and they would turn to me, says God,
and I would heal them.' "

28 And Paul concluded: "You are to know, then, that God's message of salvation has been sent to the Gentiles. They will listen!" q

30 For two years Paul lived in a place he rented for himself, and there he welcomed all who came to see him. 31 He preached about the Kingdom of God and taught about the Lord Jesus Christ, speaking with all boldness and freedom.

q Some manuscripts add verse 29: After Paul said this, the Jews left, arguing violently among themselves.

PAUL'S LETTER TO THE

ROMANS

INTRODUCTION

Paul's Letter to the Romans was written to prepare the way for a visit Paul planned to make to the church at Rome. His plan was to work among the Christians there for a while and then, with their support, to go on to Spain. He wrote to explain his understanding of the Christian faith and its practical implications for the lives of Christians. The book contains Paul's most complete statement of his message.

After greeting the people of the church at Rome and telling them of his prayers for them, Paul states the theme of the letter: "The gospel reveals how God puts people right with himself: it is through faith from beginning to end" (1.17).

Paul then develops this theme. All mankind, both Jews and Gentiles, needs to be put right with God, for all alike are under the power of sin. People are put right with God through faith in Jesus Christ. Next Paul describes the new life in union with Christ that

results from this new relation with God. The believer
has peace with God and is set free by God's Spirit
from the power of sin and death. In chapters 5—8
Paul also discusses the purpose of the Law of God
and the power of God's Spirit in the believer's life.
Then the apostle wrestles with the question of how
Jews and Gentiles fit into the plan of God for mankind.
He concludes that the Jewish rejection of Jesus is
part of God's plan for bringing all mankind within
the reach of God's grace in Jesus Christ, and he believes
that the Jews will not always reject Jesus. Finally
Paul writes about how the Christian life should be
lived, especially about the way of love in relations
with others. He takes up such themes as service to
God, the duty of Christians to the state and to one
another, and questions of conscience. He ends the letter
with personal messages and with words of praise to
God.

Outline of Contents

1 From Paul, a servant of Christ Jesus and an apostle
chosen and called by God to preach his Good
News.

2 The Good News was promised long ago by God
through his prophets, as written in the Holy Scriptures.
³It is about his Son, our Lord Jesus Christ: as to
his humanity, he was born a descendant of David;
⁴as to his divine holiness, he was shown with great
power to be the Son of God by being raised from
death. ⁵Through him God gave me the privilege of
being an apostle for the sake of Christ, in order to
lead people of all nations to believe and obey. ⁶This

also includes you who are in Rome, whom God has called to belong to Jesus Christ.

7 And so I write to all of you in Rome whom God loves and has called to be his own people:

May God our Father and the Lord Jesus Christ give you grace and peace.

Prayer of Thanksgiving

8 First, I thank my God through Jesus Christ for all of you, because the whole world is hearing about your faith. 9 God is my witness that what I say is true—the God whom I serve with all my heart by preaching the Good News about his Son. God knows that I remember you 10 every time I pray. I ask that God in his good will may at last make it possible for me to visit you now. 11 For I want very much to see you, in order to share a spiritual blessing with you to make you strong. 12 What I mean is that both you and I will be helped at the same time, you by my faith and I by yours.

13 You must remember, my brothers, that many times I have planned to visit you, but something has always kept me from doing so. I want to win converts among you also, as I have among other Gentiles. 14 For I have an obligation to all peoples, to the civilized and to the savage, to the educated and to the ignorant. 15 So then, I am eager to preach the Good News to you also who live in Rome.

The Power of the Gospel

16 I have complete confidence in the gospel; it is God's power to save all who believe, first the Jews and also the Gentiles. 17 For the gospel reveals how God puts people right with himself: it is through faith from beginning to end. As the scripture says, "The person who is put right with God through faith shall live." [a]

The Guilt of Mankind

18 God's anger is revealed from heaven against all

---

[a] put right with God through faith shall live; *or* put right with God shall live through faith.

the sin and evil of the people whose evil ways prevent the truth from being known. ¹⁹God punishes them, because what can be known about God is plain to them, for God himself made it plain. ²⁰Ever since God created the world, his invisible qualities, both his eternal power and his divine nature, have been clearly seen; they are perceived in the things that God has made. So those people have no excuse at all! ²¹They know God, but they do not give him the honour that belongs to him, nor do they thank him. Instead, their thoughts have become complete nonsense, and their empty minds are filled with darkness. ²²They say they are wise, but they are fools; ²³instead

Instead of worshipping...God, they worship images (1.23)

of worshipping the immortal God, they worship images made to look like mortal man or birds or animals or reptiles.

24 And so God has given those people over to do the filthy things their hearts desire, and they do shameful things with each other. ²⁵They exchange the truth about God for a lie; they worship and serve what God has created instead of the Creator himself, who is to be praised for ever! Amen.

26 Because they do this, God has given them over to shameful passions. Even the women pervert the natural use of their sex by unnatural acts. ²⁷In the

same way the men give up natural sexual relations with women and burn with passion for each other. Men do shameful things with each other, and as a result they bring upon themselves the punishment they deserve for their wrongdoing.

28 Because those people refuse to keep in mind the true knowledge about God, he has given them over to corrupted minds, so that they do the things that they should not do. 29 They are filled with all kinds of wickedness, evil, greed, and vice; they are full of jealousy, murder, fighting, deceit, and malice. They gossip 30 and speak evil of one another; they are hateful to God, insolent, *b* proud, and boastful; they think of more ways to do evil; they disobey their parents; 31 they have no conscience; they do not keep their promises, and they show no kindness or pity for others. 32 They know that God's law says that people who live in this way deserve death. Yet, not only do they continue to do these very things, but they even approve of others who do them.

God's Judgement

2 Do you, my friend, pass judgement on others? You have no excuse at all, whoever you are. For when you judge others and then do the same things which they do, you condemn yourself. 2 We know that God is right when he judges the people who do such things as these. 3 But you, my friend, do those very things for which you pass judgement on others! Do you think you will escape God's judgement? 4 Or perhaps you despise his great kindness, tolerance, and patience. Surely you know that God is kind, because he is trying to lead you to repent. 5 But you have a hard and stubborn heart, and so you are making your own punishment even greater on the Day when God's anger and righteous judgements will be revealed. 6 For God will reward every person according to what he has done. 7 Some people keep on doing good, and seek glory, honour, and immortal life; to them God will give eternal life. 8 Other people are selfish and reject what is right, in order to follow what is wrong;

---

b are hateful to God, insolent; *or* hate God, and are insolent.

on them God will pour out his anger and fury. [9]There will be suffering and pain for all those who do what is evil, for the Jews first and also for the Gentiles. [10]But God will give glory, honour, and peace to all who do what is good, to the Jews first and also to the Gentiles. [11]For God judges everyone by the same standard.

12 The Gentiles do not have the Law of Moses; they sin and are lost apart from the Law. The Jews have the Law; they sin and are judged by the Law. [13]For it is not by hearing the Law that people are put right with God, but by doing what the Law commands. [14]The Gentiles do not have the Law; but whenever they do by instinct what the Law commands, they are their own law, even though they do not have the Law. [15]Their conduct shows that what the Law commands is written in their hearts. Their consciences also show that this is true, since their thoughts sometimes accuse them and sometimes defend them. [16]And so, according to the Good News I preach, this is how it will be on that Day when God through Jesus Christ will judge the secret thoughts of all.

The Jews and the Law

17 What about you? You call yourself a Jew; you depend on the Law and boast about God; [18]you know what God wants you to do, and you have learnt from the Law to choose what is right; [19]you are sure that you are a guide for the blind, a light for those who are in darkness, [20]an instructor for the foolish, and a teacher for the ignorant. You are certain that in the Law you have the full content of knowledge and of truth. [21]You teach others—why don't you teach yourself? You preach, "Do not steal"—but do you yourself steal? [22]You say, "Do not commit adultery"—but do you commit adultery? You detest idols—but do you rob temples? [23]You boast about having God's law—but do you bring shame on God by breaking his law? [24]The scripture says, "Because of you Jews, the Gentiles speak evil of God."

25 If you obey the Law, your circumcision is of value; but if you disobey the Law, you might as well never have been circumcised. [26]If the Gentile,

who is not circumcised, obeys the commands of the Law, will God not regard him as though he were circumcised? 27 And so you Jews will be condemned by the Gentiles because you break the Law, even though you have it written down and are circumcised; but they obey the Law, even though they are not physically circumcised. 28 After all, who is a real Jew, truly circumcised? It is not the man who is a Jew on the outside, whose circumcision is a physical thing. 29 Rather, the real Jew is the person who is a Jew on the inside, that is, whose heart has been circumcised, and this is the work of God's Spirit, not of the written Law. Such a person receives his praise from God, not from man.

3 Have the Jews then any advantage over the Gentiles? Or is there any value in being circumcised? 2 Much, indeed, in every way! In the first place, God trusted his message to the Jews. 3 But what if some of them were not faithful? Does this mean that God will not be faithful? 4 Certainly not! God must be true, even though every man is a liar. As the scripture says,

"You must be shown to be right when you speak; you must win your case when you are being tried."

5 But what if our doing wrong serves to show up more clearly God's doing right? Can we say that God does wrong when he punishes us? (This would be the natural question to ask.) 6 By no means! If God is not just, how can he judge the world?

7 But what if my untruth serves God's glory by making his truth stand out more clearly? Why should I still be condemned as a sinner? 8 Why not say, then, "Let us do evil so that good may come"? Some people, indeed, have insulted me by accusing me of saying this very thing! They will be condemned, as they should be.

No One Is Righteous

9 Well then, are we Jews in any better condition than the Gentiles? Not at all!c I have already shown

c any better condition than the Gentiles? Not at all!; or any worse condition than the Gentiles? Not altogether.

that Jews and Gentiles alike are all under the power
of sin. ¹⁰As the Scriptures say:
  "There is no one who is righteous,
¹¹   no one who is wise
      or who worships God.
¹² All have turned away from God;
      they have all gone wrong;
      no one does what is right, not even one.
¹³ Their words are full of deadly deceit;
      wicked lies roll off their tongues,
      and dangerous threats, like snake's poison, from
          their lips;
¹⁴   their speech is filled with bitter curses.
¹⁵ They are quick to hurt and kill;
¹⁶   they leave ruin and destruction wherever they
          go
¹⁷ They have not known the path of peace,
¹⁸   nor have they learnt reverence for God."

19 Now we know that everything in the Law applies
to those who live under the Law, in order to stop
all human excuses and bring the whole world under
God's judgement. ²⁰For no one is put right in God's
sight by doing what the Law requires; what the Law
does is to make man know that he has sinned.

How God Puts Us Right with Him

21 But now God's way of putting people right with
himself has been revealed. It has nothing to do with
law, even though the Law of Moses and the prophets
gave their witness to it. ²²God puts people right
through their faith in Jesus Christ. God does this
to all who believe in Christ, because there is no difference at all: ²³everyone has sinned and is far away
from God's saving presence. ²⁴But by the free gift
of God's grace all are put right with him through
Christ Jesus, who sets them free. ²⁵⁻²⁶God offered
him, so that by his sacrificial death he should become
the means by which people's sins are forgiven through
their faith in him. God did this in order to demonstrate
that he is righteous. In the past he was patient and
overlooked people's sins; but in the present time he
deals with their sins, in order to demonstrate his
righteousness. In this way God shows that he himself

is righteous and that he puts right everyone who believes in Jesus.

27 What, then, can we boast about? Nothing! And what is the reason for this? Is it that we obey the Law? No, but that we believe. [28] For we conclude that a person is put right with God only through faith, and not by doing what the Law commands. [29] Or is God the God of the Jews only? Is he not the God of the Gentiles also? Of course he is. [30] God is one, and he will put the Jews right with himself on the basis of their faith, and will put the Gentiles right through their faith. [31] Does this mean that by this faith we do away with the Law? No, not at all; instead, we uphold the Law.

The Example of Abraham

4 What shall we say, then, of Abraham, the father of our race? What was his experience? [2] If he was put right with God by the things he did, he would have something to boast about—but not in God's sight. [3] The scripture says, "Abraham believed God, and because of his faith God accepted him as righteous." [4] A person who works is paid his wages, but they are not regarded as a gift; they are something that he has earned. [5] But the person who depends on his faith, not on his deeds, and who believes in the God who declares the guilty to be innocent, it is his faith that God takes into account in order to put him right with himself. [6] This is what David meant when he spoke of the happiness of the person whom God accepts as righteous, apart from anything that person does:

[7] "Happy are those whose wrongs are forgiven,
　　whose sins are pardoned!
[8] Happy is the person whose sins the Lord will not
　　keep account of!"

9 Does this happiness that David spoke of belong only to those who are circumcised? No indeed! It belongs also to those who are not circumcised. For we have quoted the scripture, "Abraham believed God, and because of his faith God accepted him as righteous." [10] When did this take place? Was it before or after Abraham was circumcised? It was before,

not after. [11]He was circumcised later, and his circumcision was a sign to show that because of his faith God had accepted him as righteous before he had been circumcised. And so Abraham is the spiritual father of all who believe in God and are accepted as righteous by him, even though they are not circumcised. [12]He is also the father of those who are circumcised, that is, of those who, in addition to being circumcised, also live the same life of faith that our father Abraham lived before he was circumcised.

God's Promise Is Received through Faith

13 When God promised Abraham and his descendants that the world would belong to him, he did so, not because Abraham obeyed the Law, but because he believed and was accepted as righteous by God. [14]For if what God promises is to be given to those who obey the Law, then man's faith means nothing and God's promise is worthless. [15]The Law brings down God's anger; but where there is no law, there is no disobeying of the law.

16 And so the promise was based on faith, in order that the promise should be guaranteed as God's free gift to all of Abraham's descendants—not just to those who obey the Law, but also to those who believe as Abraham did. For Abraham is the spiritual father of us all; [17]as the scripture says, "I have made you father of many nations." So the promise is good in the sight of God, in whom Abraham believed—the God who brings the dead to life and whose command brings into being what did not exist. [18]Abraham believed and hoped, even when there was no reason for hoping, and so became "the father of many nations." Just as the scripture says, "Your descendants will be as many as the stars." [19]He was then almost one hundred years old; but his faith did not weaken when he thought of his body, which was already practically dead, or of the fact that Sarah could not have children. [20]His faith did not leave him, and he did not doubt God's promise; his faith filled him with power, and he gave praise to God. [21]He was absolutely sure that God would be able to do what he had promised. [22]That is why Abraham, through faith, "was

accepted as righteous by God." 23 The words "he was accepted as righteous" were not written for him alone. 24 They were written also for us who are to be accepted as righteous, who believe in him who raised Jesus our Lord from death. 25 Because of our sins he was handed over to die, and he was raised to life in order to put us right with God.

Right with God

5 Now that we have been put right with God through faith, we have *d* peace with God through our Lord Jesus Christ. 2 He has brought us by faith into this experience of God's grace, in which we now live. And so we boast *e* of the hope we have of sharing God's glory! 3 We also boast *f* of our troubles, because we know that trouble produces endurance, 4 endurance brings God's approval, and his approval creates hope. 5 This hope does not disappoint us, for God has poured out his love into our hearts by means of the Holy Spirit, who is God's gift to us.

6 For when we were still helpless, Christ died for the wicked at the time that God chose. 7 It is a difficult thing for someone to die for a righteous person. It may even be that someone might dare to die for a good person. 8 But God has shown us how much he loves us—it was while we were still sinners that Christ died for us! 9 By his sacrificial death we are now put right with God; how much more, then, will we be saved by him from God's anger! 10 We were God's enemies, but he made us his friends through the death of his Son. Now that we are God's friends, how much more will we be saved by Christ's life! 11 But that is not all; we rejoice because of what God has done through our Lord Jesus Christ, who has now made us God's friends.

Adam and Christ

12 Sin came into the world through one man, and his sin brought death with it. As a result, death has

d we have; *some manuscripts have* let us have.
e we boast; *or* let us boast.
f We also boast; *or* Let us also boast.

spread to the whole human race because everyone has sinned. [13]There was sin in the world before the Law was given; but where there is no law, no account is kept of sins. [14]But from the time of Adam to the time of Moses death ruled over all mankind, even over those who did not sin in the same way that Adam did when he disobeyed God's command.

Adam was a figure of the one who was to come. [15]But the two are not the same, because God's free gift is not like Adam's sin. It is true that many people died because of the sin of that one man. But God's grace is much greater, and so is his free gift to so many people through the grace of the one man, Jesus Christ. [16]And there is a difference between God's gift and the sin of one man. After the one sin, came the judgement of "Guilty"; but after so many sins, comes the undeserved gift of "Not guilty!" [17]It is true that through the sin of one man death began to rule because of that one man. But how much greater is the result of what was done by the one man, Jesus Christ! All who receive God's abundant grace and are freely put right with him will rule in life through Christ.

18 So then, as the one sin condemned all mankind, in the same way the one righteous act sets all mankind free and gives them life. [19]And just as all people were made sinners as the result of the disobedience of one man, in the same way they will all be put right with God as the result of the obedience of the one man.

20 Law was introduced in order to increase wrong-doing; but where sin increased, God's grace increased much more. [21]So then, just as sin ruled by means of death, so also God's grace rules by means of righteousness, leading us to eternal life through Jesus Christ our Lord.

Dead to Sin but Alive in Union with Christ

6 What shall we say, then? Should we continue to live in sin so that God's grace will increase? [2]Certainly not! We have died to sin—how then can we go on living in it? [3]For surely you know that when we were baptized into union with Christ Jesus,

we were baptized into union with his death. ⁴By our
baptism, then, we were buried with him and shared
his death, in order that, just as Christ was raised
from death by the glorious power of the Father, so
also we might live a new life.

5 For since we have become one with him in dying
as he did, in the same way we shall be one with
him by being raised to life as he was. ⁶And we

So that we should no longer be the slaves of sin (6.6)

know that our old being has been put to death with
Christ on his cross, in order that the power of the
sinful self might be destroyed, so that we should no
longer be the slaves of sin. ⁷For when a person dies,
he is set free from the power of sin. ⁸Since we have
died with Christ, we believe that we will also live
with him. ⁹For we know that Christ has been raised
from death and will never die again—death will no
longer rule over him. ¹⁰And so, because he died, sin
has no power over him; and now he lives his life
in fellowship with God. ¹¹In the same way you are
to think of yourselves as dead, so far as sin is concerned, but living in fellowship with God through Christ
Jesus.

12 Sin must no longer rule in your mortal bodies,
so that you obey the desires of your natural self.
¹³Nor must you surrender any part of yourselves to

sin to be used for wicked purposes. Instead, give yourselves to God, as those who have been brought from
death to life, and surrender your whole being to him
to be used for righteous purposes. 14 Sin must not
be your master; for you do not live under law but
under God's grace.

Slaves of Righteousness

15 What, then? Shall we sin, because we are not
under law but under God's grace? By no means!
16 Surely you know that when you surrender yourselves
as slaves to obey someone, you are in fact the slaves
of the master you obey—either of sin, which results
in death, or of obedience, which results in being put
right with God. 17 But thanks be to God! For though
at one time you were slaves to sin, you have obeyed
with all your heart the truths found in the teaching
you received. 18 You were set free from sin and became
the slaves of righteousness. 19 (I use everyday language
because of the weakness of your natural selves.) At
one time you surrendered yourselves entirely as slaves
to impurity and wickedness for wicked purposes. In
the same way you must now surrender yourselves
entirely as slaves of righteousness for holy purposes.

20 When you were the slaves of sin, you were free
from righteousness. 21 What did you gain from doing
the things that you are now ashamed of? The result
of those things is death! 22 But now you have been
set free from sin and are the slaves of God. Your
gain is a life fully dedicated to him, and the result
is eternal life. 23 For sin pays its wage—death; but
God's free gift is eternal life in union with Christ
Jesus our Lord.

An Illustration from Marriage

7 Certainly you will understand what I am about
to say, my brothers, because all of you know
about law. The law rules over people only as long
as they live. 2 A married woman, for example, is bound
by the law to her husband as long as he lives; but
if he dies, then she is free from the law that bound
her to him. 3 So then, if she lives with another man
while her husband is alive, she will be called an

adulteress; but if her husband dies, she is legally a free woman and does not commit adultery if she marries another man. ⁴That is how it is with you, my brothers. As far as the Law is concerned, you also have died because you are part of the body of Christ; and now you belong to him who was raised from death in order that we might be useful in the service of God. ⁵For when we lived according to our human nature, the sinful desires stirred up by the Law were at work in our bodies, and all we did ended in death. ⁶Now, however, we are free from the Law, because we died to that which once held us prisoners. No longer do we serve in the old way of a written law, but in the new way of the Spirit.

Law and Sin

7 Shall we say, then, that the Law itself is sinful? Of course not! But it was the Law that made me know what sin is. If the Law had not said, "Do not desire what belongs to someone else," I would not have known such a desire. ⁸But by means of that commandment sin found its chance to stir up all kinds of selfish desires in me. Apart from law, sin is a dead thing. ⁹I myself was once alive apart from law; but when the commandment came, sin sprang to life, ¹⁰and I died. And the commandment which was meant to bring life, in my case brought death. ¹¹Sin found its chance, and by means of the commandment it deceived me and killed me.

12 So then, the Law itself is holy, and the commandment is holy, right, and good. ¹³But does this mean that what is good caused my death? By no means! It was sin that did it; by using what is good, sin brought death to me, in order that its true nature as sin might be revealed. And so, by means of the commandment sin is shown to be even more terribly sinful.

The Conflict in Man

14 We know that the Law is spiritual; but I am a mortal man, sold as a slave to sin. ¹⁵I do not understand what I do; for I don't do what I would like to do, but instead I do what I hate. ¹⁶Since

what I do is what I don't want to do, this shows that I agree that the Law is right. [17] So I am not really the one who does this thing; rather it is the sin that lives in me. [18] I know that good does not live in me—that is, in my human nature. For even though the desire to do good is in me, I am not able to do it. [19] I don't do the good I want to do; instead, I do the evil that I do not want to do. [20] If I do what I don't want to do, this means that I am no longer the one who does it; instead, it is the sin that lives in me.

21 So I find that this law is at work: when I want to do what is good, what is evil is the only choice I have. [22] My inner being delights in the law of God. [23] But I see a different law at work in my body—a law that fights against the law which my mind approves of. It makes me a prisoner to the law of sin which is at work in my body. [24] What an unhappy man I am! Who will rescue me from this body that is taking me to death? [25] Thanks be to God, who does this through our Lord Jesus Christ!

This, then, is my condition: on my own I can serve God's law only with my mind, while my human nature serves the law of sin.

Life in the Spirit

8 There is no condemnation now for those who live in union with Christ Jesus. [2] For the law of the Spirit, which brings us life in union with Christ Jesus, has set me[g] free from the law of sin and death. [3] What the Law could not do, because human nature was weak, God did. He condemned sin in human nature by sending his own Son, who came with a nature like man's sinful nature, to do away with sin. [4] God did this so that the righteous demands of the Law might be fully satisfied in us who live according to the Spirit, and not according to human nature. [5] Those who live as their human nature tells them to, have their minds controlled by what human nature wants. Those who live as the Spirit tells them to, have their minds controlled by what the Spirit wants. [6] To

[g]me; *some manuscripts have* you; *others have* us.

be controlled by human nature results in death; to be controlled by the Spirit results in life and peace. 7 And so a person becomes an enemy of God when he is controlled by his human nature; for he does not obey God's law, and in fact he cannot obey it. 8 Those who obey their human nature cannot please God.

9 But you do not live as your human nature tells you to; instead, you live as the Spirit tells you to—if, in fact, God's Spirit lives in you. Whoever does not have the Spirit of Christ does not belong to him. 10 But if Christ lives in you, the Spirit is life for you [h] because you have been put right with God, even though your bodies are going to die because of sin. 11 If the Spirit of God, who raised Jesus from death, lives in you, then he who raised Christ from death will also give life to your mortal bodies by the presence of his Spirit in you.

12 So then, my brothers, we have an obligation, but it is not to live as our human nature wants us to. 13 For if you live according to your human nature, you are going to die; but if by the Spirit you put to death your sinful actions, you will live. 14 Those who are led by God's Spirit are God's sons. 15 For the Spirit that God has given you does not make you slaves and cause you to be afraid; instead, the Spirit makes you God's children, and by the Spirit's power we cry out to God, "Father! my Father!" 16 God's Spirit joins himself to our spirits to declare that we are God's children. 17 Since we are his children, we will possess the blessings he keeps for his people, and we will also possess with Christ what God has kept for him; for if we share Christ's suffering, we will also share his glory.

The Future Glory

18 I consider that what we suffer at this present time cannot be compared at all with the glory that is going to be revealed to us. 19 All of creation waits with eager longing for God to reveal his sons. 20 For creation was condemned to lose its purpose, not of

[h] the Spirit is life for you; or your spirit is alive.

its own will, but because God willed it to be so. Yet there was the hope [21]that creation itself would one day be set free from its slavery to decay and would share the glorious freedom of the children of God. [22]For we know that up to the present time all of creation groans with pain, like the pain of childbirth. [23]But it is not just creation alone which groans; we who have the Spirit as the first of God's gifts also groan within ourselves, as we wait for God to make us his sons and[i] set our whole being free. [24]For it was by hope that we were saved; but if we see what we hope for, then it is not really hope. For who hopes for something he sees? [25]But if we hope for what we do not see, we wait for it with patience.

[26] In the same way the Spirit also comes to help us, weak as we are. For we do not know how we ought to pray; the Spirit himself pleads with God for us in groans that words cannot express. [27]And God, who sees into our hearts, knows what the thought of the Spirit is; because the Spirit pleads with God on behalf of his people and in accordance with his will.

[28] We know that in all things God works for good with those who love him,[j] those whom he has called according to his purpose. [29]Those whom God had already chosen he also set apart to become like his Son, so that the Son would be the first among many brothers. [30]And so those whom God set apart, he called; and those he called, he put right with himself, and he shared his glory with them.

God's Love in Christ Jesus

[31] In view of all this, what can we say? If God is for us, who can be against us? [32]Certainly not God, who did not even keep back his own Son, but offered him for us all! He gave us his Son—will he not also freely give us all things? [33]Who will

---

[i] *Some manuscripts do not have* make us his sons and.
[j] in all things God works for good with those who love him; *some manuscripts have* all things work for good for those who love God.

accuse God's chosen people? God himself declares them not guilty! ³⁴Who, then, will condemn them? Not Christ Jesus, who died, or rather, who was raised to life and is at the right-hand side of God, pleading with him for us! ³⁵Who, then, can separate us from the love of Christ? Can trouble do it, or hardship or persecution or hunger or poverty or danger or death? ³⁶As the scripture says,

"For your sake we are in danger of death at all
    times;
  we are treated like sheep that are going to be
    slaughtered."

³⁷No, in all these things we have complete victory through him who loved us! ³⁸For I am certain that nothing can separate us from his love: neither death nor life, neither angels nor other heavenly rulers or powers, neither the present nor the future, ³⁹neither the world above nor the world below—there is nothing in all creation that will ever be able to separate us from the love of God which is ours through Christ Jesus our Lord.

God and His People

9 I am speaking the truth; I belong to Christ and I do not lie. My conscience, ruled by the Holy Spirit, also assures me that I am not lying ²when I say how great is my sorrow, how endless the pain in my heart ³for my people, my own flesh and blood! For their sake I could wish that I myself were under God's curse and separated from Christ. ⁴They are God's people; he made them his sons and revealed his glory to them; he made his covenants*k* with them and gave them the Law; they have the true worship; they have received God's promises; ⁵they are descended from the famous Hebrew ancestors; and Christ, as a human being, belongs to their race. May God, who rules over all, be praised for ever!*l* Amen.

6 I am not saying that the promise of God has failed; for not all the people of Israel are the people

---

*k*covenants; *some manuscripts have* covenant.
*l*May God, who rules over all, be praised for ever!; *or* And may he, who is God ruling over all, be praised for ever!

of God. [7] Nor are all Abraham's descendants the children of God. God said to Abraham, "It is through Isaac that you will have the descendants I promised you." [8] This means that the children born in the usual way[m] are not the children of God; instead, the children born as a result of God's promise are regarded as the true descendants. [9] For God's promise was made in these words: "At the right time[n] I will come back, and Sarah will have a son."

10 And this is not all. For Rebecca's two sons had the same father, our ancestor Isaac. [11-12] But in order that the choice of one son might be completely the result of God's own purpose, God said to her, "The elder will serve the younger." He said this before they were born, before they had done anything either good or bad; so God's choice was based on his call, and not on anything they had done. [13] As the scripture says, "I loved Jacob, but I hated Esau."

14 Shall we say, then, that God is unjust? Not at all. [15] For he said to Moses, "I will have mercy on anyone I wish; I will take pity on anyone I wish." [16] So then, everything depends, not on what man wants or does, but only on God's mercy. [17] For the scripture says to the king of Egypt, "I made you king in order to use you to show my power and to spread my fame over the whole world." [18] So then, God has mercy on anyone he wishes, and he makes stubborn anyone he wishes.

God's Anger and Mercy

19 But one of you will say to me, "If this is so, how can God find fault with anyone? Who can resist God's will?" [20] But who are you, my friend, to answer God back? A clay pot does not ask the man who made it, "Why did you make me like this?" [21] After all, the man who makes the pots has the right to use the clay as he wishes, and to make two pots

[m] CHILDREN BORN IN THE USUAL WAY: *This refers to the descendants Abraham had through Ishmael, his son by Hagar (see Gal 4.22-23).*

[n] At the right time; *or* At this time next year.

from the same lump of clay, one for special occasions and the other for ordinary use.

22 And the same is true of what God has done. He wanted to show his anger and to make his power known. But he was very patient in enduring those who were the objects of his anger, who were doomed to destruction. 23 And he also wanted to reveal his abundant glory, which was poured out on us who are the objects of his mercy, those of us whom he has prepared to receive his glory. 24 For we are the people he called, not only from among the Jews but also from among the Gentiles. 25 This is what he says in the book of Hosea:

"The people who were not mine
  I will call 'My People.'
The nation that I did not love
  I will call 'My Beloved.'
26 And in the very place where they were told, 'You
    are not my people,'
  there they will be called the sons of the living
    God."

27 And Isaiah exclaims about Israel: "Even if the people of Israel are as many as the grains of sand by the sea, yet only a few of them will be saved; 28 for the Lord will quickly settle his full account with the world." 29 It is as Isaiah had said before, "If the Lord Almighty had not left us some descendants, we would have become like Sodom, we would have been like Gomorrah."

Paul's Prayer for Israel

30 So we say that the Gentiles, who were not trying to put themselves right with God, were put right with him through faith; 31 while God's people, who were seeking a law that would put them right with God, did not find it. 32 And why not? Because they did not depend on faith but on what they did. And so they stumbled over the "stumbling stone" 33 that the scripture speaks of:

"Look, I place in Zion a stone
  that will make people stumble,
  a rock that will make them fall.

But whoever believes in him will not be
    disappointed."

10 My brothers, how I wish with all my heart
that my own people might be saved! How I
pray to God for them! ²I can assure you that they
are deeply devoted to God; but their devotion is not
based on true knowledge. ³They have not known the
way in which God puts people right with himself, and
instead, they have tried to set up their own way;
and so they did not submit themselves to God's way
of putting people right. ⁴For Christ has brought the
Law to an end, so that everyone who believes is
put right with God.

Salvation Is for All

5 Moses wrote this about being put right with God
by obeying the Law: "Whoever obeys the commands
of the Law will live." ⁶But what the scripture says
about being put right with God through faith is this:
"You are not to ask yourself, Who will go up into
heaven?" (that is, to bring Christ down). ⁷"Nor are
you to ask, Who will go down into the world below?"
(that is, to bring Christ up from death). ⁸What it
says is this: "God's message is near you, on your
lips and in your heart"—that is, the message of faith
that we preach. ⁹If you confess that Jesus is Lord
and believe that God raised him from death, you will be
saved. ¹⁰For it is by our faith that we are put right
with God; it is by our confession that we are saved.
¹¹The scripture says, "Whoever believes in him will
not be disappointed." ¹²This includes everyone, because
there is no difference between Jews and Gentiles; God
is the same Lord of all and richly blesses all who
call to him. ¹³As the scripture says, "Everyone who
calls out to the Lord for help will be saved."

14 But how can they call to him for help if they
have not believed? And how can they believe if they
have not heard the message? And how can they hear
if the message is not proclaimed? ¹⁵And how can
the message be proclaimed if the messengers are not
sent out? As the scripture says, "How wonderful is
the coming of messengers who bring good news!"
¹⁶But not all have accepted the Good News. Isaiah

himself said, "Lord, who believed our message?" 17 So then, faith comes from hearing the message, and the message comes through preaching Christ.

18 But I ask: Is it true that they did not hear the message? Of course they did—for as the scripture says:

"The sound of their voice went out to all the world;
    their words reached the ends of the earth."

19 Again I ask: Did the people of Israel not understand? Moses himself is the first one to answer:

"I will use a so-called nation
    to make my people jealous;
and by means of a nation of fools
    I will make my people angry."

20 And Isaiah is even bolder when he says,

"I was found by those who were not looking for
    me;
I appeared to those who were not asking for me."

21 But concerning Israel he says, "All day long I held out my hands to welcome a disobedient and rebellious people."

God's Mercy on Israel

11 I ask, then: Did God reject his own people? Certainly not! I myself am an Israelite, a descendant of Abraham, a member of the tribe of Benjamin. 2 God has not rejected his people, whom he chose from the beginning. You know what the scripture says in the passage where Elijah pleads with God against Israel: 3 "Lord, they have killed your prophets and torn down your altars; I am the only one left, and they are trying to kill me." 4 What answer did God give him? "I have kept for myself seven thousand men who have not worshipped the false god Baal." 5 It is the same way now: there is a small number left of those whom God has chosen because of his grace. 6 His choice is based on his grace, not on what they have done. For if God's choice were based on what people do, then his grace would not be real grace.

7 What then? The people of Israel did not find what they were looking for. It was only the small group that God chose who found it; the rest grew

deaf to God's call. [8] As the scripture says, "God made their minds and hearts dull; to this very day they cannot see or hear." [9] And David says,

"May they be caught and trapped at their feasts;
    may they fall, may they be punished!
[10] May their eyes be blinded so that they cannot
    see;
    and make them bend under their troubles at all
    times."

11 I ask, then: When the Jews stumbled, did they fall to their ruin? By no means! Because they sinned, salvation has come to the Gentiles, to make the Jews jealous of them. [12] The sin of the Jews brought rich blessings to the world, and their spiritual poverty brought rich blessings to the Gentiles. Then, how much greater the blessings will be when the complete number of Jews is included!

The Salvation of the Gentiles

13 I am speaking now to you Gentiles: As long as I am an apostle to the Gentiles, I will take pride in my work. [14] Perhaps I can make the people of my own race jealous, and so be able to save some of them. [15] For when they were rejected, mankind was changed from God's enemies into his friends. What will it be, then, when they are accepted? It will be life for the dead!

16 If the first piece of bread is given to God, then the whole loaf is his also; and if the roots of a tree are offered to God, the branches are his also. [17] Some of the branches of the cultivated olive-tree have been broken off, and a branch of a wild olive-tree has been joined to it. You Gentiles are like that wild olive-tree, and now you share the strong spiritual life of the Jews. [18] So then, you must not despise those who were broken off like branches. How can you be proud? You are just a branch; you don't support the roots—the roots support you.

19 But you will say, "Yes, but the branches were broken off to make room for me." [20] That is true. They were broken off because they did not believe, while you remain in place because you do believe. But do not be proud of it; instead, be afraid. [21] God

did not spare the Jews, who are like natural branches; do you think he will spare you? 22 Here we see how kind and how severe God is. He is severe towards those who have fallen, but kind to you—if you continue in his kindness. But if you do not, you too will be broken off. 23 And if the Jews abandon their unbelief, they will be put back in the place where they were; for God is able to do that. 24 You Gentiles are like the branch of a wild olive-tree that is broken off and then, contrary to nature, is joined to a cultivated olive-tree. The Jews are like this cultivated tree; and it will be much easier for God to join these broken-off branches to their own tree again.

God's Mercy on All

25 There is a secret truth, my brothers, which I want you to know, for it will keep you from thinking how wise you are. It is that the stubbornness of the people of Israel is not permanent, but will last only until the complete number of Gentiles comes to God. 26 And this is how all Israel will be saved. As the scripture says,

"The Saviour will come from Zion
and remove all wickedness from the descendants
of Jacob.
27 I will make this covenant with them
when I take away their sins."

28 Because they reject the Good News, the Jews are God's enemies for the sake of you Gentiles. But because of God's choice, they are his friends because of their ancestors. 29 For God does not change his mind about whom he chooses and blesses. 30 As for you Gentiles, you disobeyed God in the past; but now you have received God's mercy because the Jews were disobedient. 31 In the same way, because of the mercy that you have received, the Jews now disobey God, in order that they also may now° receive God's mercy. 32 For God has made all people prisoners of disobedience, so that he might show mercy to them all.

° Some manuscripts do not have now.

Praise to God

33 How great are God's riches! How deep are his
wisdom and knowledge! Who can explain his decisions? Who can understand his ways? 34 As the scripture says,

"Who knows the mind of the Lord?
Who is able to give him advice?
35 Who has ever given him anything,
so that he had to pay it back?"
36 For all things were created by him, and all things
exist through him and for him. To God be the glory
for ever! Amen.

Life in God's Service

12 So then, my brothers, because of God's great
mercy to us I appeal to you: Offer yourselves
as a living sacrifice to God, dedicated to his service
and pleasing to him. This is the true worship that
you should offer. 2 Do not conform yourselves to the
standards of this world, but let God transform you
inwardly by a complete change of your mind. Then
you will be able to know the will of God—what is
good and is pleasing to him and is perfect.

3 And because of God's gracious gift to me I say
to every one of you: Do not think of yourself more
highly than you should. Instead, be modest in your
thinking, and judge yourself according to the amount
of faith that God has given you. 4 We have many
parts in the one body, and all these parts have different
functions. 5 In the same way, though we are many,
we are one body in union with Christ, and we are
all joined to each other as different parts of one
body. 6 So we are to use our different gifts in accordance with the grace that God has given us. If our
gift is to speak God's message, we should do it according to the faith that we have; 7 if it is to serve,
we should serve; if it is to teach, we should teach;
8 if it is to encourage others, we should do so. Whoever
shares with others should do it generously; whoever
has authority should work hard; whoever shows kindness to others should do it cheerfully.

9 Love must be completely sincere. Hate what is

evil, hold on to what is good. [10]Love one another warmly as Christian brothers, and be eager to show respect for one another. [11]Work hard and do not be lazy. Serve the Lord with a heart full of devotion. [12]Let your hope keep you joyful, be patient in your troubles, and pray at all times. [13]Share your belongings with your needy fellow-Christians, and open your homes to strangers.

14 Ask God to bless those who persecute you—yes, ask him to bless, not to curse. [15]Be happy with those who are happy, weep with those who weep. [16]Have the same concern for everyone. Do not be proud, but accept humble duties.[p] Do not think of yourselves as wise.

17 If someone has done you wrong, do not repay him with a wrong. Try to do what everyone considers to be good. [18]Do everything possible on your part to live in peace with everybody. [19]Never take revenge, my friends, but instead let God's anger do it. For the scripture says, "I will take revenge, I will pay back, says the Lord." [20]Instead, as the scripture says: "If your enemy is hungry, feed him; if he is thirsty, give him a drink; for by doing this you will make him burn with shame." [21]Do not let evil defeat you; instead, conquer evil with good.

Duties towards the State Authorities

13 Everyone must obey the state authorities, because no authority exists without God's permission, and the existing authorities have been put there by God. [2]Whoever opposes the existing authority opposes what God has ordered; and anyone who does so will bring judgement on himself. [3]For rulers are not to be feared by those who do good, but by those who do evil. Would you like to be unafraid of the man in authority? Then do what is good, and he will praise you, [4]because he is God's servant working for your own good. But if you do evil, then be afraid of him, because his power to punish is real. He is God's servant and carries out God's punishment on those who do evil. [5]For this reason you must obey the

[p]accept humble duties; or make friends with humble people.

authorities—not just because of God's punishment, but also as a matter of conscience.

6 That is also why you pay taxes, because the authorities are working for God when they fulfil their duties. 7 Pay, then, what you owe them; pay them your personal and property taxes, and show respect and honour for them all.

Duties towards One Another

8 Be under obligation to no one—the only obligation you have is to love one another. Whoever does this has obeyed the Law. 9 The commandments, "Do not commit adultery; do not commit murder; do not steal; do not desire what belongs to someone else"—all these, and any others besides, are summed up in the one command, "Love your neighbour as you love yourself." 10 If you love someone, you will never do him wrong; to love, then, is to obey the whole Law.

11 You must do this, because you know that the time has come for you to wake up from your sleep. For the moment when we will be saved is closer now than it was when we first believed. 12 The night is nearly over, day is almost here. Let us stop doing the things that belong to the dark, and let us take up weapons for fighting in the light. 13 Let us conduct ourselves properly, as people who live in the light of day—no orgies or drunkenness, no immorality or indecency, no fighting or jealousy. 14 But take up the weapons of the Lord Jesus Christ, and stop paying attention to your sinful nature and satisfying its desires.

Do Not Judge Your Brother

14 Welcome the person who is weak in faith, but do not argue with him about his personal opinions. 2 One person's faith allows him to eat anything, but the person who is weak in the faith eats only vegetables. 3 The person who will eat anything is not to despise the one who doesn't; while the one who eats only vegetables is not to pass judgement on the one who will eat anything; for God has accepted him. 4 Who are you to judge the servant of someone else? It is his own Master who will decide whether he succeeds or fails. And he will succeed, because the Lord is able to make him succeed.

5 One person thinks that a certain day is more important than other days, while someone else thinks that all days are the same. Each one should firmly make up his own mind. 6 Whoever thinks highly of a certain day does so in honour of the Lord; whoever will eat anything does so in honour of the Lord, because he gives thanks to God for the food. Whoever refuses to eat certain things does so in honour of the Lord, and he gives thanks to God. 7 None of us lives for himself only, none of us dies for himself only. 8 If we live, it is for the Lord that we live, and if we die, it is for the Lord that we die. So whether we live or die, we belong to the Lord. 9 For Christ died and rose to life in order to be the Lord of the living and of the dead. 10 You then, who eat only vegetables—why do you pass judgement on your brother? And you who eat anything—why do you despise your brother? All of us will stand before God to be judged by him. 11 For the scripture says,

"As surely as I am the living God, says the Lord,
    everyone will kneel before me,
    and everyone will confess that I am God."
12 Every one of us, then, will have to give an account of himself to God.

Do Not Make Your Brother Fall

13 So then, let us stop judging one another. Instead, you should decide never to do anything that would make your brother stumble or fall into sin. 14 My union with the Lord Jesus makes me certain that no food is of itself ritually unclean; but if a person believes that some food is unclean, then it becomes unclean for him. 15 If you hurt your brother because of something you eat, then you are no longer acting from love. Do not let the food that you eat ruin the person for whom Christ died! 16 Do not let what you regard as good get a bad name. 17 For God's Kingdom is not a matter of eating and drinking, but of the righteousness, peace, and joy which the Holy Spirit gives. 18 And when someone serves Christ in this way, he pleases God and is approved by others.

19 So then, we must always aim q at those things
that bring peace and that help to strengthen one
another. 20 Do not, because of food, destroy what God
has done. All foods may be eaten, but it is wrong
to eat anything that will cause someone else to fall
into sin. 21 The right thing to do is to keep from
eating meat, drinking wine, or doing anything else
that will make your brother fall. 22 Keep what you
believe about this matter, then, between yourself and
God. Happy is the person who does not feel guilty
when he does something he judges is right! 23 But
if he has doubts about what he eats, God condemns
him when he eats it, because his action is not based
on faith. And anything that is not based on faith
is sin.

Please Others, Not Yourselves

15 We who are strong in the faith ought to help
the weak to carry their burdens. We should
not please ourselves. 2 Instead, we should all please

Help the weak (15.1)

our brothers for their own good, in order to build
them up in the faith. 3 For Christ did not please himself.
Instead, as the scripture says, "The insults which are

q we must always aim; *some manuscripts have* we always aim.

hurled at you have fallen on me." [4]Everything written in the Scriptures was written to teach us, in order that we might have hope through the patience and encouragement which the Scriptures give us. [5]And may God, the source of patience and encouragement, enable you to have the same point of view among yourselves by following the example of Christ Jesus, [6]so that all of you together may praise with one voice the God and Father of our Lord Jesus Christ.

Good News for the Gentiles

[7] Accept one another, then, for the glory of God, as Christ has accepted you. [8]For I tell you that Christ's life of service was on behalf of the Jews, to show that God is faithful, to make his promises to their ancestors come true, [9]and to enable even the Gentiles to praise God for his mercy. As the scripture says,
"And so I will praise you among the Gentiles;
I will sing praises to you."
[10]Again it says,
"Rejoice, Gentiles, with God's people!"
[11]And again,
"Praise the Lord, all Gentiles;
praise him, all peoples!"
[12]And again, Isaiah says,
"A descendant of Jesse will appear;
he will come to rule the Gentiles,
and they will put their hope in him."
[13] May God, the source of hope, fill you with all joy and peace by means of your faith in him, so that your hope will continue to grow by the power of the Holy Spirit.

Paul's Reason for Writing So Boldly

[14] My brothers: I myself feel sure that you are full of goodness, that you have all knowledge, and that you are able to teach one another. [15]But in this letter I have been quite bold about certain subjects of which I have reminded you. I have been bold because of the privilege God has given me [16]of being a servant of Christ Jesus to work for the Gentiles. I serve like a priest in preaching the Good News from God, in order that the Gentiles may be an offering acceptable

to God, dedicated to him by the Holy Spirit. [17] In union with Christ Jesus, then, I can be proud of my service for God. [18] I will be bold and speak only about what Christ has done through me to lead the Gentiles to obey God. He has done this by means of words and deeds, [19] by the power of miracles and wonders, and by the power of the Spirit of God. And so, in travelling all the way from Jerusalem to Illyricum, I have proclaimed fully the Good News about Christ. [20] My ambition has always been to proclaim the Good News in places where Christ has not been heard of, so as not to build on a foundation laid by someone else. [21] As the scripture says,

"Those who were not told about him will see,
 and those who have not heard will understand."

Paul's Plan to Visit Rome

[22] And so I have been prevented many times from coming to you. [23] But now that I have finished my work in these regions and since I have been wanting for so many years to come to see you, [24] I hope to do so now. I would like to see you on my way to Spain, and be helped by you to go there, after I have enjoyed visiting you for a while. [25] Just now, however, I am going to Jerusalem in the service of God's people there. [26] For the churches in Macedonia and Achaia have freely decided to give an offering to help the poor among God's people in Jerusalem. [27] That decision was their own; but, as a matter of fact, they have an obligation to help them. Since the Jews shared their spiritual blessings with the Gentiles, the Gentiles ought to use their material blessings to help the Jews. [28] When I have finished this task and have handed over to them all the money that has been raised for them, I shall leave for Spain and visit you on my way there. [29] When I come to you, I know that I shall come with a full measure of the blessing of Christ.

[30] I urge you, brothers, by our Lord Jesus Christ and by the love that the Spirit gives: join me in praying fervently to God for me. [31] Pray that I may be kept safe from the unbelievers in Judaea and that my service in Jerusalem may be acceptable to God's

people there. ³²And so I will come to you full of
joy, if it is God's will, and enjoy a refreshing visit
to you. ³³May God, our source of peace, be with
all of you. Amen.

Personal Greetings

16 I recommend to you our sister Phoebe, who
serves the church at Cenchreae. ²Receive her
in the Lord's name, as God's people should, and give
her any help she may need from you; for she herself
has been a good friend to many people and also
to me.

3 I send greetings to Priscilla and Aquila, my fellow-
workers in the service of Christ Jesus; ⁴they risked
their lives for me. I am grateful to them—not only
I, but all the Gentile churches as well. ⁵Greetings also
to the church that meets in their house.

Greetings to my dear friend Epaenetus, who was
the first man in the province of Asia to believe in
Christ. ⁶Greetings to Mary, who has worked so hard
for you. ⁷Greetings also to Andronicus and Junias,ʳ
fellow-Jews who were in prison with me; they are
well known among the apostles, and they became
Christians before I did.

8 My greetings to Ampliatus, my dear friend in the
fellowship of the Lord. ⁹Greetings also to Urbanus,
our fellow-worker in Christ's service, and to Stachys,
my dear friend. ¹⁰Greetings to Apelles, whose loyalty to
Christ has been proved. Greetings to those who belong
to the family of Aristobulus. ¹¹Greetings to Herodion,
a fellow-Jew, and to the Christian brothers in the
family of Narcissus.

12 My greetings to Tryphaena and Tryphosa, who
work in the Lord's service, and to my dear friend
Persis, who has done so much work for the Lord. ¹³I
send greetings to Rufus, that outstanding worker in
the Lord's service, and to his mother, who has always
treated me like a son. ¹⁴My greetings to Asyncritus,
Phlegon, Hermes, Patrobas, Hermas, and all the other
Christian brothers with them. ¹⁵Greetings to Philologus
and Julia, to Nereus and his sister, to Olympas and

ʳJunias; *or* June; *some manuscripts have* Julia.

to all of God's people who are with them.

16 Greet one another with a brotherly kiss. All the churches of Christ send you their greetings.

Final Instructions

17 I urge you, my brothers: watch out for those who cause divisions and upset people's faith and go against the teaching which you have received. Keep away from them! [18]For those who do such things are not serving Christ our Lord, but their own appetites. By their fine words and flattering speech they deceive innocent people. [19]Everyone has heard of your loyalty to the gospel, and for this reason I am happy about you. I want you to be wise about what is good, but innocent in what is evil. [20]And God, our source of peace, will soon crush Satan under your feet.

The grace of our Lord Jesus be with you.[s]

21 Timothy, my fellow-worker, sends you his greetings; and so do Lucius, Jason, and Sosipater, fellow-Jews.

22 I, Tertius, the writer of this letter, send you Christian greetings.

23 My host Gaius, in whose house the church meets, sends you his greetings; Erastus, the city treasurer, and our brother Quartus send you their greetings.[t]

Concluding Prayer of Praise

25 Let us give glory to God! He is able to make you stand firm in your faith, according to the Good News I preach about Jesus Christ and according to the revelation of the secret truth which was hidden for long ages in the past. [26]Now, however, that truth has been brought out into the open through the writings of the prophets; and by the command of the eternal God it is made known to all nations, so that all may believe and obey.

27 To the only God, who alone is all-wise, be glory through Jesus Christ for ever! Amen.[u]

[s] *Some manuscripts omit this sentence.*
[t] *Some manuscripts add verse 24:* The grace of our Lord Jesus Christ be with you all. Amen; *others add this after verse 27.*
[u] *Some manuscripts have verses 25–27 here and after 14.23; others have them only after 14.23; one has them after 15.33.*

PAUL'S FIRST LETTER TO THE
CORINTHIANS

INTRODUCTION

Paul's First Letter to the Corinthians was written to
deal with problems of Christian life and faith that
had arisen in the church which Paul had established
at Corinth. At that time Corinth was a great cosmo-
politan Greek city, the capital of the Roman province
of Achaia. It was noted for its thriving commerce,
proud culture, widespread immorality, and variety of
religions.

The apostle's chief concerns are with problems such
as divisions and immorality in the church, and with
questions about sex and marriage, matters of conscience, church order, gifts of the Holy Spirit, and the
resurrection. With deep insight he shows how the Good
News speaks to these questions.

Chapter 13, which presents love as the best of God's
gifts to his people, is probably the most widely known
passage in the book.

Outline of Contents

1 From Paul, who was called by the will of God to be an apostle of Christ Jesus, and from our brother Sosthenes—

2 To the church of God which is in Corinth, to all who are called to be God's holy people, who belong to him in union with Christ Jesus, together with all people everywhere who worship our Lord Jesus Christ, their Lord and ours:

3 May God our Father and the Lord Jesus Christ give you grace and peace.

Blessings in Christ

4 I always give thanks to my God for you because of the grace he has given you through Christ Jesus. 5 For in union with Christ you have become rich in all things, including all speech and all knowledge. 6 The message about Christ has become so firmly established in you 7 that you have not failed to receive a single blessing, as you wait for our Lord Jesus Christ to be revealed. 8 He will also keep you firm to the end, so that you will be faultless on the Day of our Lord Jesus Christ. 9 God is to be trusted, the God who called you to have fellowship with his Son Jesus Christ, our Lord.

Divisions in the Church

10 By the authority of our Lord Jesus Christ I appeal to all of you, my brothers, to agree in what you say, so that there will be no divisions among you. Be completely united, with only one thought and one purpose. 11 For some people from Chloe's family have told me quite plainly, my brothers, that there are quarrels among you. 12 Let me put it this way: each one of you says something different. One says, "I follow Paul"; another, "I follow Apollos"; another, "I follow Peter"; and another, "I follow Christ." 13 Christ has been divided[a] into groups! Was it Paul who died on the cross for you? Were you baptized as Paul's disciples?

14 I thank God that I did not baptize any of you

---

[a] Christ has been divided; *some manuscripts have* Christ cannot be divided.

except Crispus and Gaius. 15 No one can say, then, that you were baptized as my disciples. 16 (Oh yes, I also baptized Stephanas and his family; but I can't remember whether I baptized anyone else.) 17 Christ did not send me to baptize. He sent me to tell the Good News, and to tell it without using the language of human wisdom, in order to make sure that Christ's death on the cross is not robbed of its power.

Christ the Power and the Wisdom of God

18 For the message about Christ's death on the cross is nonsense to those who are being lost; but for us who are being saved it is God's power. 19 The scripture says,

"I will destroy the wisdom of the wise
    and set aside the understanding of the scholars."

20 So then, where does that leave the wise? or the scholars? or the skilful debaters of this world? God has shown that this world's wisdom is foolishness!

21 For God in his wisdom made it impossible for people to know him by means of their own wisdom. Instead, by means of the so-called "foolish" message we preach, God decided to save those who believe. 22 Jews want miracles for proof, and Greeks look for wisdom. 23 As for us, we proclaim the crucified Christ, a message that is offensive to the Jews and nonsense to the Gentiles; 24 but for those whom God has called, both Jews and Gentiles, this message is Christ, who is the power of God and the wisdom of God. 25 For what seems to be God's foolishness is wiser than human wisdom, and what seems to be God's weakness is stronger than human strength.

26 Now remember what you were, my brothers, when God called you. From the human point of view few of you were wise or powerful or of high social standing. 27 God purposely chose what the world considers nonsense in order to shame the wise, and he chose what the world considers weak in order to shame the powerful. 28 He chose what the world looks down on and despises, and thinks is nothing, in order to destroy what the world thinks is important. 29 This means that no one can boast in God's presence. 30 But God has brought you into union with Christ Jesus,

and God has made Christ to be our wisdom. By him we are put right with God; we become God's holy people and are set free. ³¹So then, as the scripture says, "Whoever wants to boast must boast of what the Lord has done."

The Message about the Crucified Christ

2 When I came to you, my brothers, to preach God's secret truth,*b* I did not use big words and great learning. ²For while I was with you, I made up my mind to forget everything except Jesus Christ and especially his death on the cross. ³So when I came to you, I was weak and trembled all over with fear, ⁴and my teaching and message were not delivered with skilful words of human wisdom, but with convincing proof of the power of God's Spirit. ⁵Your faith, then, does not rest on human wisdom but on God's power.

God's Wisdom

6 Yet I do proclaim a message of wisdom to those who are spiritually mature. But it is not the wisdom that belongs to this world or to the powers that rule this world—powers that are losing their power. ⁷The wisdom I proclaim is God's secret wisdom, which is hidden from mankind, but which he had already chosen for our glory even before the world was made. ⁸None of the rulers of this world knew this wisdom. If they had known it, they would not have crucified the Lord of glory. ⁹However, as the scripture says,

"What no one ever saw or heard,
    what no one ever thought could happen,
    is the very thing God prepared for those who
        love him."

¹⁰But*c* it was to us that God made known his secret by means of his Spirit. The Spirit searches everything, even the hidden depths of God's purposes. ¹¹It is only a person's own spirit within him that knows all about him; in the same way, only God's Spirit knows

*b*God's secret truth; *some manuscripts have* the testimony about God.
*c*But; *some manuscripts have* For.

all about God. [12] We have not received this world's spirit; instead, we have received the Spirit sent by God, so that we may know all that God has given us.

13 So then, we do not speak in words taught by human wisdom, but in words taught by the Spirit, as we explain spiritual truths to those who have the Spirit. [d] [14] Whoever does not have the Spirit cannot receive the gifts that come from God's Spirit. Such a person really does not understand them; they are nonsense to him, because their value can be judged only on a spiritual basis. [15] Whoever has the Spirit, however, is able to judge the value of everything, but no one is able to judge him. [16] As the scripture says,

"Who knows the mind of the Lord?
    Who is able to give him advice?"

We, however, have the mind of Christ.

Servants of God

3 As a matter of fact, my brothers, I could not talk to you as I talk to people who have the Spirit; I had to talk to you as though you belonged to this world, as children in the Christian faith. [2] I had to feed you with milk, not solid food, because you were not ready for it. And even now you are not ready for it, [3] because you still live as the people of this world live. When there is jealousy among you and you quarrel with one another, doesn't this prove that you belong to this world, living by its standards? [4] When one of you says, "I follow Paul," and another, "I follow Apollos"—aren't you acting like worldly people?

5 After all, who is Apollos? And who is Paul? We are simply God's servants, by whom you were led to believe. Each one of us does the work which the Lord gave him to do: [6] I sowed the seed, Apollos watered the plant, but it was God who made the plant grow. [7] The one who sows and the one who waters really do not matter. It is God who matters, because he makes the plant grow. [8] There is no dif-

---

[d] to those who have the Spirit; *or* with words given by the Spirit.

God...made the plant grow (3.6)

ference between the man who sows and the man who waters; God will reward each one according to the work he has done. ⁹For we are partners working together for God, and you are God's field.

You are also God's building. ¹⁰Using the gift that God gave me, I did the work of an expert builder and laid the foundation, and another man is building on it. But each one must be careful how he builds. ¹¹For God has already placed Jesus Christ as the one and only foundation, and no other foundation can be laid. ¹²Some will use gold or silver or precious stones in building on the foundation; others will use wood or grass or straw. ¹³And the quality of each person's work will be seen when the Day of Christ exposes it. For on that Day fire will reveal everyone's work; the fire will test it and show its real quality. ¹⁴If what was built on the foundation survives the fire, the builder will receive a reward. ¹⁵But if anyone's work is burnt up, then he will lose it; but he himself will be saved, as if he had escaped through the fire.

16 Surely you know that you are God's temple and that God's Spirit lives in you! 17 So if anyone destroys God's temple, God will destroy him. For God's temple is holy, and you yourselves are his temple.

18 No one should fool himself. If anyone among you thinks that he is wise by this world's standards, he should become a fool, in order to be really wise. 19 For what this world considers to be wisdom is nonsense in God's sight. As the scripture says, "God traps the wise in their cleverness"; 20 and another scripture says, "The Lord knows that the thoughts of the wise are worthless." 21 No one, then, should boast about what men can do. Actually everything belongs to you: 22 Paul, Apollos, and Peter; this world, life and death, the present and the future—all these are yours, 23 and you belong to Christ, and Christ belongs to God.

Apostles of Christ

4 You should think of us as Christ's servants, who have been put in charge of God's secret truths. 2 The one thing required of such a servant is that he be faithful to his master. 3 Now, I am not at all concerned about being judged by you or by any human standard; I don't even pass judgement on myself. 4 My conscience is clear, but that does not prove that I am really innocent. The Lord is the one who passes judgement on me. 5 So you should not pass judgement on anyone before the right time comes. Final judgement must wait until the Lord comes; he will bring to light the dark secrets and expose the hidden purposes of people's minds. And then everyone will receive from God the praise he deserves.

6 For your sake, my brothers, I have applied all this to Apollos and me, using the two of us as an example, so that you may learn what the saying means, "Observe the proper rules." None of you should be proud of one person and despise another. 7 Who made you superior to others? Didn't God give you everything you have? Well, then, how can you boast, as if what you have were not a gift?

8 Do you already have everything you need? Are you already rich? Have you become kings, even though

we are not? Well, I wish you really were kings, so that we could be kings together with you. 9 For it seems to me that God has given the very last place to us apostles, like men condemned to die in public as a spectacle for the whole world of angels and of mankind. 10 For Christ's sake we are fools; but you are wise in union with Christ! We are weak, but you are strong! We are despised, but you are honoured! 11 To this very moment we go hungry and thirsty; we are clothed in rags; we are beaten; we wander from place to place; 12 we wear ourselves out with hard work. When we are cursed, we bless; when we are persecuted, we endure; 13 when we are insulted, we answer with kind words. We are no more than this world's refuse; we are the scum of the earth to this very moment!

14 I write this to you, not because I want to make you feel ashamed, but to instruct you as my own dear children. 15 For even if you have ten thousand guardians in your Christian life, you have only one father. For in your life in union with Christ Jesus I have become your father by bringing the Good News to you. 16 I beg you, then, to follow my example. 17 For this purpose I am sending to you Timothy, who is my own dear and faithful son in the Christian life. He will remind you of the principles which I follow in the new life in union with Christ Jesus and which I teach in all the churches everywhere.

18 Some of you have become proud because you have thought that I would not be coming to visit you. 19 If the Lord is willing, however, I will come to you soon, and then I will find out for myself the power which these proud people have, and not just what they say. 20 For the Kingdom of God is not a matter of words but of power. 21 Which do you prefer? Shall I come to you with a whip, or in a spirit of love and gentleness?

Immorality in the Church

5 Now, it is actually being said that there is sexual immorality among you so terrible that not even the heathen would be guilty of it. I am told that a man is sleeping with his stepmother! 2 How, then,

can you be proud? On the contrary, you should be filled with sadness, and the man who has done such a thing should be expelled from your fellowship. 3-4 And even though I am far away from you in body, still I am there with you in spirit; and as though I were there with you, I have in the name of our Lord Jesus already passed judgement on the man who has done this terrible thing. As you meet together, and I meet with you in my spirit, by the power of our Lord Jesus present with us, 5 you are to hand this man over to Satan for his body to be destroyed, so that his spirit may be saved in the Day of the Lord.

6 It is not right for you to be proud! You know the saying, "A little bit of yeast makes the whole batch of dough rise." 7 You must remove the old yeast of sin so that you will be entirely pure. Then you will be like a new batch of dough without any yeast, as indeed I know you actually are. For our Passover Festival is ready, now that Christ, our Passover lamb, has been sacrificed. 8 Let us celebrate our Passover, then, not with bread having the old yeast of sin and wickedness, but with the bread that has no yeast, the bread of purity and truth.

9 In the letter that I wrote you I told you not to associate with immoral people. 10 Now I did not mean pagans who are immoral or greedy or are thieves or who worship idols. To avoid them you would have to get out of the world completely. 11 What I meant was that you should not associate with a person who calls himself a brother but is immoral or greedy or worships idols or is a slanderer or a drunkard or a thief. Don't even sit down to eat with such a person.

12-13 After all, it is none of my business to judge outsiders. God will judge them. But should you not judge the members of your own fellowship? As the scripture says, "Remove the evil man from your group."

Lawsuits against Fellow-Christians

6 If one of you has a dispute with a fellow-Christian, how dare he go before heathen judges instead of letting God's people settle the matter? 2 Don't you know that God's people will judge the world? Well, then, if you are to judge the world, aren't you capable

of judging small matters? [3] Do you not know that we shall judge the angels? How much more, then, the things of this life! [4] If such matters come up, are you going to take them to be settled by people who have no standing in the church? [5] Shame on you! Surely there is at least one wise person in your fellowship who can settle a dispute between fellow-Christians. [6] Instead, one Christian goes to court against another and lets unbelievers judge the case!

7 The very fact that you have legal disputes among yourselves shows that you have failed completely. Would it not be better for you to be wronged? Would it not be better for you to be robbed? [8] Instead, you yourselves wrong one another and rob one another, even your own brothers! [9] Surely you know that the wicked will not possess God's Kingdom. Do not fool yourselves; people who are immoral or who worship idols or are adulterers or homosexual perverts [10] or who steal or are greedy or are drunkards or who slander others or are thieves—none of these will possess God's Kingdom. [11] Some of you were like that. But you have been purified from sin; you have been dedicated to God; you have been put right with God by the Lord Jesus Christ and by the Spirit of our God.

Use Your Bodies for God's Glory

12 Someone will say, "I am allowed to do anything." Yes; but not everything is good for you. I could say that I am allowed to do anything, but I am not going to let anything make me its slave. [13] Someone else will say, "Food is for the stomach, and the stomach is for food." Yes; but God will put an end to both. The body is not to be used for sexual immorality, but to serve the Lord; and the Lord provides for the body. [14] God raised the Lord from death, and he will also raise us by his power.

15 You know that your bodies are parts of the body of Christ. Shall I take a part of Christ's body and make it part of the body of a prostitute? Impossible! [16] Or perhaps you don't know that the man who joins his body to a prostitute becomes physically one with her? The scripture says quite plainly,

"The two will become one body." [17]But he who joins himself to the Lord becomes spiritually one with him.

18 Avoid immorality. Any other sin a man commits does not affect his body; but the man who is guilty of sexual immorality sins against his own body. [19]Don't you know that your body is the temple of the Holy Spirit, who lives in you and who was given to you by God? You do not belong to yourselves but to God; [20]he bought you for a price. So use your bodies for God's glory.

Questions about Marriage

7 Now, to deal with the matters you wrote about. A man does well not to marry.[e] [2]But because there is so much immorality, every man should have his own wife, and every woman should have her own husband. [3]A man should fulfil his duty as a husband, and a woman should fulfil her duty as a wife, and each should satisfy the other's needs. [4]A wife is not the master of her own body, but her husband is; in the same way a husband is not the master of his own body, but his wife is. [5]Do not deny yourselves to each other, unless you first agree to do so for a while in order to spend your time in prayer; but then resume normal marital relations. In this way you will be kept from giving in to Satan's temptation because of your lack of self-control.

6 I tell you this not as an order, but simply as a concession. [7]Actually I would prefer that all of you were as I am; but each one has a special gift from God, one person this gift, another one that gift.

8 Now, to the unmarried and to the widows I say that it would be better for you to continue to live alone as I do. [9]But if you cannot restrain your desires, go ahead and marry—it is better to marry than to burn with passion.

10 For married people I have a command which is not my own but the Lord's: a wife must not leave her husband; [11]but if she does, she must remain single

[e]A man does well not to marry; or You say that a man does well not to marry.

or else be reconciled to her husband; and a husband must not divorce his wife.

12 To the others I say (I, myself, not the Lord): if a Christian man has a wife who is an unbeliever and she agrees to go on living with him, he must not divorce her. [13] And if a Christian woman is married to a man who is an unbeliever and he agrees to go on living with her, she must not divorce him. [14] For the unbelieving husband is made acceptable to God by being united to his wife, and the unbelieving wife is made acceptable to God by being united to her Christian husband. If this were not so, their children would be like pagan children; but as it is, they are acceptable to God. [15] However, if the one who is not a believer wishes to leave the Christian partner, let it be so. In such cases the Christian partner, whether husband or wife, is free to act. God has called you to live in peace. [16] How can you be sure, Christian wife, that you will not save[f] your husband? Or how can you be sure, Christian husband, that you will not save[f] your wife?

Live as God Called You

17 Each one should go on living according to the Lord's gift to him, and as he was when God called him. This is the rule I teach in all the churches. [18] If a circumcised man has accepted God's call, he should not try to remove the marks of circumcision; if an uncircumcised man has accepted God's call, he should not get circumcised. [19] For whether or not a man is circumcised means nothing; what matters is to obey God's commandments. [20] Everyone should remain as he was when he accepted God's call. [21] Were you a slave when God called you? Well, never mind; but if you have a chance to become a free man, use it.[g] [22] For a slave who has been called by the Lord is the Lord's free man; in the same way a

---

[f] How can you be sure...that you will not save; or How do you know...that you will save.

[g] but if you have a chance to become a free man, use it; or but even if you have a chance to become a free man, choose rather to make the best of your condition as a slave.

free man who has been called by Christ is his slave. 23 God bought you for a price; so do not become slaves of men. 24 My brothers, each one should remain in fellowship with God in the same condition as he was when he was called.

Questions about the Unmarried and the Widows

25 Now, concerning what you wrote about unmarried people: I do not have a command from the Lord, but I give my opinion as one who by the Lord's mercy is worthy of trust.

26 Considering the present distress, I think it is better for a man to stay as he is. 27 Have you got a wife? Then don't try to get rid of her. Are you unmarried? Then don't look for a wife. 28 But if you do marry, you haven't committed a sin; and if an unmarried woman marries, she hasn't committed a sin. But I would rather spare you the everyday troubles that married people will have.

29 What I mean, my brothers, is this: there is not much time left, and from now on married men should live as though they were not married; 30 those who weep, as though they were not sad; those who laugh, as though they were not happy; those who buy, as though they did not own what they bought; 31 those who deal in material goods, as though they were not fully occupied with them. For this world, as it is now, will not last much longer.

32 I would like you to be free from worry. An unmarried man concerns himself with the Lord's work, because he is trying to please the Lord. 33 But a married man concerns himself with worldly matters, because he wants to please his wife; 34 and so he is pulled in two directions. An unmarried woman or a virgin concerns herself with the Lord's work, because she wants to be dedicated both in body and spirit; but a married woman concerns herself with worldly matters, because she wants to please her husband.

35 I am saying this because I want to help you. I am not trying to put restrictions on you. Instead, I want you to do what is right and proper, and to give yourselves completely to the Lord's service without any reservation.

36 In the case of an engaged couple who have decided not to marry: if the man feels that he is not acting properly towards the girl and if his passions are too strong and he feels that they ought to marry, then they should get married, as he wants to.[h] There is no sin in this. [37]But if a man, without being forced to do so, has firmly made up his mind not to marry,[i] and if he has his will under complete control and has already decided in his own mind what to do—then he does well not to marry the girl.[j] [38]So the man who marries[k] does well, but the one who doesn't marry[l] does even better.

39 A married woman is not free as long as her husband lives; but if her husband dies, then she is free to be married to any man she wishes, but only if he is a Christian. [40]She will be happier, however, if she stays as she is. That is my opinion, and I think that I too have God's Spirit.

The Question about Food Offered to Idols

8 Now, concerning what you wrote about food offered to idols.

It is true, of course, that "all of us have knowledge," as they say. Such knowledge, however, puffs a person up with pride; but love builds up. [2]Whoever thinks he knows something really doesn't know as he ought to know. [3]But the person who loves God is known by him.

4 So then, about eating the food offered to idols: we know that an idol stands for something that does not really exist; we know that there is only the one God. [5]Even if there are so-called "gods," whether in heaven or on earth, and even though there are many of these "gods" and "lords," [6]yet there is for us

[h]an engaged couple...as he wants to; or a man and his unmarried daughter: if he feels that he is not acting properly towards her, and if she is at the right age to marry, then he should do as he wishes and let her get married.
[i]not to marry; or not to let his daughter get married.
[j]marry the girl; or let her get married.
[k]marries; or lets his daughter get married.
[l]doesn't marry; or doesn't let her get married.

only one God, the Father, who is the Creator of all things and for whom we live; and there is only one Lord, Jesus Christ, through whom all things were created and through whom we live.

7 But not everyone knows this truth. Some people have been so used to idols that to this day when they eat such food they still think of it as food that belongs to an idol; their conscience is weak, and they feel they are defiled by the food. 8 Food, however, will not improve our relations with God; we shall not lose anything if we do not eat, nor shall we gain anything if we do eat.

9 Be careful, however, not to let your freedom of action make those who are weak in the faith fall into sin. 10 Suppose a person whose conscience is weak in this matter sees you, who have so-called "knowledge," eating in the temple of an idol; will not this encourage him to eat food offered to idols? 11 And so this weak person, your brother for whom Christ died, will perish because of your "knowledge"! 12 And in this way you will be sinning against Christ by sinning against your Christian brothers and wounding their weak conscience. 13 So then, if food makes my brother sin, I will never eat meat again, so as not to make my brother fall into sin.

Rights and Duties of an Apostle

9 Am I not a free man? Am I not an apostle? Haven't I seen Jesus our Lord? And aren't you the result of my work for the Lord? 2 Even if others do not accept me as an apostle, surely you do! Because of your life in union with the Lord you yourselves are proof of the fact that I am an apostle.

3 When people criticize me, this is how I defend myself: 4 Haven't I the right to be given food and drink for my work? 5 Haven't I the right to follow the example of the other apostles and the Lord's brothers and Peter, by taking a Christian wife with me on my travels? 6 Or are Barnabas and I the only ones who have to work for our living? 7 What soldier ever has to pay his own expenses in the army? What farmer does not eat the grapes from his own vineyard?

What shepherd does not use the milk from his own sheep?

8 I don't have to limit myself to these everyday examples, because the Law says the same thing. 9 We read in the Law of Moses, "Do not muzzle an ox when you are using it to thresh corn." Now, is God concerned about oxen? 10 Didn't he really mean us when he said that? Of course that was written for us. The man who ploughs and the man who reaps should do their work in the hope of getting a share of the crop. 11 We have sown spiritual seed among you. Is it too much if we reap material benefits from you? 12 If others have the right to expect this from you, haven't we an even greater right?

But we haven't made use of this right. Instead, we have endured everything in order not to put any obstacle in the way of the Good News about Christ. 13 Surely you know that the men who work in the Temple get their food from the Temple and that those who offer the sacrifices on the altar get a share of the sacrifices. 14 In the same way, the Lord has ordered that those who preach the gospel should get their living from it.

15 But I haven't made use of any of these rights, nor am I writing this now in order to claim such rights for myself. I would rather die first! Nobody is going to turn my rightful boast into empty words! 16 I have no right to boast just because I preach the gospel. After all, I am under orders to do so. And how terrible it would be for me if I did not preach the gospel! 17 If I did my work as a matter of free choice, then I could expect to be paid; but I do it as a matter of duty, because God has entrusted me with this task. 18 What pay do I get, then? It is the privilege of preaching the Good News without charging for it, without claiming my rights in my work for the gospel.

19 I am a free man, nobody's slave; but I make myself everybody's slave in order to win as many people as possible. 20 While working with the Jews, I live like a Jew in order to win them; and even though I myself am not subject to the Law of Moses, I live as though I were when working with those

who are, in order to win them. 21 In the same way, when working with Gentiles, I live like a Gentile, outside the Jewish Law, in order to win Gentiles. This does not mean that I don't obey God's law; I am really under Christ's law. 22 Among the weak in faith I become weak like one of them, in order to win them. So I become all things to all men, that I may save some of them by whatever means are possible.

23 All this I do for the gospel's sake, in order to share in its blessings. 24 Surely you know that many

Only one of them wins the prize (9.24)

runners take part in a race, but only one of them wins the prize. Run, then, in such a way as to win the prize. 25 Every athlete in training submits to strict discipline, in order to be crowned with a wreath that will not last; but we do it for one that will last for ever. 26 That is why I run straight for the finishing-line; that is why I am like a boxer who does not waste his punches. 27 I harden my body with blows and bring it under complete control, to keep myself from being disqualified after having called others to the contest.

Warnings against Idols

10 I want you to remember, my brothers, what happened to our ancestors who followed Moses. They were all under the protection of the cloud, and all passed safely through the Red Sea. ²In the cloud and in the sea they were all baptized as followers of Moses. ³All ate the same spiritual bread ⁴and drank the same spiritual drink. They drank from the spiritual rock that went with them; and that rock was Christ himself. ⁵But even then God was not pleased with most of them, and so their dead bodies were scattered over the desert.

6 Now, all this is an example for us, to warn us not to desire evil things, as they did, ⁷nor to worship idols, as some of them did. As the scripture says, "The people sat down to a feast which turned into an orgy of drinking and sex." ⁸We must not be guilty of sexual immorality, as some of them were—and in one day twenty-three thousand of them fell dead. ⁹We must not put the Lord*m* to the test, as some of them did—and they were killed by snakes. ¹⁰We must not complain, as some of them did—and they were destroyed by the Angel of Death.

11 All these things happened to them as examples for others, and they were written down as a warning for us. For we live at a time when the end is about to come.

12 Whoever thinks he is standing firm had better be careful that he does not fall. ¹³Every test that you have experienced is the kind that normally comes to people. But God keeps his promise, and he will not allow you to be tested beyond your power to remain firm; at the time you are put to the test, he will give you the strength to endure it, and so provide you with a way out.

14 So then, my dear friends, keep away from the worship of idols. ¹⁵I speak to you as sensible people; judge for yourselves what I say. ¹⁶The cup we use in the Lord's Supper and for which we give thanks to God: when we drink from it, we are sharing in the

---

*m*the Lord; *some manuscripts have* Christ.

blood of Christ. And the bread we break: when we
eat it, we are sharing in the body of Christ. [17]Because

We all share the same loaf (10.17)

there is the one loaf of bread, all of us, though many,
are one body, for we all share the same loaf.

18 Consider the people of Israel; those who eat what
is offered in sacrifice share in the altar's service to
God. [19]Do I imply, then, that an idol or the food
offered to it really amounts to anything? [20]No! What
I am saying is that what is sacrificed on pagan altars
is offered to demons, not to God. And I do not want
you to be partners with demons. [21]You cannot drink
from the Lord's cup and also from the cup of demons;
you cannot eat at the Lord's table and also at the
table of demons. [22]Or do we want to make the Lord
jealous? Do we think that we are stronger than he?

23 "We are allowed to do anything," so they say.
That is true, but not everything is good. "We are
allowed to do anything"—but not everything is helpful.
[24]No one should be looking to his own interests, but to
the interests of others.

25 You are free to eat anything sold in the meat-
market, without asking any questions because of your

conscience. [26]For, as the scripture says, "The earth and everything in it belong to the Lord."

27 If an unbeliever invites you to a meal and you decide to go, eat what is set before you, without asking any questions because of your conscience. [28]But if someone says to you, "This food was offered to idols," then do not eat that food, for the sake of the one who told you and for conscience' sake—[29]that is, not your own conscience, but the other person's conscience.

"Well, then," someone asks, "why should my freedom to act be limited by another person's conscience? [30]If I thank God for my food, why should anyone criticize me about food for which I give thanks?"

31 Well, whatever you do, whether you eat or drink, do it all for God's glory. [32]Live in such a way as to cause no trouble either to Jews or Gentiles or to the church of God. [33]Just do as I do; I try to please everyone in all that I do, not thinking of my own good, but of the good of all, so that they might

11 be saved.
Imitate me, then, just as I imitate Christ.

Covering the Head in Worship

2 I praise you because you always remember me and follow the teachings that I have handed on to you. [3]But I want you to understand that Christ is supreme over every man, the husband is supreme over his wife, and God is supreme over Christ. [4]So a man who prays or proclaims God's message in public worship with his head covered disgraces Christ. [5]And any woman who prays or proclaims God's message in public worship with nothing on her head disgraces her husband; there is no difference between her and a woman whose head has been shaved. [6]If the woman does not cover her head, she might as well cut her hair. And since it is a shameful thing for a woman to shave her head or cut her hair, she should cover her head. [7]A man has no need to cover his head, because he reflects the image and glory of God. But woman reflects the glory of man; [8]for man was not created from woman, but woman from man. [9]Nor was man created for woman's sake,

but woman was created for man's sake. [10]On account of the angels, then, a woman should have a covering over her head to show that she is under her husband's authority. [11]In our life in the Lord, however, woman is not independent of man, nor is man independent of woman. [12]For as woman was made from man, in the same way man is born of woman; and it is God who brings everything into existence.

13 Judge for yourselves whether it is proper for a woman to pray to God in public worship with nothing on her head. [14]Why, nature itself teaches you that long hair on a man is a disgrace, [15]but on a woman it is a thing of beauty. Her long hair has been given her to serve as a covering. [16]But if anyone wants to argue about it, all I have to say is that neither we nor the churches of God have any other custom in worship.

The Lord's Supper
(Matt. 26.26–29; Mark 14.22–25; Luke 22.14–20)

17 In the following instructions, however, I do not praise you, because your meetings for worship actually do more harm than good. [18]In the first place, I have been told that there are opposing groups in your meetings; and this I believe is partly true. [19](No doubt there must be divisions among you so that the ones who are in the right may be clearly seen.) [20]When you meet together as a group, it is not the Lord's Supper that you eat. [21]For as you eat, each one goes ahead with his own meal, so that some are hungry while others get drunk. [22]Haven't you got your own homes in which to eat and drink? Or would you rather despise the church of God and put to shame the people who are in need? What do you expect me to say to you about this? Shall I praise you? Of course I don't!

23 For I received from the Lord the teaching that I passed on to you: that the Lord Jesus, on the night he was betrayed, took a piece of bread, [24]gave thanks to God, broke it, and said, "This is my body, which is for you. Do this in memory of me." [25]In the same way, after the supper he took the cup and said, "This cup is God's new covenant, sealed with

my blood. Whenever you drink it, do so in memory of me."

26 This means that every time you eat this bread and drink from this cup you proclaim the Lord's death until he comes. [27]It follows that if anyone eats the Lord's bread or drinks from his cup in a way that dishonours him, he is guilty of sin against the Lord's body and blood. [28]So then, everyone should examine himself first, and then eat the bread and drink from the cup. [29]For if he does not recognize the meaning of the Lord's body when he eats the bread and drinks from the cup, he brings judgement on himself as he eats and drinks. [30]That is why many of you are weak and ill, and several have died. [31]If we would examine ourselves first, we would not come under God's judgement. [32]But we are judged and punished by the Lord, so that we shall not be condemned together with the world.

33 So then, my brothers, when you gather together to eat the Lord's Supper, wait for one another. [34]And if anyone is hungry, he should eat at home, so that you will not come under God's judgement as you meet together. As for the other matters, I will settle them when I come.

Gifts from the Holy Spirit

12 Now, concerning what you wrote about the gifts from the Holy Spirit.

I want you to know the truth about them, my brothers. [2]You know that while you were still heathen, you were led astray in many ways to the worship of lifeless idols. [3]I want you to know that no one who is led by God's Spirit can say "A curse on Jesus!" and no one can confess "Jesus is Lord," unless he is guided by the Holy Spirit.

4 There are different kinds of spiritual gifts, but the same Spirit gives them. [5]There are different ways of serving, but the same Lord is served. [6]There are different abilities to perform service, but the same God gives ability to everyone for their particular service. [7]The Spirit's presence is shown in some way in each person for the good of all. [8]The Spirit gives one person a message full of wisdom, while to another

person the same Spirit gives a message full of knowledge. [9] One and the same Spirit gives faith to one person, while to another person he gives the power to heal. [10] The Spirit gives one person the power to work miracles; to another, the gift of speaking God's message; and to yet another, the ability to tell the difference between gifts that come from the Spirit and those that do not. To one person he gives the ability to speak in strange tongues, and to another he gives the ability to explain what is said. [11] But it is one and the same Spirit who does all this; as he wishes, he gives a different gift to each person.

One Body with Many Parts

12 Christ is like a single body, which has many parts; it is still one body, even though it is made up of different parts. [13] In the same way, all of us, whether Jews or Gentiles, whether slaves or free, have been baptized into the one body by the same Spirit, and we have all been given the one Spirit to drink.

14 For the body itself is not made up of only one part, but of many parts. [15] If the foot were to say, "Because I am not a hand, I don't belong to the body," that would not keep it from being a part of the body. [16] And if the ear were to say, "Because I am not an eye, I don't belong to the body," that would not keep it from being a part of the body. [17] If the whole body were just an eye, how could it hear? And if it were only an ear, how could it smell? [18] As it is, however, God put every different part in the body just as he wanted it to be. [19] There would not be a body if it were all only one part! [20] As it is, there are many parts but one body.

21 So then, the eye cannot say to the hand, "I don't need you!" Nor can the head say to the feet, "Well, I don't need you!" [22] On the contrary, we cannot do without the parts of the body that seem to be weaker; [23] and those parts that we think aren't worth very much are the ones which we treat with greater care; while the parts of the body which don't look very nice are treated with special modesty, [24] which the more beautiful parts do not need. God himself has put the body together in such a way as to give greater

honour to those parts that need it. 25 And so there is no division in the body, but all its different parts have the same concern for one another. 26 If one part of the body suffers, all the other parts suffer with it; if one part is praised, all the other parts share its happiness.

27 All of you are Christ's body, and each one is a part of it. 28 In the church God has put all in place: in the first place apostles, in the second place prophets, and in the third place teachers; then those who perform miracles, followed by those who are given the power to heal or to help others or to direct them or to speak in strange tongues. 29 They are not all apostles or prophets or teachers. Not everyone has the power to work miracles 30 or to heal diseases or to speak in strange tongues or to explain what is said. 31 Set your hearts, then, on the more important gifts.

Best of all, however, is the following way.

Love

13 I may be able to speak the languages of men and even of angels, but if I have no love, my speech is no more than a noisy gong or a clanging bell. 2 I may have the gift of inspired preaching; I may have all knowledge and understand all secrets; I may have all the faith needed to move mountains—but if I have no love, I am nothing. 3 I may give away everything I have, and even give up my body to be burnt[n] —but if I have no love, this does me no good.

4 Love is patient and kind; it is not jealous or conceited or proud; 5 love is not ill-mannered or selfish or irritable; love does not keep a record of wrongs; 6 love is not happy with evil, but is happy with the truth. 7 Love never gives up; and its faith, hope, and patience never fail.

8 Love is eternal. There are inspired messages, but they are temporary; there are gifts of speaking in strange tongues, but they will cease; there is knowledge, but it will pass. 9 For our gifts of knowledge and

[n] to be burnt; *some manuscripts have* in order to boast.

of inspired messages are only partial; ¹⁰but when what is perfect comes, then what is partial will disappear.

11 When I was a child, my speech, feelings, and thinking were all those of a child; now that I am a man, I have no more use for childish ways. ¹²What

What we see now is like a dim image in a mirror (13.12)

we see now is like a dim image in a mirror; then we shall see face to face. What I know now is only partial; then it will be complete—as complete as God's knowledge of me.

13 Meanwhile these three remain: faith, hope, and love; and the greatest of these is love.

More about Gifts from the Spirit

14 It is love, then, that you should strive for. Set your hearts on spiritual gifts, especially the gift of proclaiming God's message. ²The one who speaks in strange tongues does not speak to others but to God, because no one understands him. He is speaking secret truths by the power of the Spirit. ³But the one who proclaims God's message speaks to people and gives them help, encouragement, and comfort. ⁴The one who speaks in strange tongues helps only himself, but the one who proclaims God's message helps the whole church.

5 I would like all of you to speak in strange tongues; but I would rather that you had the gift of proclaiming

Then we shall see face to face (13.12)

God's message. For the person who proclaims God's message is of greater value than the one who speaks in strange tongues—unless there is someone present who can explain what he says, so that the whole church may be helped. ⁶So when I come to you, my brothers, what use will I be to you if I speak in strange tongues? Not a bit, unless I bring you some revelation from God or some knowledge or some inspired message, or some teaching.

7 Take such lifeless musical instruments as the flute or the harp—how will anyone know the tune that is being played unless the notes are sounded distinctly? ⁸And if the man who plays the bugle does not sound a clear call, who will prepare for battle? ⁹In the same way, how will anyone understand what you are talking about if your message given in strange tongues is not clear? Your words will vanish in the air! ¹⁰There are many different languages in the world, yet none of them is without meaning. ¹¹But if I do not know the language being spoken, the person who uses it will be a foreigner to me and I will be a foreigner to him. ¹²Since you are eager to have the gifts of the Spirit, you must try above everything else to make greater use of those which help to build up the church.

13 The person who speaks in strange tongues, then, must pray for the gift to explain what he says. 14 For if I pray in this way, my spirit prays indeed, but my mind has no part in it. 15 What should I do, then? I will pray with my spirit, but I will pray also with my mind; I will sing with my spirit, but I will sing also with my mind. 16 When you give thanks to God in spirit only, how can an ordinary person taking part in the meeting say "Amen" to your prayer of thanksgiving? He has no way of knowing what you are saying. 17 Even if your prayer of thanks to God is quite good, the other person is not helped at all.

18 I thank God that I speak in strange tongues much more than any of you. 19 But in church worship I would rather speak five words that can be understood, in order to teach others, than speak thousands of words in strange tongues.

20 Do not be like children in your thinking, my brothers; be children so far as evil is concerned, but be grown-up in your thinking. 21 In the Scriptures it is written,

"By means of men speaking strange languages
    I will speak to my people, says the Lord.
I will speak through lips of foreigners,
    but even then my people will not listen to me."
22 So then, the gift of speaking in strange tongues is proof for unbelievers, not for believers, while the gift of proclaiming God's message is proof for believers, not for unbelievers.

23 If, then, the whole church meets together and everyone starts speaking in strange tongues—and if some ordinary people or unbelievers come in, won't they say that you are all crazy? 24 But if everyone is proclaiming God's message when some unbeliever or ordinary person comes in, he will be convinced of his sin by what he hears. He will be judged by all he hears, 25 his secret thoughts will be brought into the open, and he will bow down and worship God, confessing, "Truly God is here among you!"

Order in the Church

26 This is what I mean, my brothers. When you meet for worship, one person has a hymn, another

a teaching, another a revelation from God, another a message in strange tongues, and still another the explanation of what is said. Everything must be of help to the church. 27If someone is going to speak in strange tongues, two or three at the most should speak, one after the other, and someone else must explain what is being said. 28But if no one is there who can explain, then the one who speaks in strange tongues must be quiet and speak only to himself and to God. 29Two or three who are given God's message should speak, while the others are to judge what they say. 30But if someone sitting in the meeting receives a message from God, the one who is speaking should stop. 31All of you may proclaim God's message, one by one, so that everyone will learn and be encouraged. 32The gift of proclaiming God's message should be under the speaker's control, 33because God does not want us to be in disorder but in harmony and peace.

As in all the churches of God's people, 34the women should keep quiet in the meetings. They are not allowed to speak; as the Jewish Law says, they must not be in charge. 35If they want to find out about something, they should ask their husbands at home. It is a disgraceful thing for a woman to speak in church.

36 Or could it be that the word of God came from you? Or are you the only ones to whom it came? 37If anyone supposes he is God's messenger or has a spiritual gift, he must realize that what I am writing to you is the Lord's command. 38But if he does not pay attention to this, pay no attention to him.

39 So then, my brothers, set your heart on proclaiming God's message, but do not forbid the speaking in strange tongues. 40Everything must be done in a proper and orderly way.

The Resurrection of Christ

15 And now I want to remind you, my brothers, of the Good News which I preached to you, which you received, and on which your faith stands firm. 2That is the gospel, the message that I preached to you. You are saved by the gospel if you hold firmly to it—unless it was for nothing that you believed.

3 I passed on to you what I received, which is of the greatest importance: that Christ died for our sins, as written in the Scriptures; ⁴that he was buried and that he was raised to life three days later, as written in the Scriptures; ⁵that he appeared to Peter and then to all twelve apostles. ⁶Then he appeared to more than five hundred of his followers at once, most of whom are still alive, although some have died. ⁷Then he appeared to James, and afterwards to all the apostles.

8 Last of all he appeared also to me—even though I am like someone whose birth was abnormal.º ⁹For I am the least of all the apostles—I do not even deserve to be called an apostle, because I persecuted God's church. ¹⁰But by God's grace I am what I am, and the grace that he gave me was not without effect. On the contrary, I have worked harder than any of the other apostles, although it was not really my own doing, but God's grace working with me. ¹¹So then, whether it came from me or from them, this is what we all preach, and this is what you believe.

Our Resurrection

12 Now, since our message is that Christ has been raised from death, how can some of you say that the dead will not be raised to life? ¹³If that is true, it means that Christ was not raised; ¹⁴and if Christ has not been raised from death, then we have nothing to preach and you have nothing to believe. ¹⁵More than that, we are shown to be lying about God, because we said that he raised Christ from death—but if it is true that the dead are not raised to life, then he did not raise Christ. ¹⁶For if the dead are not raised, neither has Christ been raised. ¹⁷And if Christ has not been raised, then your faith is a delusion and you are still lost in your sins. ¹⁸It would also mean that the believers in Christ who have died are lost. ¹⁹If our hope in Christ is good for this life only

ºwhose birth was abnormal; *or* who was born at the wrong time.

and no more,*p* then we deserve more pity than anyone else in all the world.

20 But the truth is that Christ has been raised from

Those who sleep in death will also be raised (15.20)

death, as the guarantee that those who sleep in death will also be raised. ²¹For just as death came by means of a man, in the same way the rising from death comes by means of a man. ²²For just as all people die because of their union with Adam, in the same way all will be raised to life because of their union with Christ. ²³But each one will be raised in his proper order: Christ, first of all; then, at the time of his coming, those who belong to him. ²⁴Then the end will come; Christ will overcome all spiritual rulers, authorities, and powers, and will hand over the Kingdom to God the Father. ²⁵For Christ must rule until God defeats all enemies and puts them under his feet. ²⁶The last enemy to be defeated will be death. ²⁷For the scripture says, "God put *all* things under his feet." It is clear, of course, that the words "all things" do not include God himself, who puts all things under Christ. ²⁸But when all things have been placed under

*p*If our hope in Christ is good for this life only and no more; *or* If all we have in this life is our hope in Christ.

Christ's rule, then he himself, the Son, will place himself under God, who placed all things under him; and God will rule completely over all.

29 Now, what about those people who are baptized for the dead? What do they hope to accomplish? If it is true, as some claim, that the dead are not raised to life, why are those people being baptized for the dead? 30 And as for us—why would we run the risk of danger every hour? 31 My brothers, I face death every day! The pride I have in you, in our life in union with Christ Jesus our Lord, makes me declare this. 32 If I have, as it were, fought "wild beasts" here in Ephesus simply from human motives, what have I gained? But if the dead are not raised to life, then, as the saying goes, "Let us eat and drink, for tomorrow we will die."

33 Do not be fooled. "Bad companions ruin good character." 34 Come back to your right senses and stop your sinful ways. I declare to your shame that some of you do not know God.

The Resurrection Body

35 Someone will ask, "How can the dead be raised to life? What kind of body will they have?" 36 You fool! When you sow a seed in the ground, it does not sprout to life unless it dies. 37 And what you sow is a bare seed, perhaps a grain of wheat or some other grain, not the full-bodied plant that will later grow up. 38 God provides that seed with the body he wishes; he gives each seed its own proper body.

39 And the flesh of living beings is not all the same kind of flesh; human beings have one kind of flesh, animals another, birds another, and fish another.

40 And there are heavenly bodies and earthly bodies; the beauty that belongs to heavenly bodies is different from the beauty that belongs to earthly bodies. 41 The sun has its own beauty, the moon another beauty, and the stars a different beauty; and even among stars there are different kinds of beauty.

42 This is how it will be when the dead are raised to life. When the body is buried, it is mortal; when raised, it will be immortal. 43 When buried, it is ugly

and weak; when raised, it will be beautiful and strong. ⁴⁴When buried, it is a physical body; when raised, it will be a spiritual body. There is, of course, a physical body, so there has to be a spiritual body. ⁴⁵For the scripture says, "The first man, Adam, was created a living being"; but the last Adam is the life-giving Spirit. ⁴⁶It is not the spiritual that comes first, but the physical, and then the spiritual. ⁴⁷The first Adam, made of earth, came from the earth; the second Adam came from heaven. ⁴⁸Those who belong to the earth are like the one who was made of earth; those who are of heaven are like the one who came from heaven. ⁴⁹Just as we wear the likeness of the man made of earth, so we will wearᑫ the likeness of the Man from heaven.

50 What I mean, brothers, is that what is made of flesh and blood cannot share in God's Kingdom, and what is mortal cannot possess immortality.

51-52 Listen to this secret truth: we shall not all die, but when the last trumpet sounds, we shall all be changed in an instant, as quickly as the blinking of an eye. For when the trumpet sounds, the dead will be raised, never to die again, and we shall all be changed. ⁵³For what is mortal must be changed into what is immortal; what will die must be changed into what cannot die. ⁵⁴So when this takes place, and the mortal has been changed into the immortal, then the scripture will come true: "Death is destroyed; victory is complete!"

⁵⁵ "Where, Death, is your victory?
   Where, Death, is your power to hurt?"

⁵⁶Death gets its power to hurt from sin, and sin gets its power from the Law. ⁵⁷But thanks be to God who gives us the victory through our Lord Jesus Christ!

58 So then, my dear brothers, stand firm and steady. Keep busy always in your work for the Lord, since you know that nothing you do in the Lord's service is ever useless.

ᑫwe will wear; *some manuscripts have* let us wear.

The Offering for Fellow-Believers

16 Now, concerning what you wrote about the money to be raised to help God's people in Judaea. You must do what I told the churches in Galatia to do. ²Every Sunday each of you must put aside some money, in proportion to what he has earned, and save it up, so that there will be no need to collect money when I come. ³After I come, I shall give letters of introduction to the men you have approved, and send them to take your gift to Jerusalem. ⁴If it seems worth while for me to go, then they can go along with me.

Paul's Plans

5 I shall come to you after I have gone through Macedonia—for I have to go through Macedonia. ⁶I shall probably spend some time with you, perhaps the whole winter, and then you can help me to continue my journey, wherever it is I shall go next. ⁷I want to see you more than just briefly in passing; I hope to spend quite a long time with you, if the Lord allows.

8 I will stay here in Ephesus until the day of Pentecost. ⁹There is a real opportunity here for great and worthwhile work, even though there are many opponents.

10 If Timothy comes your way, be sure to make him feel welcome among you, because he is working for the Lord, just as I am. ¹¹No one should look down on him, but you must help him to continue his trip in peace, so that he will come back to me; for I am expecting him back with the brothers.

12 Now, about brother Apollos. I have often encouraged him to visit you with the other brothers, but he is not completely convinced[r] that he should go at this time. When he gets the chance, however, he will go.

Final Words

13 Be alert, stand firm in the faith, be brave, be strong. ¹⁴Do all your work in love.

[r]he is not completely convinced; *or* it is not at all God's will.

15 You know about Stephanas and his family; they are the first Christian converts in Achaia and have given themselves to the service of God's people. I beg you, my brothers, [16]to follow the leadership of such people as these, and of anyone else who works and serves with them.

17 I am happy about the coming of Stephanas, Fortunatus, and Achaicus; they have made up for your absence [18]and have cheered me up, just as they cheered you up. Such men as these deserve notice.

19 The churches in the province of Asia send you their greetings; Aquila and Priscilla and the church that meets in their house send warm Christian greetings. [20]All the brothers here send greetings.

Greet one another with a brotherly kiss.

21 With my own hand I write this: *Greetings from Paul.*

22 Whoever does not love the Lord—a curse on him!

Marana tha—Our Lord, come!

23 The grace of the Lord Jesus be with you.

24 My love be with you all in Christ Jesus.

PAUL'S SECOND LETTER TO THE
CORINTHIANS

INTRODUCTION

Paul's Second Letter to the Corinthians was written during a difficult period in his relations with the church at Corinth. Some members of the church had evidently made strong attacks against Paul, but he shows his deep longing for reconciliation and expresses his great joy when this is brought about.

In the first part of the letter Paul discusses his relationship with the church at Corinth, explaining why he had responded with severity to insult and opposition in the church and expressing his joy that this severity had resulted in repentance and reconciliation. Then he appeals to the church for a generous offering to help the needy Christians in Judaea. In the final chapters Paul defends his apostleship against a few people at Corinth who had set themselves up as true apostles, while accusing Paul of being a false one.

Outline of Contents

---

1 From Paul, an apostle of Christ Jesus by God's will, and from our brother Timothy—

To the church of God in Corinth, and to all God's people throughout Achaia:

2 May God our Father and the Lord Jesus Christ give you grace and peace.

Paul Gives Thanks to God

3 Let us give thanks to the God and Father of our Lord Jesus Christ, the merciful Father, the God from whom all help comes! ⁴He helps us in all our troubles, so that we are able to help others who

Help others who have all kinds of troubles (1.4)

have all kinds of troubles, using the same help that we ourselves have received from God. [5]Just as we have a share in Christ's many sufferings, so also through Christ we share in God's great help. [6]If we suffer, it is for your help and salvation; if we are helped, then you too are helped and given the strength to endure with patience the same sufferings that we also endure. [7]So our hope in you is never shaken; we know that just as you share in our sufferings, you also share in the help we receive.

8 We want to remind you, brothers, of the trouble we had in the province of Asia. The burdens laid upon us were so great and so heavy that we gave up all hope of staying alive. [9]We felt that the death sentence had been passed on us. But this happened so that we should rely, not on ourselves, but only on God, who raises the dead. [10]From such terrible dangers of death[a] he saved us, and will save us; and we have placed our hope in him that he will save us again, [11]as you help us by means of your prayers for us. So it will be that the many prayers for us will be answered, and God will bless us; and many will raise their voices to him in thanksgiving for us.

The Change in Paul's Plans

12 We are proud that our conscience assures us that our lives in this world, and especially our relations with you, have been ruled by God-given frankness[b] and sincerity, by the power of God's grace, and not by human wisdom. [13-14]We write to you only what you can read and understand. But even though you now understand us only in part, I hope that you will come to understand us completely, so that in the Day of our Lord Jesus you can be as proud of us as we shall be of you.

15 I was so sure of all this that I made plans at first to visit you, in order that you might be blessed twice. [16]For I planned to visit you on my way to

[a]terrible dangers of death; *some manuscripts have* terrible death.
[b]frankness; *some manuscripts have* holiness.

Macedonia and again on my way back, in order to get help from you for my journey to Judaea. [17]In planning this, did I appear fickle? When I make my plans, do I make them from selfish motives, ready to say "Yes, yes" and "No, no" at the same time? [18]As surely as God speaks the truth, my promise to you was not a "Yes" and a "No." [19]For Jesus Christ, the Son of God, who was preached among you by Silas, Timothy, and myself, is not one who is "Yes" and "No." On the contrary, he is God's "Yes"; [20]for it is he who is the "Yes" to all God's promises. This is why through Jesus Christ our "Amen" is said to the glory of God. [21]It is God himself who makes us, together with you, sure of our life in union with Christ; it is God himself who has set us apart, [22]who has placed his mark of ownership upon us, and who has given us the Holy Spirit in our hearts as the guarantee of all that he has in store for us.

[23] I call God as my witness—he knows my heart! It was in order to spare you that I decided not to go to Corinth. [24]We are not trying to dictate to you what you must believe; we know that you stand firm in the faith. Instead, we are working with you for your own happiness.

2 So I made up my mind not to come to you again to make you sad. [2]For if I were to make you sad, who would be left to cheer me up? Only the very persons I had made sad. [3]That is why I wrote that letter to you—I did not want to come to you and be made sad by the very people who should make me glad. For I am convinced that when I am happy, then all of you are happy too. [4]I wrote to you with a greatly troubled and distressed heart and with many tears; my purpose was not to make you sad, but to make you realize how much I love you all.

Forgiveness for the Offender

[5] Now, if anyone has made somebody sad, he has not done it to me but to all of you—in part at least. (I say this because I do not want to be too hard on him.) [6]It is enough that this person has been punished in this way by most of you. [7]Now, however,

you should forgive him and encourage him, in order to keep him from becoming so sad as to give up completely. [8] And so I beg you to let him know that you really do love him. [9] I wrote you that letter because I wanted to find out how well you had stood the test and whether you are always ready to obey my instructions. [10] When you forgive someone for what he has done, I forgive him too. For when I forgive—if, indeed, I need to forgive anything—I do it in Christ's presence because of you, [11] in order to keep Satan from getting the upper hand of us; for we know what his plans are.

Paul's Anxiety in Troas

12 When I arrived in Troas to preach the Good News about Christ, I found that the Lord had opened the way for the work there. [13] But I was deeply worried, because I could not find our brother Titus. So I said good-bye to the people there and went on to Macedonia.

Victory through Christ

14 But thanks be to God! For in union with Christ we are always led by God as prisoners in Christ's victory procession. God uses us to make the knowledge about Christ spread everywhere like a sweet fragrance. [15] For we are like a sweet-smelling incense offered by Christ to God, which spreads among those who are being saved and those who are being lost. [16] For those who are being lost, it is a deadly stench that kills; but for those who are being saved, it is a fragrance that brings life. Who, then, is capable of such a task? [17] We are not like so many others, who handle God's message as if it were cheap merchandise; but because God has sent us, we speak with sincerity in his presence, as servants of Christ.

Servants of the New Covenant

3 Does this sound as if we were again boasting about ourselves? Could it be that, like some other people, we need letters of recommendation to you or from you? [2] You yourselves are the letter we have, written on our hearts for everyone to know and read. [3] It is clear that Christ himself wrote this letter and

sent it by us. It is written, not with ink but with the Spirit of the living God, and not on stone tablets but on human hearts.

4 We say this because we have confidence in God through Christ. [5]There is nothing in us that allows us to claim that we are capable of doing this work. The capacity we have comes from God; [6]it is he who made us capable of serving the new covenant, which consists not of a written law but of the Spirit. The written law brings death, but the Spirit gives life.

7 The Law was carved in letters on stone tablets, and God's glory appeared when it was given. Even though the brightness on Moses' face was fading, it was so strong that the people of Israel could not keep their eyes fixed on him. If the Law, which brings death when it is in force, came with such glory, [8]how much greater is the glory that belongs to the activity of the Spirit! [9]The system which brings condemnation was glorious; how much more glorious is the activity which brings salvation! [10]We may say that because of the far brighter glory now the glory that was so bright in the past is gone. [11]For if there was glory in that which lasted for a while, how much more glory is there in that which lasts for ever!

12 Because we have this hope, we are very bold. [13]We are not like Moses, who had to put a veil over his face so that the people of Israel would not see the brightness fade and disappear. [14]Their minds, indeed, were closed; and to this very day their minds are covered with the same veil as they read the books of the old covenant. The veil is removed only when a person is joined to Christ. [15]Even today, whenever they read the Law of Moses, the veil still covers their minds. [16]But it can be removed, as the scripture says about Moses: "His veil was removed when he turned to the Lord." [c] [17]Now, "the Lord" in this passage is the Spirit; and where the Spirit of the Lord is present, there is freedom. [18]All of us, then, reflect the glory of the Lord with uncovered faces; and that

---

[c] *Verse 16 may be translated:* But the veil is removed whenever someone turns to the Lord.

same glory, coming from the Lord, who is the Spirit, transforms us into his likeness in an ever greater degree of glory.

Spiritual Treasure in Clay Pots

4 God in his mercy has given us this work to do, and so we are not discouraged. ²We put aside all secret and shameful deeds; we do not act with deceit, nor do we falsify the word of God. In the full light of truth we live in God's sight and try to commend ourselves to everyone's good conscience. ³For if the gospel we preach is hidden, it is hidden only from those who are being lost. ⁴They do not believe, because their minds have been kept in the dark by the evil god of this world. He keeps them from seeing the light shining on them, the light that comes from the Good News about the glory of Christ, who is the exact likeness of God. ⁵For it is not ourselves that we preach; we preach Jesus Christ as Lord, and ourselves as your servants for Jesus' sake. ⁶The God who said, "Out of darkness the light shall shine!" is the same God who made his light shine in our hearts, to bring us the knowledge of God's glory shining in the face of Christ.

7 Yet we who have this spiritual treasure are like common clay pots, in order to show that the supreme power belongs to God, not to us. ⁸We are often troubled, but not crushed; sometimes in doubt, but never in despair; ⁹there are many enemies, but we are never without a friend; and though badly hurt at times, we are not destroyed. ¹⁰At all times we carry in our mortal bodies the death of Jesus, so that his life also may be seen in our bodies. ¹¹Throughout our lives we are always in danger of death for Jesus' sake, in order that his life may be seen in this mortal body of ours. ¹²This means that death is at work in us, but life is at work in you.

13 The scripture says, "I spoke because I believed." In the same spirit of faith, we also speak because we believe. ¹⁴We know that God, who raised the Lord Jesus to life, will also raise us up with Jesus and take us, together with you, into his presence. ¹⁵All this is for your sake; and as God's grace reaches

more and more people, they will offer to the glory
of God more prayers of thanksgiving.

Living by Faith

16 For this reason we never become discouraged.
Even though our physical being is gradually decaying,
yet our spiritual being is renewed day after day. 17 And
this small and temporary trouble we suffer will bring
us a tremendous and eternal glory, much greater than
the trouble. 18 For we fix our attention, not on things
that are seen, but on things that are unseen. What
can be seen lasts only for a time, but what cannot
be seen lasts for ever.

5 For we know that when this tent we live in—our
body here on earth—is torn down, God will have
a house in heaven for us to live in, a home he himself
has made, which will last for ever. 2 And now we
sigh, so great is our desire that our home which
comes from heaven should be put on over us; 3 by
being clothed with it we shall not be without a body.
4 While we live in this earthly tent, we groan with
a feeling of oppression; it is not that we want to
get rid of our earthly body, but that we want to
have the heavenly one put on over us, so that what
is mortal will be transformed by life. 5 God is the
one who has prepared us for this change, and he
gave us his Spirit as the guarantee of all that he
has in store for us.

6 So we are always full of courage. We know that
as long as we are at home in the body we are away
from the Lord's home. 7 For our life is a matter of
faith, not of sight. 8 We are full of courage and would
much prefer to leave our home in the body and be
at home with the Lord. 9 More than anything else,
however, we want to please him, whether in our home
here or there. 10 For all of us must appear before
Christ, to be judged by him. Each one will receive
what he deserves, according to everything he has done,
good or bad, in his bodily life.

Friendship with God through Christ

11 We know what it means to fear the Lord, and
so we try to persuade others. God knows us completely,

and I hope that in your hearts you know me as well. [12] We are not trying again to recommend ourselves to you; rather, we are trying to give you a good reason to be proud of us, so that you will be able to answer those who boast about a man's appearance and not about his character. [13] Are we really insane? It is for God's sake. Or are we sane? Then it is for your sake. [14] We are ruled by the love of Christ, now that we recognize that one man died for everyone, which means that all share in his death. [15] He died for all, so that those who live should no longer live for themselves, but only for him who died and was raised to life for their sake.

16 No longer, then, do we judge anyone by human standards. Even if at one time we judged Christ according to human standards, we no longer do so. [17] When anyone is joined to Christ, he is a new being; the old is gone, the new has come. [18] All this is done by God, who through Christ changed us from enemies into his friends and gave us the task of making others his friends also. [19] Our message is that God was making all mankind his friends through Christ.[d] God did not keep an account of their sins, and he has given us the message which tells how he makes them his friends.

20 Here we are, then, speaking for Christ, as though God himself were making his appeal through us. We plead on Christ's behalf: let God change you from enemies into his friends! [21] Christ was without sin, but for our sake God made him share our sin in order that in union with him we might share the righteousness of God.

6 In our work together with God, then, we beg you who have received God's grace not to let it be wasted. [2] Hear what God says:

"When the time came for me to show you favour
    I heard you;
when the day arrived for me to save you
    I helped you."

Listen! This is the hour to receive God's favour; today is the day to be saved!

---

[d]God was making all mankind his friends through Christ; or God was in Christ making all mankind his friends.

3 We do not want anyone to find fault with our work, so we try not to put obstacles in anyone's way. ⁴Instead, in everything we do we show that we are God's servants by patiently enduring troubles, hardships, and difficulties. ⁵We have been beaten, imprisoned, and mobbed; we have been overworked and have gone without sleep or food. ⁶By our purity, knowledge, patience, and kindness we have shown ourselves to be God's servants—by the Holy Spirit, by our true love, ⁷by our message of truth, and by the power of God. We have righteousness as our weapon, both to attack and to defend ourselves. ⁸We are honoured and disgraced; we are insulted and praised. We are treated as liars, yet we speak the truth; ⁹as unknown, yet we are known by all; as though we were dead, but, as you see, we live on. Although punished, we are not killed; ¹⁰although saddened, we are always glad; we seem poor, but we make many people rich; we seem to have nothing, yet we really possess everything.

11 Dear friends in Corinth! We have spoken frankly to you; we have opened our hearts wide. ¹²It is not we who have closed our hearts to you; it is you who have closed your hearts to us. ¹³I speak now as though you were my children: show us the same feelings that we have for you. Open your hearts wide!

Warning against Pagan Influences

14 Do not try to work together as equals with unbelievers, for it cannot be done. How can right and wrong be partners? How can light and darkness live together? ¹⁵How can Christ and the Devil agree? What does a believer have in common with an unbeliever? ¹⁶How can God's temple come to terms with pagan idols? For we are the temple of the living God! As God himself has said,

"I will make my home with my people
　and live among them;
I will be their God,
　and they shall be my people."
¹⁷And so the Lord says,
"You must leave them
　and separate yourselves from them.

Have nothing to do with what is unclean,
   and I will accept you.
18 I will be your father,
   and you shall be my sons and daughters,
   says the Lord Almighty."

7 All these promises are made to us, my dear friends. So then, let us purify ourselves from everything that makes body or soul unclean, and let us be completely holy by living in awe of God.

Paul's Joy

2 Make room for us in your hearts. We have wronged no one; we have ruined no one, nor tried to take advantage of anyone. 3 I do not say this to condemn you; for, as I have said before, you are so dear to us that we are always together, whether we live or die. 4 I am so sure of you; I take such pride in you! In all our troubles I am still full of courage; I am running over with joy.

5 Even after we arrived in Macedonia, we had no rest. There were troubles everywhere, quarrels with others, fears in our hearts. 6 But God, who encourages the downhearted, encouraged us with the coming of Titus. 7 It was not only his coming that cheered us, but also his report of how you encouraged him. He told us how much you want to see me, how sorry you are, how ready you are to defend me; and so I am even happier now.

8 For even if that letter of mine made you sad, I am not sorry I wrote it. I could have been sorry when I saw that it made you sad for a while. 9 But now I am happy—not because I made you sad, but because your sadness made you change your ways. That sadness was used by God, and so we caused you no harm. 10 For the sadness that is used by God brings a change of heart that leads to salvation—and there is no regret in that! But sadness that is merely human causes death. 11 See what God did with this sadness of yours: how earnest it has made you, how eager to prove your innocence! Such indignation, such alarm, such feelings, such devotion, such readiness to punish wrongdoing! You have shown yourselves to be without fault in the whole matter.

12 So, even though I wrote that letter, it was not because of the one who did wrong or the one who was wronged. Instead, I wrote it to make plain to you, in God's sight, how deep your devotion to us really is. 13 That is why we were encouraged.

Not only were we encouraged; how happy Titus made us with his happiness over the way in which all of you helped to cheer him up! 14 I did boast of you to him, and you have not disappointed me. We have always spoken the truth to you, and in the same way the boast we made to Titus has proved true. 15 And so his love for you grows stronger, as he remembers how all of you were ready to obey his instructions, how you welcomed him with fear and trembling. 16 How happy I am that I can depend on you completely!

Christian Giving

8 Our brothers, we want you to know what God's grace has accomplished in the churches in Macedonia. 2 They have been severely tested by the troubles they went through; but their joy was so great that they were extremely generous in their giving, even though they are very poor. 3 I can assure you that they gave as much as they could, and even more than they could. Of their own free will 4 they begged us and pleaded for the privilege of having a part in helping God's people in Judaea. 5 It was more than we could have hoped for! First they gave themselves to the Lord; and then, by God's will they gave themselves to us as well. 6 So we urged Titus, who began this work, to continue it and help you complete this special service of love. 7 You are so rich in all you have: in faith, speech, and knowledge, in your eagerness to help and in your love for us. *e* And so we want you to be generous also in this service of love.

8 I am not laying down any rules. But by showing how eager others are to help, I am trying to find out how real your own love is. 9 You know the grace of our Lord Jesus Christ; rich as he was, he made

e your love for us; *some manuscripts have* our love for you.

himself poor for your sake, in order to make you rich by means of his poverty.

10 My opinion is that it is better for you to finish now what you began last year. You were the first, not only to act, but also to be willing to act. ¹¹On with it, then, and finish the job! Be as eager to finish it as you were to plan it, and do it with what you now have. ¹²If you are eager to give, God will accept your gift on the basis of what you have to give, not on what you haven't.

13-14 I am not trying to relieve others by putting a burden on you; but since you have plenty at this time, it is only fair that you should help those who are in need. Then, when you are in need and they have plenty, they will help you. In this way both are treated equally. ¹⁵As the scripture says, "The one who gathered much did not have too much, and the one who gathered little did not have too little."

Titus and His Companions

16 How we thank God for making Titus as eager as we are to help you! ¹⁷Not only did he welcome our request; he was so eager to help that of his own free will he decided to go to you. ¹⁸With him we are sending the brother who is highly respected in all the churches for his work in preaching the gospel. ¹⁹And besides that, he has been chosen and appointed by the churches to travel with us as we carry out this service of love for the sake of the Lord's glory, and in order to show that we want to help.

20 We are taking care not to stir up any complaints about the way we handle this generous gift. ²¹Our purpose is to do what is right, not only in the sight of the Lord, but also in the sight of man.

22 So we are sending our brother with them; we have tested him many times and found him always very eager to help. And now that he has so much confidence in you, he is all the more eager to help. ²³As for Titus, he is my partner and works with me to help you; as for the other brothers who are going with him, they represent the churches and bring glory to Christ. ²⁴Show your love to them, so that

all the churches will be sure of it and know that we are right in boasting about you.

Help for Fellow-Christians

9 There is really no need for me to write to you about the help being sent to God's people in Judaea. ²I know that you are willing to help, and I have boasted of you to the people in Macedonia. "The brothers in Achaia," I said, "have been ready to help since last year." Your eagerness has stirred up most of them. ³Now I am sending these brothers, so that our boasting about you in this matter may not turn out to be empty words. But, just as I said, you will be ready with your help. ⁴However, if the people from Macedonia should come with me and find out that you are not ready, how ashamed we would be—not to speak of your shame—for feeling so sure of you! ⁵So I thought it was necessary to urge these brothers to go to you ahead of me and get ready in advance the gift you promised to make. Then it will be ready when I arrive, and it will show that you give because you want to, not because you have to.

6 Remember that the person who sows few seeds will have a small crop; the one who sows many seeds will have a large crop. ⁷Each one should give, then, as he has decided, not with regret or out of a sense of duty; for God loves the one who gives gladly. ⁸And God is able to give you more than you need, so that you will always have all you need for yourselves and more than enough for every good cause. ⁹As the scripture says,

"He gives generously to the needy;
  his kindness lasts for ever."

¹⁰And God, who supplies seed to sow and bread to eat, will also supply you with all the seed you need and will make it grow and produce a rich harvest from your generosity. ¹¹He will always make you rich enough to be generous at all times, so that many will thank God for your gifts which they receive from us. ¹²For this service you perform not only meets the needs of God's people, but also produces an outpouring of gratitude to God. ¹³And because of the

proof which this service of yours brings, many will give glory to God for your loyalty to the gospel of Christ, which you profess, and for your generosity in sharing with them and everyone else. ¹⁴And so with deep affection they will pray for you because of the extraordinary grace God has shown you. ¹⁵Let us thank God for his priceless gift!

Paul Defends His Ministry ,

10 I, Paul, make a personal appeal to you—I who am said to be meek and mild when I am with you, but harsh with you when I am away. By the gentleness and kindness of Christ I beg you ²not to force me to be harsh when I come; for I am sure I can deal harshly with those who say that we act from worldly motives. ³It is true that we live in the world, but we do not fight from worldly motives. ⁴The weapons we use in our fight are not the world's weapons but God's powerful weapons, which we use to destroy strongholds. We destroy false arguments; ⁵we pull down every proud obstacle that is raised against the knowledge of God; we take every thought captive and make it obey Christ. ⁶And after you have proved your complete loyalty, we will be ready to punish any act of disloyalty.

7 You are looking at the outward appearance of things. Is there someone there who reckons himself to belong to Christ? Well, let him think again about himself, because we belong to Christ just as much as he does. ⁸For I am not ashamed, even if I have boasted somewhat too much about the authority that the Lord has given us—authority to build you up, not to tear you down. ⁹I do not want it to appear that I am trying to frighten you with my letters. ¹⁰Someone will say, "Paul's letters are severe and strong, but when he is with us in person, he is weak, and his words are nothing!" ¹¹Such a person must understand that there is no difference between what we write in our letters when we are away and what we will do when we are there with you.

12 Of course we would not dare to classify ourselves or compare ourselves with those who rate themselves so highly. How stupid they are! They make up their

own standards to measure themselves by, and they judge themselves by their own standards! 13 As for us, however, our boasting will not go beyond certain limits; it will stay within the limits of the work which God has set for us, and this includes our work among you. 14 And since you are within those limits, we were not going beyond them when we came to you, bringing the Good News about Christ. 15 So we do not boast about the work that others have done beyond the limits God set for us. Instead, we hope that your faith may grow and that we may be able to do a much greater work among you, always within the limits that God has set. 16 Then we can preach the

Preach the Good News in other countries beyond you (10.16)

Good News in other countries beyond you and shall not have to boast about work already done in another man's field.

17 But as the scripture says, "Whoever wants to boast must boast about what the Lord has done."

18 For it is when the Lord thinks well of a person that he is really approved, and not when he thinks well of himself.

Paul and the False Apostles

11 I wish you would tolerate me, even when I am a bit foolish. Please do! 2 I am jealous for you, just as God is; you are like a pure virgin whom I have promised in marriage to one man only, Christ himself. 3 I am afraid that your minds will be corrupted and that you will abandon your full and pure devotion to Christ—in the same way that Eve was deceived by the snake's clever lies. 4 For you gladly tolerate anyone who comes to you and preaches a different Jesus, not the one we preached; and you accept a spirit and a gospel completely different from the Spirit and the gospel you received from us!

5 I do not think that I am the least bit inferior to those very special so-called "apostles" of yours! 6 Perhaps I am an amateur in speaking, but certainly not in knowledge; we have made this clear to you at all times and in all conditions.

7 I did not charge you a thing when I preached the Good News of God to you; I humbled myself in order to make you important. Was that wrong of me? 8 While I was working among you, I was paid by other churches. I was robbing them, so to speak, in order to help you. 9 And during the time I was with you I did not bother you for help when I needed money; the brothers who came from Macedonia brought me everything I needed. As in the past, so in the future: I will never be a burden to you! 10 By Christ's truth in me, I promise that this boast of mine will not be silenced anywhere in all Achaia. 11 Do I say this because I don't love you? God knows I love you!

12 I will go on doing what I am doing now, in order to keep those other "apostles" from having any reason for boasting and saying that they work in the same way that we do. 13 Those men are not true apostles—they are false apostles, who lie about their work and disguise themselves to look like real apostles of Christ. 14 Well, no wonder! Even Satan can disguise

himself to look like an angel of light! [15] So it is no great thing if his servants disguise themselves to look like servants of righteousness. In the end they will get exactly what their actions deserve.

Paul's Sufferings as an Apostle

16 I repeat: no one should think that I am a fool. But if you do, at least accept me as a fool, so that I will have a little to boast of. [17] Of course what I am saying now is not what the Lord would like me to say; in this matter of boasting I am really talking like a fool. [18] But since there are so many who boast for merely human reasons, I will do the same. [19] You yourselves are so wise, and so you gladly tolerate fools! [20] You tolerate anyone who orders you about or takes advantage of you or traps you or looks down on you or slaps you in the face. [21] I am ashamed to admit that we were too timid to do those things!

But if anyone dares to boast about something—I am talking like a fool—I will be just as daring. [22] Are they Hebrews? So am I. Are they Israelites? So am I. Are they Abraham's descendants? So am I. [23] Are they Christ's servants? I sound like a madman—but I am a better servant than they are! I have worked much harder, I have been in prison more times, I have been whipped much more, and I have been near death more often. [24] Five times I was given the thirty-nine lashes by the Jews; [25] three times I was whipped by the Romans; and once I was stoned. I have been in three shipwrecks, and once I spent twenty-four hours in the water. [26] In my many travels I have been in danger from floods and from robbers, in danger from fellow-Jews and from Gentiles; there have been dangers in the cities, dangers in the wilds, dangers on the high seas, and dangers from false friends. [27] There has been work and toil; often I have gone without sleep; I have been hungry and thirsty; I have often been without enough food, shelter, or clothing. [28] And not to mention other things, every day I am under the pressure of my concern for all the churches. [29] When someone is weak, then I feel weak too; when someone is led into sin, I am filled with distress.

30 If I must boast, I will boast about things that show how weak I am. [31]The God and Father of the Lord Jesus—blessed be his name for ever!—knows that I am not lying. [32]When I was in Damascus, the governor under King Aretas placed guards at the city gates to arrest me. [33]But I was let down in a basket through an opening in the wall and escaped from him.

Paul's Visions and Revelations

12 I have to boast, even though it doesn't do any good. But I will now talk about visions and revelations given me by the Lord. [2]I know a certain Christian man who fourteen years ago was snatched up to the highest heaven (I do not know whether this actually happened or whether he had a vision— only God knows). [3-4]I repeat, I know that this man was snatched to Paradise (again, I do not know whether this actually happened or whether it was a vision—only God knows), and there he heard things which cannot be put into words, things that human lips may not speak. [5]So I will boast about this man—but I will not boast about myself, except the things that show how weak I am. [6]If I wanted to boast, I would not be a fool, because I would be telling the truth. But I will not boast, because I do not want anyone to have a higher opinion of me than he has as a result of what he has seen me do and heard me say.

7 But to keep me from being puffed up with pride because of the many wonderful things I saw, I was given a painful physical ailment, which acts as Satan's messenger to beat me and keep me from being proud. [8]Three times I prayed to the Lord about this and asked him to take it away. [9]But his answer was: "My grace is all you need, for my power is greatest when you are weak." I am most happy, then, to be proud of my weaknesses, in order to feel the protection of Christ's power over me. [10]I am content with weaknesses, insults, hardships, persecutions, and difficulties for Christ's sake. For when I am weak, then I am strong.

Paul's Concern for the Corinthians

11 I am acting like a fool—but you have made me do it. You are the ones who ought to show your approval of me. For even if I am nothing, I am in no way inferior to those very special "apostles" of yours. 12 The many miracles and wonders that prove that I am an apostle were performed among you with much patience. 13 How were you treated any worse than the other churches, except that I did not bother you for financial help? Please forgive me for being so unfair!

14 This is now the third time that I am ready to come to visit you—and I will not make any demands on you. It is you I want, not your money. After all, children should not have to provide for their parents, but parents should provide for their children. 15 I will be glad to spend all I have, and myself as well, in order to help you. Will you love me less because I love you so much?

16 You will agree, then, that I was not a burden to you. But someone will say that I was crafty, and trapped you with lies. 17 How? Did I take advantage of you through any of the messengers I sent? 18 I begged Titus to go, and I sent the other Christian brother with him. Would you say that Titus took advantage of you? Do he and I not act from the very same motives and behave in the same way?

19 Perhaps you think that all along we have been trying to defend ourselves before you. No! We speak as Christ would wish us to speak in the presence of God, and everything we do, dear friends, is done to help you. 20 I am afraid that when I get there I will find you different from what I would like you to be and you will find me different from what you would like me to be. I am afraid that I will find quarrelling and jealousy, hot tempers and selfishness, insults and gossip, pride and disorder. 21 I am afraid that the next time I come my God will humiliate me in your presence, and I shall weep over many who sinned in the past and have not repented of the immoral things they have done—their lust and their sexual sins.

Final Warnings and Greetings

13 This is now the third time that I am coming to visit you. "Any accusation must be upheld by the evidence of two or more witnesses"—as the scripture says. ²I want to say to those of you who have sinned in the past, and to all the others; I said it before during my second visit to you, but I will say it again now that I am away: the next time I come nobody will escape punishment. ³You will have all the proof you want that Christ speaks through me. When he deals with you, he is not weak; instead, he shows his power among you. ⁴For even though it was in weakness that he was put to death on the cross, it is by God's power that he lives. In union with him we also are weak; but in our relations with you we shall share God's power in his life.

5 Put yourselves to the test and judge yourselves, to find out whether you are living in faith. Surely you know that Christ Jesus is in you?—unless you have completely failed. ⁶I trust you will know that we are not failures. ⁷We pray to God that you will do no wrong—not in order to show that we are a success, but so that you may do what is right, even though we may seem to be failures. ⁸For we cannot do a thing against the truth, but only for it. ⁹We are glad when we are weak but you are strong. And so we also pray that you will become perfect. ¹⁰That is why I write this while I am away from you; it is so that when I arrive I will not have to deal harshly with you in using the authority that the Lord has given me—authority to build you up, not to tear you down.

11 And now, my brothers, good-bye! Strive for perfection; listen to my appeals; agree with one another; live in peace. And the God of love and peace will be with you.

12 Greet one another with a brotherly kiss.

All God's people send you their greetings.

13 The grace of the Lord Jesus Christ, the love of God, and the fellowship of the Holy Spirit be with you all.

PAUL'S LETTER TO THE
GALATIANS

INTRODUCTION

As the good news about Jesus began to be preached and welcomed among people who were not Jews, the question arose as to whether a person must obey the Law of Moses in order to be a true Christian. Paul had argued that this was not necessary—that in fact, the only sound basis for life in Christ was faith, by which all are put right with God. But among the churches of Galatia, a Roman province in Asia Minor, there had come people who opposed Paul and claimed that one must also observe the Law of Moses in order to be right with God.

Paul's Letter to the Galatians was written in order to bring back to true faith and practice those people who were being misled by this false teaching. Paul begins by defending his right to be called an apostle of Jesus Christ. He insists that his call to be an apostle came from God, not from any human authority, and that his mission was especially to the non-Jews. Then he develops the argument that it is by faith alone that people are put right with God. In the concluding chapters Paul shows that Christian conduct flows naturally from the love that results from faith in Christ.

Outline of Contents

1 From Paul, whose call to be an apostle did not come from man or by means of man, but from Jesus Christ and God the Father, who raised him from death. ²All the brothers who are here join me in sending greetings to the churches of Galatia:

3 May God our Father and the Lord Jesus Christ give you grace and peace.

4 In order to set us free from this present evil age, Christ gave himself for our sins, in obedience to the will of our God and Father. ⁵To God be the glory for ever and ever! Amen.

The One Gospel

6 I am surprised at you! In no time at all you are deserting the one who called you by the grace of Christ, ᵃ and are accepting another gospel. ⁷Actually, there is no "other gospel," but I say this because there are some people who are upsetting you and trying to change the gospel of Christ. ⁸But even if we or an angel from heaven should preach to you a gospel that is different from the one we preached to you, may he be condemned to hell! ⁹We have said it before, and now I say it again: if anyone preaches to you a gospel that is different from the one you accepted, may he be condemned to hell!

10 Does this sound as if I am trying to win man's approval? No indeed! What I want is God's approval! Am I trying to be popular with men? If I were still trying to do so, I would not be a servant of Christ.

How Paul Became an Apostle

11 Let me tell you, my brothers, that the gospel I preach is not of human origin. ¹²I did not receive it from any man, nor did anyone teach it to me. It was Jesus Christ himself who revealed it to me.

13 You have been told how I used to live when I was devoted to the Jewish religion, how I persecuted without mercy the church of God and did my best to destroy it. ¹⁴I was ahead of most fellow-Jews of my

ᵃby the grace of Christ; *some manuscripts have* by his grace.

age in my practice of the Jewish religion, and was much more devoted to the traditions of our ancestors.

15 But God in his grace chose me even before I was born, and called me to serve him. And when he decided 16 to reveal his Son to me, so that I might preach the Good News about him to the Gentiles, I did not go to anyone for advice, 17 nor did I go to Jerusalem to see those who were apostles before me. Instead, I went at once to Arabia, and then I returned to Damascus. 18 It was three years later that I went to Jerusalem to obtain information from Peter, and I stayed with him for two weeks. 19 I did not see any other apostle except James, b the Lord's brother.

20 What I write is true. God knows that I am not lying!

21 Afterwards I went to places in Syria and Cilicia. 22 At that time the members of the churches in Judaea did not know me personally. 23 They knew only what others were saying: "The man who used to persecute us is now preaching the faith that he once tried to destroy!" 24 And so they praised God because of me.

Paul and the Other Apostles

2 Fourteen years later I went back to Jerusalem with Barnabas, taking Titus along with me. 2 I went because God revealed to me that I should go. In a private meeting with the leaders I explained the gospel message that I preach to the Gentiles. I did not want my work in the past or in the present to be a failure. 3 My companion Titus, even though he is Greek, was not forced to be circumcised, 4 although some wanted it done. Pretending to be fellow-believers, these men slipped into our group as spies, in order to find out about the freedom we have through our union with Christ Jesus. They wanted to make slaves of us, 5 but in order to keep the truth of the gospel safe for you, we did not give in to them for a minute.

6 But those who seemed to be the leaders—I say this because it makes no difference to me what they

b any other apostle except James; or any other apostle; the only other person I saw was James.

were; God does not judge by outward appearances—those leaders, I say, made no new suggestions to me. 7 On the contrary, they saw that God had given me the task of preaching the gospel to the Gentiles, just as he had given Peter the task of preaching the gospel to the Jews. 8 For by God's power I was made an apostle to the Gentiles, just as Peter was made an apostle to the Jews. 9 James, Peter, and John, who seemed to be the leaders, recognized that God had given me this special task; so they shook hands with Barnabas and me, as a sign that we were all partners. We agreed that Barnabas and I would work among the Gentiles and they among the Jews. 10 All they asked was that we should remember the needy in their group, which is the very thing I have*c* been eager to do.

Paul Rebukes Peter at Antioch

11 But when Peter came to Antioch, I opposed him in public, because he was clearly wrong. 12 Before some men who had been sent by James arrived there, Peter had been eating with the Gentile brothers. But after these men arrived, he drew back and would not eat with the Gentiles, because he was afraid of those who were in favour of circumcising them. 13 The other Jewish brothers also started acting like cowards along with Peter; and even Barnabas was swept along by their cowardly action. 14 When I saw that they were not walking a straight path in line with the truth of the gospel, I said to Peter in front of them all, "You are a Jew, yet you have been living like a Gentile, not like a Jew. How, then, can you try to force Gentiles to live like Jews?"

Jews and Gentiles Are Saved by Faith

15 Indeed, we are Jews by birth and not "Gentile sinners," as they are called. 16 Yet we know that a person is put right with God only through faith in Jesus Christ, never by doing what the Law requires. We, too, have believed in Christ Jesus in order to be put right with God through our faith in Christ,

*c*have; or had.

and not by doing what the Law requires. For no one is put right with God by doing what the Law requires. 17 If, then, as we try to be put right with God by our union with Christ, we are found to be sinners as much as the Gentiles are—does this mean that Christ is serving the cause of sin? By no means! 18 If I start to rebuild the system of Law that I tore down, then I show myself to be someone who breaks the Law. 19 So far as the Law is concerned, however, I am dead—killed by the Law itself—in order that I might live for God. I have been put to death with Christ on his cross, 20 so that it is no longer I who live, but it is Christ who lives in me. This life that I live now, I live by faith in the Son of God, who loved me and gave his life for me. 21 I refuse to reject the grace of God. But if a person is put right with God through the Law, it means that Christ died for nothing!

Law or Faith

3 You foolish Galatians! Who put a spell on you? Before your very eyes you had a clear description of the death of Jesus Christ on the cross! 2 Tell me this one thing: did you receive God's Spirit by doing what the Law requires or by hearing the gospel and believing it? 3 How can you be so foolish! You began by God's Spirit; do you now want to finish by your own power? 4 Did all your experience mean nothing at all? Surely it meant something! 5 Does God give you the Spirit and work miracles among you because you do what the Law requires or because you hear the gospel and believe it?

6 Consider the experience of Abraham; as the scripture says, "He believed God, and because of his faith God accepted him as righteous." 7 You should realize then, that the real descendants of Abraham are the people who have faith. 8 The scripture predicted that God would put the Gentiles right with himself through faith. And so the scripture announced the Good News to Abraham: "Through you God will bless all mankind." 9 Abraham believed and was blessed; so all who believe are blessed as he was.

10 Those who depend on obeying the Law live under

a curse. For the scripture says, "Whoever does not always obey everything that is written in the book of the Law is under God's curse!" 11 Now, it is clear that no one is put right with God by means of the Law, because the scripture says, "Only the person who is put right with God through faith shall live."*d* 12 But the Law has nothing to do with faith. Instead, as the scripture says, "Whoever *does* everything the Law requires will live."

13 But by becoming a curse for us Christ has redeemed us from the curse that the Law brings; for the scripture says, "Anyone who is hanged on a tree is under God's curse." 14 Christ did this in order that the blessing which God promised to Abraham might be given to the Gentiles by means of Christ Jesus, so that through faith we might receive the Spirit promised by God.

The Law and the Promise

15 My brothers, I am going to use an everyday example: when two people agree on a matter and sign an agreement, no one can break it or add anything to it. 16 Now, God made his promises to Abraham and to his descendant. The scripture does not use the plural "descendants," meaning many people, but the singular "descendant," meaning one person only, namely, Christ. 17 What I mean is that God made a covenant with Abraham and promised to keep it. The Law, which was given four hundred and thirty years later, cannot break that covenant and cancel God's promise. 18 For if God's gift depends on the Law, then it no longer depends on his promise. However, it was because of his promise that God gave that gift to Abraham.

19 What, then, was the purpose of the Law? It was added in order to show what wrongdoing is, and it was meant to last until the coming of Abraham's descendant, to whom the promise was made. The Law was handed down by angels, with a man acting as a go-between. 20 But a go-between is not needed when

---

*d*put right with God through faith shall live; *or* put right with God shall live through faith.

only one person is involved; and God is one. *e*

The Purpose of the Law

21 Does this mean that the Law is against God's promises? No, not at all! For if mankind had received a law that could bring life, then everyone could be put right with God by obeying it. 22 But the scripture says that the whole world is under the power of sin; and so the gift which is promised on the basis of faith in Jesus Christ is given to those who believe.

23 But before the time for faith came, the Law kept us all locked up as prisoners until this coming faith should be revealed. 24 And so the Law was in charge of us until Christ came, in order that we might then be put right with God through faith. 25 Now that the time for faith is here, the Law is no longer in charge of us.

26 It is through faith that all of you are God's sons in union with Christ Jesus. 27 You were baptized into union with Christ, and now you are clothed, so to speak, with the life of Christ himself. 28 So there is no difference between Jews and Gentiles, between slaves and free men, between men and women; you are all one in union with Christ Jesus. 29 If you belong to Christ, then you are the descendants of Abraham and will receive what God has promised.

4 But now to continue—the son who will receive his father's property is treated just like a slave while he is young, even though he really owns everything. 2 While he is young, there are men who take care of him and manage his affairs until the time set by his father. 3 In the same way, we too were slaves of the ruling spirits of the universe before we reached spiritual maturity. 4 But when the right time finally came, God sent his own Son. He came as the son of a human mother and lived under the Jewish Law, 5 to redeem those who were under the Law, so that we might become God's sons.

6 To show that you are *f* his sons, God sent the Spirit of his Son into our hearts, the Spirit who cries

---

e and God is one; *or* and God acts alone.
f To show that you are; *or* Because you are.

You are all one in union with Christ Jesus (3.28)

out, "Father, my Father." 7 So then, you are no longer a slave but a son. And since you are his son, God will give you all that he has for his sons.

Paul's Concern for the Galatians

8 In the past you did not know God, and so you were slaves of beings who are not gods. 9 But now that you know God—or, I should say, now that God knows you—how is it that you want to turn back to those weak and pitiful ruling spirits? Why do you want to become their slaves all over again? 10 You pay special attention to certain days, months, seasons, and years. 11 I am worried about you! Can it be that all my work for you has been for nothing?

12 I beg you, my brothers, be like me. After all, I am like you. You have not done me any wrong. 13 You remember why I preached the gospel to you the first time; it was because I was ill. 14 But even

You are no longer a slave (4.7)

though my physical condition was a great trial to you, you did not despise or reject me. Instead, you received me as you would an angel from heaven; you received me as you would Christ Jesus. 15 You were so happy! What has happened? I myself can say that you would have taken out your own eyes, if you could, and given them to me. 16 Have I now become your enemy by telling you the truth?

17 Those other people show a deep interest in you, but their intentions are not good. All they want is to separate you from me, so that you will have the same interest in them as they have in you. 18 Now, it is good to have such a deep interest if the purpose is good—this is true always, and not merely when I am with you. 19 My dear children! Once again, just like a mother in childbirth, I feel the same kind of pain for you until Christ's nature is formed in you. 20 How I wish I were with you now, so that I could take a different attitude towards you. I am so worried about you!

The Example of Hagar and Sarah

21 Let me ask those of you who want to be subject to the Law: do you not hear what the Law says? 22 It says that Abraham had two sons, one by a slave-

woman, the other by a free woman. [23]His son by the slave-woman was born in the usual way, but his son by the free woman was born as a result of God's promise. [24]These things can be understood as a figure: the two women represent two covenants. The one whose children are born in slavery is Hagar, and she represents the covenant made at Mount Sinai. [25]Hagar, who stands for Mount Sinai in Arabia, is[g] a figure of the present city of Jerusalem, in slavery with all its people. [26]But the heavenly Jerusalem is free, and she is our mother. [27]For the scripture says,

"Be happy, you childless woman!
  Shout and cry with joy, you who never felt the
    pains of childbirth!
For the woman who was deserted will have more
    children
  than the woman whose husband never left her."

28 Now, you, my brothers, are God's children as a result of his promise, just as Isaac was. [29]At that time the son who was born in the usual way persecuted the one who was born because of God's Spirit; and it is the same now. [30]But what does the scripture say? It says, "Send the slave-woman and her son away; for the son of the slave-woman will not have a part of the father's property along with the son of the free woman." [31]So then, my brothers, we are not the children of a slave-woman but of a free woman.

Preserve Your Freedom

5 Freedom is what we have—Christ has set us free! Stand, then, as free people, and do not allow yourselves to become slaves again.

2 Listen! I, Paul, tell you that if you allow yourselves to be circumcised, it means that Christ is of no use to you at all. [3]Once more I warn any man who allows himself to be circumcised that he is obliged to obey the whole Law. [4]Those of you who try to be put right with God by obeying the Law have cut yourselves off from Christ. You are outside God's grace. [5]As for us, our hope is that God will put

[g]Hagar...is; *some manuscripts have* Sinai is a mountain in Arabia, and it is.

us right with him; and this is what we wait for by the power of God's Spirit working through our faith. 6 For when we are in union with Christ Jesus, neither circumcision nor the lack of it makes any difference at all; what matters is faith that works through love.

7 You were doing so well! Who made you stop obeying the truth? How did he persuade you? 8 It was not done by God, who calls you. 9 "It takes only a little yeast to make the whole batch of dough rise," as they say. 10 But I still feel confident about you. Our life in union with the Lord makes me confident that you will not take a different view and that the man who is upsetting you, whoever he is, will be punished by God.

11 But as for me, my brothers, if I continue to preach that circumcision is necessary, why am I still being persecuted? If that were true, then my preaching about the cross of Christ would cause no trouble. 12 I wish that the people who are upsetting you would go all the way; let them go on and castrate themselves!

13 As for you, my brothers, you were called to be free. But do not let this freedom become an excuse for letting your physical desires control you. Instead, let love make you serve one another. 14 For the whole Law is summed up in one commandment: "Love your neighbour as you love yourself." 15 But if you act like wild animals, hurting and harming each other, then watch out, or you will completely destroy one another.

The Spirit and Human Nature

16 What I say is this: let the Spirit direct your lives, and you will not satisfy the desires of the human nature. 17 For what our human nature wants is opposed to what the Spirit wants, and what the Spirit wants is opposed to what our human nature wants. These two are enemies, and this means that you cannot do what you want to do. 18 If the Spirit leads you, then you are not subject to the Law.

19 What human nature does is quite plain. It shows itself in immoral, filthy, and indecent actions; 20 in worship of idols and witchcraft. People become ene-

mies and they fight; they become jealous, angry, and ambitious. They separate into parties and groups; 21they are envious, get drunk, have orgies, and do other things like these. I warn you now as I have before: those who do these things will not possess the Kingdom of God.

22 But the Spirit produces love, joy, peace, patience, kindness, goodness, faithfulness, 23humility, and self-control. There is no law against such things as these. 24And those who belong to Christ Jesus have put to death their human nature with all its passions and desires. 25The Spirit has given us life; he must also control our lives. 26We must not be proud or irritate one another or be jealous of one another.

Bear One Another's Burdens

6 My brothers, if someone is caught in any kind of wrongdoing, those of you who are spiritual should set him right; but you must do it in a gentle way. And keep an eye on yourselves, so that you will not be tempted, too. 2Help to carry one another's

Help to carry one another's burdens (6.2)

burdens, and in this way you will obey[h] the law of Christ. 3If someone thinks he is somebody when really he is nobody, he is only deceiving himself. 4Each one should judge his own conduct. If it is good, then he can be proud of what he himself has done, without having to compare it with what someone else has done. 5For everyone has to carry his own load.

[h]you will obey; *some manuscripts have* obey.

6 The man who is being taught the Christian message should share all the good things he has with his teacher.

7 Do not deceive yourselves; no one makes a fool of God. A person will reap exactly what he sows. 8 If he sows in the field of his natural desires, from it he will gather the harvest of death; if he sows in the field of the Spirit, from the Spirit he will gather the harvest of eternal life. 9 So let us not become tired of doing good; for if we do not give up, the time will come when we will reap the harvest. 10 So then, as often as we have the chance, we should do good to everyone, and especially to those who belong to our family in the faith.

Final Warning and Greeting

11 See what big letters I make as I write to you now with my own hand! 12 The people who are trying to force you to be circumcised are the ones who want to show off and boast about external matters. They do it, however, only so that they may not be persecuted for the cross of Christ. 13 Even those who practise circumcision do not obey the Law; they want you to be circumcised so that they can boast that you submitted to this physical ceremony. 14 As for me, however, I will boast only about the cross of our Lord Jesus Christ; for by means of his cross the world is dead to me, and I am dead to the world. 15 It does not matter at all whether or not one is circumcised; what does matter is being a new creature. 16 As for those who follow this rule in their lives, may peace and mercy be with them—with them and with all God's people!

17 To conclude: let no one give me any more trouble, because the scars I have on my body show that I am the slave of Jesus.

18 May the grace of our Lord Jesus Christ be with you all, my brothers. Amen.

PAUL'S LETTER TO THE
EPHESIANS

INTRODUCTION

Paul's Letter to the Ephesians is concerned first of all with "God's plan...to bring all creation together, everything in heaven and on earth, with Christ as head" (1.10). It is also an appeal to God's people to live out the meaning of this great plan for the unity of mankind through oneness with Jesus Christ.

In the first part of *Ephesians* the writer develops the theme of unity by speaking of the way in which God the Father has chosen his people, how they are forgiven and set free from their sins through Jesus Christ the Son, and how God's great promise is guaranteed by the Holy Spirit. In the second part he appeals to the readers to live in such a way that their oneness in Christ may become real in their life together.

Several figures of speech are used to show the oneness of God's people in union with Christ: the church is like a body, with Christ as the head; or like a building, with Christ as the cornerstone; or like a wife, with Christ as the husband. This letter rises to great heights of expression as the writer is moved by the thought of God's grace in Christ. Everything is seen in the light of Christ's love, sacrifice, forgiveness, grace, and purity.

Outline of Contents

1 From Paul, who by God's will is an apostle of Christ Jesus—

To God's people in Ephesus,[a] who are faithful in their life in union with Christ Jesus:

2 May God our Father and the Lord Jesus Christ give you grace and peace.

Spiritual Blessings in Christ

3 Let us give thanks to the God and Father of our Lord Jesus Christ! For in our union with Christ he has blessed us by giving us every spiritual blessing in the heavenly world. [4]Even before the world was made, God had already chosen us to be his through our union with Christ, so that we would be holy and without fault before him.

.Because of his love [5]God[b] had already decided that through Jesus Christ he would make us his sons—this was his pleasure and purpose. [6]Let us praise God for his glorious grace, for the free gift he gave us in his dear Son! [7]For by the sacrificial death of Christ we are set free, that is, our sins are forgiven. How great is the grace of God, [8]which he gave to us in such large measure!

In all his wisdom and insight [9]God did what he had purposed, and made known to us the secret plan he had already decided to complete by means of Christ. [10]This plan, which God will complete when the time is right, is to bring all creation together, everything in heaven and on earth, with Christ as head.

11 All things are done according to God's plan and decision; and God chose us to be his own people in union with Christ because of his own purpose, based on what he had decided from the very beginning. [12]Let us, then, who were the first to hope in Christ, praise God's glory!

13 And you also became God's people when you heard the true message, the Good News that brought you salvation. You believed in Christ, and God put his stamp of ownership on you by giving you the

---

[a] *Some manuscripts do not have* in Ephesus.
[b] before him. Because of his love God; *or* before him, and to live in love. God.

Let us...praise God's glory! (1.12)

Holy Spirit he had promised. ¹⁴The Spirit is the guarantee that we shall receive what God has promised his people, and this assures us that God will give complete freedom to those who are his. Let us praise his glory!

Paul's Prayer

15 For this reason, ever since I heard of your faith in the Lord Jesus and your love for all God's people, ¹⁶I have not stopped giving thanks to God for you. I remember you in my prayers ¹⁷and ask the God of our Lord Jesus Christ, the glorious Father, to give you the Spirit, who will make you wise and reveal

God to you, so that you will know him. [18]I ask that your minds may be opened to see his light, so that you will know what is the hope to which he has called you, how rich are the wonderful blessings he promises his people, [19]and how very great is his power at work in us who believe. This power working in us is the same as the mighty strength [20]which he used when he raised Christ from death and seated him at his right side in the heavenly world. [21]Christ rules there above all heavenly rulers, authorities, powers, and lords; he has a title superior to all titles of authority in this world and in the next. [22]God put all things under Christ's feet and gave him to the church as supreme Lord over all things. [23]The church is Christ's body, the completion of him who himself completes all things everywhere. [c]

From Death to Life

2 In the past you were spiritually dead because of your disobedience and sins. [2]At that time you followed the world's evil way; you obeyed the ruler of the spiritual powers in space, the spirit who now controls the people who disobey God. [3]Actually all of us were like them and lived according to our natural desires, doing whatever suited the wishes of our own bodies and minds. In our natural condition we, like everyone else, were destined to suffer God's anger.

4 But God's mercy is so abundant, and his love for us is so great, [5]that while we were spiritually dead in our disobedience he brought us to life with Christ. It is by God's grace that you have been saved. [6]In our union with Christ Jesus he raised us up with him to rule with him in the heavenly world. [7]He did this to demonstrate for all time to come the extraordinary greatness of his grace in the love he showed us in Christ Jesus. [8-9]For it is by God's grace that you have been saved through faith. It is not the result of your own efforts, but God's gift, so that no one can boast about it. [10]God has made us what we are, and in our union with Christ Jesus he has created

[c]who himself completes all things everywhere; *or* who is himself completely filled with God's fullness.

us for a life of good deeds, which he has already
prepared for us to do.

One in Christ

11 You Gentiles by birth—called "the uncircumcised" by the Jews, who call themselves "the circumcised" (which refers to what men do to their
bodies)—remember what you were in the past. ¹²At
that time you were apart from Christ. You were
foreigners and did not belong to God's chosen people.
You had no part in the covenants, which were based
on God's promises to his people, and you lived in
this world without hope and without God. ¹³But now,
in union with Christ Jesus, you who used to be far
away have been brought near by the sacrificial death
of Christ. ¹⁴For Christ himself has brought us peace
by making Jews and Gentiles one people. With his
own body he broke down the wall that separated
them and kept them enemies. ¹⁵He abolished the Jewish Law with its commandments and rules, in order
to create out of the two races one new people in union
with himself, in this way making peace. ¹⁶By his death
on the cross Christ destroyed their enmity; by means
of the cross he united both races into one body and
brought them back to God. ¹⁷So Christ came and
preached the Good News of peace to all—to you Gentiles, who were far away from God, and to the Jews,
who were near to him. ¹⁸It is through Christ that
all of us, Jews and Gentiles, are able to come in
the one Spirit into the presence of the Father.

19 So then, you Gentiles are not foreigners or
strangers any longer; you are now fellow-citizens with
God's people and members of the family of God. ²⁰You,
too, are built upon the foundation laid by the apostles
and prophets,ᵈ the cornerstone being Christ Jesus himself. ²¹He is the one who holds the whole building
together and makes it grow into a sacred temple dedicated to the Lord. ²²In union with him you too are
being built together with all the others into a place
where God lives through his Spirit.

ᵈthe foundation laid by the apostles and prophets; *or* the
foundation, that is, the apostles and prophets.

Paul's Work for the Gentiles

3 For this reason I, Paul, the prisoner of Christ Jesus for the sake of you Gentiles, pray to God. ²Surely you have heard that God in his grace has given me this work to do for your good. ³God revealed his secret plan and made it known to me. (I have written briefly about this, ⁴and if you will read what I have written, you can learn about my understanding of the secret of Christ.) ⁵In past times mankind was not told this secret, but God has revealed it now by the Spirit to his holy apostles and prophets. ⁶The secret is that by means of the gospel the Gentiles have a part with the Jews in God's blessings; they are members of the same body and share in the promise that God made through Christ Jesus.

7 I was made a servant of the gospel by God's special gift, which he gave me through the working of his power. ⁸I am less than the least of all God's people; yet God gave me this privilege of taking to the Gentiles the Good News about the infinite riches of Christ, ⁹and of making all people see how God's secret plan is to be put into effect. God, who is the Creator of all things, kept his secret hidden through all the past ages, ¹⁰in order that at the present time, by means of the church, the angelic rulers and powers in the heavenly world might learn of his wisdom in all its different forms. ¹¹God did this according to his eternal purpose, which he achieved through Christ Jesus our Lord. ¹²In union with Christ and through our faith in him we have the boldness to go into God's presence with all confidence. ¹³I beg you, then, not to be discouraged because I am suffering for you; it is all for your benefit.

The Love of Christ

14 For this reason I fall on my knees before the Father, ¹⁵from whom every family in heaven and on earth receives its true name. ¹⁶I ask God from the wealth of his glory to give you power through his Spirit to be strong in your inner selves, ¹⁷and I pray that Christ will make his home in your hearts through faith. I pray that you may have your roots and foun-

dation in love, [18]so that you, together with all God's people, may have the power to understand how broad and long, how high and deep, is Christ's•love. [19]Yes, may you come to know his love—although it can never be fully known—and so be completely filled with the very nature of God.

20 To him who by means of his power working in us is able to do so much more than we can ever ask for, or even think of: [21]to God be the glory in the church and in Christ Jesus for all time, for ever and ever! Amen.

The Unity of the Body

4 I urge you, then—I who am a prisoner because I serve the Lord: live a life that measures up to the standard God set when he called you. [2]Be always humble, gentle, and patient. Show your love by being tolerant with one another. [3]Do your best to preserve the unity which the Spirit gives by means of the peace that binds you together. [4]There is one body and one Spirit, just as there is one hope to which God has called you. [5]There is one Lord, one faith, one baptism; [6]there is one God and Father of all mankind, who is Lord of all, works through all, and is in all.

7 Each one of us has received a special gift in proportion to what Christ has given. [8]As the scripture says,

"When he went up to the very heights,
  he took many captives with him;
  he gave gifts to mankind."

[9]Now, what does "he went up" mean? It means that first he came down to the lowest depths of the earth.[e] [10]So the one who came down is the same one who went up, above and beyond the heavens, to fill the whole universe with his presence. [11]It was he who "gave gifts to mankind"; he appointed some to be apostles, others to be prophets, others to be evangelists, others to be pastors and teachers. [12]He did this to prepare all God's people for the work of

[e]the lowest depths of the earth; or the lower depths, the earth itself.

Christian service, in order to build up the body of Christ. [13] And so we shall all come together to that oneness in our faith and in our knowledge of the Son of God; we shall become mature people, reaching to the very height of Christ's full stature. [14] Then we shall no longer be children, carried by the waves and blown about by every shifting wind of the teaching of deceitful men, who lead others into error by the tricks they invent. [15] Instead, by speaking the truth in a spirit of love, we must grow up in every way to Christ, who is the head. [16] Under his control all the different parts of the body fit together, and the whole body is held together by every joint with which it is provided. So when each separate part works as it should, the whole body grows and builds itself up through love.

The New Life in Christ

17 In the Lord's name, then, I warn you: do not continue to live like the heathen, whose thoughts are worthless [18] and whose minds are in the dark. They have no part in the life that God gives, for they are completely ignorant and stubborn. [19] They have lost all feeling of shame; they give themselves over to vice and do all sorts of indecent things without restraint.

20 That was not what you learnt about Christ! [21] You certainly heard about him, and as his followers you were taught the truth that is in Jesus. [22] So get rid of your old self, which made you live as you used to—the old self that was being destroyed by its deceitful desires. [23] Your hearts and minds must be made completely new, [24] and you must put on the new self, which is created in God's likeness and reveals itself in the true life that is upright and holy.

25 No more lying, then! Everyone must tell the truth to his fellow-believer, because we are all members together in the body of Christ. [26] If you become angry, do not let your anger lead you into sin, and do not stay angry all day. [27] Don't give the Devil a chance. [28] The man who used to rob must stop robbing and start working, in order to earn an honest living for himself and to be able to help the poor. [29] Do not use harmful

Do not let your anger lead you into sin (4.26)

words, but only helpful words, the kind that build up and provide what is needed, so that what you say will do good to those who hear you. ³⁰ And do not make God's Holy Spirit sad; for the Spirit is God's mark of ownership on you, a guarantee that the Day will come when God will set you free. ³¹ Get rid of all bitterness, passion, and anger. No more shouting or insults, no more hateful feelings of any sort. ³² Instead, be kind and tender-hearted to one another, and forgive one another, as God has forgiven you through Christ.

Living in the Light

5 Since you are God's dear children, you must try to be like him. ² Your life must be controlled by love, just as Christ loved us and gave his life for us as a sweet-smelling offering and sacrifice that pleases God.

3 Since you are God's people, it is not right that any matters of sexual immorality or indecency or greed should even be mentioned among you. ⁴ Nor is it fitting for you to use language which is obscene, profane, or vulgar. Rather you should give thanks to God. ⁵ You may be sure that no one who is immoral, indecent,

or greedy (for greed is a form of idolatry) will ever receive a share in the Kingdom of Christ and of God.

6 Do not let anyone deceive you with foolish words; it is because of these very things that God's anger will come upon those who do not obey him. 7 So have nothing at all to do with such people. 8 You yourselves used to be in the darkness, but since you have become the Lord's people, you are in the light. So you must live like people who belong to the light, 9 for it is the light[f] that brings a rich harvest of every kind of goodness, righteousness, and truth. 10 Try to learn what pleases the Lord. 11 Have nothing to do with the worthless things that people do, things that belong to the darkness. Instead, bring them out to the light. 12 (It is really too shameful even to talk about the things they do in secret.) 13 And when all things are brought out to the light, then their true nature is clearly revealed; 14 for anything that is clearly revealed becomes light.[g] That is why it is said,

"Wake up, sleeper,
    and rise from death,
and Christ will shine on you."

15 So be careful how you live. Don't live like ignorant people, but like wise people. 16 Make good use of every opportunity you have, because these are evil days. 17 Don't be fools, then, but try to find out what the Lord wants you to do.

18 Do not get drunk with wine, which will only ruin you; instead, be filled with the Spirit. 19 Speak to one another with the words of psalms, hymns, and sacred songs; sing hymns and psalms to the Lord with praise in your hearts. 20 In the name of our Lord Jesus Christ, always give thanks for everything to God the Father.

Wives and Husbands

21 Submit yourselves to one another because of your reverence for Christ.

22 Wives, submit to your husbands as to the Lord.

---

[f] the light; *some manuscripts have* the Spirit.
[g] anything that is clearly revealed becomes light; *or* it is light that clearly reveals everything.

23 For a husband has authority over his wife just as Christ has authority over the church; and Christ is himself the Saviour of the church, his body. 24 And so wives must submit completely to their husbands just as the church submits itself to Christ.

25 Husbands, love your wives just as Christ loved the church and gave his life for it. 26 He did this to dedicate the church to God by his word, after making it clean by washing it in water, 27 in order to present the church to himself in all its beauty—pure and faultless, without spot or wrinkle or any other imperfection. 28 Men ought to love their wives just as they love their own bodies. A man who loves his wife loves himself. 29 (No one ever hates his own body. Instead, he feeds it and takes care of it, just as Christ does the church; 30 for we are members of his body.) 31 As the scripture says, "For this reason a man will leave his father and mother and unite with his wife, and the two will become one." 32 There is a deep secret truth revealed in this scripture, which I understand as applying to Christ and the church. 33 But it also applies to you: every husband must love his wife as himself, and every wife must respect her husband.

Children and Parents

6 Children, it is your Christian duty to[h] obey your parents, for this is the right thing to do. 2 "Respect your father and mother" is the first commandment that has a promise added: 3 "so that all may go well with you, and you may live a long time in the land."

4 Parents, do not treat your children in such a way as to make them angry. Instead, bring them up with Christian discipline and instruction.

Slaves and Masters

5 Slaves, obey your human masters with fear and trembling; and do it with a sincere heart, as though you were serving Christ. 6 Do this not only when they are watching you, because you want to gain their approval; but with all your heart do what God wants,

---

[h] *Some manuscripts do not have* It is your Christian duty to.

as slaves of Christ. ⁷Do your work as slaves cheerfully, as though you served the Lord, and not merely men. ⁸Remember that the Lord will reward everyone, whether slave or free, for the good work he does.

9 Masters, behave in the same way towards your slaves and stop using threats. Remember that you and your slaves belong to the same Master in heaven, who judges everyone by the same standard.

The Whole Armour of God

10 Finally, build up your strength in union with the Lord and by means of his mighty power. ¹¹Put on all the armour that God gives you, so that you will be able to stand up against the Devil's evil tricks. ¹²For we are not fighting against human beings but against the wicked spiritual forces in the heavenly world, the rulers, authorities, and cosmic powers of this dark age. ¹³So put on God's armour now! Then when the evil day comes, you will be able to resist the enemy's attacks; and after fighting to the end, you will still hold your ground.

14 So stand ready, with truth as a belt tight round your waist, with righteousness as your breastplate, ¹⁵and as your shoes the readiness to announce the Good News of peace. ¹⁶At all times carry faith as a shield; for with it you will be able to put out all the burning arrows shot by the Evil One. ¹⁷And accept salvation as a helmet, and the word of God as the sword which the Spirit gives you. ¹⁸Do all this in prayer, asking for God's help. Pray on every occasion, as the Spirit leads. For this reason keep alert and never give up; pray always for all God's people. ¹⁹And pray also for me, that God will give me a message when I am ready to speak, so that I may speak boldly and make known the gospel's secret. ²⁰For the sake of this gospel I am an ambassador, though now I am in prison. Pray that I may be bold in speaking about the gospel as I should.

Final Greetings

21 Tychicus, our dear brother and faithful servant in the Lord's work, will give you all the news about me, so that you may know how I am getting on.

22 That is why I am sending him to you—to tell you how all of us are getting on, and to encourage you.

23 May God the Father and the Lord Jesus Christ give to all Christian brothers peace and love with faith. 24 May God's grace be with all those who love our Lord Jesus Christ with undying love.

PAUL'S LETTER TO THE
PHILIPPIANS

INTRODUCTION

Paul's Letter to the Philippians was written to the first church that Paul established on European soil, in the Roman province of Macedonia. It was written while the apostle was in prison, and at a time when he was troubled by the opposition of other Christian workers towards himself and was distressed by false teaching in the church at Philippi. Yet this letter breathes a joy and confidence that can be explained only by Paul's deep faith in Jesus Christ.

The immediate reason for writing the letter was to thank the Philippian Christians for the gift which they had sent to help him in his time of need. He uses this opportunity to reassure them, so that they may have courage and confidence in spite of all his troubles and their own as well. He pleads with them to have the humble attitude of Jesus, rather than to be controlled by selfish ambition and pride. He reminds them that their life in union with Christ is a gift of God's grace which they have received through faith, not through obedience to the ceremonies of the Jewish Law. He writes of the joy and peace that God gives to those who live in union with Christ.

This letter is marked by its emphasis on joy, confidence, unity, and perseverance in the Christian faith and life. It also reveals the deep affection Paul had for the church at Philippi.

Outline of Contents

1 From Paul and Timothy, servants of Christ Jesus—
To all God's people in Philippi who are in union with Christ Jesus, including the church leaders and helpers:

2 May God our Father and the Lord Jesus Christ give you grace and peace.

Paul's Prayer for His Readers

3 I thank my God for you every time I think of you; 4 and every time I pray for you all, I pray with joy 5 because of the way in which you have helped me in the work of the gospel from the very first day until now. 6 And so I am sure that God, who began this good work in you, will carry it on until it is finished on the Day of Christ Jesus. 7 You are always in my heart! And so it is only right for me to feel as I do about you. For you have all shared with me in this privilege that God has given me, both now that I am in prison and also while I was free to defend the gospel and establish it firmly. 8 God is my witness that I am telling the truth when I say that my deep feeling for you all comes from the heart of Christ Jesus himself.

9 I pray that your love will keep on growing more and more, together with true knowledge and perfect judgement, 10 so that you will be able to choose what is best. Then you will be free from all impurity and blame on the Day of Christ. 11 Your lives will be filled with the truly good qualities which only Jesus Christ can produce, for the glory and praise of God.

To Live Is Christ

12 I want you to know, my brothers, that the things that have happened to me have really helped the progress of the gospel. 13 As a result, the whole palace guard and all the others here know that I am in prison because I am a servant of Christ. 14 And my being in prison has given most of the brothers more confidence in the Lord, so that they grow bolder all the time to preach the message a fearlessly.

15 Of course some of them preach Christ because they are jealous and quarrelsome, but others from genuine goodwill. 16 These do so from love, because they know that God has given me the work of defending the gospel. 17 The others do not proclaim Christ sincerely, but from a spirit of selfish ambition; they think that they will make more trouble for me while I am in prison.

18 It does not matter! I am happy about it—so long as Christ is preached in every way possible, whether from wrong or right motives. And I will continue to be happy, 19 because I know that by means of your prayers and the help which comes from the Spirit of Jesus Christ I shall be set free. 20 My deep desire and hope is that I shall never fail in my duty, but that at all times, and especially just now, I shall be full of courage, so that with my whole being I shall bring honour to Christ, whether I live or die. 21 For what is life? To me, it is Christ. Death, then, will bring more. 22 But if by continuing to live I can do more worthwhile work, then I am not sure which I should choose. 23 I am pulled in two directions. I want very much to leave this life and be with Christ, which is a far better thing; 24 but for your sake it is much more important that I remain alive. 25 I am sure of this, and so I know that I will stay. I will stay on with you all, to add to your progress and joy in the faith, 26 so that when I am with you again, you will have even more reason to be proud of me in your life in union with Christ Jesus.

27 Now, the important thing is that your way of

---

a the message; *some manuscripts have* God's message.

life should be as the gospel of Christ requires, so that, whether or not I am able to go and see you, I will hear that you are standing firm with one common purpose and that with only one desire you are fighting together for the faith of the gospel. 28 Don't be afraid of your enemies; always be courageous, and this will prove to them that they will lose and that you will win, because it is God who gives you the victory. 29 For you have been given the privilege of serving Christ, not only by believing in him, but also by suffering for him. 30 Now you can take part with me in the battle. It is the same battle you saw me fighting in the past, and as you hear, the one I am fighting still.

Christ's Humility and Greatness

2 Your life in Christ makes you strong, and his love comforts you. You have fellowship with the Spirit, *b* and you have kindness and compassion for one another. 2 I urge you, then, to make me completely happy by having the same thoughts, sharing the same love, and being one in soul and mind. 3 Don't do anything from selfish ambition or from a cheap desire to boast, but be humble towards one another, always considering others better than yourselves. 4 And look out for one another's interests, not just for your own. 5 The attitude you should have is the one that Christ Jesus had:

6 He always had the nature of God,
   but he did not think that by force he should
      try to become *c* equal with God.
7 Instead of this, of his own free will he gave up
      all he had,
   and took the nature of a servant.
He became like man
   and appeared in human likeness.
8 He was humble and walked the path of obedience
      all the way to death—
   his death on the cross.

---

b You have fellowship with the Spirit; *or* The Spirit has brought you into fellowship with one another.
c become; *or* remain.

9 For this reason God raised him to the highest place
above,
and gave him the name that is greater than any
other name.
10 And so, in honour of the name of Jesus
all beings in heaven, on earth, and in the world
below[d]
will fall on their knees,
11 and all will openly proclaim that Jesus Christ is
Lord,
to the glory of God the Father.

Shining as Lights in the World

12 So then, dear friends, as you always obeyed me
when I was with you, it is even more important
that you obey me now while I am away from you.
Keep on working with fear and trembling to complete
your salvation, 13 because God is always at work in
you to make you willing and able to obey his own
purpose.

14 Do everything without complaining or arguing,
15 so that you may be innocent and pure as God's
perfect children, who live in a world of corrupt and
sinful people. You must shine among them like stars
lighting up the sky, 16 as you offer them the message
of life. If you do so, I shall have reason to be proud
of you on the Day of Christ, because it will show
that all my effort and work have not been wasted.

17 Perhaps my life's blood is to be poured out like
an offering on the sacrifice that your faith offers to
God. If that is so, I am glad and share my joy with
you all. 18 In the same way, you too must be glad and
share your joy with me.

Timothy and Epaphroditus

19 If it is the Lord's will, I hope that I will be
able to send Timothy to you soon, so that I may
be encouraged by news about you. 20 He is the only
one who shares my feelings and who really cares
about you. 21 Everyone else is concerned only with

[d] WORLD BELOW: *It was thought that the dead continued to exist
in a dark world under the ground.*

his own affairs, not with the cause of Jesus Christ. 22 And you yourselves know how he has proved his worth, how he and I, like a son and his father, have worked together for the sake of the gospel. 23 So I hope to send him to you as soon as I know how things are going to turn out for me. 24 And I trust in the Lord that I myself will be able to come to you soon.

25 I have thought it necessary to send you our brother Epaphroditus, who has worked and fought by my side and who has served as your messenger in helping me. 26 He is anxious to see you all and is very upset because you had heard that he was ill. 27 Indeed he was ill and almost died. But God had pity on him, and not only on him but on me, too, and spared me an even greater sorrow. 28 I am all the more eager, then, to send him to you, so that you will be glad again when you see him, and my own sorrow will disappear. 29 Receive him, then, with

Receive him...as a brother (2.29)

joy, as a brother in the Lord. Show respect to all such people as he, 30 because he risked his life and nearly died for the sake of the work of Christ, in order to give me the help that you yourselves could not give.

The True Righteousness

3 In conclusion, my brothers, be joyful in your union with the Lord. I don't mind repeating what I have written before, and you will be safer if I do so. ²Watch out for those who do evil things, those dogs, those men who insist on cutting the body. ³It is we, not they, who have received the true circumcision, for we worship God by means of his Spirit and rejoice in our life in union with Christ Jesus. We do not put any trust in external ceremonies. ⁴I could, of course, put my trust in such things. If anyone thinks he can trust in external ceremonies, I have even more reason to feel that way. ⁵I was circumcised when I was a week old. I am an Israelite by birth, of the tribe of Benjamin, a pure-blooded Hebrew. As far as keeping the Jewish Law is concerned, I was a Pharisee, ⁶and I was so zealous that I persecuted the church. As far as a person can be righteous by obeying the commands of the Law, I was without fault. ⁷But all those things that I might count as profit I now reckon as loss for Christ's sake. ⁸Not only those things; I reckon everything as complete loss for the sake of what is so much more valuable, the knowledge of Christ Jesus my Lord. For his sake I have thrown everything away; I consider it all as mere refuse, so that I may gain Christ ⁹and be completely united with him. I no longer have a righteousness of my own, the kind that is gained by obeying the Law. I now have the righteousness that is given through faith in Christ, the righteousness that comes from God and is based on faith. ¹⁰All I want is to know Christ and to experience the power of his resurrection, to share in his sufferings and become like him in his death, ¹¹in the hope that I myself will be raised from death to life.

Running towards the Goal

12 I do not claim that I have already succeeded or have already become perfect. I keep striving to win the prize for which Christ Jesus has already won me to himself. ¹³Of course, my brothers, I really do

not*e* think that I have already won it; the one thing
I do, however, is to forget what is behind me and
do my best to reach what is ahead. ¹⁴So I run straight

I run straight towards the goal (3.14)

towards the goal in order to win the prize, which
is God's call through Christ Jesus to the life above.

15 All of us who are spiritually mature should have
this same attitude. But if some of you have a different
attitude, God will make this clear to you. ¹⁶However
that may be, let us go forward according to the same
rules we have followed until now.

17 Keep on imitating me, my brothers. Pay attention
to those who follow the right example that we have
set for you. ¹⁸I have told you this many times before,
and now I repeat it with tears: there are many whose
lives make them enemies of Christ's death on the
cross. ¹⁹They are going to end up in hell, because
their god is their bodily desires. They are proud of
what they should be ashamed of, and they think only of
things that belong to this world. ²⁰We, however, are
citizens of heaven, and we eagerly wait for our Saviour,
the Lord Jesus Christ, to come from heaven. ²¹He
will change our weak mortal bodies and make them

*e*not; *some manuscripts have* not yet.

Their god is their bodily desires (3.19)

like his own glorious body, using that power by which
he is able to bring all things under his rule.

Instructions

4 So then, my brothers, how dear you are to me
and how I miss you! How happy you make me,
and how proud I am of you! This then, dear brothers, is
how you should stand firm in your life in the Lord.

2 Euodia and Syntyche, please, I beg you, try to
agree as sisters in the Lord. 3 And you too, my faithful
partner, I want you to help these women; for they
have worked hard with me to spread the gospel,
together with Clement and all my other fellow-workers,
whose names are in God's book of the living.

4 May you always be joyful in your union with
the Lord. I say it again: rejoice!

5 Show a gentle attitude towards everyone. The Lord
is coming soon. 6 Don't worry about anything, but
in all your prayers ask God for what you need, always
asking him with a thankful heart. 7 And God's peace,
which is far beyond human understanding, will keep
your hearts and minds safe in union with Christ Jesus.

8 In conclusion, my brothers, fill your minds with
those things that are good and that deserve praise:
things that are true, noble, right, pure, lovely, and
honourable. 9 Put into practice what you learnt and

received from me, both from my words and from my actions. And the God who gives us peace will be with you.

Thanks for the Gift

10 In my life in union with the Lord it is a great joy to me that after so long a time you once more had the chance of showing that you care for me. I don't mean that you had stopped caring for me—you just had no chance to show it. 11 And I am not saying this because I feel neglected, for I have learnt to be satisfied with what I have. 12 I know what it is to be in need and what it is to have more than enough. I have learnt this secret, so that anywhere, at any time, I am content, whether I am full or hungry, whether I have too much or too little. 13 I have the strength to face all conditions by the power that Christ gives me.

14 But it was very good of you to help me in my troubles. 15 You Philippians know very well that when I left Macedonia in the early days of preaching the Good News, you were the only church to help me; you were the only ones who shared my profits and losses. 16 More than once when I needed help in Thessalonica, you sent it to me. 17 It is not that I just want to receive gifts; rather, I want to see profit added to your account. 18 Here, then, is my receipt for everything you have given me—and it has been more than enough! I have all I need now that Epaphroditus has brought me all your gifts. They are like a sweet-smelling offering to God, a sacrifice which is acceptable and pleasing to him. 19 And with all his abundant wealth through Christ Jesus, my God will supply all your needs. 20 To our God and Father be the glory for ever and ever! Amen.

Final Greetings

21 Greetings to each one of God's people who belong to Christ Jesus. The brothers here with me send you their greetings. 22 All God's people here send greetings, especially those who belong to the Emperor's palace.

23 May the grace of the Lord Jesus Christ be with you all.

PAUL'S LETTER TO THE
COLOSSIANS

INTRODUCTION

Paul's Letter to the Colossians was written to the church at Colossae, a town in Asia Minor east of Ephesus. This church had not been established by Paul, but was in an area for which Paul felt responsible, as he sent out workers from Ephesus, the capital of the Roman province of Asia. Paul had learnt that there were false teachers in the church at Colossae who insisted that in order to know God and have full salvation one must worship certain "spiritual rulers and authorities." In addition, these teachers said, one must submit to special rites such as circumcision and must observe strict rules about foods and other matters.

Paul writes to oppose these teachings with the true Christian message. The heart of his reply is that Jesus Christ is able to give full salvation and that these other beliefs and practices actually lead away from him. Through Christ, God created the world and through him he is bringing it back to himself. Only in union with Christ is there hope of salvation for the world. Paul then spells out the implications of this great teaching for the lives of believers.

It is noteworthy that Tychicus, who took this letter to Colossae for Paul, was accompanied by Onesimus, the slave on whose behalf Paul wrote *Philemon*.

Outline of Contents

1 From Paul, who by God's will is an apostle of Christ Jesus, and from our brother Timothy—

2 To God's people in Colossae, who are our faithful brothers in union with Christ:

May God our Father give you grace and peace.

Prayer of Thanksgiving

3 We always give thanks to God, the Father of our Lord Jesus Christ, when we pray for you. 4 For we have heard of your faith in Christ Jesus and of your love for all God's people. 5 When the true message, the Good News, first came to you, you heard about the hope it offers. So your faith and love are based on what you hope for, which is kept safe for you in heaven. 6 The gospel keeps bringing blessings and is spreading throughout the world, just as it has among you ever since the day you first heard about the grace of God and came to know it as it really is. 7 You learnt of God's grace from Epaphras, our dear fellow-servant, who is Christ's faithful worker on our[a] behalf. 8 He has told us of the love that the Spirit has given you.

9 For this reason we have always prayed for you, ever since we heard about you. We ask God to fill you with the knowledge of his will, with all the wisdom and understanding that his Spirit gives. 10 Then you will be able to live as the Lord wants and will always do what pleases him. Your lives will produce all kinds of good deeds, and you will grow in your knowledge of God. 11-12 May you be made strong with all the strength which comes from his glorious power, so that you may be able to endure everything with patience. And with joy give thanks to[b] the Father, who has made you fit to have your share of what God has reserved for his people in the kingdom of light. 13 He rescued us from the power of darkness and brought us safe into the kingdom of his dear Son,

[a] our; *some manuscripts have* your.
[b] with patience. And with joy give thanks to; *or* with patience and joy. And give thanks to.

14 by whom we are set free, that is, our sins are forgiven.

The Person and Work of Christ

15 Christ is the visible likeness of the invisible God. He is the first-born Son, superior to all created things. 16 For through him God created everything in heaven and on earth, the seen and the unseen things, including spiritual powers, lords, rulers, and authorities. God created the whole universe through him and for him. 17 Christ existed before all things, and in union with him all things have their proper place. 18 He is the head of his body, the church; he is the source of the body's life. He is the first-born Son, who was raised from death, in order that he alone might have the first place in all things. 19 For it was by God's own decision that the Son has in himself the full nature of God. 20 Through the Son, then, God decided to bring the whole universe back to himself. God made peace through his Son's sacrificial death on the cross and so brought back to himself all things, both on earth and in heaven.

21 At one time you were far away from God and were his enemies because of the evil things you did and thought. 22 But now, by means of the physical death of his Son, God has made you his friends, in order to bring you, holy, pure, and faultless, into his presence. 23 You must, of course, continue faithful on a firm and sure foundation, and must not allow yourselves to be shaken from the hope you gained when you heard the gospel. It is of this gospel that I, Paul, became a servant—this gospel which has been preached to everybody in the world.

Paul's Work as a Servant of the Church

24 And now I am happy about my sufferings for you, for by means of my physical sufferings I am helping to complete what still remains of Christ's sufferings on behalf of his body, the church. 25 And I have been made a servant of the church by God, who gave me this task to perform for your good. It is the task of fully proclaiming his message, 26 which is the secret he hid through all past ages from all mankind but has now revealed to his people. 27 God's

plan is to make known his secret to his people, this rich and glorious secret which he has for all peoples. And the secret is that Christ is in you, which means that you will share in the glory of God. 28 So we preach Christ to everyone. With all possible wisdom we warn and teach them in order to bring each one into God's presence as a mature individual in union with Christ. 29 To get this done I toil and struggle, using the mighty strength which Christ supplies and which is at work in me.

2 Let me tell you how hard I have worked for you and for the people in Laodicea and for all others who do not know me personally. 2 I do this in order that they may be filled with courage and may be drawn together in love, and so have the full wealth of assurance which true understanding brings. In this way they will know God's secret, which is Christ himself. c 3 He is the key that opens all the hidden treasures of God's wisdom and knowledge.

4 I tell you, then, do not let anyone deceive you with false arguments, no matter how good they seem to be. 5 For even though I am absent in body, yet I am with you in spirit, and I am glad as I see the resolute firmness with which you stand together in your faith in Christ.

Fullness of Life in Christ

6 Since you have accepted Christ Jesus as Lord, live in union with him. 7 Keep your roots deep in him, build your lives on him, and become stronger in your faith, as you were taught. And be filled with thanksgiving.

8 See to it, then, that no one enslaves you by means of the worthless deceit of human wisdom, which comes from the teachings handed down by men and from the ruling spirits of the universe, and not from Christ. 9 For the full content of divine nature lives in Christ, in his humanity, 10 and you have been given full life

c God's secret, which is Christ himself; *some manuscripts have* God's secret; *others have* the secret of God the Father of Christ; *others have* the secret of the God and Father, and of Christ.

in union with him. He is supreme over every spiritual ruler and authority.

11 In union with Christ you were circumcised, not with the circumcision that is made by men, but with the circumcision made by Christ, which consists of being freed from the power of this sinful self. [12] For when you were baptized, you were buried with Christ, and in baptism you were also raised with Christ through your faith in the active power of God, who raised him from death. [13] You were at one time spiritually dead because of your sins and because you were Gentiles without the Law. But God has now brought you to life with Christ. God forgave us all our sins; [14] he cancelled the unfavourable record of our debts with its binding rules and did away with it completely by nailing it to the cross. [15] And on that cross Christ freed himself from the power of the spiritual rulers and authorities;[d] he made a public spectacle of them by leading them as captives in his victory procession.

16 So let no one make rules about what you eat or drink or about holy days or the New Moon Festival or the Sabbath. [17] All such things are only a shadow of things in the future; the reality is Christ. [18] Do not allow yourselves to be condemned by anyone who claims to be superior because of special visions and who insists on false humility and the worship of angels. For no reason at all, such a person is all puffed up by his human way of thinking [19] and has stopped holding on to Christ, who is the head of the body. Under Christ's control the whole body is nourished and held together by its joints and ligaments, and it grows as God wants it to grow.

Dying and Living with Christ

20 You have died with Christ and are set free from the ruling spirits of the universe. Why, then, do you live as though you belonged to this world? Why do you obey such rules as [21] "Don't handle this," "Don't taste that," "Don't touch the other"? [22] All these refer

[d]Christ freed himself from the power of the spiritual rulers and authorities; *or* Christ stripped the spiritual rulers and authorities of their power.

to things which become useless once they are used; they are only man-made rules and teachings. 23 Of course such rules appear to be based on wisdom in their forced worship of angels, and false humility, and severe treatment of the body; but they have no real value in controlling physical passions.

3 You have been raised to life with Christ, so set your hearts on the things that are in heaven, where Christ sits on his throne at the right-hand side of God. 2 Keep your minds fixed on things there, not on things here on earth. 3 For you have died, and your life is hidden with Christ in God. 4 Your real life is Christ and when he appears, then you too will appear with him and share his glory!

The Old Life and the New

5 You must put to death, then, the earthly desires at work in you, such as sexual immorality, indecency, lust, evil passions, and greed (for greed is a form of idolatry). 6 Because of such things God's anger will come upon those who do not obey him.e 7 At one time you yourselves used to live according to such desires, when your life was dominated by them.

8 But now you must get rid of all these things: anger, passion, and hateful feelings. No insults or obscene talk must ever come from your lips. 9 Do not lie to one another, for you have taken off the old self with its habits 10 and have put on the new self. This is the new being which God, its Creator, is constantly renewing in his own image, in order to bring you to a full knowledge of himself. 11 As a result, there is no longer any distinction between Gentiles and Jews, circumcised and uncircumcised, barbarians, savages, slaves, and free men, but Christ is all, Christ is in all.

12 You are the people of God; he loved you and chose you for his own. So then, you must clothe yourselves with compassion, kindness, humility, gentleness, and patience. 13 Be tolerant with one another and forgive one another whenever any of you has

e *Some manuscripts do not have* upon those who do not obey him.

a complaint against someone else. You must forgive one another just as the Lord has forgiven you. [14] And to all these qualities add love, which binds all things together in perfect unity. [15] The peace that Christ gives is to guide you in the decisions you make; for it is to this peace that God has called you together in the one body. And be thankful. [16] Christ's message in all its richness must live in your hearts. Teach and instruct each other with all wisdom. Sing psalms, hymns, and sacred songs; sing to God with thanksgiving in your hearts. [17] Everything you do or say, then, should be done in the name of the Lord Jesus, as you give thanks through him to God the Father.

Personal Relations in the New Life

18 Wives, submit to your husbands, for that is what you should do as Christians.

19 Husbands, love your wives and do not be harsh with them.

20 Children, it is your Christian duty to obey your parents always, for that is what pleases God.

21 Parents, do not irritate your children, or they will become discouraged.

22 Slaves, obey your human masters in all things, not only when they are watching you because you want to gain their approval; but do it with a sincere heart because of your reverence for the Lord. [23] Whatever you do, work at it with all your heart, as though you were working for the Lord and not for men. [24] Remember that the Lord will give you as a reward what he has kept for his people. For Christ is the real Master you serve. [25] And every wrongdoer will be repaid for the wrong things he does, because God judges everyone by the same standard.

4 Masters, be fair and just in the way you treat your slaves. Remember that you too have a Master in heaven.

Instructions

2 Be persistent in prayer, and keep alert as you pray, giving thanks to God. [3] At the same time pray also for us, so that God will give us a good opportunity to preach his message about the secret of Christ. For

that is why I am now in prison. ⁴Pray, then, that I may speak, as I should, in such a way as to make it clear.

5 Be wise in the way you act towards those who are not believers, making good use of every opportunity you have. ⁶Your speech should always be pleasant and interesting, and you should know how to give the right answer to everyone.

Final Greetings

7 Our dear brother Tychicus, who is a faithful worker and fellow-servant in the Lord's work, will give you all the news about me. ⁸That is why I am sending him to you, in order to cheer you up by telling you how all of us are getting on. ⁹With him goes Onesimus, that dear and faithful brother, who belongs to your group. They will tell you everything that is happening here.

10 Aristarchus, who is in prison with me, sends you greetings, and so does Mark, the cousin of Barnabas. (You have already received instructions to welcome Mark if he comes your way.) ¹¹Joshua, also called Justus, sends greetings too. These three are the only Jewish believers who work with me for the Kingdom of God, and they have been a great help to me.

12 Greetings from Epaphras, another member of your group and a servant of Christ Jesus. He always prays fervently for you, asking God to make you stand firm, as mature and fully convinced Christians, in complete obedience to God's will. ¹³I can personally testify to his hard work for you and for the people in Laodicea and Hierapolis. ¹⁴Luke, our dear doctor, and Demas send you their greetings.

15 Give our best wishes to the brothers in Laodicea and to Nympha and the church that meets in her house.ᶠ ¹⁶After you read this letter, make sure that it is read also in the church at Laodicea. At the same time, you are to read the letter that the brothers in Laodicea will send you. ¹⁷And say to Archippus,

ᶠNympha...her house; *some manuscripts have* Nymphas...his house.

"Be sure to finish the task you were given in the Lord's service."

18 With my own hand I write this: *Greetings from Paul.* Do not forget my chains!

May God's grace be with you.

PAUL'S FIRST LETTER TO THE

THESSALONIANS

INTRODUCTION

Thessalonica was the capital city of the Roman province of Macedonia. Paul established a church there after he left Philippi. Soon, however, there was opposition from Jews who were jealous of Paul's success in preaching the Christian message among the non-Jews who had become interested in Judaism. Paul was forced to leave Thessalonica and go on to Berea. Later on, after he reached Corinth, Paul received a personal report from his companion and fellow-worker Timothy about the situation in the church at Thessalonica.

Paul's First Letter to the Thessalonians was then written to encourage and reassure the Christians there. He gives thanks for the news about their faith and love; he reminds them of the kind of life he had lived while he was with them, and then answers questions that had arisen in the church about the return of Christ: Could a believer who died before Christ's return still share in the eternal life that his return will bring? And when will Christ come again? Paul takes this occasion to tell them to go on working quietly while waiting in hope for Christ's return.

Outline of Contents

1 From Paul, Silas, and Timothy—
To the people of the church in Thessalonica, who belong to God the Father and the Lord Jesus Christ:
May grace and peace be yours.

The Life and Faith of the Thessalonians

2 We always thank God for you all and always mention you in our prayers. 3 For we remember before our God and Father how you put your faith into practice, how your love made you work so hard, and how your hope in our Lord Jesus Christ is firm. 4 Our brothers, we know that God loves you and has chosen you to be his own. 5 For we brought the Good News to you, not with words only, but also with power and the Holy Spirit, and with complete conviction of its truth. You know how we lived when we were with you; it was for your own good. 6 You imitated us and the Lord; and even though you suffered much, you received the message with the joy that comes from the Holy Spirit. 7 So you became an example to all believers in Macedonia and Achaia. 8 For not only did the message about the Lord go out from you throughout Macedonia and Achaia, but the news about your faith in God has gone everywhere. There is nothing, then, that we need to say. 9 All those people speak about how you received us when we visited you, and how you turned away from idols to God, to serve the true and living God 10 and to wait for his Son to come from heaven—his Son Jesus, whom he raised from death and who rescues us from God's anger that is coming.

Paul's Work in Thessalonica

2 Our brothers, you yourselves know that our visit to you was not a failure. 2 You know how we had already been ill-treated and insulted in Philippi before we came to you in Thessalonica. And even though there was much opposition, our God gave us courage to tell you the Good News that comes from him. ³Our appeal to you is not based on error or impure motives, nor do we try to trick anyone. ⁴Instead, we always speak as God wants us to, because he has judged us worthy to be entrusted with the Good News. We do not try to please men, but to please God, who tests our motives. ⁵You know very well that we did not come to you with flattering talk, nor did we use words to cover up greed—God is our witness! ⁶We did not try to get praise from anyone, either from you or from others, ⁷even though as apostles of Christ we could have made demands on you. But we were gentle when we were with you, like a mother*a* taking care of her children. ⁸Because of our love for you we were ready to share with you not only the Good News from God but even our own lives. You were so dear to us! ⁹Surely you remember, our brothers, how we worked and toiled! We worked day and night so that we would not be any trouble to you as we preached to you the Good News from God.

10 You are our witnesses, and so is God, that our conduct towards you who believe was pure, right, and without fault. ¹¹You know that we treated each one of you just as a father treats his own children. ¹²We encouraged you, we comforted you, and we kept urging you to live the kind of life that pleases God, who calls you to share in his own Kingdom and glory.

13 And there is another reason why we always give thanks to God. When we brought you God's message, you heard it and accepted it, not as man's message but as God's message, which indeed it is. For God is at work in you who believe. ¹⁴Our brothers, the same things happened to you that happened to the churches of God in Judaea, to the people there who belong to Christ Jesus. You suffered the same persecutions from your own countrymen that they suffered from the Jews, ¹⁵who killed the Lord Jesus and the

---

*a*we were gentle when we were with you, like a mother; *some manuscripts have* we were like children when we were with you; we were like a mother.

prophets, and persecuted us. How displeasing they are to God! How hostile they are to everyone! [16]They even tried to stop us from preaching to the Gentiles the message that would bring them salvation. In this way they have brought to completion all the sins they have always committed. And now God's anger has at last come down on them!

Paul's Desire to Visit Them Again

17 As for us, brothers, when we were separated from you for a little while—not in our thoughts, of course, but only in body—how we missed you and how hard we tried to see you again! [18]We wanted to return to you. I myself tried to go back more than once, but Satan would not let us. [19]After all, it is you—you, no less than others!—who are our hope, our joy, and our reason for boasting of our victory in the presence of our Lord Jesus when he comes. [20]Indeed, you are our pride and our joy!

3 Finally, we could not bear it any longer. So we decided to stay on alone in Athens [2]while we sent Timothy, our brother who works with us for God in preaching the Good News about Christ. We sent him to strengthen you and help your faith, [3]so that none of you should turn back because of these persecutions. You yourselves know that such persecutions are part of God's will for us. [4]For while we were still with you, we told you beforehand that we were going to be persecuted; and as you well know, that is exactly what happened. [5]That is why I had to send Timothy. I could not bear it any longer, so I sent him to find out about your faith. Surely it could not be that the Devil had tempted you and all our work had been for nothing!

6 Now Timothy has come back, and he has brought us the welcome news about your faith and love. He has told us that you always think well of us and that you want to see us just as much as we want to see you. [7]So, in all our trouble and suffering we have been encouraged about you, brothers. It was your faith that encouraged us, [8]because now we really live if you stand firm in your life in union with the Lord. [9]Now we can give thanks to our God for you.

We thank him for the joy we have in his presence because of you. ¹⁰Day and night we ask him with all our heart to let us see you personally and supply what is needed in your faith.

11 May our God and Father himself and our Lord Jesus prepare the way for us to come to you! ¹²May the Lord make your love for one another and for all people grow more and more and become as great as our love for you. ¹³In this way he will strengthen you, and you will be perfect and holy in the presence of our God and Father when our Lord Jesus comes with all who belong to him.*b*

A Life that Pleases God

4 Finally, our brothers, you learnt from us how you should live in order to please God. This is, of course, how you have been living. And now we beg and urge you in the name of the Lord Jesus to do even more. ²For you know the instructions we gave you by the authority of the Lord Jesus. ³God wants you to be holy and completely free from sexual immorality. ⁴Each of you men should know how to live with his wife*c* in a holy and honourable way, ⁵not with a lustful desire, like the heathen who do not know God. ⁶In this matter, then, no man should do wrong to his fellow-Christian or take advantage of him. We have told you this before, and we strongly warned you that the Lord will punish those who do that. ⁷God did not call us to live in immorality, but in holiness. ⁸So then, whoever rejects this teaching is not rejecting man, but God, who gives you his Holy Spirit.

9 There is no need to write to you about love for your fellow-believers. You yourselves have been taught by God how you should love one another. ¹⁰And you have, in fact, behaved like this towards all the brothers in all Macedonia. So we beg you, our brothers, to do even more. ¹¹Make it your aim to live a quiet life, to mind your own business, and to earn your own living, just as we told you before. ¹²In this way

*b*all who belong to him; *or* all his angels.
*c*live with his wife; *or* control his body.

you will win the respect of those who are not believers, and you will not have to depend on anyone for what you need.

The Lord's Coming

13 Our brothers, we want you to know the truth about those who have died, so that you will not be sad, as are those who have no hope. 14 We believe that Jesus died and rose again, and so we believe that God will take back with Jesus those who have died believing in him.

15 What we are teaching you now is the Lord's teaching: we who are alive on the day the Lord comes will not go ahead of those who have died. 16 There will be the shout of command, the archangel's voice, the sound of God's trumpet, and the Lord himself will come down from heaven. Those who have died believing in Christ will rise to life first; 17 then we who are living at that time will be gathered up along with them in the clouds to meet the Lord in the air. And so we will always be with the Lord. 18 So then, encourage one another with these words.

Be Ready for the Lord's Coming

5 There is no need to write to you, brothers, about the times and occasions when these things will happen. 2 For you yourselves know very well that the Day of the Lord will come as a thief comes at night. 3 When people say, "Everything is quiet and safe," then suddenly destruction will hit them! It will come as suddenly as the pains that come upon a woman in labour, and people will not escape. 4 But you, brothers, are not in the darkness, and the Day should not take you by surprise like a thief. 5 All of you are people who belong to the light, who belong to the day. We do not belong to the night or to the darkness. 6 So then, we should not be sleeping like the others; we should be awake and sober. 7 It is at night that people sleep; it is at night that they get drunk. 8 But we belong to the day, and we should be sober. We must wear faith and love as a breastplate, and our hope of salvation as a helmet. 9 God did not choose us to suffer his anger, but to possess

salvation through our Lord Jesus Christ, [10]who died for us in order that we might live together with him, whether we are alive or dead when he comes. [11]And so encourage one another and help one another, just as you are now doing.

Final Instructions and Greetings

12 We beg you, our brothers, to pay proper respect to those who work among you, who guide and instruct you in the Christian life. [13]Treat them with the greatest respect and love because of the work they do. Be at peace among yourselves.

14 We urge you, our brothers, to warn the idle, encourage the timid, help the weak, be patient with everyone. [15]See that no one pays back wrong for wrong, but at all times make it your aim to do good to one another and to all people.

16 Be joyful always, [17]pray at all times, [18]be thankful in all circumstances. This is what God wants from you in your life in union with Christ Jesus.

19 Do not restrain the Holy Spirit; [20]do not despise inspired messages. [21]Put all things to the test: keep what is good [22]and avoid every kind of evil.

23 May the God who gives us peace make you holy in every way and keep your whole being—spirit, soul, and body—free from every fault at the coming of our Lord Jesus Christ. [24]He who calls you will do it, because he is faithful.

25 Pray also for us, brothers.

26 Greet all the believers with a brotherly kiss.

27 I urge you by the authority of the Lord to read this letter to all the believers.

28 The grace of our Lord Jesus Christ be with you.

PAUL'S SECOND LETTER TO THE

THESSALONIANS

INTRODUCTION

Confusion over the expected return of Christ continued
to cause disturbances in the church at Thessalonica.
Paul's Second Letter to the Thessalonians deals with
the belief that the day of the Lord's coming had already
arrived. Paul corrects this idea, pointing out that before
Christ returns, evil and wickedness will reach a climax
under the leadership of a mysterious figure called "the
Wicked One," who would be opposed to Christ.

The apostle emphasizes the need for his readers
to remain steady in their faith in spite of trouble
and suffering, to work for a living as did Paul and
his fellow-workers, and to persevere in doing good.

Outline of Contents

1 From Paul, Silas, and Timothy—
To the people of the church in Thessalonica, who
belong to God our Father and the Lord Jesus Christ:

2 May God our Father and the Lord Jesus Christ
give you grace and peace.

The Judgement at Christ's Coming

3 Our brothers, we must thank God at all times
for you. It is right for us to do so, because your
faith is growing so much and the love each of you

has for the others is becoming greater. [4]That is why we ourselves boast about you in the churches of God. We boast about the way you continue to endure and believe through all the persecutions and sufferings you are experiencing.

5 All of this proves that God's judgement is just and as a result you will become worthy of his Kingdom, for which you are suffering. [6]God will do what is right: he will bring suffering on those who make you suffer, [7]and he will give relief to you who suffer and to us as well. He will do this when the Lord Jesus appears from heaven with his mighty angels, [8]with a flaming fire, to punish those who reject God and who do not obey the Good News about our Lord Jesus. [9]They will suffer the punishment of eternal destruction, separated from the presence of the Lord and from his glorious might, [10]when he comes on that Day to receive glory from all his people and honour from all who believe. You too will be among them, because you have believed the message that we told you.

11 That is why we always pray for you. We ask our God to make you worthy of the life he has called you to live. May he fulfil by his power all your desire for goodness and complete your work of faith. [12]In this way the name of our Lord Jesus will receive glory from you, and you from him, by the grace of our God and of the Lord[a] Jesus Christ.

The Wicked One

2 Concerning the coming of our Lord Jesus Christ and our being gathered together to be with him: I beg you, my brothers, [2]not to be so easily confused in your thinking or upset by the claim that the Day of the Lord has come. Perhaps it is thought that we said this while prophesying or preaching, or that we wrote it in a letter. [3]Do not let anyone deceive you in any way. For the Day will not come until the final Rebellion takes place and the Wicked One appears, who is destined for hell. [4]He will oppose every so-called god or object of worship and will

[a]our God and of the Lord; *or* our God and Lord.

put himself above them all. He will even go in and sit down in God's Temple and claim to be God.

5 Don't you remember? I told you all this while I was with you. ⁶Yet there is something that keeps this from happening now, and you know what it is. At the proper time, then, the Wicked One will appear. ⁷The Mysterious Wickedness is already at work, but what is going to happen will not happen until the one who holds it back is taken out of the way. ⁸Then the Wicked One will be revealed, but when the Lord Jesus comes, he will kill him with the breath from his mouth and destroy him with his dazzling presence. ⁹The Wicked One will come with the power of Satan and perform all kinds of false miracles and wonders, ¹⁰and use every kind of wicked deceit on those who will perish. They will perish because they did not welcome and love the truth so as to be saved. ¹¹And so God sends the power of error to work in them so that they believe what is false. ¹²The result is that all who have not believed the truth, but have taken pleasure in sin, will be condemned.

You Are Chosen for Salvation

13 We must thank God at all times for you, brothers, you whom the Lord loves. For God chose you as the first ᵇ to be saved by the Spirit's power to make you his holy people and by your faith in the truth. ¹⁴God called you to this through the Good News we preached to you; he called you to possess your share of the glory of our Lord Jesus Christ. ¹⁵So then, our brothers, stand firm and hold on to those truths which we taught you, both in our preaching and in our letter.

16 May our Lord Jesus Christ himself and God our Father, who loved us and in his grace gave us unfailing courage and a firm hope, ¹⁷encourage you and strengthen you to always do and say what is good.

Pray for Us

3 Finally, our brothers, pray for us, that the Lord's message may continue to spread rapidly and be

ᵇas the first; *some manuscripts have* from the beginning.

received with honour, just as it was among you. ²Pray also that God will rescue us from wicked and evil people; for not everyone believes the message.

3 But the Lord is faithful, and he will strengthen you and keep you safe from the Evil One. ⁴And the Lord gives us confidence in you, and we are sure that you are doing and will continue to do what we tell you.

5 May the Lord lead you into a greater understanding of God's love and the endurance that is given by Christ.

The Obligation to Work

6 Our brothers, we command you in the name of our Lord Jesus Christ to keep away from all brothers who are living a lazy life and who do not follow the instructions that we gave them. ⁷You yourselves know very well that you should do just what we did. We were not lazy when we were with you. ⁸We did not accept anyone's support without paying for it. Instead, we worked and toiled; we kept working day and night so as not to be an expense to any of you. ⁹We did this, not because we have no right to demand our support; we did it to be an example for you to follow. ¹⁰While we were with you, we used to say to you, "Whoever refuses to work is not allowed to eat."

11 We say this because we hear that there are some people among you who live lazy lives and who do nothing except meddle in other people's business. ¹²In the name of the Lord Jesus Christ we command these people and warn them to lead orderly lives and work to earn their own living.

13 But you, brothers, must not get tired of doing good. ¹⁴It may be that someone there will not obey the message we send you in this letter. If so, take note of him and have nothing to do with him, so that he will be ashamed. ¹⁵But do not treat him as an enemy; instead, warn him as a brother.

Final Words

16 May the Lord Himself, who is our source of

Do not treat him as an enemy (3.15)

peace, give you peace at all times and in every way. The Lord be with you all.

17 With my own hand I write this: *Greetings from Paul.* This is the way I sign every letter; this is how I write.

18 May the grace of our Lord Jesus Christ be with you all.

PAUL'S FIRST LETTER TO
TIMOTHY

INTRODUCTION

Timothy, a young Christian from Asia Minor, was the son of a Jewish mother and a Greek father. He became a companion and assistant to Paul in his missionary work. *Paul's First Letter to Timothy* deals with three main concerns.

The letter is first of all a warning against false teaching in the church. This teaching, a mixture of Jewish and non-Jewish ideas, was based on the belief that the physical world is evil and that one can attain salvation only by special secret knowledge and by

practices such as avoiding certain foods and not marrying. The letter also contains instructions about church administration and worship, with a description of the kind of character that church leaders and helpers should have. Finally, Timothy is advised how to be a good servant of Jesus Christ and about the responsibilities that he has towards various groups of believers.

Outline of Contents

---

1 From Paul, an apostle of Christ Jesus by order of God our Saviour and Christ Jesus our hope—
2 To Timothy, my true son in the faith:
May God the Father and Christ Jesus our Lord give you grace, mercy, and peace.

Warnings against False Teaching

3 I want you to stay in Ephesus, just as I urged you when I was on my way to Macedonia. Some people there are teaching false doctrines, and you must order them to stop. 4 Tell them to give up those legends and those long lists of ancestors, which only produce arguments; they do not serve God's plan, which is known by faith. 5 The purpose of this order is to arouse the love that comes from a pure heart, a clear conscience, and a genuine faith. 6 Some people have turned away from these and have lost their way in foolish discussions. 7 They want to be teachers of God's law, but they do not understand their own words or the matters about which they speak with so much confidence.

8 We know that the Law is good if it is used as it should be used. 9 It must be remembered, of course, that laws are made, not for good people, but for lawbreakers and criminals, for the godless and sinful, for those who are not religious or spiritual,

for those who kill their fathers or mothers, for murderers, 10for the immoral, for sexual perverts, for kidnappers, for those who lie and give false testimony or who do anything else contrary to sound doctrine. 11That teaching is found in the gospel that was entrusted to me to announce, the Good News from the glorious and blessed God.

Gratitude for God's Mercy

12 I give thanks to Christ Jesus our Lord, who has given me strength for my work. I thank him for considering me worthy and appointing me to serve him, 13even though in the past I spoke evil of him and persecuted and insulted him. But God was merciful to me because I -did not yet have faith and so did not know what I was doing. 14And our Lord poured out his abundant grace on me and gave me the faith and love which are ours in union with Christ Jesus. 15This is a true saying, to be completely accepted and believed: Christ Jesus came into the world to save sinners. I am the worst of them, 16but God was merciful to me in order that Christ Jesus might show his full patience in dealing with me, the worst of sinners, as an example for all those who would later believe in him and receive eternal life. 17To the eternal King, immortal and invisible, the only God—to him be honour and glory for ever and ever! Amen.

18 Timothy, my child, I entrust to you this command, which is in accordance with the words of prophecy spoken in the past about you. Use those words as weapons in order to fight well, 19and keep your faith and a clear conscience. Some men have not listened to their conscience and have made a ruin of their faith. 20Among them are Hymenaeus and Alexander, whom I have punished by handing them over to the power of Satan; this will teach them to stop their blasphemy.

Church Worship

2 First of all, then, I urge that petitions, prayers, requests, and thanksgivings be offered to God for all people; 2for kings and all others who are in authority, that we may live a quiet and peaceful life

Christ Jesus came into the world to save sinners (1.15)

with all reverence towards God and with proper conduct. ³This is good and it pleases God our Saviour, ⁴who wants everyone to be saved and to come to know the truth. ⁵For there is one God, and there is one who brings God and mankind together, the man Christ Jesus, ⁶who gave himself to redeem all mankind. That was the proof at the right time that God wants everyone to be saved, ⁷and that is why I was sent as an apostle and teacher of the Gentiles, to proclaim the message of faith and truth. I am not lying; I am telling the truth!

8 In every church service I want the men to pray, men who are dedicated to God and can lift up their hands in prayer without anger or argument. ⁹I also want the women to be modest and sensible about their clothes and to dress properly; not with fancy hair styles or with gold ornaments or pearls or expensive dresses, ¹⁰but with good deeds, as is proper for

women who claim to be religious. [11]Women should learn in silence and all humility. [12]I do not allow them to teach or to have authority over men; they must keep quiet. [13]For Adam was created first, and then Eve. [14]And it was not Adam who was deceived; it was the woman who was deceived and broke God's law. [15]But a woman will be saved through having children,[a] if she perseveres[b] in faith and love and holiness, with modesty.

Leaders in the Church

3 This is a true saying: If a man is eager to be a church leader, he desires an excellent work. [2]A church leader must be without fault; he must have only one wife,[c] be sober, self-controlled, and orderly; he must welcome strangers in his home; he must be able to teach; [3]he must not be a drunkard or a violent man, but gentle and peaceful; he must not love money; [4]he must be able to manage his own family well and make his children obey him with all respect. [5]For if a man does not know how to manage his own family, how can he take care of the church of God? [6]He must be mature in the faith, so that he will not swell up with pride and be condemned, as the Devil was. [7]He should be a man who is respected by the people outside the church, so that he will not be disgraced and fall into the Devil's trap.

Helpers in the Church

[8] Church helpers must also have a good character and be sincere; they must not drink too much wine or be greedy for money; [9]they should hold to the revealed truth of the faith with a clear conscience. [10]They should be tested first, and then, if they pass the test, they are to serve. [11]Their wives[d] also must be of good character and must not gossip; they must

[a]will be saved through having children; *or* will be kept safe through childbirth.
[b]if she perseveres; *or* if they persevere.
[c]have only one wife; *or* be married only once.
[d]Their wives; *or* Women helpers.

be sober and honest in everything. ¹²A church helper must have only one wife,ᵉ and be able to manage his children and family well. ¹³Those helpers who do their work well win for themselves a good standing and are able to speak boldly about their faith in Christ Jesus.

The Great Secret

14 As I write this letter to you, I hope to come and see you soon. ¹⁵But if I am delayed, this letter will let you know how we should conduct ourselves in God's household, which is the church of the living God, the pillar and support of the truth. ¹⁶No one can deny how great is the secret of our religion:

He appeared in human form,
　　was shown to be right by the Spirit,ᶠ
　　　　and was seen by angels.
He was preached among the nations,
　　was believed in throughout the world,
　　　　and was taken up to heaven.

False Teachers

4 The Spirit says clearly that some people will abandon the faith in later times; they will obey lying spirits and follow the teachings of demons. ²Such teachings are spread by deceitful liars, whose consciences are dead, as if burnt with a hot iron. ³Such people teach that it is wrong to marry and to eat certain foods. But God created those foods to be eaten, after a prayer of thanks, by those who are believers and have come to know the truth. ⁴Everything that God has created is good; nothing is to be rejected, but everything is to be received with a prayer of thanks, ⁵because the word of God and the prayer make it acceptable to God.

A Good Servant of Christ Jesus

6 If you give these instructions to the brothers, you will be a good servant of Christ Jesus, as you feed

---

ᵉhave only one wife; *or* be married only once.
ᶠwas shown to be right by the Spirit; *or* and, in spiritual form, was shown to be right.

yourself spiritually on the words of faith and of the true teaching which you have followed. 7 But keep away from those godless legends, which are not worth telling. Keep yourself in training for a godly life. 8 Physical exercise has some value, but spiritual exercise is valuable in every way, because it promises life both for the present and for the future. 9 This is a true saying, to be completely accepted and believed. 10 We struggle[g] and work hard, because we have placed our hope in the living God, who is the Saviour of all and especially of those who believe.

11 Give them these instructions and these teachings. 12 Do not let anyone look down on you because you are young, but be an example for the believers in your speech, your conduct, your love, faith, and purity. 13 Until I come, give your time and effort to the public reading of the Scriptures and to preaching and teaching. 14 Do not neglect the spiritual gift that is in you, which was given to you when the prophets spoke and the elders laid their hands on you. 15 Practise these things and devote yourself to them, in order that your progress may be seen by all. 16 Watch yourself and watch your teaching. Keep on doing these things, because if you do, you will save both yourself and those who hear you.

Responsibilities towards Believers

5 Do not rebuke an older man, but appeal to him as if he were your father. Treat the younger men as your brothers, 2 the older women as mothers, and the younger women as sisters, with all purity.

3 Show respect for widows who really are all alone. 4 But if a widow has children or grandchildren, they should learn first to carry out their religious duties towards their own family and in this way repay their parents and grandparents, because that is what pleases God. 5 A widow who is all alone, with no one to take care of her, has placed her hope in God and continues to pray and ask him for his help night and day. 6 But a widow who gives herself to pleasure has already died, even though she lives. 7 Give them

g struggle; *some manuscripts have* are reviled.

these instructions, so that no one will find fault with them. 8 But if anyone does not take care of his relatives, especially the members of his own family, he has denied the faith and is worse than an unbeliever.

9 Do not add any widow to the list of widows unless she is over sixty years of age. In addition, she must have been married only once[h] 10 and have a reputation for good deeds: a woman who brought up her children well, received strangers in her home, performed humble duties for fellow-Christians, helped people in trouble, and devoted herself to doing good.

11 But do not include younger widows in the list; because when their desires make them want to marry, they turn away from Christ, 12 and so become guilty of breaking their earlier promise to him. 13 They also learn to waste their time in going round from house to house; but even worse, they learn to be gossips and busybodies, talking of things they should not. 14 So I would prefer that the younger widows get married, have children, and take care of their homes, so as to give our enemies no chance of speaking evil of us. 15 For some widows have already turned away to follow Satan. 16 But if any Christian woman has widows in her family, she must take care of them and not put the burden on the church, so that it may take care of the widows who are all alone.

17 The elders who do good work as leaders should be considered worthy of receiving double pay, especially those who work hard at preaching and teaching. 18 For the scripture says, "Do not muzzle an ox when you are using it to thresh corn" and "A worker should be given his pay." 19 Do not listen to an accusation against an elder unless it is brought by two or more witnesses. 20 Rebuke publicly all those who commit sins, so that the rest may be afraid.

21 In the presence of God and of Christ Jesus and of the holy angels I solemnly call upon you to obey these instructions without showing any prejudice or favour to anyone in anything you do. 22 Be in no hurry to lay hands on someone to dedicate him to the Lord's

---

[h] married only once; or faithful to her husband.

service. Take no part in the sins of others; keep
yourself pure.

23 Do not drink water only, but take a little wine
to help your digestion, since you are ill so often.

24 The sins of some people are plain to see, and
their sins go ahead of them to judgement; but the
sins of others are seen only later. 25 In the same way
good deeds are plainly seen, and even those that are
not so plain cannot be hidden.

6 Those who are slaves must consider their masters
worthy of all respect, so that no one will speak
evil of the name of God and of our teaching. 2 Slaves
belonging to Christian masters must not despise them,
for they are their brothers. Instead, they are to serve
them even better, because those who benefit from
their work are believers whom they love.

False Teaching and True Riches

You must teach and preach these things. 3 Whoever
teaches a different doctrine and does not agree with
the true words of our Lord Jesus Christ and with
the teaching of our religion 4 is swollen with pride
and knows nothing. He has an unhealthy desire to
argue and quarrel about words, and this brings on
jealousy, disputes, insults, evil suspicions, 5 and con-
stant arguments from people whose minds do not
function and who no longer have the truth. They
think that religion is a way to become rich.

6 Well, religion does make a person very rich, if
he is satisfied with what he has. 7 What did we bring
into the world? Nothing! What can we take out of
the world? Nothing! 8 So then, if we have food and
clothes, that should be enough for us. 9 But those
who want to get rich fall into temptation and are
caught in the trap of many foolish and harmful desires,
which pull them down to ruin and destruction. 10 For
the love of money is a source of all kinds of evil.
Some have been so eager to have it that they have
wandered away from the faith and have broken their
hearts with many sorrows.

Personal Instructions

11 But you, man of God, avoid all these things.

What did we bring into the world? Nothing! What can we take out of the world? Nothing! (6.7)

Strive for righteousness, godliness, faith, love, endurance, and gentleness. ¹²Run your best in the race of faith, and win eternal life for yourself; for it was to this life that God called you when you firmly professed your faith before many witnesses. ¹³Before God, who gives life to all things, and before Christ Jesus, who firmly professed his faith before Pontius Pilate, I command you ¹⁴to obey your orders and keep them faithfully until the Day when our Lord Jesus Christ will appear. ¹⁵His appearing will be brought about at the right time by God, the blessed and only Ruler, the King of kings and the Lord of lords. ¹⁶He alone is immortal; he lives in the light that no one can approach. No one has ever seen him; no one can ever see him. To him be honour and eternal dominion! Amen.

17 Command those who are rich in the things of this life not to be proud, but to place their hope, not in such an uncertain thing as riches, but in God, who generously gives us everything for our enjoyment. ¹⁸Command them to do good, to be rich in good works, to be generous and ready to share with others. ¹⁹In this way they will store up for themselves a treasure which will be a solid foundation for the future.

And then they will be able to win the life which
is true life.

20 Timothy, keep safe what has been entrusted to
your care. Avoid the profane talk and foolish arguments of what some people wrongly call "Knowledge."
21 For some have claimed to possess it, and as a result
they have lost the way of faith.

God's grace be with you all.

PAUL'S SECOND LETTER TO

TIMOTHY

INTRODUCTION

Paul's Second Letter to Timothy consists largely of
personal advice to Timothy, as a younger colleague
and assistant. The main theme is endurance. Timothy
is advised and encouraged to keep on witnessing faithfully to Jesus Christ, to hold to the true teaching
of the Good News and the Old Testament, and to
do his duty as teacher and evangelist, all in the face
of suffering and opposition.

Timothy is especially warned about the dangers of
becoming involved in "foolish and ignorant arguments"
that do no good, but only ruin the people who listen
to them.

In all this, Timothy is reminded of the example
of the writer's own life and purpose—his faith, patience,
love, endurance, and suffering in persecution.

Outline of Contents

1 From Paul, an apostle of Christ Jesus by God's will, sent to proclaim the promised life which we have in union with Christ Jesus—

2 To Timothy, my dear son:

May God the Father and Christ Jesus our Lord give you grace, mercy, and peace.

Thanksgiving and Encouragement

3 I give thanks to God, whom I serve with a clear conscience, as my ancestors did. I thank him as I remember you always in my prayers night and day. [4]I remember your tears, and I want to see you very much, so that I may be filled with joy. [5]I remember the sincere faith you have, the kind of faith that your grandmother Lois and your mother Eunice also had. I am sure that you have it also. [6]For this reason I remind you to keep alive the gift that God gave you when I laid my hands on you. [7]For the Spirit that God has given us does not make us timid; instead, his Spirit fills us with power, love, and self-control.

8 Do not be ashamed, then, of witnessing for our Lord; nor be ashamed of me, a prisoner for Christ's sake. Instead, take your part in suffering for the Good News, as God gives you the strength to do it. [9]He saved us and called us to be his own people, not because of what we have done, but because of his own purpose and grace. He gave us this grace by means of Christ Jesus before the beginning of time, [10]but now it has been revealed to us through the coming of our Saviour, Christ Jesus. He has ended the power of death and through the gospel has revealed immortal life.

11 God has appointed me as an apostle and teacher to proclaim the Good News, [12]and it is for this reason that I suffer these things. But I am still full of confidence, because I know whom I have trusted, and I am sure that he is able to keep safe until that Day what he has entrusted to me.[a] [13]Hold firmly to the true words that I taught you, as the example for you to follow, and remain in the faith and love

---

[a]what he has entrusted to me; *or* what I have entrusted to him.

that are ours in union with Christ Jesus. 14 Through the power of the Holy Spirit, who lives in us, keep the good things that have been entrusted to you.

15 You know that everyone in the province of Asia, including Phygelus and Hermogenes, has deserted me. 16 May the Lord show mercy to the family of Onesiphorus, because he cheered me up many times. He was not ashamed that I am in prison, 17 but as soon as he arrived in Rome, he started looking for me until he found me. 18 May the Lord grant him his mercy on that Day! And you know very well how much he did for me in Ephesus.

A Loyal Soldier of Christ Jesus

2 As for you, my son, be strong through the grace that is ours in union with Christ Jesus. 2 Take the teachings that you heard me proclaim in the presence of many witnesses, and entrust them to reliable people, who will be able to teach others also.

3 Take your part in suffering, as a loyal soldier of Christ Jesus. 4 A soldier on active service wants to please his commanding officer and so does not get mixed up in the affairs of civilian life. 5 An athlete who runs in a race cannot win the prize unless he obeys the rules. 6 The farmer who has done the hard work should have the first share of the harvest. 7 Think about what I am saying, because the Lord will enable you to understand it all.

8 Remember Jesus Christ, who was raised from death, who was a descendant of David, as is taught in the Good News I preach. 9 Because I preach the Good News, I suffer and I am even chained like a criminal. But the word of God is not in chains, 10 and so I endure everything for the sake of God's chosen people, in order that they too may obtain the salvation that comes through Christ Jesus and brings eternal glory. 11 This is a true saying:

"If we have died with him,
    we shall also live with him.
12 If we continue to endure,
    we shall also rule with him.
If we deny him,
    he also will deny us.

13 If we are not faithful,
    he remains faithful,
    because he cannot be false to himself."

An Approved Worker

14 Remind your people of this, and give them a solemn warning in God's presence not to fight over words. It does no good, but only ruins the people who listen. 15 Do your best to win full approval in God's sight, as a worker who is not ashamed of his work, one who correctly teaches the message of God's truth. 16 Keep away from profane and foolish discussions, which only drive people further away from God. 17 Such teaching is like an open sore that eats away the flesh. Two men who have taught such things are Hymenaeus and Philetus. 18 They have left the way of truth and are upsetting the faith of some believers by saying that our resurrection has already taken place. 19 But the solid foundation that God has laid cannot be shaken; and on it are written these words: "The Lord knows those who are his" and "Whoever says that he belongs to the Lord must turn away from wrongdoing."

20 In a large house there are dishes and bowls of all kinds: some are made of silver and gold, others of wood and clay; some are for special occasions, others for ordinary use. 21 If anyone makes himself clean from all those evil things, he will be used for special purposes, because he is dedicated and useful to his Master, ready to be used for every good deed. 22 Avoid the passions of youth, and strive for righteousness, faith, love, and peace, together with those who with a pure heart call out to the Lord for help. 23 But keep away from foolish and ignorant arguments; you know that they end up in quarrels. 24 The Lord's servant must not quarrel. He must be kind towards all, a good and patient teacher, 25 who is gentle as he corrects his opponents, for it may be that God will give them the opportunity to repent and come to know the truth. 26 And then they will come to their senses and escape from the trap of the Devil, who had caught them and made them obey his will.

The Last Days

3 Remember that there will be difficult times in
the last days. [2] People will be selfish, greedy, boastful, and conceited; they will be insulting, disobedient
to their parents, ungrateful, and irreligious; [3] they will
be unkind, merciless, slanderers, violent, and fierce;
they will hate the good; [4] they will be treacherous,
reckless, and swollen with pride; they will love pleasure
rather than God; [5] they will hold to the outward form
of our religion, but reject its real power. Keep away
from such people. [6] Some of them go into people's
houses and gain control over weak women who are
burdened by the guilt of their sins and driven by
all kinds of desires, [7] women who are always trying
to learn but who can never come to know the truth.
[8] As Jannes and Jambres were opposed to Moses, so
also these people are opposed to the truth—people
whose minds do not function and who are failures
in the faith. [9] But they will not get very far, because
everyone will see how stupid they are. That is just
what happened to Jannes and Jambres.

Last Instructions

10 But you have followed my teaching, my conduct,
and my purpose in life; you have observed my faith,
my patience, my love, my endurance, [11] my persecutions, and my sufferings. You know all that happened
to me in Antioch, Iconium, and Lystra, the terrible
persecutions I endured! But the Lord rescued me from
them all. [12] Everyone who wants to live a godly life
in union with Christ Jesus will be persecuted; [13] and
evil persons and impostors will keep on going from
bad to worse, deceiving others and being deceived
themselves. [14] But as for you, continue in the truths
that you were taught and firmly believe. You know
who your teachers were, [15] and you remember that
ever since you were a child, you have known the
Holy Scriptures, which are able to give you the wisdom
that leads to salvation through faith in Christ Jesus.

[16] All Scripture is inspired by God and is useful [b] for teaching the truth, rebuking error, correcting faults, and giving instruction for right living, [17] so that the person who serves God may be fully qualified and equipped to do every kind of good deed.

4 In the presence of God and of Christ Jesus, who will judge the living and the dead, and because he is coming to rule as King, I solemnly urge you [2] to preach the message, to insist upon proclaiming it (whether the time is right or not), to convince, reproach, and encourage, as you teach with all patience. [3] The time will come when people will not listen to sound doctrine, but will follow their own desires and will collect for themselves more and more teachers who will tell them what they are itching to hear. [4] They will turn away from listening to the truth and give their attention to legends. [5] But you must keep control of yourself in all circumstances; endure suffering, do the work of a preacher of the Good News, and perform your whole duty as a servant of God.

[6] As for me, the hour has come for me to be sacrificed; the time is here for me to leave this life. [7] I have done my best in the race, I have run the full distance, and I have kept the faith. [c] [8] And now there is waiting for me the victory prize of being put right with God, which the Lord, the righteous Judge, will give me on that Day—and not only to me, but to all those who wait with love for him to appear.

Personal Words

[9] Do your best to come to me soon. [10] Demas fell in love with this present world and has deserted me, going off to Thessalonica. Crescens went to Galatia, and Titus to Dalmatia. [11] Only Luke is with me. Get Mark and bring him with you, because he can help me in the work. [12] I sent Tychicus to Ephesus. [13] When you come, bring my coat that I left in Troas with

---

[b] All Scripture is inspired by God and is useful; *or* Every scripture inspired by God is also useful.
[c] kept the faith; *or* been true to my promise.

The prize which the Lord...will give me on that Day (4.8)

Carpus; bring the books too, and especially the ones made of parchment.

14 Alexander the metal-worker did me much harm; the Lord will reward him according to what he has done. 15 Be on your guard against him yourself, because he was violently opposed to our message.

16 No one stood by me the first time I defended myself; all deserted me. May God not count it against them! 17 But the Lord stayed with me and gave me strength, so that I was able to proclaim the full message for all the Gentiles to hear; and I was rescued from being sentenced to death. 18 And the Lord will rescue me from all evil and take me safely into his heavenly Kingdom. To him be the glory for ever and ever! Amen.

Final Greetings

19 I send greetings to Priscilla and Aquila and to the family of Onesiphorus. 20 Erastus stayed in Corinth, and I left Trophimus in Miletus, because he was ill. 21 Do your best to come before winter.

Eubulus, Pudens, Linus, and Claudia send their greetings, and so do all the other Christian brothers.

22 The Lord be with your spirit.

God's grace be with you all.

PAUL'S LETTER TO

TITUS

INTRODUCTION

Titus was a Gentile convert to Christianity who became a fellow-worker and assistant to Paul in his missionary work. *Paul's Letter to Titus* is addressed to his young helper in Crete, who had been left there to supervise the work of the church. The letter expresses three main concerns.

First, Titus is reminded of the kind of character that church leaders should have, especially in view of the bad character of many Cretans. Next, Titus is advised how to teach the various groups in the church, the older men, the older women (who are, in turn, to teach the younger women), the young men, and the slaves. Finally, the writer gives Titus advice regarding Christian conduct, especially the need to be peaceful and friendly, and to avoid hatred, argument, and division in the church.

Outline of Contents

1 From Paul, a servant of God and an apostle of Jesus Christ.

I was chosen and sent to help the faith of God's chosen people and to lead them to the truth taught by our religion, [2] which is based on the hope for eternal life. God, who does not lie, promised us this life before the beginning of time, [3] and at the right time he revealed it in his message. This was entrusted to me, and I proclaim it by order of God our Saviour.

4 I write to Titus, my true son in the faith that we have in common.

May God the Father and Christ Jesus our Saviour give you grace and peace.

Titus' Work in Crete

5 I left you in Crete, so that you could put in order the things that still needed doing and appoint church elders in every town. Remember my instructions: [6] an elder must be blameless; he must have only one wife,[a] and his children must be believers and not have the reputation of being wild or disobedient. [7] For since a church leader is in charge of God's work, he should be blameless. He must not be arrogant or quick-tempered, or a drunkard or violent or greedy for money. [8] He must be hospitable and love what is good. He must be self-controlled, upright, holy, and disciplined. [9] He must hold firmly to the message which can be trusted and which agrees with the doctrine. In this way he will be able to encourage others with the true teaching and also to show the error of those who are opposed to it.

10 For there are many, especially converts from Judaism, who rebel and deceive others with their nonsense. [11] It is necessary to stop their talk, because they are upsetting whole families by teaching what they should not, and all for the shameful purpose of making money. [12-13] It was a Cretan himself, one of their own prophets, who spoke the truth when he said, "Cretans are always liars, wicked beasts, and lazy gluttons." For this reason you must rebuke them sharply, so that they may have a healthy faith [14] and no longer hold on to Jewish legends and to human commandments which come from people who have rejected the truth. [15] Everything

---

[a] have only one wife; or be married only once.

is pure to those who are themselves pure; but nothing is pure to those who are defiled and unbelieving, for their minds and consciences have been defiled. 16They claim that they know God, but their actions deny it. They are hateful and disobedient, not fit to do anything good.

Sound Doctrine

2 But you must teach what agrees with sound doctrine. 2Instruct the older men to be sober, sensible, and self-controlled; to be sound in their faith, love, and endurance. 3In the same way instruct the older women to behave as women should who live a holy life. They must not be slanderers or slaves to wine. They must teach what is good, 4in order to train the younger women to love their husbands and children, 5to be self-controlled and pure, and to be good housewives who submit to their husbands, so that no one will speak evil of the message that comes from God.

6 In the same way urge the young men to be self-controlled. 7In all things you yourself must be an example of good behaviour. Be sincere and serious in your teaching. 8Use sound words that cannot be criticized, so that your enemies may be put to shame by not having anything bad to say about us.

9 Slaves are to submit to their masters and please them in all things. They must not answer them back 10or steal from them. Instead, they must show that they are always good and faithful, so as to bring credit to the teaching about God our Saviour in all they do.

11 For God has revealed his grace for the salvation of all mankind. 12That grace instructs us to give up ungodly living and worldly passions, and to live self-controlled, upright, and godly lives in this world, 13as we wait for the blessed Day we hope for, when the glory of our great God and Saviour Jesus Christ*b* will appear. 14He gave himself for us, to rescue us

*b*our great God and Saviour Jesus Christ; *or* the great God and our Saviour Jesus Christ.

from all wickedness and to make us a pure people who belong to him alone and are eager to do good.

15 Teach these things and use your full authority as you encourage and rebuke your hearers. Let none of them look down on you.

Christian Conduct

3 Remind your people to submit to rulers and authorities, to obey them, and to be ready to do good in every way. [2]Tell them not to speak evil of anyone, but to be peaceful and friendly, and always to show a gentle attitude towards everyone. [3]For we ourselves were once foolish, disobedient, and wrong. We were slaves to passions and pleasures of all kinds. We spent our lives in malice and envy; others hated us and we hated them. [4]But when the kindness and love of God our Saviour was revealed, [5]he saved us. It was not because of any good deeds that we ourselves had done, but because of his own mercy that he saved us, through the Holy Spirit, who gives us new birth and new life by washing us. [6]God poured out the Holy Spirit abundantly on us through Jesus Christ our Saviour, [7]so that by his grace we might be put right with God and come into possession of the eternal life we hope for. [8]This is a true saying.

I want you to give special emphasis to these matters, so that those who believe in God may be concerned with giving their time to doing good deeds, which are good and useful for everyone. [9]But avoid stupid arguments, long lists of ancestors, quarrels, and fights about the Law. They are useless and worthless. [10]Give at least two warnings to the person who causes divisions, and then have nothing more to do with him. [11]You know that such a person is corrupt, and his sins prove that he is wrong.

Final Instructions

12 When I send Artemas or Tychicus to you, do your best to come to me in Nicopolis, because I have decided to spend the winter there. [13]Do your best to help Zenas the lawyer and Apollos to get started on their travels, and see to it that they have everything they need. [14]Our people must learn to spend their

time doing good, in order to provide for real needs; they should not live useless lives.

15 All who are with me send you greetings. Give our greetings to our friends in the faith.

God's grace be with you all.

PAUL'S LETTER TO
PHILEMON

INTRODUCTION

Philemon was a prominent Christian, probably a member of the church at Colossae and the owner of a slave named Onesimus. This slave had run away from his master, and then somehow he had come in contact with Paul, who was then in prison. Through Paul, Onesimus became a Christian. *Paul's Letter to Philemon* is an appeal to Philemon to be reconciled to his slave, whom Paul is sending back to him, and to welcome him not only as a forgiven slave but as a Christian brother.

Outline of Contents

1 From Paul, a prisoner for the sake of Christ Jesus, and from our brother Timothy—

To our friend and fellow-worker Philemon, 2 and the church that meets in your house, and our sister Apphia, and our fellow-soldier Archippus:

3 May God our Father and the Lord Jesus Christ give you grace and peace.

Philemon's Love and Faith

4 Brother Philemon, every time I pray, I mention you and give thanks to my God. 5 For I hear of your love for all God's people and the faith you have in the Lord Jesus. 6 My prayer is that our fellowship with you as believers will bring about a deeper understanding of every blessing which we have in our life in union with Christ. 7 Your love, dear brother, has brought me great joy and much encouragement! You have cheered the hearts of all God's people.

A Request for Onesimus

8 For this reason I could be bold enough, as your brother in Christ, to order you to do what should be done. 9 But because I love you, I make a request instead. I do this even though I am Paul, the ambassador of Christ Jesus, and at present also a prisoner for his sake.[a] 10 So I make a request to you on behalf of Onesimus, who is my own son in Christ; for while in prison I have become his spiritual father. 11 At one time he was of no use to you, but now he is useful[b] both to you and to me.

12 I am sending him back to you now, and with him goes my heart. 13 I would like to keep him here with me, while I am in prison for the gospel's sake, so that he could help me in your place. 14 However, I do not want to force you to help me; rather, I would like you to do it of your own free will. So I will not do anything unless you agree.

15 It may be that Onesimus was away from you for a short time so that you might have him back for all time. 16 And now he is not just a slave, but much more than a slave: he is a dear brother in Christ. How much he means to me! And how much more he will mean to you, both as a slave and as a brother in the Lord!

17 So, if you think of me as your partner, welcome him back just as you would welcome me. 18 If he

[a] the ambassador of Christ Jesus, and at present also a prisoner for his sake; or an old man, and at present a prisoner for the sake of Christ Jesus.
[b] The Greek name Onesimus means "useful".

Welcome him back (17)

has done you any wrong or owes you anything, charge it to my account. ¹⁹Here, I will write this with my own hand: *I, Paul, will pay you back.* (I should not have to remind you, of course, that you owe your very self to me.) ²⁰So, my brother, please do me this favour for the Lord's sake; as a brother in Christ, cheer me up!

21 I am sure, as I write this, that you will do what I ask—in fact I know that you will do even more. ²²At the same time, get a room ready for me, because I hope that God will answer the prayers of all of you and give me back to you.

Final Greetings

23 Epaphras, who is in prison with me for the sake of Christ Jesus, sends you his greetings, ²⁴and so do my fellow-workers Mark, Aristarchus, Demas, and Luke.

25 May the grace of the Lord Jesus Christ be with you all.

THE LETTER TO THE
HEBREWS

INTRODUCTION

The Letter to the Hebrews was written to a group of Christians who, faced with increasing opposition, were in danger of abandoning the Christian faith. The writer encourages them in their faith primarily by showing that Jesus Christ is the true and final revelation of God. In doing this he emphasizes three truths: (1) Jesus is the eternal Son of God, who learnt true obedience to the Father through the suffering that he endured. As the Son of God, Jesus is superior to the prophets of the Old Testament, to the angels, and to Moses himself. (2) Jesus has been declared by God to be an eternal priest, superior to the priests of the Old Testament. (3) Through Jesus the believer is saved from sin, fear, and death; and Jesus, as High Priest, provides the true salvation, which was only foreshadowed by the rituals and animal sacrifices of the Hebrew religion.

By citing the example of the faith of some famous persons in Israel's history (chapter 11), the writer appeals to his readers to remain faithful, and in chapter 12 he urges his readers to continue faithful to the end, with eyes fixed on Jesus, and to endure whatever suffering and persecution may come to them. The book closes with words of advice and warning.

Outline of Contents

God's Word through His Son

1 In the past, God spoke to our ancestors many times and in many ways through the prophets, ²but in these last days he has spoken to us through his Son. He is the one through whom God created the universe, the one whom God has chosen to possess all things at the end. ³He reflects the brightness of God's glory and is the exact likeness of God's own being, sustaining the universe with his powerful word. After achieving forgiveness for the sins of mankind, he sat down in heaven at the right-hand side of God, the Supreme Power.

The Greatness of God's Son

4 The Son was made greater than the angels, just as the name that God gave him is greater than theirs. ⁵For God never said to any of his angels,

"You are my Son;
    today I have become your Father."

Nor did God say about any angel,

"I will be his Father,
    and he will be my Son."

⁶But when God was about to send his first-born Son into the world, he said,

"All God's angels must worship him."

⁷But about the angels God said,

"God makes his angels winds,
    and his servants flames of fire."

⁸About the Son, however, God said:

"Your kingdom, O God, will last *a* for ever and ever!
    You rule over your *b* people with justice.

⁹ You love what is right and hate what is wrong.

---

*a*Your kingdom, O God, will last; *or* God is your kingdom.
*b*Your; *some manuscripts have* his.

That is why God, your God, has chosen you
and has given you the joy of an honour far greater
than he gave to your companions."

10 He also said,
"You, Lord, in the beginning created the earth,
and with your own hands you made the heavens.
11 They will disappear, but you will remain;
they will all wear out like clothes.
12 You will fold them up like a coat,
and they will be changed like clothes.
But you are always the same,
and your life never ends."
13 God never said to any of his angels:
"Sit here on my right
until I put your enemies
as a footstool under your feet."

14 What are the angels, then? They are spirits who serve God and are sent by him to help those who are to receive salvation.

The Great Salvation

2 That is why we must hold on all the more firmly to the truths we have heard, so that we will not be carried away. 2 The message given to our ancestors by the angels was shown to be true, and anyone who did not follow it or obey it received the punishment he deserved. 3 How, then, shall we escape if we pay no attention to such a great salvation? The Lord himself first announced this salvation, and those who heard him proved to us that it is true. 4 At the same time God added his witness to theirs by performing all kinds of miracles and wonders and by distributing the gifts of the Holy Spirit according to his will.

The One Who Leads Us to Salvation

5 God has not placed the angels as rulers over the new world to come—the world of which we speak. 6 Instead, as it is said somewhere in the Scriptures:
"What is man, O God, that you should think of
him;
mere man, that you should care for him?
7 You made him for a little while lower than the
angels;

you crowned him with glory and honour, *c*

8   and made him ruler over all things."

It says that God made man "ruler over all things"; this clearly includes everything. We do not, however, see man ruling over all things now. 9But we do see Jesus, who for a little while was made lower than the angels, so that through God's grace he should die for everyone. We see him now crowned with glory and honour because of the death he suffered. 10It was only right that God, who creates and preserves all things, should make Jesus perfect through suffering, in order to bring many sons to share his glory. For Jesus is the one who leads them to salvation.

11 He purifies people from their sins, and both he and those who are made pure all have the same Father. That is why Jesus is not ashamed to call them his brothers. 12He says to God,

"I will tell my brothers what you have done;
     I will praise you in their meeting."

13He also says, "I will put my trust in God." And he also says, "Here I am with the children that God has given me."

14 Since the children, as he calls them, are people of flesh and blood, Jesus himself became like them and shared their human nature. He did this so that through his death he might destroy the Devil, who has the power over death, 15and in this way set free those who were slaves all their lives because of their fear of death. 16For it is clear that it is not the angels that he helps. Instead, as the scripture says, "He helps the descendants of Abraham." 17This means that he had to become like his brothers in every way, in order to be their faithful and merciful High Priest in his service to God, so that the people's sins would be forgiven. 18And now he can help those who are tempted, because he himself was tempted and suffered.

---

c Many manuscripts add: You made him ruler over everything you made *(see Ps 8.6).*

Jesus Is Greater than Moses

3 My Christian brothers, who also have been called by God! Think of Jesus, whom God sent to be the High Priest of the faith we profess. ²He was faithful to God, who chose him to do this work, just as Moses was faithful in his work in God's house. ³A man who builds a house receives more honour than the house itself. In the same way Jesus is worthy of much greater honour than Moses. ⁴Every house, of course, is built by someone—and God is the one who has built all things. ⁵Moses was faithful in God's house as a servant, and he spoke of the things that God would say in the future. ⁶But Christ is faithful as the Son in charge of God's house. We are his house if we keep up our courage and our confidence in what we hope for.

A Rest for God's People

7 So then, as the Holy Spirit says,
  "If you hear God's voice today,
8   do not be stubborn, as your ancestors were when
        they rebelled against God,
      as they were that day in the desert
      when they put him to the test.
⁹ There they put me to the test and tried me, says
        God,
      although they had seen what I did for forty years.
¹⁰ And so I was angry with those people and said,
      'They are always disloyal
      and refuse to obey my commands.'
¹¹ I was angry and made a solemn promise:
      'They will never enter the land where I would
        have given them rest!' "

12 My fellow-believers, be careful that no one among you has a heart so evil and unbelieving that he will turn away from the living God. ¹³Instead, in order that none of you be deceived by sin and become stubborn, you must help one another every day, as long as the word "Today" in the scripture applies to us. ¹⁴For we are all partners with Christ if we hold firmly to the end the confidence we had at the beginning.

15 This is what the scripture says:

"If you hear God's voice today,
do not be stubborn, as your ancestors were
when they rebelled against God."

16 Who were the people who heard God's voice and rebelled against him? All those who were led out of Egypt by Moses. 17 With whom was God angry for forty years? With the people who sinned, who fell down dead in the desert. 18 When God made his solemn promise, "They will never enter the land where I would have given them rest"—of whom was he speaking? Of those who rebelled. 19 We see, then, that they were not able to enter the land, because they did not believe.

4 Now, God has offered us the promise that we may receive that rest he spoke about. Let us take care, then, that none of you will be found to have failed to receive that promised rest. 2 For we have heard the Good News, just as they did. They heard the message, but it did them no good, because when they heard it, they did not accept it with faith. 3 We who believe, then, do receive that rest which God promised. It is just as he said,

"I was angry and made a solemn promise:
'They will never enter the land where I would
have given them rest!' "

He said this even though his work had been finished from the time he created the world. 4 For somewhere in the Scriptures this is said about the seventh day: "God rested on the seventh day from all his work." 5 This same matter is spoken of again: "They will never enter that land where I would have given them rest." 6 Those who first heard the Good News did not receive that rest, because they did not believe. There are, then, others who are allowed to receive it. 7 This is shown by the fact that God sets another day, which is called "Today." Many years later he spoke of it through David in the scripture already quoted:

"If you hear God's voice today,
do not be stubborn."

8 If Joshua had given the people the rest that God had promised, God would not have spoken later about another day. 9 As it is, however, there still remains

for God's people a rest like God's resting on the seventh day. [10] For whoever receives that rest which God promised will rest from his own work, just as God rested from his. [11] Let us, then, do our best to receive that rest, so that no one of us will fail as they did because of their lack of faith.

12 The word of God is alive and active, sharper than any double-edged sword. It cuts all the way through, to where soul and spirit meet, to where joints and marrow come together. It judges the desires and thoughts of man's heart. [13] There is nothing that can be hidden from God; everything in all creation is exposed and lies open before his eyes. And it is to him that we must all give an account of ourselves.

Jesus the Great High Priest

14 Let us, then, hold firmly to the faith we profess. For we have a great High Priest who has gone into the very presence of God—Jesus, the Son of God. [15] Our High Priest is not one who cannot feel sympathy for our weaknesses. On the contrary, we have a High Priest who was tempted in every way that we are, but did not sin. [16] Let us have confidence, then, and approach God's throne, where there is grace. There we will receive mercy and find grace to help us just when we need it.

5 Every high priest is chosen from his fellow-men and appointed to serve God on their behalf, to offer sacrifices and offerings for sins. [2] Since he himself is weak in many ways, he is able to be gentle with those who are ignorant and make mistakes. [3] And because he is himself weak, he must offer sacrifices not only for the sins of the people but also for his own sins. [4] No one chooses for himself the honour of being a high priest. It is only by God's call that a man is made a high priest—just as Aaron was.

5 In the same way, Christ did not take upon himself the honour of being a high priest. Instead, God said to him,

"You are my Son;
today I have become your Father."

[6] He also said in another place,

"You will be a priest for ever,

in the priestly order of Melchizedek." c

7 In his life on earth Jesus made his prayers and requests with loud cries and tears to God, who could save him from death. Because he was humble and devoted, God heard him. 8But even though he was God's Son, he learnt through his sufferings to be obedient. 9When he was made perfect, he became the source of eternal salvation for all those who obey him, 10and God declared him to be high priest, in the priestly order of Melchizedek. c

Warning against Abandoning the Faith

11 There is much we have to say about this matter, but it is hard to explain to you, because you are so slow to understand. 12There has been enough time for you to be teachers—yet you still need someone to teach you the first lessons of God's message. Instead of eating solid food, you still have to drink milk. 13Anyone who has to drink milk is still a child, without any experience in the matter of right and wrong. 14Solid food, on the other hand, is for adults, who through practice are able to distinguish between good and evil.

6 Let us go forward, then, to mature teaching and leave behind us the first lessons of the Christian message. We should not lay again the foundation of turning away from useless works and believing in God; 2of the teaching about baptismsd and the laying on of hands; of the resurrection of the dead and the eternal judgement. 3Let us go forward! And this is what we will do, if God allows.

4 For how can those who abandon their faith be brought back to repent again? They were once in God's light; they tasted heaven's gift and received their share of the Holy Spirit; 5they knew from experience that God's word is good, and they had felt the powers of the coming age. 6And then they abandoned their faith! It is impossible to bring them back to repent again, because they are again crucifying the Son of God and exposing him to public shame.

7 God blesses the soil which drinks in the rain that

---

cin...Melchizedek; or like Melchizedek; or in the line of succession to Melchizedek.
dbaptisms; or purification ceremonies.

often falls on it and which grows plants that are useful to those for whom it is cultivated. [8]But if it grows thorns and weeds, it is worth nothing; it is in danger of being cursed by God and will be destroyed by fire.

9 But even if we speak like this, dear friends, we feel sure about you. We know that you have the better blessings that belong to your salvation. [10]God is not unfair. He will not forget the work you did or the love you showed for him in the help you gave and are still giving to your fellow-Christians. [11]Our great desire is that each one of you keep up his eagerness to the end, so that the things you hope for will come true. [12]We do not want you to become lazy, but to be like those who believe and are patient, and so receive what God has promised.

God's Sure Promise

13 When God made his promise to Abraham, he made a vow to do what he had promised. Since there was no one greater than himself, he used his own name when he made his vow. [14]He said, "I promise you that I will bless you and give you many descendants." [15]Abraham was patient, and so he received what God had promised. [16]When a person makes a vow, he uses the name of someone greater than himself, and the vow settles all arguments. [17]To those who were to receive what he promised, God wanted to make it very clear that he would never change his purpose; so he added his vow to the promise. [18]There are these two things, then, that cannot change and about which God cannot lie. So we who have found safety with him are greatly encouraged to hold firmly to the hope placed before us. [19]We have this hope as an anchor for our lives. It is safe and sure, and goes through the curtain of the heavenly temple into the inner sanctuary. [20]On our behalf Jesus has gone in there before us, and has become a high priest for ever, in the priestly order of Melchizedek.[e]

The Priest Melchizedek

7 This Melchizedek was king of Salem and a priest of the Most High God. As Abraham was coming

[e]in...Melchizedek (see 5.6).

back from the battle in which he defeated the four kings, Melchizedek met him and blessed him, ²and Abraham gave him a tenth of all he had taken. (The first meaning of Melchizedek's name is "King of Righteousness"; and because he was king of Salem, his name also means "King of Peace.") ³There is no record of Melchizedek's father or mother or of any of his ancestors; no record of his birth or of his death. He is like the Son of God; he remains a priest for ever.

4 You see, then, how great he was. Abraham, our famous ancestor, gave him a tenth of all he got in the battle. ⁵And those descendants of Levi who are priests are commanded by the Law to collect a tenth from the people of Israel, that is, from their own countrymen, even though their countrymen are also descendants of Abraham. ⁶Melchizedek was not descended from Levi, but he collected a tenth from Abraham and blessed him, the man who received God's promises. ⁷There is no doubt that the one who blesses is greater than the one who is blessed. ⁸In the case of the priests the tenth is collected by men who die; but as for Melchizedek the tenth was collected by one who lives, as the scripture says. ⁹And, so to speak, when Abraham paid the tenth, Levi (whose descendants collect the tenth) also paid it. ¹⁰For Levi had not yet been born, but was, so to speak, in the body of his ancestor Abraham when Melchizedek met him.

11 It was on the basis of the levitical priesthood that the Law was given to the people of Israel. Now, if the work of the levitical priests had been perfect, there would have been no need for a different kind of priest to appear, one who is in the priestly order of Melchizedek,ᵉ not of Aaron. ¹²For when the priesthood is changed, there also has to be a change in the law. ¹³And our Lord, of whom these things are said, belonged to a different tribe, and no member of his tribe ever served as a priest. ¹⁴It is well known that he was born a member of the tribe of Judah; and Moses did not mention this tribe when he spoke of priests.

Another Priest, like Melchizedek

15 The matter becomes even plainer; a different priest has appeared, who is like Melchizedek. [16] He was made a priest, not by human rules and regulations, but through the power of a life which has no end. [17] For the scripture says, "You will be a priest for ever, in the priestly order of Melchizedek." [e] [18] The old rule, then, is set aside, because it was weak and useless. [19] For the Law of Moses could not make anything perfect. And now a better hope has been provided through which we come near to God.

20 In addition, there is also God's vow. There was no such vow when the others were made priests. [21] But Jesus became a priest by means of a vow when God said to him,

"The Lord has made a solemn promise
  and will not take it back:
  'You will be a priest for ever.' "

[22] This difference, then, also makes Jesus the guarantee of a better covenant.

23 There is another difference: there were many of those other priests, because they died and could not continue their work. [24] But Jesus lives on for ever, and his work as priest does not pass on to someone else. [25] And so he is able, now and always, to save those who come to God through him, because he lives for ever to plead with God for them.

26 Jesus, then, is the High Priest that meets our needs. He is holy; he has no fault or sin in him; he has been set apart from sinners and raised above the heavens. [27] He is not like other high priests; he does not need to offer sacrifices every day for his own sins first and then for the sins of the people. He offered one sacrifice, once and for all, when he offered himself. [28] The Law of Moses appoints men who are imperfect to be high priests; but God's promise made with the vow, which came later than the Law, appoints the Son, who has been made perfect for ever.

Jesus Our High Priest

8 The whole point of what we are saying is that we have such a High Priest, who sits at the

[e] in...Melchizedek (see 5.6).

right of tne throne of the Divine Majesty in heaven.
² He serves as High Priest in the Most Holy Place,
that is, in the real tent which was put up by the
Lord, not by man.

3 Every High Priest is appointed to present offerings
and animal sacrifices to God, and so our High Priest
must also have something to offer. ⁴ If he were on
earth, he would not be a priest at all, since there
are priests who offer the gifts required by the Jewish
Law. ⁵ The work they do as priests is really only
a copy and a shadow of what is in heaven. It is the
same as it was with Moses. When he was about to
build the Covenant Tent, God said to him, "Be sure
to make everything according to the pattern you were
shown on the mountain." ⁶ But now, Jesus has been
given priestly work which is superior to theirs, just
as the covenant which he arranged between God and
his people is a better one, because it is based on
promises of better things.

7 If there had been nothing wrong with the first
covenant, there would have been no need for a second
one. ⁸ But God finds fault with his people when he
says,

"The days are coming, says the Lord,
    when I will draw up a new covenant with the
        people of Israel and with the people of Judah.
⁹ It will not be like the covenant that I made with
        their ancestors
    on the day I took them by the hand and led
        them out of Egypt.
They were not faithful to the covenant I made with
        them,
    and so I paid no attention to them.
¹⁰ Now, this is the covenant that I will make with
        the people of Israel
    in the days to come, says the Lord:
I will put my laws in their minds
    and write them on their hearts.
I will be their God,
    and they will be my people.
¹¹ None of them will have to teach his fellow-citizen
        or say to his fellow-countryman,
    'Know the Lord.'

For they will all know me,
from the least to the greatest.
12 I will forgive their sins
and will no longer remember their wrongs."
13 By speaking of a new covenant, God has made the first one old; and anything that becomes old and worn out will soon disappear.

Earthly and Heavenly Worship

9 The first covenant had rules for worship and a man-made place for worship as well. 2 A Tent was put up, the outer one, which was called the Holy Place. In it were the lampstand and the table with the bread offered to God. 3 Behind the second curtain was the Tent called the Most Holy Place. 4 In it were the gold altar for the burning of incense and the Covenant Box all covered with gold and containing the gold jar with the manna in it, Aaron's stick that had sprouted leaves, and the two stone tablets with the commandments written on them. 5 Above the Box were the winged creatures representing God's presence, with their wings spread over the place where sins were forgiven. But now is not the time to explain everything in detail.

6 This is how those things have been arranged. The priests go into the outer Tent every day to perform their duties, 7 but only the High Priest goes into the inner Tent, and he does so only once a year. He takes with him blood which he offers to God on behalf of himself and for the sins which the people have committed without knowing they were sinning. 8 The Holy Spirit clearly teaches from all these arrangements that the way into the Most Holy Place has not yet been opened as long as the outer Tent still stands. 9 This is an illustration which points to the present time. It means that the offerings and animal sacrifices presented to God cannot make the worshipper's heart perfect, 10 since they have to do only with food, drink, and various purification ceremonies. These are all outward rules, which apply only until the time when God will establish the new order.

11 But Christ has already come as the High Priest

of the good things that are already here.[e] The tent in which he serves is greater and more perfect; it is not a man-made tent, that is, it is not a part of this created world. [12] When Christ went through the tent and entered once and for all into the Most Holy Place, he did not take the blood of goats and bulls to offer as a sacrifice; rather, he took his own blood and obtained eternal salvation for us. [13] The blood of goats and bulls and the ashes of a burnt calf are sprinkled on the people who are ritually unclean, and this purifies them by taking away their ritual impurity. [14] Since this is true, how much more is accomplished by the blood of Christ! Through the eternal Spirit he offered himself as a perfect sacrifice to God. His blood will purify our consciences from useless rituals, so that we may serve the living God.

15 For this reason Christ is the one who arranges a new covenant, so that those who have been called by God may receive the eternal blessings that God has promised. This can be done because there has been a death which sets people free from the wrongs they did while the first covenant was in force.

16 In the case of a will it is necessary to prove that the person who made it has died, [17] for a will means nothing while the person who made it is alive; it comes into effect only after his death. [18] That is why even the first covenant[f] came into effect only with the use of blood. [19] First, Moses proclaimed to the people all the commandments as set forth in the Law. Then he took the blood of bulls and goats, mixed it with water, and sprinkled it on the book of the Law and all the people, using a sprig of hyssop and some red wool. [20] He said, "This is the blood which seals the covenant that God has commanded you to obey." [21] In the same way Moses also sprinkled the blood on the Covenant Tent and over all the things used in worship. [22] Indeed, according to the Law almost everything is purified by blood, and sins are forgiven only if blood is poured out.

[e] already here; *some manuscripts have* coming.
[f] COVENANT: *In Greek the same word means "will" and "covenant."*

Christ's Sacrifice Takes Away Sins

23 Those things, which are copies of the heavenly originals, had to be purified in that way. But the heavenly things themselves require much better sacrifices. 24 For Christ did not go into a man-made Holy Place, which was a copy of the real one. He went into heaven itself, where he now appears on our behalf in the presence of God. 25 The Jewish High Priest goes into the Most Holy Place every year with the blood of an animal. But Christ did not go in to offer himself many times, 26 for then he would have had to suffer many times ever since the creation of the world. Instead, now when all ages of time are nearing the end, he has appeared once and for all, to remove sin through the sacrifice of himself. 27 Everyone must die once, and after that be judged by God. 28 In the same manner Christ also was offered in sacrifice once to take away the sins of many. He will appear a second time, not to deal with sin, but to save those who are waiting for him.

10 The Jewish Law is not a full and faithful model of the real things; it is only a faint outline of the good things to come. The same sacrifices are offered for ever, year after year. How can the Law, then, by means of these sacrifices make perfect the people who come to God? 2 If the people worshipping God had really been purified from their sins, they would not feel guilty of sin any more, and all sacrifices would stop. 3 As it is, however, the sacrifices serve year after year to remind people of their sins. 4 For the blood of bulls and goats can never take away sins.

5 For this reason, when Christ was about to come into the world, he said to God:

"You do not want sacrifices and offerings,
    but you have prepared a body for me.
6 You are not pleased with animals burnt whole on
        the altar
    or with sacrifices to take away sins.
7 Then I said, 'Here I am,
    to do your will, O God,

just as it is written of me in the book of the
    Law.' "

8 First he said, "You neither want nor are you pleased
with sacrifices and offerings or with animals burnt
on the altar and the sacrifices to take away sins."
He said this even though all these sacrifices are offered
according to the Law. 9 Then he said, "Here I am,
O God, to do your will." So God does away with
all the old sacrifices and puts the sacrifice of Christ
in their place. 10 Because Jesus Christ did what God
wanted him to do, we are all purified from sin by
the offering that he made of his own body once and
for all.

11 Every Jewish priest performs his services every
day and offers the same sacrifices many times; but
these sacrifices can never take away sins. 12 Christ,
however, offered one sacrifice for sins, an offering that
is effective for ever, and then he sat down at the
right-hand side of God. 13 There he now waits until
God puts his enemies as a footstool under his feet.
14 With one sacrifice, then, he has made perfect for ever
those who are purified from sin.

15 And the Holy Spirit also gives us his witness.
First he says,
16 "This is the covenant that I will make with them
    in the days to come, says the Lord:
I will put my laws in their hearts
    and write them on their minds."
17 And then he says, "I will not remember their sins
and evil deeds any longer." 18 So when these have
been forgiven, an offering to take away sins is no
longer needed.

Let Us Come Near to God

19 We have, then, my brothers, complete freedom
to go into the Most Holy Place by means of the
death of Jesus. 20 He opened for us a new way, a
living way, through the curtain—that is, through his
own body. 21 We have a great priest in charge of
the house of God. 22 So let us come near to God
with a sincere heart and a sure faith, with hearts that
have been purified from a guilty conscience and with
bodies washed with clean water. 23 Let us hold on

firmly to the hope we profess, because we can trust God to keep his promise. ²⁴Let us be concerned for one another, to help one another to show love and to do good. ²⁵Let us not give up the habit of meeting

Let us not give up the habit of meeting together (10.25)

together, as some are doing. Instead, let us encourage one another all the more, since you see that the Day of the Lord is coming nearer.

26 For there is no longer any sacrifice that will take away sins if we purposely go on sinning after the truth has been made known to us. ²⁷Instead, all that is left is to wait in fear for the coming Judgement and the fierce fire which will destroy those who oppose God! ²⁸Anyone who disobeys the Law of Moses is put to death without any mercy when judged guilty on the evidence of two or more witnesses. ²⁹What, then, of the person who despises the Son of God? who treats as a cheap thing the blood of God's covenant which purified him from sin? who insults the Spirit of grace? Just think how much worse is the punishment he will deserve! ³⁰For we know who said, "I will take revenge, I will repay"; and who also said, "The Lord will judge his people." ³¹It is a terrifying thing to fall into the hands of the living God!

32 Remember how it was with you in the past.

In those days, after God's light had shone on you, you suffered many things, yet were not defeated by the struggle. ³³You were at times publicly insulted and ill-treated, and at other times you were ready to join those who were being treated in this way. ³⁴You shared the sufferings of prisoners, and when all your belongings were seized, you endured your loss gladly, because you knew that you still possessed something much better, which would last for ever. ³⁵Do not lose your courage, then, because it brings with it a great reward. ³⁶You need to be patient, in order to do the will of God and receive what he promises. ³⁷For, as the scripture says,

"Just a little while longer,
  and he who is coming will come;
  he will not delay.
³⁸My righteous people, however, will believe and
    live;
  but if any of them turns back,
  I will not be pleased with him."

³⁹We are not people who turn back and are lost. Instead, we have faith and are saved.

Faith

11 To have faith is to be sure of the things we hope for, to be certain of the things we cannot see. ²It was by their faith that people of ancient times won God's approval.

3 It is by faith that we understand that the universe was created by God's word, so that what can be seen was made out of what cannot be seen.

4 It was faith that made Abel offer to God a better sacrifice than Cain's. Through his faith he won God's approval as a righteous man, because God himself approved of his gifts. By means of his faith Abel still speaks, even though he is dead.

5 It was faith that kept Enoch from dying. Instead, he was taken up to God, and nobody could find him, because God had taken him up. The scripture says that before Enoch was taken up, he had pleased God. ⁶No one can please God without faith, for whoever comes to God must have faith that God exists and rewards those who seek him.

7 It was faith that made Noah hear God's warnings about things in the future that he could not see. He obeyed God and built a boat in which he and his family were saved. As a result, the world was condemned, and Noah received from God the righteousness that comes by faith.

8 It was faith that made Abraham obey when God called him to go out to a country which God had promised to give him. He left his own country without knowing where he was going. 9 By faith he lived as a foreigner in the country that God had promised him. He lived in tents, as did Isaac and Jacob, who received the same promise from God. 10 For Abraham was waiting for the city which God has designed and built, the city with permanent foundations.

11 It was faith that made Abraham able to become a father, even though he was too old and Sarah herself could not have children. He*g* trusted God to keep his promise. 12 Though Abraham was practically dead, from this one man came as many descendants as there are stars in the sky, as many as the numberless grains of sand on the sea-shore.

13 It was in faith that all these persons died. They did not receive the things God had promised, but from a long way off they saw them and welcomed them, and admitted openly that they were foreigners and refugees on earth. 14 Those who say such things make it clear that they are looking for a country of their own. 15 They did not keep thinking about the country they had left; if they had, they would have had the chance to return. 16 Instead, it was a better country they longed for, the heavenly country. And so God is not ashamed for them to call him their God, because he has prepared a city for them.

17 It was faith that made Abraham offer his son Isaac as a sacrifice when God put Abraham to the test. Abraham was the one to whom God had made the promise, yet he was ready to offer his only son as a sacrifice. 18 God had said to him, "It is through

g It was faith...children. He; *some manuscripts have* It was faith that made Sarah herself able to conceive, even though she was too old to have children. She.

Isaac that you will have the descendants I promised."
19 Abraham reckoned that God was able to raise Isaac from death—and, so to speak, Abraham did receive Isaac back from death.

20 It was faith that made Isaac promise blessings for the future to Jacob and Esau.

21 It was faith that made Jacob bless each of the sons of Joseph just before he died. He leaned on the top of his walking-stick and worshipped God.

22 It was faith that made Joseph, when he was about to die, speak of the departure of the Israelites from Egypt, and leave instructions about what should be done with his body.

23 It was faith that made the parents of Moses hide him for three months after he was born. They saw that he was a beautiful child, and they were not afraid to disobey the king's order.

24 It was faith that made Moses, when he had grown up, refuse to be called the son of the king's daughter. 25 He preferred to suffer with God's people rather than to enjoy sin for a little while. 26 He reckoned that to suffer scorn for the Messiah was worth far more than all the treasures of Egypt, for he kept his eyes on the future reward.

27 It was faith that made Moses leave Egypt without being afraid of the king's anger. As though he saw the invisible God, he refused to turn back. 28 It was faith that made him establish the Passover and order the blood to be sprinkled on the doors, so that the Angel of Death would not kill the first-born sons of the Israelites.

29 It was faith that made the Israelites able to cross the Red Sea as if on dry land; when the Egyptians tried to do it, the water swallowed them up.

30 It was faith that made the walls of Jericho fall down after the Israelites had marched round them for seven days. 31 It was faith that kept the prostitute Rahab from being killed with those who disobeyed God, for she gave the Israelite spies a friendly welcome.

32 Should I go on? There isn't enough time for me to speak of Gideon, Barak, Samson, Jephthah, David, Samuel, and the prophets. 33 Through faith they fought whole countries and won. They did what was

right and received what God had promised. They shut the mouths of lions, ³⁴put out fierce fires, escaped being killed by the sword. They were weak, but became strong; they were mighty in battle and defeated the armies of foreigners. ³⁵Through faith women received their dead relatives raised back to life.

Others, refusing to accept freedom, died under torture in order to be raised to a better life. ³⁶Some were mocked and whipped, and others were put in chains and taken off to prison. ³⁷They were stoned, they were sawn in two, they were killed by the sword. They went round clothed in skins of sheep or goats— poor, persecuted, and ill-treated. ³⁸The world was not good enough for them! They wandered like refugees in the deserts and hills, living in caves and holes in the ground.

39 What a record all of these have won by their faith! Yet they did not receive what God had promised, ⁴⁰because God had decided on an even better plan for us. His purpose was that only in company with us would they be made perfect.

God Our Father

12 As for us, we have this large crowd of witnesses round us. So then, let us rid ourselves of everything that gets in the way, and of the sin which holds on to us so tightly, and let us run with determination the race that lies before us. ²Let us keep our eyes fixed on Jesus, on whom our faith depends from beginning to end. He did not give up because of the cross! On the contrary, because of the joy that was waiting for him, he thought nothing of the disgrace of dying on the cross, and he is now seated at the right-hand side of God's throne.

3 Think of what he went through; how he put up with so much hatred from sinners! So do not let yourselves become discouraged and give up. ⁴For in your struggle against sin you have not yet had to resist to the point of being killed. ⁵Have you forgotten the encouraging words which God speaks to you as his sons?

"My son, pay attention when the Lord corrects you,
    and do not be discouraged when he rebukes you.

[6] Because the Lord corrects everyone he loves,
    and punishes everyone he accepts as a son."
[7] Endure what you suffer as being a father's punishment; your suffering shows that God is treating you as his sons. Was there ever a son who was not punished by his father? [8] If you are not punished, as all his sons are, it means you are not real sons, but bastards. [9] In the case of our human fathers, they punished us and we respected them. How much more, then, should we submit to our spiritual Father and live! [10] Our human fathers punished us for a short time, as it seemed right to them; but God does it for our own good, so that we may share his holiness. [11] When we are punished, it seems to us at the time something to make us sad, not glad. Later, however, those who have been disciplined by such punishment reap the peaceful reward of a righteous life.

Instructions and Warnings

12 Lift up your tired hands, then, and strengthen your trembling knees! [13] Keep walking on straight paths, so that the lame foot may not be disabled, but instead be healed.

14 Try to be at peace with everyone, and try to live a holy life, because no one will see the Lord without it. [15] Guard against turning back from the grace of God. Let no one become like a bitter plant that grows up and causes many troubles with its poison. [16] Let no one become immoral or unspiritual like Esau, who for a single meal sold his rights as the elder son. [17] Afterwards, you know, he wanted to receive his father's blessing; but he was turned away, because he could not find any way to change what he had done, even though in tears he looked for it. [h]

18 You have not come, as the people of Israel came, to what you can feel, to Mount Sinai with its blazing fire, the darkness and the gloom, the storm, [19] the blast of a trumpet, and the sound of a voice. When the people heard the voice, they begged not to hear another word, [20] because they could not bear the order which

[h] he looked for it; *or* he tried to get the blessing.

said, "If even an animal touches the mountain, it must be stoned to death." 21 The sight was so terrifying that Moses said, "I am trembling and afraid!"

22 Instead, you have come to Mount Zion and to the city of the living God, the heavenly Jerusalem, with its thousands of angels. 23 You have come to the joyful gathering of God's first-born sons, whose names are written in heaven. You have come to God, who is the judge of all mankind, and to the spirits of good people made perfect. 24 You have come to Jesus, who arranged the new covenant, and to the sprinkled blood that promises much better things than does the blood of Abel.

25 Be careful, then, and do not refuse to hear him who speaks. Those who refused to hear the one who gave the divine message on earth did not escape. How much less shall we escape, then, if we turn away from the one who speaks from heaven! 26 His voice shook the earth at that time, but now he has promised, "I will once more shake not only the earth but heaven as well." 27 The words "once more" plainly show that the created things will be shaken and removed, so that the things that cannot be shaken will remain.

28 Let us be thankful, then, because we receive a kingdom that cannot be shaken. Let us be grateful and worship God in a way that will please him, with reverence and awe; 29 because our God is indeed a destroying fire.

How to Please God

13 Keep on loving one another as Christian brothers. 2 Remember to welcome strangers in your homes. There were some who did that and welcomed angels without knowing it. 3 Remember those who are in prison, as though you were in prison with them. Remember those who are suffering, as though you were suffering as they are.

4 Marriage is to be honoured by all, and husbands and wives must be faithful to each other. God will judge those who are immoral and those who commit adultery.

5 Keep your lives free from the love of money,

Keep your lives free from the love of money (13.5)

and be satisfied with what you have. For God has said, "I will never leave you; I will never abandon you." ⁶Let us be bold, then, and say,

"The Lord is my helper,
 I will not be afraid.
What can anyone do to me?"

7 Remember your former leaders, who spoke God's message to you. Think back on how they lived and died, and imitate their faith. ⁸Jesus Christ is the same yesterday, today, and for ever. ⁹Do not let all kinds of strange teachings lead you from the right way. It is good to receive inner strength from God's grace, and not by obeying rules about foods; those who obey these rules have not been helped by them.

10 The priests who serve in the Jewish place of worship have no right to eat any of the sacrifice on our altar. ¹¹The Jewish High Priest brings the blood of the animals into the Most Holy Place to offer it as a sacrifice for sins; but the bodies of the animals are burnt outside the camp. ¹²For this reason Jesus also died outside the city, in order to purify the people from sin with his own blood. ¹³Let us, then, go to him outside the camp and share his shame. ¹⁴For there is no permanent city for us here on earth; we are looking for the city which is to

come. [15] Let us, then, always offer praise to God as our sacrifice through Jesus, which is the offering presented by lips that confess him as Lord. [16] Do not forget to do good and to help one another, because these are the sacrifices that please God.

17 Obey your leaders and follow their orders. They watch over your souls without resting, since they must give God an account of their service. If you obey them, they will do their work gladly; if not, they will do it with sadness, and that would be of no help to you.

18 Keep on praying for us. We are sure we have a clear conscience, because we want to do the right thing at all times. [19] And I beg you even more earnestly to pray that God will send me back to you soon.

Closing Prayer

20-21 God has raised from death our Lord Jesus, who is the Great Shepherd of the sheep as the result of his sacrificial death, by which the eternal covenant is sealed. May the God of peace provide you with every good thing you need in order to do his will, and may he, through Jesus Christ, do in us what pleases him. And to Christ be the glory for ever and ever! Amen.

Final Words

22 I beg you, my brothers, to listen patiently to this message of encouragement; for this letter I have written to you is not very long. [23] I want you to know that our brother Timothy has been let out of prison. If he comes soon enough, I will have him with me when I see you.

24 Give our greetings to all your leaders and to all God's people. The brothers from Italy send you their greetings.

25 May God's grace be with you all.

THE LETTER FROM
JAMES

INTRODUCTION

The Letter from James is a collection of practical instructions, written to "all God's people scattered over the whole world." The writer uses many vivid figures of speech to present instructions regarding practical wisdom and guidance for Christian attitudes and conduct. From the Christian perspective he deals with a variety of topics such as riches and poverty, temptation, good conduct, prejudice, faith and actions, the use of the tongue, wisdom, quarrelling, pride and humility, judging others, boasting, patience, and prayer.

The letter emphasizes the importance of actions along with faith, in the practice of the Christian religion.

1 From James, a servant of God and of the Lord Jesus Christ:

Greetings to all God's people scattered over the whole world.

Faith and Wisdom

2 My brothers, consider yourselves fortunate when all kinds of trials come your way, ³for you know that when your faith succeeds in facing such trials, the result is the ability to endure. ⁴Make sure that your endurance carries you all the way without failing, so that you may be perfect and complete, lacking nothing. ⁵But if any of you lacks wisdom, he should pray to God, who will give it to him; because God gives generously and graciously to all. ⁶But when you pray, you must believe and not doubt at all. Whoever doubts is like a wave in the sea that is driven and blown about by the wind. ⁷⁻⁸A person like that, unable to make up his mind and undecided in all he does, must not think that he will receive anything from the Lord.

Poverty and Riches

9 The Christian who is poor must be glad when God lifts him up, ¹⁰and the rich Christian must be glad when God brings him down. For the rich will pass away like the flower of a wild plant. ¹¹The sun rises with its blazing heat and burns the plant; its flower falls off, and its beauty is destroyed. In the same way the rich man will be destroyed while he goes about his business.

Testing and Tempting

12 Happy is the person who remains faithful under trials, because when he succeeds in passing such a test, he will receive as his reward the life which God has promised to those who love him. ¹³If a person is tempted by such trials, he must not say, "This temptation comes from God." For God cannot be tempted by evil, and he himself tempts no one. ¹⁴But a person is tempted when he is drawn away and trapped by his own evil desire. ¹⁵Then his evil desire conceives and gives birth to sin; and sin, when it is full-grown, gives birth to death.

16 Do not be deceived, my dear brothers! ¹⁷Every good gift and every perfect present comes from heaven; it comes down from God, the Creator of the heavenly lights, who does not change or cause darkness by

turning. ¹⁸By his own will he brought us into being
through the word of truth, so that we should have
first place among all his creatures.

Hearing and Doing

19 Remember this, my dear brothers! Everyone must
be quick to listen, but slow to speak and slow to
become angry. ²⁰Man's anger does not achieve God's
righteous purpose. ²¹So get rid of every filthy habit and
all wicked conduct. Submit to God and accept the
word that he plants in your hearts, which is able
to save you.

22. Do not deceive yourselves by just listening to
his word; instead, put it into practice. ²³Whoever
listens to the word but does not put it into practice
is like a man who looks in a mirror and sees himself as
he is. ²⁴He takes a good look at himself and then
goes away and at once forgets what he looks like.
²⁵But whoever looks closely into the perfect law that
sets people free, who keeps on paying attention to
it and does not simply listen and then forget it, but
puts it into practice—that person will be blessed by
God in what he does.

26 Does anyone think he is religious? If he does
not control his tongue, his religion is worthless and
he deceives himself. ²⁷What God the Father considers
to be pure and genuine religion is this: to take care
of orphans and widows in their suffering and to keep
oneself from being corrupted by the world.

Warning against Prejudice

2 My brothers, as believers in our Lord Jesus Christ,
the Lord of glory, you must never treat people
in different ways according to their outward appearance. ²Suppose a rich man wearing a gold ring and
fine clothes comes to your meeting, and a poor man
in ragged clothes also comes. ³If you show more
respect to the well-dressed man and say to him, "Have
this best seat here," but say to the poor man, "Stand
over there, or sit here on the floor by my feet,"
⁴then you are guilty of creating distinctions among
yourselves and of making judgements based on evil
motives.

5 Listen, my dear brothers! God chose the poor people of this world to be rich in faith and to possess the kingdom which he promised to those who love him. 6 But you dishonour the poor! Who are the ones who oppress you and drag you before the judges? The rich! 7 They are the ones who speak evil of that good name which has been given to you.

8 You will be doing the right thing if you obey the law of the Kingdom, which is found in the scripture, "Love your neighbour as you love yourself." 9 But if you treat people according to their outward appearance, you are guilty of sin, and the Law condemns you as a law-breaker. 10 Whoever breaks one commandment is guilty of breaking them all. 11 For the same one who said, "Do not commit adultery," also said, "Do not commit murder." Even if you do not commit adultery, you have become a law-breaker if you commit murder. 12 Speak and act as people who will be judged by the law that sets us free. 13 For God will not show mercy when he judges the person who has not been merciful; but mercy triumphs over judgement.

Faith and Actions

14 My brothers, what good is it for someone to say that he has faith if his actions do not prove it? Can that faith save him? 15 Suppose there are brothers or sisters who need clothes and don't have enough to eat. 16 What good is there in your saying to them, "God bless you! Keep warm and eat well!"— if you don't give them the necessities of life? 17 So it is with faith: if it is alone and includes no actions, then it is dead.

18 But someone will say, "One person has faith, another has actions." My answer is, "Show me how anyone can have faith without actions. I will show you my faith by my actions." 19 Do you believe that there is only one God? Good! The demons also believe—and tremble with fear. 20 You fool! Do you want to be shown that faith without actions is useless?[a] 21 How was our ancestor Abraham put right with God? It was through his actions, when he offered

---

[a] useless; *some manuscripts have* dead.

his son Isaac on the altar. 22 Can't you see? His faith and his actions worked together; his faith was made perfect through his actions. 23 And the scripture came true that said, "Abraham believed God, and because of his faith God accepted him as righteous." And so Abraham was called God's friend. 24 You see, then, that it is by his actions that a person is put right with God, and not by his faith alone.

25 It was the same with the prostitute Rahab. She was put right with God through her actions, by welcoming the Israelite spies and helping them to escape by a different road.

26 So then, as the body without the spirit is dead, so also faith without actions is dead.

The Tongue

3 My brothers, not many of you should become teachers. As you know, we teachers will be judged with greater strictness than others. 2 All of us often make mistakes. But if a person never makes a mistake in what he says, he is perfect and is also able to control his whole being. 3 We put a bit into the mouth of a horse to make it obey us, and we are able to make it go where we want. 4 Or think of a ship: big as it is and driven by such strong winds, it can be steered by a very small rudder, and it goes wherever the pilot wants it to go. 5 So it is with the tongue: small as it is, it can boast about great things.

Just think how large a forest can be set on fire by a tiny flame! 6 And the tongue is like a fire. It is a world of wrong, occupying its place in our bodies and spreading evil through our whole being. It sets on fire the entire course of our existence with the fire that comes to it from hell itself. 7 Man is able to tame and has tamed all other creatures—wild animals and birds, reptiles and fish. 8 But no one has ever been able to tame the tongue. It is evil and uncontrollable, full of deadly poison. 9 We use it to give thanks to our Lord and Father and also to curse our fellow-man, who is created in the likeness of God. 10 Words of thanksgiving and cursing pour out from the same mouth. My brothers, this should not happen! 11 No spring of water pours out sweet water and bitter water from the same opening. [12] A fig-tree, my brothers, cannot bear olives; a grapevine cannot bear figs, nor can a salty spring produce sweet water.

The Wisdom from Above

13 Is there anyone among you who is wise and understanding? He is to prove it by his good life, by his good deeds performed with humility and wisdom. [14] But if in your heart you are jealous, bitter, and selfish, don't sin against the truth by boasting of your wisdom. [15] Such wisdom does not come down from heaven; it belongs to the world, it is unspiritual and demonic. [16] Where there is jealousy and selfishness, there is also disorder and every kind of evil. [17] But the wisdom from above is pure first of all; it is also peaceful, gentle, and friendly; it is full of compassion and produces a harvest of good deeds; it is free from prejudice and hypocrisy. [18] And goodness is the harvest that is produced from the seeds the peacemakers plant in peace.

Friendship with the World

4 Where do all the fights and quarrels among you come from? They come from your desires for pleasure, which are constantly fighting within you. [2] You want things, but you cannot have them, so you are ready to kill; you strongly desire things, but you cannot get them, so you quarrel and fight. You do not have what you want because you do not ask God for it. [3] And when you ask, you do not receive it, because your motives are bad; you ask for things to use for your own pleasures. [4] Unfaithful people! Don't you know that to be the world's friend means to be God's enemy? Whoever wants to be the world's friend makes himself God's enemy. [5] Don't think that there is no truth in the scripture that says, "The spirit that God placed in us is filled with fierce desires."[b] [6] But the grace that God gives is even stronger. As the scripture says, "God resists the proud, but gives grace to the humble."

[b] The spirit...fierce desires; *or* God yearns jealously over the spirit that he placed in us.

7 So then, submit to God. Resist the Devil, and he will run away from you. 8Come near to God, and he will come near to you. Wash your hands, you sinners! Purify your hearts, you hypocrites! 9Be sorrowful, cry, and weep; change your laughter into crying, your joy into gloom! 10Humble yourselves before the Lord, and he will lift you up.

Warning against Judging a Christian Brother

11 Do not criticize one another, my brothers. Whoever criticizes a Christian brother or judges him, criticizes the Law and judges it. If you judge the Law, then you are no longer one who obeys the Law, but one who judges it. 12God is the only lawgiver and judge. He alone can save and destroy. Who do you think you are, to judge your fellow-man?

Warning against Boasting

13 Now listen to me, you that say, "Today or tomorrow we will travel to a certain city, where we will stay a year and go into business and make a lot of money." 14You don't even know what your life tomorrow will be! You are like a puff of smoke, which appears for a moment and then disappears. 15What you should say is this: "If the Lord is willing, we will live and do this or that." 16But now you are proud, and you boast; all such boasting is wrong.

17 So then, the person who does not do the good he knows he should do is guilty of sin.

Warning to the Rich

5 And now, you rich people, listen to me! Weep and wail over the miseries that are coming upon you! 2Your riches have rotted away, and your clothes have been eaten by moths. 3Your gold and silver are covered with rust, and this rust will be a witness against you and will eat up your flesh like fire. You have piled up riches in these last days. 4You have not paid any wages to the men who work in your fields. Listen to their complaints! The cries of those who gather in your crops have reached the ears of God, the Lord Almighty. 5Your life here on earth has been full of luxury and pleasure. You have made yourselves

fat for the day of slaughter. 6 You have condemned and murdered innocent people, and they do not resist you.[c]

Patience and Prayer

7 Be patient, then, my brothers, until the Lord comes. See how patient a farmer is as he waits for his land to produce precious crops. He waits patiently for the autumn and spring rains. 8 You also must be patient. Keep your hopes high, for the day of the Lord's coming is near.

9 Do not complain against one another, my brothers, so that God will not judge you. The Judge is near, ready to appear. 10 My brothers, remember the prophets who spoke in the name of the Lord. Take them as examples of patient endurance under suffering. 11 We call them happy because they endured. You have heard of Job's patience, and you know how the Lord provided for him in the end. For the Lord is full of mercy and compassion.

12 Above all, my brothers, do not use an oath when you make a promise. Do not swear by heaven or by earth or by anything else. Say only "Yes" when you mean yes, and "No" when you mean no, and then you will not come under God's judgement.

13 Is anyone among you in trouble? He should pray. Is anyone happy? He should sing praises. 14 Is there anyone who is ill? He should send for the church elders, who will pray for him and rub olive-oil on him in the name of the Lord. 15 This prayer made in faith will heal the sick person; the Lord will restore him to health, and the sins he has committed will be forgiven. 16 So then, confess your sins to one another and pray for one another, so that you will be healed. The prayer of a good person has a powerful effect. 17 Elijah was the same kind of person as we are. He prayed earnestly that there would be no rain, and no rain fell on the land for three and a half years. 18 Once again he prayed, and the sky poured out its rain and the earth produced its crops.

[c]people, and they do not resist you; or people. Will God not resist you?

This prayer made in faith will heal the sick person (5.15)

19 My brothers, if one of you wanders away from the truth and another one brings him back again, 20 remember this: whoever turns a sinner back from his wrong way will save that sinner's soul*d* from death and bring about the forgiveness of many sins.

*d*that sinner's soul; *or* his own soul.

THE FIRST LETTER FROM
PETER

INTRODUCTION

The First Letter from Peter was addressed to Christians, here called "God's chosen people," who were scattered throughout the northern part of Asia Minor. The main purpose of the letter is to encourage the readers, who were facing persecution and suffering for their faith. The writer does this by reminding his readers of the Good News about Jesus Christ, whose death, resurrection, and promised coming give them hope. In the light of this they are to accept and endure their suffering, confident that it is a test of the genuineness of their faith and that they will be rewarded on "the Day when Jesus Christ is revealed."

Along with his encouragement in time of trouble, the writer also urges his readers to live as people who belong to Christ.

---

1 From Peter, apostle of Jesus Christ—
To God's chosen people who live as refugees scattered throughout the provinces of Pontus, Galatia, Cappadocia, Asia, and Bithynia. ²You were chosen according to the purpose of God the Father and were

made a holy people by his Spirit, to obey Jesus Christ and be purified by his blood.

May grace and peace be yours in full measure.

A Living Hope

3 Let us give thanks to the God and Father of our Lord Jesus Christ! Because of his great mercy he gave us new life by raising Jesus Christ from death. This fills us with a living hope, 4and so we look forward to possessing the rich blessings that God keeps for his people. He keeps them for you in heaven, where they cannot decay or spoil or fade away. 5They are for you, who through faith are kept safe by God's power for the salvation which is ready to be revealed at the end of time.

6 Be glad about this, even though it may now be necessary for you to be sad for a while because of the many kinds of trials you suffer. 7Their purpose is to prove that your faith is genuine. Even gold, which can be destroyed, is tested by fire; and so your faith, which is much more precious than gold, must also be tested, so that it may endure. Then you will receive praise and glory and honour on the Day when Jesus Christ is revealed. 8You love him, although you have not seen him, and you believe in him, although you do not now see him. So you rejoice with a great and glorious joy which words cannot express, 9because you are receiving the salvation of your souls, which is the purpose of your faith in him.

10 It was concerning this salvation that the prophets made careful search and investigation, and they prophesied about this gift which God would give you. 11They tried to find out when the time would be and how it would come.[a] This was the time to which Christ's Spirit in them was pointing, in predicting the sufferings that Christ would have to endure and the glory that would follow. 12God revealed to these prophets that their work was not for their own benefit, but for yours, as they spoke about those things which you have now heard from the messengers who

[a] when the time would be and how it would come; or who the person would be and when he would come.

announced the Good News by the power of the Holy Spirit sent from heaven. These are things which even the angels would like to understand.

A Call to Holy Living

13 So then, have your minds ready for action. Keep alert and set your hope completely on the blessing which will be given you when Jesus Christ is revealed. 14 Be obedient to God, and do not allow your lives to be shaped by those desires you had when you were still ignorant. 15 Instead, be holy in all that you do, just as God who called you is holy. 16 The scripture says, "Be holy because I am holy."

17 You call him Father, when you pray to God, who judges all people by the same standard, according to what each one has done; so then, spend the rest of your lives here on earth in reverence for him. 18 For you know what was paid to set you free from the worthless manner of life handed down by your ancestors. It was not something that can be destroyed, such as silver or gold; 19 it was the costly sacrifice of Christ, who was like a lamb without defect or flaw. 20 He had been chosen by God before the creation of the world and was revealed in these last days for your sake. 21 Through him you believe in God, who raised him from death and gave him glory; and so your faith and hope are fixed on God.

22 Now that by your obedience to the truth you have purified yourselves and have come to have a sincere love for your fellow-believers, love one another earnestly with all your heart. b 23 For through the living and eternal word of God you have been born again as the children of a parent who is immortal, not mortal. 24 As the scripture says,

"All mankind are like grass,
    and all their glory is like wild flowers.
The grass withers, and the flowers fall,
25   but the word of the Lord remains for ever."
This word is the Good News that was proclaimed to you.

b with all your heart; *some manuscripts have* with a pure heart.

The Living Stone and the Holy Nation

2 Rid yourselves, then, of all evil; no more lying or hypocrisy or jealousy or insulting language. ²Be like new-born babies, always thirsty for the pure spiritual milk, so that by drinking it you may grow up and be saved. ³As the scripture says, "You have found out for yourselves how kind the Lord is."

4 Come to the Lord, the living stone rejected by man as worthless but chosen by God as valuable. ⁵Come as living stones, and let yourselves be used in building the spiritual temple, where you will serve as holy priests to offer spiritual and acceptable sacrifices to God through Jesus Christ. ⁶For the scripture says,

"I chose a valuable stone,
which I am placing as the cornerstone in Zion;
and whoever believes in him will never be
disappointed."

⁷This stone is of great value for you that believe; but for those who do not believe:

"The stone which the builders rejected as worthless
turned out to be the most important of all."

⁸And another scripture says,

"This is the stone that will make people stumble,
the rock that will make them fall."

They stumbled because they did not believe in the word; such was God's will for them.

9 But you are the chosen race, the King's priests, the holy nation, God's own people, chosen to proclaim the wonderful acts of God, who called you out of darkness into his own marvellous light. ¹⁰At one time you were not God's people, but now you are his people; at one time you did not know God's mercy, but now you have received his mercy.

Slaves of God

11 I appeal to you, my friends, as strangers and refugees in this world! Do not give in to bodily passions, which are always at war against the soul. ¹²Your conduct among the heathen should be so good that when they accuse you of being evildoers, they

will have to recognize your good deeds and so praise God on the Day of his coming.

13 For the sake of the Lord submit to every human authority: to the Emperor, who is the supreme authority, 14 and to the governors, who have been appointed by him to punish the evildoers and to praise those who do good. 15 For God wants you to silence the ignorant talk of foolish people by the good things you do. 16 Live as free people; do not, however, use your freedom to cover up any evil, but live as God's slaves. 17 Respect everyone, love your fellow-believers, honour God, and respect the Emperor.

The Example of Christ's Suffering

18 You servants must submit to your masters and show them complete respect, not only to those who are kind and considerate, but also to those who are harsh. 19 God will bless you for this, if you endure the pain of undeserved suffering because you are conscious of his will. 20 For what credit is there if you endure the beatings you deserve for having done wrong? But if you endure suffering even when you have done right, God will bless you for it. 21 It was to this that God called you, for Christ himself suffered for you and left you an example, so that you would follow in his steps. 22 He committed no sin, and no one ever heard a lie come from his lips. 23 When he was insulted, he did not answer back with an insult; when he suffered, he did not threaten, but placed his hopes in God, the righteous Judge. 24 Christ himself carried our sins in his body to the cross, so that we might die to sin and live for righteousness. It is by his wounds that you have been healed. 25 You were like sheep that had lost their way, but now you have been brought back to follow the Shepherd and Keeper of your souls.

Wives and Husbands

3 In the same way you wives must submit to your husbands, so that if any of them do not believe God's word, your conduct will win them over to believe. It will not be necessary for you to say a word, 2 because they will see how pure and reverent your conduct

is. ³You should not use outward aids to make yourselves beautiful, such as the way you do your hair,
or the jewellery you put on, or the dresses you wear.
⁴Instead, your beauty should consist of your true inner
self, the ageless beauty of a gentle and quiet spirit,
which is of the greatest value in God's sight. ⁵For
the devout women of the past who placed their hope
in God used to make themselves beautiful by sub-
mitting to their husbands. ⁶Sarah was like that; she
obeyed Abraham and called him her master. You are
now her daughters if you do good and are not afraid
of anything.

7 In the same way you husbands must live with
your wives with the proper understanding that they
are the weaker sex. Treat them with respect, because
they also will receive, together with you, God's gift
of life. Do this so that nothing will interfere with
your prayers.

Suffering for Doing Right

8 To conclude: you must all have the same attitude
and the same feelings; love one another as brothers,
and be kind and humble with one another. ⁹Do not
pay back evil with evil or cursing with cursing; instead,
pay back with a blessing, because a blessing is what
God promised to give you when he called you. ¹⁰As
the scripture says,
"Whoever wants to enjoy life
    and wishes to see good times,
    must keep from speaking evil
    and stop telling lies.
¹¹ He must turn away from evil and do good;
    he must strive for peace with all his heart.
¹² For the Lord watches over the righteous
    and listens to their prayers;
    but he opposes those who do evil."
13 Who will harm you if you are eager to do what
is good? ¹⁴But even if you should suffer for doing
what is right, how happy you are! Do not be afraid
of anyone, and do not worry. ¹⁵But have reverence for
Christ in your hearts, and honour him as Lord. Be
ready at all times to answer anyone who asks you
to explain the hope you have in you, ¹⁶but do it

with gentleness and respect. Keep your conscience clear, so that when you are insulted, those who speak evil of your good conduct as followers of Christ will be ashamed of what they say. ¹⁷For it is better to suffer for doing good, if this should be God's will, than for doing evil. ¹⁸For Christ died*c* for sins once and for all, a good man on behalf of sinners, in order to lead you to God. He was put to death physically, but made alive spiritually, ¹⁹and in his spiritual existence he went and preached to the imprisoned spirits. ²⁰These were the spirits of those who had not obeyed God when he waited patiently during the days that Noah was building his boat. The few people in the boat—eight in all—were saved by the water, ²¹which was a symbol pointing to baptism, which now saves you. It is not the washing away of bodily dirt, but the promise made to God from a good conscience. It saves you through the resurrection of Jesus Christ, ²²who has gone to heaven and is at the right-hand side of God, ruling over all angels and heavenly authorities and powers.

Changed Lives

4 Since Christ suffered physically, you too must strengthen yourselves with the same way of thinking that he had; because whoever suffers physically is no longer involved with sin. ²From now on, then, you must live the rest of your earthly lives controlled by God's will and not by human desires. ³You have spent enough time in the past doing what the heathen like to do. Your lives were spent in indecency, lust, drunkenness, orgies, drinking parties, and the disgusting worship of idols. ⁴And now the heathen are surprised when you do not join them in the same wild and reckless living, and so they insult you. ⁵But they will have to give an account of themselves to God, who is ready to judge the living and the dead. ⁶That is why the Good News was preached also to the dead, to those who had been judged in their physical existence as everyone is judged; it was preached to

*c*died; *many manuscripts have* suffered.

them so that in their spiritual existence they may
live as God lives.

Good Managers of God's Gifts

7 The end of all things is near. You must be self-
controlled and alert, to be able to pray. 8 Above everything, love one another earnestly, because love covers
over many sins. 9 Open your homes to each other
without complaining. 10 Each one, as a good manager
of God's different gifts, must use for the good of
others the special gift he has received from God. 11 Whoever preaches must preach God's messages; whoever
serves must serve with the strength that God gives
him, so that in all things praise may be given to
God through Jesus Christ, to whom belong glory and
power for ever and ever. Amen.

Suffering as a Christian

12 My dear friends, do not be surprised at the painful
test you are suffering, as though something unusual
were happening to you. 13 Rather be glad that you
are sharing Christ's sufferings, so that you may be full
of joy when his glory is revealed. 14 Happy are you
if you are insulted because you are Christ's followers;
this means that the glorious Spirit, the Spirit of God,
is resting on you. 15 If any of you suffers, it must
not be because he is a murderer or a thief or a
criminal or a meddler in other people's affairs. 16 However, if you suffer because you are a Christian, don't
be ashamed of it, but thank God that you bear Christ's
name.

17 The time has come for judgement to begin, and
God's own people are the first to be judged. If it
starts with us, how will it end with those who do
not believe the Good News from God? 18 As the scripture says,

"It is difficult for good people to be saved;
    what, then, will become of godless sinners?"
19 So then, those who suffer because it is God's will
for them, should by their good actions trust themselves
completely to their Creator, who always keeps his
promise.

The Flock of God

5 I, who am an elder myself, appeal to the church elders among you. I am a witness of Christ's sufferings, and I will share in the glory that will be revealed. I appeal to you ²to be shepherds of the flock that God gave you and to take care of it willingly, as God wants you to, and not unwillingly. Do your work, not for mere pay, but from a real desire to serve. ³Do not try to rule over those who have been put in your care, but be examples to the flock. ⁴And when the Chief Shepherd appears, you will receive the glorious crown which will never lose its brightness.

5 In the same way you younger men must submit to the older men. And all of you must put on the apron of humility, to serve one another; for the scripture says, "God resists the proud, but shows favour to the humble." ⁶Humble yourselves, then, under God's mighty hand, so that he will lift you up in his own good time. ⁷Leave all your worries with him, because he cares for you.

8 Be alert, be on the watch! Your enemy, the Devil, roams round like a roaring lion, looking for someone to devour. ⁹Be firm in your faith and resist him, because you know that your fellow-believers in all the world are going through the same kind of sufferings. ¹⁰But after you have suffered for a little while, the God of all grace, who calls you to share his eternal glory in union with Christ, will himself perfect you and give you firmness, strength, and a sure foundation. ¹¹To him be the power for ever! Amen.

Final Greetings

12 I write you this brief letter with the help of Silas, whom I regard as a faithful Christian brother. I want to encourage you and give my testimony that this is the true grace of God. Stand firm in it.

13 Your sister church in Babylon,*d* also chosen by

---

*d*BABYLON: *As in the book of Revelation, this probably refers to Rome.*

The kiss of Christian love (5.14)

God, sends you greetings, and so does my son Mark.
¹⁴Greet one another with the kiss of Christian love.
May peace be with all of you who belong to Christ.

THE SECOND LETTER FROM

PETER

INTRODUCTION

The Second Letter from Peter is addressed to a wide
circle of early Christians. Its main concern is to combat
the work of false teachers and the immorality which
results from such teaching. The answer to these problems is found in holding to the true knowledge of
God and of the Lord Jesus Christ, knowledge which
has been conveyed by persons who themselves have
seen Jesus and have heard him teach. The writer is
especially concerned with the teaching of those who
claim that Christ will not return again. He says that
the apparent delay in Christ's return is due to the
fact that God "does not want anyone to be destroyed,
but wants all to turn away from their sins."

Outline of Contents

Introduction 1.1–2
The Christian calling 1.3–21
False teachers 2.1–22
The final coming of Christ 3.1–18

---

1 From Simon Peter, a servant and apostle of Jesus Christ—

To those who through the righteousness of our God and Saviour Jesus Christ have been given a faith as precious as ours:

2 May grace and peace be yours in full measure through your knowledge of God and of Jesus our Lord.

God's Call and Choice

3 God's divine power has given us everything we need to live a truly religious life through our knowledge of the one who called us to share in his own[a] glory and goodness. 4 In this way he has given us the very great and precious gifts he promised, so that by means of these gifts you may escape from the destructive lust that is in the world, and may come to share the divine nature. 5 For this very reason do your best to add goodness to your faith; to your goodness add knowledge; 6 to your knowledge add self-control; to your self-control add endurance; to your endurance add godliness; 7 to your godliness add brotherly affection; and to your brotherly affection add love. 8 These are the qualities you need, and if you have them in abundance, they will make you active and effective in your knowledge of our Lord Jesus Christ. 9 But whoever does not have them is so short-sighted that he cannot see and has forgotten that he has been purified from his past sins.

10 So then, my brothers, try even harder to make God's call and his choice of you a permanent experi-

---

[a] to share in his own; *some manuscripts have* through his.

To make God's call...a permanent experience (1.10)

ence; if you do so, you will never abandon your faith.[b] 11 In this way you will be given the full right to enter the eternal Kingdom of our Lord and Saviour Jesus Christ.

12 And so I will always remind you of these matters, even though you already know them and are firmly grounded in the truth you have received. 13 I think it only right for me to stir up your memory of these matters as long as I am still alive. 14 I know that I shall soon put off this mortal body, as our Lord Jesus Christ plainly told me. 15 I will do my best, then, to provide a way for you to remember these matters at all times after my death.

Eye-Witnesses of Christ's Glory

16 We have not depended on made-up stories in making known to you the mighty coming of our Lord Jesus Christ. With our own eyes we saw his greatness.

[b] abandon your faith; *or* fall into sin.

¹⁷We were there when he was given honour and glory by God the Father, when the voice came to him from the Supreme Glory, saying, "This is my own dear Son, with whom I am pleased!" ¹⁸We ourselves heard this voice coming from heaven, when we were with him on the holy mountain.

19 So we are even more confident of the message proclaimed by the prophets. You will do well to pay attention to it, because it is like a lamp shining in a dark place until the Day dawns and the light of the morning star shines in your hearts. ²⁰Above all else, however, remember that no one can explain by himself a prophecy in the Scriptures. ²¹For no prophetic message ever came just from the will of man, but men were under the control of the Holy Spirit as they spoke the message that came from God.

False Teachers

2 False prophets appeared in the past among the people, and in the same way false teachers will appear among you. They will bring in destructive, untrue doctrines, and will deny the Master who redeemed them, and so they will bring upon themselves sudden destruction. ²Even so, many will follow their immoral ways; and because of what they do, others will speak evil of the Way of truth. ³In their greed these false teachers will make a profit out of telling you made-up stories. For a long time now their Judge has been ready, and their Destroyer has been wide awake!

4 God did not spare the angels who sinned, but threw them into hell, where they are kept chained in darkness,ᶜ waiting for the Day of Judgement. ⁵God did not spare the ancient world, but brought the flood on the world of godless people; the only ones he saved were Noah, who preached righteousness, and seven other people. ⁶God condemned the cities of Sodom and Gomorrah, destroying them with fire, and made them an example of what will happen to the godless. ⁷He rescued Lot, a good man, who was distressed by the immoral conduct of lawless people.

ᶜchained in darkness; *some manuscripts have* in dark pits.

⁸That good man lived among them, and day after day he suffered agony as he saw and heard their evil actions. ⁹And so the Lord knows how to rescue godly people from their trials and how to keep the wicked under punishment for the Day of Judgement, ¹⁰especially those who follow their filthy bodily lusts and despise God's authority.

These false teachers are bold and arrogant, and show no respect for the glorious beings above; instead, they insult them. ¹¹Even the angels, who are so much stronger and mightier than these false teachers, do not accuse them with insults in the presence of the Lord. ¹²But these men act by instinct, like wild animals born to be captured and killed; they attack with insults anything they do not understand. They will be destroyed like wild animals, ¹³and they will be paid with suffering for the suffering they have caused. Pleasure for them is to do anything in broad daylight that will satisfy their bodily appetites; they are a shame and a disgrace as they join you in your meals, all the while enjoying their deceitful ways! ¹⁴They want to look at nothing but immoral women; their appetite for sin is never satisfied. They lead weak people into a trap. Their hearts are trained to be greedy. They are under God's curse! ¹⁵They have left the straight path and have lost their way; they have followed the path taken by Balaam son of Beor, who loved the money he would get for doing wrong ¹⁶and was rebuked for his sin. His donkey spoke with a human voice and stopped the prophet's insane action.

17 These men are like dried-up springs, like clouds blown along by a storm; God has reserved a place for them in the deepest darkness. ¹⁸They make proud and stupid statements, and use immoral bodily lusts to trap those who are just beginning to escape from among people who live in error. ¹⁹They promise them freedom while they themselves are slaves of destructive habits—for a person is a slave of anything that has conquered him. ²⁰If people have escaped from the corrupting forces of the world through their knowledge of our Lord and Saviour Jesus Christ, and then are again caught and conquered by them, such people are in a worse state at the end than they were at

the beginning. 21 It would have been much better for them never to have known the way of righteousness than to know it and then turn away from the sacred command that was given them. 22 What happened to them shows that the proverbs are true: "A dog goes back to what it has vomited" and "A pig that has been washed goes back to roll in the mud."

The Promise of the Lord's Coming

3 My dear friends, this is now the second letter I have written to you. In both letters I have tried to arouse pure thoughts in your minds by reminding you of these things. 2 I want you to remember the words that were spoken long ago by the holy prophets, and the command from the Lord and Saviour which was given you by your apostles. 3 First of all, you must understand that in these last days some people will appear whose lives are controlled by their own lusts. They will mock you 4 and will ask, "He promised to come, didn't he? Where is he? Our fathers have already died, but everything is still the same as it was since the creation of the world!" 5 They purposely ignore the fact that long ago God gave a command, and the heavens and earth were created. The earth was formed out of water and by water, 6 and it was also by water, the water of the flood, that the old world was destroyed. 7 But the heavens and the earth that now exist are being preserved by the same command of God, in order to be destroyed by fire. They are being kept for the day when godless people will be judged and destroyed.

8 But do not forget one thing, my dear friends! There is no difference in the Lord's sight between one day and a thousand years; to him the two are the same. 9 The Lord is not slow to do what he has promised, as some think. Instead, he is patient with you, because he does not want anyone to be destroyed, but wants all to turn away from their sins.

10 But the Day of the Lord will come like a thief. On that Day the heavens will disappear with a shrill noise, the heavenly bodies will burn up and be destroyed, and the earth with everything in it will

vanish.*d* 11 Since all these things will be destroyed in this way, what kind of people should you be? Your lives should be holy and dedicated to God, 12 as you wait for the Day of God and do your best to make it come soon—the Day when the heavens will burn up and be destroyed, and the heavenly bodies will be melted by the heat. 13 But we wait for what God has promised: new heavens and a new earth, where righteousness will be at home.

14 And so, my friends, as you wait for that Day, do your best to be pure and faultless in God's sight and to be at peace with him. 15 Look on our Lord's patience as the opportunity he is giving you to be saved, just as our dear brother Paul wrote to you, using the wisdom that God gave him. 16 This is what he says in all his letters when he writes on the subject. There are some difficult things in his letters which ignorant and unstable people explain falsely, as they do with other passages of the Scriptures. So they bring on their own destruction.

17 But you, my friends, already know this. Be on your guard, then, so that you will not be led away by the errors of lawless people and fall from your safe position. 18 But continue to grow in the grace and knowledge of our Lord and Saviour Jesus Christ. To him be the glory, now and for ever! Amen.

*d*vanish; *some manuscripts have* be found; *others have* be burnt up; *one has* be found destroyed.

THE FIRST LETTER OF
JOHN

INTRODUCTION

The First Letter of John has two main purposes: to encourage its readers to live in fellowship with God and with his Son, Jesus Christ, and to warn them against following false teaching that would destroy this fellowship. This teaching was based on the belief that evil results from contact with the physical world, and so Jesus, the Son of God, could not really have been a human being. Those teachers claimed that to be saved was to be set free from concern with life in this world; and they also taught that salvation had nothing to do with matters of morality or of love for one's fellow-man.

In opposition to this teaching the writer clearly states that Jesus Christ was a real human being, and he emphasizes that all who believe in Jesus and love God must also love one another.

Outline of Contents

The Word of Life

1 We write to you about the Word of life, which has existed from the very beginning. We have heard it, and we have seen it with our eyes; yes,

we have seen it, and our hands have touched it.
2 When this life became visible, we saw it; so we
speak of it and tell you about the eternal life which
was with the Father and was made known to us.
3 What we have seen and heard we announce to you
also, so that you will join with us in the fellowship
that we have with the Father and with his Son Jesus
Christ. 4 We write this in order that our[a] joy may
be complete.

God Is Light

5 Now the message that we have heard from his
Son and announce is this: God is light, and there
is no darkness at all in him. 6 If, then, we say that
we have fellowship with him, yet at the same time
live in the darkness, we are lying both in our words
and in our actions. 7 But if we live in the light—just
as he is in the light—then we have fellowship with
one another, and the blood of Jesus, his Son, purifies
us from every sin.

8 If we say that we have no sin, we deceive ourselves, and there is no truth in us. 9 But if we confess
our sins to God, he will keep his promise and do
what is right: he will forgive us our sins and purify us
from all our wrongdoing. 10 If we say that we have
not sinned, we make God out to be a liar, and his
word is not in us.

Christ Our Helper

2 I am writing this to you, my children, so that
you will not sin; but if anyone does sin, we have
someone who pleads with the Father on our behalf—
Jesus Christ, the righteous one. 2 And Christ himself is
the means by which our sins are forgiven, and not
our sins only, but also the sins of everyone.

3 If we obey God's commands, then we are sure
that we know him. 4 If someone says that he knows
him, but does not obey his commands, such a person
is a liar and there is no truth in him. 5 But whoever
obeys his word is the one whose love for God has
really been made perfect. This is how we can be

[a] our; *some manuscripts have* your.

sure that we are in union with God: [6] whoever says that he remains in union with God should live just as Jesus Christ did.

The New Command

7 My dear friends, this command I am writing to you is not new; it is the old command, the one you have had from the very beginning. The old command is the message you have already heard. [8] However, the command I am now writing to you is new, because its truth is seen in Christ and also in you. For the darkness is passing away, and the real light is already shining.

9 Whoever says that he is in the light, yet hates his brother, is in the darkness to this very hour. [10] Whoever loves his brother lives in the light, and

Whoever loves his brother...whoever hates his brother (2.10–11)

so there is nothing in him that will cause someone else[b] to sin. [11] But whoever hates his brother is in the

[b] someone else; *or* him.

darkness; he walks in it and does not know where he is going, because the darkness has made him blind.

12 I am writing to you, my children, because your sins are forgiven for the sake of Christ. [13] I am writing to you, fathers, because you know him who has existed from the beginning. I am writing to you, young men, because you have defeated the Evil One.

14 I am writing to you, my children, because you know the Father. I am writing to you, fathers, because you know him who has existed from the beginning. I am writing to you, young men, because you are strong; the word of God lives in you, and you have defeated the Evil One.

15 Do not love the world or anything that belongs to the world. If you love the world, you do not love the Father. [16] Everything that belongs to the world— what the sinful self desires, what people see and want, and everything in this world that people are so proud of—none of this comes from the Father; it all comes from the world. [17] The world and everything in it that people desire is passing away; but he who does the will of God lives for ever.

The Enemy of Christ

18 My children, the end is near! You were told that the Enemy of Christ would come; and now many enemies of Christ have already appeared, and so we know that the end is near. [19] These people really did not belong to our fellowship, and that is why they left us; if they had belonged to our fellowship, they would have stayed with us. But they left so that it might be clear that none of them really belonged to us.

20 But you have had the Holy Spirit poured out on you by Christ, and so all of you know the truth. [21] I am writing to you, then, not because you do not know the truth; instead, it is because you do know it, and you also know that no lie ever comes from the truth.

22 Who, then, is the liar? It is anyone who says that Jesus is not the Messiah. Such a person is the Enemy of Christ—he rejects both the Father and the

Son. 23 For whoever rejects the Son also rejects the Father; whoever accepts the Son has the Father also.

24 Be sure, then, to keep in your hearts the message you heard from the beginning. If you keep that message, then you will always live in union with the Son and the Father. 25 And this is what Christ himself promised to give us—eternal life.

26 I am writing this to you about those who are trying to deceive you. 27 But as for you, Christ has poured out his Spirit on you. As long as his Spirit remains in you, you do not need anyone to teach you. For his Spirit teaches you about everything, and what he teaches is true, not false. Obey the Spirit's teaching, then, and remain in union with Christ.

28 Yes, my children, remain in union with him, so that when he appears we may be full of courage and need not hide in shame from him on the Day he comes. 29 You know that Christ is righteous; you should know, then, that everyone who does what is right is God's child.

Children of God

3 See how much the Father has loved us! His love is so great that we are called God's children—and so, in fact, we are. This is why the world does not know us: it has not known God. 2 My dear friends, we are now God's children, but it is not yet clear what we shall become. But we know that when Christ appears, we shall be like him, because we shall see him as he really is. 3 Everyone who has this hope in Christ keeps himself pure, just as Christ is pure.

4 Whoever sins is guilty of breaking God's law, because sin is a breaking of the law. 5 You know that Christ appeared in order to take away sins,c and that there is no sin in him. 6 So everyone who lives in union with Christ does not continue to sin; but whoever continues to sin has never seen him or known him.

7 Let no one deceive you, my children! Whoever does what is right is righteous, just as Christ is righteous. 8 Whoever continues to sin belongs to the Devil,

c sins; *some manuscripts have* our sins.

because the Devil has sinned from the very beginning. The Son of God appeared for this very reason, to destroy what the Devil had done.

9 Whoever is a child of God does not continue to sin, for God's very nature is in him; and because God is his Father, he cannot continue to sin. 10 This is the clear difference between God's children and the Devil's children: anyone who does not do what is right or does not love his brother is not God's child.

Love One Another

11 The message you heard from the very beginning is this: we must love one another. 12 We must not be like Cain; he belonged to the Evil One and murdered his own brother Abel. Why did Cain murder him? Because the things he himself did were wrong, but the things his brother did were right.

13 So do not be surprised, my brothers, if the people of the world hate you. 14 We know that we have left death and come over into life; we know it because we love our brothers. Whoever does not love is still under the power of death. 15 Whoever hates his brother is a murderer, and you know that a murderer has not got eternal life in him. 16 This is how we know what love is: Christ gave his life for us. We too, then, ought to give our lives for our brothers! 17 If a rich person sees his brother in need, yet closes his heart against his brother, how can he claim that he loves God? 18 My children, our love should not be just words and talk; it must be true love, which shows itself in action.

Courage before God

19 This, then, is how we will know that we belong to the truth; this is how we will be confident in God's presence. 20 If our conscience condemns us, we know that God is greater than our conscience and that he knows everything. 21 And so, my dear friends, if our conscience does not condemn us, we have courage in God's presence. 22 We receive from him whatever we ask, because we obey his commands and do what pleases him. 23 What he commands is that we believe in his Son Jesus Christ and love

one another, just as Christ commanded us. 24 Whoever obeys God's commands lives in union with God and God lives in union with him. And because of the Spirit that God has given us we know that God lives in union with us.

The True Spirit and the False

4 My dear friends, do not believe all who claim to have the Spirit, but test them to find out if the spirit they have comes from God. For many false prophets have gone out everywhere. 2 This is how you will be able to know whether it is God's Spirit: anyone who acknowledges that Jesus Christ came as a human being has the Spirit who comes from God. 3 But anyone who denies this about Jesus does not have the Spirit from God. The spirit that he has is from the Enemy of Christ; you heard that it would come, and now it is here in the world already.

4 But you belong to God, my children, and have defeated the false prophets, because the Spirit who is in you is more powerful than the spirit in those who belong to the world. 5 Those false prophets speak about matters of the world, and the world listens to them because they belong to the world. 6 But we belong to God. Whoever knows God listens to us; whoever does not belong to God does not listen to us. This, then, is how we can tell the difference between the Spirit of truth and the spirit of error.

God Is Love

7 Dear friends, let us love one another, because love comes from God. Whoever loves is a child of God and knows God. 8 Whoever does not love does not know God, for God is love. 9 And God showed his love for us by sending his only Son into the world, so that we might have life through him. 10 This is what love is: it is not that we have loved God, but that he loved us and sent his Son to be the means by which our sins are forgiven.

11 Dear friends, if this is how God loved us, then we should love one another. 12 No one has ever seen God, but if we love one another, God lives in union with us, and his love is made perfect in us.

13 We are sure that we live in union with God and that he lives in union with us, because he has given us his Spirit. ¹⁴And we have seen and tell others that the Father sent his Son to be the Saviour of the world. ¹⁵If anyone declares that Jesus is the Son of God, he lives in union with God and God lives in union with him. ¹⁶And we ourselves know and believe the love which God has for us.

God is love, and whoever lives in love lives in union with God and God lives in union with him. ¹⁷Love is made perfect in us in order that we may have courage on Judgement Day; and we will have it because our life in this world is the same as Christ's. ¹⁸There is no fear in love; perfect love drives out

Perfect love drives out all fear (4.18)

all fear. So then, love has not been made perfect in anyone who is afraid, because fear has to do with punishment.

19 We love because God first loved us. ²⁰If someone says he loves God, but hates his brother, he is a liar. For he cannot love God, whom he has not seen, if he does not love his brother, whom he has seen.

²¹ The command that Christ has given us is this: whoever loves God must love his brother also.

Our Victory over the World

5 Whoever believes that Jesus is the Messiah is a child of God; and whoever loves a father loves his child also. ² This is how we know that we love God's children: it is by loving God and obeying his commands. ³ For our love for God means that we obey his commands. And his commands are not too hard for us, ⁴ because every child of God is able to defeat the world. And we win the victory over the world by means of our faith. ⁵ Who can defeat the world? Only the person who believes that Jesus is the Son of God.

The Witness about Jesus Christ

6 Jesus Christ is the one who came with the water of his baptism and the blood of his death. He came not only with the water, but with both the water and the blood. And the Spirit himself testifies that this is true, because the Spirit is truth. ⁷ There are three witnesses: ⁸ the Spirit, the water, and the blood; and all three give the same testimony. ⁹ We believe man's testimony; but God's testimony is much stronger, and he has given this testimony about his Son. ¹⁰ So whoever believes in the Son of God has this testimony in his own heart; but whoever does not believe God, has made him out to be a liar, because he has not believed what God has said about his Son. ¹¹ The testimony is this: God has given us eternal life, and this life has its source in his Son. ¹² Whoever has the Son has this life; whoever does not have the Son of God does not have life.

Eternal Life

13 I am writing this to you so that you may know that you have eternal life—you that believe in the Son of God. ¹⁴ We have courage in God's presence, because we are sure that he hears us if we ask him for anything that is according to his will. ¹⁵ He hears us whenever we ask him; and since we know

this is true, we know also that he gives us w
we ask from him.

16 If you see your brother commit a sin that does
not lead to death, you should pray to God, who will
give him life. This applies to those whose sins do
not lead to death. But there is sin which leads to
death, and I do not say that you should pray to
God about that. ¹⁷All wrongdoing is sin, but there
is sin which does not lead to death.

18 We know that no child of God keeps on sinning,
for the Son of God keeps him safe, and the Evil
One cannot harm him.

19 We know that we belong to God even though
the whole world is under the rule of the Evil One.

20 We know that the Son of God has come and
has given us understanding, so that we know the
true God. We live in union with the true God—in
union with his Son Jesus Christ. This is the true
God, and this is eternal life.

21 My children, keep yourselves safe from false gods!

THE SECOND LETTER OF
JOHN

INTRODUCTION

The Second Letter of John was written by "the Elder"
to "the dear Lady and to her children," probably meaning a local church and its members. The brief message
is an appeal to love one another and a warning against
false teachers and their teachings.

Outline of Contents

1 From the Elder—
To the dear Lady and to her children,[a] whom I truly love. And I am not the only one, but all who know the truth love you, [2]because the truth remains in us and will be with us for ever.

3 May God the Father and Jesus Christ, the Father's Son, give us grace, mercy, and peace; may they be ours in truth and love.

Truth and Love

4 How happy I was to find that some of your children live in the truth, just as the Father commanded us. [5]And so I ask you, dear Lady: let us all love one another. This is no new command I am writing to you; it is the command which we have had from the beginning. [6]This love I speak of means that we must live in obedience to God's commands. The command, as you have all heard from the beginning, is that you must all live in love.

7 Many deceivers have gone out all over the world, people who do not acknowledge that Jesus Christ came as a human being. Such a person is a deceiver and the Enemy of Christ. [8]Be on your guard, then, so that you will not lose what we[b] have worked for, but will receive your reward in full.

9 Anyone who does not stay with the teaching of Christ, but goes beyond it, does not have God. Whoever does stay with the teaching has both the Father and the Son. [10]So then, if someone comes to you who does not bring this teaching, do not welcome him in your homes; do not even say, "Peace be with you." [11]For anyone who wishes him peace becomes his partner in the evil things he does.

Final Words

12 I have so much to tell you, but I would rather not do it with paper and ink; instead, I hope to

---

[a]LADY AND...HER CHILDREN: *This probably refers to a church and its members (also in verses 4-5).*
[b]we; *some manuscripts have* you.

visit you and talk with you personally, so that we shall be completely happy.

13 The children of your dear Sister[c] send you their greetings.

[c]CHILDREN OF YOUR DEAR SISTER: *This probably refers to the members of the church to which the writer belonged.*

THE THIRD LETTER OF

JOHN

INTRODUCTION

The Third Letter of John was written by "the Elder" to a church leader named Gaius. The writer praises Gaius because of his help to other Christians, and warns against a man named Diotrephes.

---

1 From the Elder—
To my dear Gaius, whom I truly love.

2 My dear friend, I pray that everything may go well with you and that you may be in good health—as I know you are well in spirit. 3 I was so happy when some Christian brothers arrived and told me how faithful you are to the truth—just as you always live in the truth. 4 Nothing makes me happier than to hear that my children live in the truth.

Gaius Is Praised

5 My dear friend, you are so faithful in the work you do for your fellow-Christians, even when they are strangers. 6They have spoken to the church here about your love. Please help them to continue their journey in a way that will please God. 7For they set out on their journey in the service of Christ without accepting any help from unbelievers. 8We Christians, then, must help these people, so that we may share in their work for the truth.

Diotrephes and Demetrius

9 I wrote a short letter to the church; but Diotrephes, who likes to be their leader, will not pay any attention to what I say. 10When I come, then, I will call attention to everything he has done: the terrible things he says about us and the lies he tells! But that is not enough for him; he will not receive the Christian brothers when they come, and even stops those who want to receive them and tries to drive them out of the church!

11 My dear friend, do not imitate what is bad, but imitate what is good. Whoever does good belongs to God; whoever does what is bad has not seen God.

12 Everyone speaks well of Demetrius; truth itself speaks well of him. And we add our testimony, and you know that what we say is true.

Final Greetings

13 I have so much to tell you, but I do not want to do it with pen and ink. 14I hope to see you soon, and then we will talk personally.

15 Peace be with you.

All your friends send greetings. Greet all our friends personally.

THE LETTER FROM
JUDE

INTRODUCTION

The Letter from Jude was written to warn against false teachers who claimed to be believers. In this brief letter, which is similar in content to *2 Peter,* the writer encourages his readers "to fight on for the faith which once and for all God has given to his people."

Outline of Contents

---

1 From Jude, servant of Jesus Christ, and brother of James—

To those who have been called by God, who live in the love of God the Father and the protection of Jesus Christ:

2 May mercy, peace, and love be yours in full measure.

False Teachers

3 My dear friends, I was doing my best to write to you about the salvation we share in common, when I felt the need of writing at once to encourage you to fight on for the faith which once and for all God has given to his people. ⁴For some godless people have slipped in unnoticed among us, persons who distort the message about the grace of our God in order

to excuse their immoral ways, and who reject Jesus Christ, our only Master and Lord. Long ago the Scriptures predicted the condemnation they have received.

5 For even though you know all this, I want to remind you of how the Lord[a] once rescued the people of Israel from Egypt, but afterwards destroyed those who did not believe. 6 Remember the angels who did not stay within the limits of their proper authority, but abandoned their own dwelling place: they are bound with eternal chains in the darkness below, where God is keeping them for that great Day on which they will be condemned. 7 Remember Sodom and Gomorrah, and the nearby towns, whose people acted as those angels did and indulged in sexual immorality and perversion: they suffer the punishment of eternal fire as a plain warning to all.

8 In the same way also, these people have visions which make them sin against their own bodies; they despise God's authority and insult the glorious beings above. 9 Not even the chief angel Michael did this. In his quarrel with the Devil, when they argued about who would have the body of Moses, Michael did not dare to condemn the Devil with insulting words, but said, "The Lord rebuke you!" 10 But these people attack with insults anything they do not understand; and those things that they know by instinct, like wild animals, are the very things that destroy them. 11 How terrible for them! They have followed the way that Cain took. For the sake of money they have given themselves over to the error that Balaam committed. They have rebelled as Korah rebelled, and like him they are destroyed. 12 With their shameless carousing they are like dirty spots in your fellowship meals. They take care only of themselves. They are like clouds carried along by the wind, but bringing no rain. They are like trees that bear no fruit, even in autumn, trees that have been pulled up by the roots and are completely dead. 13 They are like wild waves of the sea, with their shameful deeds showing up like foam.

---

[a] the Lord; *some manuscripts have* Jesus, *which in Greek is the same as* Joshua.

They are like wandering stars, for whom God has reserved a place for ever in the deepest darkness.

14 It was Enoch, the sixth direct descendant from Adam, who long ago prophesied this about them: "The Lord will come with many thousands of his holy angels 15 to bring judgement on all, to condemn them all for the godless deeds they have performed and for all the terrible words that godless sinners have spoken against him!"

16 These people are always grumbling and blaming others; they follow their own evil desires; they boast about themselves and flatter others in order to get their own way.

Warnings and Instructions

17 But remember, my friends, what you were told in the past by the apostles of our Lord Jesus Christ. 18 They said to you, "When the last days come, people will appear who will mock you, people who follow their own godless desires." 19 These are the people who cause divisions, who are controlled by their natural desires, who do not have the Spirit. 20 But you, my friends, keep on building yourselves up on your most sacred faith. Pray in the power of the Holy Spirit, 21 and keep yourselves in the love of God, as you wait for our Lord Jesus Christ in his mercy to give you eternal life.

22 Show mercy towards those who have doubts; 23 save others by snatching them out of the fire; and to others show mercy mixed with fear, but hate their very clothes, stained by their sinful lusts.

Prayer of Praise

24 To him who is able to keep you from falling, and to bring you faultless and joyful before his glorious presence—25 to the only God our Saviour, through Jesus Christ our Lord, be glory, majesty, might, and authority, from all ages past, and now, and for ever and ever! Amen.

THE REVELATION

TO JOHN

INTRODUCTION

The Revelation to John was written at a time when Christians were being persecuted because of their faith in Jesus Christ as Lord. The writer's main concern is to give his readers hope and encouragement, and to urge them to remain faithful during times of suffering and persecution.

For the most part the book consists of several series of revelations and visions presented in symbolic language that would have been understood by Christians of that day, but would have remained a mystery to all others. As with the themes of a symphony, the themes of this book are repeated again and again in different ways through the various series of visions. Although there are differences of opinion regarding the details of interpretation of the book, the central theme is clear: through Christ the Lord, God will finally and totally defeat all his enemies, including Satan, and will reward his faithful people with the blessings of a new heaven and a new earth when this victory is complete.

Outline of Contents

1 This book is the record of the events that Jesus Christ revealed. God gave him this revelation in order to show his servants what must happen very soon. Christ made these things known to his servant John by sending his angel to him, ²and John has told all that he has seen. This is his report concerning the message from God and the truth revealed by Jesus Christ. ³Happy is the one who reads this book, and happy are those who listen to the words of this prophetic message and obey what is written in this book! For the time is near when all these things will happen.

Greetings to the Seven Churches

4 From John to the seven churches in the province of Asia:

Grace and peace be yours from God, who is, who was, and who is to come, and from the seven spirits in front of his throne, ⁵and from Jesus Christ, the faithful witness, the first to be raised from death and who is also the ruler of the kings of the world.

He loves us, and by his sacrificial death he has freed us from our sins ⁶and made us a kingdom of priests to serve his God and Father. To Jesus Christ be the glory and power for ever and ever! Amen.

7 Look, he is coming on the clouds! Everyone will see him, including those who pierced him. All peoples on earth will mourn over him. So shall it be!

8 "I am the first and the last," says the Lord God Almighty, who is, who was, and who is to come.

A Vision of Christ

9 I am John, your brother, and as a follower of Jesus I am your partner in patiently enduring the suffering that comes to those who belong to his Kingdom. I was put on the island of Patmos because

I had proclaimed God's word and the truth that Jesus revealed. ¹⁰On the Lord's day the Spirit took control of me, and I heard a loud voice, that sounded like a trumpet, speaking behind me. ¹¹It said, "Write down what you see, and send the book to the churches in these seven cities: Ephesus, Smyrna, Pergamum, Thyatira, Sardis, Philadelphia, and Laodicea."

12 I turned round to see who was talking to me, and I saw seven gold lamp-stands, ¹³and among them there was what looked like a human being, wearing a robe that reached to his feet, and a gold belt round his chest. ¹⁴His hair was white as wool, or as snow, and his eyes blazed like fire; ¹⁵his feet shone like brass that has been refined and polished, and his voice sounded like a roaring waterfall. ¹⁶He held seven stars in his right hand, and a sharp two-edged sword came out of his mouth. His face was as bright as the midday sun. ¹⁷When I saw him, I fell down at his feet like a dead man. He placed his right hand on me and said, "Don't be afraid! I am the first and the last. ¹⁸I am the living one! I was dead, but now I am alive for ever and ever. I have authority over death and the world of the dead. ¹⁹Write, then, the things you see, both the things that are now and the things that will happen afterwards. ²⁰This is the secret meaning of the seven stars that you see in my right hand, and of the seven gold lamp-stands: the seven stars are the angels of the seven churches, and the seven lamp-stands are the seven churches.

The Message to Ephesus

2   "To the angel of the church in Ephesus write:

"This is the message from the one who holds the seven stars in his right hand and who walks among the seven gold lamp-stands. ²I know what you have done; I know how hard you have worked and how patient you have been. I know that you cannot tolerate evil men and that you have tested those who say they are apostles but are not, and have found out that they are liars. ³You are patient, you have

suffered for my sake, and you have not given up.
⁴But this is what I have against you: you do not
love me now as you did at first. ⁵Think how far
you have fallen! Turn from your sins and do what
you did at first. If you don't turn from your sins,
I will come to you and take your lamp-stand from
its place. ⁶But this is what you have in your favour:
you hate what the Nicolaitans do, as much as I do.

7 "If you have ears, then, listen to what the Spirit
says to the churches!

"To those who win the victory I will give the right
to eat the fruit of the tree of life that grows in
the Garden of God.

The Message to Smyrna

8 "To the angel of the church in Smyrna write:

"This is the message from the one who is the first
and the last, who died and lived again. ⁹I know your
troubles; I know that you are poor—but really you
are rich! I know the evil things said against you by
those who claim to be Jews but are not; they are
a group that belongs to Satan! ¹⁰Don't be afraid of
anything you are about to suffer. Listen! The Devil
will put you to the test by having some of you thrown
into prison, and your troubles will last ten days. Be
faithful to me, even if it means death, and I will
give you life as your prize of victory.

11 "If you have ears, then, listen to what the Spirit
says to the churches!

"Those who win the victory will not be hurt by
the second death.

The Message to Pergamum

12 "To the angel of the church in Pergamum write:

"This is the message from the one who has the
sharp two-edged sword. ¹³I know where you live, there
where Satan has his throne. You are true to me,
and you did not abandon your faith in me even during
the time when Antipas, my faithful witness, was killed
there where Satan lives. ¹⁴But there are a few things
I have against you: there are some among you who
follow the teaching of Balaam, who taught Balak how

to lead the people of Israel into sin by persuading them to eat food that had been offered to idols and to practise sexual immorality. 15 In the same way you have people among you who follow the teaching of the Nicolaitans. 16 Now turn from your sins! If you don't, I will come to you soon and fight against those people with the sword that comes out of my mouth.

17 "If you have ears, then, listen to what the Spirit says to the churches!

"To those who win the victory I will give some of the hidden manna. I will also give each of them a white stone on which is written a new name that no one knows except the one who receives it.

The Message to Thyatira

18 "To the angel of the church in Thyatira write:

"This is the message from the Son of God, whose eyes blaze like fire, whose feet shine like polished brass. 19 I know what you do. I know your love, your faithfulness, your service, and your patience. I know that you are doing more now than you did at first. 20 But this is what I have against you: you tolerate that woman Jezebel, who calls herself a messenger of God. By her teaching she misleads my servants into practising sexual immorality and eating food that has been offered to idols. 21 I have given her time to repent of her sins, but she does not want to turn from her immorality. 22 And so I will throw her on to a bed where she and those who committed adultery with her will suffer terribly. I will do this now unless they repent of the wicked things they did with her. 23 I will also kill her followers, and then all the churches will know that I am the one who knows everyone's thoughts and wishes. I will repay each one of you according to what he has done.

24 "But the rest of you in Thyatira have not followed this evil teaching; you have not learnt what the others call 'the deep secrets of Satan.' I say to you that I will not put any other burden on you. 25 But until I come, you must hold firmly to what you have. 26-28 To those who win the victory, who continue to the end to do what I want, I will give the same authority that I received from my Father: I will give them

authority over the nations, to rule them with an iron
rod and to break them to pieces like clay pots. I
will also give them the morning star.

29 "If you have ears, then, listen to what the Spirit
says to the churches!

The Message to Sardis

3 "To the angel of the church in Sardis write:

"This is the message from the one who has
the seven spirits of God and the seven stars. I know
what you are doing; I know that you have the reputation of being alive, even though you are dead! 2 So
wake up, and strengthen what you still have before
it dies completely. For I find that what you have
done is not yet perfect in the sight of my God. 3 Remember, then, what you were taught and what you heard;
obey it and turn from your sins. If you do not wake
up, I will come upon you like a thief, and you will
not even know the time when I will come. 4 But a
few of you there in Sardis have kept your clothes
clean. You will walk with me, clothed in white, because
you are worthy to do so. 5 Those who win the victory
will be clothed like this in white, and I will not
remove their names from the book of the living. In
the presence of my Father and of his angels I will
declare openly that they belong to me.

6 "If you have ears, then, listen to what the Spirit
says to the churches!

The Message to Philadelphia

7 "To the angel of the church in Philadelphia write:

"This is the message from the one who is holy
and true. He has the key that belonged to David,
and when he opens a door, no one can close it,
and when he closes it, no one can open it. 8 I know
what you do; I know that you have a little power;
you have followed my teaching and have been faithful
to me. I have opened a door in front of you, which
no one can close. 9 Listen! As for that group that
belongs to Satan, those liars who claim that they
are Jews but are not, I will make them come and
bow down at your feet. They will all know that I
love you. 10 Because you have kept my command to

endure, I will also keep you safe from the time of trouble which is coming upon the world to test all the people on earth. [11]I am coming soon. Keep safe what you have, so that no one will rob you of your victory prize. [12]I will make him who is victorious a pillar in the temple of my God, and he will never leave it. I will write on him the name of my God and the name of the city of my God, the new Jerusalem, which will come down out of heaven from my God. I will also write on him my new name.

13 "If you have ears, then, listen to what the Spirit says to the churches!

The Message to Laodicea

14 "To the angel of the church in Laodicea write:

"This is the message from the Amen, the faithful and true witness, who is the origin[b] of all that God has created. [15]I know what you have done; I know that you are neither cold nor hot. How I wish you were either one or the other! [16]But because you are lukewarm, neither hot nor cold, I am going to spit you out of my mouth! [17]You say, 'I am rich and well off; I have all I need.' But you do not know how miserable and pitiful you are! You are poor, naked, and blind. [18]I advise you, then, to buy gold from me, pure gold, in order to be rich. Buy also white clothing to dress yourself and cover up your shameful nakedness. Buy also some ointment to put on your eyes, so that you may see. [19]I rebuke and punish all whom I love. Be in earnest, then, and turn from your sins. [20]Listen! I stand at the door and knock; if anyone hears my voice and opens the door, I will come into his house and eat with him, and he will eat with me. [21]To those who win the victory I will give the right to sit beside me on my throne, just as I have been victorious and now sit by my Father on his throne.

22 "If you have ears, then, listen to what the Spirit says to the churches!"

---

[b]origin: or ruler.

*If anyone...opens the door, I will come into his house
(3.20)*

Worship in Heaven

4 At this point I had another vision and saw an
open door in heaven. And the voice that sounded
like a trumpet, which I had heard speaking to me
before, said, "Come up here, and I will show you
what must happen after this." ²At once the Spirit
took control of me. There in heaven was a throne
with someone sitting on it. ³His face gleamed like
such precious stones as jasper and carnelian, and all
round the throne there was a rainbow the colour
of an emerald. ⁴In a circle round the throne were
twenty-four other thrones, on which were seated
twenty-four elders dressed in white and wearing
crowns of gold. ⁵From the throne came flashes of
lightning, rumblings, and peals of thunder. In front
of the throne seven lighted torches were burning, which
are the seven spirits of God. ⁶Also in front of the
throne there was what looked like a sea of glass,
clear as crystal.

Surrounding the throne on each of its sides, were
four living creatures covered with eyes in front and
behind. ⁷The first one looked like a lion; the second
looked like a bull; the third had a face like a man's

face; and the fourth looked like an eagle in flight.
8 Each one of the four living creatures had six wings,
and they were covered with eyes, inside and out.
Day and night they never stop singing:

"Holy, holy, holy, is the Lord God Almighty,
    who was, who is, and who is to come."

9 The four living creatures sing songs of glory and
honour and thanks to the one who sits on the throne,
who lives for ever and ever. When they do so, 10 the
twenty-four elders fall down before the one who sits
on the throne, and worship him who lives for ever
and ever. They throw their crowns down in front
of the throne and say,

11 "Our Lord and God! You are worthy
    to receive glory, honour, and power.
For you created all things,
    and by your will they were given existence and
    life."

The Scroll and the Lamb

5 I saw a scroll in the right hand of the one who
sits on the throne; it was covered with writing
on both sides and was sealed with seven seals. 2 And
I saw a mighty angel, who announced in a loud voice,
"Who is worthy to break the seals and open the
scroll?" 3 But there was no one in heaven or on earth
or in the world below c who could open the scroll and
look inside it. 4 I cried bitterly because no one could
be found who was worthy to open the scroll or look
inside it. 5 Then one of the elders said to me, "Don't
cry. Look! The Lion from Judah's tribe, the great
descendant of David, has won the victory, and he
can break the seven seals and open the scroll."

6 Then I saw a Lamb standing in the centre of
the throne, surrounded by the four living creatures
and the elders. The Lamb appeared to have been
killed. It had seven horns and seven eyes, which are
the seven spirits of God that have been sent throughout
the whole earth. 7 The Lamb went and took the scroll
from the right hand of the one who sits on the throne.
8 As he did so, the four living creatures and the twenty-

c WORLD BELOW: *the world of the dead (see 1.18).*

four elders fell down before the Lamb. Each had a harp and gold bowls filled with incense, which are the prayers of God's people. 9They sang a new song:

"You are worthy to take the scroll
    and to break open its seals.
For you were killed, and by your sacrificial death you
        bought for God
    people from every tribe, language, nation, and race.
10 You have made them a kingdom of priests to
        serve our God,
    and they shall rule on earth."

11 Again I looked, and I heard angels, thousands and millions of them! They stood round the throne, the four living creatures, and the elders, 12and sang in a loud voice:

"The Lamb who was killed is worthy
    to receive power, wealth, wisdom, and strength,
    honour, glory, and praise!"

13And I heard every creature in heaven, on earth, in the world below, and in the sea—all living beings in the universe—and they were singing:

"To him who sits on the throne and to the Lamb,
    be praise and honour, glory and might,
    for ever and ever!"

14The four living creatures answered, "Amen!" And the elders fell down and worshipped.

The Seals

6 Then I saw the Lamb break open the first of the seven seals, and I heard one of the four living creatures say in a voice that sounded like thunder, "Come!" 2I looked, and there was a white horse. Its rider held a bow, and he was given a crown. He rode out as a conqueror to conquer.

3 Then the Lamb broke open the second seal; and I heard the second living creature say, "Come!" 4Another horse came out, a red one. Its rider was given the power to bring war on the earth, so that men should kill each other. He was given a large sword.

5 Then the Lamb broke open the third seal; and I heard the third living creature say, "Come!" I looked, and there was a black horse. Its rider held a pair

of scales in his hand. 6I heard what sounded like a voice coming from among the four living creatures, which said, "A litre of wheat for a day's wages, and three litres of barley for a day's wages. But do not damage the olive-trees and the vineyards!"

7 Then the Lamb broke open the fourth seal; and I heard the fourth living creature say, "Come!" 8I looked, and there was a pale-coloured horse. Its rider was named Death, and Hades*d* followed close behind. They were given authority over a quarter of the earth, to kill by means of war, famine, disease, and wild animals.

9 Then the Lamb broke open the fifth seal. I saw underneath the altar the souls of those who had been killed because they had proclaimed God's word and had been faithful in their witnessing. 10They shouted in a loud voice, "Almighty Lord, holy and true! How long will it be until you judge the people on earth and punish them for killing us?" 11Each of them was given a white robe, and they were told to rest a little while longer, until the complete number of their fellow-servants and brothers had been killed, as they had been.

12 And I saw the Lamb break open the sixth seal. There was a violent earthquake, and the sun became black like coarse black cloth, and the moon turned completely red like blood. 13The stars fell down to the earth, like unripe figs falling from the tree when a strong wind shakes it. 14The sky disappeared like a scroll being rolled up, and every mountain and island was moved from its place. 15Then the kings of the earth, the rulers and the military chiefs, the rich and the powerful, and all other men, slave and free, hid themselves in caves and under rocks on the mountains. 16They called out to the mountains and to the rocks, "Fall on us and hide us from the eyes of the one who sits on the throne and from the anger of the Lamb! 17The terrible day of their anger is here, and who can stand against it?"

*d*HADES: *The world of the dead (see 1.18).*

The 144,000 People of Israel

7 After this I saw four angels standing at the four corners of the earth, holding back the four winds so that no wind should blow on the earth or the sea or against any tree. ²And I saw another angel coming up from the east with the seal of the living God. He called out in a loud voice to the four angels to whom God had given the power to damage the earth and the sea. ³The angel said, "Do not harm the earth, the sea, or the trees, until we mark the servants of our God with a seal on their foreheads." ⁴And I was told that the number of those who were marked with God's seal on their foreheads was 144,000. They were from the twelve tribes of Israel, ⁵⁻⁸twelve thousand from each tribe: Judah, Reuben, Gad, Asher, Naphtali, Manasseh, Simeon, Levi, Issachar, Zebulun, Joseph, and Benjamin.

The Enormous Crowd

9 After this I looked, and there was an enormous crowd—no one could count all the people! They were from every race, tribe, nation, and language, and they stood in front of the throne and of the Lamb, dressed in white robes and holding palm branches in their hands. ¹⁰They called out in a loud voice: "Salvation comes from our God, who sits on the throne, and from the Lamb!" ¹¹All the angels stood round the throne, the elders, and the four living creatures. Then they threw themselves face downwards in front of the throne and worshipped God, ¹²saying, "Amen! Praise, glory, wisdom, thanksgiving, honour, power, and might belong to our God for ever and ever! Amen!"

13 One of the elders asked me, "Who are these people dressed in white robes, and where do they come from?"

14 "I don't know, sir. You do," I answered.

He said to me, "These are the people who have come safely through the terrible persecution. They have washed their robes and made them white with the blood of the Lamb. ¹⁵That is why they stand before God's throne and serve him day and night in his temple. He who sits on the throne will protect them with his presence. [16]Never again will they hunger or thirst; neither sun nor any scorching heat will burn them, [17]because the Lamb, who is in the centre of the throne, will be their shepherd, and he will guide them to springs of life-giving water. And God will wipe away every tear from their eyes."

The Seventh Seal

8 When the Lamb broke open the seventh seal, there was silence in heaven for about half an hour. [2]Then I saw the seven angels who stand before God, and they were given seven trumpets.

3 Another angel, who had a gold incense-burner, came and stood at the altar. He was given a lot of incense to add to the prayers of all God's people and to offer it on the gold altar that stands before the throne. [4]The smoke of the burning incense went up with the prayers of God's people from the hands of the angel standing before God. [5]Then the angel took the incense-burner, filled it with fire from the altar, and threw it on the earth. There were rumblings and peals of thunder, flashes of lightning, and an earthquake.

The Trumpets

6 Then the seven angels with the seven trumpets prepared to blow them.

7 The first angel blew his trumpet. Hail and fire, mixed with blood, came pouring down on the earth. A third of the earth was burnt up, a third of the trees, and every blade of green grass.

8 Then the second angel blew his trumpet. Something that looked like a huge mountain on fire was thrown into the sea. A third of the sea was turned into blood, [9]a third of the living creatures in the sea died, and a third of the ships were destroyed.

10 Then the third angel blew his trumpet. A large star, burning like a torch, dropped from the sky and fell on a third of the rivers and on the springs of water. [11](The name of the star is "Bitterness.") A third of the water turned bitter, and many people

died from drinking the water, because it had turned bitter.

12 Then the fourth angel blew his trumpet. A third of the sun was struck, and a third of the moon, and a third of the stars, so that their light lost a third of its brightness; there was no light during a third of the day and a third of the night.

13 Then I looked, and I heard an eagle that was flying high in the air say in a loud voice, "O horror! horror! How horrible it will be for all who live on earth when the sound comes from the trumpets that the other three angels must blow!"

9 Then the fifth angel blew his trumpet. I saw a star which had fallen down to the earth, and it was given the key to the abyss.*e* ²The star opened the abyss, and smoke poured out of it, like the smoke from a large furnace; the sunlight and the air were darkened by the smoke from the abyss. ³Locusts came down out of the smoke upon the earth, and they were given the same kind of power that scorpions have. ⁴They were told not to harm the grass or the trees or any other plant; they could harm only the people who did not have the mark of God's seal on their foreheads. ⁵The locusts were not allowed to kill these people, but only to torture them for five months. The pain caused by the torture is like the pain caused by a scorpion's sting. ⁶During those five months they will seek death, but will not find it; they will want to die, but death will flee from them.

7 The locusts looked like horses ready for battle; on their heads they had what seemed to be crowns of gold, and their faces were like men's faces. ⁸Their hair was like women's hair, their teeth were like lions' teeth. ⁹Their chests were covered with what looked like iron breastplates, and the sound made by their wings was like the noise of many horse-drawn chariots rushing into battle. ¹⁰They have tails and stings like those of a scorpion, and it is with their tails that they have the power to hurt people for five months. ¹¹They have a king ruling over them, who is the

*e*ABYSS: *The place in the depths of the earth where the demons were imprisoned until their final punishment.*

angel in charge of the abyss. His name in Hebrew is Abaddon; in Greek the name is Apollyon (meaning "The Destroyer").

12 The first horror is over; after this there are still two more horrors to come.

13 Then the sixth angel blew his trumpet. I heard a voice coming from the four corners of the gold altar standing before God. 14 The voice said to the sixth angel, "Release the four angels who are bound at the great river Euphrates!" 15 The four angels were released; for this very hour of this very day of this very month and year they had been kept ready to kill a third of all mankind. 16 I was told the number of the mounted troops: it was two hundred million. 17 And in my vision I saw the horses and their riders: they had breastplates red as fire, blue as sapphire, and yellow as sulphur. The horses' heads were like lions' heads, and from their mouths came out fire, smoke, and sulphur. 18 A third of mankind was killed by those three plagues: the fire, the smoke, and the sulphur coming out of the horses' mouths. 19 For the power of the horses is in their mouths and also in their tails. Their tails are like snakes with heads, and they use them to hurt people.

20 The rest of mankind, all those who had not been killed by these plagues, did not turn away from what they themselves had made. They did not stop worshipping demons, nor the idols of gold, silver, bronze, stone, and wood, which cannot see, hear, or walk. 21 Nor did they repent of their murders, their magic, their sexual immorality, or their stealing.

The Angel and the Little Scroll

10 Then I saw another mighty angel coming down out of heaven. He was wrapped in a cloud and had a rainbow round his head; his face was like the sun, and his legs were like pillars of fire. 2 He had a small scroll open in his hand. He put his right foot on the sea and his left foot on the land, 3 and called out in a loud voice that sounded like the roar of lions. After he had called out, the seven thunders answered with a roar. 4 As soon as they spoke, I was about to write. But I heard a voice speak from heaven, "Keep secret what the seven thunders have said; do not write it down!"

5 Then the angel that I saw standing on the sea and on the land raised his right hand to heaven 6 and took a vow in the name of God, who lives for ever and ever, who created heaven, earth, and the sea, and everything in them. The angel said, "There will be no more delay! 7 But when the seventh angel blows his trumpet, then God will accomplish his secret plan, as he announced to his servants, the prophets."

8 Then the voice that I had heard speaking from heaven spoke to me again, saying, "Go and take the open scroll which is in the hand of the angel standing on the sea and on the land."

9 I went to the angel and asked him to give me the little scroll. He said to me, "Take it and eat it; it will turn sour in your stomach, but in your mouth it will be sweet as honey."

10 I took the little scroll from his hand and ate it, and it tasted sweet as honey in my mouth. But after I swallowed it, it turned sour in my stomach. 11 Then I was told, "Once again you must proclaim God's message about many nations, races, languages, and kings."

The Two Witnesses

11 I was then given a stick that looked like a measuring-rod, and was told, "Go and measure the temple of God and the altar, and count those who are worshipping in the temple. 2 But do not measure the outer courts, because they have been given to the heathen, who will trample on the Holy City for forty-two months. 3 I will send my two witnesses dressed in sackcloth, and they will proclaim God's message during those 1,260 days."

4 The two witnesses are the two olive-trees and the two lamps that stand before the Lord of the earth. 5 If anyone tries to harm them, fire comes out of their mouths and destroys their enemies; and in this way, whoever tries to harm them will be killed. 6 They have authority to shut up the sky so that there will be no rain during the time they proclaim God's message. They have authority also over the

springs of water, to turn them into blood; they have authority also to strike the earth with every kind of plague as often as they wish.

7 When they finish proclaiming their message, the beast that comes up out of the abyss will fight against them. He will defeat them and kill them, 8 and their bodies will lie in the street of the great city, where their Lord was crucified. The symbolic name of that city is Sodom, or Egypt. 9 People from all nations, tribes, languages, and races will look at their bodies for three and a half days and will not allow them to be buried. 10 The people of the earth will be happy because of the death of these two. They will celebrate and send presents to each other, because those two prophets brought much suffering upon mankind. 11 After three and a half days a life-giving breath came from God and entered them, and they stood up; and all who saw them were terrified. 12 Then the two prophets heard a loud voice say to them from heaven, "Come up here!" As their enemies watched, they went up into heaven in a cloud. 13 At that very moment there was a violent earthquake; a tenth of the city was destroyed, and seven thousand people were killed. The rest of the people were terrified and praised the greatness of the God of heaven.

14 The second horror is over, but the third horror will come soon!

The Seventh Trumpet

15 Then the seventh angel blew his trumpet, and there were loud voices in heaven, saying, "The power to rule over the world belongs now to our Lord and his Messiah, and he will rule for ever and ever!" 16 Then the twenty-four elders who sit on their thrones in front of God threw themselves face downwards and worshipped God, 17 saying:

"Lord God Almighty, who is and who was!
We thank you that you have taken your great power
  and have begun to rule!
18 The heathen were filled with rage,
  because the time for your anger has come,
  the time for the dead to be judged.

The time has come to reward your servants, the
  prophets,
    and all your people, all who have reverence for you,
    great and small alike.
The time has come to destroy those who destroy
    the earth!"

19 God's temple in heaven was opened, and the Covenant Box was seen there. Then there were flashes of lightning, rumblings and peals of thunder, an earthquake, and heavy hail.

The Woman and the Dragon

12 Then a great and mysterious sight appeared in the sky. There was a woman, whose dress was the sun and who had the moon under her feet and a crown of twelve stars on her head. ²She was soon to give birth, and the pains and suffering of childbirth made her cry out.

3 Another mysterious sight appeared in the sky. There was a huge red dragon with seven heads and ten horns and a crown on each of his heads. ⁴With his tail he dragged a third of the stars out of the sky and threw them down to the earth. He stood in front of the woman, in order to eat her child as soon as it was born. ⁵Then she gave birth to a son, who will rule over all nations with an iron rod. But the child was snatched away and taken to God and his throne. ⁶The woman fled to the desert, to a place God had prepared for her, where she will be taken care of for 1,260 days.

7 Then war broke out in heaven. Michael and his angels fought against the dragon, who fought back with his angels; ⁸but the dragon was defeated, and he and his angels were not allowed to stay in heaven any longer. ⁹The huge dragon was thrown out—that ancient serpent, called the Devil, or Satan, that deceived the whole world. He was thrown down to earth, and all his angels with him.

10 Then I heard a loud voice in heaven saying, "Now God's salvation has come! Now God has shown his power as King! Now his Messiah has shown his authority! For the one who stood before our God and accused our brothers day and night has been

thrown out of heaven. [11] Our brothers won the victory over him by the blood of the Lamb and by the truth which they proclaimed; and they were willing to give up their lives and die. [12] And so be glad, you heavens, and all you that live there! But how terrible for the earth and the sea! For the Devil has come down to you, and he is filled with rage, because he knows that he has only a little time left."

13 When the dragon realized that he had been thrown down to the earth, he began to pursue the woman who had given birth to the boy. [14] She was given the two wings of a large eagle in order to fly to her place in the desert, where she will be taken care of for three and a half years, safe from the dragon's attack. [15] And then from his mouth the dragon poured out a flood of water after the woman, so that it would carry her away. [16] But the earth helped the woman; it opened its mouth and swallowed the water that had come from the dragon's mouth. [17] The dragon was furious with the woman and went off to fight against the rest of her descendants, all those who obey God's commandments and are faithful to the truth revealed by Jesus. [18] And the dragon stood[f] on the sea-shore.

The Two Beasts

13 Then I saw a beast coming up out of the sea. It had ten horns and seven heads; on each of its horns there was a crown, and on each of its heads there was a name that was insulting to God. [2] The beast looked like a leopard, with feet like a bear's feet and a mouth like a lion's mouth. The dragon gave the beast his own power, his throne, and his vast authority. [3] One of the heads of the beast seemed to have been fatally wounded, but the wound had healed. The whole earth was amazed and followed the beast. [4] Everyone worshipped the dragon because he had given his authority to the beast. They worshipped the beast also, saying, "Who is like the beast? Who can fight against it?"

[f] And the dragon stood; *some manuscripts have* And I stood, *connecting this verse with what follows.*

5 The beast was allowed to make proud claims which were insulting to God, and it was permitted to have authority for forty-two months. 6 It began to curse God, his name, the place where he lives, and all those who live in heaven. 7 It was allowed to fight against God's people and to defeat them, and it was given authority over every tribe, nation, language, and race. 8 All people living on earth will worship it, except those whose names were written before the creation of the world in the book of the living which belongs to the Lamb that was killed.

9 "Listen, then, if you have ears! 10 Whoever is meant to be captured will surely be captured; whoever is meant to be killed by the sword will surely be killed by the sword. This calls for endurance and faith on the part of God's people."

11 Then I saw another beast, which came up out of the earth. It had two horns like a lamb's horns, and it spoke like a dragon. 12 It used the vast authority of the first beast in its presence. It forced the earth and all who live on it to worship the first beast, whose wound had healed. 13 This second beast performed great miracles; it made fire come down out of heaven to earth in the sight of everyone. 14 And it deceived all the people living on earth by means of the miracles which it was allowed to perform in the presence of the first beast. The beast told them to build an image in honour of the beast that had been wounded by the sword and yet lived. 15 The second beast was allowed to breathe life into the image of the first beast, so that the image could talk and put to death all those who would not worship it. 16 The beast forced all the people, small and great, rich and poor, slave and free, to have a mark placed on their right hands or on their foreheads. 17 No one could buy or sell unless he had this mark, that is, the beast's name or the number that stands for the name.

18 This calls for wisdom. Whoever is intelligent can work out the meaning of the number of the beast, because the number stands for a man's name. Its number is 666.

The Lamb and His People

14 Then I looked, and there was the Lamb standing on Mount Zion; with him were 144,000 people who have his name and his Father's name written on their foreheads. ²And I heard a voice from heaven that sounded like a roaring waterfall, like a loud peal of thunder. It sounded like the music made by musicians playing their harps. ³The 144,000 people stood before the throne, the four living creatures, and the elders; they were singing a new song, which only they could learn. Of all mankind they are the only ones who have been redeemed. ⁴They are the men who have kept themselves pure by not having sexual relations with women; they are virgins. They follow the Lamb wherever he goes. They have been redeemed from the rest of mankind and are the first ones to be offered to God and to the Lamb. ⁵They have never been known to tell lies; they are faultless.

The Three Angels

6 Then I saw another angel flying high in the air, with an eternal message of Good News to announce to the peoples of the earth, to every race, tribe, language, and nation. ⁷He said in a loud voice, "Honour God and praise his greatness! For the time has come for him to judge mankind. Worship him who made heaven, earth, sea, and the springs of water!"

8 A second angel followed the first one, saying, "She has fallen! Great Babylon has fallen! She made all peoples drink her wine—the strong wine of her immoral lust!"

9 A third angel followed the first two, saying in a loud voice, "Whoever worships the beast and its image and receives the mark on his forehead or on his hand ¹⁰will himself drink God's wine, the wine of his fury, which he has poured at full strength into the cup of his anger! All who do this will be tormented in fire and sulphur before the holy angels and the Lamb. ¹¹The smoke of the fire that torments them goes up for ever and ever. There is no relief day or night for those who worship the beast and its image, for anyone who has the mark of its name."

12 This calls for endurance on the part of God's people, those who obey God's commandments and are faithful to Jesus.

13 Then I heard a voice from heaven saying, "Write this: Happy are those who from now on die in the service of the Lord!"

"Yes indeed!" answers the Spirit. "They will enjoy rest from their hard work, because the results of their service go with them."

The Harvest of the Earth

14 Then I looked, and there was a white cloud, and sitting on the cloud was what looked like a human being, with a crown of gold on his head and a sharp sickle in his hand. 15 Then another angel came out from the temple and cried out in a loud voice to the one who was sitting on the cloud, "Use your sickle and reap the harvest, because the time has come; the earth is ripe for the harvest!" 16 Then the one who sat on the cloud swung his sickle on the earth, and the earth's harvest was reaped.

17 Then I saw another angel come out of the temple in heaven, and he also had a sharp sickle.

18 Then another angel, who is in charge of the fire, came from the altar. He shouted in a loud voice to the angel who had the sharp sickle, "Use your sickle, and cut the grapes from the vineyard of the earth, because the grapes are ripe!" 19 So the angel swung his sickle on the earth, cut the grapes from the vine, and threw them into the winepress of God's furious anger. 20 The grapes were squeezed out in the winepress outside the city, and blood came out of the winepress in a flood three hundred kilometres long and nearly two metres deep.

The Angels with the Last Plagues

15 Then I saw in the sky another mysterious sight, great and amazing. There were seven angels with seven plagues, which are the last ones, because they are the final expression of God's anger.

2 Then I saw what looked like a sea of glass mixed with fire. I also saw those who had won the victory over the beast and its image and over the one whose

name is represented by a number. They were standing by the sea of glass, holding harps that God had given them ³and singing the song of Moses, the servant of God, and the song of the Lamb:

"Lord God Almighty,
  how great and wonderful are your deeds!
King of the nations,ᵍ
  how right and true are your ways!
⁴ Who will not stand in awe of you, Lord?
  Who will refuse to declare your greatness?
  You alone are holy.
All the nations will come
  and worship you,
  because your just actions are seen by all."

5 After this I saw the temple in heaven open, with the Tent of God's presence in it. ⁶The seven angels who had the seven plagues came out of the temple, dressed in clean shining linen and with gold belts tied around their chests. ⁷Then one of the four living creatures gave the seven angels seven gold bowls full of the anger of God, who lives for ever and ever. ⁸The temple was filled with smoke from the glory and power of God, and no one could go into the temple until the seven plagues brought by the seven angels had come to an end.

The Bowls of God's Anger

16 Then I heard a loud voice speaking from the temple to the seven angels: "Go and pour out the seven bowls of God's anger on the earth!"

2 The first angel went and poured out his bowl on the earth. Terrible and painful sores appeared on those who had the mark of the beast and on those who had worshipped its image.

3 Then the second angel poured out his bowl on the sea. The water became like the blood of a dead person, and every living creature in the sea died.

4 Then the third angel poured out his bowl on the rivers and the springs of water, and they turned into blood. ⁵I heard the angel in charge of the waters say, "The judgements you have made are just, O

ᵍnations; *some manuscripts have* ages.

Holy One, you who are and who were! 6 They poured
out the blood of God's people and of the prophets,
and so you have given them blood to drink. They are
getting what they deserve!" 7 Then I heard a voice
from the altar saying, "Lord God Almighty! True and
just indeed are your judgements!"

8 Then the fourth angel poured out his bowl on
the sun, and it was allowed to burn people with
its fiery heat. 9 They were burnt by the fierce heat, and
they cursed the name of God, who has authority over
these plagues. But they would not turn from their
sins and praise his greatness.

10 Then the fifth angel poured out his bowl on
the throne of the beast. Darkness fell over the beast's
kingdom, and people bit their tongues because of their
pain, 11 and they cursed the God of heaven for their
pains and sores. But they did not turn from their
evil ways.

12 Then the sixth angel poured out his bowl on
the great river Euphrates. The river dried up, to provide
a way for the kings who come from the east. 13 Then
I saw three unclean spirits that looked like frogs.
They were coming out of the mouth of the dragon,
the mouth of the beast, and the mouth of the false
prophet. 14 They are the spirits of demons that perform
miracles. These three spirits go out to all the kings
of the world, to bring them together for the battle
on the great Day of Almighty God.

15 "Listen! I am coming like a thief! Happy is
he who stays awake and guards his clothes, so that
he will not walk around naked and be ashamed in
public!"

16 Then the spirits brought the kings together in
the place that in Hebrew is called Armageddon.

17 Then the seventh angel poured out his bowl in
the air. A loud voice came from the throne in the
temple, saying, "It is done!" 18 There were flashes
of lightning, rumblings and peals of thunder, and a
terrible earthquake. There has never been such an
earthquake since the creation of man; this was the
worst earthquake of all! 19 The great city was split
into three parts, and the cities of all countries were
destroyed. God remembered great Babylon and made

her drink the wine from his cup—the wine of his
furious anger. [20] All the islands disappeared, all the
mountains vanished. [21] Huge hailstones, each weighing
as much as fifty kilogrammes, fell from the sky on
people, who cursed God on account of the plague
of hail, because it was such a terrible plague.

The Famous Prostitute

17 Then one of the seven angels who had the
seven bowls came to me and said, "Come, and
I will show you how the famous prostitute is to be punished, that great city that is built near many rivers.
[2] The kings of the earth practised sexual immorality
with her, and the people of the world became drunk
from drinking the wine of her immorality."

[3] The Spirit took control of me, and the angel carried
me to a desert. There I saw a woman sitting on
a red beast that had names insulting to God written
all over it; the beast had seven heads and ten horns.
[4] The woman was dressed in purple and scarlet, and
covered with gold ornaments, precious stones, and
pearls. In her hand she held a gold cup full of obscene
and filthy things, the result of her immorality. [5] On
her forehead was written a name that has a secret
meaning: "Great Babylon, the mother of all the prostitutes and perverts in the world." [6] And I saw that
the woman was drunk with the blood of God's people
and the blood of those who were killed because they
had been loyal to Jesus.

When I saw her, I was completely amazed. [7] "Why
are you amazed?" the angel asked me. "I will tell
you the secret meaning of the woman and of the
beast that carries her, the beast with seven heads
and ten horns. [8] That beast was once alive, but lives
no longer; it is about to come up from the abyss
and will go off to be destroyed. The people living
on earth whose names have not been written before
the creation of the world in the book of the living,
will all be amazed as they look at the beast. It was
once alive; now it no longer lives, but it will reappear.

[9] "This calls for wisdom and understanding. The
seven heads are seven hills, on which the woman
sits. They are also seven kings: [10] five of them have

fallen, one still rules, and the other one has not yet come; when he comes, he must rule only a little while. 11 And the beast that was once alive, but lives no longer, is itself an eighth king who is one of the seven and is going off to be destroyed.

12 "The ten horns you saw are ten kings who have not yet begun to rule, but who will be given authority to rule as kings for one hour with the beast. 13 These ten all have the same purpose, and they give their power and authority to the beast. 14 They will fight against the Lamb; but the Lamb, together with his called, chosen, and faithful followers, will defeat them, because he is Lord of lords and King of kings."

15 The angel also said to me, "The waters you saw, on which the prostitute is sitting, are nations, peoples, races, and languages. 16 The ten horns you saw, and the beast, will hate the prostitute; they will take away everything she has and leave her naked; they will eat her flesh and destroy her with fire. 17 For God has placed in their hearts the will to carry out his purpose by acting together and giving the beast their power to rule until God's words come true.

18 "The woman you saw is the great city that rules over the kings of the earth."

The Fall of Babylon

18 After this I saw another angel coming down out of heaven. He had great authority, and his splendour brightened the whole earth. 2 He cried out in a loud voice: "She has fallen! Great Babylon has fallen! She is now haunted by demons and unclean spirits; all kinds of filthy and hateful birds live in her. 3 For all the nations have drunk her wine—the strong wine of her immoral lust. The kings of the earth practised sexual immorality with her, and the businessmen of the world grew rich from her unrestrained lust."

4 Then I heard another voice from heaven, saying,
"Come out, my people! Come out from her!
  You must not take part in her sins;
  you must not share in her punishment!
5 For her sins are piled up as high as heaven,
  and God remembers her wicked ways.

6 Treat her exactly as she has treated you;
   pay her back double for all she has done.
Fill her cup with a drink twice as strong
   as the drink she prepared for you.
7 Give her as much suffering and grief
   as the glory and luxury she gave herself.
For she keeps telling herself:
'Here I sit, a queen!
   I am no widow,
   I will never know grief!'
8 Because of this, in one day she will be struck with
   plagues—
   disease, grief, and famine.
And she will be burnt with fire,
   because the Lord God, who judges her, is mighty."

9 The kings of the earth who took part in her immorality and lust will cry and weep over the city when they see the smoke from the flames that consume her. 10 They stand a long way off, because they are

This great and mighty city Babylon! (18.10)

afraid of sharing in her suffering. They say, "How terrible! How awful! This great and mighty city Babylon! In just one hour you have been punished!"

11 The businessmen of the earth also cry and mourn for her, because no one buys their goods any longer;

12 no one buys their gold, silver, precious stones, and pearls; their goods of linen, purple cloth, silk, and scarlet cloth; all kinds of rare woods and all kinds of objects made of ivory and of expensive wood, of bronze, iron, and marble; 13 and cinnamon, spice, incense, myrrh, and frankincense; wine and oil, flour and wheat, cattle and sheep, horses and carriages, slaves, and even human lives. 14 The businessmen say to her, "All the good things you longed to own have disappeared, and all your wealth and glamour are gone, and you will never find them again!" 15 The businessmen, who became rich from doing business in that city, will stand a long way off, because they are afraid of sharing in her suffering. They will cry and mourn, 16 and say, "How terrible! How awful for the great city! She used to dress herself in linen, purple, and scarlet, and cover herself with gold ornaments, precious stones, and pearls! 17 And in one hour she has lost all this wealth!"

All the ships' captains and passengers, the sailors and all others who earn their living on the sea, stood a long way off, 18 and cried out as they saw the smoke from the flames that consumed her: "There never has been another city like this great city!" 19 They threw dust on their heads, they cried and mourned, saying, "How terrible! How awful for the great city! She is the city where all who have ships sailing the seas became rich on her wealth! And in one hour she has lost everything!"

20 Be glad, heaven, because of her destruction! Be glad, God's people and the apostles and prophets! For God has condemned her for what she did to you!

21 Then a mighty angel picked up a stone the size of a large millstone and threw it into the sea, saying, "This is how the great city Babylon will be violently thrown down and will never be seen again. 22 The music of harps and of human voices, of players of the flute and the trumpet, will never be heard in you again! No workman in any trade will ever be found in you again; and the sound of the millstone will be heard no more! 23 Never again will the light of a lamp be seen in you; no more will the voices

of brides and grooms be heard in you. Your business-men were the most powerful in all the world, and with your false magic you deceived all the peoples of the world!"

24 Babylon was punished because the blood of pro-phets and of God's people was found in the city; yes, the blood of all those who have been killed on earth.

19 After this I heard what sounded like the roar of a large crowd of people in heaven, saying, "Praise God! Salvation, glory, and power belong to our God! ²True and just are his judgements! He has condemned the prostitute who was corrupting the earth with her immorality. God has punished her because she killed his servants." ³Again they shouted, "Praise God! The smoke from the flames that consume the great city goes up for ever and ever!" ⁴The twenty-four elders and the four living creatures fell down and worshipped God, who was seated on the throne. They said, "Amen! Praise God!"

The Wedding-Feast of the Lamb

5 Then there came from the throne the sound of a voice, saying, "Praise our God, all his servants and all people, both great and small, who have reverence for him!" ⁶Then I heard what sounded like a large crowd, like the sound of a roaring waterfall, like loud peals of thunder. I heard them say, "Praise God! For the Lord, our Almighty God, is King! ⁷Let us rejoice and be glad; let us praise his greatness! For the time has come for the wedding of the Lamb, and his bride has prepared herself for it. ⁸She has been given clean shining linen to wear." (The linen is the good deeds of God's people.)

9 Then the angel said to me, "Write this: Happy are those who have been invited to the wedding-feast of the Lamb." And the angel added, "These are the true words of God."

10 I fell down at his feet to worship him, but he said to me, "Don't do it! I am a fellow-servant of yours and of your brothers, all those who hold to the truth that Jesus revealed. Worship God!"

For the truth that Jesus revealed is what inspires the prophets.

The Rider on the White Horse

11 Then I saw heaven open, and there was a white horse. Its rider is called Faithful and True; it is with justice that he judges and fights his battles. 12 His eyes were like a flame of fire, and he wore many crowns on his head. He had a name written on him, but no one except himself knows what it is. 13 The robe he wore was covered with blood. His name is "The Word of God." 14 The armies of heaven followed him, riding on white horses and dressed in clean white linen. 15 Out of his mouth came a sharp sword, with which he will defeat the nations. He will rule over them with a rod of iron, and he will trample out the wine in the winepress of the furious anger of the Almighty God. 16 On his robe and on his thigh was written the name: "King of kings and Lord of lords."

17 Then I saw an angel standing on the sun. He shouted in a loud voice to all the birds flying in midair: "Come and gather together for God's great feast! 18 Come and eat the flesh of kings, generals, and soldiers, the flesh of horses and their riders, the flesh of all people, slave and free, great and small!"

19 Then I saw the beast and the kings of the earth and their armies gathered to fight against the one who was riding the horse and against his army. 20 The beast was taken prisoner, together with the false prophet who had performed miracles in his presence. (It was by those miracles that he had deceived those who had the mark of the beast and those who had worshipped the image of the beast.) The beast and the false prophet were both thrown alive into the lake of fire that burns with sulphur. 21 Their armies were killed by the sword that comes out of the mouth of the one who was riding the horse; and all the birds ate all they could of their flesh.

The Thousand Years

20 Then I saw an angel coming down from heaven, holding in his hand the key of the abyss and a heavy chain. ²He seized the dragon, that ancient serpent—that is, the Devil, or Satan—and chained him up for a thousand years. ³The angel threw him into the abyss, locked it, and sealed it, so that he could not deceive the nations any more until the thousand years were over. After that he must be let loose for a little while.

4 Then I saw thrones, and those who sat on them were given the power to judge. I also saw the souls of those who had been executed because they had proclaimed the truth that Jesus revealed and the word of God. They had not worshipped the beast or its image, nor had they received the mark of the beast on their foreheads or their hands. They came to life and ruled as kings with Christ for a thousand years. ⁵(The rest of the dead did not come to life until the thousand years were over.) This is the first raising of the dead. ⁶Happy and greatly blessed are those who are included in this first raising of the dead. The second death has no power over them; they shall be priests of God and of Christ, and they will rule with him for a thousand years.

The Defeat of Satan

7 After the thousand years are over, Satan will be let loose from his prison, ⁸and he will go out to deceive the nations scattered over the whole world, that is, Gog and Magog. Satan will bring them all together for battle, as many as the grains of sand on the sea-shore. ⁹They spread out over the earth and surrounded the camp of God's people and the city that he loves. But fire came down from heaven and destroyed them. ¹⁰Then the Devil, who deceived them, was thrown into the lake of fire and sulphur, where the beast and the false prophet had already been thrown; and they will be tormented day and night for ever and ever.

The Final Judgement

11 Then I saw a great white throne and the one who sits on it. Earth and heaven fled from his presence and were seen no more. ¹²And I saw the dead, great and small alike, standing before the throne. Books were

opened, and then another book was opened, the book of the living. The dead were judged according to what they had done, as recorded in the books. 13 Then the sea gave up its dead. Death and the world of the dead also gave up the dead they held. And all were judged according to what they had done. 14 Then death and the world of the dead were thrown into the lake of fire. (This lake of fire is the second death.) 15 Whoever did not have his name written in the book of the living was thrown into the lake of fire.

The New Heaven and the New Earth

21 Then I saw a new heaven and a new earth. The first heaven and the first earth disappeared, and the sea vanished. 2 And I saw the Holy City, the new Jerusalem, coming down out of heaven from God, prepared and ready, like a bride dressed to meet her husband. 3 I heard a loud voice speaking from the throne: "Now God's home is with mankind! He will live with them, and they shall be his people. God himself will be with them, and he will be their God. 4 He will wipe away all tears from their eyes. There will be no more death, no more grief or crying or pain. The old things have disappeared."

5 Then the one who sits on the throne said, "And now I make all things new!" He also said to me, "Write this, because these words are true and can be trusted." 6 And he said, "It is done! I am the first and the last, the beginning and the end. To anyone who is thirsty I will give the right to drink from the spring of the water of life without paying for it. 7 Whoever wins the victory will receive this from me: I will be his God, and he will be my son. 8 But cowards, traitors, perverts, murderers, the immoral, those who practise magic, those who worship idols, and all liars— the place for them is the lake burning with fire and sulphur, which is the second death."

The New Jerusalem

9 One of the seven angels who had the seven bowls full of the seven last plagues came to me and said,

"Come, and I will show you the Bride, the wife of the Lamb." 10 The Spirit took control of me, and the angel carried me to the top of a very high mountain. He showed me Jerusalem, the Holy City, coming down out of heaven from God 11 and shining with the glory of God. The city shone like a precious stone, like a jasper, clear as crystal. 12 It had a great, high wall with twelve gates and with twelve angels in charge of the gates. On the gates were written the names of the twelve tribes of the people of Israel. 13 There were three gates on each side: three on the east, three on the south, three on the north, and three on the west. 14 The city's wall was built on twelve foundation-stones, on which were written the names of the twelve apostles of the Lamb. 15 The angel who spoke to me had a gold measuring-rod to measure the city, its gates, and its wall. 16 The city was perfectly square, as wide as it was long. The angel measured the city with his measuring-rod: it was 2,400 kilometres long and was as wide and as high as it was long. 17 The angel also measured the wall, and it was sixty metres high, *h* according to the standard unit of measure which he was using. *i* 18 The wall was made of jasper, and the city itself was made of pure gold, as clear as glass. 19 The foundation-stones of the city wall were adorned with all kinds of precious stones. The first foundation-stone was jasper, the second sapphire, the third agate, the fourth emerald, 20 the fifth onyx, the sixth carnelian, the seventh yellow quartz, the eighth beryl, the ninth topaz, the tenth chalcedony, the eleventh turquoise, the twelfth amethyst. 21 The twelve gates were twelve pearls; each gate was made from a single pearl. The street of the city was of pure gold, transparent as glass.

22 I did not see a temple in the city, because its temple is the Lord God Almighty and the Lamb. 23 The city has no need of the sun or the moon to shine on it, because the glory of God shines on it, and the Lamb is its lamp. 24 The peoples of the world will walk by its light, and the kings of the earth

h high; *or* thick.
i In verses 16 and 17 the Greek text speaks of "12,000 furlongs" and "144 cubits" which may have symbolic significance.

will bring their wealth into it. ²⁵The gates of the city will stand open all day; they will never be closed, because there will be no night there. ²⁶The greatness and the wealth of the nations will be brought into the city. ²⁷But nothing that is impure will enter the city, nor anyone who does shameful things or tells lies. Only those whose names are written in the Lamb's book of the living will enter the city.

22 The angel also showed me the river of the water of life, sparkling like crystal, and coming from the throne of God and of the Lamb ²and flowing down the middle of the city's street. On each side of the river was the tree of life, which bears fruit twelve times a year, once each month; and its leaves are for the healing of the nations. ³Nothing that is under God's curse will be found in the city.

The throne of God and of the Lamb will be in the city, and his servants will worship him. ⁴They will see his face, and his name will be written on their foreheads. ⁵There shall be no more night, and they will not need lamps or sunlight, because the Lord God will be their light, and they will rule as kings for ever and ever.

The Coming of Jesus

6 Then the angel said to me, "These words are true and can be trusted. And the Lord God, who gives his Spirit to the prophets, has sent his angel to show his servants what must happen very soon."

7 "Listen!" says Jesus. "I am coming soon! Happy are those who obey the prophetic words in this book!"

8 I, John, have heard and seen all these things. And when I finished hearing and seeing them, I fell down at the feet of the angel who had shown me these things, and I was about to worship him. ⁹But he said to me, "Don't do it! I am a fellow-servant of yours and of your brothers the prophets and of all those who obey the words in this book. Worship God!" ¹⁰And he said to me, "Do not keep the prophetic words of this book a secret, because the time is near when all this will happen. ¹¹Whoever is evil must go on doing evil, and whoever is filthy must go on being filthy; whoever is good must go on doing good,

and whoever is holy must go on being holy."

12 "Listen!" says Jesus. "I am coming soon! I will bring my rewards with me, to give to each one according to what he has done. 13 I am the first and the last, the beginning and the end."

14 Happy are those who wash their robes clean and so have the right to eat the fruit from the tree of life and to go through the gates into the city. 15 But outside the city are the perverts and those who practise magic, the immoral and the murderers, those who worship idols and those who are liars both in words and deeds.

16 "I, Jesus, have sent my angel to announce these things to you in the churches. I am descended from the family of David; I am the bright morning star."

17 The Spirit and the Bride say, "Come!"

Everyone who hears this must also say, "Come!"

Come, whoever is thirsty; accept the water of life as a gift, whoever wants it.

Conclusion

18 I, John, solemnly warn everyone who hears the prophetic words of this book: if anyone adds anything to them, God will add to his punishment the plagues described in this book. 19 And if anyone takes anything away from the prophetic words of this book, God will take away from him his share of the fruit of the tree of life and of the Holy City, which are described in this book.

20 He who gives his testimony to all this says, "Yes indeed! I am coming soon!"

So be it. Come, Lord Jesus!

21 May the grace of the Lord Jesus be with everyone.*j*

*j*everyone; *some manuscripts have* God's people; *others have* all God's people.

Word List

(See Index for further New Testament references)

A

Aaron The brother of Moses, who was chosen by God to be the chief priest in Israel (Exodus 28.1—30.10).

Abel One of Adam's sons who was murdered by his brother Cain (Genesis 4.1–16).

Achaia A Roman province covering what is now the southern half of Greece (the northern half of modern Greece was known as Macedonia). The capital city of the province was Corinth; other cities in Achaia mentioned in the New Testament are Cenchreae and Athens.

Agate A semi-precious stone of different colours, but usually white and brown.

Agrippa Herod Agrippa II, great-grandson of Herod the Great, was king of Chalcis, a small country north of Palestine, and ruler of nearby territories. Paul made his defence before him and his sister Bernice (Acts 25.13—26.32).

Alabaster A soft stone, usually of light creamy colour, from which vases and jars were made.

Aloes A sweet-smelling liquid, produced from a plant. It was used as medicine and as a perfume.

Altar The place where sacrifices were offered to God.

Amen A Hebrew word which means "it is so" or "may it be so". It can also be translated "certainly", "truly", or "surely". In Revelation 3.14 it is used as a name for Christ.

Amethyst A semi-precious stone, usually purple or violet in colour.

Ancestor Someone who lived in the past, from whom a person is descended.

Anoint To pour or rub olive-oil on someone in order to honour him or to appoint him to some special work. The Israelite kings were anointed when they took office, and so the king could be called "the anointed one". Christ, the Greek word for "The Anointed One", is the title of the one whom God chose and appointed as Saviour and Lord.

Apostle Usually one of the group of twelve men whom Jesus chose to be his special followers and helpers. It is also used in the New Testament to refer to Paul and other Christian workers. The word means "messenger".

Areopagus A hill in Athens where the city council used to meet. For this reason the council itself was called Areopagus, even after it no longer met on the hill.

Armageddon The place mentioned in Revelation 16.16; it is not certain whether the name refers to an actual place ("the hill of Megiddo"), or is used as a symbol.

Artemis The Greek name of an ancient goddess of fertility, worshipped especially in Asia Minor.

Asia A Roman province in the western part of what was later known as Asia Minor, and is today part of the country of Turkey. Besides the seven cities of Asia listed in the book of Revelation (1.4,11; 2.1—3.22), other cities in the province mentioned in the New Testament are Colossae, Hierapolis, and Miletus. The capital of the province was Ephesus.

Atonement, Day of The most important of Israel's holy days, when the High Priest would offer sacrifice for the sins of the people of Israel (Leviticus 16). It was held on the 10th day of the seventh month of the Hebrew calendar (about October 1st). The Jewish name for this day is Yom Kippur.

Augustus One of the titles of Gaius Octavius, who was Roman Emperor from 27 B.C. to A.D. 14 (Luke 2.1).

B

Baal The god of fertility worshipped by the Canaanites (1 Kings 18).

Babylon The capital city of the ancient land of Babylonia, east of Palestine, on the rivers Tigris and Euphrates. In 1 Peter 5.13 and Revelation the name Babylon probably refers to the city of Rome.

Balaam A native of Pethor, near the River Euphrates, who was asked by Balak, king of Moab, to curse the people of Israel. Instead, Balaam obeyed God's command and blessed Israel (Numbers 22.1—24.25).

Balak The king of Moab, a country on the southeast side of the Dead Sea. He led the people of Israel to worship idols (Numbers 22.1—24.25).

Bastard A person born of parents who are not legally married.

Beelzebul A New Testament name given to the Devil as the chief of the evil spirits.

Beryl A semi-precious stone, usually green or bluish green in colour.

Breastplate Part of a soldier's armour, made of leather or metal; it covered the chest and sometimes the back, to protect him against arrows and the blows of a sword.

C

Carnelian A semi-precious stone, usually red in colour.

Census The registration of citizens and their property, to determine how much tax they had to pay.

Chalcedony A semi-precious stone, usually milky or grey in colour.

Christ The Greek word for the Hebrew "Messiah". It means "the anointed one". Jesus was called the Christ because he was the one whom God chose and sent as Saviour and Lord.

Circumcise To cut off the foreskin of the penis. As a sign of God's covenant with his people Israelite boys were circumcised eight days after they were born (Genesis 17.9–14).

Claudius Roman Emperor A.D. 41–54 (Acts 11.28; 18.2).

Convert A person who is converted, or turned, from one belief or faith to another.

Council The highest religious court of the Jews. It was made up of seventy leaders of the Jewish people. Its president was the High Priest.

Covenant An agreement, either between people, or between God and a person or a group of people. God made a covenant with Noah (Genesis 9.8–17) and with Abraham (Genesis 17.1–8), but in the Old Testament the term usually refers to the covenant made between God and the people of Israel at the time of Moses (Exodus 24.4–8). In Hebrews 8 the writer refers to a new covenant and quotes Jeremiah 31.31–34.

Covenant Box A wooden chest covered with gold. The two stone tablets with the Ten Commandments written on them were kept in it. It is often called "the Ark of the Covenant".

Cumin A small plant whose seeds are crushed and used for seasoning foods.

D

Dalmatia The southern half of the province of Illyricum.

David's City In the Old Testament it usually refers to the part of Jerusalem which was captured from the Jebusites by King David. In the New Testament Bethlehem, David's boyhood home where Jesus was born, is referred to as David's town.

Dedication, Festival of A Jewish festival in which people remembered how Judas Maccabeus rededicated the altar in the Temple in 165 B.C. The festival began on the 25th day of the month Kislev (about December 10th) and lasted eight days. The Jewish name for this festival is Hanukkah.

Defile To make a person unfit to worship God. Some foods and actions were forbidden by the Law of Moses. If people broke these laws they were not allowed into the place where they worshipped God. Such people could not take part in worship until they had gone through certain rituals.

Demon An evil spirit with the power to harm people; it was regarded as a messenger and servant of the Devil.

Descendant A person who is related by family line to someone who lived a long time before him.

Dill A small plant whose stems, leaves, and seeds are used for seasoning food.

Disciple A person who follows and learns from someone else. In the New Testament the word is used of the followers of John the Baptist and especially of the followers of Jesus, particularly the twelve apostles.

Dragon A beast in old legends, thought to be like a huge lizard. It is also called a serpent and appears as a picture of the Devil (Revelation 12.3—13.4; 20.2–3).

E

Elders In the New Testament three different groups are called elders: (1) in the Gospels the elders are important Jewish religious leaders, some of whom were members of their highest Council; (2) in Acts 11—21 and the Letters, the elders are Christian church officers who were responsible for the work of the church; (3) in Revelation the twenty-four elders are part of God's court in heaven, perhaps as representatives of God's people.

Elijah The Old Testament prophet who was expected to appear to announce the coming of the Messiah (1 Kings 17.1—2 Kings 2.15; Malachi 4.5-6).

Elisha The Old Testament prophet who followed Elijah (2 Kings 2—9).

Emerald A very valuable stone, green in colour.

Epicureans Those who followed the teaching of Epicurus (died 270 B.C.), a Greek philosopher who taught that happiness is the highest good in life.

Epileptic A person who suffers from a nervous disease which causes fits and fainting.

Eunuch A man who has had an operation which prevents him from having normal sexual relations. Eunuchs were often important officials in the courts of ancient kings, and the word may have come to be used of such officials, even if they had not had the operation.

F

Fast To go without food for a while as a religious duty.

Felix The Roman governor of Judaea A.D. 52-60, before whom Paul defended himself (Acts 23.24—24.27).

Festus The Roman governor of Judaea A.D. 60-62, before whom Paul defended himself and made his appeal to the Roman Emperor (Acts 25.1—26.32).

Frankincense A valuable substance made from the sap of a certain tree, probably brought from Arabia. It was burnt to give a pleasant smell.

G

Gabriel One of God's chief angels, who was sent to Zechariah, father of John the Baptist (Luke 1.11-20), and to Mary, mother of Jesus (Luke 1.26-38).

Galatia A Roman province in the eastern part of what was later known as Asia Minor, and is today part of the country of Turkey. The cities of Antioch of Pisidia, Iconium, Lystra, and Derbe were in the province of Galatia.

Gallio The Roman governor of Greece A.D. 51-52 (Acts 18.12-17).

Generation The average period, about 30 years in length, from the time a man becomes an adult to the time his son becomes an adult.

Gennesaret Another name for Lake Galilee (Luke 5.1).

Gentile A person who is not a Jew.

H

Hades The Greek name used in the New Testament to refer to the world of the dead.

Hermes The name of a Greek god who served as messenger of the gods.

Herod (1) Herod the Great was king of all the country of the Jews 37-4 B.C. He was responsible for the killing of the baby boys in Bethlehem soon after Jesus was born. (2) Herod (whose full name was Herod Antipas) was ruler of Galilee 4 B.C.-A.D. 39. He was son of Herod the Great, and although called a king (Mark 6.14), he was not a king as his father had been. He was responsible for the death of John the Baptist. (3) Herod (whose full name was Herod Agrippa I) was ruler of Judaea, with the title of king, A.D. 41-44. He was grandson of Herod the Great. He put the apostle James to death and arrested Peter.

Herodias The wife of Herod Antipas, ruler of Galilee. Before marrying Herod she had been the wife of his half-brother Philip.

Herod's Party A political party in New Testament times made up of Jews who wanted to be ruled by one of the family of Herod the Great rather than by the Roman governor.

High Priest The chief Jewish priest and president of their supreme Council. Once a year (on the Day of Atonement) he would enter the Most Holy Place in the Temple and offer a sacrifice for himself and for the sins of the people of Israel.

Homosexual A man who has sexual relations with another man.

Hyssop A small bushy plant used in religious ceremonies to sprinkle liquids.

I

Illyricum A province on the coast of the Adriatic Sea, north of the province of Macedonia, in what is now Yugoslavia.

Incense Material which is burnt in order to produce a pleasant smell. The Israelites used it in their worship.

J

Jasper A semi-precious stone of various colours. The jasper mentioned in the Bible was probably green, or else clear.

Jesse The father of Kind David (1 Samuel 16), one of the ancestors of Jesus.

K

Kingdom of God, Kingdom of heaven The titles used to describe God's ruling over the world as king. There is no difference between the two titles, both of which refer primarily to God's possession and exercise of his power, not to a place or time in history. This Kingdom is spoken of as being already present and also as coming in the future.

L

Lady The recipient of 2 John (verses 1, 5), probably a church, not an individual. Under this interpretation, her "children" (verses 1, 4) are the church members, and her "Sister" (verse 13) is also a church to which the writer belongs.

Law The name which the Jews applied to the first five books of the Old Testament, also called "The Books of Moses". Sometimes, however, the name is used in a more general way for the entire Old Testament.

Levite (1) A member of the tribe of Levi (Exodus 6.16–25); (2) a man who helped the priest to perform religious duties (Numbers 1.47–53).

Living Creatures Symbols of God's majesty and his presence. For a description of them, see Exodus 25.18–20; Ezekiel 1.5–13; 10; Revelation 4.6–9. Older translations call them cherubim.

Locust A winged insect extremely harmful to plants; locusts fly in huge swarms and eat crops and other plants.

Lot The nephew of Abraham who escaped with his daughters from the city of Sodom when it was destroyed by God (Genesis 19.12-29).

M

Macedonia A Roman province covering what is now the northern half of Greece. Its capital city was Thessalonica. Other cities in the province mentioned in the New Testament are Neapolis, Philippi, Amphipolis, Apollonia, and Berea.

Magdalene Mary Magdalene, a follower of Jesus, was one of those to whom Jesus appeared after he was raised from death (Mark 15.40-47; John 20.1-18). Her name indicates that she was born in Magdala, a town on the west side of Lake Galilee.

Manna A food eaten by the Isrealites during their travels in the wilderness. It was white and flaky, and looked like small seeds (Exodus 16.14-21; Numbers 11.7-9).

Messiah A Hebrew title (meaning "the anointed one") given to the Saviour whose coming was promised by the Hebrew prophets; the Greek word "the Christ" has the same meaning.

Michael One of God's chief angels (Jude 9; Revelation 12.7).

Mint A small garden plant whose leaves are used for seasoning foods.

Molech One of the gods of the ancient people of Canaan.

Most Holy Place The innermost room of the Tent of the LORD's presence or the Temple. The Covenant Box was kept there. Only the High Priest could enter the Most Holy Place, and he did so only once a year, on the Day of Atonement.

Mustard A large plant which grows from a very small seed. The seeds are ground into powder and used as spice on food.

Myrrh A sweet-smelling resin that was very valuable. It served as a medicine (Mark 15.23) and was used by the Jews in preparing bodies for burial (John 19.39).

N

Nard An expensive perfume made from a plant.

Nazarene Someone from the town of Nazareth. The name was used as a title for Jesus and also as a name for the early Christians (Acts 24.5).

Nicolaitans A group referred to in Revelation 2.6,15 whose teachings and actions are condemned. They apparently practised idolatry and immorality, but nothing definite is known as to when, where, and by whom the group was started.

Nineveh The ancient capital of Assyria, on the east side of the river Tigris, where the prophet Jonah preached (Jonah 3.1-10).

Noah The Old Testament patriarch who built a boat in which he, his family, and the animals were saved from the flood that God sent on the earth (Genesis 6.5—9.28).

O

Onyx A semi-precious stone of various colours.

Outcasts In other Bibles this word is translated "sinners". In the Gospels it refers to Jews who were not allowed to attend synagogue worship because they had broken rules about foods that should not be eaten, and about being friendly with people who were not Jews. Such outcasts were looked down on by many of their fellow-Jews, and Jesus was criticized for being friendly with them (Mark 2.15-17; Luke 7.34; 15.1-2).

P

Parable A story which teaches spiritual truth. It was often used by Jesus.

Paradise A name for heaven (Luke 23.43; 2 Corinthians 12.3).

Parchment The skin of an animal, usually a sheep or a goat, which was prepared to be written on (2 Timothy 4.13).

Passover The Israelite festival, on the 14th day of the month Nisan (about April 1st), which celebrated the freeing of the Hebrews from their captivity in Egypt. The Angel of Death killed the first-born in the Egyptian homes but passed over the Hebrew homes (Exodus 12.23-27). The Jewish name for this festival is Pesach.

Pentecost, Day of The Greek name for the Israelite festival of wheat harvest (see Harvest Festival). The name Pentecost (meaning "fiftieth") comes from the fact that the feast was held fifty days after Passover.

Pervert One who commits unnatural sexual acts.

Pharaoh The title of the kings of ancient Egypt. Two different kings of Egypt are mentioned in the New Testament: the one who ruled during the time of Joseph, the son of Jacob (Genesis 40.1—50.26; Acts 7.10-13), and the one who ruled during the time of Moses (Exodus 1.8—14.31; Acts 7.21; Romans 9.17; Hebrews 11).

Pharisees A Jewish religious party during the time of Jesus. They were strict in obeying the Law of Moses and other regulations which had been added to it through the centuries.

Pilate Pontius Pilate was the Roman governor of Judaea, Samaria, and Idumea, A.D. 26-36 (Mark 15.1-15; Luke 3.1; Acts 3.13; 1 Timothy 6.13).

Preparation, Day of The sixth day of the week (Friday), on which the Jews got ready to keep the Sabbath (Saturday).

Prophet A person who proclaims a message from God. The word usually refers to certain men in the Old Testament, but the New Testament speaks of prophets in the early church. John the Baptist is also called a prophet.

Q

Quartz A semi-precious stone of various colours, but usually clear.

R

Rabbi A Hebrew word which means "my teacher".

Red Sea The sea which separated Egypt from the desert and which the Israelites crossed under the leadership of Moses, as described in Exodus 14.

Rephan The name of an ancient god who was worshipped as the ruler of the planet Saturn.

Rue A small garden plant whose leaves are used for seasoning food.

S

Sabbath The seventh day of the week (from sunset on Friday to sunset on Saturday), a holy day on which no work was permitted.

Sackcloth A coarse cloth made of goats' hair, which was worn as a sign of mourning or distress.

Sadducees A small Jewish religious party in New Testament times. Most of them were priests. They based their beliefs mainly on the first five books of the Old Testament. They had several beliefs and practices which were different from those of the larger party of the Pharisees.

Samaritan A name used to refer to a native of Samaria, the region between Judaea and Galilee. Because of differences in politics, race, customs, and religion (including especially the central place of worship), there was much bad feeling between the Jews and the Samaritans.

Sanctuary A building dedicated to the worship of God. Sometimes the word refers to the central place of worship and not to the whole building.

Sapphire A very valuable stone, usually blue in colour.

Saul (1) The first king of Israel (1 Samuel 13—31); (2) the Hebrew name of the apostle Paul.

Scorpion A small creature which has eight legs and a long tail with a poisonous sting. It can inflict a very painful, and sometimes fatal, wound.

Scribe A person who wrote documents for others or copied written material. Some scribes were employed by ancient kings to prepare official documents, and so became important officials.

Scriptures In the New Testament the word refers to the Hebrew sacred writings, known to Christians as the Old Testament. Various names are used: the Law (or the Law of Moses) and the prophets (Matthew 5.17; 7.12; Luke 2.22; 24.44; Acts 13.15; 28.23); the Holy Scriptures (Romans 1.2; 2 Timothy 3.15); the old covenant (2 Corinthians 3.14). The singular "scripture" refers to a single passge of the Old Testament.

Serpent A name given to the dragon, which appears in the New Testament as a picture of the Devil (Revelation 12.3-17; 20.2-3).

Sheepfold An enclosure where sheep were kept, usually at night, to protect then from wild animals and thieves.

Shelters, Festival of A happy festival celebrated by the Israelites in the autumn after the harvest was complete. In order to help them remember the years when their ancestors wandered through the winderness, the Israelites built rough shelters to live in during the festival. The Jewish name for this festival is Sukkoth. It is also called the Feast of Tabernacles or the Feast of Booths.

Sickle A tool consisting of a curved metal blade and a wooden handle, used for cutting wheat and other crops.

Sodom and Gomorrah Cities near the Dead Sea which God destroyed by fire because of the great wickedness of their people (Genesis 19.24-28).

Solomon's Porch A covered court on the east side of the Temple in Jerusalem.

Son of David A title which the Jews used of the expected Messiah as the descendant and successor of Kind David.

Son of Man The title used by Jesus to refer to himself as the one chosen by God to be the Saviour (Mark 10.45). As used by Jesus, this title emphasized both his present lowly condition (Mark 8.31; Luke 9.58) and his future glory (Matthew 25.31; Mark 8.38).

Spice One of several pleasant-smelling vegetable products which were used by the Jews in preparing bodies for burial.

Stoics Those who followed the teachings of the Greek philosopher Zeno (died 265 B.C.), who taught that happiness is to be found in being free from pleasure and pain.

Sulphur In the Bible this refers to a chemical which burns with great heat and produces an unpleasant smell.

Synagogue The place where Jews met every Sabbath day for their public worship; it was also used as a social centre and as a school for Jewish children during week days.

T

Teachers of the Law Men who in New Testament times taught and explained the teachings of the Old Testament, especially the first five books.

Tenant In Bible times, a man who grew crops on land owned by someone else, and handed over a part of the harvest to the owner to pay for the use of his land.

Tent of the LORD's Presence The large tent described in detail in Exodus 26, where the Israelites worshipped God until Solomon built the Temple. It is also called the Tabernacle or Tent of Meeting.

Ten Towns A group of ten Gentile towns, most of which were to the east and southeast of Lake Galilee.

Theophilus The one to whom the Gospel of Luke and the book of Acts (Luke 1.1; Acts 1.1) are dedicated. Nothing is known about him, and it is not certain that he is a real person; the name means "God's friend," and may designate the Christian readers of the books.

Tiberius Roman Emperor A.D. 14–37. It was in the 15th year of his rule (about A.D. 29) that John the Baptist began his work (Luke 3.1).

Topaz A semi-precious stone, usually yellow in colour.

Turquoise A semi-precious stone, blue or bluish green in colour.

U

Unleavened Bread, Festival of The Israelite festival, lasting seven days after Passover; it also celebrated the deliverance of the ancient Hebrews from Egypt. The name came from the practice of not using leaven (yeast) in making bread during that week (Exodus 12.14–20). It was held from the 15th to the 22nd day of the month Nisan (about the first week of April).

V

Vow A strong statement or promise, often made by calling upon God to punish the speaker if the statement should prove to be untrue or if the promise was not kept.

W

Winnowing Shovel A tool like a shovel or a large fork, used to separate the grains from the husks.

Wreath Flowers or leaves arranged in a circle, to be placed on a person's head. In ancient times a wreath of leaves was the prize given to winners in athletic games.

Y

Yeast A substance, also called leaven, which is added to dough made from flour of wheat or barley to make it rise before being baked into bread.

Yoke A heavy bar of wood which is fitted over the necks of two oxen to make it possible for them to pull a plough or a cart. The word is used to describe the rules for living that a teacher passes on to his pupils.

Z

Zeus The name of the supreme god of the Greeks.

Zion Originally a name for "David's City", the Jebusite stronghold captured by King David's men. The word "Zion" was later used to refer to the hill on which the Temple stood.

Index

The numbers in heavy type are the page numbers. The verses containing the reference are given after the page numbers.

Reading Plan

The Bible is mostly presented to us in unconnected bits.
Readings in church are often chosen in a random manner
and if people dip into the Bible many read just where it falls
open. Yet the Bible is intelligent writing by intelligent men
written for real situations under the inspiration of God. Its
real benefit comes when we approach it like this and read it
all in a sensible way looking for God to speak to us as we
read.

The Reading plan is designed to help you to get to know the
whole New Testament in one year in this clear new translation. Each day's reading is only about one and a half pages
and follows the clear section headings in the Good News
New Testament.

The plan has four cycles based on the four different portraits
of Jesus in the Gospels. It begins with the Gospel of Luke, to
give a comprehensive run through of Jesus' life, death and
resurrection. It follows on to get a comprehensive picture of
the first Christians in Acts and the letters of Paul. The second
cycle takes you through Matthew's Gospel and with it are
grouped the more Jewish bits of the New Testament like
Hebrews and James. Your third conductor through the life
of Jesus is Mark, who gave us Peter's picture, and with him
therefore are grouped the two letters of Peter. Towards the
end John takes over and tells us his memories of Jesus in his
Gospel and letters. Logically the plan ends with the finale,
the book of Revelation.

FIRST MONTH

DAY	BOOK	CHAPTER	Tick when read
1	Luke	1. 1-25	☐
2	Luke	1. 26-56	☐
3	Luke	1. 57-80	☐
4	Luke	2. 1-21	☐
5	Luke	2. 22-40	☐
6	Luke	2. 41-52	☐
7	Luke	3. 1-38	☐
8	Luke	4. 1-15	☐
9	Luke	4. 16-30	☐
10	Luke	4. 31-44	☐
11	Luke	5. 1-26	☐
12	Luke	5. 27 - 6. 11	☐
13	Luke	6. 12-36	☐
14	Luke	6. 37-49	☐
15	Luke	7. 1-28	☐
16	Luke	7. 29-50	☐
17	Luke	8. 1-21	☐
18	Luke	8. 22-39	☐
19	Luke	8. 40-56	☐
20	Luke	9. 1-27	☐
21	Luke	9. 28-62	☐
22	Luke	10. 1-24	☐
23	Luke	10. 25-42	☐
24	Luke	11. 1-23	☐
25	Luke	11. 24-36	☐
26	Luke	11. 37-54	☐
27	Luke	12. 1-21	☐
28	Luke	12. 22-40	☐
29	Luke	12. 41-59	☐
30	Luke	13. 1-21	☐

SECOND MONTH

DAY	BOOK	CHAPTER	Tick when read
1	Luke	13. 22-35	☐
2	Luke	14. 1-24	☐
3	Luke	14. 25-35	☐
4	Luke	15. 1-32	☐
5	Luke	16. 1-18	☐
6	Luke	16. 19 - 17. 10	☐
7	Luke	17. 11-37	☐
8	Luke	18. 1-17	☐
9	Luke	18. 18-43	☐
10	Luke	19. 1-27	☐
11	Luke	19. 28-48	☐
12	Luke	20. 1-26	☐
13	Luke	20. 27 - 21. 6	☐
14	Luke	21. 7-38	☐
15	Luke	22. 1-38	☐
16	Luke	22. 39-71	☐
17	Luke	23. 1-25	☐
18	Luke	23. 26-56	☐
19	Luke	24. 1-35	☐
20	Luke	24. 36-53	☐
21	Acts	1. 1-26	☐
22	Acts	2. 1-21	☐
23	Acts	2. 22-47	☐
24	Acts	3. 1-26	☐
25	Acts	4. 1-22	☐
26	Acts	4. 23-37	☐
27	Acts	5. 1-16	☐
28	Acts	5. 17-42	☐
29	Acts	6. 1-15	☐
30	Acts	7. 1-29	☐

THIRD MONTH

DAY	BOOK	CHAPTER	Tick when read
1	Acts	7. 30 - 8. 1a	☐
2	Acts	8. 1b-25	☐
3	Acts	8. 26-40	☐
4	Acts	9. 1-31	☐
5	Acts	9. 32-43	☐
6	Acts	10. 1-33	☐
7	Acts	10. 34 - 11. 18	☐
8	Acts	11. 19-30	☐
9	Acts	12. 1-25	☐
10	Acts	13. 1-12	☐
11	Acts	13. 13-52	☐
12	Acts	14. 1-28	☐
13	Acts	15. 1-35	☐
14	Galatians	1. 1-24	☐
15	Galatians	2. 1-21	☐
16	Galatians	3. 1-20	☐
17	Galatians	3. 21 - 4. 7	☐
18	Galatians	4. 8-31	☐
19	Galatians	5. 1-26	☐
20	Galatians	6. 1-18	☐
21	Acts	15. 36 - 16. 15	☐
22	Acts	16. 16-40	☐
23	Acts	17. 1-15	☐
24	Acts	17. 16-34	☐
25	1 Thessalonians	1. 1 - 2. 16	☐
26	1 Thessalonians	2. 17 - 4. 12	☐
27	1 Thessalonians	4. 13 - 5. 28	☐
28	2 Thessalonians	1. 1 - 2. 12	☐
29	2 Thessalonians	2. 13 - 3. 18	☐
30	Acts	18. 1-23	☐

FOURTH MONTH

DAY	BOOK	CHAPTER	Tick when read
1	Acts	18. 24 - 19. 20	☐
2	Acts	19. 21-41	☐
3	1 Corinthians	1. 1-17	☐
4	1 Corinthians	1. 18 - 2. 16	☐
5	1 Corinthians	3. 1-23	☐
6	1 Corinthians	4. 1-21	☐
7	1 Corinthians	5. 1-13	☐
8	1 Corinthians	6. 1-20	☐
9	1 Corinthians	7. 1-24	☐
10	1 Corinthians	7. 25-40	☐
11	1 Corinthians	8. 1-13	☐
12	1 Corinthians	9. 1-27	☐
13	1 Corinthians	10. 1 - 11. 1	☐
14	1 Corinthains	11. 2-34	☐
15	1 Corinthians	12. 1-31	☐
16	1 Corinthians	13. 1-13	☐
17	1 Corinthians	14. 1-25	☐
18	1 Corinthians	14. 26-40	☐
19	1 Corinthians	15. 1-34	☐
20	1 Corinthians	15. 35-58	☐
21	1 Corinthians	16. 1-24	☐
22	Acts	20. 1-16	☐
23	2 Corinthians	1. 1 - 2. 4	☐
24	2 Corinthians	2. 5-17	☐
25	2 Corinthians	3. 1-18	☐
26	2 Corinthians	4. 1 - 5. 10	☐
27	2 Corinthians	5. 11 - 6. 13	☐
28	2 Corinthians	6. 14 - 7. 16	☐
29	2 Corinthians	8. 1-24	☐
30	2 Corinthians	9. 1-15	☐

FIFTH MONTH

DAY	BOOK	CHAPTER	Tick when read
1	2 Corinthians	10. 1-18	☐
2	2 Corinthians	11. 1-33	☐
3	2 Corinthians	12. 1-21	☐
4	2 Corinthians	13. 1-13	☐
5	Romans	1. 1-17	☐
6	Romans	1. 18-32	☐
7	Romans	2. 1-16	☐
8	Romans	2. 17 - 3. 8	☐
9	Romans	3. 9-31	☐
10	Romans	4. 1-25	☐
11	Romans	5. 1-21	☐
12	Romans	6. 1-23	☐
13	Romans	7. 1-25	☐
14	Romans	8. 1-17	☐
15	Romans	8. 18-39	☐
16	Romans	9. 1-29	☐
17	Romans	9. 30 - 10. 21	☐
18	Romans	11. 1-12	☐
19	Romans	11. 13-36	☐
20	Romans	12. 1-21	☐
21	Romans	13. 1-14	☐
22	Romans	14. 1-23	☐
23	Romans	15. 1-33	☐
24	Romans	16. 1-27	☐
25	Acts	20. 17-38	☐
26	Acts	21. 1-26	☐
27	Acts	21. 27 - 22. 5	☐
28	Acts	22. 6-29	☐
29	Acts	22. 30 - 23. 22	☐
30	Acts	23. 23 - 24. 9	☐
31	Acts	24. 10-27	☐

SIXTH MONTH

DAY	BOOK	CHAPTER	Tick when read
1	Acts	25. 1-27	☐
2	Acts	26. 1-32	☐
3	Acts	27. 1-44	☐
4	Acts	28. 1-15	☐
5	Acts	28. 16-31	☐
6	Philippians	1. 1-30	☐
7	Philippians	2. 1-30	☐
8	Philippians	3. 1-21	☐
9	Philippians	4. 1-23	☐
10	Ephesians	1. 1-23	☐
11	Ephesians	2. 1-22	☐
12	Ephesians	3. 1-21	☐
13	Ephesians	4. 1-32	☐
14	Ephesians	5. 1-33	☐
15	Ephesians	6. 1-24	☐
16	Colossians	1. 1-23	☐
17	Colossians	1. 24 - 2. 19	☐
18	Colossians	2. 20 - 3. 17	☐
19	Colossians	3. 18 - 4. 18	☐
20	Philemon	1-25	☐
21	1 Timothy	1. 1-20	☐
22	1 Timothy	2. 1 - 3. 16	☐
23	1 Timothy	4. 1-16	☐
24	1 Timothy	5. 1-6. 2a	☐
25	1 Timothy	6. 2b-21	☐
26	Titus	1. 1-16	☐
27	Titus	2. 1 - 3. 15	☐
28	2 Timothy	1. 1-18	☐
29	2 Timothy	2. 1-26	☐
30	2 Timothy	3. 1-17	☐

SEVENTH MONTH

DAY	BOOK	CHAPTER	Tick when read
1	2 Timothy	4. 1-22	☐
2	Matthew	1. 1-25	☐
3	Matthew	2. 1-23	☐
4	Matthew	3. 1-17	☐
5	Matthew	4. 1-25	☐
6	Matthew	5. 1-20	☐
7	Matthew	5. 21-48	☐
8	Matthew	6. 1-18	☐
9	Matthew	6. 19-34	☐
10	Matthew	7. 1-29	☐
11	Matthew	8. 1-27	☐
12	Matthew	8. 28 - 9. 17	☐
13	Matthew	9. 18-38	☐
14	Matthew	10. 1-25	☐
15	Matthew	10. 26-42	☐
16	Matthew	11. 1-30	☐
17	Matthew	12. 1-21	☐
18	Matthew	12. 22-37	☐
19	Matthew	12. 38-50	☐
20	Matthew	13. 1-23	☐
21	Matthew	13. 24-52	☐
22	Matthew	13. 53 - 14. 21	☐
23	Matthew	14. 22-36	☐
24	Matthew	15. 1-28	☐
25	Matthew	15. 29 - 16. 12	☐
26	Matthew	16. 13-28	☐
27	Matthew	17. 1-23	☐
28	Matthew	17. 24 - 18. 14	☐
29	Matthew	18. 15-35	☐
30	Matthew	19. 1-15	☐
31	Matthew	19. 16-30	☐

EIGHTH MONTH

DAY	BOOK	CHAPTER	Tick when read
1	Matthew	20. 1-16	☐
2	Matthew	20. 17-34	☐
3	Matthew	21. 1-22	☐
4	Matthew	21. 23-46	☐
5	Matthew	22. 1-22	☐
6	Matthew	22. 23-46	☐
7	Matthew	23. 1-28	☐
8	Matthew	23. 29 - 24. 2	☐
9	Matthew	24. 3-31	☐
10	Matthew	24. 32 - 25. 13	☐
11	Matthew	25. 14-30	☐
12	Matthew	25. 31-46	☐
13	Matthew	26. 1-16	☐
14	Matthew	26. 17-35	☐
15	Matthew	26. 36-56	☐
16	Matthew	26. 57-75	☐
17	Matthew	27. 1-26	☐
18	Matthew	27. 27-44	☐
19	Matthew	27. 45-66	☐
20	Matthew	28. 1-20	☐
21	Hebrews	1. 1-14	☐
22	Hebrews	2. 1-18	☐
23	Hebrews	3. 1 - 4. 13	☐
24	Hebrews	4. 14 - 5. 10	☐
25	Hebrews	5. 11 - 6. 20	☐
26	Hebrews	7. 1-28	☐
27	Hebrews	8. 1-13	☐
28	Hebrews	9. 1-22	☐
29	Hebrews	9. 23 - 10. 18	☐
30	Hebrews	10. 19-39	☐
31	Hebrews	11. 1-22	☐

NINTH MONTH

DAY	BOOK	CHAPTER	Tick when read
1	Hebrews	11. 23-40	☐
2	Hebrews	12. 1-29	☐
3	Hebrews	13. 1-25	☐
4	James	1. 1-18	☐
5	James	1. 19 - 2. 13	☐
6	James	2. 14-26	☐
7	James	3. 1-18	☐
8	James	4. 1-17	☐
9	James	5. 1-20	☐
10	Mark	1. 1-20	☐
11	Mark	1. 21-45	☐
12	Mark	2. 1-17	☐
13	Mark	2. 18 - 3. 6	☐
14	Mark	3. 7-35	☐
15	Mark	4. 1-20	☐
16	Mark	4. 21-41	☐
17	Mark	5. 1-20	☐
18	Mark	5. 21-43	☐
19	Mark	6. 1-13	☐
20	Mark	6. 14-29	☐
21	Mark	6. 30-56	☐
22	Mark	7. 1-23	☐
23	Mark	7. 24-37	☐
24	Mark	8. 1-26	☐
25	Mark	8. 27 - 9. 1	☐
26	Mark	9. 2-13	☐
27	Mark	9. 14-29	☐
28	Mark	9. 30-50	☐
29	Mark	10. 1-16	☐
30	Mark	10. 17-31	☐

TENTH MONTH

DAY	BOOK	CHAPTER	Tick when read
1	Mark	10. 32-52	☐
2	Mark	11. 1-19	☐
3	Mark	11. 20-33	☐
4	Mark	12. 1-17	☐
5	Mark	12. 18-34	☐
6	Mark	12. 35 - 13. 2	☐
7	Mark	13. 3-23	☐
8	Mark	13. 24-36	☐
9	Mark	14. 1-11	☐
10	Mark	14. 12-31	☐
11	Mark	14. 32-52	☐
12	Mark	14. 53-72	☐
13	Mark	15. 1-20	☐
14	Mark	15. 21-47	☐
15	Mark	16. 1-20	☐
16	1 Peter	1. 1-12	☐
17	1 Peter	1. 13-25	☐
18	1 Peter	2. 1-10	☐
19	1 Peter	2. 11-25	☐
20	1 Peter	3. 1-22	☐
21	1 Peter	4. 1-19	☐
22	1 Peter	5. 1-14	☐
23	2 Peter	1. 1-21	☐
24	2 Peter	2. 1-22	☐
25	2 Peter	3. 1-18	☐
26	Jude	1-25	☐
27	John	1. 1-18	☐
28	John	1. 19-34	☐
29	John	1. 35-51	☐
30	John	2. 1-25	☐
31	John	3. 1-21	☐

ELEVENTH MONTH

DAY	BOOK	CHAPTER	Tick when read
1	John	3. 22-36	☐
2	John	4. 1-26	☐
3	John	4. 27-54	☐
4	John	5. 1-18	☐
5	John	5. 19-47	☐
6	John	6. 1-24	☐
7	John	6. 25-59	☐
8	John	6. 60-71	☐
9	John	7. 1-24	☐
10	John	7. 25-52	☐
11	John	8. 1-30	☐
12	John	8. 31-59	☐
13	John	9. 1-41	☐
14	John	10. 1-21	☐
15	John	10. 22-42	☐
16	John	11. 1-27	☐
17	John	11. 28-57	☐
18	John	12. 1-19	☐
19	John	12. 20-50	☐
20	John	13. 1-20	☐
21	John	13. 21-38	☐
22	John	14. 1-31	☐
23	John	15. 1-27	☐
24	John	16. 1-15	☐
25	John	16. 16-33	☐
26	John	17. 1-26	☐
27	John	18. 1-27	☐
28	John	18. 28 - 19. 16	☐
29	John	19. 17-42	☐
30	John	20. 1-18	☐

TWELFTH MONTH

DAY	BOOK	CHAPTER	Tick when read
1	John	20. 19-31	☐
2	John	21. 1-25	☐
3	1 John	1. 1 - 2. 6	☐
4	1 John	2. 7-29	☐
5	1 John	3. 1-24	☐
6	1 John	4. 1-21	☐
7	1 John	5. 1-21	☐
8	2 John	1-13	☐
9	3 John	1-15	☐
10	Revelation	1. 1-20	☐
11	Revelation	2. 1-17	☐
12	Revelation	2. 18 - 3. 6	☐
13	Revelation	3. 7-22	☐
14	Revelation	4. 1-11	☐
15	Revelation	5. 1-14	☐
16	Revelation	6. 1-17	☐
17	Revelation	7. 1 - 8. 5	☐
18	Revelation	8. 6 - 9. 21	☐
19	Revelation	10. 1-11	☐
20	Revelation	11. 1-19	☐
21	Revelation	12. 1-18	☐
22	Revelation	13. 1-18	☐
23	Revelation	14. 1-20	☐
24	Revelation	15. 1-8	☐
25	Revelation	16. 1-21	☐
26	Revelation	17. 1-18	☐
27	Revelation	18. 1 - 19. 4	☐
28	Revelation	19. 5-21	☐
29	Revelation	20. 1-15	☐
30	Revelation	21. 1 - 22. 5	☐
31	Revelation	22. 6-21	☐

Maps

To help the reader the following pages
contain the maps as found on pages
2, 156, 302, 334, 342, 372

JERUSALEM IN NEW TESTAMENT TIMES

To Caesarea

Present City Wall

To Jericho

Damascus Gate

Pool of Bethzatha

PRAETORIUM

Ancient City Wall

FORT

To Bethany

Golgotha

Gate

TEMPLE

Gethsemane

Gate

Beautiful Gate

Gate

Solomon's Porch

Court of Gentiles

To Joppa

Gennath Gate

Bridge

Gates

To Bethlehem

HEROD'S PALACE

Pool

Present City Wall

Pool of Siloam

KIDRON VALLEY

VALLEY

Gate

OF HINNOM

To Dead Sea

0   250   500 Metres

Roads

PALESTINE IN THE TIME OF JESUS

MEDITERRANEAN SEA

Sidon

Zarephath

Tyre

PHOENICIA

ITUREA

ABILENE

Caesarea Philippi

GALILEE

TRACHONITIS

Chorazin

Capernaum

Bethsaida

LAKE GALILEE

Cana

Tiberias

Mount Carmel

Nazareth

Nain

Gadara

D E C A P O L I S (The Ten Towns)

Caesarea

Salim

Aenon

Samaria

Mount Gerizim

Sychar

Gerasa

SAMARIA

Arimathea

River Jordan

PEREA

Ephraim

Emmaus

Jericho

Bethphage

Jerusalem

Bethany

JUDAEA

Qumran

Bethlehem

DEAD SEA

IDUMEA

0 10 20 30 40

Kilometres

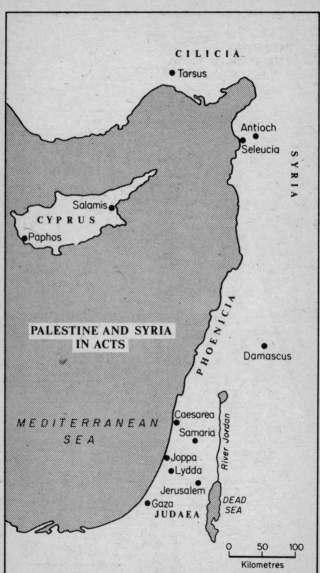

CILICIA

● Tarsus

Antioch

● Seleucia

SYRIA

Salamis ●

CYPRUS

● Paphos

PHOENICIA

Damascus ●

PALESTINE AND SYRIA
IN ACTS

MEDITERRANEAN
SEA

Caesarea ●

Samaria ●

River Jordan

● Joppa

● Lydda

Jerusalem ●

DEAD
SEA

● Gaza

JUDAEA

0   50   100

Kilometres

PAUL'S FIRST MISSIONARY JOURNEY

PAUL'S
SECOND AND THIRD
JOURNEYS

Paul's Second Journey
Paul's Third Journey

0   100   200   300 Kilometres

PAUL'S JOURNEY
TO ROME

BLACK SEA

MACEDONIA
Thessalonica
Philippi

Corinth

ITALY
Rome
Three Inns
Market
of Appius
Puteoli
Rhegium

SICILY
Syracuse

MALTA

MEDITERRANEAN SEA

GALATIA

ASIA
Adramyttium
Ephesus
Colossae

Cnidus

CRETE
Safe
Harbours
Cauda

Cape
Salmone

PAMPHYLIA
Myra

CILICIA

CYPRUS

SYRIA
Antioch
Sidon
Caesarea
Jerusalem

0 100 200 300
Kilometres